This Land Is Your Land

Introduction to American Government and Politics
Version 1.1

Martin Saiz and Jennifer L. De Maio

FlatWorld

This Land Is Your Land: Introduction to American Government and Politics
Version 1.1

Martin Saiz and Jennifer L. De Maio

Published by:

FlatWorld
292 Newbury Street
Suite #282
Boston, MA 02115-2832

Gen: 202102011811

Brief Contents

Contents

About the Authors

Martin Saiz

Martin Saiz (Ph.D. University of Colorado at Boulder, 1992) is Professor of Political Science and the former Chair of the Political Science Department at California State University, Northridge. Professor Saiz joined the CSUN faculty in 1999 after teaching for seven years with the Department of Government and International Studies at the University of Notre Dame. Prior to teaching, Professor Saiz directed small town and neighborhood community service centers for the Center for Community Development and Design at the University of Colorado at Denver. There he helped local organizations develop problem-solving capacities doing neighborhood revitalization projects together with graduate design and planning students. He was appointed to the Denver Planning Commission and served two four-year terms during which he developed insights into the political process gained only from the inside.

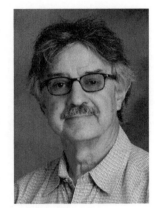

Martin has taught American government and politics for 27 years. He writes extensively on issues of urban politics, political parties, economic development, and education policy. His articles have been published in the *Journal of Politics*, *Urban Affairs Review*, *Political Research Quarterly*, *Policy Studies Journal*, *Economic Development Quarterly*, *The Journal of Urban Affairs*, *California Policy Issues Annual*, *Thought & Action*, and the *Higher Education Journal of the National Education Association*, as well as in other books and journals.

Jennifer L. De Maio

Jennifer De Maio (Ph.D. University of California, Los Angeles, 2005) is Professor of Political Science at California State University, Northridge. She holds a MSc in International Relations from the London School of Economics and a BA in English and History from Georgetown University. Professor De Maio's research focuses on African Politics, specifically on ethnic civil wars and conflict management. She has also published and presented papers on elections and the use of social media, transnationalized violence, the relationship between urban space and conflict management, women and conflict, and sustainable development in Africa, including the 2019 co-edited volume *Sustainability in Sub-Saharan Africa: Problems, Perspectives, and Prospects*. Professor De Maio's first book, *Confronting Ethnic Conflict: The Role of Third Parties in Managing Africa's Civil Wars*, was published in 2009. Professor De Maio is also working on a NIH funded project on the ethical considerations of prevention and treatment efforts for HIV/AIDS among members of the African diaspora in the United States. Before beginning a career in academia, she worked as a journalist for ABC News and NHK Japan Broadcasting Corporation.

Photograph by Tara Shriner

Jennifer has taught Introduction to American Politics for over thirteen years and brings a unique perspective to the subject that allows her to incorporate research from the comparative politics and international relations fields. She regularly participates in teaching conferences and workshops focused on pedagogy. She uses the classroom as a stage, on which the students are "spect-actors" actively involved in the learn

Acknowledgements

We are grateful to many for their help in bringing this text to life. Sean Wakely of FlatWorld has championed this book from the beginning. His experience and steady editorial guidance are visible throughout. Nikki Ross of FlatWorld has expertly shepherded the project through its many drafts and has kept us on track with revisions and deadlines. We owe an enormous debt of gratitude to Steve Paradis, our brilliant and thorough copy-editor, who caught errors, checked for cohesion across the chapters, and offered excellent editorial advice. We also thank the many reviewers who provided feedback and useful comments at many different stages of this project. In particular, we would like to thank the following:

- William James, Henderson State University
- Jeffrey Callen, Idaho State University
- Carolyn Myers, Southwestern Illinois College
- Amanda Rosen, Webster University
- Jolly Emery, University of Wisconsin-Whitewater
- Bradford Young, Snow College
- James Nelson, Lamar College
- Julie Hershenberg, Collin College—Preston Campus

Our colleagues in the Political Science Department at California State University, Northridge have cheered us on throughout this process. We thank them and the College of Social and Behavioral Studies for their support.

We owe an endless debt of gratitude to our families. Anne, Sarah, Laura, Dan, Giulia, Jacob, and Matteo, thank you so much for your love and care throughout this process.

Preface

The original title we proposed for this book was *The Accidental Citizen*. It was inspired by Anne Tyler's award-winning novel and, like her fictional character who writes guidebooks for business travelers who would rather stay home, we proposed a book for people who prefer to avoid politics but who end up voting out of a sense of civic duty. This approach works well for our students, mostly non-political science majors compelled to take an introductory course in American government to complete a general education requirement. For these students and others, we offer a comprehensive assessment of the American political system to help citizens understand and participate effectively in democratic governance without an unreasonable expenditure of time and effort.

Inspiring active civic engagement, which is a major goal of this book, has a long history. At the turn of the nineteenth century, Progressive Movement reformers sought to wrest control of government from political parties whose power was based on personal and ethnic loyalties, reinforced by political favoritism and patronage. The replacement values were objective, impersonal moral standards with an orientation toward the larger community. These principles were to be taught in the newly created public schools as a means of indoctrinating the children of immigrants. The result of this effort is the idealized civics-book citizen: a rational, objective individual, who closely follows political events, understands the workings of public policy, and who grasps the true consequences of his or her decisions. As we mention in our first chapter, however, the problem with this notion is that it assigns rather heroic characteristics to average people who, like our students, would rather be doing or learning something that can be more directly used to improve their individual lives or career prospects.

Because we were taught to view civic engagement as it should be rather than how it actually works, we are led toward an unrealistic understanding of the incentives and capacities of ordinary citizens and away from an appreciation for how political institutions (like campaigns, parties, and public interest groups) help voters by providing free and accessible information and cues to make participation cost effective. It is this cost-effective and realistic approach to politics that is at the heart of this text.

One of the most difficult challenges of teaching an introductory course in American politics lies in the fact that no robust, theoretically based framework has been developed to integrate the various parts of the discipline into an understandable whole. Approaches based on systems theory and political culture were deemed excessively vague. Pluralism was forsaken as naively optimistic. Since the 1960s, American political science has been practiced in sub-disciplines. Presidential scholars have developed their own theories somewhat separately from those who study Congress. Those who study interest groups, political parties, public opinion, voting behavior, the judiciary, the media, and the bureaucracy have done much the same. The result is a fine grained and nuanced understanding of the parts of the American political system, but only rough notions about how it works together. Some textbook writers, seeking to integrate American politics for their readers, have adopted the old systems and political culture frameworks. Others take the theories developed in the sub-disciplines at their face, but only within each chapter. Still others discard a theoretical framework altogether in favor of pure description. In our view, the result of all these attempts is the same–the student is unable to relate one part of the system with others because the framework is imprecise or missing, or the theoretical basis of one chapter is incompatible with the others.

We attempt to integrate the American political system through the idea of self-interest, a common and accepted theory of individual behavior used across the social sciences. It is well developed, scientifically defensible, and cutting-edge. We understand, however, that rational action by itself does not explain all political behavior; thus, the full range of influences, institutions, history, and culture are integrated to convey an understanding of the American political system.

Beyond theory, the organization of the text is an important tool in conveying the notion that the system operates as a cohesive whole. We begin with the overall legal framework, starting with the Constitution, its origins, and its key features. We follow with fundamental elements of the Constitution in chapters on federalism, civil liberties, and civil rights to provide an understanding of the rules by which the games of government and politics are played.

The heart of the text is a bottom-up or "individual-up" view of the political system. Like other democracies, our system attempts to put ordinary citizens in control by connecting the self-interests of voters to the careers of leaders who want to maintain power. In chapters on public opinion, citizen participation, and voting, we show how cognitive or collective action problems lead many to free-ride on the work of others, either not participating at all or voting with scant information. We acknowledge that most citizens have little reason to bear the costs associated with being a civics-book citizen. The implication is that citizens need help in the form of linking institutions to control their leaders. The following chapters on political parties, interest groups, and the media illuminate how these institutions join citizens to each other and their representatives, making participation cost effective. Because they have the potential to increase the influence of average citizens, we argue that many of their functions are underappreciated. Chapters on Congress and the presidency offer important details on how these institutions work to provide, or fail to provide, representation. The courts, on the other hand, work to keep the various institutions in balance and provide individual justice as envisioned by the Constitution. The two chapters on domestic and foreign policy provide insight into what the government does and how it accomplishes its goals. Lastly, two features at the end of each chapter summarize the chapter's main points, help readers critically assess its implications, and challenge readers to imagine how our institutions can be rearranged to make the system more democratic.

What's New in Version 1.1?

Version 1.1 includes updates to the Introduction, Public Opinion, Citizen Participation and Voting, Parties, Congress and Presidency chapters, including new names, dates, examples, and data on attitudes and voting patterns related to race, ethnicity, gender, relation and party affiliation. A new 2,500-word introduction to the Presidency chapter summarizes the political context of the 2020 election including the Muller investigation; two impeachments of the President and his acquittal by the US Senate; the COVID-19 pandemic, the shootings of George Floyd and Breonna Taylor and the Black Lives Matter social protest movement; the death of Justice Ruth Bader Ginsberg and the confirmation of Amy Coney Barrett; the results of the 2020 presidential election; and its legal challenges. The chapter on Congress is updated to include the results of the run-off elections in Georgia and the future of the US Congress.

CHAPTER 1
Introduction: Principles of American Government and Politics

Chapter Objectives

1. Identify the ways government can affect daily life.
2. Read about the land, the people, and the economy of the United States.
3. Explore the idea of popular sovereignty.
4. Examine how The Declaration of Independence implies a contract for popular sovereignty.
5. Understand the idea of democracy.
6. Learn how this book will help you understand American government and politics.

Introduction

© Shutterstock, Inc.

"This land is your land, this land is my land" declares in a very personal way that the United States belongs to the people. Woody Guthrie's famous song was written in 1940 as the country was emerging from the Great Depression, the worst economic downturn in the history of the industrialized world. Like today, our grandparents and great-grandparents saw poverty amid great wealth and anger produced by unfairness. Also like today, people asked if democracy itself was in jeopardy. But in the darkest of times, Americans came together to choose new leadership and move forward.

"This Land is Your Land" was meant to inspire collective ownership. Prior to the twentieth century, the skies, valleys, deserts, waters, and forests that Guthrie mentions in his song were considered inexhaustible and to be exploited for personal gain. The development of the national parks system at the turn of the century was an early acknowledgement that preservation demanded that some things be held in common. Today, we know that even the skies are vulnerable to degradation and that it costs everyone to keep them clean and breathable. The same could be said for less tangible endowments like justice, security, pubic welfare, and the blessings of liberty. We evoke the title to remind ourselves that the people own America and, as responsible owners, we need to work together to sustain a healthy and prosperous society.

Unfortunately, many Americans have been led to believe that the burdens of active citizenship are onerous. This perspective is understandable. Democracy places greater moral requirements on ordinary citizens than less inclusive forms of government. Indeed, modern ideals about what it means to be a good citizen were formulated as replacements for a social order based on aristocracy and monarchy. Because authority was to be placed in the hands of ordinary citizens, it was thought that social and political harmony could be realized only if citizens were willing to sacrifice their private interests for the sake of the community. Centuries of political socialization have led to the idealized "civics book" citizen who actively approaches government as a fair-minded individual, regularly follows current events, and understands the workings of public policy and the consequences of his or her political decisions. Americans want to be good citizens, yet are torn by doubt that they can live up to this ideal. Still, being a good and responsible citizen is actually easier than most people assume. We believe that American politics can be made intelligible and satisfying to the average American such that the duties of citizenship can be met with relative ease. In short, our book is written for citizens looking to understand the American government and satisfy their citizen duties, but without an unreasonable expenditure of time and effort. To do this, however, requires a different understanding of government, politics, and citizenship than found in most books.

We wrote this book for students like you who find yourselves in a situation similar to that of the average citizen. Most students in our classes are obligated to take a course in American government to complete a general education requirement. Yes, many enroll out of a genuine interest and are eager to engage in politics, but most feel that government is mysterious and corrupt; that ordinary citizens cannot make much of an impact. Other texts recognize this problem but attempt to foster motivation by inflicting guilt or simply by insisting that politics is relevant. Our approach, which has been refined over decades teaching this subject, recognizes that students vary widely in their knowledge of and motivation to learn about American politics. We attempt to instill interest by asking our readers to identify with average citizens who, like our students, would probably rather be doing or learning something that can be more directly used to improve their individual life or career prospects.

Our approach centers on two well-established observations from political science research that have yet to be incorporated into the teaching of this subject, namely (1) that politics is remote from the concerns of most Americans most of the time, and (2) that politics is inherently ambiguous. Both of these observations are at odds with accepted notions about the role and motivations of average citizens in a democratic society. The prevailing view is that civic participation is the very basis of republican governance and that the impetus to participate comes not from lofty notions of devotion to the common good, but from individual self-interest. Citizen participation and responsiveness are expected to happen more or less automatically because people are assumed to be inherently self-regarding. In other words, people participate to protect their interests. Voters express their self-interest by selecting representatives whom they believe best satisfy their personal needs, while elected officials respond faithfully out of their self-interest in maintaining their power to represent. This formulation puts people in charge by connecting their self-interest to the jobs of leaders who want to maintain power. However, the problem with this notion is that it assigns rather heroic characteristics to average people, namely that voters sum the positive and negative attributes of candidate characteristics and vote for those with the greatest net qualities. It also assumes that voters communicate their policy preferences after consideration of the candidates' positions on salient issues relative to their own. Ideas about democratic accountability or responsiveness make similar assumptions about the watchful eyes of voters, who understand how well they have been helped or harmed by their representatives' actions while in office.

The notion that citizen participation is motivated by self-interest also ignores long established findings that voters face collective action problems when selecting representatives in elections. In technical terms, the product produced by an election is simply representation. Like any public good, the outcome (the public official who is elected) is non-excludable and non-rival, meaning that one's enjoyment of the good does not take away from another person's enjoyment of that same good. Once the election is over, non-voters cannot be denied representation, nor can their access to representation be diminished by those who did vote. Why vote, then, if the benefits of voting are also available to non-voters? This logic (along with the more obvious observation that a single vote has little chance of determining the outcome of an election) has long tempted some citizens to "free ride" on the efforts of others by not voting.

However, contrary to expectations regarding strict rational self-interest, most Americans do vote—and they do so in large numbers. In the 2020 presidential election, some 155 million Americans (or about 66 percent of eligible voters) showed up at the polls. Moreover, the most accepted social scientific explanation of voter turnout is not rational self-interest but citizen duty. For most voters, the personal satisfaction derived from expressing themselves politically outweighed the typically low cost of participating in the election. This explains why seemingly modest social pressures play a large part in stimulating voter turnout—from coworkers who note who is performing their duty, to the deliberate efforts of political activists and institutions of all kinds to get people to vote. If participation is caused by self-interested behavior, why are these external motivations effective or even necessary?

A person can satisfy his or her civic duty at low cost (or with a little prodding), but the real problem is that most citizens vote with scant information. In truth, they have little reason to bear the information costs associated with discerning the candidates' true characteristics, where they stand on the issues, or how competent the incumbents may have been as political leaders. What follows from this observation is the idea that citizens are in the paradoxical position of being "in charge" of government but, for reasons related to the real consequences of individual self-interest (rather than the optimistic assumptions made by the Framers of the Constitution), they are hardly motivated to make choices based on policy or candidate research. On the other hand, public officials, corporations, interest groups, and others who seek private goods from government—power, perquisites of office, or selective policy benefits—find it cost-effective to bear the costs of rational decision-making. This also explains why these groups (which often represent small numbers of people) can satisfy their interests, often at the expense of the majority of citizens.

In this text, we start from the realistic position that most people take up their responsibilities as citizens somewhat reluctantly (or at least superficially). What makes this approach especially innovative is that it explains how government and politics really work and looks for answers in more appropriate places. Americans are very much casual citizens, not only because most are here by chance, but because they are typically engaged for symbolic reasons rather than from an innate love of politics or robust self-interest.

We are not claiming there is little the average citizens can do to influence government. To the contrary, we contend that the American public is more aware of and engaged in political affairs than strict rational self-interest would predict. There is ample evidence that involvement by ordinary citizens makes a great deal of difference. On the other hand, those in leadership positions, whether they are engaged in electoral politics or interest groups, political parties or the media, understand the incentive structure of popular politics and use these insights to their advantage. Our point is that self-interest on the part of citizens cannot be taken for granted. In particular, the link between citizens and their representatives is fragile, not robust; tentative, not secure. This understanding should be incorporated into the teaching of American politics and citizenship. The implication is that political engagement, like much else in life, must be cost-effective for the ordinary citizen to be sustainable and satisfying.

Our approach also suggests that, just like one does not need to be a computer scientist to use the internet or an automotive engineer to drive a car, one does not need to be a political scientist to be a competent citizen or to have a meaningful effect on government. Strangely, despite hard evidence that average citizens show scant knowledge about governmental institutions and policies, political scientists are actually less cynical about the state of American politics than the general public. We believe that this is because we are trained to see things empirically—that is, we are taught to view politics as it is rather than how we imagine it should be. This perspective not only leads to a realistic understanding of the limited incentives and capacities of voters, but to an appreciation for how political institutions like campaigns, parties, and public interest groups, among other things, aid citizen engagement by providing free and accessible information and cues to make participation cost effective. Many of these practices are similar to ones that consumers use to compare goods and services–from cell phones to doctors–before they purchase.

Thus, this book is very much a guide to American citizenship. It describes how the system of American government and politics works empirically. This book will help you to be critical, to understand how the political system can be made more democratic, and to evaluate how you can use your limited time and resources to participate most efficiently. Our goal is to encourage you to engage in politics and learn that politics can be interesting, useful, and rewarding. It need not be burdensome if viewed from a realistic perspective.

1.1 The Land, the People, and the Economy

The Land

The United States is composed of 50 states and several self-governing territories and possessions. Its land reaches through nine official time zones across the Western Hemisphere, the Pacific Ocean, and the Caribbean Sea. At 3.8 million square miles, the country is the third largest in the world by size and has the third largest population with about 325 million people. On the North American continent, the hills, low mountains, and broad river valleys in the east give way to vast plains west of the Mississippi River. Rugged mountains and deserts mark the western landscape. The county encompasses the world's largest coal reserves but also substantial stocks of minerals, ores, oil, natural gas, forests, arable land, fresh water, and people.[1] These resources determine the vigor of our economy and affect the laws and priorities we set as a country. We are free to exploit our resources for our own needs, or we can export them to bring in money from other parts of the world.

© Shutterstock, Inc.

The land can also be a basis of political conflict. For example, in the western part of the country, the public owns much of the land that has been a long-standing source of disagreements between the people living there and the federal government. Lately, oil and natural gas extraction, aided by a process called hydraulic fracturing or fracking, has led to controversies over its contribution to water and air pollution, global warming, and the triggering of earthquakes. The large size of the country continues to present a challenge to the provision of transportation, water, electricity, sanitation, and communications infrastructure, especially for rural and remote areas.

The People

The most fundamental determinate of politics and public policy is the population. For most of the country's history, the U.S. population increased steadily along with its physical territory. Natural increase (the greater number of births over deaths) was the major contributor to population growth in early America given the needs of an agricultural economy, early marriage, and large families. After 1830, with the beginnings of immigration and industrialization, urban populations started to grow and continued high levels of population growth (over 20 percent per decade) until World War I and the Great Depression. Since then, natural population increase has declined (with the exception of the Baby Boom era) and the country's population has been sustained by immigration from Latin America, Asia, and other regions.

© Shutterstock, Inc.

Population growth and decline has political consequences. In the years of rapid growth, the country struggled to provide roads, bridges, and schools. Cities strained to provide housing, law enforcement, and manage waste. But today's slow population growth also brings problems. With fewer working-age people, there will be fewer tax dollars to support a growing retired population with a high life expectancy. If we pursue a policy to reduce immigration by limiting immigration and deporting undocumented workers and their families, we will exacerbate the problem.

The composition of the population also matters. From the beginning of the country until about 1940, more than 80 percent of Americans were non-Hispanic whites. Since then, the white population has been declining relative to other racial groups, but still comprises the majority of the population in every region and every state except Hawaii. The percentage of black Americans has held steady, but the percentage of Latina/o and Asian Americans has increased significantly. The percentage of Native Americans has grown since the 1940s, but still only amounts to about 1 percent of the total.[2]

The United States is becoming more diverse every year and, by the middle of the twenty-first century, whites may cease to be the majority as a combination of black Americans, Latinas/os, Asians, and other groups account for slightly more. If trends continue such that Democrats remain the dominant choice among minority groups and Republicans build strength among whites in general and working-class whites in particular, an increasingly diverse population could provide a basis for political conflict. According to the 2015 American Values Survey, most supporters of Republican candidates (56 percent) say that immigrants are a burden to the United States because they take

American jobs, housing, and health care. Nearly 80 percent of the supporters of President Donald Trump agreed with these sentiments and added that discrimination against whites has become as big a problem as discrimination against blacks and other minorities.[3]

The Economy

The United States has the most robust and powerful economy in the world. The country is home to some of the most technologically advanced firms in the areas of computers, pharmaceuticals, aerospace, medical, communications, and military equipment. Individuals and businesses in the United States buy most goods and services from the private marketplace. Even federal, state, and local governments buy most of their goods and contract many of their services from private firms. Decisions to invest in a new factory, develop new products, or to close a facility and lay off workers are mostly in private hands.

economic globalization

The increasing movement of goods, labor, and services across borders due to interdependence of the world economies.

New technologies and increasing interdependence of world economies has caused the development of a "two-tier" labor market in which people lacking technical skills and education fail to get comparable pay, health insurance coverage, and other benefits relative to those with higher education and professional/technical skills. At the same time, **economic globalization** has forced low-wage workers in the United States to compete with low-wage workers in other parts of the world. Since the mid-1970s, practically all the gains in household income and wealth have gone to the top 20 percent of households. Incomes for the top 10 percent of Americans now average more than nine times the bottom 90 percent, while the top 1 percent averages more than 40 times the bottom 90 percent.[4] Other economic problems for the Unites States include inadequate investment in deteriorating infrastructure and rapidly rising medical and pension costs.

1.2 The Idea of Popular Sovereignty

popular sovereignty

The doctrine that sovereign power should be vested in the people.

Back in the day, the king was sovereign, meaning that he had supreme and absolute power within his territory. In the United States, we got rid of the king and made the people sovereign. It says so in the very first line of the Constitution: "We the People of the United States, in Order to form a more perfect Union, establish Justice, insure domestic Tranquility, provide for the common defense, promote the general Welfare, and secure the Blessings of Liberty to ourselves and our Posterity ..."[5] In this country, the people are not subordinate nor responsible to any other earthly authority. Together, we can do what we wish. If we decide our president should be a real estate developer from New York City with no political or military experience, then so be it. If we resolve that all Americans deserve to be healthy and cared for when they are sick, we can make it so. Alternatively, we can declare that it's every person for themselves when it comes to public welfare. Together, Americans developed a democratic government, grew as a nation, abolished slavery, dug the Panama Canal, helped save the world from certain tyranny (at least twice), built the first nuclear reactor, explored the moon, and developed the internet among many, many other accomplishments. In the future we can do more or fewer of these things; it is up to us. That is **popular sovereignty**.

The Contract: The Declaration of Independence

The theory under which sovereign power was taken from the king and given to the people is articulated in the Declaration of Independence. The claim was that the king had failed in his responsibility to protect the safety and well-being of all citizens under his domain, namely those living in the American colonies. The implication was that a new contract could be created under the assumption that the state arose, not from God, who gave the king and his descendants a "divine right" to rule, but out of a voluntary act of a free people where the government exists to serve their will. At the end of the Declaration, the 56 delegates made a solemn vow: "we mutually pledge to each other, our lives, our Fortunes, and our sacred Honor." With the signing of the document, the 13 colonies declared themselves to be independent states and began their quest for self-governance.

After almost 250 years, should we pledge our lives, fortunes, and sacred honor to each other as our forefathers did? Most states require children in public schools to recite the Pledge of Allegiance but not all states do so. The Supreme Court ruled that no student can be compelled to recite the Pledge.[6] No American alive today signed the Declaration of Independence, nor has anyone been asked to. Most of us are here by the chance of birth. If so, are we morally obligated to obey the law, pay our taxes, participate in government, and serve on juries and in the military if necessary? The answer is yes, but not because we actually signed away our individual freedoms in exchange for the protections and the benefits of government. We are obligated to do our part, to obey the law, and participate in government out of respect for our fellow citizens and for those who founded and protected our country.

1.3 The Impact of Government on Daily Life

We agree to follow the rules and abide by laws that limit what we can do. For example, we agree not to drive over the speed limit, to pay our taxes, and to respect private property. We agree to these things because, in return, we get security, protection, and resources that we could not provide for ourselves. We would not be able to transport and deliver our own mail, build highways and maintain roads, run a judiciary, preserve the national parks, or operate our health care and education systems. The government works to keep the peace and defends the nation and its people. It provides order and stability. It also provides essential public services, law enforcement, fire protection, and safety programs. Without government, we would have chaos. Thus, the exchange of some of our freedoms is a small cost in exchange for all the benefits the government provides.

American government is defined by its political culture. This culture is rooted in western European ideas and focuses on the principles of individualism, private property, and equal protection under the law. Other cultural heritages prioritize family and community over the individual and place less emphasis on materialism. While other nations have identities that are defined by shared languages, religions, or common ethnic heritages, diversity in the United States has meant that the nation needed to rely on a set of ideas rather than on cultural realities to unite it. Thus, political culture has come to represent the notion of what it means to be American. The set of ideals that constitutes the nation's identity is embodied in the values of liberty, equality, self-government, individualism, unity, and diversity. At the core of the political culture is the concept of the American Dream: with hard work and determination, anything is possible for anyone in the United States. While the American Dream certainly has its appeal and has come true for many, those who grew up in poverty or without access to adequate resources know all too well the limits on opportunity. And while the United States holds equality as one of its fundamental values, the country's experiences with slavery, segregation, and institutionalized discrimination suggest the limits of its ideals. Not all people are created equal in the United States and not everyone has access to the American Dream. But, the reason these ideals do not always match reality is that they are not rules of conduct; instead, they are general principles intended to unite the country and establish a national identity. As you will see throughout this book, conflicts about these principles and figuring out how ideals like equality, democracy, and liberty should be carried out have been important parts of the country's history. Politics is how we resolve these conflicts.

1.4 What Is Politics?

Imagine a big pie sliced into portions of unequal sizes. Some pieces are bigger; others are smaller. Now imagine it is your job to hand out the pieces to people at a party. How do you decide who gets what piece? There may be people who ask for a bigger or smaller piece, but what happens when you have people asking for the same size? And what if your supply of that size is limited? Figuring out who gets what can be a challenge.

© Shutterstock, Inc.

Imagine that government is like a pie made up of institutions, benefits, and resources. How do we slice that pie? How much should we allocate to the various components? And once it is sliced, how do we do we decide who should get what piece? Politics is the process of how we slice the governmental pie. It is about determining who gets what, when, and how. When people argue about how the pie should be sliced (because they value institutions or benefits differently), and when they compete for the slices (a limited or scarce resource), it is to politics that they turn for help.

Politics helps resolve conflicts that arise between differences in values and due to scarcity of resources. By scarcity, we mean there are not enough resources to satisfy everyone's needs or desires; by differences in values, we mean people have different beliefs and interests. Consider, for example, the different opinions that people hold about issues like abortion and the death penalty. Who decides how the resources should be divided and whose opinions will prevail? Politics decides.

In many ways, politics is a game. Like football, baseball, and chess, there are clear players and teams, strategies and techniques, winners and losers. But because politics can determine things like how much of your paycheck you get to keep, how much assistance you will get to pay for school and health care, and even what you can do legally during your free time, the game is played for extremely high stakes. While the game is played continuously, the scores are only really calculated during elections. Few games are so entertaining and play such an important role in your life.

Politics exists whenever individuals come together to make decisions. These groups can include, for example, school boards, churches, businesses, and government agencies. While politics are used to settle many of the conflicts that arise in society, one of the most interesting and important places to see the political process play out is in government.

1.5 What Is Democracy?

Democracy is rule by the people. The idea comes from the Athenian Greeks, who thought of democracy as self-government in which citizens gathered in face-to-face forums, debated, and voted directly on legislation. Democracy is an ideal in which the governed actively participate in a government that represents the people, such that its actions are determined by their involvement and it produces policies that reflect their interests. In Abraham Lincoln's words from his Gettysburg Address, democracy is "government of the people, by the people, and for the people." To make matters somewhat confusing, democracy also refers to governments that fall considerably short of the ideal. For example, we note in Chapter 11 that American democracy falls short of Lincoln's "of the people" ideal given Congress' underrepresentation of women, minorities, working class people, and certain religious groups. The degree to which the American government's policies are reflective of the interests, needs, and desires of the people is a matter of debate, but most scholars agree the government falls somewhat short of this criterion. Many scholars argue that wide disparities evident today in material conditions among people are incompatible with democracy.[7] Much of American political history, as you will learn, is a struggle to reach the ideals of democracy. In practice, perfectly democratic governments do not exist—and probably never will.

The Athenian Greeks practiced democracy directly in face-to-face forums. Some towns in New England still follow this method of governance, but geographically large nations with millions of citizens find direct democracy impractical on a day-to-day basis. In large societies, such as the United States, the people rule indirectly through representatives. To preserve the democratic ideal, all citizens should have an adequate and equal opportunity to express their preferences and have an equal voice in choosing their representatives in free and fair elections. It is important to note that this grant of authority from the people to their representatives is revocable when the representatives' terms of office expire. This provision allows people to hold their leaders accountable for conduct in office. In theory, control of the representatives equates to control of government and puts the people in charge.

© Shutterstock, Inc.

A major assumption behind democracy is that all people are equal. This sentiment is powerfully expressed in the second paragraph of the Declaration of Independence: "We hold these truths to be self-evident, that all men are created equal, that they are endowed by their Creator with certain unalienable Rights, that among these are Life, Liberty and the Pursuit of Happiness." Of course, when the country was founded, many members of Congress owned slaves, and women, Native Americans, and men without property were not allowed to vote in most states. While this ideal was not fully put into practice, the belief in equality among the American people has helped overcome practices that deviated from the democratic ideal. In the context of democracy, equality means that individuals should have the opportunity to fully develop their potential and, within the limits of decency and fairness to others, the opportunity to satisfy those interests they themselves deem important. Thus, with respect to collective decision making, all votes are considered equal.

majority rule

The principle that the greater number should exercise greater influence.

Making decisions based on unanimous consent is consistent with the principle of equal consideration, but in a large society unanimity is not feasible. Compromise is an important feature of democracy, with groups engaging in give and take to advance their agendas. As a practical matter, democracies normally make decisions on the basis of a majority vote, a rule that declares the greater number should determine the outcome.[8] This decision rule necessarily means that the interests of the minority on any given vote or issue will not be satisfied, but consider that any feasible alternative to **majority rule** permits a minority to decide.

supermajority

The principle that more than half the total should determine the outcome of a vote.

In special circumstances, such as when Congress votes to propose an amendment to the Constitution (Chapter 2) or to override a presidential veto (see Chapter 11 and Chapter 12), a **supermajority**, or more than a majority vote, is required to determine the outcome. If the majority vote is a good rule, why isn't a supermajority better? Why shouldn't we insist on supermajorities on every vote? The answer is simply that supermajorities allow a minority to block the preference of the majority. Requiring supermajorities may be important when the Constitutional rights of the minority are at stake, but only majority rule maximizes the preferences of the entire electorate. Simply put, more citizens benefit more consistently under majority rule because fewer people lose. Keep in mind that majorities normally change depending on the issue. Thus, citizens who lose one issue have a reasonable expectation of being part of the majority and winning on the next issue.

Majority rule does not mean that democracies give majorities unlimited power. The Constitution protects the unalienable Rights of "life, liberty and the pursuit of happiness" of the minority from the actions of the majority. Political liberty—the right to speak, write, assemble, and publish freely—are necessary conditions for democracy to exist. After all, how are majorities to be formed justly and challenged unless the people have unrestricted freedoms to propose, argue, persuade, and decide? It wouldn't be a democracy if those in power could jail or otherwise silence their opponents. On the other hand, majorities and indeed all citizens have the responsibility to listen to the views of the minority and consider their wishes. This is also a necessary condition for democracy to exist.

1.6 Understanding American Politics: The Analytical Framework

Our approach to understanding the American political system begins with the simple assumption that most people act in their own self-interest, whether they be voters, members of Congress, judges, bureaucrats, or the president of the United States. This is the most common assumption regarding human behavior used across the various social sciences. It allows us to draw upon a vast reservoir of empirical findings and present them with theoretical consistency. However, we also acknowledge that self-interest is not necessarily rational, nor does it fully explain political behavior—especially with regard to low-cost conduct (such as voting) or within highly constrained institutional environments (such as the courts). In context, seemingly intangible factors such as age, gender, race, region, friendship, ideology, allegiance to a political party, and culture matter, sometimes a great deal. We thus incorporate various theoretical models, including rational choice, political culture, and political psychology to help us understand political behavior. Social and institutional context also matter. Individuals make political choices in the midst of millions of others doing the same. Presidential campaigns commit resources according to election rules determined by the distribution of Electoral College votes and state election laws. Presidents, legislators, and judges make public policy according to complex procedures outlined in constitutions shaped by history and tradition. The full range of political behaviors, institutions, history, and relationships needs to be covered to convey an understanding of how the American political system works as a whole. In this regard, individual self-interest is a starting point, an assumption rather than an explanation. When such actions are viewed as shaped by historical and institutional contexts, they can provide answers to complex political events.

Unfortunately, all this seems to leave little room for us to say that as an individual you can make a big difference. Indeed, the central paradox of democracy is that individual action is necessary (even critical) for democracy to work well, but collective action matters most. Still, we find from experience that this honest assessment is welcomed by students looking to reconcile the guilt they feel over falling short of the civics book ideal of the good citizen. Unlike other books, we do not insist that you become politically active (beyond voting) or even expend resources above those necessary to achieve your individual political goals. We assume that, like other Americans, you want to fulfill your citizen duties and do so without incurring undue costs. Our approach only asks that you identify with the political perspective of the average citizen—someone with a busy life and priorities beyond politics.

Of course, our subject is compelling. Politics has long been the focus of literature, theater, movies, and television, but like the average citizen, we assume that most students would rather be learning something that can be more easily to improve their individual lives or career prospects—goals that do not normally require overcoming barriers to collective action. Thus, we feel no remorse when suggesting that you use "shortcuts" such as party identification and consulting interest group ratings to guide voting choices. This is no different than relying on brand names or reviews to make consumer choices. More importantly, this is what the science tells us about how ordinary citizens make political choices. Indeed, research consistently shows that when individuals use heuristics such as ideology and party identification, the political system remains stable, responsive, and coherent. We believe that each citizen has an obligation to participate, but also the right to choose the level at which to participate. This is consistent with the wide range of political motivations coming from our students. Some are eager to run for political office, while others are satisfied with simply voting.

Two features at the end of each chapter summarize the chapter's main points and will help you critically assess what you can do should you choose to engage yourself in the political process. The first feature, "What Can I Do?" challenges you to draw out the implications of our analysis, be a more critical consumer of political information, and to be more informed and involved. A second feature titled, "What's the Alternative?" discusses how political institutions can be redesigned to make the system more democratic.

1.7 What Can I Do?

This feature opens opportunities for thinking about a wide variety of individual political engagement. Most social scientists assume politicians respond to their constituents in much the same way business owners respond to their customers—they respond to the threat of exit, or the ability to "vote with one's feet," as the economists say. In the political realm, threat of exit is represented by your ability to withdraw your vote from an incumbent, to withdraw your membership from a political party or group, or, in the case of the media, the ability to tune out or switch networks. Exiting is an easy option, but quitting keeps citizens from using their actions and voices by working for a group, party, or candidate or attempting to influence their leaders or fellow citizens.[9] As a college student with multiple constraints on your time, the easiest way to engage in politics is to vote. This book should help increase your knowledge of American politics and institutions so you can participate more effectively. Fortunately, for those wanting to become more engaged, the more demanding forms of political participation, such as writing letters or working for a candidate, usually have greater impacts on political outcomes and hence greater political pay-offs. Those who have the time and energy can participate actively through interest groups, political parties, or social movements. With less effort, one can be a loyal supporter of a particular group, party, or individual politician. Lastly, one can stay mostly aloof from political involvement by remaining independent. Like a picky customer, one can show approval or displeasure of the system's outcomes by giving or withdrawing support from the candidates and parties. Each of these levels of involvement can be valid in their own context.

Most Americans, whether through a process of socialization or experience, develop a sense of attachment to the society and its government. Unlike attachments based on blind faith, political loyalty is grounded in the belief that, over time, the right turns made by government will more than balance the wrong turns. Of course, this optimism may simply be a rationalization (it's not easy to move to another country), but whether it is a consequence of reasoned calculation or hopefulness, we acknowledge that some features of the American political system are resistant to popular control. That is to say, when it comes to the decisions of the Supreme Court, the bureaucracy, or the consequences of federalism, a sensible strategy is to stay informed, remain loyal, and hope for the best. Fortunately, plenty of research demonstrates that despite its dysfunctions, the American political system performs remarkably well. Over time, social and economic changes, partisan realignments, and social movements have moved the society closer to its democratic ideals. More often than not, politics often works like a competitive market such that there is some value in allowing political entrepreneurs to do their jobs while citizens stand ready to hold their representatives accountable. Sooner or later, things work out or become subject to a popular referendum when citizens can use their voices to change things for the better.

1.8 What's the Alternative?

The second set of features offers suggestions for how political institutions can be redesigned to help lower the costs of engagement, such that biases favoring those segments of society with greater resources would be reduced. This feature gives us the opportunity to learn about the relationship between the design of political institutions and the quality of democracy. For example, the passage and the enforcement of civil rights and voting rights acts were enormously costly, but the acts expanded participation and made the political system more equal and responsive to previously underrepresented groups. Similarly, institutional change, such as lowering the cost of voting by easing registration requirements, would increase voter participation and presumably the political power of people from lower socio-economic classes. We also engage in comparative analyses between institutions in the United States and other democracies to explore the idea that there are multiple ways that democracies can be designed. The goal of these comparative analyses is to encourage students to think critically about the efficacy of American political institutions, know what other options are out there that we could adopt, and evaluate the advantages and disadvantages of various alternatives.

Throughout these sections, we take care to avoid suggestions that are closely identified with one side of the ideological or partisan divide. Still, freedom of choice is considered a given good because in most cases it leads to increased competition and enhanced efficiency in public policy. Democracy embodies freedom by allowing people to choose their leaders and hold them accountable for their actions. The fact that the majority should prevail in most cases maximizes individual preferences. Our founding principle that all people are born equal—embodied by the principle of one person, one vote—personifies the value of equality that has been a driving force for much of our nation's.history. Our analysis and suggestions are not value free, but are grounded in the principles of freedom, equality, and democracy that lie above any particular party or ideology.

Endnotes

1. "The World Factbook: UNITED STATES," Central Intelligence Agency, April 24, 2018, Accessed May 1, 2018, https://www.cia.gov/library/publications/the-world-factbook/geos/us.html.

2. Data Access and Dissemination Systems (DADS), "Your Geography Selections." American FactFinder – Results, October 5, 2010, accessed May 1, 2018, https://factfinder.census.gov/faces/tableservices/jsf/pages/productview.xhtml?pid=ACS_16_1YR_CP05&prodType=table.

3. Robert P. Jones, Daniel Cox, Betsy Cooper, and Rachel Lienesch, *Anxiety, Nostalgia, And Mistrust: Findings from the 2015 American Values Survey* (Public Religion Research Institute).

4. "Income Inequality," Inequality.org, accessed May 1, 2018, https://inequality.org/facts/income-inequality/.

5. U.S. Congress,. *The Constitution of the United States and the Declaration of Independence* (Cong, Washington, D.C.: U.S. G.P.O., 2009).

6. Amy Crawford, "How the Pledge of Allegiance Went From PR Gimmick to Patriotic Vow," Smithsonian.com, September 1, 2015, accessed May 1, 2018, https://www.smithsonianmag.com/history/pledge-allegiance-pr-gimmick-patriotic-vow-180956332/.

7. M. Gilens, *Affluence and Influence: Economic Inequality and Political Power in America* (Princeton, NJ: Princeton Univ. Press/Russell Sage Found, 2012).

8. Robert Alan Dahl, *Democracy and Its Critics* (New Haven: Yale University Press, 2011).

9. Albert O. Exit Hirschman, Voice, and Loyalty: *Responses to Decline in Firms*, Organizations, and States, (Cambridge, MA: Harvard Univ. Press, 2007).

CHAPTER 2
The Founding and the Constitution: Creating a Nation

Chapter Objectives

1. Explain the origins of the Constitution in colonial and revolutionary America.
2. Understand the reasons why the United States declared independence from England.
3. Highlight the shortcomings of the Articles of Confederation and explain why the document was replaced by the Constitution.
4. Describe the debates that characterized the Constitutional Convention and explain the various arguments and compromises that produced the final document.
5. Recognize the Constitution as a living document that is both stable and open to change.

checks and balances

The power of the legislative, executive, and judicial branches of government to block some acts by the other two branches.

Introduction: A Love Story

The typical love story goes something like this: Two people meet. They fall in love. They live happily ever after. For Jack Baker and Michael McConnell, happily ever after included them getting married. The problem was that they were gay, in the United States, in the 1970s. Baker and McConnell knew within four months of meeting at a Halloween party in 1966 that they wanted to marry. But same-sex marriage was illegal. Marrying legally became a mission that would define their lives.

One of the most iconic representations of the United States of America is the Constitution. The document opens with the words "We the People." It provides the blueprint for governing the country and protecting the rights of citizens.

© Shutterstock, Inc.

The two men first applied for a marriage license in a Minnesota courthouse in 1970. The county clerk refused their request, telling them that marriage licenses were only for people of opposite sexes. The couple sued in state court, noting that nothing in the Minnesota marriage statute mentioned gender. Moreover, Baker, who had gone to the University of Minnesota Law School in order to figure out how the couple could get married, argued that to limit marriage to opposite-sex couples would violate their constitutional rights, specifically their Fourteenth Amendment right to equal protection and due process. The situation, Baker claimed, was similar to that of *Loving v. Virginia* (1967), the landmark civil rights case in which the U.S. Supreme Court overturned laws banning interracial marriage. The state court dismissed the men's claim and the Minnesota Supreme Court upheld the decision. In 1972, Baker and McConnell appealed to the U.S. Supreme Court, which refused to hear the case of *Baker v. Nelson* on the basis that it did not present an important constitutional question. With its dismissal, the Court blocked same-sex couples from having the constitutional right to marry. In 1996, Congress passed, and President Bill Clinton signed, the Defense of Marriage Act (DOMA), which defined marriage as between a man and woman. With DOMA, the federal government had further institutionalized the notion that marriage was a constitutional right reserved for citizens who were the opposite sex.

It was not until 2015 that the U.S. Supreme Court reversed its decision and legalized same-sex marriage. With *Obergefell v. Hodges*, the justices determined that the Constitution grants same-sex couples the right to marry. The arguments in *Obergefell* were similar to those made by Baker and McConnell in the 1970s. So how did the United States go from deciding same-sex marriage was not serious enough to warrant a Supreme Court hearing in 1972 to judging it constitutionally protected in 2015? The Constitution did not change, but our understanding of it did.

> On June 26, 2015, the Supreme Court ruled that the Due Process Clause and the Equal Protection Clause of the Constitution's 14th Amendment guarantee the fundamental right to marry for same-sex couples. With this ruling, all 50 states were legally obligated to perform and recognize the marriages of same-sex couples.

Ted Eytan from Washington, DC, USA (SCOTUS Marriage Equality 2015 58151) [CC BY-SA 2.0 (https://creativecommons.org/licenses/by-sa/2.0)], via Wikimedia Commons. https://bit.ly/2MHveKe.

The Constitution is a living document, meaning that even though the words themselves do not change, our understanding of them evolves as the country changes. In the 1970s, when Baker and McConnell first began their struggle to marry legally, sodomy was a crime in almost every state. There was also widespread discrimination against the LGBTQ community. Before the Supreme Court could make its ruling in 2015, the nation had to be ready. In order for that to happen, states needed to start allowing same-sex marriage and public opinion on the issue had to shift. It took time and a committed political campaign for the American public to alter its views of LGBTQ citizens. In 1999, California passed a domestic partnership statute and, in 2000, Vermont became the first state to legalize same-sex civil unions. Massachusetts legalized gay marriage in 2003, but in 2004, 11 states passed constitutional amendments to ban gay marriage. Over the next 10 years, states across the nation passed laws legalizing same-sex marriage. By the time the case reached the Supreme Court, there was widespread support both at the state level and among the public for gay marriage. In 1996, 27 percent of Americans supported the idea, but by 2015, 60 percent supported it. The LGBTQ community had become normalized and humanized to the point at which its equality being guaranteed by the Constitution seemed obvious.

The Framers of the Constitution likely could not predict that the issue of same-sex marriage would one day divide the nation. They did, however, know that challenges would arise that would force the country to go back to the document that defines its values and provides the framework for governance. The Framers were familiar with conflict. They knew differences in values, lifestyles, and opinions would generate tension. With the Constitution, the Framers had to reconcile the interests of small farmers, shopkeepers, and laborers with those of rich merchants and planters, of big states with small states, and northern and southern concerns. Most importantly, they had to engineer a strong central government with the desire to keep it from becoming an instrument of the majority while protecting the autonomy of the states. For four months, the Framers negotiated and crafted. What they came up with was a true feat of political engineering. The document they introduced proposed a political system in which power would be shared between the national and state governments. A system of **checks and balances** would ensure that no single branch of government would become too strong. The Framers knew they had to write a document that would be flexible and could adapt to changing times. In this way, they ensured that citizens across multiple generations would feel ownership over the document, while that document remained relevant and legitimate for years to come.

When thinking about the development of the Constitution, it is important to keep in mind that it was created by a political process in response to concrete political problems. The document, however, was also written in general terms so as to apply to future generations. In many ways, the Framers were like today's politicians— public officials working to produce solutions to public problems. They were also driven by private objectives, such as their careers and their personal fortunes (not to mention those of their benefactors). The Framers' conception of the common good was also influenced by the dominant culture and prejudices of the time. Consequently, the Constitution should not be seen as an object of perfection. As an outcome of politics, it reflects the compromises that needed to be made to reach agreement. Indeed, an important part of the Constitution is a provision for amendments to correct its flaws and to account for the uncertainties of the future.

This chapter explores the political engineering that resulted in the Constitution. We consider the events that led to the colonies' decision to split from England and ultimately to fight for independence. We also examine the predecessor to the Constitution—the Articles of Confederation—and evaluate the limitations of a government in which there is no centralized power. Next, we turn to the Constitutional Convention and the compromises brokered between various factions with competing interests. We conclude by thinking about the reasons why a document that was written in 1787 has endured for more than 230 years.

2.1 Constitutional Engineering

What is the U.S. Constitution? Is it a living document open to change and modern interpretation, or is it static and fixed? Does it grant rights or take them away? Does it provide order, stability, and structure or does it guarantee liberty and freedom? Does it bring American citizens into the political process or keep them out?

The Constitution is all these things. It is a record of the founders' intentions and decisions. It is also a document that adapts and changes with the times. It keeps the wheels of government turning and it ensures order and stability. At the same time, it safeguards our rights. The **Constitution** is an outline for civil society and defines the United States and its people. It helps preserve the laws and policies in defense of the American society and to enhance its welfare. It is also where we go to find support and rationale for changes to existing laws and public policies.

Constitution

An outline for civil society that defines the United States and its people.

natural rights

A philosophical belief expressed in the Declaration of Independence that certain rights are ordained by God, are discoverable in nature and history, and are essential to human progress. The perception that these rights were violated by Great Britain contributed to the American Revolution.

The Constitution is the embodiment of the social contract we make with our government. We agree to give up some **natural rights** in exchange for the protection, order, security, and services that the government provides. Of course, none of us were actually asked to sign a contract to give up our rights in exchange for government. In theory, this was something the original authors of the Constitution asked the people of the United States to do. This point may seem minor, but the issue is problematic for those Americans whose ancestors were brought here by force and who were excluded from any contract. Further, most Americans are citizens simply because they were born here. Because we are in a sense "accidental citizens," our obligations to government are more fragile than consent theory assumes. Yet we benefit today from the blood and sweat that it took to build and develop our society. Out of respect for what earlier generations have built, we are obliged to work together to understand and protect the Constitution and to do our best to keep our government functioning well. In the same vein, we should pay forward to future generations what was given to us. All this implies a responsibility to be critical, to preserve and enhance what is good, and to change things for the better.

The word constitution comes from the Latin *constituere*, which means to appoint or establish. If we think about the origins of the term, we can recognize the Constitution as the document that establishes the precedents according to which the United States and its people are governed. One hundred fifty-five countries in the world have constitutions (the U.S. Constitution is the oldest). For almost all of those nations, their constitutions are the means through which government can be controlled. Constitutions derive from a desire to change existing governmental practices and reflect a belief in limited government. Countries differ, however, in how many limitations to impose on government. Governments also differ on how closely they adhere to the rules established by their respective constitutions. Nevertheless, constitutions represent an effort to resolve political conflict.

Politics is the process of resolving conflict that arises over differences in values and scarcity of resources. The story of how the U.S. Constitution came into being is very much one about resolving conflict, rational decision-making, and compromise. When the Framers met at the Constitutional Convention in Philadelphia in 1787, they brought with them valuable assets that would help them navigate the political conflicts they knew would arise. One such asset was their English political heritage. In addition, they brought their experience with governance that they had acquired during the colonial era. Their political knowledge and experience prepared them for negotiating a constitution that could meet the needs of their time as well as generations to come.

2.2 Politics in the Colonies

America was first established as a series of colonies by settlers coming from England, France, Spain, the Netherlands, Sweden, and Norway, among others. The majority of the colonists came from England. Some came to the colonies to escape religious persecution. Others sought to expand political power and private wealth. Few if any came with the goal of creating a new, independent country.

mercantilism

An economic system under which empires built their economic power by monopolizing sources of raw materials from their colonies.

The 13 British colonies were established by private individuals and trading companies and were under the rule of the British crown. In the beginning, relations with England were good and colonists were proud to be members of the British Empire. Wealthy colonists sent their children to school in England. They read books and newspapers published in the homeland. They drank tea imported on British ships from India. Most manufactured products and many other goods were imported from across the empire. On the other hand, the colonies exported timber, tobacco, indigo, rice, and other raw materials to England. This was common economic practice in the 18th century as guided by the ideas of **mercantilism**. Under this system, empires built their economic power by monopolizing sources of raw materials from their colonies. England protected its domestic industries through taxation and legislation that prohibited the manufacture of items such as hats, shoes, and other finished goods in the colonies. This kept them dependent on British goods. This uneven economic relationship was an ongoing source of contention among colonial merchants and would-be manufacturers.

The colonies represented not only an extension of the British economy but also an extension of the English government. Still, the reality was that England was thousands of miles away. It took two months to sail across the Atlantic Ocean. Day-to-day governance was therefore handled by colonial administrators. Courts enforced English common law. Each colony had an appointed royal governor who worked with a body of advisers called the Governor's Council or Governor's Court. There was a legislative, or law-making body, in each colony that was elected by colonists who could vote (by 1750, most free white men could vote if they owned property). Town hall meetings were held every year and the colonists were invited to participate and share ideas. Participation gave the colonists critical experience with politics and administration. Thus, while American politics is steeped in the English political tradition, the colonists' ideas about the rights of people, social contracts, limited government, and representative democracy derived from their own experiences with governance.

This picture shows three colonies serving gold, silver, foodstuffs, and raw materials to the mother country. The mother country, or colonial power, controlled the colonies and exploited them in order to extract resources for its own economic enrichment.

The Mercantilist Argument for Colonial Expansion

Dorf, Philip. Our Early Heritage: a Visualized Text In Ancient And Medieval History. New York: Oxford book company, 1940.

In the sections that follow, we explain how colonial leaders learned to handle the practical problems of governing, such as levying taxes and drafting budgets. We also discuss how their experience with self-governance allowed these leaders to develop techniques for managing political conflict by creating coalitions of people with diverse interests and ideas about how resources should be allocated and power should be shared. They also learned to use decision-making strategies such as compromising and consensus-building. Given their hands-on experience, the colonists were able to establish their own constitutions and organize state systems of government when they declared their independence from England in 1776.

The Ideological Split from England

For the majority of American colonists, England was their homeland and loyalty to the British crown was strong. Many did not want to be independent of England. Why, then, did the American colonists decide to revolt against King George III and declare their independence?

In pre-revolutionary America, there were considerable social inequalities. While the people in the colonies were by today's standards a relatively homogenous society, there were substantial differences within and across the 13 colonies. Farming was the primary means of material support for most colonists in both the North and South. Most farms were subsistence farms, meaning that the yearly harvest would provide a family with food and seed for the following year. If the family worked hard, the farm might yield a small surplus that could be sold or traded for manufactured goods, including shoes and cooking pots. They could also buy luxury goods such as coffee, tea, and sugar. Some farms near larger settlements were commercial farms, which supplied goods to local markets. These could support a more affluent class of farmer. The large plantations in the southern and mid-Atlantic states used slave labor to produce commercial crops for export and were owned by wealthy farmers. Finally, there were a few urban, seaport communities located around natural harbors, such as in Boston, Massachusetts, and Charleston, South Carolina. The largest of these urban centers in 1750 was Philadelphia with 25,000 inhabitants; others had fewer than 10,000. Like urban areas of today, these seaport populations were diverse. Laborers, sailors, and indentured servants made up the lower class. It is estimated that in 1750, between 40 and 50 percent of Philadelphia's population was composed of servants and slaves.[1] A class of urban professionals, shop owners, and crafts people were in the middle class. Wealthy merchants and ship owners were at the top and dominated urban society. Across the colonies, the largest landowners and most successful merchants possessed nearly half the wealth of pre-revolutionary America. Slaves constituted about one-third of the total colonial population and an estimated one-fifth of all whites were property-less.[2] These differences would translate into diverse interests regarding taxation, motivations to fight for independence, and demands for representation, protection, and civil liberties after the Revolution.

The rules of monarchy and aristocracy determined one's social status and political power. This reality became a source of tension between English and colonial societies. One's position was determined not by merit and ability, but by family connections. In the minds of the ruling gentry of England, all colonists were commoners and looked down upon. This view created a sense that members of the colonial elite were inferior and at best should be thought of as men of commercial wealth. This notion of social hierarchy was also evident in colonial society. There was a separation between ordinary and extraordinary people, patricians and plebeians, commoners and gentlemen. People at the time believed that this was normal in society and nature—that those who were wealthy were superior to people in the middle class and those in the middle class were better than the poor. Social status within the colonies had political consequences. Ordinary colonists were considered commoners by the colonial elite and, as such, did not have the capacity for political thought. Farmers, craftsmen, shop keepers, and artisans were expected to step aside and allow their superiors to lead. This social hierarchy in the colonies would be challenged as average working people participated in the protest movements leading to the Revolution and did the bulk of the fighting during the war.

The Issue of Representation

Several events took place in the mid-1700s that changed the attitudes of colonists toward England. The first of these events was the French and Indian War (1756-1763), a global conflict that included England and France. It is sometimes called the Seven Years War. After the war, 10,000 English troops remained in the colonies to protect the land that had been newly won from the French. The "Redcoats," as they were known, were able to enforce policies on behalf of the British crown, and the colonists found their freedoms greatly reduced. In particular, the Proclamation of 1763 prevented settlement west of the watershed of rivers flowing into the Atlantic, in effect containing the colonies to areas east of the Appalachian Mountains. This erected a barrier to westward expansion of farmers and the activities of land speculators. The Navigation Acts had already prohibited merchants in the colonies from trading directly with the other empires (France, Spain, and the Netherlands) and their colonies as a way to keep the benefits of trade flowing to England. In addition, the English found themselves in massive debt after the war. England decided to alleviate some of the debt by imposing taxes on the American colonies and exercising more direct control over colonial trade.

This decision to tax the colonies as a means of obtaining revenue did not sit well with the colonists. From the time the colonies were established, both England and the colonies knew that trade and taxation would be difficult to control from across the Atlantic. The long-standing agreement was that England would regulate trade and in exchange would allow the colonies to tax themselves to provide for local services. Direct taxation by England not only altered this understanding, but threatened the social status of colonial citizens. Since 1688, it had been illegal for the king to impose taxes on English citizens without the consent of Parliament. Since the colonists had no representation in Parliament and were subject to taxation without their consent, to them this meant that they were politically reduced to the level of women, slaves, and servants. This reduction in social status was taken as an insult. The colonists also felt that because they had fought alongside the English in the French and Indian War, they deserved credit rather than punishment in the form of taxes for helping the British win.

In 1764, the British government passed the **Sugar Act**, which imposed a tax on all sugar imported into the colonies. New England merchants who used sugar and molasses to make rum for export saw their revenues decline. They feared they would be priced out of the market. The following year, the British imposed the **Stamp Act**, which declared that all legal documents, newspapers, and other items had to be printed on specially stamped paper that was purchased from the government. This tax affected larger segments of colonial society, from printers, publishers, and lawyers to gamblers who had to spend more for dice and cards.

Sugar Act

This act imposed a tax on all sugar imported into the colonies. New England merchants who used sugar and molasses to make rum for export saw their revenues decline and feared that they would be priced out of the market.

Stamp Act

This act asserted that all legal documents, newspapers, and other items had to be printed on specially stamped paper that was purchased from the government.

The Stamp Act was met with widespread hostility in the colonies. This cartoon shows supporters of the act gathering at a dock to carry a small coffin containing the remains of the bill toward an open vault. Because it imposed a tax on paper, the act directly affected the most politically active in colonial society, including newspaper publishers, academics, lawyers, and judges. These people in turn organized widespread protests to the act, giving rise to the battle cry, "No Taxation without Representation."

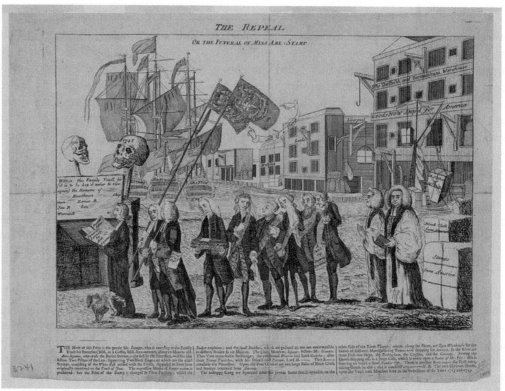

Library of Congress: http://www.loc.gov/pictures/item/2006678564/.

Declaratory Act

This act asserted that the power of Parliament was unlimited and that it had the right to make laws for the colonies.

Townshend Acts

Taxes on a wide range of goods imported from England, such as paper, glass, and tea. The Townshend Acts also established a new colonial authority called the American Board of Customs, which collected taxes independently from the colonial assemblies.

Leaders representing the interests of New England merchants and southern planters—the two groups most heavily affected by the Sugar Act—broke from royal authorities and encouraged shopkeepers, artisans, and laborers to demonstrate and boycott British goods. In Massachusetts, mobs intimidated royal stamp distributors and forced some to resign. Mob action spread to other colonies and stamp paper was seized. Two years after its passage, Parliament repealed the Stamp Act. The colonists had won a big victory, but many in Parliament felt that they were setting a dangerous precedent by conceding–and doing so in a way that would encourage more disobedience. Thus, at the same time that Parliament repealed the Stamp Act, it passed the **Declaratory Act**, patterned after a similar law that was used to subjugate Ireland. This act asserted that the power of Parliament was unlimited and that they had the right to make laws for the colonies "in all cases whatsoever." To reinforce the point, in 1767, Parliament passed the **Townshend Acts**, which taxed a wide range of goods imported from England such as paper, glass, and tea. The Townshend Acts also established a new colonial authority, the American Board of Customs, which collected taxes independently from the colonial assemblies, essentially stripping them of power. Colonial self-rule took another hit when the New York State Assembly was suspended for refusing to house and supply British troops.

The taxes were seen by the colonists as violations of their rights and prompted the beginnings of the conversation about taxation without representation—the colonists could not vote in British elections and were not represented in the British government. They felt it was unfair to be taxed without a voice in determining the laws and policies that governed them. The colonists responded with protests, petitions, meetings, mobs, and a further boycott of British goods, this time across all 13 colonies. As they organized the boycott, colonial society began to change. Throughout the colonies, local groups continued to confront tax collectors, some of whom were tarred and feathered. Organizations such as the Sons of Liberty, the Daughters of Liberty, and the even more radical Committees of Correspondence were formed to enforce the boycott. On a widespread basis, ordinary people participated not only in protest activities, but in the decisions and strategies of action. So unusual was this participation of commoners and women in the processes of government that they become the subjects of ridicule in English newspapers.

In the most famous gesture of protest against the Tea Act of 1773, a group of about 50 colonists dressed as Native Americans dumped 342 chests of British tea worth about £90,000 (between $1 million and $3 million today) into Boston Harbor. This ultimate act of protest against taxation became known as the **Boston Tea Party**. The British were furious and responded by passing the **Coercive Acts** (called the Intolerable Acts by the colonists), which closed Boston Harbor and put the government of Massachusetts under direct control of the British military.

The Boston Tea Party was a political protest against the Tea Act that allowed the British East India Company to sell tea from China in the colonies without paying any taxes. As a result, local tea merchants could not compete with the imported tea. On December 16, 1773, demonstrators (some of whom disguised themselves as Native Americans) dumped an entire shipment of tea sent by the East India Company into Boston Harbor. The British government responded with the Coercive Acts. Tensions between the two sides escalated, ultimately leading to the American Revolution.

THE DESTRUCTION OF TEA AT BOSTON HARBOR.

Nathaniel Currier [Public domain], via Wikimedia Commons. https://bit.ly/2FZ8jcU.

The Development of an American Identity

As resentment toward England was mounting, the colonists also started to develop an identity separate from the British. The colonists started to believe that British politicians were corrupt and that the English constitution did not do enough to safeguard the liberty of citizens. Educated elites among the colonists started to look more closely at the writings of Hobbes, Locke, and Roseau. They came to value a higher law of natural rights, which included life, liberty, and property. In particular, they looked to Locke's *Two Treatises on Government* and found the basis for their belief that citizens give up some of their natural rights and freedoms in exchange for the safety, stability, and order that government can provide. It was during this time that the colonists began to use the term *Americans* to describe themselves. They firmly believed in the principle that in order to be legitimate, government requires the consent of the governed.

Talk of independence grew, which led the colonists to come together at the First and Second Continental Congresses in 1774 and 1775. For both Congresses, each colony sent their most important political leaders, professionals, merchants, and planters. The group only knew each other by reputation, but members would form a core of leaders that we have come to know as the Founding Fathers: people like planters George Washington and Thomas Jefferson, merchant John Hancock, lawyer John Adams, and his brewer cousin, Samuel Adams. At the First Continental Congress, delegates agreed to fully support Massachusetts. They passed resolutions reasserting home rule and condemned British taxes and the military occupation of Boston. They also proposed the continuation of the boycott and called for the formation of "committees of observation" to ensure compliance. These committees would begin to investigate "treasonous" acts, thereby separating British loyalists from patriots in their communities. Eventually, they would collect taxes and take over control of the local militias. In short, they would become de facto governments. The Congress also passed a resolution advising the colonies to arm and prepare to defend themselves.

Boston Tea Party

In the most famous gesture of protest against the Tea Act of 1773, a group of about 50 colonists dressed as Native Americans dumped 342 chests of British tea worth about £90,000 (between $1 million and $3 million today) into Boston Harbor.

Coercive Acts

The British response to the Boston Tea Party, which closed Boston Harbor and put the government of Massachusetts under direct control of the British military.

Two Treatises on Government

A book by John Locke in which he argued that citizens give up some of the rights and freedoms that they have in the state of nature in exchange for the safety, stability, and order that government can provide.

Common Sense

The pamphlet written in 1775-76 by Thomas Paine arguing that the colonies could survive economically on their own and no longer needed to be tied to England. The document is considered to be the single most important publication of the American Revolution.

The First Continental Congress marked the moment that the colonies started working together. The Congress created an organizational structure for unified action, and by advising the colonies to arm themselves, directly threatened British sovereignty. The colonies also came to the important realization that they could survive economically without being tied to England. This idea was embodied in Thomas Paine's 1775-76 pamphlet **Common Sense**, considered the single most important publication of the American Revolution. Paine argued that Britain ruled the colonies for her own benefit and did not take into consideration the best interests of the colonists. He also wrote that it was absurd for an island to rule the continent and that America was not a British nation. Instead, it was composed of influences and people from all of Europe. If Britain were the mother country of America, that made her actions all the more horrendous, for no mother would treat her children so brutally. If America were to remain part of Britain, it would be dragged into unnecessary wars and would be prevented from excelling in international commerce. Furthermore, the distance between the two nations made governing the colonies from England unwieldy. Responses to petitions of wrongdoings to Parliament could take over a year to receive. Paine also drew upon the Puritanical belief that the colonies were created by God as a safe haven from the persecution of British rule. With its accessible language and writing style, *Common Sense* appealed to the masses and won popular support for the idea of independence. Paine also popularized the idea that ordinary people can understand and participate in government. This idea for transformation from monarchy to a government in which the people would govern themselves was truly revolutionary.

First published on January 10, 1776, the pamphlet made the case for American independence using a style of writing that was accessible to the average person. By the end of 1776, 250,000 copies had been sold, the equivalent of 35 million today. Almost half of the nation had either read the pamphlet or had it read to them. *Common Sense* sold for a shilling and, in what turned out to be an effective marketing strategy, Paine pledged that all proceeds would be used to purchase supplies for the Continental Army. [3]

Auguste Millière [Public domain] PD-US, via Wikimedia Commons. https://commons.wikimedia.org/wiki/File:Thomas_Paine.jpg; By Scanned by uploader, originally by Thomas Paine. [Public domain], via Wikimedia Commons. https://commons.wikimedia.org/wiki/File:Commonsense.jpg. Caption source: Feurerherd, Peter, "How Thomas Paine Marketed the Revolution," *JStor Daily*. January 10, 2017. https://daily.jstor.org/how-thomas-paine-marketed-the-revolution/.

Common Sense alarmed the American gentry. It was one thing to encourage ordinary people to involve themselves in protests and boycotts or even vote for representatives; it was something else to spread the idea that they could be elected leaders and participate in the making of policy. As one loyalist wrote in response to Thomas Paine: "I find no Common Sense in this pamphlet, but much uncommon frenzy. It is an outrageous insult on the common sense of Americans, an insidious attempt to poison their minds and seduce them from their loyalty and truest interest. The principles of government laid down in it are not only false but as such scarcely ever entered the head of a crazy politician. Even Hobbes would blush to own the author for a disciple. He unites the violence of a republican with all the folly of a fanatic.... I think it a duty which I owe to God, to my King and country, to counteract in this manner the poison it contains...."[4] Still, the idea of political and social equality would be the most compelling force of the American Revolution. To this day, *Common Sense* is the single best-selling title in American publishing history. During the war, officers would read it to their troops to remind them of what they were fighting for—freedom from monarchy and the benefits of democracy.

The American Revolution began on April 19, 1775, when British soldiers fought with colonial citizen soldiers in Lexington and Concord in Massachusetts. At the Second Continental Congress, which met less than a month later, an army was created with George Washington as its commander in chief. It was also suggested at the meeting that the colonies establish state governments separate from England. However, the colonists were still hopeful that they would reconcile with Britain. It was not their original intention to foment rebellion or create a republic. They became revolutionaries despite themselves.[5]

In 1776, Thomas Jefferson was encouraged by a committee of the Continental Congress to write a declaration of independence that would dissolve political ties between the United States and Britain. When he was drafting the document, Thomas Jefferson wrote, "Believe me, dear Sir: there is not in the British empire a man who more cordially loves a union with Great Britain than I do. But, by the God that made me, I will cease to exist before I yield to a connection on such terms as the British Parliament propose; and in this, I think I speak the sentiments of America."[6] On July 4, 1776, after the 13 colonies and Britain had been at war for more than a year, 50 members of the Continental Congress signed the **Declaration of Independence**. It is essentially a list of 27 grievances the colonists had against King George III. It explained why they wanted a legal separation and was an announcement to the international community that the colonies were striking out on their own. Politically, it followed the logic of *Common Sense* by identifying common grievances and promoting political equity to inspire national unity; it also asserted certain natural and legal rights, including a right of revolution.

The second sentence of the Declaration of Independence contains the most powerful words in American history: "We hold these truths to be self-evident, that all men are created equal, that they are endowed by their Creator with certain unalienable Rights, that among these are Life, Liberty, and the pursuit of Happiness." These words came to represent the moral standards which the United States should strive to follow. They also established the set of principles through which the Constitution should be interpreted. The words also form the basis of the belief in **American exceptionalism**, the idea that America is morally superior to other nations and is derived from a uniquely American ideology based on core values including liberty, equality, unity, and individualism. Of course, these terms, as understood by Jefferson and his cohorts, applied to white men living in the colonies. Jefferson himself was a slave owner and the document he drafted refers to the "merciless Indian savages." The concept of all people being created equal has been expanded over time to include disenfranchised groups, but the battle for true equality continues to this day, as we will see in chapters to come.

Declaration of Independence

A list of 27 grievances the colonists had against the King of England detailing why they wanted a legal separation, signed on July 4, 1776, by 50 members of the Continental Congress. Politically it followed the logic of Common Sense by identifying common grievances and promoting political equity to inspire national unity. The document asserted certain natural and legal rights, including a right of revolution.

American exceptionalism

A term first used by Alexis de Tocqueville in the 1800s to describe America as morally superior to other nations and as a nation derived from a uniquely American ideology, based on core values including liberty, equality, unity, and individualism.

2.3 The Articles of Confederation

confederation

A voluntary association of independent states who agree to let the central government undertake a limited number of activities, such as forming an army. The states do not allow the central government to place restrictions on many of the states' own actions.

Articles of Confederation

The 1777 document establishing the functions of the national government of the newly independent United States. It set forth an agreement. The government under the Articles proved too weak to rule effectively and it was replaced by the current Constitution.

Upon signing the Declaration of Independence, the colonists realized that there was power in numbers and they needed to organize. The 13 colonies—now states—formed a **confederation**, a voluntary association of independent states in which the central government undertakes a limited number of activities, such as forming an army. The states do not allow the central government to place restrictions on many of the states' own actions. Member states governed most of their own affairs. The first constitution governing the United States was called the **Articles of Confederation**, which was approved by the Second Continental Congress in November 1777. Before they were ratified, the Continental Congress used the Articles of Confederation to guide the Revolutionary War, conduct diplomatic relations with Europe and Native American territories, and deal with land issues. Once they were ratified, the Articles were intended to organize the colonies into states and establish the laws of the land. Under the Articles, power rested with the states and not with a centralized government. The Articles set up a common legislature, but there were no executive or judiciary branches. The absence of a strong central government ultimately rendered the Articles of Confederation ineffective and futile. Without a powerful national government, the Articles were limited. These limitations manifested themselves primarily in lack of economic power, absence of effective leadership, and legislative weaknesses.

Before the Constitution was written, the colonies were organized under the Articles of Confederation, which loosely bound the confederation of 13 sovereign states in a "league of friendship." The document, which consists of six pages of parchment stitched together, opens with the words: "To all to whom these Presents shall come, we the under signed Delegates of the States affixed to our Names, send greeting."

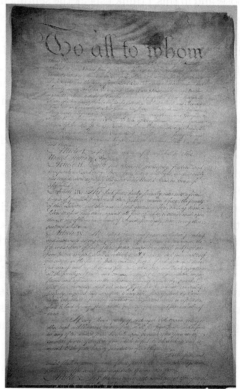

The U.S. National Archives (Articles of Confederation) [No restrictions or Public domain], via Wikimedia Commons. https://bit.ly/2RuhSBZ.

Limitations of the Articles of Confederation

Under the Articles of Confederation, the states retained their sovereignty and independence. Congress had some formal powers, but all of these were rendered ineffectual due to the power of the states. Without effective enforcement mechanisms, there was little motivation for states to fulfill their obligations and maximum incentives for them to free ride (letting others bear the costs). Because so many states were free riding, no one was contributing. It soon became apparent that the Articles of Confederation suffered serious limitations that would ultimately make them untenable.

Lack of Economic Power

The Articles of Confederation granted the national government limited economic power; thus, Congress had no way of financing its activities. Congress could not regulate trade between the states or negotiate trade agreements with foreign countries. States could therefore enforce any trade restrictions they wanted, meaning that import and export policies varied from state to state. There was little economic coordination among the states: Congress could coin money, but it could not establish a unitary and stable monetary system based on a single currency. States were permitted to issue their own currencies, which eventually led to inflation.

Congress also could not impose taxes. It was forced to rely on each state's willingness to pay its annual tax assessments and requisitions. Very few states cooperated. Requisitions were requests made by the national government for state resources to pay primarily for defense initiatives, including soldiers and supplies. Congress had the authority to request these resources from the states, but there was no enforcement mechanism to ensure the payment. Because national defense is a public good—meaning everyone can enjoy its benefits without having to contribute to its cost—it suffered from collective action problems. Why pay the cost for something you will ultimately get for free?

Under the Articles of Confederation, each state could issue its own currency, as seen here in this image of a three-dollar bill issued by Pennsylvania in 1776.

Continental Congress, United States of America(Lifetime: n.a.) [Public domain or Public domain], via Wikimedia Commons. https://bit.ly/2Wxfuhy.

The Articles of Confederation struggled with these collective action problems from 1775-1789. States either ignored requisitions entirely, or if they did comply, the payments were almost always partial and incomplete. Early accounts of the Continental Army leaving bloody footprints in the snow, living for days on a handful of chestnuts, being outnumbered by the British and short on arms, warm clothing, and ammunition were only too true. Indeed, about 10,000 American soldiers died in camps from exposure, wounds, starvation, and disease.[7] Much of this could have been avoided if the army had received the requisitions that Congress had requested from the states. The Articles faced similar problems with coordinating attendance at the confederation congress, enforcing a unified response to trade barriers imposed by foreign countries, and getting states to comply with legal rulings.[8]

The Articles of Confederation created a union of states that was not economically viable. Without revenue and without knowing whether states would contribute their share, Congress could not pay off the country's debts or even establish a national budget. The result was a disorganized and weak economy that prevented the national government from coordinating activities and implementing policies. By 1784, the new nation was suffering from serious economic depression.

Absence of Effective Leadership

In an effort to prevent the type of tyrannical authority exercised by the British crown, the Articles of Confederation intentionally did not establish a strong central government. Instead, it gave sovereign power to the states. What this decision meant was that the national government had no judiciary system and no way to enforce laws. States could choose to ignore national laws and not comply with national policies. In addition, because there were no federal courts, citizens had no place where they could file suit against the national government.

Captured in this 1787 portrait are Daniel Shays and Job Shattuck, leaders of the Massachusetts protest against the taxation and collection of debts from farmers that became known as Shays' Rebellion.

Cover of Bickerstaff's Boston Almanack [Public domain], via Wikimedia Commons. https://bit.ly/2D0mPzO.

Shays' Rebellion

A rebellion in 1787 by ex-Revolutionary War soldiers who feared losing their property over indebtedness. The former soldiers disrupted the trials of debtors in Massachusetts. The inability of the government to deal effectively with the rebellion showed the weakness of the political system at the time and led to support for revision of the Articles of Confederation.

The lack of an executive meant no one could represent the nation in its dealings with foreign countries. The absence of effective diplomatic representation put the nation at a disadvantage in its interactions abroad. Moreover, Congress could declare war but it could not dispatch an armed force. The government had to rely on state militias, which severely limited its capacity to respond to threats both at home and abroad. Congress was unable, for example, to react effectively when rebels protested the collection of debts and taxes from impoverished farmers.

Tempers of angry farmers in western Massachusetts reached a boiling point in August 1786 in what is known as **Shays' Rebellion**. Farmers led by former revolutionary war captain Daniel Shays seized county courthouses and disrupted debtors' trials. The 4,000 rebels under Shays' command went on to attempt to capture the United States' national weapons arsenal at the U.S. Armory in Springfield, Massachusetts. When Congress requested money from the states to form an army to suppress the rebellion, only Virginia paid a portion of its share, while the other states contributed nothing. Ultimately, Congress funded a smaller force, while Massachusetts raised its own force with funds borrowed from merchants and bankers from Boston. The rebels were ultimately crushed, but Shays' Rebellion called attention to concerns about the stability and strength of the nation. Fears of chaos and anarchy spread as the country found itself in true crisis. It became clear to leaders that they needed to get control over the states and that the country needed stronger centralized leadership. When the Framers drafted the Constitution and created the executive branch, they were drawing directly upon the lessons learned in Shays' Rebellion.

Legislative Weakness

In addition to the absence of strong centralized leadership, the Articles of Confederation suffered from rules that rendered Congress inefficient. Each state had one vote, meaning that small and large states had equal representation in Congress. This detail mattered because states differed vastly in population. Virginia, for example, had more than 10 times the number of people compared to Delaware and more than the populations of Delaware, Rhode Island, New Jersey, New Hampshire, and Georgia combined. Each state, however, had an equal vote in Congress. This system raised questions about fairness and accurate representation of the will of the people. It also made passing laws difficult because, for any law to pass, nine of 13 states had to agree. It took just five of the 13 states to block legislation. Five states with smaller populations could effectively band together in opposition to one state whose population was greater than theirs combined. Again, this raised concerns about equity and the possibility of overriding majority rule. Furthermore, the consent of all 13 states was required to make any revisions to the Articles of Confederation, which meant that any state had veto power over any proposed change. This requirement rendered the amendment process virtually useless, as it was extremely difficult to get a unanimous vote on any proposed change. There was essentially no way to fix any of the shortcomings of the Articles through an amendment process.

The end of the Revolutionary War on October 18, 1781, and the signing of the Treaty of Paris in 1783, confirmed the colonies' independence from Britain. While they had the Articles of Confederation as a blueprint for how to coexist, there were ultimately more weaknesses than strengths under the Articles. Because there were no executive or judicial branches except within the states, the states maintained autonomy and authority over every issue that was not specifically assigned to the Continental Congress. The states were united in a "firm league of friendship," but because of collective action problems, the states were reluctant to pay the costs of providing for that alliance. The limited power of the Continental Congress essentially stripped the national government of any real authority. Congress could pass laws but could not enforce them. Moreover, because Congress had no power to levy taxes or regulate trade, it was unable to finance any national initiatives. Being able to enforce mandates is critical for effective governance. The Articles of Confederation made it clear that enforcement would be impossible without a federal judiciary or executive leader. As the United States emerged as an independent country, addressing the shortcomings of the Articles became a priority.

2.4 The Constitutional Convention

Fifty-five representatives from 12 of the 13 states met in Philadelphia in May 1787 for the first **Constitutional Convention**. Their purpose in coming together was to amend the Articles of Confederation. The delegates ended up writing an entirely new constitution that established a federal form of government to replace the system created by the Articles of Confederation. What emerged from the Convention was an important lesson in decision-making and the strategies of compromise and consensus-building.

Constitutional Convention

A meeting of delegates in 1787 to revise the Articles of Confederation, which produced a new Constitution still in use today.

The Constitutional Convention took place in Independence Hall (then known as the Pennsylvania State House) in Philadelphia, PA.

Ritu Manoj Jethani / Shutterstock.com

Who Was There?

For 100 days, delegates debated about how the United States should be governed. They convened in the Pennsylvania State House from May 14 to September 17, 1787, and though they had originally gathered to revise the Articles of Confederation, they soon found themselves drafting a new Constitution. George Washington was elected to preside over the Constitutional Convention to which 70 delegates had been appointed. Only 55 were able to attend. Every state except Rhode Island sent delegates.

PHOTOGRAPH OF FIRST PAGE OF SECRETARY'S RECORD OF VOTES *
The original uploader was Tarmstro99 at English Wikisource. (Transferred from en.wikisource to Commons.) [Public domain], via Wikimedia Commons. https://bit.ly/2G2Du6Y.

The delegates used the lessons of experience, state constitutions, and English law to draft the Constitution. The states had originally appointed 70 representatives to the Constitutional Convention, but only 55 delegates were able to attend. The delegates who did come were men who hailed from the best-educated and wealthiest classes, including Continental Army veterans and members of the Congress of the Confederation. Their average age was 42. Of the 74 delegates, 31 had attended college. At least 19 owned slaves. It was an elite, male-only assembly—no common laborers, skilled craftspeople, small farmers, women, or racial minorities were present. Most of the delegates were landowners with significant holdings. The economic background of the majority of the delegates has led to the suggestion that the Constitution was drafted primarily by wealthy property owners who wanted a stronger government that could protect their property rights. In his 1913 book, *An Economic Interpretation of the Constitution*, Charles Beard claimed that the Framers were motivated by their desire to safeguard their economic interests. He suggested that the convention and the ratification process were controlled by three categories of people: 1) those who owned public securities and wanted a government that could pay its debts; 2) merchants who wanted to protect commerce; and 3) land speculators who wanted to protect property rights. While Beard might have underestimated the more noble intentions of the Framers and downplayed their genuine desire for self-governance, his story about the broad economic and social-class motives was probably accurate. The Framers were people in positions of power and their decisions were motivated by the rational action of protecting their property and wealth. They were likely guided by their concern about the instability and economic chaos of the confederation. They were also concerned about the effect it would have on their own wealth as well as the rise of a democratic and egalitarian culture among the common people–and their increasing control of the state legislatures.

The only state that did not send delegates was Rhode Island. Rhode Island was concerned that one of the aims of the Convention was to nationalize the currency and that this would be detrimental to the state's economy. Rhode Islanders also had a fierce sense of independence and were suspicious of calls for a stronger national government. Several of the most famous patriots did not attend the Convention, including John Hancock, Samuel Adams, Thomas Jefferson, and John Adams. Patrick Henry turned down the invitation because he "smelt a rat in Philadelphia tending toward the monarchy."[9]

Conflicts

The delegates met for four months in the sweltering summer heat of Philadelphia. The Constitutional Convention was intended to be a closed-door meeting about institutional design. The Framers were deliberate about who was included and who was excluded. Even though they were creating a government whose power would ultimately reside with the people, their mistrust of popular passions kept them from opening up negotiations to a wider public. In order to protect the secrecy of the meetings, the windows and doors of Convention Hall were sealed despite the heat and humidity that rose rapidly in the airless rooms. Because the meetings were conducted in secret, we do not have many records of the proceedings. Most of what we know about the convention comes from the notes taken by James Madison.

Strength of the Central Government

One of the first conflicts to be resolved at the Convention was the decision about how strong the central government should be vis-à-vis the states. Those like James Madison and Alexander Hamilton argued for a strong central government because they were concerned that human impulses, greed, and personal interests would override the efforts of state governments. They were worried that the states had given too much power to the people, whose involvement–which derived from misinformation and lack of experience–would only lead to chaos. Therefore, they wanted a document that would provide for a strong central government with formal authority that would answer to the public, but which would not be overly responsive or accessible to the people.

Others were concerned about the central government taking away too much autonomy from the states. They argued instead for a constitution that would establish a decentralized government with informal authority. The delegates ultimately agreed that they would create a system of shared powers between a central government and state governments. This system, known as **federalism**, differs from a confederation in which the states retain power over the whole, and it differs from a unitary system in which all the power rests with the central government. Federalism was viewed as an effective compromise because it protected states' rights while at the same time giving the central government its own source of power and legitimacy.

Large States vs. Small States

Federalism provided the basic framework for the new government, but the delegates still had to work through several other issues that divided them, including how to protect the rights of small states while at the same time acknowledging the representative power of large states. Two plans were proposed to resolve this issue. The **Virginia Plan**, drafted by James Madison and presented by Edmund Randolph, provided for a strong national government organized into three branches. It had two houses in the legislature, an executive chosen by the legislature, a national judiciary also appointed by the legislature, and a council of revision comprising the executive and some judiciary branch members with veto power to override state laws. There were two key features of the plan: 1) a national legislature with supreme powers in which the lower legislative house would be elected directly by the people in proportion to each state's population; and 2) members of the lower house would elect the upper house. The Virginia Plan favored large states because they would have more representatives and therefore would have more power in the legislature.

Smaller states responded with the **New Jersey Plan**, presented by William Paterson. This plan sought to amend rather than replace the Articles of Confederation. It called for a multi-person executive so that no one person would have too much power. More importantly, the plan proposed one vote per state in the legislature, thereby protecting smaller states' interests while enhancing the power of the national government.

federalism

A political system in which authority is shared between a central government and state or regional governments.

Virginia Plan

A plan submitted to the Constitutional Convention that proposed a new form of government, not a mere revision of the Articles of Confederation. The plan envisioned a much stronger national government structured around three branches. James Madison prepared the initial draft.

New Jersey Plan

A plan of government proposed by William Paterson as a substitute for the Virginia Plan in an effort to provide greater protection for the interests of small states. It recommended that the Articles of Confederation be amended, not replaced, with a single house in Congress, in which each state would have an equal vote.

Great Compromise

The agreement that prevented the collapse of the Constitutional Convention because of friction between large and small states. It reconciled their interests by awarding states representation in the Senate on a basis of equality and in the House of Representatives in proportion to each state's population.

separation of powers

A principle of the Constitution that declares that political power is to be shared among the three branches of government.

What ultimately resulted was one of the most significant compromises in American political decision-making. The Connecticut Plan, or **Great Compromise**, kept much of the framework of the Virginia Plan and proposed a strong central government that could tax its citizens, regulate commerce, conduct foreign affairs, and organize the military. It would consist of a single executive, a national judiciary, and a legislature that would be divided into a House of Representatives (based on population size and elected directly by the people) and a Senate (composed of two members per state, elected by state legislatures). With its plan for two legislative houses, the Great Compromise reconciled the interests of large and small states. Legislation would require the approval of both houses, so that neither large states nor small states could be over or under represented (or have too much influence on the entire government). Further, the **separation of powers** would allow the Senate, whose members were elected by the state legislatures, to cool the passions of members of the House of Representatives, who would be elected directly by the people. Similarly, the president, who would be chosen indirectly by the Electoral College, would have veto power to serve as an additional check on the excesses of democracy.

FIGURE 2.1 The Virginia Plan vs. The New Jersey Plan

Virginia Plan	The Great Compromise	New Jersey Plan
• Favored by large states • Two houses of Congress • Representation based on population • A strong central government	• Two houses of Congress • Equal representation in the Senate • Representation based on population in the House of Representatives	• Favored by small states • One house of Congress • Each state would have equal representation • Similar to the Articles of Confederation

North vs. South

Three-Fifths Compromise

Presented as a solution to the conflict of whether slaves should be counted as part of the population. As the result of the compromise, slaves were counted as three-fifths of a person (every five slaves counted as three people) in determining a state's representation in Congress.

The next challenge the delegates had to confront was how to account for slaves when determining a state's population size. At the time of the Constitutional Convention, slavery was still legal in the North and the South. There were significantly more slaves in the South, however, where they comprised 40 percent of the population. If slaves were counted as part of the population, the number of representatives from the South would increase significantly. Delegates from the South wanted slaves to be fully counted as persons because this calculation would benefit their representative power in the national legislature. Delegates from the North disagreed with counting the slaves as persons because doing so would disadvantage them. The **Three-Fifths Compromise** was presented to resolve the conflict: each slave would count as three-fifths of a person (or every five slaves would count as three people) in determining representation in Congress. This decision, while certainly a low point from a humanitarian and moral perspective, was another example of compromise.

The counting of slaves was one of the most contentious topics that the delegates to the Constitutional Convention debated. The issue was not whether slavery should be abolished, but rather how slaves would be counted in determining a state's population for representation in Congress and for taxing purposes. In what became known as the Three-Fifths Compromise, the delegates decided that every five slaves would count as three people.

Davis, Theodore R., Artist. A slave auction at the south / from an original sketch by Theodore R. Davis. , 1861. Photograph. https://www.loc.gov/item/98510250/.

Many delegates were concerned about the issue of slavery more broadly. Several proposed that it be banned. Slavery was an extremely divisive topic and, in order to move the debate forward, the delegates compromised by agreeing that the importation of slaves could continue until 1808. With this decision, the South won 20 more years of unrestricted slave trade. Moreover, it was also decided that slaves who had escaped to the North would be returned to their owners. It is interesting to note that the word *slavery* did not actually appear in the Constitution until more than 80 years after the document was written. Slavery was made illegal by the Thirteenth Amendment, passed in 1865.

The Presidency

The Great Compromise suggested that cooperation at the Convention was possible. The delegates agreed to follow the Virginia Plan's proposal of a single executive. The delegates reasoned that during times of war, it would be ineffective to have a plural executive. Once they had settled on a single executive, the delegates had to decide how this person would be elected. They did not want to follow the Virginia Plan's idea about choosing the executive based on a vote of state legislatures. They also rejected the idea of a direct election by the people because this would be "too much upon the democratic order." They thus developed the idea of the Electoral College, in which the president would be selected according to votes from each state equal to its number of representatives and senators in Congress. In the event of a tie when the members of the Electoral College cast their vote for president, the House of Representatives would choose the president, with each state having one vote.

2.5 What the Framers Framed

On September 17, 1787, three months after the Constitutional Convention convened, the delegates signed the Constitution and the meeting adjourned. Most of the delegates agreed that the new Constitution was not perfect, but it was the best they could produce given the urgency and the compromises that needed to be made. Hamilton and Madison, who came from large states had pushed for a strong central government with broad power. Leaders from smaller states advocated for states to be supreme under a Constitution that corrected the weaknesses of the Articles of Confederation, but did not significantly expand the authority of a central government. The document that emerged from their contentious debates was the product of compromise and the desire for balance. It was at its very core a political process that produced a government with a separation of powers.[10]

republic

A government in which power resides with representatives elected by the people at large.

sovereign

The ultimate authority to rule a land and its people.

amendment

A change in, or addition to, a constitution. Amendments are proposed by a two-thirds vote of both houses of Congress or by a convention called by Congress at the request of two-thirds of the state legislatures and ratified by approval of three-fourths of the states.

The Framers created a **republic**, a government based on the principles of popular sovereignty, representative democracy, and limits on the power of government. These principles were widely discussed throughout the eighteenth century among educated people concerned about the nature of government and how best to constitute one. Given Shays' rebellion and other events in the states, the Framers were anxious about putting too much power in the hands of ordinary citizens. It would be wrong, however, to suggest that they intended to create another aristocracy. There is no greater evidence of this than the preamble of the Constitution itself. The words "We the people of the United States, … do ordain and establish this Constitution for the United States of America," makes crystal clear that the people as a whole, not the states or any other institution, individual, or group, are **sovereign**. What "the people" create, they may also alter, via a formal change or **amendment** through their representatives. They can also destroy the Constitution and create a new one through a properly established convention, such as the one that created the Constitution in the first place. Alexander Hamilton, the framer most fearful of "the people," said as much when he wrote "that fundamental principle of republican government, which admits the right of the people to alter or abolish the established Constitution, whenever they find it inconsistent with their happiness."[11]

Given the debate that resulted in the Three-Fifths Compromise, however, it was not entirely clear who "the people" were. If slaves were not fully counted as persons, what about women, free black men, or servants? For the most part, these matters were left to the individual states to establish, but republican principles of the time determined that "the people" meant those eligible to vote and men who owned property. Only independent citizens were thought to have the virtues necessary to participate in government. Women were assumed to be dependent. Similarly, men who worked with their hands and sold their labor were thought to be dependent on their patrons. It followed that only autonomous individuals with no master were qualified to be citizens. Men who owned property, presumably self-sufficient farmers and landed gentry, would be sufficiently free from market interests and could be trusted to avoid the temptations of power. Thus, "the people" were defined narrowly as independent men who were disinterested in the privileges of power and could sacrifice their private interests for those of the public interest.[12] Of course, there were few truly independent and disinterested men; as a practical matter, the states used male gender and property classifications to define who were citizens and therefore eligible to vote.

The intent of the Framers was to create a government with a system of representation designed to temper the power of the people. Madison in particular argued that with regard to public affairs, the people would be motivated by self-interest rather than that of the common good. A "well-constructed Union" would control the effects of self-interest if the people govern indirectly through representatives, rather than directly. As he put it, "representatives would refine and enlarge the public views, by passing them through the medium of a chosen body of citizens, whose wisdom may best discern the true interest of their country."[13] This system of representation was embodied in the Constitution along with the following obstacles placed in the path of democracy.

Indirect Elections

Initially, the members of the Senate were to be chosen by the state legislatures (this was changed to direct election in 1913 by the Seventeenth Amendment), the president was to be elected by members of the Electoral College, and the entire federal judiciary was to be appointed by the president and approved only by the Senate. Therefore, voters could only influence the actions of these office holders indirectly through their representatives. This form of indirect influence is different from a system of direct democracy, in which every citizen actively and directly participates in every political decision that is made.

Separation of Powers

Because governmental power would be divided among the legislative, executive, and judicial branches of government, this created a *separation of powers*. Majorities would need to be formed in each of these institutions before the people at large could express power. As a result, the system of *checks and balances* was born in order to regulate the actions of each branch. For example, the president can reject legislation and return it to Congress, acting as a check on the legislature. However, Congress can override vetoed legislation, which requires a supermajority, or a two-thirds majority vote, and this can potentially prevent popular bills from becoming laws. Congress can also check the power of the executive branch by rejecting presidential nominations, such as Supreme Court justices or Cabinet members. The power of the courts to rule congressional or presidential actions unconstitutional was added by the Supreme Court itself in the case of *Marbury v. Madison*, which established the power of **judicial review**. This is the power of the judicial branch of the federal government to rule actions unconstitutional. Another check is the **filibuster,** a procedure adopted by the Senate designed to enable a minority of members to delay and often prevent popular bills from being brought to a vote.

judicial review

The power of courts to declare an act of Congress unconstitutional. It is also a way of limiting the power of popular majorities.

filibuster

A parliamentary procedure used in the Senate designed to enable a minority of members to delay and often prevent popular bills from being brought to a vote. The practice followed from the tradition of unlimited debate in the senate. Those holding the floor would do so continuously until the majority backed down or organized a vote of three-fifths of the members to end debate.

Ratification

While the delegates had signed the Constitution, it still needed to be ratified, or approved and voted into law, by state conventions in at least nine of the 13 states. It is important to note that the decision rule in each of these conventions was simple majority rule. In some states, such as Delaware and New Jersey, the vote among the delegates for adoption was unanimous. In others, such as Massachusetts, New York, and New Hampshire, the final vote was a bare majority in favor. The Constitution was eventually ratified by all 13 states, but only after significant debate about the distribution of power between the central government and the states.

2.6 Federalists vs. Anti-Federalists

Federalists

Supporters of the Constitution during ratification debates in state legislatures.

Anti-Federalists

Opponents to the ratification of the Constitution who valued liberty above all else and believed it could be protected only in a small republic. They emphasized states' rights and worried that the new central government was too strong.

Federalist Papers

A series of 85 essays written in support of the new Constitution.

Federalist No. 10

An essay composed by James Madison that argues that liberty is safest in a large republic because many interests (factions) exist. Such diversity makes tyranny by the majority more difficult because it would be difficult for any one faction to assume total control.

factions

A term used by James Madison to refer to groups of people who come together based on their interests, such as farmers and merchants, Northerners and Southerners, debtors and creditors.

Ratification rested on a debate between **Federalists** (those who favored the new Constitution and a strong central government) and the **Anti-Federalists** (those who opposed the new Constitution and a strong central government). The Anti-Federalists' opposition to a strong central government came from their aversion to a monarchical system like the one under which the colonies were previously ruled. They argued that liberty could only be secured in small republics. Otherwise the national government would be distant from the people and risked becoming tyrannical. They also feared that a strong national government would use its powers to appropriate and eventually annihilate state functions. The Anti-Federalists believed that there should be many more restrictions on the national government than were contained in the proposed Constitution. They presented these arguments in a series of 16 papers published under the name *Brutus*. This was in honor of the Roman republican who was one of the participants in the assassination of Emperor Julius Caesar to prevent him from overthrowing the Roman Republic.

The Federalist Papers

Federalists wrote their own series of 85 essays known as the ***Federalist Papers***. The Federalists published their editorials in New York newspapers under the name "Publius." Alexander Hamilton authored Federalist No. 1 and then recruited James Madison and John Jay for the project. Together they organized an effective ratification campaign, targeting those states where the ratification struggle was close. Two of the most important *Federalist Papers* are **Federalist No. 10** and No. 51, written by James Madison. In Federalist No. 10, Madison argued that personal liberty is safest in large (extended) republics. A nation's size was actually an advantage in controlling **factions**, or groups of people: in a large nation, there would be so many diverse interests and different factions that no one faction would be able to gain control of the government. In No. 51, Madison contends that the institutions proposed in the Constitution would not lead to corruption or tyranny. The system of checks and balances and the principle of shared powers would prevent any one unit of government from becoming too powerful and overtaking the others.

In the late 1780s, Alexander Hamilton, James Madison, and John Jay wrote a series of 85 letters to newspapers in support of the Constitution. They wrote the names under the pseudonym "Publius" and argued that the new Constitution would empower the federal government to act effectively and coherently in the national interest. The Federalist Papers were published in 1788 as book titled *The Federalist*.

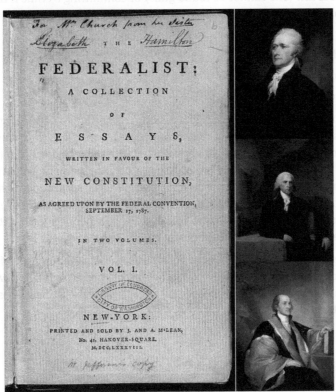

Publius (pseudonym) [Alexander Hamilton, John Jay, James Madison]. [Public domain], via Wikimedia Commons. https://commons. wikimedia.org/wiki/File:The_Federalist_(1st_ed,_1788,_vol_I,_title_page).jpg; The Federalist (vol. 1) J and A M'Lean, publisher, New York, 1788. From Rare Books and Special Collections Division in Madison's Treasures ; John Trumbull [Public domain], via Wikimedia Commons. https://commons.wikimedia.org/wiki/File:Alexander_Hamilton_by_John_Trumbull,_1806.png PD-US; Gilbert Stuart [Public domain], via Wikimedia Commons. https://commons.wikimedia.org/wiki/File:James_Madison_by_Gilbert_Stuart.jpg; Gilbert Stuart [Public domain], via Wikimedia Commons. https://commons.wikimedia.org/wiki/File:John_Jay_(Gilbert_Stuart_portrait).jpg PD-US.

The Bill of Rights

The Anti-Federalists also took issue with the fact that the Constitution did not have a bill of rights. As Patrick Henry put it, "A Bill of Rights may be summed up in a few words. What do they tell us? That our rights are reserved. Why not say so? Is it because it will consume too much paper?"[14] The Federalists responded in Federalist No. 84 with reasons for the absence of a bill of rights. Written by Hamilton, Federalist No. 84 argued that there were several guarantees in the Constitution already, including:

writ of habeas corpus

A court order directing a police officer, sheriff, or warden who has a person in custody to bring the prisoner before a judge to show sufficient cause for his or her detention. The purpose of the order is to prevent illegal arrests and unlawful imprisonment. Under the Constitution, the writ cannot be suspended, except during invasion or rebellion.

bill of attainder

A law that declares a person, without trial, to be guilty of a crime.

ex post facto law

A law which makes criminal an act that was legal when it was committed, that increases the penalty for a crime after it has been committed, or that changes the rules of evidence to make conviction easier. The state legislatures and Congress are forbidden to pass such laws according to Article 1, Sections 9 and 10, of the Constitution.

Bill of Rights

The first 10 amendments of the U.S. Constitution, containing a list of individual rights and liberties, such as freedom of speech, religion, and the press.

- **Writ of habeas corpus** (one cannot be unlawfully imprisoned);
- No **bill of attainder** (one cannot be found guilty and punished without a trial);
- No **ex post facto law** (one cannot be found guilty of committing a crime if the act was legal at the time it was committed);
- Trial by jury;
- Privileges and immunities;
- No religious tests for political office;
- Obligation of contracts

Furthermore, most states had bills of rights making the need for a national one less immediate. The Federalists also feared that no list of rights could ever be complete or exhaustive and that the government would therefore be invited to abridge or ignore the "excluded" rights. To address this concern, Madison proposed what would become the Ninth Amendment, which declares that citizens have additional rights beyond those enumerated. When he introduced the amendment to Congress, Madison said, "This is one of the most plausible arguments that I have ever heard urged against the admission of a bill of rights into this system; but, I conceive, that it may be guarded against. I have attempted it, as the gentlemen may see."[15]

Despite the reassurances provided by the Federalists, the Anti-Federalists refused to ratify the Constitution without a bill of rights. Twelve amendments, or specific rights that would be protected by the government, were eventually proposed and 10 of these were ratified. These became known as the **Bill of Rights**.

The Final Vote

The ratification process ended when the final state, Rhode Island, ratified the Constitution on May 29, 1790, almost three years after the delegates to the Constitutional Convention approved it. Once the Bill of Rights had been included and the Constitution was sent to individual states for ratification, economic interests played a major role in determining who was in favor and who was against adopting the new document. In general, merchants who lived in urban areas, owned land, held IOUs issued by the government to pay for the Revolutionary War, and did not have slaves were in favor of the Constitution. Farmers and slave owners who did not hold government IOUs tended to oppose ratification.[16]

Small states ratified the Constitution quickly and unanimously. By January 2, 1788, Delaware, New Jersey, and Georgia had all signed. Pennsylvania, Massachusetts, Maryland, and South Carolina also came on board fairly quickly despite some internal debates. The battle for ratification was hardest fought in Virginia and New York. Virginia was the largest of the states. The Anti-Federalists, led by Patrick Henry, and joined by Governor William Randolph and George Mason, refused to sign the Constitution. After 22 days of debate, Virginia ratified the Constitution in an 89 to 79 vote. In New York, the situation was even more tense. New York City supported the Constitution, but the rest of the state opposed it. The debate that raged in New York led to the writing of the *Federalist Papers* and the Anti-Federalist response, *The Federalist Farmer*. New York eventually signed the Constitution in a 30 to 27 vote. For its part, Rhode Island refused to even have a Constitutional Convention and only joined the union two months after George Washington became president. New Hampshire became the ninth state to ratify the Constitution in June 1789, and with that, the Constitution had the majority it needed to be the law of the land.

TABLE 2.1 Ratification Votes for the U.S. Constitution

State	Date	Vote For	Vote Against
Delaware	December 8, 1787	30	9
Pennsylvania	December 12, 1787	46	23
New Jersey	December 18, 1787	38	0
Georgia	January 2, 1788	26	0
Connecticut	January 9, 1788	128	40
Massachusetts	February 16, 1788	187	168
Maryland	April 26, 1788	63	11
South Carolina	May 23, 1788	149	73
New Hampshire	June 21, 1788	57	47
Virginia	June 25, 1788	89	79
New York	June 26, 1788	30	27
North Carolina	November 21, 1789	194	77
Rhode Island	May 29, 1790	34	32

Despite the debates that delayed ratification, the states ultimately agreed that the Constitution addressed several problems that the Articles of Confederation had not resolved and shifted many powers from the states to the central government. To be sure, the Constitution has proven to be an enduring document, in part because it is a short, flexible one providing for broad principles of government. This allows it to be adapted to the changing needs of the nation over the years. Its brevity and breadth have also provided for enduring debates about how its provisions should be interpreted. Close to 10,000 amendments have been proposed in Congress since 1789. These have included a wide range of issues such as equal rights for women, prayer in public schools, abolishing the Electoral College, and limiting personal wealth to $1 million. Some amendments get passed, but the vast majority of them do not receive enough support to make it through the constitutional ratification process. In fact, only 17 amendments have been passed since the original 10 amendments were included in the Bill of Rights. Part of the reason why most amendments do not pass is that the Framers made the formal amendment process very difficult. Article V of the Constitution provides for two methods for the proposal and two methods for the ratification of an amendment. A constitutional amendment may be proposed by either a two-thirds vote in each house of Congress or by a national convention called by Congress at the request of two-thirds of the state legislatures. The latter method has never been used. Ratification can then occur either by a positive vote by three-fourths of the state legislatures (38 states) or by a positive vote in the special conventions called in three-fourths of the states. Congress has the power to decide which method of ratification to adopt.

2.7 The Living Constitution

The Constitution is the rulebook for the game of American politics. It provides the framework and the foundation for the sources of political power and for how institutions and policies respond to the will of the people. The rules of the game can and have changed over time as the result of amendments, judicial interpretation (as we will see in Chapter 14), and political practices, which is why we often refer to it as the "living Constitution." These changes suggest that the Constitution can be flexible, adaptable, and responsive. But these changes are not easily won. Only 17 amendments have been added in more than 200 years for two main reasons: the road to the Supreme

Court for judicial (re)interpretation of the Constitution is long and arduous, and changing political practices occur over many years and across several administrations.

While our system remains heavily influenced by the eighteenth-century principles that guided the Framers, the United States is far more democratic and responsive to popular will than the Framers intended it to be. The American citizen has a loud voice in what the government does. But those pressing for change and political innovation often find themselves up against the obstacles designed to slow, block, or veto action. The existence of these barriers does not absolutely prevent change from occurring, but efforts to alter the system require time, money in many cases, and high levels of commitment, pressure, and participation.

2.8 What Can I Do?

We refer to the Constitution as a living document. Yes, it is a record of decisions that were made when the country was founded, but it is also a blueprint for government that was designed to be adapted and modified as the United States expanded. While you cannot change the Constitution directly, you can take important actions to influence its direction.

1. It is important to read the Constitution and understand what it says about your rights and about the government's obligations to you. As we have said in this chapter, the Constitution is the blueprint for American government. If you have questions about why we have certain policies and laws, the best place to look for answers is the Constitution. Do yourself the favor of reading it at least once in your lifetime. Some people carry a pocket size copy of the Constitution with them as reminder of where we come from and as reference for decoding political decision-making.

2. The Framers of the Constitution were primarily concerned with striking the right balance between representation, state autonomy, and federal responsibility. The tension between state rights and national rights continues to play out in the courtroom. There are those who continue to argue that political decision-making should rest first and foremost with the states and that there should be limits on the size and scope of the national government. Others argue that the federal government should be the locus of power and should delegate to the states. Which side you take in this debate stems from your ideas about democracy. When you vote in elections, you may find yourself drawn to a candidate who supports a particular side in the debate. By supporting that candidate, you can advance your beliefs about the role the national government should play.

If the Constitution is particularly interesting to you, you could take classes in Constitutional law and even consider becoming an attorney or policymaker. Becoming an expert on the Constitution is a highly valued trait in the United States. Being directly involved in how the document is modified to fit current needs in society can be immensely rewarding. While this seems to be a lot of work, remember that becoming an attorney or public official can be a well-paying career. The personal benefits, knowledge, prestige, and salary are yours to keep.

2.9 What's the Alternative?

In order to make the United States more democratic we could 1) move to a parliamentary system, and/or 2) move toward proportional representation.

In all democracies, there is an inherent trade-off between representation and governability. The government must come up with ways to ensure that it represents the diversity of interests in society, while at the same time allowing for majority rule. Our system of presidential democracy means that we have one office with a national constituency. This can make it easier to govern a diverse population. But it can also create a system that is not as representative of different political beliefs. An alternative to a presidential system is a parliamentary government. In a parliamentary government, the executive and legislative branches are fused together, which means that the government needs the confidence of a majority in the legislature to come to and remain in power. Some scholars argue that this system is more democratic because it increases accountability for the Prime Minister and members of the Cabinet, who are called upon to justify their actions and decisions at regular Parliamentary sessions. Supporters of parliamentary democracies also contend that the quality of leaders is better because it is up to the parties to choose the best among them to become party leader. In presidential systems, elections can become popularity contests in which the winner may not be the most qualified to lead. On the other hand, in presidential systems, it is the citizens themselves who get to choose their leader.

The following figure shows the key differences and similarities between Presidential and Parliamentary systems.

FIGURE 2.2 Presidential vs. Parliamentary Systems

Parliamentary System

- Leader is prime minister
- Citizens vote for representatives
- Representatives vote for leader
- Fusion between executive and legislative branches
- Citizens elect members of Parliament
- Most common form of Democracy
- One political party in control
- Executive and legislative both in Parliament
- Can have ceremonial head of state (i.e., the Queen of England), but has no real power
- Examples include the United Kingdom and Canada

Presidential System

- Leader is president
- Citizens vote for leader
- Citizens vote for representatives
- Separation between executive and legislative branches
- System of checks and balances
- Judges appointed by executive
- Different political parties control
- Examples include the United States and France

Similarities

- Both are republics
- Citizens vote directly and indirectly for their leaders
- Can have one or more main branches of government
- One main leader who is the head of the military and government

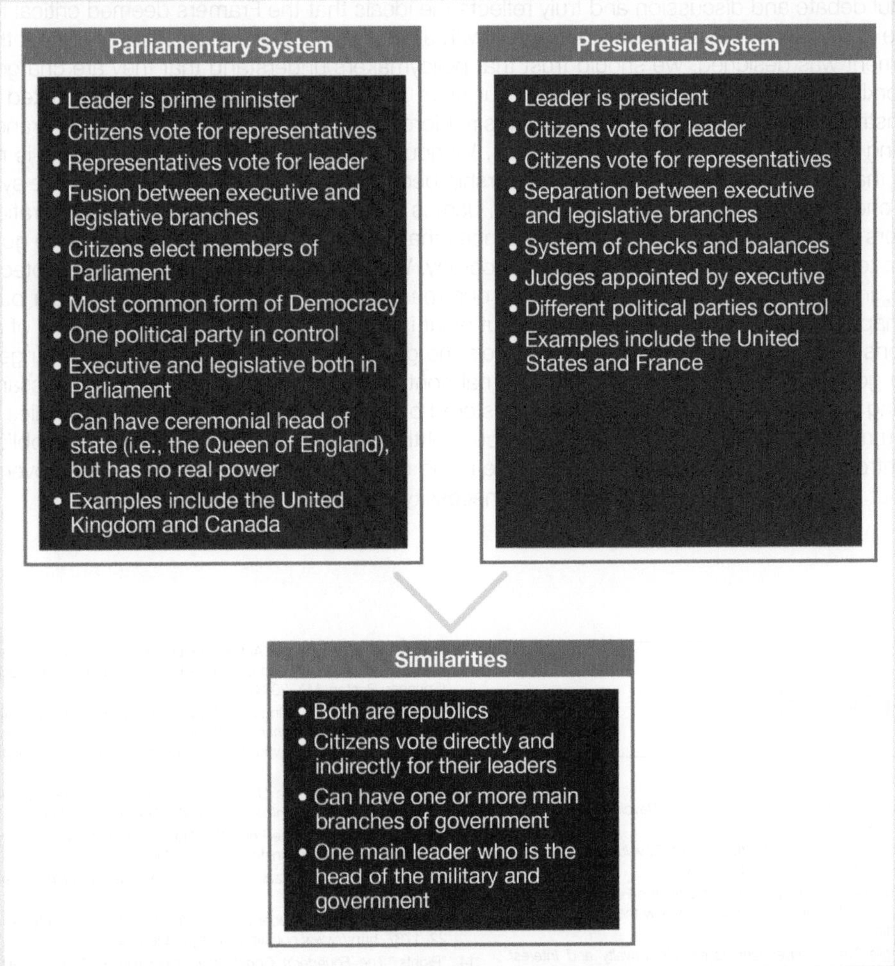

The fact that in presidential systems it is the citizens who choose the leader can make the government more democratic. But the role that money plays in elections can undermine representation. Without money, it is very hard if not impossible to win a campaign in the United States. The role of money in elections has increased the likelihood that incumbents, or those already holding office, get reelected. This can make it difficult for new people and those who come from lower socioeconomic situations to enter into politics. In parliamentary systems, money does not play a significant role in elections. Campaigns tend to be shorter and candidates are guaranteed media time.

The way we vote for our president can also be challenged for not being as democratic as possible. The United States has a winner-take-all election system, which means that all the Electoral College votes for a particular state go to the candidate who received the most votes in that state, even if it was 50.01 to 49.99 percent. The Electoral College vote may also not always align with the popular vote, so you could end up with a leader who got the most Electoral College votes but who did not win the majority of votes of the American people. There have been many suggestions offered for revising the Electoral College, but none of these have been adopted.

To make our system more responsive to the majority, some have proposed moving Congress to proportional representation. In their current form, congressional elections follow the same winner-takes-all formula as presidential elections. Under proportional representation, the congressional seats would be allocated based on the percentage of votes they received. This suggests that even a minority political party could win a seat in Congress, thus giving third parties and independent candidates a chance to win representation. There is nothing in the Constitution that would prevent a state from moving to proportional representation. While this could increase representation of views in the legislature, it would be an important departure from established political behavior. Moreover, the U.S. Senate is not democratic. Citizens are not represented proportionally, and this violates the principle of one person, one vote. Modest modifications could include giving Washington, D.C. a vote in the Senate or electing its members according to population.

The U.S. Constitution was drafted by some of the best political minds in history. It was the result of careful debate and discussion and truly reflects the ideals that the Framers deemed critical for effective governance. While we may not agree with all aspects of the Constitution or of how the government was designed, we should trust that policymakers understand that they are charged with working on behalf of the public good. Our strict separation of powers that is stipulated in the Constitution also ensures that democracy is reinforced. There is no danger of any one branch becoming too powerful and overtaking others. Without discarding the Constitution, there is no chance that the president could form a dictatorship because democracy is protected by the system of checks and balances. In *Federalist 51*, James Madison argues that it is this separation of powers and the system of checks and balances that guarantee our freedom, enable the government to act on our behalf, and ensure democracy. We also have a Bill of Rights that protects citizens, limits governmental encroachment on our freedoms, and allows us to maximize our pursuit of happiness. As Madison reminds us: "But what is government itself, but the greatest of all reflections on human nature? If men were angels, no government would be necessary. If angels were to govern men, neither external nor internal controls on government would be necessary. In framing a government which is to be administered by men over men, the great difficulty lies in this: you must first enable the government to control the governed; and in the next place oblige it to control itself. A dependence on the people is, no doubt, the primary control on the government; but experience has taught mankind the necessity of auxiliary precautions."[17]

Endnotes

1. Gordon S. Wood, *The Radicalism of the American Revolution* (New York: Alfred A. Knopf, 1992).

2. Jackson Turner Main, *The Social Structure of Revolutionary America* (Princeton, N.J.: Princeton University Press, 1965).

3. Peter Feurerherd, "How Thomas Paine Marketed the Revolution," *JStor Daily*, January 10, 2017, https://daily.jstor.org/how-thomas-paine-marketed-the-revolution/.

4. Rev. Charles Inglis, *The Deceiver Unmasked; Or, Loyalty and Interest United: In Answer to a Pamphlet Entitled Common Sense* (1776), http://americainclass.org/sources/makingrevolution/rebellion/text7/inglis-deceiverunmasked.pdf

5. Jack Rakove, *Revolutionaries: A New History of the Invention of America* (Houghton Mifflin Harcourt, 2010).

6. Letter from Thomas Jefferson to John Randolph. Philadelphia Pennsylvania, November 1775. (Retrieved at American Achieves Documents of the American Revolution, 1774-1776.) http://dig.lib.niu.edu/amarch/Series 4,Volume 3, Page 1706.

7. Keith L. Dougherty, *Collective Action Under the Articles of Confederation* (Cambridge: Cambridge University Press, 2001).

8. K. Dougherty, "Collective Action Under the Articles of Confederation," *The Encyclopedia of Public Choice*, eds. C. K. Rowley and F. Schneider (Springer, Boston, MA, 2004).

9. Christopher Klein., "7 Things You May Not Know About the Constitutional Convention," *History Channel*, September 17, 2012, http://www.history.com/news/7-things-you-may-not-know-about-the-constitutional-convention.

10. David B. Robertson, *The Original Compromise: What the Constitution's Framers Were Really Thinking* (New York: Oxford University Press, 2013).

11. Alexander Hamilton, "The Federalist No. 78," Constitution Society, June 14, 1788, http://www.constitution.org/fed/federa78.htm.

12. Gordon S. Wood, *The Radicalism of the American Revolution* (New York: Alfred A. Knopf, 1992).

13. James Madison, "The Federalist No. 10," Constitution Society, November 22, 1787, http://www.constitution.org/fed/federa10.htm.

14. "Rights," *The Founder's Constitution*, University of Chicago, accessed December 30, 2015, http://presspubs.uchicago.edu/founders/print_documents/v1ch14s39.html.

15. *James Madison: Writings*, ed. Jack N. Rakove (New York: Library of America, 1999), 437-452.

16. Charles A. Beard, *An Economic Interpretation of the Constitution* (Dover Publications, 2004).

17. James Madison, "Federalist #51: The Structure of the Government Must Furnish the Proper Checks and Balances Between the Different Departments," *Independent Journal* (February 6, 1788): http://constitution.org/fed/federa51.htm.

CHAPTER 3
Federalism: Two Governments in the Same Area

Introduction: Is Marijuana Legal or Illegal?

Under federalism, both the state and federal governments can write their own marijuana laws.

© Shutterstock, Inc.

controlled substance

A drug or substance whose manufacture, sale, and distribution is regulated by government and represents a potential for abuse.

sovereignty

The full right and power of a governing body over itself without interference from an outside government.

autonomy

The right of self-government or the freedom from external control or influence by another government.

A majority of states (29) and Washington, D.C. allow the possession and use of marijuana for medical purposes. Eight have legalized it for recreational use and another dozen effectively decriminalized the possession of small amounts.[1] The federal government, however, considers marijuana a **controlled substance** with no medical value, like methamphetamine and heroin. Marijuana remains illegal under federal law even in states that legalized it. In the recent past, casual users did not need to worry much because in 2013, Deputy U.S. Attorney General James Cole issued a memorandum saying federal prosecutors and law enforcement officials should only focus on preventing what it considered the more serious marijuana crimes. These include inter-state trafficking, distribution to minors, the associated use of firearms, driving under the influence, and growing or possessing marijuana on federal property.[2] In other words, the Obama administration chose not to enforce the letter of the law. However, Jeff Sessions, Donald Trump's attorney general, repealed Cole's memo, signaling that federal marijuana laws would again be fully enforced by federal authorities in the states that legalized it.

The two sets of marijuana laws cause confusion and put the states in direct confrontation with the federal government. Users risk being arrested and losing their jobs, parental rights, and federal benefits.[3] Banks are reluctant to do business with marijuana growers and dispensaries because doing so makes them potentially liable for aiding and abetting illegal activity under federal law. Not being able to bank or accept credit cards forces the industry to operate on a cash-only basis—a dangerous situation that attracts criminals. Furthermore, what one state does often affects its neighbors. The states of Oklahoma and Nebraska filed a federal lawsuit against Colorado, claiming that pot purchased legally in Colorado is being transported illegally into their states, overwhelming the police and courts.[4]

In the United States, constitutional authority exists among both the national and state governments. Both levels of government have some degree of **sovereignty** and **autonomy,** meaning states can enact laws independent of the national government and vice versa. Because both units of governments exist within the same territory, two layers of law and policy are superimposed on the same area.[5] As a result, citizens are subject to the laws of the state governments and the laws of the federal government, even if some laws, such as those regarding the possession of marijuana, contradict each other. This is federalism and the arrangement has advantages and disadvantages. Federalism encourages policy innovation and brings government closer to the people, but it also causes confusion, conflict, and duplication of effort. Perhaps there is no better example of this than the controversy over marijuana laws.

3.1 Why Federalism?

The system of federalism in the United States is the product of compromise. Recall from Chapter 2 that the first constitution of the United States was the Articles of Confederation, which was approved by the Second Continental Congress in 1777—a little more than a year after the 13 colonies declared their independence from Great Britain. In doing so, the colonies referred to themselves in the plural as "free and independent states."[6] Then, as now, the word "state" refers to a nation as a whole, especially one that is sovereign.[7] During the colonial period, Americans did not call themselves Americans; that term was used by British officials to refer to the colonists. The colonies of Virginia, Pennsylvania, and Massachusetts had histories of 150 years. The youngest colony, Georgia, was established nearly 100 years prior to the adoption of the Articles. Americans identified their states as their countries and themselves as citizens of whatever state in which they resided.[8] The Articles created only a weak form of union. The words used in the document make clear that "each state retains its sovereignty" and that "as Free and Independent States, they have full Power to levy War, conclude Peace, contract Alliances, establish Commerce, and to do all other Acts and Things which Independent States may of right do."[9] Taking the words seriously in 1778, France asked each of the 13 states to individually ratify the commercial and the military alliance signed in Paris with the United States.[10]

It would be ten years before the Articles would be scrapped for a new federal constitution, but in the meantime, the states took individual action. Each state printed its own money; some states used British pounds as standard while others used Spanish dollars. Even in states that used the British standard, the definition of the pound varied from 1,547 grains of silver in Georgia to 1,289 grains in Virginia, Connecticut, Rhode Island, Massachusetts and New Hampshire, to 966 grains in North Carolina and New York.[11] Congress could coin money, but it could not establish a single currency. The monetary system became a patchwork of coins and paper currencies minted by the states, the national government, and foreign countries. Some states refused to recognize other states' money, while others declared their own currency to be legal tender for all purposes, forcing out-of-state buyers to exchange money and allowing their citizens and governments to pay out-of-state creditors with questionable currency.[12]

George Washington presiding at the Convention of 1787 to revise the Articles of Confederation, 1787.

© Shutterstock, Inc.

The absence of a uniform currency disrupted trade among the states and made both public and private finance risky. Under the Articles, the national government could not regulate commerce between the states. Soon economic warfare erupted. States used tax policy to promote manufactured goods produced in their states by taxing products coming from out-of-state, effectively raising the price of their competitor's goods. "Gateway" states with the best harbors and rivers, such as New York, Pennsylvania, Massachusetts, and Maryland, taxed goods moving through their states, shifting the tax burden to out-of-state customers. In New York's case, taxes paid on items going to Connecticut covered about a third of New York's budget.[13] Connecticut retaliated by giving foreign manufacturers advantages over goods produced in adjoining states. When Britain banned American ships from trading with its remaining colonies, the national government declared a boycott. New Hampshire, Massachusetts, and Rhode Island followed by banning British ships from their harbors, but Connecticut, South Carolina, and Delaware welcomed British ships and the tariffs they paid while breaking the national boycott.[14] Britain, France, and other European governments began to conduct trade negotiations with individual states, bypassing the national government altogether and pitting the states against each other. When John Adams offered to resolve the issue by negotiating a commercial treaty with Great Britain, Britain declined, saying that the individual states would not be bound by it. The national government could not levy taxes; it was forced instead to rely on each state's willingness to pay its annual tax assessments. Very few states cooperated. As a result, the bonds and notes of the U.S. government were essentially worthless. Georgia declared war on the Creek Indian nation and Massachusetts raised a private army to quell Shays' rebellion.

As fears of chaos and anarchy spread, it became clear to national leaders that they needed to get control over the states. The lawyers, merchants, and southern planters, such as James Madison, John Adams, Alexander Hamilton, and George Washington, sought to create a stronger central government. They also understood that unifying power into a single national government would be unpopular. At issue was how to balance authority between state and national governments. Some of the delegates wanted to continue as a confederation of states but with increased national powers restricted to foreign affairs and national defense. Others wanted to diminish the power of the states. The system they created is known as federalism, a hybrid arrangement that mixes elements from a confederation, in which the states retain power over the whole, and a unitary system, in which all the power rests with the central government (see Figure 3.1). Federalism was viewed as an effective compromise because it protected states' sovereignty while at the same time giving the central government its own source of power and legitimacy. Both federal and state governments would exist in the same territory, yet have independent authority and some leverage over the other.

FIGURE 3.1 Comparing Unitary, Federal, and Confederal Governments

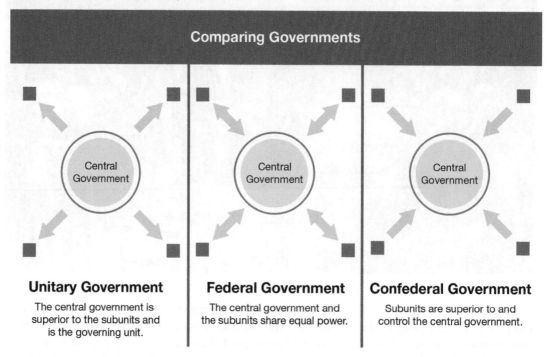

Unitary Government

The central government is superior to the subunits and is the governing unit.

Federal Government

The central government and the subunits share equal power.

Confederal Government

Subunits are superior to and control the central government.

To ensure ratification, the federalists offered to draft a Bill of Rights in the form of the first 10 amendments as its first order of business should the Constitution be adopted. Most of the proposed amendments guaranteed the protection of individual liberties, such as free speech and religious freedom, but the Tenth Amendment was intended to protect the sovereignty of the states. It says: "The powers not delegated to the United States by the Constitution, nor prohibited by it to the States, are reserved to the States respectively, or to the people." The federalists got a central government whose power was independent of the states and capable of dealing more effectively with national problems, while the states remained independent decision makers across a wide range of policy areas. The compromise offered the possibility of merging the virtues of small, flexible governments with a large unified government while avoiding the pitfalls of each. However, the Constitution was not entirely clear as to exactly which powers were reserved to the states. Also unclear was the right of the people to delegate their reserved powers to the national government. The precise balance of power would be left to future generations to work out, a process that continues today.

3.2 Federalism and The Constitution

exclusive powers

The powers given only to the federal government.

The idea of federalism is embodied in the U.S. Constitution in more places than the Tenth Amendment. The Constitution gives some powers only to the national government. Among other powers, the U.S. Congress has **exclusive powers** to regulate commerce between the states (later this would be interpreted by the Supreme Court as within states as well) and with foreign countries, to coin money, make treaties, raise and maintain an army and navy, and declare war. The states are denied the authority to tax imports and exports and make compacts (agreements) with other states without the consent of Congress.

The Constitution gives other powers to the states, namely the power to tax, borrow money, charter banks and corporations, regulate business within their states, and make and enforce laws to protect the general welfare of their citizens. These are considered **concurrent powers,** and as such, they belong to both the national government and the states. Other powers are **implied powers**. At the end of Article I, section 8 is language that allows Congress to "make all Laws which shall be necessary and proper for carrying into Execution the Powers, and all other Powers vested by this Constitution ...." This statement is referred to as the **elastic** or the **necessary and proper clause**. It gives the federal government flexibility to, for example, create departments, punish counterfeiters, establish a national bank, or to pass its own laws to protect the general welfare of the public even though these powers are not specifically listed in the Constitution.

The **reserved powers** not delegated to the national government by the Constitution are held in reserve to the states by the Tenth Amendment, although it is not clear what powers are left. There is no list of specific powers such as those listed in Article I, but those implied by the amendment include the power to tax, borrow, and spend; to make and enforce laws; to regulate business within their borders; and to practice **eminent domain**, which is the power to take private property for public use with compensation. If there is any doubt which government is superior, the national **supremacy clause** in Article VI, paragraph 2 says the "Constitution, and the laws of the United States which shall be made in pursuance thereof ... shall be the supreme law of the land; and the judges in every state shall be bound thereby...." In other words, the federal Constitution and laws take precedence over state laws and their constitutions. **Police powers** or the power to make laws to protect the health, safety, and morals of the public are by tradition reserved to the states. However, the current controversy over marijuana laws shows that there exists ambiguity as to which level of government has the primary authority for such laws. As a result, the U.S. Supreme Court is often called upon to settle disputes between national and state powers.

concurrent powers

Powers exercised by both the federal and state governments.

implied powers

Powers not explicitly listed in the Constitution but assumed to exist given the necessary and proper clause.

necessary and proper clause

Congress has the power to make laws to carry out its other powers vested in the Constitution. It grants Congress flexibility to create laws the Constitution does not explicitly grant or list.

reserved powers

Powers not listed or enumerated by the Constitution.

eminent domain

The power of government to take private property for public use with fair compensation.

supremacy clause

A passage in the U.S. Constitution stating that the Constitution and the laws made under its authority constitute the supreme law of the land.

police powers

Powers of government to make laws that protect the health, safety, and morals of the public.

College students can save money by attending a local university and paying in-state tuition.

© Shutterstock, Inc.

full faith and credit clause

Part of the U.S. Constitution that requires states to respect the public acts, records, and judicial proceedings of every other state.

privileges and immunities clause

Prevents states from discriminating against citizens from other states.

interstate compacts

An agreement between two or more states to ensure cooperative action.

The Constitution also specifies obligations of the states to each other. Article IV, section 1 requires each state to grant "Full Faith and Credit" the "public Acts, Records, and judicial Proceedings of every other State." Also known as the **full faith and credit clause**, this section of the Constitution means that wills, contracts, marriages, and judicial decisions made in one state are valid in all other states. If you are living in California and plan to drive to New Mexico, for example, you don't need to obtain driver's licenses from Arizona and New Mexico; your California license will be honored by the other states. Should you move to another state, your marriage license, wills, and other contracts will be similarly valid. This also means that the money you borrowed in California to pay tuition or to buy the car you drove will still be owed. You can't escape your debts or other obligations imposed by the state courts by fleeing to another state.

A similar provision called the **comity** or the **privileges and immunities clause** says: "Citizens of each State shall be entitled to all Privileges and Immunities of Citizens in the several States." This prevents states from discriminating against citizens from other states. In the above-mentioned road trip to New Mexico, neither Arizona nor New Mexico can prevent you from entering or leaving their states, nor can they deny your basic rights such as freedom of speech and assembly just because you are from California. Of course, states do give special privileges to their own residents, such as when they require out-of-state students to pay higher tuition at state colleges and universities or when they charge higher fees for fishing and hunting to out-of-state residents. The Supreme Court allows such differences if the state has a compelling interest in doing so (such as protecting the educational investments residents made in their state universities) and as long as such rules and regulations do not deny the fundamental rights of another state's citizens.

The Constitution also allows the states to make agreements or treaties with other states called **interstate compacts**. There are many such agreements, but one of the more long-standing agreements is the Colorado River Compact signed in 1922. This governs the water rights in the Colorado River and its tributaries. This agreement ensures that the states in the upper portion of the river basin, including Colorado, New Mexico, Utah, and Wyoming, do not deplete the flow of water. They must leave sufficient amounts in the river for the states in the lower portion of the river basin, namely California, Arizona, and Nevada. Interstate compacts require the explicit or implicit consent of Congress to avoid unfair collusion between states against other states or the national government.

3.3 The Slow Growth of The National Government's Power

The U.S. Constitution leaves considerable room for disagreement between the states and the federal government over which level of government has the power to do what. Often it is the duty of the Supreme Court to determine the balance of power. One of the first such cases began when Alexander Hamilton, then Secretary of the U.S. Treasury, established a national bank as part of his plan to assume the national and state Revolutionary War debts and improve the nation's finances. Hamilton argued that the power to charter a national bank was allowed under the Constitution by the Necessary and Proper Clause because it would help the government manage its finances and was essential to carry out Congress's authority to tax and spend. Secretary of State Thomas Jefferson believed that no such power existed because the Constitution did not explicitly list a power to charter a bank. However, Congress and President George Washington agreed with Hamilton and the bank was established.

In 1816, Congress chartered a second bank which established a branch in the state of Maryland. Not wanting the national bank to compete with its state-chartered banks, Maryland imposed a tax on the bank's operations. The bank cashier, James McCulloch, refused to pay the tax and was then sued by the State of Maryland. The case was appealed to the Maryland Court of Appeals and then to the U.S. Supreme Court. In the 1819 case of *McCulloch v. Maryland*, the Court decided that Congress did have the power to create the bank by invoking the Necessary and Proper Clause. The Court argued that means such as a bank which are adapted to legitimate goals are constitutional unless specifically prohibited by the Constitution. In Chief Justice John Marshall's majority opinion, the purpose of the Necessary and Proper Clause was "to enlarge, not diminish the powers vested in the government."[15] The court also decreed that Maryland did not have the power to tax the bank, because federal laws have supremacy over state laws. In Marshall's words, "the power to tax involves the power to destroy," and thus the supremacy clause exempts the federal government from state taxes.

Dual Federalism

Even though the decision in *McCulloch v. Maryland* expanded the powers of the federal government and confirmed federal supremacy, the early rulings of the court would favor a more limited role of the federal government. In 1833, in the case of *Barron v. Baltimore*, the Supreme Court would establish the doctrine of **dual federalism**, the idea that there is a clear division between the constitutional powers established for federal and state governments. The case involved the City of Baltimore, which modified the flow of water in local streams for street construction and, in the process, deposited mounds of sand and other debris near a wharf in Baltimore harbor owned by John Barron. The deposits ruined Barron's business because boats could no longer access the wharf due to the resulting shallow water levels. Reading the text of the Fifth Amendment of the U.S. Constitution, Barron concluded that value of his property had been unconstitutionally taken from him by the city because he had not been compensated. Barron won his case in trial court but lost on appeal and finally ended up in the U.S. Supreme Court. In another of Chief Justice John Marshall's opinions, the court ruled that "The Constitution was ordained and established by the people of the United States for themselves, for their own government, and not for the government of individual States .... the Fifth Amendment must be understood as restraining the power of the General Government, not as applicable to the States."[16]

John Marshall, Chief Justice of United States Supreme Court from 1801 to 1835.

© Shutterstock, Inc.

Barron would not be compensated because it was the City of Baltimore, not the national government, that took the value of his property. Because the city was under the jurisdiction of the State of Maryland, and its constitution had no provision requiring the government to compensate land owners when the state took their property, Barron was out of luck. *Barron v. Baltimore* confirmed the notion that Americans were citizens of two separate governments and the provisions listed in the Bill of Rights did not apply to the state governments.

dual federalism

The idea that there is a clear division of policy areas between the federal and state government such that each level of government has distinct responsibilities. Usually represented by the metaphor of a layer cake. Also known as layer-cake federalism.

Missouri Compromise

Legislation passed by Congress in 1820 that prohibited slavery north of the 36° 30′parallel, excluding Missouri.

The ideal of dual federalism would be strengthened by the Supreme Court under Chief Justice Roger Taney from 1835 to 1864. One of the most infamous cases during this time was *Scott v. Stanford* (1857). The case involved Dred Scott, a slave taken from Missouri, which allowed slavery, to Illinois, a state where slavery was not allowed because of the **Missouri Compromise**. The Missouri Compromise was passed by Congress in 1820 and prohibited slavery north of the 36° 30′ parallel, excluding Missouri. After returning to Missouri, Scott sued for his freedom after his master died, claiming that his residency in Illinois made him a free man under federal law. The Supreme Court ruled that Scott be returned to slavery because the federal government had no power to regulate slavery in the territories. We discuss this case again in Chapter 5 with regard to its implications for civil rights.

Roger B. Taney, Chief Justice of United States Supreme Court from 1836 through 1864.

© Shutterstock, Inc.

freedom of contract doctrine

Supreme Court doctrine based on the freedom of private individuals to form contracts without government restrictions.

Even after the passage of the Fourteenth Amendment in 1868, which makes clear that all persons born or naturalized in the United States are citizens of both the national and state governments wherein they reside, the U.S. Supreme Court continued to view the state and national constitutions separately. In the Slaughterhouse Cases, the Louisiana state legislature granted a monopoly to a single slaughterhouse in New Orleans, effectively taking the property rights from the other slaughterhouses in the area without compensation as required by the Fifth Amendment. The Court's majority ruled that the purpose of the Fourteenth Amendment was to protect newly emancipated slaves and did not extend to the property rights of private business. Similarly, the freedoms of speech, press, religion, and other liberties mentioned in the Bill of Rights applied to laws passed by Congress and actions of the federal government, but did not apply to the states.[17]

Throughout the nineteenth century the federal government was allowed to regulate shipping between states on roads, rivers, and railroads under the Commerce Clause, which states that Congress has the power to "regulate Commerce with foreign Nations and among the several States." However, many commercial activities, including manufacturing and mining, and most services were considered within state commercial activities. This was because the products produced had yet to be transported across state borders and thus were beyond the powers of Congress to regulate. During this time, the Supreme Court acted to protect business from federal government regulation by striking down attempts by Congress to regulate child labor, dangerous working conditions, long work hours, minimum wages, fraud, and the production of impure foods as a violation of the concept of interstate commerce. Such laws were also considered a violation of the Court's **freedom of contract doctrine** and thus the states were also denied the power to regulate business.

Things changed during the Great Depression after President Franklin Roosevelt and Congress threatened to pass the Judicial Procedures Reform Bill of 1937, which would allow the president to appoint new justices for every sitting justice over the age of 70. This legislation would have allowed Roosevelt to appoint up to six new Supreme Court justices, presumably making the Court more sympathetic to national concerns and shift the balance of the Court in Roosevelt's favor. Shortly after Roosevelt's court packing scheme, the Court changed its position on business regulation. In the case of *West Coast Hotel Co. v. Parrish*, a hotel maid from Wenatchee, Washington, sued her employer asking for back pay of $216.19 owed to her given the state's minimum wage law. A year earlier the Court declared New York State's minimum wage law unconstitutional. The West Coast Hotel's representatives argued that it had the right to pay Elsie Parrish less than the minimum $14.50 per week under the liberty of contract doctrine. But in a decision that became known as "the switch in time that saved nine," the Court changed its mind. Chief Justice Evans Hughes' majority opinion announced that the economic conditions of the Depression made it imperative that the Court uphold the Washington state minimum wage law. Parrish would get her back pay and the public would no longer have to endure "unscrupulous" employers who are "exploiting" their employees by denying them a "living wage."[18] This and other cases at the time are referred to as ushering in the "constitutional revolution" of 1937.[19]

Regulating Commerce After 1937

A few years later in the case of *United States v. Darby Lumber Co* (1941), the Court would uphold the Fair Labor Standards Act, which allows the federal government to regulate wages related to the manufacturing of goods shipped across state lines. In this case, the Supreme Court deemed that the Tenth Amendment was "but a truism that all is retained which has not been surrendered."[20] In other words, the Tenth Amendment was a declaration that the states would be able to exercise their reserve powers, not a limitation on federal powers. The court would go further in *Wikard v. Filburn* (1942) by concluding there would be no limits on what could be construed as interstate commerce. The case concerned Roscoe Filburn, an Ohio farmer who was growing wheat to feed the animals on his own farm. The U.S. government had established limits on wheat production in order to stabilize prices, but Filburn refused to pay the penalties for growing more than he was permitted. He argued that his feed was not sold on the market, let alone transported for sale across state lines. However, the Court ruled that the farmer was undermining Congress's ability to regulate interstate commerce because, in exceeding his growing quota, his actions reduced the amount of feed he would buy on the open market, which was normally traded across state lines.

With the distinction between interstate and intrastate commerce gone, the commerce clause would be converted from a barrier to a source of federal power. Over the next 30 years, the courts would allow Congress to protect the rights of employees to bargain collectively with their employers, set minimum wages, set working hours, preclude child labor, regulate workplace conditions, prevent monopolies and price fixing among business competitors, regulate farm land, prohibit fraud and insider trading in the stock market, and make businesses comply with product labeling laws, among many other regulations.

LBGPF6-016a, Lane Brothers Commercial Photographers Photographic Collection, 1920-1976. Photographic Collection, Special Collections and Archives, Georgia State University Library.

In 1964, the Court would allow the federal government to prevent private acts of racial discrimination in places of public accommodation. In the *Heart of Atlanta Motel v. United States* (1964), the owners were following local traditions backed by law that allowed businesses to refuse service to blacks. In denying the motel's right to discriminate, the Court found that the business was clearly related to interstate travel, and thus subject to regulation under the Commerce Clause. The Civil Rights Act of 1964 also allowed the federal government to regulate within state businesses as part of its police power to protect the general welfare of the country's citizens.[21]

Moving Some Power Back to The States: *United States v. Lopez*

From the time of the Great Depression until the end of the twentieth century, power moved toward the national level. However, the trend moderated as Republican presidents began shaping the legal outlook of the court. In 1972, President Richard Nixon nominated William Rehnquist as an associate justice to fill the seat vacated by John Marshall Harlan II. He would be part of the Court's conservative minority, believing that whenever possible, conflicts between state and federal authority should be resolved in favor of the states. In 1986, he was elevated to Chief Justice by President Ronald Reagan to succeed Warren Burger. In 1990 and 1991, two liberal justices, William Brennan and Thurgood Marshall, retired and their replacements (appointed by President George H. W. Bush) would give the conservatives on the Court a clear majority.

The case of the *United States v. Lopez* (1994) gave the court the opportunity to move power back to the states. The case involved Alfonzo Lopez, a twelfth-grade high school student who violated the Gun-Free School Zones Act of 1990 when he brought a concealed revolver into his school in San Antonio, Texas. The law was justified by Congress under the Commerce Clause, so the question before the Rehnquist Court was: What did keeping guns away from schools have to do with interstate commerce? The theory used by Congress was that guns near schools would have a disruptive influence on the educational experience of the students. If students' educations are disturbed, they will do poorly in the workforce and the economy will suffer. The additive effects of schools being disrupted by handguns will affect the national economy. The majority on the Court decided that Congress had stretched the Commerce Clause too far because banning guns near schools "has nothing to do with 'commerce' or any sort of economic enterprise, however broadly one might define those terms."[22] They declared the law unconstitutional, thereby reversing a 50-year history of interpreting Congress's authority under the Commerce Clause as effectively unlimited. Six years later, the court reinforced their decision in *Lopez* when, in *United States v. Morrison*, the justices struck down as another unconstitutional extension of the Commerce Clause part of the Violence Against Women Act, which gave victims of gender-motivated violence the right to sue their attackers in federal court.[23]

Cooperative Federalism

Dual federalism, or the notion that there is a clear division of policy areas between the national and state governments, is also known as layer-cake federalism. The idea is that each level of government has distinct responsibilities. For example, the national government delivers Social Security and Medicare for the elderly, protects the borders and the environment, and provides for national defense. Alternatively, the state governments oversee education, build and maintain roads, bridges, and other public works projects, and provide for public safety. Unfortunately, this orderly arrangement is at odds with actual practice. To illustrate the point, political scientist Matthew Grodzins asks us to consider the job of a "sanitarian" of a rural county. Part of his salary comes from state funds, but the other is provided by a federal grant. His office is in the local county courthouse, and the vehicle he uses has a large county seal on the door. At any given time, it is difficult to tell under which government he is working. When he is inspecting poultry, he is implementing federal standards, but when he is inspecting commodities or restaurant cleanliness, he is enforcing state laws. According to Grodzins, the sanitarian cannot think of himself as having distinct responsibilities owed to each level of government: it's just one job, protecting the public from food contaminants.[24]

Most public goods and services in the United States are provided through partnerships made between state and federal governments. The basic pattern was set during Roosevelt's New Deal program. The federal government would identify a problem and set basic goals and make funds available to administer the problem, but then turn over much of the responsibility for implementing the program to the state governments. For example, the giant Medicaid program which provides medical care to low-income people who are aged, blind, or disabled, to poor families with children, and to certain pregnant women and children is a shared responsibility of the state and federal governments. The federal government sets program standards, defines eligibility guidelines, and provides much of the funding, while the state governments give their share of funding and administer the program. The federal government requires all states to provide certain hospital and physician services, but states can offer additional services such as eye or psychiatric care. They may also place limits on recipients' use of services. The obvious advantage of the arrangement is that many national problems span state boundaries yet defy any single national "one-size-fits-all" solution. Federalism, among other things, allows the achievement of national goals through the joint participation of state governments. At the same time, federalism permits local differences to be considered and lets the state governments experiment with their own policy solutions.

This arrangement is often described as **cooperative federalism** or marble-cake federalism, where there is a mixing of national and state resources and powers such that it is almost impossible to separate the layers of authority. Such partnerships have been common since the Civil War, when the U.S. government began to provide support for war veterans, give land and research assistance through land-grant colleges, and lend the assistance of the U.S. Army engineers to help states build dams and bridges.[25] When the states ratified the Sixteenth Amendment in 1913 authorizing a federal income tax, they made it easier for Congress to give grants to the states. During the Great Depression, spending by the national government in the states accelerated rapidly, as did the mixing of responsibilities and resources of state and national governments. Before this time, local governments spent more on public goods and services than the state and national governments combined. By 1970, spending by the national government outpaced the amounts spent by state and local governments.[26] Today, nearly three-quarters of all state agencies receive grants from national agencies, and more than a quarter depend on those grants for a least half of their revenues.[27]

cooperative federalism

A relationship between federal and state governments characterized by a mixing of state and federal resources and powers usually represented by the metaphor of a marble cake. Also known as marble-cake federalism.

FIGURE 3.2 Layer-Cake Federalism vs. Marble-Cake Federalism

Programs and authority are clearly divided among the national, state, and local governments.

Programs and authority are mixed among the national, state, and local governments.

Federal Grants

Offering **grants-in-aid** is a common method used by the national government to get the independent states to enact federal programs. They encourage voluntary compliance with federal policy because, by accepting assistance, the states also accept mandates to observe national goals or standards. For example, traditionally the states have had responsibility for laws regarding safety on roads and highways throughout the United States, including the setting of standards for driving under the influence of alcohol. In the 1980s, groups under the leadership of Mothers against Drunk Driving lobbied Congress to pass a law that offered the states a large grant if they adopted the use of breathalyzers for administering roadside tests for drunk driving and accepted a national standard of .08 percent blood alcohol concentration (BAC) or higher as proof of intoxication. Thirty-eight states qualified for incentive grants under the program, but all states had not yet complied with the .08 standard. In 2000, Congress added language to the Department of Transportation's Appropriations Act providing that states must pass the .08 BAC standard or risk losing some of their federal highway construction funds. By the end of 2001, all 50 states had adopted the national standard and the federal government achieved its goal of making the roads safer.[28]

FIGURE 3.3 Total Federal Outlays for Grants to State and Local Governments and Medicaid, Fiscal Years 1980-2016

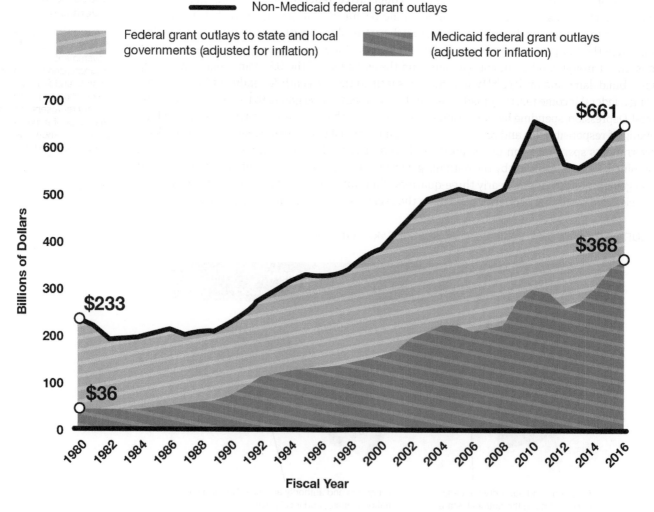

Based on "Federal Grants to State and Local Governments." U.S. Government Accountability Office: https://www.gao.gov/key_issues/management_of_federal_grants_to_state_local/issue_summary#t=0.

The example of the establishment of the national .08 BAC standard illustrates how cash incentives are used to entice states to comply with national priorities, but it also serves as an example of a **cross-over sanction** because the loss of federal highway construction funds was used as leverage to induce the remaining states to conform to the national standard. The federal government uses a similar method for compliance when it attaches requirements or "strings" to its grants. Often referred to as **cross-cutting requirements**, virtually any project that uses a federal funds for a brick-and-mortar type project, such as a new library addition or highway expansion, requires an environmental impact assessment of the new project, including the mitigation of any impact uncovered by the assessment. Title VI of the 1964 Civil Rights Act decrees that agencies using federal funds are prohibited from discriminating against any person based on race, color, or national origin. Title IX of the same act says "no person in the United States shall, on the basis of sex, be excluded from participation in, be denied the benefits of, or be subjected to discrimination under any education program or activity receiving federal financial assistance."

Federal requirements often include compliance with policies for equal access in employment and contracting, historic preservation, fair or prevailing wages, asbestos and lead-based paint removal, care of experimental animals, and the treatment of human subjects in research, among other conditions. The Family Educational Rights and Privacy Act requires that your college or university (if it accepts federal funds) protect the privacy of your grades, even from your parents.[29]

Federal agencies offer more than 1,000 grant programs each year ranging from health care to the arts.[30] In 2018, the national government is expected to spend more than $703 billion worth of grants-in-aid to state and local governments. More than half of the money is for medical assistance, social services, cash assistance, food stamps, and housing subsidies for disadvantaged populations. The remainder is for agriculture, education, transportation, law enforcement, and homeland security. On average, federal grants-in-aid represent one-third of the general revenue of state governments.[31] More than half of the total state spending for health care and public assistance comes from the federal government. Some states are more dependent on federal spending than others. Louisiana and Mississippi, for example, receive almost 42 percent of their general revenue from the federal government, whereas North Dakota and Virginia receive only about 20 percent.[32] Because much of federal domestic policy is implemented through grants to the states rather than through the federal bureaucracy, paradoxically, state governments have grown because of, rather than despite of, the federal government.

Federal grants are arranged into categorical or block grants. The difference is that block grants are not project specific and have a much broader range of uses. About 90 percent of federal aid dollars are spent for **categorical grants**, in which federal dollars are targeted narrowly and tied to particular programs, or categories, of spending. For example, the Department of Health and Human Services offers the Head Start program, which helps local communities fund educational, health, nutrition, and parental involvement programs for low-income children under 5 years old. Grant recipients can be public or private non-profit organizations, but they must meet financial, curricula, enrollment, attendance, health, safety, and nutrition requirements, among other conditions established by the program. Agency staff and management must meet minimum professional qualifications and submit to background checks. Some staffers must agree to alcohol and drug testing. Recipients are often required to match a portion of the federal funds with non-federal dollars. In addition, grant recipients must provide yearly reports to the Department of Health and Human Services and submit to financial audits. In 2014, Congress awarded more than $500 million to 275 Head Start programs.

The Head Start program is considered a competitive grant because the grant is for a specific time and purpose. Such grants are discretionary on the part of the federal agency, which often chooses recipients after a competitive selection process, but 33 percent of all categorical grants are **formula grants**. They are given on the bases of a formula set by legislation or regulation often based on a states' population, need, or other conditions related to the purpose of the grant. The formula tells potential recipients, usually state and local governments, how much they are entitled to under the provisions of the grant. Medicaid is a categorical grant in which the amounts going to state governments are determined by a formula. The grant varies by state depending on its need as

cross-over sanction

A penalty attached to a federal grant that affects federal money from one program to influence policy in another program.

cross-cutting requirements

Requirements or strings attached to federal grants that may or may not directly relate to the purpose of the grant.

categorical grants

Grants from the federal government that are tied to specific purposes outlined in the grant proposal.

formula grants

Non-competitive federal grants based on a predetermined formula. Usually based on the need or population of the government recipient.

measured by its per-capita income. It ranges from the federal government matching 50 percent of program expenses in wealthier states such as Connecticut and California, to a 75 percent match in Mississippi.[33]

block grants

Grants of money that come with few requirements from the federal government and that allow recipients flexibility with regard to spending.

Block grants, on the other hand, permit recipients to determine how grants are used, within broad limits. The Community Development Block Grant is offered by the Department of Housing and Urban Development to help states and local governments address a wide range of urban problems. Under the program, cities with populations of at least 50,000, and urban counties with 200,000 or more, are entitled to federal funds based on a formula that reflects local need. Smaller communities are offered grants through their state government. The funds must be used to benefit low- and moderate-income people, so if local communities can meet this goal, they can spend the money as they wish. Some communities use the money to provide affordable housing or expand economic opportunities. The money can go to real-estate developers to subsidize the building of low-cost apartments or condominiums, or the community can set funds aside for a loan program to help local entrepreneurs revitalize a neighborhood commercial area. Other communities choose to give some of their grants to social service agencies to provide mental health services to the homeless. Still others use the federal money to fix streets and sidewalks or to plant trees. Communities can use the money any way they choose as long as they show that the money was used to benefit low- and moderate-income individuals directly, or was spent in a low- and moderate-income area. Naturally, state and local policymakers prefer block grants, which come with fewer strings attached.

Regulated Federalism

unfunded mandates

Congress simply imposes its will on the states and passes on the costs. Sometimes referred to as regulated federalism.

Congress also uses mandates, in the form of a direct orders, to achieve its policy objectives in areas where national power is well-established under the Supremacy Clause. Congress uses what are sometimes referred to as **unfunded mandates** to impose its will on the states and pass on the costs. One of the more controversial mandates is the Endangered Species Act of 1973, designed to protect species of fish, wildlife, and plants from extinction. Beyond listing engendered species, the act seeks to protect "the ecosystems upon which they depend" whether such lands are public or private. In 1978, Congress amended the law to allow the U.S. Fish and Wildlife Service and National Marine Fisheries Service to make critical habitat designation a mandatory requirement for all threatened and endangered species. More than half of these critical habitats are on non-federal property. When the Fish and Wildlife Service began to reintroduce gray wolves into central Idaho, the state protested. Idaho farmers and ranchers claimed the wolves were a direct threat to their livelihoods. The state backed their claims and objected to the fact that the national government expected the state to assume responsibility for managing the wolves after they were released. Despite protests from the state, the wolves were released. In 2016, the total annual costs to the 39 states covered by the gray wolf project was under $500,000. For its part, the federal government spent a little more than $2.25 million on the recovery program.[34]

Similarly, the Clean Air Act (1970) established national air quality standards but required the states to develop and implement plans to meet those standards. The Americans with Disabilities Act (1990), which prohibits discrimination against individuals with disabilities, is also an unfunded mandate because it requires state and local governments to remove architectural barriers and provide accommodations for people with hearing, vision, and speech disabilities without federal compensation. Normally, mandates are enforced with cross-over sanctions such as the loss of federal funds, but states also risk civil and criminal sanctions if they fail to comply.[35] Since the 1980s, tight federal budget deficits have led national politicians to rely more heavily on mandates to achieve their policy objectives.

3.4 The Policy Effects of Federalism

When the 50 states are left on their own, the laws and policies of one state often affect the others. Recall that Oklahoma and Nebraska filed a lawsuit claiming that marijuana purchased legally in neighboring Colorado was being transported into their states, overwhelming the police and courts. A similar problem occurred when the state governments had different drinking age requirements. The National Minimum Drinking Age Act ended that practice with cross-cutting sanctions that pushed states to set a uniform minimum drinking age of 21 years. But before 1984, minimum drinking ages varied across the states from 18 to 21. Differences between neighboring states would cause vehicle fatalities, as teenagers from a state where the drinking age was set at 21, for example, would drive across state lines to purchase alcohol in a state with an 18-year-old minimum. Today, a state's efforts to control the purchase of guns can be undermined by its neighbors' lax gun laws.

Environmental Shirking and Blackmail

Problems arise when states attempt to reduce pollution or conserve natural resources. One state's efforts to reduce air and water pollution can be undermined by their up-wind or up-river neighbors, who allow citizens and businesses to dump pollution into the air or water and let it drift out of their jurisdiction to do damage across state lines. Indeed, states have a strong incentive to adopt lax environmental regulations even if the state's residents want a cleaner environment. Why burden your own citizens with expensive environmental legislation knowing that one state acting on its own cannot restore a pristine environment? Further, a state contemplating strict environmental standards will assume that its citizens will pay the costs of environmental improvement while its neighbors reap the benefits. Better to free ride and let other states clean the environment while your citizens save the costs.

A more likely outcome happens as states compete with other states for jobs and industry and the taxes they bring. Polluting businesses can take their jobs from one state to another if the difference between states in costs of doing business, due to environmental regulation, is sufficiently large. Thus, states wishing to clean their environments through regulation risk losing jobs to states with weaker environmental laws. States considering new environmental legislation often become targets of "economic-environmental blackmail" as companies play one state against another with threats to locate to the state with the most permissive pollution standards.[36] Across the states, the tendency is for states to settle for weaker environmental standards than their citizens would prefer to avoid repelling business investment.

Cut-Throat Competition Between the States

States care deeply about their economies, but federalism places limits on the types of policies states can adopt to promote economic development. States cannot control the movement of raw materials, capital, or workers across borders. Unlike the federal government, they cannot affect the supply of money or the rate of interest on borrowed funds. Most importantly, state governments cannot command business to invest; they can only hope to induce interest in their state by offering business incentives to promote investment. All states offer low-interest loans, loan guarantees, and outright grants of cash and land to attract, retain, and stimulate private businesses in their state. States also induce investment by granting tax breaks to businesses. They may also reduce personal taxes to entice corporate managers and entrepreneurs to come to (or remain in) the state.[37]

Yet, when states offer incentives to retain and attract companies, they do so in a competitive environment. They are uncertain of the deals being offered by other states as well as the needs of the firms they are trying to attract. Given the intense competition, states often promise more than is wise or necessary to secure the deal, often with no guarantee that the benefits will outweigh the costs. State incentive packages ratchet upward because businesses play states off each other to get the best deal. Only the firm knows what it really needs. States do not want to make a bid that is too low to attract the firm.[38] This competitive environment of bidding up incentives across states sometimes resembles the spiral of decisions in an arms race.[39] City Planner and Mayor of Ventura, California, William Fulton, writes of watching governors of seven states on the Phil Donahue Show begging General Motors to build a new Saturn plant in their state. "It was, to put it bluntly, a pretty pathetic excuse for an economic development campaign."[40]

In 1993, more than 35 states vied to be the site for Mercedes-Benz's sport utility vehicle plant. Alabama's $300 million winning package included tax breaks, promises to buy the vehicles for the state fleet, payments to workers while in training; commitments to develop the new site and construct a welcome center for visitors to the plant, as well as more traditional infrastructure development like roads and utility connections.[41] Computer maker Dell got several states to bid for its relocation and ended up with more than $242 million in grants and tax credits from North Carolina.[42] Dell also initiated a bidding war between counties within the state and came up with an additional $37 million. In addition, Dell was exempted from state minimum wage laws, allowing the company to reduce its annual average pay from $31,000 to $28,000 and pay only 50 percent of the cost of health insurance for its employees.[43]

Recently, the e-commerce giant Amazon started a bidding war by announcing that it was soliciting bids for its new corporate headquarters. It received 238 bids from cities and states across the country, including a bid from California that offered $1 billion in tax incentives and another from Newark, New Jersey, that offered $7 billion in tax incentives over the next 10 years.[44] Such policies imply a beggar-thy-neighbor outcome in which one state seeks to gain at the expense of the others. Such a practice has led many observers to conclude that traditional state economic development policies merely shift economic activity from one location to another and do not really create new wealth or distribute it more equitably.[45] Such competition also shifts the tax burden from mobile companies to more rooted businesses and citizens, distorts market decisions as corporate managers seek incentives rather than competitive advantage, and has resulted in the movement of much of the automobile industry and many of its workers from the Midwest to the South.[46]

welfare magnet

A factual claim based on evidence that higher welfare benefits in one state act as a magnet for poor people seeking higher public benefits or that public officials act in a way that assumes higher benefits will attract more poor to their area.

Competition also leads states to consider the costs of their residents. Since childless residents are both more mobile and less likely to consume educational services, states compete to recruit upper-income retirees to their states. One study found that the absence of an income tax was worth an extra 25 sunny days a year as a lure to seniors.[47] On the other hand, state legislators might believe their current welfare grants are too meager to help poor families deal effectively with the problems of poverty, but are reluctant to increase payments out of fear of attracting the poor from other states. Since every state fears becoming a "**welfare magnet**," benefit levels remain lower than they would be if they were set by the national government.[48] Whether poor people move in search of higher benefits is an open question, but state officials believe they do as demonstrated by a distinctive pattern of deteriorating standards across the states often characterized as a "race to the bottom." In the past, some states gave welfare recipients free, one-way bus tickets to relocate to another state.[49] Today some cities (including San Francisco) are doing the same thing by relocating their homeless populations to other jurisdictions.[50]

3.5 The Advantages and Disadvantages of Federalism

A federalist system has advantages and disadvantages, but it is not always clear how federalism helps one's political cause. Liberals tend to favor strong national powers to fight discrimination against minorities, women, disabled people, gays, and the elderly. Liberals also favor the use of national power to protect the environment and promote economic opportunity. Conservatives, on the other hand, favor allowing the states to deal with their environmental, social, and regulatory problems in their own way without intrusion from the national government. However, things are not that simple. Today, liberals are about as likely as conservatives to argue for state's rights when it comes to the decriminalization of marijuana, assisted suicide, and protections for LGBT individuals. How these matters pan out will be a matter for the Supreme Court to decide, but given the Court's lean toward a more state-centered federalism, it is likely the justices will uphold liberal state laws in the name of local control. Whether the division of federal-state authority is decided based on ideology or pragmatism remains to be seen. The fact is that any assessment of federalism must consider its advantages and disadvantages.

Advantages of Federalism

The advantages of federalism can be summarized in four points. Federalism helps keep government closer to the people, manages social and political conflict, encourages administrative efficiency, and encourages innovation. The United States is an enormously diverse society. Across the country, citizens differ in their circumstances and reflect distinct cultural values and policy preferences. According to political scientist Daniel Elazar, across New England and the upper Midwest, migration patterns created a political culture in which government is a positive force for addressing social problems and politics is a legitimate means to achieving a greater good. Settlement patterns of immigrants in search of individual opportunity from the middle Atlantic states and extending west produced a political culture that views politics like a business. Government in these areas plays a more limited role, primarily to keep services operating smoothly. Across the South, where state populations tend to be rural and engaged in agriculture and natural resource extraction, Elazar identifies a more traditionalist political culture in which politics is fundamentally conservative, concerned with preserving the existing social order.[51]

Across political cultures, federalism works to accommodate political diversity. It is not far-fetched to assume that local politicians know their constituents, and what they want, better than representatives living in Washington. People with common interests tend to cluster. Local politics can keep levels of taxation and services close to local desires. Such local control encourages citizen involvement because citizens can more easily see their effect on public policies. The states and local governments also represent many opportunities to participate through elections and public hearings. They also serve as political training camps for aspiring leaders. This accommodation of local differences reduces conflict. Rather than trying to resolve regional policy differences at the national level, where majorities win at the expense of the minority, both sets of preferences can be accommodated.

Federalism promotes administrative efficiency. The federal government represents economies of scale when it controls air-traffic, maintains standard weights and measures, and establishes uniform product labeling, but the larger size brings complexity and a greater need for coordination and communication. At the same time, the opportunities for waste and confusion multiply at the larger scale. As discussed above, national goals are often accomplished through the participation of the states and local governments. The Medicaid program is one of many national programs administered by the states, which constitute a geographically dispersed delivery system with roots to local communities.

Lastly, federalism allows for innovation and experimentation in policy. Supreme Court Justice Louis Brandeis wrote that "a single courageous state may, if its citizens choose, serve as a laboratory, and try social and economic experiments without risk to the rest of the country."[52] As the states and localities customize their policies to accommodate diverse demands and needs, new policies are constantly being developed and tested. Because the states often deal with the same problems, they are always on the lookout for successful innovations, developed by their counterparts, that can be copied. Innovations can also be adopted by the federal government, such as when Massachusetts developed a program that delivered universal health coverage, which served as the model for President Obama's Affordable Care Act.

Disadvantages of Federalism

But federalism also has its disadvantages. It can lead to inequality in services, it can cause complexity, confusion, and difficulty in coordinating national policy, and it can promote duplication and reduce accountability. Federalism can accommodate diversity, but there are tremendous differences between the sizes of states' economies and thus their abilities to provide public services. Even after accounting for the sizes of their populations, the economy of Massachusetts is more than twice the size of Mississippi's. This means Massachusetts can more easily pay for the services it provides to its citizens. If the two states were to provide the same level of services at the same costs, Mississippi would have to tax its citizens at twice the rate as Massachusetts. Across the nation, wealthy states can spend more on their schools, highways, and public health services and still enjoy lower tax rates. One important role of the national government is to make sure poor states get extra resources to help them provide a minimum level of services. Prior to the passage of the Civil Rights Act in 1964, some states were unwilling to protect the civil rights of their citizens.

Policy innovation and flexibility is a major advantage of federalism, but different laws and policies across state, local, and national governments add complexity and confusion. The interdependence that has developed between the federal and state government means most citizens have only a vague idea which level of government is responsible for what. This lack of clear distinctions in jurisdiction makes it difficult for voters to assign responsibility when programs fail or succeed. When programs fail, state politicians often blame the federal government, but when programs succeed, state leaders quickly claim credit. Moreover, inconsistencies among state laws makes it very difficult for companies that operate nationwide. At times, the greatest supporters of national regulation are corporations that otherwise would be required to meet 50 sets of standards, laws, and bureaucracies. In practice, states with smaller markets often differ from larger states in setting safety and emission standards for automobile manufacturers. To do otherwise would require them to produce a different model for each state. There is also significant overlap with regard to some services. In the same area, the city police, the county sheriff, the Federal Bureau of Investigation, and the Drug Enforcement Agency may all respond to the same crime. During national emergencies, the need for a quick response can lead to massive coordination problems among first responders, like those experienced during Hurricane Katrina and the terrorist attacks on 9/11. During both disasters, teams of rescue workers from different jurisdictions and levels of government were unable to communicate effectively because each had radios that operated at different frequencies.

At some point, the proliferation of governments begins to strain the capacities of local citizens and the media to keep up. In addition to the 50 states, there are more than 89,000 governments in the United States, including counties, towns, cities, school boards, and special districts.[53] Each has its own ability set policies and levy taxes. Media outlets have largely given up coverage of state legislatures, preferring to focus on national and local political events. As a result, the average citizen cares about and understands national politics to a much greater degree than in the past. About 60 percent of eligible voters show up and vote during a U.S. presidential election, but in 15 of the 30 most populous U.S. cities, voter turnout for local elections averages less than 20 percent.

TABLE 3.1 Advantages and Disadvantages of Federalism

Advantages	Disadvantages
Helps keep government closer to the people	Can lead to inequality in services
Manages social and political conflict	Can cause complexity, confusion, and difficulty in coordinating national policy
Encourages administrative efficiency	Can promote duplication
Encourages innovation	Reduces accountability

Yet, as the example of the state's marijuana laws illustrates, federalism often manages to accommodate both sides of a political conflict. Some states manage to accommodate those seeking relief from serious medical conditions while others experiment with marijuana for recreational use. Still other states can wait in the wings to see if the positive effects of legalization outweigh the costs. In the meantime, the nation's citizens remain subject to two levels of government simultaneously. The debate as to the proper balance of power between the states and the federal government continues.

3.6 What Can I Do?

Because federalism allows a large measure of local and regional self-government, the likelihood that you can make a difference at the local level is very good, especially when compared to the probability of making a national impact. Tired of living with your parents because apartments are too expensive? Many communities have controls that regulate the amounts landlords can charge for rented housing and limit how much rent can be increased annually. Other communities require housing developers to include a certain proportion of their residential units be offered at prices that people with modest incomes can afford. Care about the ethical treatment of animals? Some communities have banned puppy mills in which dogs are bred and their offspring are packed into tiny cages. These puppies are often neglected and raised in unsanitary conditions with little human interaction or affection. Without puppy mills, people looking for four-legged companions are more apt to rescue unwanted pets from animal shelters or to buy their puppies from reputable breeders. Care about the natural environment? Those lightweight plastic bags used to carry your groceries get blown around and litter the landscape and water ways and work their way into the world's oceans. They consume non-renewal resources to produce and refuse to degrade over time. Many communities prevent grocery stores from giving away free lightweight plastic bags and require them to offer more robust bags for a tiny price that can be reused. Customers can save money and help save the planet by bringing their own bags. On the other hand, you can work to make your community a haven from interfering do-gooders and give the people the freedom to do what they want within the limits of common decency. Think *Footloose*, the 1980s movie classic in which Kevin Bacon teaches an entire town of uptight citizens that dancing is the greatest thing there is.[54]

With so many governments, the chances for getting into politics as a career multiply. Federalism offers the real possibility for training in state and local government decision-making. Most elected positions have no qualifications, other than age and residency. Most politicians get their experience "on-the-job" from being on city councils, school boards, and local commissions before moving up the political ladder to state and national office. As a member of a local governing body, you will be exposed to a wide range of public policies. If you feel less than qualified, you will be briefed before each decision by your community's top professionals, including engineers, attorneys, planners, accountants, educators, and public managers. The job may not pay well (if at all) but it usually comes with a great deal of respect and gratitude. Besides, exercising power can be fun and intoxicating.

3.7 What's the Alternative?

competitive federalism

When states and local governments compete, usually for economic advantage.

The alternative to federalism is unitary government, a system in which all the power rests with the central government, or a confederacy, which is a voluntary association of independent states. The former is the most common system of government and has been shown to be workable in democratic nations across the world, whereas the latter is rare and inefficient, as our experience with the Articles of Confederation showed.

From our nation's history we know that federalism did not cure the country's sectional divisions. Even after a series of compromises with the slave states in the first half of the nineteenth century, the country did not manage to avoid a bloody civil war, which took the lives of more than 600,000 Americans. Nor did concessions to states' rights do much to settle the issue after the southern states instituted a system of racial apartheid after the war. Rather, it took conflict and the assertion of national power to make progress in the area of human trafficking and civil rights.

Competitive federalism leads state leaders to think within their own borders rather than of the national good. The fact that pollution fails to respect state borders and strict environmental legislation puts a state at an economic disadvantage relative to its competitors leads one to look to the federal government when it comes to regulating polluters and cleaning the environment. Similarly, even poor states feel compelled by competition to offer tax incentives to retain or attract jobs. Such behavior transfers much needed tax revenues from schools and hospitals to otherwise healthy businesses with no new wealth produced. The very thought that states must subdue their compassion for the less fortunate for fear of becoming welfare magnets is depressing. Unified national government is thus needed to set reasonable standards for economic efficiency, human dignity, and environmental quality.

Still, should everything be decided in Washington? Federalism does provide robust training and experience for politicians that is hard to reproduce in schools or within the national political parties. Most politicians gain valuable political experience and knowledge about the intricacies of public policies by working up the ranks of the federal system. Quite often, one of the nation's governors, like Franklin Roosevelt or Ronald Reagan, rises to become an effective president. The plethora of governments also provides opportunities for policy innovation. Much of the reduction in the national welfare rolls was made after Washington began allowing the states to experiment with job training and child care subsidies that allowed single mothers to return to work. California has been successful in reducing air pollution and Massachusetts managed to cover 90 percent of its residents with health insurance before Obamacare. Finally, the nation's state attorneys general on their own won an estimated $246 billion settlement from the tobacco companies in 1998. Today, the attorneys general are actively suing opioid manufacturers over drug addiction and the Federal Communications Commission over the issue of net neutrality.

Endnotes

1. Karmen Hanson Alise Garcia, "State Medical Marijuana Laws", National Conference of State Legislators, accessed February 27, 2018, http://www.ncsl.org/research/health/state-medical-marijuana-laws.aspx.

2. James M. Cole, "Memorandum for All United States Attorneys," U.S. Department of Justice, August 29, 2013, www.justice.gov/iso/opa/resources/3052013829132756857467.pdf.

3. "Cooperative Federalism and Marijuana Regulation," UCLA Law Review, January 11, 2015, accessed February 27, 2018, https://www.uclalawreview.org/cooperative-federalism-and-marijuana-regulation-2/.

4. John Ingold, "Nebraska and Oklahoma sue Colorado over marijuana legalization," The Denver Post, October 2, 2016, accessed February 27, 2018, https://www.denverpost.com/2014/12/18/nebraska-and-oklahoma-sue-colorado-over-marijuana-legalization/.

5. Ivo D. Duchacek, Comparative Federalism: The Territorial Dimension of Politics (University Press of America, 1987).

6. "The Declaration of Independence: Full text - US History," accessed February 27, 2018, https://www.archives.gov/founding-docs/declaration-transcript.

7. "State," Merriam-Webster, accessed February 27, 2018, https://www.merriam-webster.com/dictionary/state.

8. Catolica Instituto de Estudios Politicos, http://www.iep.lisboa.ucp.pt/resources/documentos/estoril-political-forum-2013/gordon-wood.pdf.

9. "Articles of Confederation," History.com, accessed February 27, 2018, http://www.history.com/topics/articles-of-confederation/videos/articles-of-confederation.

10. The Oxford Handbook of the American Revolution, ed. Jane Kamensky and Edward G. Gray, (Oxford University Press, 2012), 392.

11. Thomas Jefferson, The Works of Thomas Jefferson: Notes on Virginia II, Correspondence 1782-1786 (Washington: Taylor & Maury, 1853).

12. John D. Donahue, Disunited States (New York: Basic Books, 1997).

13. Ibid.

14. Ibid.

15. The Judicial Branch of Federal Government: People, Process, and Politics, ed. Charles L. Zelden (Santa Barbara, CA: ABC-CLIO, 2007).

16. "U.S. Constitution"

17. Note 14 in cannon.

18. "West Coast Hotel Co. v. Parrish, 300 U.S. 379 (1937)," Justia Law, accessed February 27, 2018, https://supreme.justia.com/cases/federal/us/300/379/case.html.

19. "Inside the 'Constitutional Revolution' of 1937," NDLScholarship, accessed February 27, 2018, https://scholarship.law.nd.edu/law_faculty_scholarship/1287/.

20. United States v. Darby, 312 U.S. 100, 124 (U.S. 1941).

21. Key Supreme Court Cases: Heart of Atlanta Motel v. U.S., ABA Division for Public Education, accessed February 27, 2018, https://www.americanbar.org/groups/public_education/initiatives_awards/students_in_action/atlanta.html.

22. United States v. Lopez, 514 U.S. 549 (U.S. 1995).

23. "United States v. Morrison," Oyez, https://www.oyez.org/cases/1999/99-5.

24. Morton Grodzins, "The Federal System," Classic Readings in American Politics, eds. Pietro S. Nivola and David H. Rosenbloom (New York: St. Martin's Press, 1990).

25. Laurence J. OToole, and Robert K. Christensen, American Intergovernmental Relations: Foundations, Perspectives, and Issues (Washington, DC: CQ Press, 2013).

26. Virginia, Russell L. Hanson Gray and Thad Kousser, Politics in the American States: A Comparative Analysis (Los Angeles: Sage/CQ Press, 2018).

27. Cho and Wright, Politics in the American States (2007).

28. "Introduction," U.S. Department of Transportation - NHTSA - Final Report - Legislative History of .08 per se Laws - DOT HS 809 286, July 2001- 1 Introduction, accessed February 27, 2018, https://one.nhtsa.gov/people/injury/research/pub/alcohol-laws/08History/1_introduction.htm.

29. "Family Educational Rights and Privacy Act (FERPA)," U.S. Department of Education, June 26, 2015, accessed February 27, 2018, https://www2.ed.gov/policy/gen/guid/fpco/ferpa/index.html.

30. "Categorical Grants - Definition, Examples, Cases, Processes," Legal Dictionary, April 28, 2016, accessed February 27, 2018, https://legaldictionary.net/categorical-grants/.

31. Robert Jay Dilger, "Federal Grants to State and Local Governments: A Historical Perspective on Contemporary Issues," Congressional Research Service, May 7, 2018, https://fas.org/sgp/crs/misc/R40638.pdf.

32. "How Much Do States Rely on Federal Funding?" Governing, accessed February 27, 2018, http://www.governing.com/topics/finance/gov-state-budgets-federal-funding-2015-2018-trump.html.

33. "Financing & Reimbursement," Medicaid.gov, accessed February 27, 2018, https://www.medicaid.gov/medicaid/financing-and-reimbursement/.

34. "Federal and State Endangered and Threatened Species Expenditures," U.S. Fish & Wildlife Service, 2016, https://www.fws.gov/endangered/esa-library/pdf/2016_Expenditures_Report.pdf.

35. Virginia Gray, Russell L. Hanson, and Thad Kousser, Politics in the American States: A Comparative Analysis (Los Angeles: Sage/CQ Press, 2018).

36. John D. Donahue, Disunited States (New York: Basic Books, 1997).

37. Martin Saiz and Susan Clarke, "Economic Development and Infrastructure Policy," Politics in the American States: A Comparative Analysis (Los Angeles: Sage/CQ Press, 2018).

38. Bryan D. Jones and Lynn W. Bachelor, The Sustaining Hand: Community Leadership and Corporate Power, (Lawrence: University Press of Kansas, 1993).

39. Susan B. Hansen, Globalization and the Politics of Pay: Policy Choices in the American States (Washington, D.C.: Georgetown University Press, 2007).

40. Martin Saiz and Susan Clarke, "Economic Development and Infrastructure Policy," Politics in the American States: A Comparative Analysis (Los Angeles: Sage/CQ Press, 2018).

41. Charles Mahtesian, "Romancing the Smokestack," Governing, November 1994, 36–40.

42. Amy Martinez, "Motion Challenges Dell Incentives," News & Observer (Raleigh, N.C.) June 24, 2005.

43. Irwin Speizer, "Dell Pickle," Business North Carolina, 2005, 25-46.

44. Leanna Garfield, "Amazon has announced the top contenders in its $5 billion bidding war for HQ2 – here are their craziest proposals," Business Insider, January 18, 2018, http://www.businessinsider.com/amazon-headquarters-city-proposals-hq2-2017-10#philadelphia-three-sites-that-would-span-a-total-of-28-million-square-feet-7.

45. Alan Peters and Peter Fisher, "Commentary: The Failures of Economic Development Incentives," Journal of the American Planning Association 70 (2004): 27–37.

46. Ibid.

47. John D. Donahue, Disunited States (New York: Basic Books, 1997).

48. Paul E. Peterson and Mark C. Rom, Welfare Magnets: A New Case for a National Standard (Washington, D.C: Brookings Books, 1990).

49. Virginia Gray, Russell L. Hanson, and Thad Kousser, Politics in the American States: A Comparative Analysis (Los Angeles: Sage/CQ Press, 2018).

50. "Bussed Out: How America Moves Thousands of Homeless People Around the Country," The Guardian, December 20, 2017, accessed February 27, 2018, https://www.theguardian.com/us-news/ng-interactive/2017/dec/20/bussed-out-america-moves-homeless-people-country-study.

51. Daniel Judah Elazar, American Federalism: A View from the States (New York: Harper and Row, 1984).

52. "New State Ice Co. v. Liebmann, 285 U.S. 262 (1932)," Justia Law, accessed February 27, 2018, https://supreme.justia.com/cases/federal/us/285/262/case.html.

53. "Census Bureau Reports There Are 89,004 Local Governments in the United States," U.S. Census Bureau, May 19, 2016, accessed February 27, 2018, https://www.census.gov/newsroom/releases/archives/governments/cb12-161.html.

54. This line was adapted from the movie "Guardians of the Galaxy" while the screenplay for "Footloose" was based on Elmore City, Oklahoma, which banned public dancing until local high schoolers petitioned to change the law so they could have a prom. http://mentalfloss.com/article/73151/18-catchy-facts-about-footloose

CHAPTER 4
Civil Liberties: Necessary for Democracy to Exist

Chapter Objectives

1. Know the difference between civil liberties and civil rights and understand the rise of civil liberties.
2. Appreciate the importance of First Amendment rights.
3. Understand the Second Amendment and the right to bear arms.
4. Consider the rights of those accused of crimes.
5. Think critically about the debate between government responsibilities and individual freedoms.

Introduction: Freedom of Speech

On March 3, 2006, while serving his country as a U.S. Marine, 20-year-old Lance Corporal Matthew A. Snyder was killed in a non-combat vehicle accident in Iraq. A week later, his family held a military funeral for him in Westminster, Maryland. His father, Albert Snyder, recalls "being presented the flag at the graveyard. I remember saluting the coffin."[1]

The First Amendment's protection of freedom of speech safeguards the rights of protesters like those who belong to the Westboro Baptist Church. The church conducts anti-gay protests at military funerals.

a katz / Shutterstock.com

Albert Snyder also remembers the demonstrators at the funeral from Westboro Baptist Church who carried signs that read, "Thank God for Dead Soldiers," "You're Going to Hell," and "God Hates Fags." These protesters were members of a small church based in Topeka, Kansas, who regularly picket at funerals of U.S. soldiers killed in action. They claim that military deaths are God's punishment for the expanding acceptance of homosexuality in the United States. Albert Snyder sued Fred Phelps, the founder of Westboro Baptist Church, and two of his daughters for intrusion upon seclusion, intentional infliction of emotional distress, and civil conspiracy. Snyder testified at trial that the church members had "turned this funeral into a media circus and they wanted to hurt my family. They wanted their message heard and they didn't care who they stepped over. My son should have been buried with dignity, not with a bunch of clowns outside."[2] A Maryland jury awarded Snyder $10 million in damages for emotional distress and invasion of privacy.

It may be difficult to find many people who would agree with the message espoused by Westboro Baptist Church, or the appropriateness of carrying such hateful signs at the funerals of military personnel. However, when Maryland court's decision was appealed, the First Amendment was invoked and the actions of Phelps and Westboro Baptist Church were determined to be protected by freedom of speech. The Fourth Circuit Court ruled in favor of the church, threw out the $10 million award, and ordered that Snyder pay $16,000 of the defendant's legal costs. In 2011, the case made its way to the Supreme Court where, in a nearly unanimous decision, the Court ruled that these demonstrations are fully protected under the U.S. Constitution. The Court determined that the First Amendment's protections of freedom of speech "are so central to the nation that the Constitution protects cruel and unpopular protests, even, as in this case, at the moment of a family's most profound grief. Chief Justice John Roberts wrote that Westboro Baptist Church's picketing at the funerals of fallen soldiers is "certainly hurtful and its contribution to public discourse may be negligible,"[3] but the reaction may not be "punishing the speaker." Thus, no matter how upsetting it was for Snyder to see signs at his son's funeral claiming that his son's death was deserved, the First Amendment protected the church members' speech.

As this example illustrates, conflict is inevitable when discussing civil liberties. Some of the basic American values we studied earlier in the book frequently lead to fundamental disagreements. For example, values such as liberty versus security come into conflict when examining issues like freedom of expression. Conflicts arise over other questions, such as, should skinheads be permitted to call for attacks against blacks, Muslims, and Jews? Should pornography be legal? Should a woman have the right to terminate a pregnancy? Should a public school display a prayer in its auditorium? These difficult questions have all appeared before the Supreme Court. The Court turns to the Constitution for answers. Civil liberties have long been a source of conflict in the United States. Even restructuring the Constitution to include a Bill of Rights was contentious. As discussed in Chapter 2, the original text of the Constitution did not address individual or states' rights. By agreeing to adopt the Bill of Rights, the Federalist supporters of the Constitution were able to convince many of the Anti-Federalists to ratify it.

This chapter defines the term civil liberties and distinguishes it from a discussion of civil rights. It then looks at the rise of civil liberties in American discourse and examines the amendments in the Bill of Rights. Throughout the chapter, we consider cases that have challenged the courts' and the public's understanding of civil liberties and extended established freedoms into new domains.

4.1 Civil Liberties vs. Civil Rights

civil liberties

Those freedoms that the government cannot take away.

The easiest way to distinguish between **civil liberties** and civil rights is to think of civil liberties as those freedoms that the government *cannot* take away and to think of civil rights as those freedoms that the government *must* provide. It may seem like these definitions make opposite demands on the government. In fact, the two concepts can at times be at odds. For example, it is possible that by enforcing civil rights for some, the government may actually limit the civil liberties of others. For example, when *Brown v. the Board of Education of Topeka* determined that schools had to be desegregated, the decision limited the freedom of citizens to attend white-only or black-only schools. However, more often than not, civil liberties and civil rights work together. Battles for civil rights, for example, generate the expansion of civil liberties. The Fourteenth Amendment, which has become the foundation of modern civil liberties, came about as the result of the fight to abolish slavery.

While civil liberties are established in the Bill of Rights, they have become increasingly important to current political discourse and culture in the United States. This next section examines how they have evolved and expanded.

4.2 Civil Liberties as a National Discourse

In the *Federalist Papers*, Alexander Hamilton argued that a bill of rights was unnecessary because of the existing provisions in the Constitution and because of the impossibility of producing an exhaustive list of rights. Some rights would inevitably and inadvertently be omitted and could potentially create future conflict. James Madison initially agreed with Hamilton that a bill of rights was not necessary, but he was ultimately convinced by Thomas Jefferson to add it. Madison remained persuaded, however, by Hamilton's concern about the infeasibility of producing a complete list of rights and thus proposed the Ninth Amendment.

The Ninth Amendment requires that the American government not infer that citizens possess only those rights listed in the Bill of Rights. The amendment was not invoked for a long time until it became relevant to the consideration of privacy rights, which we discuss later in the chapter.

The Bill of Rights, the first 10 amendments to the Constitution, originally applied only to the national government. The struggle for civil rights eventually extended the Bill of Rights to the states. Indeed, before the Civil War, the Bill of Rights did not play a significant role in American politics. When the war ended and slavery was abolished, the government was faced with the issue of what to do about freed slaves. The Fourteenth Amendment was adopted in 1868 with the intention of extending citizenship rights to newly freed slaves. The Amendment also included a **"due process" clause** directed at state governments. Every discussion of civil liberties highlights one passage in the Fourteenth Amendment. This passage has, in fact, made the Fourteenth Amendment the most frequently cited amendment at Supreme Court hearings:

> *No state shall ... deprive any person of life, liberty, or property, without due process of law; nor deny any person within its jurisdiction the equal protection of the laws.*

due process clause

The government must respect all of the legal rights that are owed to a person according to the law and cannot deprive people of their life, liberty, or property without certain legal steps being taken.

While the language of the Fourteenth Amendment seemed directly aimed at states, the Supreme Court ruled in 1873 that the amendment applied only to freed slaves. It was not until 1897 that the Court changed its mind and began extending the Bill of Rights to states one at a time. This process is called **selective incorporation**.

The doctrine first emerged after the Constitution had already been signed. Concerns remained about the extent to which federal laws would apply to the states. Congress responded to these concerns with the Fourteenth Amendment. A clause in the amendment prevents states from limiting the rights enshrined in the Constitution. The Supreme Court ruled on the Fourteenth Amendment and selective incorporation for the first time in 1873 in the Slaughterhouse cases. The Court determined in a 5 to 4 decision that Louisiana's law granting a monopoly on the slaughter of livestock to

selective incorporation

Refers to the extension of protections from the Bill of Rights to state governments, one right at a time.

one New Orleans slaughterhouse was constitutional because there was nothing in the Constitution that explicitly forbade states from granting monopolies.

The Supreme Court gradually broadened its position on selective incorporation and has consistently ruled in favor of extending Bill of Rights protections to state governments. With *Gitlow v. New York* (1925), the Supreme Court incorporated, or applied, freedom of speech to the states. Benjamin Gitlow, a member of the Socialist Party of America, had been charged with criminal anarchy for publishing his "Left Wing Manifesto." He was convicted under New York's Criminal Anarchy Law for publishing material that called for the violent overthrow of the government. The U.S. Supreme Court held that while state and local governments could not infringe upon freedom of speech, Gitlow was in fact guilty. The Court upheld his conviction on the grounds that the government may limit or punish speech that advocates the unlawful overthrow of the government by force. Two more examples that helped apply the first 10 amendments to the states included *Gideon v. Wainwright* (1963), in which the Court determined that states could not infringe upon an indigent citizen's right to an attorney, and *Brown v. the Board of Education* (1954), in which the Court ruled that a state could not segregate public schools on the basis of race. The Supreme Court has since incorporated almost every phrase of the Bill of Rights to ensure that both national *and* state governments recognize those rights and privileges.

4.3 First Amendment Rights

The First Amendment contains the rights the Framers of the Constitution thought to be the most fundamental: freedom of religion, freedom of speech, freedom of the press, the right to assemble, and the right to petition the government for a redress of grievances. This section presents each of these rights and considers the issues they raise.

Freedom of Religion

What happens when a person's religious practices clash with norms like school dress codes? This question was at the center of a lawsuit filed on behalf of Ariana Iacono, a high school student whose nose piercing violated her school's dress code. Iacono claimed her piercing was a religious symbol mandated by her church.

© Shutterstock, Inc.

In 2010, freshman Ariana Iacono was suspended four times from her high school in Raleigh, North Carolina for violating her school's dress code. Specifically, it was the piercing in her nose that school administrators found objectionable. What ensued was a battle over Iacono's First Amendment right to freedom of religion.

Iacono claimed that she was a member of the Church of Body Modification and her nose stud was an essential part of her faith. Her nose piercing was a religious symbol, she said, not a fashion statement. The Church of Body Modification is small, with just over 3,500 members nationwide, but it has a clergy, a statement of beliefs, and a formal process for accepting new members.

The American Civil Liberties Union filed a lawsuit against the school system on behalf of Iacono, stating that her rights had been violated by the suspension. Officials with the Johnston County Schools agreed to settle out of court and allowed Iacono to wear the nose piercing. While the dress code continues to forbid facial piercings, school officials amended their policy to make exceptions for students who have "sincerely held" religious beliefs.

Iacono's arguments about her religious rights can be found in two clauses in the text of the First Amendment: the "establishment" clause and the "free exercise" clause.

Establishment Clause

The **Establishment Clause** is the first clause of the First Amendment. It states that "Congress shall make no law respecting an establishment of religion." The clause was intended to prevent the federal government from imposing a national religion. But what does this mean in practice? The debates began almost immediately. Should there be no established national religion? Should the government not give preference to one established religion over another? Should the government not regulate the actual physical establishment of a church? Should the government not interfere with an established religion?

In rejecting President Washington's proposal for an annual day of prayer, Thomas Jefferson wrote that the First Amendment builds "a wall of separation between church and state" and that a national day of prayer would constitute the government encouraging religion. The Supreme Court incorporated the Establishment Clause to the states in 1947, citing Jefferson's wall of separation.

In practice, the wall of separation is not so clearly defined. "In God We Trust" is inscribed on the national currency; U.S. presidents are sworn in with their hand on the Bible; students pledge allegiance to "one nation, under God"; Congress opens its sessions with a prayer. What is clear, however, is that government should not meddle in religious and church affairs. The Supreme Court has also said that the Establishment Clause requires government neutrality and no government favoritism when it comes to religion. In one of its most unpopular decisions, *Engel v. Vitale* (1962), the Court ruled that teacher-led prayer in public schools was unconstitutional. In *Lemon v. Kurtzman* (1971), the Court established criteria to determine where there might be possible violations to the Establishment Clause. The **Lemon Test**, named for the lead plaintiff in the case, Alton Lemon, was adopted to help judge what government actions are permissible. In applying the Lemon Test, the Court must ask three questions:

1. Does the legislation reflect a secular legislative purpose?
2. Does the legislation neither advance nor inhibit religion?
3. Does the legislation avoid excessive entanglement with religion, including sponsorship, financial support, and active involvement in religious activities?

The Lemon Test has been used in a string of controversial decisions. May tax dollars be used to set up nativity scenes in public spaces at Christmas? Yes, because the nativity is a historical event and not just a religious one. It cannot, however, be a nativity scene by itself. There must also be secular and other religious decorations present, such as Christmas trees and Jewish menorahs, to demonstrate a diversity of messages rather than an endorsement of Christianity alone. May there be voluntary or silent prayers by individual students at school? Yes, but a public school cannot introduce a minute of silent prayer or meditation. Football games and graduations also cannot include prayers. Prayers are allowed in Congressional, state legislature, and other government meetings because the individuals attending the meetings are adults who have already formed their religious views and will not be intimidated.

Advocates of the Lemon Test are those who call for a strict separation between church and state. An alternative view to strict separation is accommodation, which argues that the government does not violate the Establishment Clause as long as it does not privilege one religion over another.

Establishment Clause

The first clause of the First Amendment, which states that Congress shall make no law respecting an establishment of religion.

Lemon Test

A test adopted to help judge what government actions are permissible concerning religion. In applying the Lemon Test, the Court must ask three questions: 1) Does the legislation reflect a secular legislative purpose? 2) Does the legislation neither advance nor inhibit religion? 3) Does the legislation avoid excessive entanglement with religion, including sponsorship, financial support, and active involvement in religious activities?

Members of the Air Force and their families observe a Religious Display Interfaith Ceremony at the Friendship Chapel at Shaw Air Force Base, South Carolina. Four holiday displays were lit: a yule log, menorah, nativity scene, and Christmas tree.

Airman 1st Class Jensen Stidham [Public domain], via Wikimedia Commons. https://bit.ly/2S1Cp62.

Free Exercise Clause

Free Exercise clause

Prohibits government from interfering with the "free exercise" of religion.

Sherbert Test

Used by the Supreme Court to determine whether the First Amendment right to free exercise of religion has been violated. When using the Sherbert Test, the Court asks two questions: 1) is the government imposing a significant burden on an individual's ability to exercise his or her faith; and 2) does the government have a compelling reason or interest for imposing the burden?

The **Free Exercise clause** is the second clause of the First Amendment and prohibits government from interfering with the "free exercise" of religion. Does this mean that anyone can establish and practice any religion he or she wants? The Supreme Court has ruled that people can practice any religion in any way as long as it does not violate laws regarding peace, prosperity, and morality. This view has evolved and developed over time.

In 1963, the Supreme Court ruled in favor of free exercise when it heard the case of Adell Sherbert, a Seventh-Day Adventist who was fired for refusing to work on Saturdays because it violated her religious faith. South Carolina denied her unemployment benefits because she had been offered other jobs but rejected them because they also required her to work on Saturdays. Sherbert argued that her free exercise of religion had been violated and sued South Carolina for her benefits. The Supreme Court ruled in favor of Sherbert and, in doing so, introduced the **Sherbert Test** to determine whether the First Amendment right to free exercise of religion has been violated. When using the Sherbert Test, the Court asks two questions: 1) is the government imposing a significant burden on an individual's ability to exercise his or her faith; and 2) does the government have a compelling reason or interest for imposing the burden? In the case of Sherbert, the Court ruled that her free exercise of religion had been significantly burdened and that there was no compelling state interest for doing so.

The Court relied on the Sherbert Test until 1990 when it ruled on *Employment Division v. Smith*. In this case, two men in Oregon were fired and were subsequently denied unemployment benefits for using peyote, a hallucinogenic drug they took as part of their Native American spiritual rituals. Here, the Court ruled that Oregon *did* have a compelling interest to infringe upon the men's free exercise of religion because peyote is an illegal drug in Oregon and everyone in the state is prohibited from smoking it, regardless of religion. It is therefore a neutral law applied in a neutral way. The case replaced the Sherbert Test with the *neutrality test*, which only asks whether the same law applies to everyone, irrespective of religion. If a law does not target a specific group, then the Court will not stop the law. The neutrality test has made it much more difficult to sue the government for violations of the Free Exercise clause.

The Free Exercise clause was invoked in another landmark decision, *Burwell v. Hobby Lobby* (2014). In this case, the owners of Hobby Lobby, a private chain store, argued against the Affordable Care Act's requirement that they provide contraception for their employees. Hobby Lobby claimed that providing contraception violated the company owners' religious beliefs. The Court ruled in favor of Hobby Lobby and stated that the government's contraception mandate infringed upon the owners' free exercise of religion with no compelling interest for doing so.

Groups that have found protection under the Free Exercise clause include Jehovah's Witnesses, who are allowed to refuse life-saving blood transfusions because these transfusions violate their religious beliefs; Quakers, who do not believe in killing, even in war, and can therefore be exempt from a military draft as conscientious objectors; and practitioners of Santeria, who sacrifice animals (primarily chickens), because this practice does not endanger other people.

In examining cases about the freedom of religion, the Court also considers whether the individual right to not practice religion is being violated. In 2012, 16-year-old Jessica Ahlquist, sued her public high school in Cranston, Rhode Island, over the display of a prayer in the school's auditorium (shown here https://centerforinquiry.org/blog/federal_judge_orders_removal_of_prayer_banner_in_rhode_island_high_school/). Ahlquist, an atheist, argued that the presence of the prayer, which had been hanging in the auditorium for 49 years, was unconstitutional because it violated the principle of government neutrality in religion. The District Court in Rhode Island ruled in favor of Ahlquist asserting that the Establishment Clause had been violated. The prayer was removed.

Freedom of Speech

The next part of the First Amendment addresses freedom of speech. It states:

> *Congress shall make no law ... abridging the freedom of speech.*

Freedom of speech is protected because our democratic system requires that we have the ability to express our opinions and beliefs, no matter how unpopular they may be. What do we mean by speech? Speech, as understood in the First Amendment, refers to words, images, symbols, pictures, or gestures intended to convey an idea. And while the courts are skeptical of attempts to limit or curb speech, there have been times when Americans have suffered from not being allowed to express their views and when individual liberties have in fact been infringed by the government. In 1798, the Federalists passed the Alien and Sedition Acts, which made it illegal to speak out against the government. President John Adams signed the bills into law in an effort to strengthen national security. More specifically, the four laws were intended to target foreigners and gave the president the authority to deport noncitizens who did not agree with the Adams administration. President Jefferson repealed three of the acts, arguing that they were unconstitutional. The one law that remained in place was the Alien Enemies Act, which was revised and codified during World War I. The act, which is still in effect today, was invoked during World War II to identify, detain, and later deport enemies from Germany, Italy, and Japan. During the twentieth century, the Supreme Court supported restrictions on speech in times of war because security was valued as a higher priority than liberty. During World War I, for example, socialist leader Eugene Debs was sentenced to 10 years in prison for declaring during a speech at a convention in Ohio: "If war is right, let it be declared by the people!"[4] It is rare, however, that speech is prohibited. Much of the debate about the freedom of speech focuses on the boundaries of what is protected.

Types of Speech

How the courts deal with speech depends on which type of speech is involved. Political speech is the most protected type of speech because it has to do with government policy, elections, campaigns, and debating political ideas. The **Clear and Present Danger Rule** applies here, as speech can only be limited or outlawed if it causes substantive evils (rioting, destruction of property, lawlessness) that are so imminent that no opportunity exists for discussion. In order to invoke the Clear and Present Danger Rule, the government must prove that the speech presents an immediate danger. The rule was established in the case *Schenck v. United States* (1919). Charles Schenck, the general secretary of the Socialist Party in Philadelphia, was found guilty of violating the Espionage Act by printing and distributing a document that urged men to resist being recruited to fight in World War I. According to Schenck, it was a war designed to profit Wall Street. The Court ruled that because it was wartime, Schenck's speech was likely to cause imminent threat to peace and security. Based on the Clear and Present Danger Rule, judges consider what was said (the actual words); how it was said (the tone used); the intent of the speaker (the words, tone, the speaker's prior speeches, statements, etc.); and where it was said (was a deliberately confrontational location chosen to perhaps incite trouble?).

After 50 years of the Clear and Present Danger Rule, the Court decided that "puny" threats, which no one took seriously, should not be considered as clear and present dangers. In *Brandenburg v. Ohio* (1969), the Court formally declared the preferred position of free speech and made it very difficult to limit political speech for clear and present danger. The case arose when Clarence

Clear and Present Danger Rule

Doctrine espousing that speech can only be limited or outlawed if it causes substantive evils (rioting, destruction of property, lawlessness) that are so imminent and immediate that no opportunity exists for discussion.

Brandenburg, a Ku Klux Klan leader, organized a rally in which Klan members burned crosses, waved guns, and called for "revengence" against black and Jewish Americans. The Supreme Court ruled in favor of Brandenburg's freedom of speech, finding that his speech was unlikely to incite or actually produce imminent lawless action.

Pure speech, or conversations among family, friends, and neighbors, is almost always protected because it does not deal with public policy. It is personal, intimate, and private; therefore the government does not have any business regulating it.

Commercial speech refers to advertising of any kind. In order to be protected by the First Amendment, it must be truthful—or at least not deliberately deceptive. Also, the courts allow it to be regulated by the captive audience rule: if the advertising is aimed at people who cannot get up and leave, then advertising can be restricted and regulated.

Symbolic speech refers to nonverbal communication or actions that express an idea. Examples of symbolic speech include draft card burning, wearing an armband or peace symbol, burning the American flag, and wearing a t-shirt or other article of clothing bearing a political slogan or symbol. The First Amendment protects most forms of symbolic speech, even when controversial. In *Texas v. Johnson* (1989), the Court determined that burning the American flag is a protected form of symbolic speech. Flag-burning, at the time, was banned by 48 states and by the federal government. In writing the majority opinion, the Supreme Court wrote: "If there is a bedrock principle underlying the First Amendment it is that government may not prohibit the expression of an idea simply because society finds the idea offensive or disagreeable."[5] Congress passed legislation to protect the flag, but the Court overturned it.

The Court determined, however, that limits do apply to what can be protected as symbolic speech. The Ku Klux Klan practice of burning crosses as a form of intimidation of their black neighbors is not protected. While individuals may burn crosses to express their ideas, they may not burn crosses to terrorize or intimidate others, acts that are not protected by the First Amendment. In *R.A.V v. City of St. Paul* (1992), the Supreme Court heard the case of a Minnesota teenager who, along with several others, had allegedly burned a crudely fashioned cross on the front lawn of a black family. Local police charged the teen with having violated the city's Bias-Motivated Crime Ordinance, which prevents displaying a symbol that arouses "anger, alarm, or resentment in others on the basis of race, color, creed, religion, or gender."[6] The charge was dismissed in trial court but then reversed by the Minnesota State supreme court. R.A.V. appealed to the U.S. Supreme Court, which ruled that St. Paul's ordinance violated the defendant's First Amendment freedom of speech rights because "it prohibits otherwise permitted speech solely on the basis of the subjects the speech addresses." In order words, just because government disapproves of the ideas expressed, under the rights guaranteed by the First Amendment, it cannot punish speech and expression.

The Ku Klux Klan are shown here at a cross burning in Knoxville, Tennessee, in 1948. The practice of burning crosses dates back to Medieval Europe, among Scottish clans who set fire to crosses on hillsides to rally troops or as symbols of defiance. The Klan looks to Medieval Europe as an icon of moral purity and racial homogeny, but did not burn crosses until a scene in the 1905 novel *The Clansman* included a cross-burning to link the Klan to the Scottish clans. The scene was included in the film *The Birth of a Nation*. Klansmen started burning crosses soon after to intimidate and terrorize minorities. Klansmen refer to the practice as "cross lighting" and claim it symbolizes their Christian faith.[7]

Everett Historical / Shutterstock.com

Some types of speech are considered dangerous, such as yelling, "Fire!" in a crowded theater, advocating the violent overthrow of government, or using fighting words. **Fighting words** are statements or expressions that are likely to provoke a violent reaction and are not always protected by the First Amendment. Racial slurs and some forms of hate speech fall into the category of fighting words. Student speech is another area that is less protected by the First Amendment. In the case of *Tinker v. Des Moines Independent School District* (1969), the Supreme Court ruled that school officials could not prevent students from wearing black armbands to school as a form of government protest. If, however, the speech interfered with the appropriate discipline and operation of the school, then officials had the right to regulate student speech.

False speech, including libel and slander, is also limited in its protection under the First Amendment. **Libel**, written statements that defame a person's character, and **slander**, spoken statements that defame a person's character, are difficult to prosecute, however. Victims of libel or slander must demonstrate that not only was the statement false and that it caused them harm, but also that it was made with malice and was intended to destroy their reputations. This condition, that libel or slander must be made with malice, is what makes it especially challenging for celebrities and public officials to win libel and slander judgments.

fighting words

Statements or expressions that are likely to provoke a violent reaction and are not always protected by the First Amendment.

libel

Written statements that defame the character of a person.

slander

Spoken statements that defame the character of a person.

Freedom of the Press

One of the most important features of a democracy is using the written word to freely express ideas about politics. These written expressions have played an integral part in American history since the country's founding. They have taken the form of pamphlets, brochures, newspapers, magazines, periodicals, journals, and digital media. Like speech, written words are protected with very few limits.

prior restraint

Action that prohibits speech prior to publication. The First Amendment limits any advanced government censoring of the news, with minor exceptions.

In an effort to protect the press, the courts established the rule of no **prior restraint**, which mandates that the government cannot stop the presses and there cannot be any advanced censoring of the news. There are three minor exceptions, however. The published words must:

1. cause "irreparable harm" to national security

2. impinge upon a defendant's right to a fair trial (in this case, the courts can issue a gag order and limit what is published about the case)

3. harm vital national interests, such as in the case of copyright information or economic or national trade secrets.

One of the most famous attempts to invoke the principle of irreparable harm to national security occurred in 1971. The Nixon administration attempted to stop the publication of what was known as the Pentagon Papers, a report on the history of U.S. involvement in Vietnam during 1945-1967. The report criticized several top political leaders for their handling of the Vietnam War. In the case of *New York Times Company v. United States* (1971), the Nixon administration lost because it failed to prove irreparable harm. *The New York Times* published the then-classified report without the risk of being punished by the federal government.

Today, digital media presents a new and complicated challenge to the prior restraint rule. WikiLeaks is a prime example. The website for anonymous whistleblowing allows users to publish sensitive and private internal documents from sources such as banks and government agencies. While the Supreme Court has an interest in limiting the publication of these documents, it has been difficult to stop new media sites like WikiLeaks because the company operates globally across national borders and out of reach of the Court's jurisdiction.[8] The challenges of regulating digital media leave the government vulnerable and struggling to balance civil liberties with national security.

Obscenity

Obscenity is not protected by freedom of the press because, according to the Supreme Court, it is speech that has no redeeming social importance. The Court struggles, however, with determining what is actually obscene. As Justice Potter Stewart famously said, "I know it when I see it."[9]

In order to better determine what "it" is and judge whether a work is obscene, the Supreme Court has used the **Miller Test** since 1973. In *Miller v. California* (1973), the Court created the three-part test, which holds that speech is not protected by the First Amendment if: 1) the average person applying contemporary community standards finds the work, taken as a whole, appeals to prurient interests (is meant to be sexually stimulating); 2) the work depicts, in a patently offensive way, sexual conduct that is defined and prohibited by state law; and 3) the work as a whole lacks serious literary, artistic, political, or scientific value.

How pornography should be evaluated remains a heavily debated issue. For example, some feminists argue that pornography is a form of hate speech that subordinates women. Other feminists contend that pornography should be viewed as a medium for women's sexual expression. The Court struggles with regulating pornography in the era of the internet where it can flow freely across borders and into communities with differing standards. One area that is absolutely not protected by the First Amendment is child pornography. It is considered to be abuse of minors and is prosecuted as a criminal act.

The entertainment industry and the Court have tried to compromise and balance freedom of expression with protecting communities by using rating systems and warning labels for movies, television shows, and music. While the internet again makes these ratings and warnings difficult to implement, there are at least guidelines that leave some room for the public to make its own choice about what is socially important.

Miller Test

A three-part test created by the Supreme Court, which holds that speech is not protected by the First Amendment if: 1) the average person applying contemporary community standards finds the work, taken as a whole, appeals to prurient interests (is meant to be sexually stimulating); 2) the work depicts, in a patently offensive way, sexual conduct that is defined and prohibited by state law; and 3) the work as a whole lacks serious literary, artistic, political, or scientific value.

The Freedom to Assemble and the Freedom to Petition Government for a Redress of Grievances

The First Amendment includes two other civil liberties: the freedom to assemble and the freedom to petition the government for a redress of grievances.

The freedom to assemble allows people to gather in public places, but gatherings must be peaceful in order to be protected and there is no right to assemble on private property without the consent of the property owner. Further limitations include time restrictions, which are used to prevent disturbing other people; place restrictions, which hold that assembly is not allowed in locations where quiet is necessary to operate; and management restrictions which require that essential services such as medical personnel, parking, restrooms, etc. be provided to those assembling.

The freedom to petition for a redress of grievances protects the right to complain to the government. This part of the First Amendment protects lobbyists, interest groups, and citizens.

There are also implied rights that flow from the freedom to assemble and the freedom to petition. These include the right of association (individuals have the constitutional right to belong to or form a club or organization of their choice, no matter how radical or unpopular) and the right to demonstrate (individuals have the constitutional right to march, picket, and participate in sit-ins). These rights follow the same rules and regulations as freedom of assembly.

4.4 The Second Amendment and Right to Bear Arms

One of the most hotly debated amendments in the Bill of Rights is the Second Amendment, which states that:

A well regulated militia, being necessary to the security of a free State, the right of the people to keep and bear Arms, shall not be infringed.

In the context of a country emerging from the Articles of Confederation and the absence of an effective national military, it makes sense that the Bill of Rights should include a provision about the right for militias to be able to provide for the defense of the people with weapons. In the context of a country that has the most powerful military in the world, militias are obsolete and irrelevant. In such a world, is the right to keep and bears arms still necessary? Many would argue that the Second Amendment is a relic of the Revolution and that the right to bear arms should be replaced with concerns about public safety and gun control laws. Others argue that gun rights are deeply rooted in American culture and are fundamental to personal protection.

Beginning in the 1870s, the Supreme Court has interpreted the Second Amendment to apply to a collective right to bear arms, not an individual right. The amendment was intended to apply to the defense of the nation and not to the personal protection of our families or ourselves. The Supreme Court has, however, tended to defend gun rights. In 2010, the Court incorporated the Second Amendment in *McDonald v. Chicago*, which protects an individual right to possess firearms for lawful use, such as self-defense, in the home.

On March 24, 2018, inspired to take action in the aftermath of the school shooting in Parkand, Florida, protesters around the country participated in the March for Our Lives Rally to call for stricter gun control regulations.

Eva Hawker / Shutterstock.com

Gun rights are a major source of political conflict in this country. Those who argue for gun control legislation tend to be liberals who believe that laws are necessary to eliminate crimes of passion; restrict access from mentally unstable people; limit dangerous types of guns that are owned (including assault weapons); and prevent domestic disputes from turning deadly and accidental shootings from occurring. These advocates for gun control cite the significantly lower murder rates in countries that do have restrictions on gun ownership (see Table 4.1). On the other side of the debate are those who defend gun rights. They point out that countries with lower murder rates had those lower murder rates before enacting gun control legislation. They contend that criminals will still find weapons and arm themselves, and they argue that guns ultimately produce more safety in one's own home. Gun rights advocates assert that the Second Amendment keeps the government in check. If you are armed, they would say, you can resist government tyranny, and if the government begins chipping away at the Bill of Rights, what liberties might be taken away next?

TABLE 4.1 Murder Rates in Countries with Restrictions on Gun Ownership

Country	Gun Control Legislation	Firearm Homicides per 100,000 People
Japan	The only guns permitted are shotguns, air guns, guns that have research or industrial purposes, or those used for competitions. To use these weapons, one must undergo formal instruction and pass a series of written, mental, and drug tests and a rigorous background check. Owners must let authorities know how the weapon and ammunition is stored and provide the firearm for annual inspection.	0.0
United Kingdom	Government ban on handguns (with few exceptions) and on certain semiautomatic rifles.	0.06
Norway	Applicants for firearms must be at least 18 years old, specify a "valid reason" for gun ownership, and obtain a government license.	0.10
Australia	The government restricts the legal possession of automatic and semi-automatic firearms and limits the legal importation of non-military self-loading firearms to those with a maximum magazine capacity of five rounds. Citizens must register their firearms and be licensed to possess and use them. They must also demonstrate a genuine need for a particular type of gun and take a firearm safety course.	0.16
Canada	Federal regulations require all gun owners, who must be at least 18 years old, to obtain a license that includes a background check and a public safety course.	0.38
Israel	Regulations include an assault-weapons ban and a requirement to register ownership with the government. To become licensed, an applicant must be an Israeli citizen or a permanent resident, be at least 21 years old, and speak at least some Hebrew. Applicants must also show genuine cause to carry a firearm, such as self-defense or hunting.	1.04
United States	Federal law sets the minimum standards for firearm regulation in the United States, but individual states have their own laws, some of which provide further restrictions, others of which are more lenient. The Gun Control Act of 1968 prohibited the sale of firearms to people under the age of 18, those with criminal records, the mentally disabled, unlawful aliens, dishonorably discharged military personnel, and others. The law was amended in 1993 by the Brady Handgun Violence Prevention Act, which mandated background checks for all unlicensed persons purchasing a firearm from a federally licensed dealer. *McDonald v. Chicago* (2010) extends the right to keep and bear arms to individuals in each of the 50 U.S. states.	3.54

Based on Jonathan Masters, U.S. Gun Policy: Global Comparison, Council on Foreign Relations, November 14, 2017. https://www.cfr.org/backgrounder/us-gun-policy-global-comparisons

In the aftermath of tragic school shootings, there has been increased pressure on the government to keep the debate about the Second Amendment at the top of the political agenda. Some of those shootings include the 2018 killing of 17 people at Marjory Stoneman Douglas High School in Parkland, Florida; the 2017 shooting at an outdoor concert in Las Vegas that left 58 people dead and 851 injured; the mass shooting in the Pulse nightclub in Orlando, Florida, in 2016 that killed 49; the 2012 shooting deaths of 20 children and six adults at Sandy Hook elementary school in Newtown, Connecticut; and the killing of 12 people in a movie theater in Aurora, Colorado, in 2012.

4.5 Rights of the Accused

Four of the 10 amendments in the Bill of Rights address the rights of those accused of crimes. These amendments (Four, Five, Six, and Eight) detail 31 different rights for those suspected of criminal activity. There is debate about whether those accused of crimes are overly protected by the Constitution as we try to balance the basic value of security, often expressed as "law and order," and protecting the rights of individuals accused of a crime.

The rights of the accused were further expanded during the 1960s when a liberal Supreme Court led by Chief Justice Earl Warren issued landmark judgments in cases like *Mapp v. Ohio* (1961), *Miranda v. Arizona* (1966), and *Gideon v. Wainwright* (1963). We will discuss these in the following sections. Some of the rights recognized by the Warren Court were later taken away, first by the Burger Court (1969-1985), then by the Rehnquist Court (1985-2006).

The Fourth Amendment: No Unreasonable Search and Seizure

The Fourth Amendment requires that police have a warrant before they can search a private dwelling. It states that:

> *The right of the people to be secure in their persons, houses, papers, and effects, against unreasonable searches and seizures, shall not be violated, and no Warrants shall issue, but upon probable cause, supported by Oath or affirmation, and particularly describing the place to be searched, and the persons or things to be seized.*

The Supreme Court has interpreted the Fourth Amendment's protections against unreasonable search and seizure to require one of the following for a search to be legal:

1. A valid search warrant listing the address to be searched and the items to be seized;
2. Probable cause—something about the suspect's behavior or appearance that suggests a crime is about to be committed, is being committed, or will be committed;
3. A limited search of the suspect's clothing, body, and immediate surroundings can be conducted in conjunction with an arrest to ensure that evidence will not be destroyed and a weapon will not be used against the law enforcement officer.

In 1961, the Court established the exclusionary rule, which stipulates that illegally seized evidence cannot be used in court and must be thrown out. The intention of the ruling was to deter illegal searches. It came about as the result of the 1957 case *Mapp v. Ohio*. The case centered around the search of Dollree Mapp's apartment for a bombing suspect. When the police came to Mapp's apartment, they waved a piece of paper—not a warrant—in the air when Mapp demanded to see one before allowing them to enter. There was no bombing suspect in the apartment, but the police did find a suitcase full of pornographic material in Mapp's basement. Possession of pornography was illegal at this time. Mapp was convicted on obscenity charges. The Supreme Court determined that the conviction was unconstitutional and that evidence obtained in an illegal search cannot be used in a trial.

Supporters of the exclusionary rule argue that this decision deters illegal searches and seizures and promotes more legal and professional conduct for police officers. On the other hand, critics argue that if evidence that can lead to an indictment or a conviction is thrown out, and a guilty suspect is either not indicted or not convicted, then the suspect could end up back on the streets and thus commit more crimes. They also argue that this loophole encourages more crime. The Rehnquist Court began making exceptions to the exclusionary rule for these very reasons. It revisited the Mapp ruling to allow officers to present illegally seized evidence if, when the evidence was obtained, the police were acting in "good faith." In other words, if they thought that the seizure of the evidence was legal, it should be considered admissible.

The Fifth Amendment: The Right to Remain Silent

The Fifth Amendment focuses primarily on criminal trials and states that:

No person shall be held to answer for a capital, or otherwise infamous crime, unless on a presentment or indictment of a Grand Jury ...; nor shall any person be subject for the same offence to be twice put in jeopardy of life or limb; nor shall be compelled in any criminal case to be a witness against himself, nor be deprived of life, liberty, or property, without due process of law; nor shall private property be taken for public use, without just compensation.

In order for the government to take a suspect to trial, there must be a grand jury indictment or formal charge of a felony crime. This provision protects suspects from politically motivated charges being brought against them. It takes nine of 12 grand jurors voting that there is sufficient evidence to hand down an indictment.

The no **Double Jeopardy clause** means that a person cannot be tried twice for the same crime (unless he or she commits the crime a second time), even after the person was acquitted and evidence is uncovered indicating guilt. This prevents the government from bringing a suspect to trial again and again until it finally gains a conviction.

The Fifth Amendment establishes the right to remain silent. This clause is the origin of the phrase "pleading the fifth" or "taking the fifth" and states that a suspect or defendant has the right to remain silent and not answer questions. The person has also the right not to take the stand in his or her trial. The purpose of this provision is to protect suspects from self-incrimination and to prevent coerced confessions.

Double Jeopardy clause

A person cannot be tried twice for the same crime (unless he or she commits the crime a second time) even if after an acquittal, evidence is uncovered indicating that person's guilt.

Miranda rights

An explanation of rights for criminal suspects in police custody that include the right to silence, the right to an attorney, and the right to have an attorney appointed if a suspect cannot afford one. These rights emerged from the 1966 Miranda v. Arizona case, in which the Supreme Court ruled that any evidence acquired before a suspect's rights were read would be inadmissible in court.

Under the due process provision, a person cannot be executed, jailed, imprisoned, or have property confiscated without following due process, or fair procedures. The courts have interpreted due process to require one phone call when a suspect is taken into custody and the reading to a suspect of his or her **Miranda rights**. These rights emerged from the 1966 *Miranda v. Arizona* case in which the Court ruled that any evidence acquired before a suspect's rights were read would be inadmissible in court. When a suspect is taken into custody and questioned, police must inform the suspect of his or her rights by saying:

- You have the right to remain silent.
- Anything you say can be used against you.
- You have the right to an attorney; if you cannot afford an attorney, the court will provide one for you.
- You can stop questioning at any time and request to see an attorney.

Over time, the Miranda rights have been relaxed, but they still remain part of our national culture.

As the result of *Miranda v Arizona*, a person cannot be taken into police custody without first being "Mirandized," or read their rights clearly and directly: *"You have the right to remain silent. Anything you say can and will be used against you in a court of law. You have the right to an attorney. If you cannot afford an attorney, one will be provided for you. Do you understand the rights I have just read to you? With these rights in mind, do you wish to speak to me?"*

© Shutterstock, Inc.

The Sixth Amendment: The Right to a Fair Trial

The Sixth Amendment guarantees a speedy and public trial by an impartial jury as well as the right to an attorney. The amendment states:

In all criminal prosecutions, the accused shall enjoy the right to a speedy and public trial, by an impartial jury of the State and district wherein the crime shall have been committed, which district shall have been previously ascertained by law, and to be informed of the nature and cause of the accusation; to be confronted with the witnesses against him; to have compulsory process for obtaining witnesses in his favor, and to have the Assistance of Counsel for his defense.

The right to a speedy trial has been defined by the courts as a trial being held "without unreasonable delay." The courts have never defined it in terms of a specific number of days or months. Many states (including Texas and California) have speedy trial laws requiring that criminal trials begin within a certain time period after charges have been filed. In Texas, it is 180 days; in California it is 60 days.

In terms of the right to a public trial, this means that the trial must be open to the public and press to guarantee its fairness. Public and media scrutiny make it less likely that the government could prosecute someone hastily and without public scrutiny to obtain a guilty verdict.

A makeshift memorial was set up for the four victims of the Boston Marathon bombing in April 2013. The media covered the bombing extensively. People across the country were deeply impacted by the event and the arrest of one of the two bombers, making the bomber's access to an impartial jury nearly impossible.

Hang Dinh / Shutterstock.com

The right to an impartial jury has been interpreted to mean a jury with "randomly selected" jurors (no one group deliberately excluded) and composed of jurors who can be objective and have not yet formed a prejudicial opinion about the case. However, it is becoming increasingly difficult to find impartial juries in an era of cases being so extensively covered by the media (for example, the O.J. Simpson trial in 1995, the Kobe Bryant case in 2003, and the trial of Dzhokhar Tsarnaev, one of the two Boston Marathon bombers, in 2015).

When Clarence Earl Gideon was accused of stealing from a poolroom in Florida in 1961, he was too poor to hire a lawyer and he asked the court to appoint one for him. His request was denied by the state court, so at trial, Gideon (who had an eighth-grade education) represented himself. He was found guilty and was sentenced to five years in prison. Gideon filed a handwritten petition with the Supreme Court, claiming his constitutional right to an attorney had been violated. The Court found that the right to counsel guaranteed under the 6th Amendment of the Constitution is essential to a fair trial and applies to state courts.

Wisner, Woody. *Portrait of Clarence Earl Gideon*. 1961?. Black & white photoprint, 7 x 5 in. State Archives of Florida, Florida Memory. <https://www.floridamemory.com/items/show/35169>, accessed 18 January 2019.

The right to a trial in the state and district where the crime was committed can be modified if the trial judge orders a change of venue, moves the location of the trial to another jurisdiction where there has been less media coverage, or moves the trial to a location where it might be easier to select an impartial jury. When Timothy McVeigh was tried in 1997 for the Oklahoma City bombing, the trial was moved to Denver for the very reason that it would be difficult to find an impartial jury in the city where such a devastating attack occurred.

Defendants have the right to be informed about the charges brought against them so that an adequate response can be prepared. They also have the right to confront and cross-examine witnesses against them. This right holds even in child molestation cases. Precautions are taken, however, to minimize the trauma to younger victims, such as placing the child behind a screen or a one-way mirror. Defendants also have the same right as the prosecution to subpoena reluctant witnesses to testify on their behalf.

The Sixth Amendment includes the right to counsel, or to an attorney. This right was expanded to the states in 1963 when the Supreme Court ruled in the landmark case, *Gideon v. Wainwright*, that all defendants have the right to an attorney even if they cannot afford one. In cases where defendants cannot afford counsel, court-appointed attorneys will be provided at the taxpayers' expense. The fact that tax revenues are spent on lawyers for those accused of crimes may not sit easily with some members of the public. Also, public defenders who provide the counsel carry enormous caseloads and earn small salaries compared to other trial lawyers. Despite these challenges, the right to counsel and access to publicly funded criminal defense is an essential civil liberty for all citizens accused of crimes.

The Eighth Amendment: Cruel and Unusual Punishment

The Eighth Amendment is important because it raises the question about what constitutes cruel and unusual punishment. The Amendment states:

Excessive bail shall not be required, nor excessive fines imposed, nor cruel and unusual punishments inflicted.

Bail is the money put up by defendants to guarantee that if they are released, they will appear at the trial. If they fail to appear, then the money is forfeited. The bail amount must be proportionate to the crime: the more serious the crime, the higher the bail. Bail can be denied to defendants who may be a flight risk or who pose a danger to the community.

With regard to cruel and unusual punishment, the Supreme Court has ruled that "cruel and unusual" is an "evolving standard," changing as society's attitudes change. Punishments that may have been constitutional and permissible in the past may not be today or in the future. "Cruel and unusual" has been defined as no torturous, barbarous, or injurious punishments and no punishment too excessive for the crime committed. The death penalty cannot be used unless certain guidelines are followed. Prison conditions cannot be too extreme or severe. But even in this language, there is space for debate and room for multiple interpretations.

FIGURE 4.1 Countries with the Death Penalty
This map shows which countries have the death penalty (shown in red) and which ones do not. The United States is the only Western country that currently imposes the death penalty. It is one of 54 nations worldwide that apply it. Thirty-one states, the federal government, and the military use capital punishment as a legal penalty.

COUNTRIES WITH DEATH PENALTY

■ Retentionist countries (58)   ■ Abolitionist countries except crimes committed under exceptional circumstances (6)
■ Abolitionist in practice countries – no executions in the last 10 years (34)   ■ Completely abolished in 102 countries

© Shutterstock, Inc.

One of the most controversial practices in the United States is the death penalty, whose justification follows from the Eighth Amendment. The U.S. Supreme Court has established guidelines for states using the death penalty to ensure that it is used fairly and evenly (and not randomly and capriciously used, as the Supreme Court ruled it was prior to 1976). The Court has determined that there can be no mandatory death penalty; a capital crime has to involve taking a human life. Consideration must be given to the defendant's character, record, and relevant mitigating circumstances. Ninety-seven countries have abolished the death penalty, including all nations of Western Europe. The number of executions has fallen in recent years, yet public support for the death penalty remains around 60 percent.

Supporters argue that the death penalty protects society. If those who commit the most heinous of crimes are executed, then they cannot be released to walk the streets and threaten society by killing again. According to some, there are violent murderers who just cannot be rehabilitated. They also contend that the death penalty has a deterrent effect: if a would-be murderer knows he or she will be executed, then he or she will be less likely to commit the crime. Old Testament justice of "an eye for an eye" is invoked to uphold the position that the punishment should fit the crime. What could be more fitting or fair than executing someone who has taken another's life? Moreover, advocates claim that because the Framers of the Constitution did not view the death penalty as cruel and unusual, it should not be viewed as such today.

Those who oppose the death penalty cite its expense, arguing that it actually costs more to execute a defendant than to keep the person locked up for the rest of his or her life. The high cost is the result of all the legal fees and court costs that accrue from the defendant's appeals. These appeals also tie up the courts and create a larger backlog of cases. Opponents claim that by twenty-first century standards, the death penalty is cruel and unusual. The United States should follow the example of its allies in Western Europe who consider the death penalty a human rights violation. Most criminals can be rehabilitated, according to those against the death penalty. Furthermore, there is the possibility of making a mistake and actually killing an innocent person. They also argue against the deterrent effect, pointing out that most murders are crimes of passion and are committed by people who have never murdered. In terms of a religious argument, opponents hold that God creates all life and only God should take someone's life. Perhaps the most compelling concern about the death penalty is that it

FIGURE 4.2 Americans' Views on the Death Penalty
Notes: Survey conducted March 25-29, 2015. 1936-1995 data from Gallup.

% who favor/oppose the death penalty for persons convicted of murder

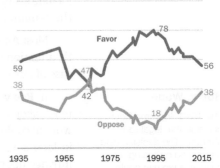

Adapted from "Less Support for Death Penalty, Especially Among Democrats." Pew Research Center, Washington, D.C. (April 16, 2017) http://www.pewresearch.org/wp-content/uploads/sites/4/2015/04/04-16-15-Death-penalty-release.pdf.

is applied unevenly based on race and socioeconomic status. People of color have accounted for a disproportionate 43 percent of total executions since 1976. They represent 55 percent of those currently awaiting execution. As of October 2002, the ACLU reports that 12 people have been executed in cases involving white defendants and black murder victims, compared with 178 black defendants executed for murdering white victims.[10]

In recent history, the Supreme Court has imposed some limits on the death penalty. For example, it can be used only in cases of murder and not in cases of child rape (2008); mentally challenged individuals cannot be executed (2002); and juvenile offenders cannot be sentenced to death (2005). Yet, despite these limits and the debates about whether it constitutes cruel and unusual punishment, the death penalty remains an important feature of the U.S. justice system.

4.6 Right to Privacy

The right to privacy is a recent addition to American constitutional law. Unlike the other liberties discussed in this chapter, the right to privacy is not specifically mentioned in the Bill of Rights. The Supreme Court has ruled that it is an implied right that follows from the First, Third, Fourth, Fifth, and Ninth Amendments.

The notion of the right to privacy as implied can be traced to the 1965 case *Griswold v. Connecticut*, in which the Supreme Court struck down a ban on contraception. In writing the opinion of the Court, Justice William O. Douglas said married couples had a right to acquire contraceptives because they had a constitutional right to privacy. According to Douglas, the right to privacy was to be found in the *penumbras* or the shadows of rights that are listed in the Bill of Rights. Penumbras suggest that there are rights that exist even if they are not explicitly stated in the Constitution. The First Amendment, for example, creates "zones of privacy" for people to make their own choices independent of government involvement. Douglas quoted Justice Louis Brandeis, who in a dissenting opinion in 1928, stated that the right to be left alone was "the most comprehensive of rights and the right most valued by civilized men.[11]

The Third Amendment's ban on quartering soldiers in private homes is also intended to protect privacy, according to Douglas. More significantly, the Ninth Amendment was noted because it states that Americans have more rights than those listed in the Bill of Rights. This Amendment was added by the Framers, who were concerned that no bill of rights could be exhaustive enough to include every possible right. It stands to reason, therefore, that the Framers intended for us to find the penumbras, the body of rights guaranteed by implication, in the language of the Bill of Rights.

Most Americans agreed that married couples should have access to contraceptives and paid little attention to the Griswold decision. But when the right to privacy was applied again in the 1973 case of *Roe v. Wade*, it quickly became one of the most controversial cases in U.S. history.

Roe v. Wade

The 1973 Supreme Court decision that legalized abortion. The decision held that based on the right to privacy, a woman could choose to terminate a pregnancy in the first trimester without legal restrictions and in later stages with restrictions.

In **Roe v. Wade**, the Supreme Court overturned a Texas law banning abortion and in doing so made abortion legal in the United States. The decision held that, based on the right to privacy, a woman could choose to terminate a pregnancy in the first trimester without legal restrictions (and in later stages with restrictions). What this essentially means is that state governments cannot infringe upon a woman's right to an abortion, at least in the first three months of pregnancy. In deciding the case, the lower court invoked the Ninth Amendment's declaration that "the enumeration in the Constitution, of certain rights, shall not be construed to deny or disparage others retained by the people" protected a person's right to privacy. The Supreme Court, however, instead based its decision on the due process clause of the Fourteenth Amendment and argued the right of privacy can be traced to the Amendment's concept of personal liberty and restrictions on state action.

Abortion is one of the key issues that divide Americans. On one side are those who support the legalization of abortion. These individuals are collectively identified under the label *pro-choice*. They argue that the *Roe v. Wade* decision is critical for gender equality and career advancement because it gives women control over the decision of when and whether to have children. By making abortions safe and legal, women's health is also protected because they do not have to resort to dangerous methods for terminating a pregnancy. Most importantly, the decision restricts the power of the government and gives women control over their own bodies. On the other side of the debate are those who are *pro-life*. They contend that life begins at the moment of conception; therefore, abortion is murder. Opponents of the *Roe v. Wade* ruling champion the rights of the unborn and use religious and moral justifications to support their position.

The legal justifications for "right to privacy" have also been used to protect rights concerning sexuality between consenting adults. The Supreme Court struck down the Texas anti-sodomy law in 2003 with *Lawrence v. Texas*. In doing so, it invalidated sodomy laws in 13 other states, making same-sex sexual activity legal in every U.S. state. The Court ruled that the due process clause of the Fourteenth Amendment protects intimate sexual conduct between consenting adults. In 2015, the Supreme Court made the landmark decision in *Obergefell v. Hodges* that same-sex couples have the fundamental right to marry as guaranteed by both the due process clause and the equal protection clause of the Fourteenth Amendment. The next chapter considers this important case and its implications for civil rights.

In addition, the courts have recently faced the question of the right to die. The Supreme Court's first right-to-die case came in 1990 with *Cruzan v. Director, Missouri Department of Health*. In this case, the Court heard the story of Nancy Cruzan, a young woman who was left in a persistent vegetative state after a car accident. Her parents had been fighting to remove their daughter from life support. However, there was no clear and convincing evidence that Nancy wished to be removed from life support in such a situation. The state of Missouri and later the Supreme Court ruled that the Cruzans could not stop life support and allow their daughter to die. The Supreme Court did rule that a competent adult has the constitutional right to die based on the Fourteenth Amendment's definition of liberty in the due process clause; however, states may regulate this process and establish guidelines.

Seven years after *Cruzan*, the Court faced right-to-die issues again in two cases involving physician-assisted suicide. In each case, the lower courts involved—one in Washington and the other in New York—ruled that laws penalizing physicians who helped terminally ill patients end their lives were unconstitutional on the basis of the due process right to privacy and of the right to equal protection. The Supreme Court reversed the lower courts' decisions in both cases, holding that the laws were constitutional and that the rights of privacy do not extend to assisted suicide. The right to die is currently being fought at the state level where states, including Oregon and more recently California, have passed legislation allowing terminally ill patients to end their lives.

While many Americans value their right to privacy, there are times when the need for security and protecting personal liberties clash. In the aftermath of the September 11, 2001, terrorist attacks, the **USA PATRIOT Act** was introduced. The Act allowed the government to use roving wiretaps, intercept emails, obtain access to library records and bookstore purchases, and hold immigrants suspected of terrorist activity for up to seven days (and sometimes indefinitely) without being charged. (It should be noted that USA PATRIOT is an acronym that stands for "Uniting and Strengthening America by Providing Appropriate Tools Required to Intercept and Obstruct Terrorism.") Initially, the Act was widely supported in an effort to give the government greater power and authority to protect the country in the War on Terror. What this has meant is that the government can infringe upon Americans' freedoms of privacy and now has greater powers of detention. The Supreme Court has not yet tested many of these policy changes, but can be expected based on past

FIGURE 4.3 Public Support for Roe v. Wade Over Past 20 Years
Abortion remains one of the most divisive topics in the United States. According to the Pew Research Center, 69 percent of Americans support the historic ruling in *Roe v. Wade,* which established the constitutional right to terminate a pregnancy in the first three months. Twenty-eight percent would like the ruling to be overturned. [12] Source: Pew Research Center. Jan. 9-13, 2013. 1992 Figures based on registered voters.

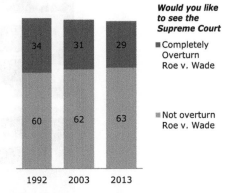

Would you like to see the Supreme Court

■ Completely Overturn Roe v. Wade

■ Not overturn Roe v. Wade

	1992	2003	2013
Completely Overturn	34	31	29
Not overturn	60	62	63

"Millennials Far Less Aware of Historic Ruling Roe v. Wade at 40: Most Oppose Overturning Abortion Decision." Pew Research Center, Washington, D.C. (January 16, 2013) http://www.pewresearch.org/wp-content/uploads/sites/7/2013/01/Roe-v-wade-full.pdf.

USA PATRIOT Act

An act of Congress introduced in 2001 that allowed the government to use roving wiretaps, intercept emails, obtain access to library records and bookstore purchases, and hold immigrants suspected of terrorist activity for up to seven days (and sometimes indefinitely) without being charged.

decisions to continue the practice of granting the federal government extraordinary powers in wartime–even at the expense of civil liberties.

In the aftermath of 9/11, airport security screenings conducted by the Transportation Security Administration (TSA) are carried out across the country to prevent prohibited items and other threats to transportation security from entering the sterile area of the airport. In this image, a TSA agent scans a passenger at Seattle-Tacoma International Airport, which serves over 30 million people a year.

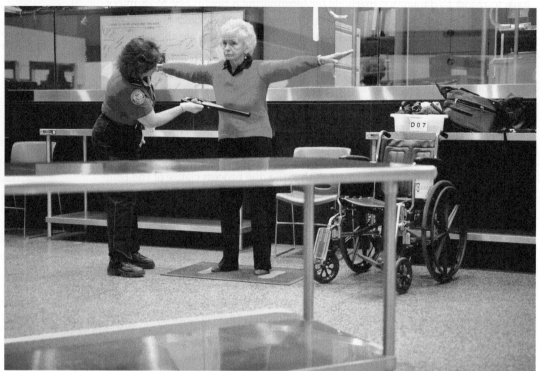

Carolina K. Smith MD / Shutterstock.com

4.7 Government Responsibility vs. Individual Freedoms

Our liberties are the basis of our power as American citizens. They are what the government cannot infringe upon or take away. Like all forms of power, our liberties can be a source of conflict. The government treads a fine line between protecting civil liberties and keeping the public safe. At times, the interests and needs of the community clash with the rights of individuals. We look to the government to arbitrate these conflicts. In some cases, like the one detailed at the beginning of this chapter, the government will protect individual freedoms and uphold rights such as freedom of speech even when that speech inflicts emotional harm on others in the community. In other cases, the government will prioritize security and safety of the community over individual liberties, as it did with the PATRIOT Act.

The topic of vaccinations highlights the challenges that the government faces when the rights of individuals are pitted against the needs of society. The decision to vaccinate one's child may seem like one that should be left up to individuals, but society also has an interest in ensuring that all people are vaccinated in order to prevent the return of fatal diseases and safeguard the collective health of the community. Thus, the decision to vaccinate may seem like a private choice, but it is one that has important implications for the public.

While we look to the government to balance individual rights and the needs of the community, we need to be mindful of the power that civil liberties give us. Civil liberties are our check on the government. They keep the government from intruding too far into our personal and private decisions. The Framers of the Constitution intended that the federal government would not be able to do anything without constitutional authority, but those who pushed for a bill of rights acknowledged that government has a natural tendency toward intrusion. The Bill of Rights restrains the government and limits its control over citizens. It also limits the government's ability to monitor us and predict who among us is likely to endanger our communities. The trade-off between safety and freedom is the ongoing result. We look to our government to provide order and security, but to do that perfectly, the government would need us to give up many of our liberties. If we were to sacrifice our civil liberties, then we would sacrifice protection from government itself.

4.8 What Can I Do?

When we enter into a social contract with the government, we agree to give up some of the freedoms we would naturally have in exchange for the security, services, and protections the government can provide. While we give up some of our freedoms, there are certain rights that we refuse to relinquish and instead require that the government safeguard. In this chapter, we have discussed those rights or civil liberties that the government cannot take away from us. One of the ways we can ensure that the government safeguards those rights is to educate ourselves about what the Constitution tells us we are entitled to and what we cannot be deprived of. We also need to be aware of the limits of those rights and identify opportunities to expand or alter the interpretation of those rights. By understanding the rights guaranteed by the Constitution, we can become empowered and capable of identifying when our rights are being violated and when the government is overstepping its bounds. When we know what our rights are, we can better protect ourselves and our families.

The American Civil Liberties Union provides up to date and easily accessible information about your rights (https://www.aclu.org/know-your-rights). This resource, along with others, can help you know what to do if, for example, you are stopped by the police, are detained at an airport, are photographed without your consent, or have questions about your religious liberties in the workplace. Knowledge is power. When it comes to your civil liberties, knowing what freedoms the government cannot take away can help you exercise your rights in an informed and responsible manner.

How we interpret our civil liberties depends largely on norms or accepted standards of behavior. Norms shape our interactions, both with our communities and with the government. Challenges arise because identifying norms can be difficult. They are not always clear and, occasionally, they can be contradictory. For example, if you observe a friend cheating on an exam, you may be conflicted between the norms of loyalty to your friend and seeing that academic honesty is upheld. The Constitution and the Bill of Rights help us navigate norms and provide guidelines about what is acceptable behavior. But sometimes norms are no longer accepted. We must update our interpretation of the Bill of Rights accordingly. Slavery, for example, was once an agreed upon standard of behavior in society. It became an institutionalized norm that was widely accepted. Over time, attitudes toward slavery changed and amendments to the Constitution were added to reflect the new norm that slavery was wrong and violated civil liberties.

Norms have lifecycles. They begin when standards of behavior are accepted as morally right and appropriate by a large proportion of the population. A necessary degree of acceptance is not always clear, but once a critical mass has been convinced to embrace a norm, the next step is a norm cascade, or spreading of the norm. Finally, the norm is internalized so that it becomes taken for granted. We take for granted, for example, that slavery is wrong.

You play an important role in the norm lifecycle. Your interactions with your family, friends, neighbors, and communities are all impacted by norms. If there are norms that you would like to see changed, you can be part of the movement to identify and spread the norm. In the aftermath of shootings like the one in Parkland, Florida, students across the country are coming together to advocate for changes to norms about gun ownership and use. Other groups work to change our norms about terminating pregnancies, imposing the death penalty, and allowing prayer in public schools. Our policies and laws reflect these norms, so one of the most critical ways that you can engage in politics and civil society is by evaluating norms and whether our accepted standards of behavior adequately reflect current values.

4.9 What's the Alternative?

The alternative to a government that does not provide civil liberties is one that dictates all aspects of economic, social, and political behavior. Citizens could be subject to the arbitrary imposition of rules and laws, unwarranted seizures of land and property, or false imprisonment. The state would matter more than the individual and notions of justice and equality would likely be aspirational at best.

The civil liberties adopted in the United States are rooted in Western values that may not be universally relevant. Individualism, for example, is a core value in American political culture. The interpretation and application of civil liberties in the United States reflect that value. Rights are conferred upon the *individual* as he or she is the primary unit in society. This understanding of rights differs from societies that instead value group or collective rights. In societies that emphasize the group over the individual, identity is defined by group membership and one's rights are determined by one's participation in the group.[13] By contrast, in the United States, rights flow from the individual to the group rather than the other way around.

All democratic governments have to balance the demands of groups against the rights of the individual. Getting it right can be tricky. Even in the United States, where the individual is traditionally given priority over the group, debates about individual and group rights create conflict. Consider, for example, the issue of affirmative action, which we explore in greater detail in the next chapter. Affirmative action policies intend to correct for past discrimination by privileging underrepresented groups in school admissions and employment. By privileging specific groups, these policies may deny access to jobs and universities to individuals who are not part of those groups. Protecting the rights of one person or group may involve violating those of another. Thus, even though the guarantee of civil liberties is a fundamental political value, the process of determining whose rights should prevail can be challenging.

While there are compelling arguments on both sides of the debate between group and individual rights, what is critical is that there are policies in place to deliver justice and equality. It is especially important that the government protect the weak and vulnerable. Critics of the Bill of Rights express concerns that the document protects the rights of those accused of crimes rather than the victims. If the government is supposed to protect the weak and vulnerable, these critics allege, then it should be focused on the rights of the victims rather than the freedoms of the accused. The Framers of the Constitution knew that the safeguards in the Bill of Rights would perhaps lead to the release or acquittal of people who were guilty. But they were willing to accept that risk in exchange for ensuring that innocent people were not wrongly convicted. Most of us are not likely to commit crimes; thus, protections for the accused are actually designed to safeguard the majority of Americans who are innocent.

Civil liberties limit the reach of government. The United States was founded on the idea that government exists not for the pursuit of its own goals, but instead *for* the people in order to help facilitate individual lives. The knowledge that the government will be kept in check and that our inalienable, individual rights will be maintained provides security and order.

Endnotes

1. Joan Biskupic, "Protest at Military Funeral Ignites a Test of Free Speech: High Court to Weigh Claim of Harassment," *USA TODAY US Edition*, August 30, 2010.

2. Melody Simmons, "Marine's Father Sues Church for Cheering Son's Death," *New York Times*, October 26, 2007, https://www.nytimes.com/2007/10/26/us/26funeral.html.

3. *Snyder v. Phelps*, 562 U.S. 443, no. 09-751 (U.S. 2011).

4. "Eugene V. Deb's Canton Speech 1918," (speech, Chicago, 1918), Socialist Party of the United States, http://college.cengage.com/history/ayers_primary_sources/eugene_cantonspeech_1918.htm.

5. *Texas v. Johnson*, 109 S. Ct. 2544 (U.S. 1989).

6. *R.A.V. v. City of St. Paul*, 505 US 377 (Minn. 1992), Oyez, https://www.oyez.org/cases/1991/90-7675.

7. Brendan Koerner, "Why Does the Ku Klux Klan Burn Crosses?" *Slate Magazine*, December 17, 2002, http://www.slate.com/articles/news_and_politics/explainer/2002/12/why_does_the_ku_klux_klan_burn_crosses.html.

8. Julian Assange, the founder and publisher of WikiLeaks, has been holed up in the Ecuadorian Embassy in London since 2012 out of fear of being extradited to Sweden and subsequently the United States.

9. *Jacobellis v. Ohio*, 173 Ohio St. 22, 179 N.E.2d 777 (U.S. 1964).

10. "Race and the Death Penalty," American Civil Liberties Union, https://www.aclu.org/race-and-death-penalty.

11. *Olmstead v. United States*, 277 U.S. 438 (U.S. 1928).

12. Hannah Fingerhut, "About Seven-in-Ten Americans Oppose Overturning Roe v. Wade," Pew Research Center, January 3, 2017, http://www.pewresearch.org/fact-tank/2017/01/03/about- seven-in-ten-americans-oppose-overturning-roe-v-wade/.

13. For an example of a case where group rights conflict with individual rights, see Stephen N. Ndegwa's article about Kenya: Stephen N. Ndegwa, "Citizenship and Ethnicity: An Examination of Two Transition Moments in Kenyan Politics," *The American Political Science Review* 91. no. 3 (Sep.,1997): 599-616.

CHAPTER 5
Civil Rights: Necessary for Equal Treatment

Chapter Objectives

1. Define the term civil rights, explain the constitutional basis for laws prohibiting discrimination, and discern the basis for the judiciary overturning of laws that allow or require discrimination.
2. Discuss the reasons for the civil rights movement and the changes it effected in American politics and government.
3. Explain what affirmative action is and why it has been so controversial in the United States.
4. Describe the political and economic achievements of women in this country over time and identify the obstacles to equality they continue to face.
5. Summarize the struggles faced by minority groups in America.

Introduction: Two Steps Forward, One Step Back

The United States elected its first black president in 2008. Six years later, on August 9, 2014, Michael Brown, an unarmed, 18-year-old black man, was killed by a white police officer in Ferguson, Missouri. His death set off a series of protests in Ferguson. Just a few weeks before Brown's shooting, a widely circulated video showed a New York Police Department officer choking to death another unarmed black man named Eric Garner. With his final words, "I can't breathe, I can't breathe," Garner left no room for debate about what caused his death.[1] Even though it was clear that Brown and Garner had been killed because of their skin color and not because of any threat that they posed, the officers involved in the deaths were not convicted.[2] The decisions to not indict the officers set off even larger protests across the United States. In November 2014, a 12-year-old black boy named Tamir Rice was playing with a toy gun in a playground in Cleveland, Ohio, when he was shot and killed by police. Video showed that police fired at Rice within a couple of seconds after arriving at the park. Over the next several months, the media covered more police shootings of unarmed black men. Together, these deaths unleashed the "Black Lives Matter" movement—a multiracial, multigenerational effort to put police reform on the policy agenda and issue a call to American society to reconsider how it values black lives.

In January 2015, activists gathered in Union Square in New York City to march in honor of Martin Luther King, Jr's birthday. They carried banners calling for justice for Eric Garner and Michael Brown.

a katz/Shutterstock.com

The story of civil rights in American history is one of progress. It is also a story about struggle and the fight for equality. It is a story about discrimination against various groups—blacks, women, Latinas/os, Native Americans, immigrants, members of the LGBTQ community, people with disabilities, and older people.

In its very first sentence, the Declaration of Independence establishes one of the core American values: "We hold these truths to be self-evident, that all men are created equal, that they are endowed by their Creator with certain unalienable rights, that among these are life, liberty, and the pursuit of happiness." When Thomas Jefferson wrote these words, he intended for the idea of equality to apply to white, property-owning men. The notion of equality was later extended to include all white men. It was extended further to include white women and later, blacks. Each expansion of the ideal came as the result of a struggle for inclusion, a struggle for acknowledgment that indeed all people are created equal, regardless of their race, gender, ethnicity, sexual orientation, religion, disabilities, or age. The struggles for equality also underscored the gaps that exist between American ideals and American institutions. In order to make our institutions better reflect the values of freedom, democracy, and equality, citizens have had to demand change. That change has often been slow and incremental, but when you consider where we started, progress toward equality in the United States has been significant.

The National Memorial for Peace and Justice, which opened in Montgomery, Alabama, in April 2018, is dedicated to the thousands of black people who were victims of lynching during the United States' decades-long campaign of racist terror. The memorial consists of 800 weathered steel columns that hang from the roof above a floor that slowly descends until the visitor is left looking up at the columns dangling above. Each column bears the name of an American county and the people who were lynched there. The walk is lined with some of the stories and photographs of the people who were killed, each one a reminder that racial discrimination continued long after the Civil War and evolved into decades of injustice and torture.

Soniakapadia [CC BY-SA 4.0 (https://creativecommons.org/licenses/by-sa/4.0)], from Wikimedia Commons. https://commons.wikimedia.org/wiki/File:Memorial_Corridor_at_The_National_Memorial_for_Peace_and_Justice.jpg

The long battle to win civil rights is perhaps the most powerful story in American history. In this chapter, we consider the struggles of underrepresented groups to gain equal rights. We start by looking at what the Constitution tells us about equality. We then trace the struggle for racial equality and the Civil Rights Movement. We also consider the battle for gender equality and the struggles waged by Native Americans, Latinas/os Asian Americans, and the LGBTQ community to access rights denied to them of the basis of race, ethnicity, or sexual orientation.

5.1 Inequality and the Law

The terms civil liberties and civil rights are often used interchangeably. But as we saw in the last chapter, civil liberties refer to those freedoms that the government cannot take away. **Civil rights** instead are the freedoms and protections that the government must provide. The critical difference is that civil rights require government action, whereas civil liberties are best protected when the government does not intervene.[3]

Civil rights refer to the rights of all Americans to equal treatment under the law, as provided for by the Fourteenth Amendment. One of the primary jobs of the government is to ensure—through legislation or other actions—that this constitutional mandate is upheld. The Fourteenth Amendment states:

civil rights

The freedoms and protections that the government must provide.

All persons born or naturalized in the United States, and subject to the jurisdiction thereof, are citizens of the United States and of the State wherein they reside. No State shall make or enforce any law which shall abridge the privileges or immunities of citizens of the United States; nor shall any State deprive any person of life, liberty, or property, without due process of law; nor deny to any person within its jurisdiction the equal protection of the laws.

Equal Protection Clause

The part of the Fourteenth Amendment requiring states to to treat all people in an equal manner. It says that states may not deprive citizens of their unalienable rights to life, liberty, or property without due process of law.

strict scrutiny

A test used by the Court in cases of racial discrimination that looks carefully at the law and at the government interest involved.

suspect classification

Ways of classifying people that are so rarely constitutional that they are immediately labeled "suspect."

intermediate standard of review

Tests used by the Court to determine whether there is an important state purpose for treating people differently on the basis of gender.

rational basis test

Tests used by the Court to determine whether discrimination on the basis of age, wealth, or sexual orientation is a reasonable way to achieve a legitimate government objective.

Central to the discussion of civil rights is the interpretation of the Equal Protection Clause of the Fourteenth Amendment. The courts have interpreted the **Equal Protection Clause** to mean that states must treat all persons in an equal manner. They may not deprive citizens of their unalienable rights to life, liberty, or property without due process of law. That means no one should be discriminated against without some type of legal justification. An example is the decision of states to prohibit convicted felons from voting.[4] The courts have determined that states may not discriminate unreasonably against a particular group unless there is sufficient reason to do so. The question is, how do we distinguish between reasonable and unreasonable discrimination? It usually falls to the Supreme Court to decide. The Court weighs the constitutional rights of individuals against the need to protect the safety and welfare of citizens.

The Supreme Court has determined that there are times when racial discrimination is permissible. Using a test called **strict scrutiny**, the justices look carefully at the law and at the government interest involved. Strict scrutiny is used in cases where there is **suspect classification.** This refers to ways of classifying people that are so questionably constitutional that they are immediately labeled "suspect." In order for the state to discriminate on the basis of race, it must demonstrate that it has a compelling interest to do so. If this all sounds very subjective, that is because it is. What qualifies as a compelling interest? During World War II, there was a compelling state interest (national security) to round up Japanese Americans on the West Coast and relocate them to internment camps. The Supreme Court determined in *Korematsu v. United States* (1944) that it was constitutional to deny civilian Japanese Americans their right to liberty because they were perceived to be a threat to U.S. national security while the country was fighting Japan during the war. Strict scrutiny can also be used to strike down discrimination, as was the case with *Brown v. the Board of Education* (1954). In that case, the Court determined that there was no compelling state interest to segregate schools.

When cases arise that deal with discrimination on the basis of gender, the Supreme Court uses the **intermediate standard of review**. In these quasi-suspect categories, the Court considers whether there is an important state purpose for treating people differently. An *important* interest is not as hard to meet as a *compelling* interest. This test was used when the Court decided in *Rostker v. Goldberg* (1981) that men have to register for the military draft but women do not. It was also used to strike down a law in Alabama that required men but not women to pay alimony after divorce in the case *Orr v. Orr* (1979).

Issues of discrimination based on age, wealth, or sexual orientation fall under nonsuspect categories and are considered using the **rational basis test.** When confronted with a law that treats certain groups differently, the Supreme Court asks whether the discrimination is a reasonable way to achieve a legitimate government objective. Data suggest that most crimes committed by young people occur after 10 p.m.; therefore, states have a rational interest in imposing curfews for young people. In *Gregory v. Ashcroft* (1991), the Court upheld a Missouri law that requires public officials to retire at the age of 70, citing that the law had a rational basis. There may also be rational reasons for states to have different tax rates for people. And like the other tests, the Court can use rational basis to strike down discrimination, as it did in *Obergefell v. Hodges* (2015), when it determined the state had no rational basis for preventing same-sex marriage.

Civil rights law is rooted in these classifications. Groups that have been discriminated against have lobbied, protested, and sued to have the Supreme Court classify them as suspect so they could be treated with stricter scrutiny. Once the Court has determined that a group is suspect, it is unlikely to allow any law to treat the group differently. That is why groups who are struggling for equal rights fight so hard to gain suspect status. Race finally gained suspect status in the 1950s, but women's groups have failed to convince the Court to make gender a suspect classification. Thus, gender remains a quasi-suspect category. Some groups, like the LGBTQ community, have not even obtained quasi-suspect classification. This means that they can be discriminated against as long as states demonstrate a rational reason for doing so. These classifications also translate into how much power and access to resources a particular group has. If a group is denied equal protection, it can find itself deprived of other political rights and unable to use legislation to safeguard and advances its interests. In Arkansas, for example, the state legislature passed the "Intrastate Commerce Improvement Act" in 2015 with the aim of attracting business to the state. In order to do so, each city and county must follow the same rules about whom they permit discrimination against. This provision essentially prevents local governments from extending any civil rights protections against discrimination to gay people.[5]

5.2 The Struggle for Racial Equality

When Jefferson penned the words "all men are created equal," Americans were engaged in the slave trade, forcing Africans onto ships in chains and shackles, raping them at will, separating them from their families, selling them at auction, and murdering them for disobeying their masters. The era of slavery is one of the darkest times in U.S. history and illustrates the sharpest disconnect between the ideals our Founding Fathers espoused and the realities they practiced. It also ushered in the first battle for civil rights in the United States and paved the way for other groups fighting for equality.

One of the major early challenges for blacks in the United States came with the Supreme Court 1857 declaration in *Dred Scott v. Sanford*. It said that all blacks, regardless of their status of free or slave, were not American citizens. Dred Scott was a slave from Missouri who lived from 1833 to 1843 in the slave-free state of Illinois and in a section of the Louisiana Territory where the Missouri Compromise of 1820 forbade slavery. After his owner died and Scott had returned to Missouri, he sued his owner's widow, Eliza Sanford, for his freedom, arguing that because he had lived in a free state, he should now be a free man. The lower court ruled in favor of Scott, but the Missouri Supreme Court overturned the decision when Sanford's brother appealed the original decision. Scott then appealed this decision to the Supreme Court. The Court decided that it could not rule in the case because Scott was not a U.S. citizen. Chief Justice Taney wrote that Scott is "a negro, whose ancestors were imported into this country and sold as slaves [and therefore he is not a] member of the political community formed and brought into existence by the Constitution."[6] The Court also ruled that Congress does not have the authority to ban slavery because slaves are categorized as property and the rights of slave-owners to property are protected by the Fifth Amendment. The Court's decision exacerbated tensions between northern and southern states and was ultimately rendered invalid by the three Reconstruction amendments to the Constitution—the Thirteenth, Fourteenth, and Fifteenth Amendments.

Background to the Civil Rights Movement

When it was written, the Equal Protection Clause of the Fourteenth Amendment was intended to protect newly freed slaves after the Civil War. Its purpose was to extend citizenship rights to freed slaves and, in doing so, entitle them to protections under the Constitution. But segregation laws passed by southern legislatures in the late 1880s thwarted any progress toward equal treatment under the law. These laws separated the white community from the black and became known as

Jim Crow laws

Policies of racial segregation.

the **Jim Crow laws**. The term Jim Crow was meant as a racial slur and comes from a song that was popular in black minstrel shows.[7] These laws applied to public and private facilities such as housing, restaurants, hotels, swimming pools, and buses.

The Supreme Court, in its 1896 decision in ***Plessy v. Ferguson***, institutionalized segregation. In 1892, Homer Plessy, a man who was seventh-eighths white and one-eighth black, boarded a train in New Orleans and sat in car reserved for white passengers. The conductor told Plessy to move and, when he refused, he was arrested for breaking the law. When the case reached the Supreme Court, the justices ruled that the law did not violate the Equal Protection Clause because separate facilities provided for blacks were equal to those for whites. This decision established the constitutional basis for the "separate but equal" doctrine that was used to justify segregation in America for the next 60 years.

Plessy v. Ferguson

1896 Supreme Court decision that institutionalized racial segregation.

Segregated movie theater for blacks in Leland, Mississippi, in November 1939. Segregated theaters were part of the Jim Crow laws that, beginning in the 1880s, physically separated blacks and whites in public spaces such as restaurants and theaters. The Supreme Court case *Plessy v. Fergurson* (1896) upheld the Jim Crow laws under the mandate "separate but equal."

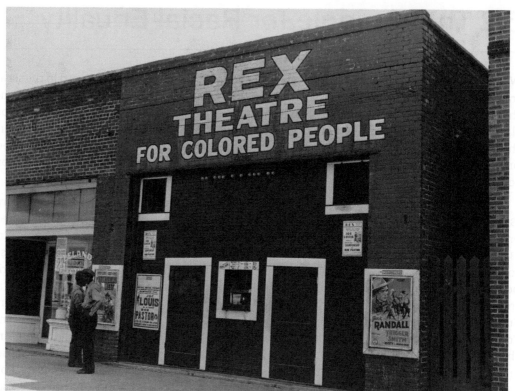

Everett Historical / Shutterstock.com

In 1870, blacks won the right to vote with the Fifteenth Amendment to the Constitution. The amendment declared that the "right of citizens of the United States to vote shall not be denied or abridged by the United States or by any state on account of race, color, or previous condition of servitude."

While blacks legally had the right to vote, the legacy of slavery and the institutionalization of segregation meant that it would take almost a century for the promise of the Fifteenth Amendment to be fully realized. Poll taxes, literacy tests, and other obstacles were used to disenfranchise blacks and keep them from voting. It was not until the passage of the Voting Rights Act of 1965 that the majority of blacks in the South were registered to vote.

Rights in the Early Twentieth Century

Even though there were small pockets of resistance to segregation laws, civil rights did not become a national issue until the 1920s. Blacks from the South had been migrating to cities in the North and West. This movement was steady during the 1920s and continued throughout the Great Depression. Blacks from the South now made more contact with blacks in other communities and developed a heightened awareness of racial discrimination. The number of migrants increased exponentially in the 1940s when World War II and wartime production required more factory workers in urban areas. During this decade alone, one million blacks moved from the South to the North, and by 1950, a third of all blacks lived outside of the South. Black ghettos emerged in northern and western cities. These ghettos perpetuated the separation of blacks and whites, but they also allowed for black culture to flourish. The 1920s and 1930s, for example, witnessed the **Harlem Renaissance**, a literary and intellectual movement that was centered in the New York City neighborhood of Harlem. The movement celebrated black cultural identity and traditions. Some of the most important writers in American literature emerged from the movement, including Langston Hughes, Zora Neale Hurston, Claude McKay, and W.E.B. Du Bois.

In addition to being culturally significant, the migration of blacks was important because, as more and more blacks moved into northern and western cities, they became a powerful voting bloc who captured the attention of white politicians. The migration also sparked a national movement for civil rights as many Americans began to realize that segregation and discrimination were no longer uniquely Southern issues.

As the civil rights movement gained national attention in the 1930s, the **National Association for the Advancement of Colored People** (NAACP) mobilized blacks and whites to fight for equal rights. The oldest U.S. civil rights organization, the NAACP was founded in 1909 by a group of Americans committed to greater racial equality. The NAACP followed two main strategies: 1) its message had to penetrate the consciences of northern white civilians; and 2) it had to make its work appeal to the interests of northern white politicians. The efforts of the NAACP were bolstered by the actions of key individuals like A. Philip Randolph.

Philip Randolph and the March on Washington Movement

Most blacks migrated out of the South by train. Black sleeping car porters staffed these trains and became important links as they traveled the country and made connections in black communities in the rural South and in northern cities. A. Philip Randolph was the president of the Brotherhood of Sleeping Car Porters, a primarily black union. A well-known civil rights leader and labor activist, Randolph worked tirelessly to improve conditions for black workers. His most significant contribution came with his proposal in 1941 of a massive march on Washington, D.C. The purpose would be to demand an end to discrimination in employment and the armed forces. The march would be a new civil rights strategy and, because it would be held in Washington, it would demand the attention of politicians.

Randolph's proposal did indeed attract the attention of political leaders, including President Franklin D. Roosevelt, who was greatly disturbed by the plan. The United States had just entered World War II and Roosevelt was trying to get support for his efforts to stop Hitler and his brutal treatment of ethnic minorities. To shine a spotlight on America's own discrimination and mistreatment of minorities would be a major embarrassment for the administration. In order to stop the march from taking place, Roosevelt called a meeting with Randolph, who made three demands. Randolph requested: 1) the immediate end to segregation and discrimination in federal government hiring; 2) an end to segregation in the armed forces; and 3) government support for an end to discrimination and segregation in all American employment. The president refused to meet Randolph's demands, but he agreed to issue Executive Order 8802 in exchange for Randolph calling off

Harlem Renaissance

A literary and intellectual movement in the 1920s and 1930s that was centered in the New York City neighborhood of Harlem and celebrated black cultural identity and traditions.

National Association for the Advancement of Colored People

The country's oldest civil rights organization, founded in 1909 by a group of Americans committed to greater racial equality.

the march. The Executive Order created the Fair Employment Practices Committee (FEPC), which stated that the federal government would not discriminate on the basis of race, creed, color, or national origin in hiring. While the FEPC was intended to enforce the order to ban discriminatory hiring, in reality it did very little. The committee's mandate was such that it could not act proactively. The committee could only investigate cases after allegations of discrimination had already been made. Roosevelt was not very sympathetic to the call for racial equality. He was more concerned with maintaining the support of southern Democrats and he did not push for a revision of the FEPC. He was also more worried about military issues than minority rights. Midway through World War II, he said: "I don't think, quite frankly, that we can bring about the millennium at this time." His Secretary of War, Henry L. Stimson, believed that blacks were inferior and declared that, "Leadership is not embedded in the Negro race yet and to try to make commissioned officers to lead men into battle—colored men—is only to bring disaster to both."[8]

While discrimination in the federal government and armed forces continued, the wartime economy and the demand for labor helped generate momentum for the civil rights movement. But as more and more blacks moved into northern and western cities in search of work, racial tensions increased. In the summer of 1943, race riots erupted in the Army training camps and in the cities of Detroit and Harlem. More than one million blacks had fought in World War II. They returned from the war as champions of democracy to a society that treated them as second-class citizens.

The Congress of Racial Equality

A civil rights organization that was founded in 1942 on the University of Chicago campus. Its creation marked the beginning of a mass movement for civil rights.

In 1942, a civil rights organization was founded on the University of Chicago campus. **The Congress of Racial Equality** (CORE) was started by a group of primarily white civil rights activists, but eventually it became a largely black organization. Its creation marked the beginning of a mass movement for civil rights. The group took an active role in the Montgomery bus boycott, in lunch counter sit-ins, and in Freedom Rides. CORE worked closely with the NAACP and joined black and white allies in resisting the status quo.

Civil Rights After World War II

By the end of World War II, there was a greater sense of optimism surrounding the civil rights movement. Events in popular culture were changing opinions about race. Jackie Robinson, for example, was the first black American to play major league baseball when he joined the Brooklyn Dodgers in 1947. Blacks were also beginning to be seen as a viable political group that could determine elections. By this time, the number of black registered voters in the South had increased to 12 percent.

But while blacks were establishing themselves as a political constituency on par with labor, business, agriculture, and other groups, southern whites posed stiff opposition. There were cases of blacks turning up at the polls and being driven away at gunpoint. In Georgia, several blacks who attempted to vote were killed. When war veteran Etoy Fletcher tried to register to vote in Mississippi, the registrar told him: "Niggers are not allowed to vote in Rankin County, and if you don't want to get into serious trouble, get out of this building."[9] Fletcher was then abducted by four white men while waiting for a bus at the local bus station. He was taken into the woods, where he was forced to strip. He was beaten with a large cable wire.[10] These acts of violence created a climate of fear among black voters. The most effective strategy for dealing with the rising political power of blacks, however, was to prevent them from registering to vote in the first place. Residency requirements, poll taxes, and literacy tests were the most common of these methods. Literacy tests like this one (https://www.businessinsider.com/reading-test-given-to-black-louisiana-voters-in-1964-2014-11) from Louisiana were used to suppress the black vote. Those wishing to vote who could not prove a certain level of education had to take and pass the test. The test was applicable to both white and black would-be voters, but it was disproportionately administered to blacks. The test had to be taken in 10 minutes and one wrong answer meant a failing grade. The questions were confusingly worded and the registrar (who was white) would determine whether an answer was correct.

The legislative branch did little to advance the rights of blacks in the postwar era. President Harry Truman, however, was angered by the treatment of blacks, and in particular war veterans. Truman was the first twentieth-century president to actively support civil rights legislation. His administration was marked by several important milestones in the struggle for civil rights. Truman was the first president to address the NAACP, and in December 1946, he established by executive order the President's Committee on Civil Rights. The committee was tasked with investigating the status of civil rights. It proposed measures to strengthen the civil rights of American citizens, including improving existing law; establishing a permanent Civil Rights Commission, a Joint Congressional Committee on Civil Rights, and a Civil Rights Division in the Department of Justice; making lynching a federal crime; creating a permanent Fair Employment Practices Commission (FEPC); and abolishing poll taxes. Truman requested that Congress implement all of the committee's recommendations, and in July 1948, he issued **Executive Order 9981**, which banned segregation in the armed forces.

Congress rejected Truman's policy recommendations, so Truman's efforts—while important for symbolic reasons—failed to advance the civil rights of black Americans. Discrimination and the denial of voting rights continued unabated. World War II army veteran Isaac Nixon was lynched on the doorstep of his own home in 1948 for exercising his voter rights. His murder was intended to warn other blacks to not vote in the future.[11] Two white men were charged in the murder but were acquitted by an all-white jury.

In response to events like the murder of Isaac Nixon, CORE and the NAACP worked tirelessly to advance the civil rights of black Americans and fought to reform the legal and justice systems in the United States. President Dwight Eisenhower followed Truman, and while he showed little interest in civil rights legislation, the civil rights campaign had gained momentum on its own. CORE and the NAACP had a series of what would become landmark cases already in the legal pipeline when Eisenhower took office. The most important of these cases was ***Brown v. Board of Education*** (1954) of Topeka, Kansas. The parents of Linda Brown, supported by the NAACP, sued the school board of Topeka because their daughter had been denied admission to the all-white school that was closer to their home than the black schools. By the time the case reached the Supreme Court, other cases had joined it, which increased the scope and the impact of the decision. On May 17, 1954, the Supreme Court came to the unanimous decision that "in the field of public education the doctrine of 'separate but equal' has no place. Separate educational facilities are inherently unequal." The decision in *Plessy v. Ferguson*, that separate but equal was acceptable had finally been overturned. The Court ordered school boards across the country to desegregate their schools "with all deliberate speed." The vague wording, however, actually allowed many school districts to delay desegregation for years. Eisenhower disagreed with the decision to desegregate, but he knew that he was constitutionally bound to enforce the Supreme Court's decision.

More than 100 U.S. congressmen from the former Confederate states signed a "Southern Manifesto" in response to the *Brown v. Board of Education* decision. They vowed to fight desegregation. In 1957, the governor of Arkansas deployed the state's National Guard to Little Rock to prevent the entry of nine black students who had been admitted to Central High School. President Eisenhower felt a constitutional duty to intervene and responded by sending in federal troops to put the Arkansas National Guard under federal control. He did remark though that: "I don't believe you can change the hearts of men with laws or decisions."[12] Regarding his nomination of Earl Warren, the Supreme Court justice who led the unanimous decision, he lamented that it was "the biggest damn fool mistake I ever made."[13] The black students in Little Rock entered the school, but there were so many threats against them that school officials decided to take them out. They then closed the school for a time in order to avoid having to follow the Court's ruling to desegregate.

Executive Order 9981

Legislation passed in 1948 which banned segregation in the armed forces.

Brown v. Board of Education

The 1954 Supreme Court decision that ended segregation in schools.

Montgomery Bus Boycott

A boycott of public transportation in Montgomery, Alabama, that lasted 381 days and ultimately led to the successful desegregation of public transportation.

The civil rights movement also gained momentum with the challenging of segregation in public transportation. In December 1955 in Montgomery, Alabama, 42-year-old Rosa Parks, a black civil rights activist, boarded a bus home from work and sat in the first row of the "colored" section in the middle of the bus. As the bus continued on its route, the white section filled up and the driver noted that there were some whites who were standing. The driver demanded that Parks and several other blacks give up their seats. Parks refused and she was arrested. That night, a group named the Montgomery Improvement Association, composed of local activists and ministers, convened in a Montgomery church to decide their next move. They agreed to boycott the city bus system, a move which would essentially bring the public transport system in Montgomery to a halt because blacks made up 75 percent of the total ridership. The **Montgomery Bus Boycott** lasted 381 days and posed a serious economic threat to the transportation company. It also posed a social threat to white rule in the city. It ultimately led to the successful desegregation of public transportation when, in December 1956, the Supreme Court ruled that the segregation law was unconstitutional. The Montgomery Bus Boycott marked the beginning of a revolutionary era of non-violent mass protests in support of civil rights.

The events in Montgomery and Little Rock prompted several white liberals in Congress to propose the Civil Rights Act in 1957. Despite the fact that President Eisenhower did little to support the legislation, it passed due in large part to the efforts of Senate Majority Leader Lyndon B. Johnson of Texas. The Act was primarily a voting rights bill that gave the Justice Department the authority to go to court to ensure that blacks could vote. This was not a huge step, but it was the first civil rights legislation passed by Congress since the 1870s.

Martin Luther King, Jr. and Nonviolent Resistance

nonviolent resistance

A civil rights strategy that uses methods of peaceful protest.

Civil Rights Act of 1964

Enforced desegregation of public accommodations and outlawed discrimination on the basis of race, sex, religion, or national origin.

The Montgomery bus boycott represented a new, dynamic style of leadership embodied by Martin Luther King, Jr. King, a 27-year-old Baptist minister, was selected by the boycott's organizers to be their spokesperson because, while he was new to the community, he was young and well-trained. He also had solid family connections and good professional standing. King introduced a new strategy to the civil rights movement: **nonviolent resistance**, a method of peaceful protest that combined the teachings of Mahatma Gandhi and Jesus. In January 1957, King, together with other civil rights activists, founded the Southern Christian Leadership Conference (SCLC) to draw on the moral authority and organizational power of churches. The SCLC gave King a national platform from which to lead nonviolent protests to promote civil rights. The organization focused on voting rights for blacks and worked to register black voters in the South. By 1960, King was gaining national notoriety. He organized a protest in Birmingham, Alabama, in 1963 during which police unleashed dogs and fire hoses on the protesters. King was arrested. While in jail, he wrote about his theory of non-violent resistance: "Nonviolent direct action seeks to create such a crisis and foster such a tension that a community, which has constantly refused to negotiate, is forced to confront the issue."[14] In August 1963, King organized a massive demonstration in Washington, D.C. More than 200,000 people converged in front of the Lincoln Memorial and heard King's famous "I have a Dream" speech, which emphasized his belief that one day all men could be brothers. In 1964, King won the Nobel Peace Prize and the attention he brought to the civil rights struggle began to sway public opinion. Many people in cities that were not experiencing racial tension started to question segregation laws and discrimination toward blacks. This increasing awareness of racial inequality helped garner support for the **Civil Rights Act of 1964**, which authorized the federal government to enforce desegregation of public accommodations and outlawed discrimination in publicly owned facilities.

On the 50th anniversary of the March on Washington and Martin Luther King Jr.'s "I Have a Dream" speech, marchers carry signs drawing attention to the ongoing battle for freedom, justice, and voting rights.

Joseph Sohm / Shutterstock.com

But as was characteristic of the battle for civil rights, the pattern of progress was two steps forward and one step back. In March 1965, a march planned from Selma to Montgomery in Alabama turned violent when police used nightsticks and tear gas against the protesters. Images of the bloodied and injured bodies of the protesters appeared on television. The event was renamed "Bloody Sunday." King led another march and, this time, when state troopers confronted the protesters, the protesters knelt in prayer and turned back. King was criticized by young black activists for not taking a more forceful stance against the police, but the march is credited for arousing support for the passage of the Voting Rights Act of 1965. King worked tirelessly for civil rights until his assassination in 1968 by James Earl Ray.

King's strategy of nonviolent resistance stood in sharp contrast to the tactics of Malcolm X, a civil rights leader who encouraged blacks to cast off the shackles of racism by any means necessary, including violence. Malcolm X was born Malcolm Little in Omaha, Nebraska, and was the son of Baptist preacher. When he was a child, Malcolm's father was murdered by a group of white supremacists. Malcolm dropped out of school when he was 15 and moved to Boston, where he quickly became involved with drugs and crime. He was arrested in 1946 and sentenced to 10 years in jail. While in prison, Malcolm was introduced to the religious teachings of the Nation of Islam, known popularly as the Black Muslims. These teachings argued against integration and said that blacks had to address their social problems alone. Malcolm Little converted to the Nation of Islam. Upon his release from prison in 1952, he dropped the name "Little," which he considered a relic of slavery, and took "X" as a tribute to the unknown names of his African ancestors. Malcolm X emerged as the leader of a more militant branch of the civil rights movement. His strategy of agitating for change stood in sharp contrast to King's method of nonviolent resistance. In 1963, Malcolm X made a pilgrimage to Mecca. There, he changed his view that Islam and integration were incompatible. He returned to the United States more optimistic about the prospects for peaceful resolution to inequality and racism in America. He took the name El-Hajj Malik El-Shabazz and started the Organization of Afro-American Unity. He was leading a rally when he was assassinated on February 21, 1965, by followers of the black Muslim movement.

Civil Rights in the 1960s

freedom riders

A group of black and white activists from the North who traveled by bus down South to test the effectiveness of a 1960 Supreme Court decision that prohibited racial segregation in public facilities.

The push for civil rights increased during President John Kennedy's administration. Civil rights, however, were not a priority for Kennedy. He was more concerned with maintaining support from southern Democrats, who controlled many congressional committees. But Kennedy could not ignore the building momentum. He eventually sent a civil rights bill to Congress in response to three events: 1) In 1960, four black college students in Greensborough, North Carolina, sat at segregated lunch counter. The students, who were followers of King's nonviolent resistance, were arrested, but their action inspired a series of sit-ins and similar protests at lunch counters throughout the South. 2) In 1961, a group of CORE members and college students from the North traveled by bus to the South to test the effectiveness of a 1960 Supreme Court decision that prohibited racial segregation in public facilities, such as bathrooms, waiting rooms, and restaurants. These so-called **freedom riders** clashed time and again with angry white Southerners. In Alabama, a mob of whites set a bus on fire and attacked the passengers as they tried to escape the flames. The attack was broadcast on television and as a result drew national attention. 3) The 1963 police attack against peaceful protesters in Birmingham, Alabama occured. The three events encouraged Kennedy to introduce the Civil Rights Bill in the summer of 1963. The bill was still in committee in Congress when Kennedy was assassinated in November 1963.

Great Society

A set of domestic programs introduced by President Johnson to eliminate poverty and racial injustice.

President Johnson, who had been instrumental in passing the Civil Rights Act in 1957 when he was Senate majority leader, made passing the new Civil Rights Bill one of his first policy goals. Johnson's commitment to civil rights stemmed from his desire to create a "Great Society" in the United States. Johnson's **Great Society** was a set of domestic programs designed to eliminate poverty and racial injustice.

Johnson's legislative agenda was helped by changing national public opinion toward civil rights. King's "I Have a Dream" speech touched many people, who became committed to supporting equality. Also, shock over Kennedy's assassination translated into support for Johnson's efforts to pass civil rights legislation as a memorial to Kennedy. In the 1964 elections, Democrats took control of Congress and liberal northern Democrats outnumbered southern Democrats who resisted civil rights reform. Congress passed the Civil Rights Act of 1964, a landmark piece of legislation that outlawed discrimination on the basis of race, color, religion, sex, or national origin. It ended the unequal application of voter registration requirements and racial segregation in schools, in the workplace, and in public facilities. The 1964 Civil Rights Act created the Equal Employment Opportunity Commission to end discrimination in the workplace. The poll tax was abolished in 1964 and literacy tests in 1975, thereby advancing voting rights. In 1968, Congress passed the Fair Housing Act, which ended discrimination based on race, color, religion, or national origin in the terms, conditions, or privilege of the sale or rental of a residence.

Affirmative Action

affirmative action

A policy designed to equalize opportunity by eliminating discriminatory barriers.

Civil rights had finally become a national issue and synonymous with political development and economic progress. In 1965, President Johnson issued Executive Order 11246, which prohibited discrimination in hiring for firms doing business with the federal government. It also took the fight against discrimination one step further by ordering the firms to take **affirmative action** to compensate for past discrimination. Firms now had to actively recruit and hire blacks. The goal of affirmative action was to equalize opportunity by eliminating discriminatory barriers. The percentage of jobs that companies put aside for blacks was ideally a reflection of the percentage of blacks in the workforce. It was used not only in employment decisions but college admissions as well. Universities reserved spaces for minorities and, at times, would admit minority applicants even if their grades and test scores were lower than those of whites.

Advocates argue that affirmative action is an effective political strategy for addressing the issue of equality. Policies that eliminate discriminatory barriers can help level the playing field and ensure everyone, regardless of their racial background, can have access to the same opportunities. Affirmative action programs are rooted in the idea that if equal opportunity were a reality, blacks and other groups who have faced discrimination would be represented fairly in the workforce and in academic institutions. By reserving spaces for blacks in companies and universities, advocates posit, we can ensure that those who have been marginalized in the past and are coming from behind have a chance to catch up and be equal.

The idea of making hiring and admissions decisions based on race, even though the goal of doing so is to eliminate discrimination, has proved controversial for those who may agree with the end result of promoting equality, but disagree with having to treat people differently to get there.

The Supreme Court first addressed the issue of affirmative action in 1978 in *Regents of the University of California v. Bakke*. Alan Bakke, a white male, was denied admission to the University of California Davis medical school. The school had reserved 16 of 100 spaces for minority applicants. Some of the minority students admitted had lower test scores than Bakke. Bakke argued he was a victim of reverse discrimination and sued the university. He claimed that use of a **quota system** in which a specific number of seats were set aside for minority applicants violated the Equal Protection Clause. The Court agreed with Bakke's assessment of the quota system and he was able to be admitted to the UC medical school. The Court, however, did not reject affirmative action in principle and acknowledged that universities may have an interest in creating a diversified student body. They can therefore use race in admissions.[15]

> **quota system**
>
> The affirmative action practice of setting aside a specific number of seats for minority applicants.

Affirmative action remains a contentious and divisive issue in American politics. As discussed earlier in the chapter, any policy that treats people differently based on race is subject to strict scrutiny. That means that even if a policy has been implemented to help a racial minority, it still must demonstrate that it serves a *compelling* government interest and must be narrowly tailored to that interest. With regard to affirmative action, it can be difficult to determine what government interest should prevail, as the topic pits individual rights against group rights. Many support the goal of affirmative action, but not if it gives preferential treatment to minorities.[16] A recent opinion poll found that the majority of Americans agree that affirmative action programs designed to increase the number of black and minority students on college campuses are a "good thing," but there is a racial and partisan divide behind those numbers. Fifty-five percent of whites support affirmative action on campuses, but that compares to 84 percent of blacks and 80 percent of Latinas/os who support it.[17]

Despite public support for affirmative action, the policy faces legal challenges at the state level. In 1996, a referendum in California passed that made affirmative action illegal. Washington, Michigan, and Arizona have also banned affirmative action programs. Laws governing affirmative action are complex and confusing. For example, in 2003 in *Grutter v. Bollinger*, the Supreme Court upheld the constitutionality of race-conscious admissions policies used by the University of Michigan Law School to create a diverse student body. However, in the case of *Gratz v. Bollinger* that same year, the Court ruled that Michigan's undergraduate admissions policy, which awarded 20 points toward admission to underrepresented minorities, was unconstitutional and tantamount to racial quotas. In 2016, the Supreme Court considered the issue of affirmative action once again in *Fisher v. University of Texas*. This time, the Court ruled in favor of affirmative action by holding that university admissions officials may continue to consider race as a factor among many to promote a diverse student body.

Debates about affirmative action are examples of the conflict between differences in values and scarcity of resources that define the political process. While the majority of Americans agree that discrimination and racism are wrong, they disagree about the fairest way to address inequality. On one hand are those who argue we should not make up for past discrimination against minorities by discriminating against non-minorities in the present. On the other hand is the argument that affirmative action programs have produced tangible results that have equalized opportunities for many minorities in employment and education. This is one issue in American politics where your opinion matters and can sway future policy and legislation on how we should deal with ensuring and enforcing equality.

5.3 The Struggle for Gender Equality

While black Americans have had to fight for equality against laws that made them inferior, women have had to battle against laws that claimed to be there to protect them. From the founding of the country, women have been excluded from the political process. Their place was at home where they would be safe from the ugliness of the outside world. Women were not invited to participate in the Constitutional Convention or in the design of the country's legal traditions and institutions. And while the Declaration of Independence promised equality, the Constitution did not follow through on this and failed to guarantee women the right to vote and to protect them from discriminatory laws in the states. Women who had played a critical role during the American Revolution felt betrayed by the new government that was forming. It was not until the 1840s that women's rights groups began to mobilize to reshape the political landscape of the country.

The Battle for Voting Rights

suffrage

The right to vote.

The first women's rights convention was held in 1848 in Seneca Falls, New York. The meeting started the discussion about extending constitutional rights to women. The participants at the convention adopted a Declaration of Principles that revisited the Declaration of Independence to state that "we hold these truths to be self-evident: that all men and women are created equal; that they are endowed by their Creator with certain inalienable rights; that among these are life, liberty, and the pursuit of happiness." The convention also issued a demand for **suffrage**, or the right to vote.

In May 1914, five thousand supporters of suffrage marched from Lafayette Square down Pennsylvania Avenue to the U.S. Capitol to deliver to Congress stacks of petitions from states across the nation.

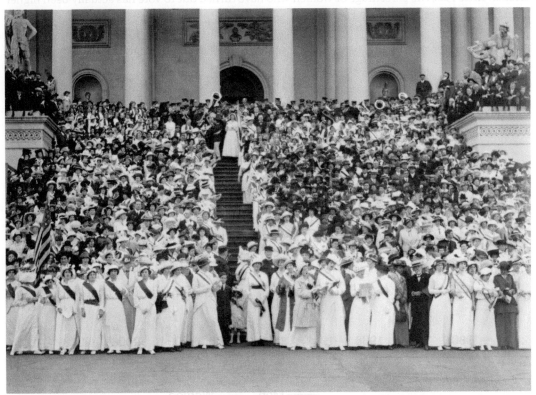

© Shutterstock, Inc.

These early efforts were put on hold when the Civil War broke out and consumed the country's political energy. The conversation about suffrage resumed and gained momentum in 1869 when Susan B. Anthony and Elizabeth Cady Stanton formed the National Suffrage Association. Their first step toward achieving equal rights for women was getting the right to vote. As had been the case for black Americans, the courts were closed to women, so women had to adopt different strategies to effect change. In addition to voting rights, the National Suffrage Association also focused on job discrimination, labor conditions, and divorce law. The organization tried repeatedly from 1878 to 1896 and after 1913 to put through Congress a suffrage amendment called the Susan B. Anthony Amendment. The amendment failed to pass. Another women's rights organization also formed in 1869 and took a different approach to suffrage. The American Woman Suffrage Association set its sights on changing voting laws at the state level. This strategy proved to be effective: while the national government did not support the women's cause, some state governments were sympathetic to the suffrage movement and allowed women to vote at the state level. Women won their first right to vote in the Wyoming territory in 1869. Utah followed the next year and, by 1916, women were able to capitalize on the support of enough states to have the necessary momentum and credibility for the federal government to listen. In 1890, the National and American Woman Suffrage Associations merged to become the National American Woman Suffrage Association (NAWSA). Their efforts were also helped by World War I, which offered opportunities for women to serve as volunteers and fill jobs left vacant by men who were fighting.

In 1920, 72 years after that first conference, the Nineteenth Amendment to the Constitution was ratified, declaring that "the right of citizens of the United States to vote shall not be denied or abridged by the United States or by any State on account of sex." For women, the passing of the Nineteenth Amendment meant an immediate enforcement of the right to vote. Some women early on were reluctant to exercise their right, but all constitutional challenges to the enfranchisement of women in the political process were over.

Since 1920, women have made important strides in American politics. In every presidential election since 1980, the percentage of women who have turned out to vote has actually been higher than the percentage of men (see Figure 5.1).

FIGURE 5.1 Proportion of Eligible Adult Population Who Reported Voting

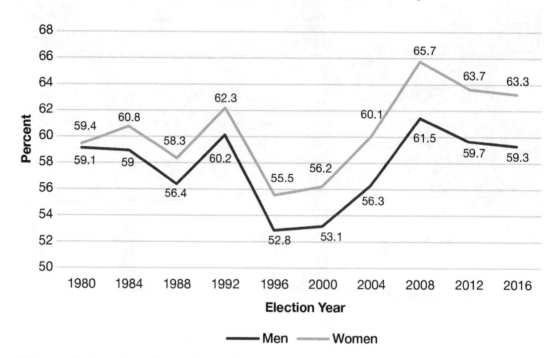

U.S. Bureau of the Census Current Population Reports, Series P-20, "Voting and Registration in the Election of November 1964" and subsequent reports for all years through 2016 as compiled by the Center for American Women and Politics at Rutgers University. Report available at: http://www.cawp.rutgers.edu/sites/default/files/resources/genderdiff.pdf.

More and more women have been elected to government positions. Women have served as governors, senators, and representatives. They have held the office of Speaker of the House of Representatives, Secretary of State, and National Security Advisor. The 116th Congress includes 127 women, or 24 percent. That number is far less than the overall American population, which is 50 percent female. Of the 438 representatives in the House, 106 are women, and there are 25 female senators. Three of the nine Supreme Court justices are women. In 2016, Hillary Clinton became the first woman to win a presidential nomination from a major political party.

Women in the Workplace

The Nineteenth Amendment gave women the right to vote, but it did not end gender discrimination. The Fourteenth Amendment applied to both genders, but the courts often did not interpret it this way. Americans were treated differently depending on their sex. This inequality was felt in the workplace especially.

Equal Rights Amendment

An amendment drafted in 1923 and submitted to Congress every year until 1972 that stated: "equality of rights ... shall not be denied or abridged ... on account of sex."

Since 1924, women's groups have struggled to pass the **Equal Rights Amendment** (ERA) that would end discrimination on the basis of sex. Progress was made in the 1960s, however, when Congress in 1963 passed the Equal Pay Act, which requires equal pay for equal work, and again in 1964, when Title VII of the Civil Rights Act was amended to prohibit discrimination on the basis of race, color, national origin, gender, and religion. In 1967, the National Organization for Women (NOW) was created to promote equal rights and to get the ERA passed. NOW succeeded in expanding women's rights with the passage of Title IX in 1972, which banned sex discrimination in public schools. In 1972, the Revenue Act gave tax credits for childcare. The ERA was introduced again in Congress in

1972, but by 1977, only 35 states had ratified it, which was three states short of the necessary 38. The ratification deadline was extended to 1982, but the ERA failed to obtain the two-thirds vote it needed to pass.

The ERA failed for several reasons. Many opponents of the bill viewed the amendment as a threat to societal norms. It also came to be associated with the Supreme Court case *Roe v. Wade*, which gave women the right to an abortion in the first three months of pregnancy. For some conservatives, the ERA became a symbol of the rejection of motherhood and traditional values. During this time, the Supreme Court was overturning laws that treated women differently from men. Many felt that the Court's rulings were adequate for addressing the issue of gender inequality.

While some barriers to equality for women have been eliminated, women continue to face discrimination when it comes to salaries. For every dollar earned by a man, a woman makes 77 cents. The National Committee on Pay Equity estimates that the wage gap may cost women almost half a million dollars over the course of their employment.[18] This wage gap is especially large for women in management positions and for older women. In 2007, the Supreme Court ruled in the case of *Lilly Ledbetter v. Goodyear Tire Co.* Ledbetter sued Goodyear after a 19-year career as a supervisor because she had been paid less than men in the same position. A jury ruled in her favor and found Goodyear guilty of pay discrimination. When the case reached the Supreme Court, the court overturned the ruling in a 5-4 decision, stating that Ledbetter should have sued Goodyear within 180 days after the company set her pay.[19] Of course, Ledbetter was not aware at that time of the wage differential. The first piece of legislation that President Barack Obama signed into law after his inauguration in 2009 was the Lilly Ledbetter Act.[20] This law allows an employee to sue up to 180 days after the last paycheck.

Women also deal with the **glass ceiling**, the often subtle obstacles to advancement that professional women encounter in the workplace. The presence of a glass ceiling has meant the underrepresentation of women in upper management positions and in political office.

An additional challenge that women face in employment is **sexual harassment**, or unwanted physical and/or verbal advances or abuse of a sexual nature that interferes with job performance and creates a hostile work environment. The Supreme Court has upheld the right of people to be free from sexual harassment, including harassment by members of the same sex. Sexual harassment can be difficult to prove, however, and the threat of retribution from employers keeps many victims silent. The recent #MeToo and Time's Up movements have focused the conversation on the professional and personal obstacles that women face. The #MeToo effort started on social media in October 2017 and invited women and men to share their experiences of sexual violence, hoping to increase awareness of the issue by showing just how widespread it is. Time's Up centers on equity in the workplace and creating equal economic opportunities for women and people of color. The Time's Up movement seeks to combat sexual harassment and assault in an effort to promote safety and equity in the workplace. Advocates are also working to raise awareness of sexual assault on college campuses. According to the U.S. Department of Justice, one out of every four college undergraduates will be a victim of some form of sexual assault before graduation. The ACLU notes that 95 percent of campus rapes go unreported. These statistics reflect the culture of rape that pervades American society and demands increased campus prevention and support from colleges to raise awareness and combat the issue. Attention is also being drawn to the issue of sexual harassment in the U.S. military. In 2017, a survey of 1,300 service women conducted by the Service Women's Action Network (SWAN) identified military sexual trauma (MST) as the number one factor negatively affecting the mental wellness of women in the military.[21]

glass ceiling

The often subtle obstacles to advancement that professional women encounter in the workplace.

sexual harassment

Unwanted physical and/or verbal advances or abuse of a sexual nature that interferes with job performance and creates a hostile work environment.

Marchers turned out again on the one-year anniversary of President Trump's inauguration, this time focused on the #MeToo and Time's Up movements to fight sexual harassment and sexual misconduct in the workplace.

Sundry Photography / Shutterstock.com

5.4 The Struggle for Ethnic and Cultural Equality

We have focused on the struggles for equality of black Americans and of women. But the battle for civil rights in the United States has been waged by other groups who have also faced discrimination based on their racial, ethnic, and/or cultural identity. In this section, we consider the efforts of Latina/o, Asian Americans, and Native Americans to gain equal representation.

Latinas/os

Latinas/os are the largest ethnic minority in United States, comprising more than 17 percent of the population. Their numbers are growing by about 2.1 percent per year. By 2060, it is estimated they will be 28.6 percent of the country's population.[22] Between 2000 and 2012, the Latina/o population grew by 50 percent. The overall U.S. population grew by just 12 percent in that same period.[23] Latinas/os are already the largest minority in California and New Mexico. The population explosion means Latinas/os are going to be increasingly crucial to the discussion about politics and economics in the United States. For now, however, Latinas/os remain entrenched in the country's working poor. About 22 percent live below the poverty line, compared to 8 percent of whites. As we shall see in the chapter on voting, their economic status translates to lower voter turnout; 48 percent versus 64 percent for non-Hispanic whites. Latinas/os are also younger than the general U.S. population. Their median age is almost 10 years younger than Americans as a whole. This means that fewer

Latinas/os are old enough to vote relative to other groups in the electorate. In 2014, Latinas/os were 17 percent of the population, yet made up only 8 percent of the nation's voters.[24]

While Latinas/os have not faced the same challenges as blacks in America, they have been marginalized and disenfranchised. They have also been the victims of discriminatory and segregationist policies. Latinas/os have fought hard against marginalization. Eight years before the Supreme Court ruled in *Brown v. The Board of Education* that segregation in schools was unconstitutional, Latinas/os won a court case in California that ended segregation in the state's schools. The 1946 *Mendez v. Westminster* case was important not only because it paved the way for *Brown v. The Board of Education*, but because it put a face on the issue of racism and brought attention to its potentially devastating psychological costs to children. The case was about a 9-year-old girl named Sylvia Mendez who was turned away from a California public school that was for "whites only." Her parents, along with four other families, fought the rejection and used school, civic, and legal channels to win a class action lawsuit. In his decision, U.S. District Court Judge Paul J. McCormick wrote that, "[T]he equal protection of the laws pertaining to the public school system in California is not provided by furnishing in separate schools the same technical facilities, textbooks and courses of instruction to children of Mexican ancestry that are available to the other public school children regardless of their ancestry. A paramount requisite in the American system of public education is social equality. It must be open to all children by unified school association regardless of lineage."[25] The school districts appealed the decision to the U.S. Court of Appeals for the Ninth Circuit, claiming that Mexican American children were inferior to white children: they carried contagious diseases and were limited by their "language deficiency." The Court of Appeals upheld Judge McCormick's ruling and California Governor Earl Warren signed a bill that ended segregation in schools in California. With that bill, California became the first state to desegregate its public schools. While the *Mendez* case was pending, several organizations, including the National Association for the Advancement of Colored People, supported the Mendez families and wrote amicus briefs. Thurgood Marshall, who later used the same arguments before the Supreme Court in *Brown v. The Board of Education*, wrote the briefs. When the Supreme Court voted in favor of Linda Brown and ended school segregation across the United States, it was Chief Justice Earl Warren (the former California governor) who wrote the majority opinion.

Civil rights advocate and labor leader Dolores Huerta was presented with the Presidential Medal of Freedom on May 29, 2012, at the White House in Washington, D.C. Huerta cofounded the National Farmworkers Association (which later became the United Farm Workers) with Cesar Chavez and helped organize the Delano grape strike in 1965. She was the lead negotiator for the workers' contract that was drafted after the strike.

Rena Schild / Shutterstock.com

Latinas/os have also fought to improve labor conditions for minority workers. In the 1960s, the United Farm Workers (UFW) led by Cesar Chavez called attention to the mistreatment of migrant workers who picked crops along the west coast. Chavez espoused the same principles as the civil rights movement and used norms of social justice to challenge discrimination and call for a national boycott of grapes and lettuce that were picked by nonunion labor. Chavez and the UFW became symbols of the Latina/o battle for equality. Other groups such as the Mexican American Legal Defense and Education Fund (MALDEF) and the League of United Latin American Citizens (LULAC) have also emerged to fight for an end to discrimination against Latinas/os. Their combined efforts have paved the way for Latina/o elected officials at every level of government.

While *Mendez v. Westminster* and the work of Cesar Chavez, MALDEF, and LULAC represent major steps forward, Latinas/os continue to struggle against racist and discriminatory policies. Their experience is unique because of diversity within the population and the politics over language and immigration.

The Politics of Diversity

One of the most important features of the Latina/o population is its diversity. Latinas/os share a common Spanish heritage, but they come from different racial and ethnic backgrounds. To classify them therefore as a single minority group can be misleading. Many Latinas/os tend to identify themselves by country of origin rather than by the term Hispanic American. The majority of Latinas/os in the United States come from Mexico, but even within this group, there is a difference between Americans with Mexican backgrounds (called Chicanos/Chicanas) and more recent Mexican-born immigrants. Mexican Americans tend to be concentrated in California, Texas, Arizona, and New Mexico. Many have been living in these areas since before they were part of the United States. Their cultural ties with more recent immigrants from Mexico have therefore weakened over time. Other Latina/o groups, such Puerto Ricans, are found in New York, New Jersey, and other northern states, while Cuban Americans are largely based in Florida (where they represent a major political constituency).

The groups vary not only in geographic location, but also in their party affiliations. Mexican Americans and Puerto Ricans tend to be Democrats. Cuban Americans, many of whom came to the United States as refugees fleeing the Communist regime of Fidel Castro in Cuba, tend to be Republicans. What this means is that Latinas/os do not represent an entirely cohesive political unit with common interests. They are a significant portion of the population located mainly in the most populous states. If they did unite and act together, they could potentially have an enormous influence on politics, but their diversity has kept them fragmented and, as a result, unable to mobilize as effectively as they might.

Recent efforts to rally voters have focused on the issue of unity. The Congressional Hispanic Caucus has used the notion of a pan-Latina/o identity as a way to attract and mobilize voters. The strategy has been successful and, according to the National Association of Latino Elected and Appointed Officials (NALEO), as of 2017 the caucus has 34 representatives in the House and four in the Senate (Bob Menendez, Marco Rubio, Ted Cruz, and Catherine Cortez Masto). There is one Latina governor (Michelle Lujan Grisham in New Mexico) and, in 2009, President Obama appointed the first Latina, Sonia Sotomayor, to the Supreme Court.

Some Latinas/os worry that forging a pan-Latina/o identity will detract from individual cultures and national pride. Others see a collective identity as critical for gaining political influence. Based on their rising numbers alone, Latinas/os could become a formidable power in American politics. If they are able to overcome their coordination problems and unite under the banner of shared identity, they could become one of the most important groups in government with the capacity to reshape the political conversation in the United States.

The Politics of Language

English-only movements

Efforts that seek to make English the official language of the United States.

The Supreme Court's 1974 ruling in *Lau v. Nichols* mandated protection for students whose first language was not English. As a result, many school districts introduced bilingual education. Opponents argue that the policy is divisive and can create long-term disadvantages for students who are not exposed to enough English (and, as a result, fail to learn it). These concerns have led to **English-only movements** that seek to make English the official language of the United States. Not only would English be the language used in schools, but it would also be the only language to appear on ballots and other official documents. Within the Latina/o community, there is widespread support for English-language education. There is also, however, the desire to ensure that Spanish-only speakers will not continue to be disenfranchised because they cannot read ballots that are only printed in English. Moreover, given the fact that the U.S. ranks sixth in the world in the number of people for whom Spanish is a first language, the question arises about how appropriate it is for English to serve as the sole voice of national and cultural identity.

The Politics of Immigration

At the heart of the Latina/o struggle for civil rights is the controversy over immigration. The United States is a country of immigrants. With the exception of Native Americans, everyone in the United States has arrived here from somewhere else. While the nation celebrates its rich cultural diversity, there is also an inherent fear of what immigrants might bring—their own languages and customs that could undermine the American way of life—and what they might take away—jobs that would otherwise go to Americans. Because Latinas/os are currently the largest group of immigrants to the United States, most of these fears are directed against them and have led to staunch anti-immigration policies and **racial profiling**, or singling out of people on the basis of their race, ethnicity, or religion. The toughest immigration measure was introduced in 2010 in Arizona when the state passed law SB 1070. The law requires individuals to carry immigration documents and authorizes law enforcement officials to stop and question anyone they suspect of being in the country illegally. Other states, including Alabama and Utah, have introduced similar measures. In 2012, the Supreme Court ruled on Arizona's SB 1070 in *Arizona v. United States*. The question before the Court was whether SB 1070 usurps the federal government's authority to regulate and enforce immigration laws. The Court ruled that federal law preempts some sections of SB 1070, but that other aspects of it were constitutional, including the right for law enforcement to verify a person's citizenship status.

Immigrants who are in the United States illegally face the constant threat of deportation. Undocumented immigrants have also struggled to access health care and education. The **DREAM Act** (**D**evelopment, **R**elief, and **E**ducation for **A**lien **M**inors) was introduced in 2001 as a means for undocumented immigrants who have been in the country since before they were 16 years old and have lived here for at least five years to acquire first conditional residency and then eventually permanent residency. In 2012, President Obama signed an executive order known as Deferred Action for Childhood Arrivals Program (DACA) that removed the threat of deportation for some DREAMers. Under DACA, undocumented youth who were under the age of 31 by June 2012 and who had been brought to the United States before they were 16 received work permits and were deemed a low priority for deportation. Nearly 800,000 undocumented youth applied for the program. In September 2017, President Trump ended the DACA program and allowed only a subset of current recipients to apply for renewal of protections, leaving hundreds of thousands of people vulnerable to detention and deportation. DACA was scheduled to be phased out beginning in March 2018, but U.S. District Court judges in New York and California issued nationwide injunctions which prevented the program from ending. The Trump Administration continues to approve DACA applications, but until there is a law in place, the future of the program remains unknown and the debate about undocumented immigrants continues.

racial profiling
Singling out of people on the basis of their race, ethnicity, or religion.

DREAM Act
Legislation introduced in 2001 as a means for undocumented immigrants who have been in the United States since before they were 16 years old and who have lived here for at least five years to acquire first conditional residency and then eventually permanent residency.

Asian Americans

Like Latinas/os and black Americans, Asian Americans have experienced racism and discrimination. Asian Americans are the third largest minority group in the United States. Like Latinas/os, they come from various countries, each with its own culture and traditions. But unlike Latinas/os, who share a common language (with the exception of Brazilians who speak Portuguese), Asian Americans speak a variety of languages. They also do not share a common history like blacks do. The lack of shared national and linguistic identity has meant that it has been even more difficult for Asian Americans to mobilize as a group. Asian Americans do not comprise an electoral majority in any congressional district except Hawaii, so they have to form coalitions with other groups in order to win elections and be politically effective.

Cultural Diversity and Discrimination

Asian Americans come from countries such as China, Japan, India, Korea, the Philippines, Vietnam, Laos, and Cambodia. As a young nation, the United States passed the Naturalization Act of 1790, which allowed only white immigrants to become naturalized citizens. The earliest Asian Americans came from China and Japan in the 1800s. They came seeking work opportunities in the frontier West. Because immigrants would accept lower wages than white workers, resentment built quickly. Congress eventually responded by passing the Chinese Exclusion Act in 1882, which stopped immigration from China and denied citizenship rights to Chinese immigrants. In 1925, Congress passed the National Origin Act, which banned Japanese immigrants. The California Alien Land Act of 1913 made it illegal for Asian immigrants who were "aliens ineligible for citizenship" to own land. Congress finally repealed the Chinese Exclusion Act in 1943 and the Naturalization Act in 1952, but it was not until 1965 that Asian immigrants were treated the same as Americans of other nationalities. The fastest growing immigrant group in America today are Asians and Pacific Islanders, with most coming from Vietnam, Laos, and Cambodia.

© Shutterstock, Inc.

Asian Americans have suffered from discrimination throughout their history in the United States. Because Asian Americans were ineligible for citizenship and in many states could not own or rent property, they were disenfranchised and marginalized. A great deal of hostility toward Asian Americans was perhaps most evident in the treatment of Japanese Americans during World War II. After the Japanese bombing of Pearl Harbor in December 1941, President Franklin Roosevelt ordered the Army to move Japanese Americans into internment camps in an effort to safeguard against the threat that some Japanese Americans could be spies. Their property, bank accounts, and possessions were seized. Many lost their jobs and/or were forced to leave college. The Supreme Court upheld the internments with the landmark decision in *Korematsu v. United States* in 1944. The Court ruled that national security concerns and the need to protect against spying were more important than the plaintiff Fred Korematsu's individual rights and the rights of Japanese Americans.[26] While they were in the camps, young Japanese men were forced to pledge their loyalty to the United States so they could be drafted for military service. They were imprisoned if they refused. During this period, the United States government stripped its own citizens of their rights because of their cultural identity. The government eventually apologized for its mistreatment of Japanese Americans and in 1988, Congress paid $1.25 billion in reparations to former camp inhabitants who were still alive.

Japanese Americans were brought by train, processed, and held in hastily constructed barracks before being assigned to remote inland Internment Camps.

The original uploader was Shep182 at English Wikipedia. (File:SanPedro to SantaAnita.gif) [Public domain], via Wikimedia Commons. https://bit.ly/2FXBnBH.

Today, Japanese and Chinese Americans lead other ethnic groups in median income and median education. In fact, Asian Americans are labeled as the most highly skilled immigrant group in United States. They are characterized as the "model minority"—a paragon of hard work and patience whose example other minority groups should follow. The problem with this label is that it again reduces Asian Americans to a stereotype and illustrates how Asian identity has been once again recast to serve various political agendas."[27]

Political Presence

Kamala Harris is the first woman, Black, and South Asian American to serve as Vice President.

Office of Senator Kamala Harris (https://www.harris. senate.gov/news#photos) [Public domain], via Wikimedia Commons. https://bit.ly/2UYE4X8.

While voter turnout rates usually rise with education and income levels, those rates for Asian Americans are among the lowest in the United States. The legacy of discrimination and the denial of citizenship rights early on have meant that some Asian American do not feel a historical connection to the American political process. Moreover, many Asian Americans have focused their attention on building economic security rather than advancing political rights.[28] Recent data suggests that this trend may be changing. Asian American voter turnout is slowly rising, though it remains a small share of the electorate. As of 2017, there are three Asian governors (David Ige in Hawaii, Bobby Jindal in Louisiana, and Nikki Haley in South Carolina). In the 117th Congress, there are 18 Asian Americans in the House and three in the Senate (Harris, Tammy Duckworth, and Mazie Hirono).

Asian Americans are becoming more politically visible and, while they tend to split their votes more or less equally between Republicans and Democrats, they are increasingly vocal about issues like welfare reform (which affects elderly legal immigrants), changes in immigration laws, and affirmative action policies.

Native Americans

The tension between the desire to protect tribal sovereignty and the need to protest against political and economic marginalization has characterized the civil rights struggle for the nation's 2.5 million Native Americans. Also referred to as American Indians, Native Americans were the earliest inhabitants of what would become the United States. They lived in well-organized, agriculturally based communities with rich cultural and artistic traditions and complex societal hierarchies. The arrival of the Europeans brought disease, war, and ultimately the alienation from their territory and disenfranchisement of their political rights.

Interactions between the U.S. Government and Native Americans

When we broadly classify the different tribes under the labels "Native American" or "American Indian," we are assuming that they constitute a uniform group sharing the same goals. This oversimplification fails to recognize the vast cultural diversity that exists among the 548 federally recognized American Indian tribes in the United States.[29] To comprehend the history of the civil rights movement for Native Americans, it is necessary to understand that each of these tribes has its own culture, language, religions, history, and political structure. This diversity has often been an obstacle for tribes to unite in common cause efforts. In this sense, the Native American struggle for civil rights is similar to that of Asian Americans. As we read earlier, Asian Americans come from a variety of backgrounds, each with its own distinct culture. What that means is that the effort to mobilize as a collective is more challenging. Linguistic barriers must be overcome, as well as cultural and political norms that divide the groups. The divisions between Native American tribes have also been reified by the unique and special relationship tribes have with the U.S. government. The federal government has signed 367 treaties, 73 agreements, and more than 100 individual statutes with American Indian tribes.[30] The differences in rights and privileges combined with the contours of cultural pluralism has formed a barrier against uniting Native Americans in a shared struggle for suffrage and citizenship rights.

One of the first challenges the government of the newly established United States of America had to confront was what to do with Native American tribes and land. The federal government did not deem Native Americans to be civilized enough to become citizens. For their part, many American Indians did not actively seek citizenship in the eighteenth century because they were citizens of powerful tribal groups who owned and controlled most of the territory in North America.[31] The nineteenth century ushered in the idea of Manifest Destiny as central to consolidating power for the federal government. Central to the notion of Manifest Destiny is the push for territorial expansion. As the United States moved westward and tried to acquire more land, the result was warfare and tension between the government and the tribes who owned and occupied the territory. In 1830, Congress passed the **Indian Removal Act**, which authorized the government to relocate 80,000 American Indians from their land to territory west of the Mississippi River. Many tribes resisted. The government responded with a policy of ethnic cleansing and brutal, forced marches that became known as the Trail of Tears. Violence increased as Americans pushed further west. Great Basin and Great Plains tribes fought against the expansion and subsequent alienation from their lands in a series of wars. Indians were able to win some of the battles, but these victories proved temporary as the government grew stronger and more powerful. With each defeat and conquest, the federal government would force a series of treaties and land cessations by the tribes, establishing reservations in many western states. In 1831, the government determined that Indian tribes were **domestic dependent nations**, thereby granting them local sovereignty but not giving them the full control they would need to have the rights of an independent nation. By essentially making them members of foreign nations, the government stripped Native Americans of any claims to civil rights under U.S. laws. This meant the tribes were unable to use legal channels to challenge the acquisition of their land. The policy of separating Native Americans was later replaced by attempts to assimilate them.

The government eventually began to offer citizenship to specific tribes in exchange for their lands. In 1887, the Dawes Act extended the offer to all Native American tribes. By the early twentieth century, millions of acres of Indian homelands had been traded for citizenship. In 1924, all American Indians who were not already citizens were granted citizenship by Congress with the Indian Citizenship Act. Native Americans were still, however, not given the civil rights guaranteed to other U.S. citizens. They were not allowed to vote in state and federal elections, testify in court, serve on juries, attend public schools, or buy alcohol (because it was illegal to sell alcohol to Indians).[32] Until the Voting Rights Act was passed in 1965, many states excluded American Indians from voting by using poll taxes and literacy tests. While amendments to the Voting Rights Act passed in 1975 and 1982, preventing states from blocking Native Americans' right to vote, the legal status of Native Americans remains an issue today. Of the two million Native Americans in the United States, about half live on tribal reservations that are considered to be independent territories that are not subject to state laws. But these American Indians are citizens of the United States and must adhere to federal regulations and laws. The unique ambiguous legal status of American Indians has allowed some tribes to build highly profitable gambling businesses, with about half of the country's tribes operating casinos. Because tribes are sovereign territories, they are exempt from state restrictions on gaming. Whether tribes should be allowed to own and operate casinos remains controversial and policies on gaming appear frequently on state ballots.

> **Indian Removal Act**
>
> Authorized the government to relocate 80,000 American Indians from their land to territory west of the Mississippi River.
>
> **domestic dependent nations**
>
> Special status given to Native American tribal nations that grants them local sovereignty but does not give them the full sovereignty they would need to have the rights of an independent nation.

Entrance sign for the Choctaw Casino and Resort in Durant, Oklahoma. The casino is owned by the Choctaw Nation of Oklahoma.

Eblis / Shutterstock.com

Cultural and Socioeconomic Dimensions

Addressing the advancement of civil rights of American Indians also requires examining their access to education and employment opportunities. Like other groups who have experienced long-term discrimination, Native Americans suffer from high poverty rates that are about three times higher than the national rate. They also have experienced high levels of unemployment, low high school completion rates, high infant mortality, and poor health care. Affirmative action programs have benefited some Native Americans, arguably, while others contend there still exists endemic racism that prevents American Indians from changing their socioeconomic status.

There is also a tension between preserving Native American culture, languages, and social practices and integrating into mainstream society. American Indians have frequently had to fight the government to keep it from suppressing their freedom to exercise their culture, including the denial of access to religious sites, restrictions on the use or ownership of certain items used for worship, and limitations on their ceremonial practices. The Supreme Court ruled in the 1988 case *Lyng v. Northwest Indian Cemetery Protection Association* that the construction of a service road through a sacred site did not violate the First Amendment Freedom of Religion rights of Native Americans. In 1991, in the case *Employment Division of Oregon v. Smith*, the Court ruled that the state of Oregon did not infringe on the freedom of religion rights of two men who were denied unemployment benefits after they took peyote as part of a religious ceremony for their Native American church. The decision was overturned in 1994 when President Bill Clinton signed a bill that prohibited discrimination against those who use peyote for religious reasons.

American Indians continue to fight against other forms of discrimination, including offensive and stereotypical mascots and team names used by sports organizations. Cultural activism on the part of Native Americans has led to an effort to teach and preserve indigenous languages and to create an expanded cultural infrastructure. Independent newspapers, a television channel, and online media have been created to serve Native American communities. Universities have established Native American Studies programs. The works of American Indian artists and writers are gaining prominence.

American Indians have made important political advances despite the challenges of mobilizing as a collective group. The National Congress of American Indians (NCAI) was established in 1944 to unite Native Americans behind a common purpose. The NCAI's goal has been to educate the public about Indian culture, language, and history as well as secure and preserve treaty rights. Another organization, the Native American Rights Fund (NARF) provides legal protection for American Indians. Together, NCAI and NARF ensure that the issue of Native American rights remains on the policy agenda.

5.5 The Struggle for Marginalized Groups

The civil rights movement for racial, gender, and ethnic equality inspired other marginalized and disenfranchised groups to demand an end to discrimination.

Age

In 1976, the Supreme Court ruled that if the government has rational reasons for doing so, it can pass laws that treat people of various ages differently. For example, the government can pass laws which make it illegal for people under the age of 21 to drink. It can also impose curfews on younger people and set the minimum age to vote at 18. Different laws based on age also apply to those who commit crimes. Young people are often tried as minors and are not subject to the same forms of punishment as older adults. We accept most of these discrepancies in treatment because they are designed to protect younger Americans.

What is more controversial, however, is age discrimination in employment. Some companies have mandatory retirement at a certain age despite an individual's capacities. The Supreme Court has tended to uphold compulsory retirement requirements. In 1967, Congress passed the Discrimination in Employment Act, which protected Americans over the age of 40 from not being hired because of their age. The law also prohibits discrimination against people up to the age of 70 in employment or in the provision of benefits. The law was amended in 1978 to stop the forced retirement of people younger than 70. In 1986, the law was further revised to prohibit all age-based compulsory retirements.

Older Americans are among the most well-organized political coalitions in the United States. They are represented by AARP (the American Association of Retired Persons), a powerful interest group with over 30 million members. AARP has been extremely effective in lobbying the government to pass policies that benefit older Americans, such as Social Security and Medicare. Preserving these services sometimes comes at the expense of cutting services that would benefit younger Americans, such as school voucher programs.

Americans with Disabilities

Americans with disabilities have also developed into a powerful coalition that has worked for better treatment and conditions. Until the 1970s, people with disabilities were limited in the schools they could attend and were discriminated against in employment. There was also limited access provided on public transportation and in public facilities. While there were no laws that discriminated against people with disabilities, these physical barriers kept many from voting and participating in mainstream society. This changed in 1973 when liberal Congressional staffers added a provision to a bill. The provision was Section 504 of the Rehabilitation Act and stated that: "No ... handicapped individual ... shall, solely by reason of his handicap, be excluded from participation in, or be denied the benefits of ... any program or activity conducted by an executive agency." That implied that all universities that received federal funds and government agencies had to build infrastructure that would accommodate people with disabilities.

The passage of Section 504 proved to have more important implications: it served to mobilize Americans with disabilities into a powerful interest group that demanded civil rights. Their biggest political success came in 1990 with the passage of the **Americans with Disabilities Act** (ADA). The ADA requires companies to provide reasonable accommodations for people with disabilities and details guidelines for access to access to buildings, public transit facilities, and communication and education systems. The ADA also made it illegal for businesses with 25 or more employees to discriminate against people who are handicapped. Companies can refuse to make accommodations, such as installing ramps or elevators, if they would be too expensive or inconvenient. Advocates for making the accommodations argue that by installing the necessary ramps or elevators, the companies will actually make more money because people with disabilities will be able to access their facilities and frequent their businesses. It is often left up to the courts to decide whether these accommodations should be made despite their cost and inconvenience. The Supreme Court limited what the ADA can do when, in 2001, it ruled that state employees could not sue their states for damages under the ADA because of the Eleventh Amendment's limits on lawsuits that can be filed against states.[33] Despite this ruling, the ADA has changed how society, schools, businesses, and the government treat Americans with special needs.

Americans with Disabilities Act

Legislation passed in 1990 that requires companies to provide reasonable accommodations for people with disabilities. It details guidelines for access to buildings and public transit facilities as well as communication and education systems.

Sexual Orientation

Since 1969, gay rights groups have become a significant political force advocating for an end to discrimination based on sexual orientation. What started the modern-day gay rights movement was the Stonewall Riot in 1969, when the gay community erupted into a violent protest after police raided the Stonewall Inn, a gay bar in New York City. The LGBTQ community immediately began to agitate for change and, in 1973, their first major success came when the American Psychiatric Association removed homosexuality from the list of mental disorders.

LGBTQ activists further developed their political skills when the AIDS epidemic forced them to mobilize and establish relationships with doctors, local governments, and social services. They have also had to work to change social and cultural norms that have discriminated against them. They have fought long, hard battles against laws that dictated what type of sex they could engage in and who they could marry. In 2003, the Supreme Court struck down sodomy laws in *Lawrence v. Texas* and, in 2015, the Court ruled in *Obergefell v. Hodges* that the fundamental right to marry is guaranteed to same sex couples by the Due Process Clause and the Equal Protection Clause of the Fourteenth Amendment. Other important changes have resulted from gay rights advocacy, including an end to the "don't ask, don't tell" policy that allowed gays to serve in the military as long as they did not make their sexual orientation known.

In many ways, the LGBTQ struggle has been the civil rights battle for the current generation. Most states and cities now have laws protecting the rights of gay men and women, but stereotypes and bullying remain critical issues as the fight for equality and security continues. This battle is currently being waged by the transgender community, whose movement for equality uses many of the same arguments adopted by advocates for gay rights, women's rights, and the rights of racial minorities.[34] The term *transgender* describes people whose gender identity differs from the sex they were assigned at birth. The legal arguments surrounding transgender rights are rooted in the idea that gender identity is an immutable characteristic of a human being. The issues surrounding transgender rights have recently played out in court cases regarding the use of public restrooms. Consider, for example, the case of Gavin Grimm, a transgender teen who sued his school board for the right to use the boys' bathroom, winning in the Fourth Circuit Court of Appeals. The Fourth Circuit based its decision on the Obama Administration's interpretation of the 1972 law known as Title IX that prohibits public schools from discriminating "on the basis of sex." The Obama Administration understood this law to mean that schools must treat transgender students according to their gender identity. When President Donald Trump took office in 2017, he changed the interpretation. Grimm had appealed his case to the Supreme Court and urged the Court to clarify Title IX. The Court instead sent the case back to the lower court for reconsideration. The divisive social issue continues to play out in the legal arena, schools, and communities. At issue is whether the 1975 federal regulation implementing Title IX and calling for "separate toilet, locker room, and shower facilities on the basis of sex" can be used as a basis for schools to keep transgender students out of bathrooms that align with their gender identities.[35] North Carolina banned transgender students from using gender-corresponding bathrooms. Thirteen other states challenged the Obama Administration's interpretation of Title IX in a Texas federal district court. The suit was later dropped after Trump declared he would not follow the Obama guidance on the issue. Most Americans support allowing transgender people to use the bathroom that is consistent with their gender identity. Civil rights activists have mounted strong opposition to those states who challenge bathroom access. The National Basketball Association and National Collegiate Athletic Association both pulled events out of North Carolina in response to its bathroom law. In addition, former North Carolina Republican Governor Pat McCrory's support for the bathroom law is believed to have cost him his reelection bid.[36] The rights of transgendered individuals, of course, extend beyond bathroom access and, as Title IX and equal protection continue to be debated at the state level, it will ultimately be up to the Supreme Court to establish the contemporary meaning of sex and gender. In the meantime, according to the National Center for Transgender Equality, transgender people are four times more likely to live in poverty and their unemployment rate is double that for the general population.

5.6 Slow But Steady Progress

From the very founding of the United States, some groups have either been marginalized or completely disenfranchised from the political process. As a result, they have had to fight for representation and equal opportunity. Their civil rights battles have been fraught with setbacks but have ultimately led to slow, steady progress. Each of the groups discussed in this chapter has faced unique challenges, but they are united in their goal: to ensure that Thomas Jefferson's words apply to all Americans, regardless of their race, ethnicity, gender, sexual orientation, religion, age, or abilities.

What their struggles for civil rights also demonstrate is the power of civic participation. Each of the groups won greater recognition and rights for its constituents because of the efforts of civil society. Most of the changes started with grassroots mobilization and pressure applied from the public on the country's leadership. The most successful groups recognized the importance of political pressure to the realization of constitutional rights. They are also the ones who realize that, in order to effect change at the federal level, you need to start at the state level. Winning civil rights is a game of changing hearts and minds. In order to put pressure on the government effectively, you need popular support. To get this, you have to break down stereotypes and address the issues of culture and traditions. This can be a long and arduous process. Success depends in large part on how a group deals with collective action problems.

As we saw with some of the groups discussed in this chapter, it can be hard to mobilize people who come from a common geographic area but who differ widely in their culture and language. It can also be hard to rally under a common banner those people who have different goals and strategies. In addition, the free rider problem complicates a group's ability to organize because civil rights are a public good—meaning they are nonexcludable and nonrival—but some people realize that they will be able to enjoy the rights without contributing to the obtainment of those rights. This means that it can be difficult to recruit participants and collect adequate funds to wage an effective battle for civil rights. Groups that have more members willing to devote time and resources to the cause are most likely to be successful. All of this illustrates, however, that civil rights is one part of government that people have power over and can change. Civil society is vital to the civil rights movement. The more people participate, the more likely they will be able to challenge discrimination and achieve equality for all.

5.7 What Can I Do?

This chapter has explored the struggles, victories, and challenges that remain with regards to achieving equality for all. The most important thing you can do is pay attention to the role you play in promoting civil rights. Do not become comfortable with inequity. Many students who observe inequalities around them and see that they and/or others are not treated fairly still do not consider themselves in a fight for their civil rights. Yet, institutional racism and structural inequality continue to present a threat to civil rights. It is critical that you speak out about the inequalities and injustices you experience and observe. Be an advocate for protecting the civil and constitutional rights of all Americans. Stand up for the civil rights of racial, ethnic, and religious minorities, women, persons with disabilities, people of all sexual orientations and gender identifications, and individuals who come from other nations and speak other languages. Address discrimination where you see it and promote equal opportunity in school, the workplace, housing, courts, prisons and detention facilities, police departments, mental health facilities, and in voting and immigration-related practices.

You can advocate for equality and justice by participating in campaigns, standing up for underrepresented or marginalized groups, and working to make all aspects of our society more inclusive. You can harness the skills of your generation to make today's civil rights movement your own. You can use art and culture as voices to describe your realities and share them with your peers and others. While you certainly can, you do not have to march or protest. Instead, you can create a song, act out an experience, and utilize other cultural media to bring attention to civil rights. You can use social media to connect with others and raise awareness of injustice. But be selective with the media you promote and consume. Social media can be a critical tool for fighting inequality, but it can also perpetuate stereotypes and discriminatory behavior. Think critically about the message you are sending before you post, comment, or retweet. While it may not be intentional, you may find yourselves reinforcing discrimination and marginalization. You can also engage in silent protest. You can choose not to participate in activities or practices that you find unfair. Of course, you can communicate more loudly and add your voice to that of others pushing for equality and change.

You can become part of a social movement for change and work with a broad coalition of organizations as well as individuals who share a common purpose and interact with political elites, opponents, and authorities. Social movements are particularly effective in democracies because they aggregate the desires of multiple organizations and individuals and provide access to people who might otherwise be ignored in American politics. Social movements have been effective in ending slavery, advocating for suffrage, protesting economic inequality, and drawing attention to present-day injustices with campaigns, such as Black Lives Matter. Social movements push for change by lobbying members of Congress their state legislatures, or their local city councils. They can also use the courts and direct action. Each of these paths has been successful for the civil rights movement in the United States.

FIGURE 5.2 Ways to Get Involved

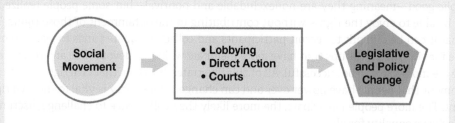

You do not have to get so directly involved to make an impact. In fact, you can contribute to promoting civil rights by listening to the experiences of others and being open to hearing their stories. Appreciate that their experience is different from yours and, even though they may express ideas that contradict your own beliefs, listen to them and try to understand their perspective. This practice will help you build empathy and awareness for the lives of others so that you can be a better advocate for civil rights.

5.8 What's the Alternative?

Each year, the National Urban League uses its Equality Index to track the gap between whites, blacks, and Latinas/os in America in five key areas: education, health, social justice, economics, and civic engagement. The index also looks at unemployment and income inequality. In its 2017 publication, the National Urban League reported that the Equality Index of Black America was 72.3 percent–up 1 percent from the year before (an index of 100 percent would mean full equality between blacks and whites). The area of greatest increase was education, which rose from 77.4 percent in 2015 to 78.2 percent in 2016. This increase is likely due to improved literacy rates for black Americans, a higher number of blacks between the ages of 18 and 24 earning associate's degrees, and a decline in the number of black students who have teachers with less than three years of experience.[37] Slight improvements were also seen in unemployment rates, wage gaps, the share of black-owned businesses, and the number of high-priced loans for black consumers. Inequities in health care also decreased slightly partly due to greater access in health care and a lower number of overweight children. The report showed that blacks are more civically engaged than whites.

Perhaps the area that requires our greatest attention is the criminal justice system. Blacks remain more likely than whites to be convicted for the same crimes and serve longer sentences than whites for committing the same crime. Minority groups are also more frequently the victims of hate crimes compared to whites. The Equality Index reports that social justice went from 60.9 percent in 2015 to 57.4 percent in 2016. Part of the decrease is due to a change in how the Bureau of Justice Statistics reports data on traffic stops, but part of the decrease reflects a growing number of black Americans incarcerated after an arrest.

The gap between whites and Latinas/os went from 77.9 percent in 2015 to 78.4 percent in 2016. The Urban League reports that this was the result of a major improvement in the health index (from 105.5 percent to 108.8 percent, meaning Latinas/os are healthier than whites) and smaller gains in the education (from 74.2 percent to 75.3 percent) and economics indexes (from 61.9 percent to 62.1 percent). Gaps remain in the areas of social justice where the index went from 75.9 percent to 69.7 percent, and in civic engagement, which fell from 67.6 percent to 67.3 percent.

Reports like these help us measure how far we have come and how much work remains in promoting civil rights. Each of the five areas documented in the report is an area that could be made more democratic. We have decades of inequality that we are still trying to address. We must work to ensure that legislative and policy changes further decrease the gaps between whites and other groups. Greater representation and the extension of civil rights to other marginalized groups must also top the political agenda. These groups have seen their rights increase in recent years, but we must ensure that these rights remain protected and guaranteed by the Constitution. Legislative changes are critical in extending civil rights to all Americans.

In the area of women's rights, consider the following map, which shows women's political rights around the world as of 2011. The map illustrates women's rights to vote, run for office, hold appointed office, join political parties, and petition government officials. What is remarkable about the map is how the United States ranks in terms of political rights guaranteed to women. While the country is in the company of Canada and several European nations, access to politics for women in the United States ranks below several African, South American, and northern European countries. This evidence suggests that the nation could be more democratic when it comes to women's political rights. Wage gaps remain between men and women. Efforts must be made to ensure women are not discriminated against, that they have equal access to employment opportunities, and that they earn pay comparable to their male colleagues.

FIGURE 5.3 Women's Political Rights, 2011

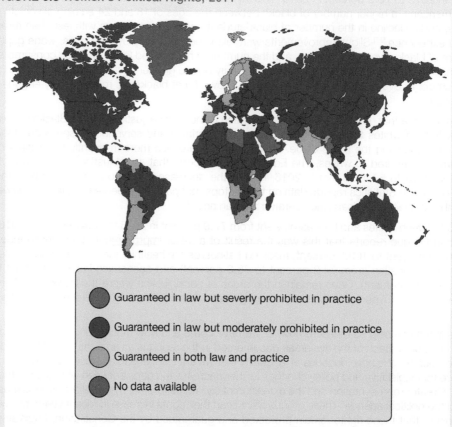

Based on David L. Cingranelli and David L. Richards, *The Cingranelli-Richards Human Rights Dataset*, http://humanrightsdata.com.

While we can certainly note how far we have come with regard to civil rights, this is one area of American politics where we do not want to sit back and trust the institutions to do the work for us. There are constitutional guarantees that protect citizens from discrimination, but the concern here is that relying too much on those guarantees will make us complacent and disconnected from the structural problems that remain. Discrimination, racism, and sexism are still very much a part of the American experience. We cannot stop fighting to ensure that citizens—regardless of their faith, skin color, gender, sexual orientation, or country of origin—feel safe, respected, and equal.

Endnotes

1. Joseph Goldstein and Nate Schweber, "Man's Death after Chokehold Raises Old Issue for the Police," *The New York Times*, July 18, 2014.

2. In July 2018, the New York Police Department filed formal departmental charges against the Officer Daniel Pantaleo who choked Eric Garner. https://www.cnn.com/2018/07/21/us/nypd-eric-garner-departmental-charges/index.html.

3. Harold Sullivan, *Civil Rights and Liberties: Provocative Questions and Evolving Answers* (New York: Prentice Hall, 2001), 1-2.

4. "Felon Voting Rights," National Conference of State Legislators, April 30, 2017, http://www.ncsl.org/research/elections-and-campaigns/felon-voting-rights.aspx.

5. Jeff Guo, "Arkansas Wants to Attract Businesses by Allowing Them to Discriminate Against Gay People," *The Washington Post*, February 17, 2015, https://www.washingtonpost.com/blogs/govbeat/wp/2015/02/17/arkansas-wants-to-attract-businesses-by-allowing-them-to-discriminate-against-gay-people/?utm_term=.be3771255b3f.

6. *Dred Scott v. Sandford*, 60 US 393 (U.S. 1857).

7. For more on this, see the Jim Crow Museum of Racist Memorabilia hosted by Ferris State University. https://ferris.edu/jimcrow/.

8. John Morton Blum, *V Was for Victory: Politics and American Culture During World War II* (New York: Harcourt Brace Jovanovich, 1976), 185.

9. Etoy Fletcher Affidavit (June 15, 1946), id. pt. IV, reel 8, fr. 894.

10. John Ditmer, *Local People: The Struggle for Civil Rights in Mississippi* (University of Illinois Press, 1995).

11. Jennifer E. Brooks, *Defining the Peace: World War II Veterans, Race, and the Remaking of Southern Political Tradition* (The University of North Carolina Press, 2004), 161.

12. Steven F. Lawson, *Black Ballots: Voting Rights in the South, 1944-1969* (Lanham: Lexington Books, 1999), 179.

13. Juan Williams, *Eyes on the Prize: America's Civil Rights Years, 1954-1965* (New York: Viking Penguin, Inc., 1987), 38.

14. Martin Luther King, Jr., *Letter from a Birmingham Jail*, April 16, 1963.

15. *Regents of the University of California v. Bakke*, 438 U.S. 265 (U.S. 1978).

16. "Public Backs Affirmative Action, But Not Minority Preferences," Pew Research Center, June 2, 2009, http://www.pewresearch.org/2009/06/02/public-backs-affirmative-action-but-not-minority-preferences/.

17. "Public strongly backs affirmative action programs on campus," Pew Research Center, April 22, 2014, http://www.pewresearch.org/fact-tank/2014/04/22/public-strongly-backs-affirmative-action-programs-on-campus/.

18. "The Wage Gap Over Time; in Real Dollars, Women See a Continuing Decline," National Committee on Pay Equity, www.pay-equity.org/info-time.html.

19. *Ledbetter v. Goodyear Tire & Rubber Co.*, 550 U.S. 618 (U.S. 2007).

20. Sheryl Gay Stolberg, "Obama Signs Equal-Pay Legislation," *The New York Times* (New York City, NY), January 29, 2009.

21. Antonieta Rico, "Why Military Women Are Missing from the #MeToo Movement," *Time*, December 12, 2017, http://time.com/5060570/military-women-sexual-assault/.

22. "Hispanic Americans by the Numbers," U.S. Census Bureau, 2014, http://www.infoplease.com/spot/hhmcensus1.html.

23. Anna Brown, "The U.S. Hispanic Population has Increased Sixfold Since 1970," The Pew Research Center, February 26, 2014, http://www.pewresearch.org/fact-tank/2014/02/26/the-u-s-hispanic-population-has-increased-sixfold-since-1970/.

24. Jens Krogstad and Mark Lope, "5 Takeaways about the 2014 Latino Vote," The Pew Research Center, November 19, 2014, http://www.pewresearch.org/fact-tank/2014/11/10/5-takeaways-about-the-2014-latino-vote/.

25. *Mendez v. Westminister School Dist.*, 64 F. Supp. 544 (S.D. Cal. 1946).

26. *Korematsu v. United States*, 323 U.S. 214 (U.S. 1944).

27. Ellen D. Wu, "Asian Americans and the 'Model Minority' Myth," *Los Angeles Times* (Los Angeles, CA), January 23, 2014.

28. K. Connie Kang, "Asian Americans Slow to Flex their Political Muscle," *Los Angeles Times* (Los Angeles, CA), October 31, 1996.

29. Willard Hughes Rollings, "Citizenship and Suffrage: The Native American Struggle for Civil Rights in the American West, 1830-1965," *Nevada Law Journal* Vol. 5 (Fall 2004): 126.

30. Francis Paul Prucha, *American Indian Treaties: The History of a Political Anomaly*, (University of California Press, 1997).

31. Willard Hughes Rollings, "Citizenship and Suffrage: The Native American Struggle for Civil Rights in the American West, 1830-1965," *Nevada Law Journal* Vol. 5 (Fall 2004): 126.

32. Willard Hughes Rollings, "Citizenship and Suffrage: The Native American Struggle for Civil Rights in the American West, 1830-1965," *Nevada Law Journal* Vol. 5 (Fall 2004): 127.

33. *Alabama v. Garrett*, 531 U.S. 356 (U.S. 2001).

34. Jeannie Suk Gerson, "A New Phase of Chaos on Transgender Rights," *The New Yorker*, March 13, 2017, https://www.newyorker.com/news/news-desk/a-new-phase-of-chaos-on-transgender-rights.

35. Ibid.

36. Ibid.

37. "Locked Out: Education, Jobs & Justice Black-White Equality Index," National Urban League, 2016, http://nul.iamempowered.com/sites/nul.iamempowered.com/files/black-white-index-051316.pdf.

CHAPTER 6
Public Opinion: Even the Busiest American Has One

Introduction: Public Opinion and the War in Iraq

The National September 11 Memorial in New York City.

© Shutterstock, Inc.

On September 11, 2001, two airliners filled with fuel and passengers flew into the twin towers of the World Trade Center in downtown Manhattan. Millions saw the death, devastation, and chaos on television as the skyscrapers burned and then collapsed. The attacks killed nearly 3,000 people, injured more than 6,000, and caused billions of dollars in property damage. It was the deadliest terrorist attack in world history.[1] The next day Americans displayed flags, donated blood, and expressed gratitude to the public safety workers who gave their lives to save others. By the end of the year, *Time* magazine would name New York City Mayor Rudy Giuliani the Person of the Year. President George W. Bush's job approval rating would climb to 90 percent as

Americans rallied around their president.[2] Soon after the attack, federal and international authorities would find video evidence showing Osama bin Laden and the hijackers preparing for the attacks.[3] At the time, al-Qaeda had established a base of operations in Afghanistan under the protection of the Taliban. In October 2001, U.S. troops invaded Afghanistan to remove the Taliban from power and to deny al-Quada a safe haven. Eighty percent of Americans would express approval for the use of ground troops against al-Qaeda in Afghanistan.[4]

But the Bush administration would use the patriotic fervor to fuel another war. Within hours after the attacks on 9/11, notes taken by aides to Defense Secretary Donald Rumsfeld would say "Hit S.H" [Saddam Hussein] @ same time, not only UBL [Osama bin Laden]". For years, Rumsfeld and a group of prominent conservatives both in and outside of the Bush administration had been seeking to remove Hussein, the Iraqi president, from power. The attacks on 9/11 and the wave of national loyalty would give them the opportunity they had been waiting for, but first they would need to convince the American public that the attacks had been supported and perhaps even arranged by Saddam Hussein. The notes from Rumsfeld would direct his aides, "Sweep it all up. Things related and not."[5]

The idea that Saddam Hussein supported the terrorists was spread by the president's inner circle. They would visit the daily news shows to make the case that the United States should preemptively invade Iraq. They even suggested that Iraq was making nuclear, chemical, and biological weapons to evoke the specter of ultimate annihilation. United Nations inspectors had been scrutinizing Iraq's weapons facilities for years and had found no evidence that the country was manufacturing or stockpiling weapons of mass destruction (WMDs). Nevertheless, the president's advisors repeated common points that this was about "disarming Saddam, not about weapons inspectors hunting and pecking all over the country." They warned Hussein should be disarmed before "the smoking gun becomes a mushroom cloud."[6] The campaign was extremely effective. Well after it was established that there was no link between al-Qaeda and the Saddam regime, public opinion polls continued to show that a substantial number of Americans still believed Hussein was responsible for the 9/11 attacks.[7] The president's advisors also promised a quick war, that the United States would be greeted as liberators, and that U.S. occupation would lead the Arab world toward democracy.

With little evidence of a tie between Iraq and the attacks on 9/11, but with support from the public, Congress voted to give the president the authority to use military action to force Saddam Hussein from office. Six months later, the president delivered a televised speech from the aircraft carrier USS Abraham Lincoln under a banner that read, "Mission Accomplished." At the time, polls showed that 72 percent of Americans thought the Iraq War was justified.[8] Yet, after the Bush administration failed to find WMDs in Iraq or establish a plausible link between Iraq and the al Qaeda terrorists, most of the public would conclude that the decision to invade Iraq was a mistake. The proportion saying so would increase over time, but support for the war would remain stronger among Republicans than Democrats.[9] George W. Bush's job approval ratings would steadily decline to only 25 percent just before the presidential election in 2008.[10]

The public's reaction to the terrorist attacks on 9/11 and the subsequent invasions of Afghanistan and Iraq show how events and circumstances affect the opinions of the American people. The story not only demonstrates how public opinion can have a strong impact on government policy, but that government officials often lead and manipulate public opinion. A close look at the polling data confirms how public opinion can be shaped by individual predispositions, such as the political party with which one chooses to identify.

Perhaps most importantly, as the events played out over several years, they show how public opinion changed in understandable ways. As circumstances unfolded and new information came to light, the public's reaction can be interpreted as sensible. Given the horror of the 9/11 attack, it was reasonable to come together and rally around the nation's leaders. Given the strong evidence that al-Qaeda had carried out the attacks and was being protected by the Taliban, it made sense to support the invasion of Afghanistan. It was even understandable to trust the Bush administration officials and to support a new war in Iraq when they claimed that Saddam Hussein supported the terrorists and was intending to use WMDs against the United States. But when evidence came to light that challenged the very premises upon which the invasion of Iraq was based, when the war proved costlier than promised, and when the campaign did not result in a more politically stable region, it was reasonable for people to reconsider their support and conclude that the invasion was a mistake. It also made sense to hold the president and his advisors responsible for their actions.

6.1 A Mob or a Whole Greater Than Its Parts?

In creating the republic, the Framers of the Constitution acknowledged an important place for public opinion in the framework of government and politics. They gave the people the power to elect whoever they believed would best represent their interests to serve as members of the House of Representatives. Through recurring elections, ordinary citizens could hold their members accountable to their wishes. Still, the U.S. Senate, with its indirect elections, designed to produce experienced politicians, was bound to statewide or national interests, and was given the right to check legislation coming from the more democratic House.[11] According to Federalist Paper No. 63, the Senate would function as "an anchor against popular fluctuations," thereby shielding the government from the people's "errors and delusions."[12] Similarly, the president would be chosen indirectly by members of the electoral college and would also be able to veto legislation. These two features, together with the lack of an electoral connection between the citizens and members of the Supreme Court, shows that the Framers of the Constitution harbored a deep-seated distrust of the political judgment of ordinary citizens. Indeed, in early American society it was common to believe that the wealthy merchants, planters, and lawyers who made up the bulk of the Founding Fathers were inherently superior to the small farmers, tradesmen, and shopkeepers who were the vast majority of citizens. For example, Benjamin Rush, a signer of the Declaration of Independence, believed that ordinary citizens were too emotional and lacked self-control to govern themselves. In a world with no king, regular people would need training in public schools to become rational and objective "republican machines."[13]

Skepticism regarding the abilities of average people to play their role in democratic governance has persisted throughout American history, and so have efforts to educate the people in the proper exercise of citizenship. Ideals about what it means to be a good citizen were formulated during the American Revolution as society moved away from aristocracy and monarchy toward a social order based on political equality and individual merit. Because ultimate authority was to be placed in the hands of the people, it was thought that social and political harmony could only be realized if citizens were willing to sacrifice their private interests for the sake of the community. At the turn of the twentieth century these ideas were reinforced when reformers took control of local politics away from the urban Democratic "party machines." Immigrant voters were the base of the party's support and loyalty was built on ethnic solidarity. To re-educate the children of immigrants, the reformers created public schools and insisted students be taught impersonal, objective moral values with an orientation toward the larger community. The result is the idealized civics-book citizen who actively approaches government as a fair-minded individual, regularly follows current events, and understands the workings of public policy as well as the consequences of his or her political decisions.

Still, when modern public opinion research developed a half century later, surveys indicated that most citizens fell far short of the ideal. Early research showed most Americans knew little about current events or even basic facts about government, such as the names of their representatives in the state or national legislatures. The average American also did not spend much time or energy understanding the issues, much less their consequences.[14] More recent research, however, has determined that the early studies were based on vague, confusing, or complicated questions asked by the researchers. Newer research shows more stability and considerable coherence on the issues, even from respondents with low levels of education.[15] This does not mean citizens have an in-depth knowledge of of government or that they follow political events closely. The reason political scientists consider public opinion reasonable, despite evidence of low individual political knowledge, has to do with what James Stimson calls "the magic of aggregation."[16] An individual's lack of political knowledge will lead to "mistakes," but when all opinions are added together, "errors" average out. Together, the public shows wisdom.

Seen in this light, public reaction to the war in Iraq is reasonable in the aggregate. The people had little reason not to support the invasion of Iraq until evidence of stockpiles of WMDs failed to materialize and the casualties and the costs of the war came to light. Still, when it comes to complicated issues, research shows that most people use mental shortcuts such as ideology and party identification to interpret the political world. Thus, when dealing with the larger question about whether going to war to depose a hostile dictator was worth the human casualties and other costs of the war, Democrats are much more willing to agree that the invasion of Iraq was a mistake than Republicans.[17]

What Is Public Opinion?

We define public opinion as the sum or aggregation of individuals' views about government and politics. This includes their evaluation of candidates running for public office, but also extends to public reaction to events like the attacks of September 11 and the policies the government creates to solve the nation's problems. Public opinion also includes what citizens know about government, how much they trust and support political institutions, and how likely they are to obey the laws made by their representatives. Pollsters not only measure how likely it is that citizens will vote, but how much they believe their voice will count. Polls are sometimes taken among political leaders, such as members of Congress, but, for the most part, public opinion is about the views of ordinary people. In this regard, public opinion is like voting; each person's opinion counts the same. It is also like an election, as researchers are mostly interested in the total, adding up the collective views of individuals as a measure of what the people think. Researchers also learn a lot by separating opinions and looking at differences among groups within the population. For example, it is instructive to know how and why opinions differ between blacks and whites, men and women, and old versus young.

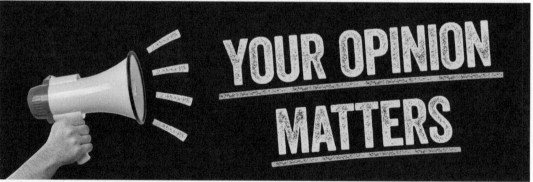

© Shutterstock, Inc.

The Role of Public Opinion

The value of public opinion comes from the idea that representative democracy works best when people express their concerns and, in turn, when public officials respond with laws or policies designed to deal with the people's issues. For example, there was no more honorable time in American politics than when President John F. Kennedy responded to citizens' distress over events in Birmingham, Alabama. Dogs and fire hoses were used to prevent black Americans from marching to protest their lack of civil rights. Kennedy addressed the nation, saying that no state or legislative body could ignore these cries for equality. A short time later the Civil Rights Act gave all Americans federal government protection from discrimination in housing, jobs, and education regardless of their race, color, religion, gender, national origin, or disabilities. Of course, not all things people want should automatically become law. It is the role of the representatives to consider public wishes and use their judgment as to what is best for the common good. Things work best, however, if politicians do not have to guess or rely on their advisors to know what the people want.

There are other means of political communication besides public opinion polls. As we shall see in Chapter 11, some members of Congress hold town meetings, while others rely on letters and emails or campaign contributions to get a sense of the attitude of voters. There are also more active ways to participate. Chapter 9, for example, discusses the ways individuals work in groups to lobby government officials or contribute to campaigns. Chapter 8 will show how others work with a political party to elect like-minded individuals to office. However, research shows that active means of participation, such as going to meetings, writing letters, or working with groups and political parties, disproportionately represent better-educated citizens with higher incomes. Research also shows that when people are placed in a situation where they need to be publicly persuasive, many feel frustrated and powerless.[18] Public opinion polls can allow average people to speak frankly and have their voices counted equally. Among the many ways that people can participate in governmental affairs, simply having opinions is perhaps the most democratic.

6.2 Measuring Public Opinion

When pollsters ask people about their opinions, they are looking for an expression of an attitude about government and politics captured with a verbal or written expression. The respondent can offer a response to a question or choose a statement given by the pollster. Investigators are asking their respondents to express how they feel about an issue and, because feelings are hard to put into words, the response can only approximate their true sentiments. As such, opinions in polls are imperfect indicators of unobserved attitudes. For example, if a pollster wants to know whether people value political freedom, the interviewer might ask if respondents agree with this statement: "I believe in free speech for all no matter what their views might be." Researchers have found that 89 percent of Americans agree with that statement, although it is not entirely clear how respondents really understand the statement.[19] Those agreeing with the sentence probably understand it to mean that government interference with free speech should be kept to a minimum. However, others may interpret the statement to mean that people should be able to say anything they want. Could this include, for example, protecting the right of white supremacists to declare that some black Americans should be lynched to keep the rest of the black community under control? Had the poll statement included that kind of harmful hate speech, it is likely that support for free speech would have declined. To the extent that a question or statement falls short of capturing the real political attitudes of individuals, public opinion polls will show inconsistent results or contradictions between different polls using dissimilar questions and statements.

Question Wording

Because poll answers depend on how the poll's questions are asked, practiced organizations screen their questions and statements carefully and pre-test them in an effort not to create confusing or misleading polls. Writers of questionnaires must take care to ask about issues in different ways and in varying degrees of detail. For example, to get a better measure of the respondent's true attitudes about free speech, the pollster might ask, "Suppose an admitted white supremacist wanted to make a speech in your community. Should the person be allowed to speak?" Worded this way, support for free speech falls to about 60 percent because respondents can recall a specific problem arising from unrestrained political discourse.[20]

Social Desirability

Even though the interviewer is a stranger and answers will be kept confidential, respondents still care how their answers reflect on them. Thus, they are unlikely to agree that people should be free to engage in hate speech regardless of their true feelings because they suspect their tolerance could be interpreted as offensive by the interviewer. This bias toward social desirability leads some to give inaccurate or "politically correct" answers to socially sensitive questions. When pollsters in California asked voters if they intended to vote for African-American Tom Bradley for governor in 1982, many more said they would than actually did. Confronted with inaccurate polls, pollsters concluded that some white voters had not given their true preferences out of fear that they would be viewed as racist. While this "Bradley effect" did not surface in 2008 when Barack Obama was elected president, **social desirability bias** remains an issue.[21] The most common response to the question, "Did you vote in the last presidential election?" is "yes" whether the respondent voted or not. This is why estimates of voter turnout that use public opinion polls usually exceed the actual turnout observed during the election. Similarly, people want the interviewer to know that they are good citizens and have opinions regarding the important issues of the day. Thus, they tend to offer opinions on topics they know little or nothing about.[22]

Complex Questions, Ordering, and Balance

© Shutterstock, Inc.

At other times pollsters ask complex or "double-barreled" questions. For example, the question, "How much confidence do you have in President Biden to handle domestic and foreign policy?" is difficult to answer because there are really two questions. The respondent may have confidence in Biden's domestic policy, but not his foreign strategy (or vice versa). This query can be broken into two questions, but the order in which questions are asked may also make a difference. Suppose the question about Biden's foreign policy is followed by the question, "Do you approve or disapprove of the way Joe Biden is handling his job as president?" If the respondent just expressed lack of confidence in the president's foreign policy in the first question, his or her answer to the job question would have to be "disapprove." And, if asked about Biden's job after expressing confidence in the president's domestic policy, the answer would be the opposite: "approve."[23] In general, people judge a president's job approval more harshly if the question comes after the respondent has been asked (and reminded) about of all the problems of the country and the president's handling of the issues.[24]

Methods of Polling

Even if questionnaire developers ask valid questions, problems can result from the way the respondents are selected. When the Gallup polling organization asks people, "Do you approve or disapprove of the way Joe Biden is handling his job as president?", the organization does not ask all 200 million or so of the country's eligible voters. Rather, the organization only asks a statistically valid sample of about 1,000 U.S. adults. The reason for this is mostly practical: it would be prohibitively expensive and time consuming to ask everyone. Every 10 years, the federal government administers the census to count every resident in the United States. The census gets most of its answers through the mail, but census takers also go into the community to find people who may have moved since the last census, to identify people who are homeless, and to find and help residents unable or reluctant to full out the forms. The periodic enterprise is expensive. The 2010 census cost taxpayers about $13 billion to survey the 116.7 million American households. It took about one year for basic population counts to be made available.[25] In contrast, a single national opinion poll only costs about $25,000 to $30,000 to produce.[26]

Still, surveys drawn from unrepresentative samples remain common. When local news organizations interview "persons on the street" from a downtown corner, they are more likely to get the opinions of shoppers and office workers than if they interviewed people at a suburban park. It would be a mistake to assume that the opinions gathered at either of these locations accurately reflect those of the city's entire population. Polls conducted scientifically use **random sampling** techniques to choose respondents representative of the entire country.

> **random sampling**
>
> A method of selecting a sample whereby any member in the population has an equal chance of being selected.

Sampling

When done correctly and interpreted carefully, a relatively small sample can provide an accurate estimate of the political opinions of a very large population. This conclusion is based on the idea that each person in the population has the same chance of being picked for the sample as any other. Random sampling is much like the numbered ball procedure to determine the winner of the Powerball lottery.

When the Gallup polling organization wanted to know what the American public thought about the job President Biden was doing, it used random-digit dialing to randomly select and call their respondents. This technique includes everyone with a phone, including the 91 percent of adults with cell phones and the remaining 8 percent with only landlines (about 40 percent of households have both).[27] Imagine it as if everyone with a phone number had purchased a ticket for Gallup's lottery. The "winners" were the 1,000 people whose phone numbers were picked at random.

Sampling Error

While random-digit dialing is a fair and valid way to select survey respondents, there will always be some error in approximating the opinions of many from a sample. Fortunately, probability mathematics can calculate precisely the magnitude of error due to the sampling size relative to the population. Generally, the larger the sample, the more it will meet the researcher's expectations of a random outcome. This can be demonstrated by flipping a coin. Assuming a coin is balanced and flipped high into the air, the odds are 50/50 that either side will come up. Hence, flipping a coin once is a fair solution for deciding which team gets the ball first. However, if one flips the coin twice, the likelihood of both coins being heads (or both being tails) is 25 percent, or 1 chance in 4, while the probability of getting one head and one tail remains 50 percent. If one flips the coin 100 times, the probability of getting an equal number of heads and tails, stays at the expected 50 percent, but there is only a 1 percent chance that all 100 tosses will be all heads (or all tails). In other words, the more flips, the more the sample will meet the researcher's expectations of a 50/50 split between heads and tails.

Still, just because large samples are more accurate than small ones, this does not mean that sample sizes need to be enormously large. Surveys conducted by reputable research organizations typically sample only 1,000 to 1,500 respondents. While this seems like a small number relative to the entire population mathematically, the sampling error due to using a selection of this size is only about plus or minus 2.5 percent (see Table 6.1). This number shows how close the result is relative to the one that would result if the entire population were asked. In other words, when the Gallup organization reports that 40 percent of adult Americans approve of Joe Biden's job performance, the actual number lies somewhere within that margin of error. With a 95 percent level of confidence, the Gallup organization is saying the actual number could be as high as 42 percent or as low as 38 percent.

TABLE 6.1 Sample Size and Confidence Level

Population Size	Confidence Level = 95%			Confidence Level = 99%		
	Margin of Error			Margin of Error		
	5%	2.5%	1%	5%	2.5%	1%
100	80	94	99	87	96	99
500	217	377	475	285	421	485
1,000	278	606	906	399	727	943
10,000	370	1,332	4,899	622	2,098	6,239
100,000	383	1,513	8,762	659	2,585	14,227
500,000	384	1,532	9,423	663	2,640	16,055
1,000,000	384	1,534	9,512	663	2,647	16,317

Based on SurveyAnyplace.com: https://surveyanyplace.com/docs/sample-size/.

Table 6.1 shows that surveyors can increase or lower their sampling error by interviewing fewer or more people. Note that the gain in accuracy from interviewing more people increases slowly compared to a rapid growth in sample size. If Gallup interviews 2,500 people instead of 1,000, it reduces its sampling error by only about 1 percent. Thus, sample sizes for everyday national polls do not get much larger than about 1,500 because, to reduce error rates significantly, samples sizes and the costs of doing surveys would increase exponentially.

To improve the chances that the opinions of small samples will approximate those of the larger population, polling organizations introduce a number of techniques into their sampling methods to improve accuracy. For example, in their national polls, Gallup wants its sample to include persons living in all 50 states and the District of Columbia. Knowing that many more people live in California than Wyoming, it makes sure that those in the larger states are more likely to be selected for interviews than those living in smaller states. In other words, the organization makes sure that the likelihood of being chosen roughly matches the distribution of the population across the country. Similar adjustments are made for other demographic factors such as age and gender. In their presidential job approval survey, Gallup included a minimum quota of 60 percent cellphone and 40 percent landline respondents. The organization also added quotas for time zones within regions. It also oversampled blacks and Latinas/os (but included them proportionally in the sample) to generate reliable estimates of these key subgroups. Lastly, it conducted interviews in Spanish for Spanish-only speakers.[28]

For telephone and other surveys, the response rate is the number of people successfully interviewed divided by the total number of people contacted. Sometimes the surveyor attempts to contact a person on the list and gets no response, such as when a caller gets a ring, but no one answers or an answering machine answers. To counter this problem, the survey organizations spend a good deal of time attempting to reach contacts or at different time of day. This is one reason it takes several days to conduct a poll. While these techniques minimize low response rates, not much can be done with people who simply refuse to answer questions.

Most pollsters and researchers agree that non-responses and refusals are increasing, although few consider it a serious problem.[29] To the extent that pollsters know who is likely to refuse to answer, the sample can be corrected by weighting. For example, Jack Brehm found that because some types of people are less likely to respond to surveys, polls tend to over represent the elderly, blacks, women, the poor, and the less educated.[30] As a correction, surveys simply add weight to the groups underrepresented in their sample. To make sure respondents do not differ systematically from the non-respondents, another set of studies is done to test this assumption. In one case, the Pew Research Center contacted those who initially refused to participate and convinced them to participate, sometimes by offering an additional incentive such as cash.[31] Their findings showed that there was no significant difference in opinions between those who refuse to participate in survey research and those who do.[32]

Internet Polls

Internet polls can be inexpensive to administer because there is no interviewer and organizations can take advantage of larger sample sizes with higher levels of confidence and low error rates. Respondents can also answer the survey at their own convenience. Online surveys also allow the respondent more time to answer complex questions, which can include links to detailed information about issues. Questions and statements can also be combined with visual information. Currently, about 87 percent of the American public say they use the internet.[33] However, the elderly, people with lower incomes, and people with lower levels of education are less likely to use or have access to the internet. Remote areas of the country often lack internet access as well, so online surveys will underrepresent these groups. Even if such problems can be resolved, valid sampling remains a problem because there is no standard convention for assigning email addresses and thus no substitute for random-digit dialing. Online respondents must still be contacted by phone or mail before they can be asked to complete the online survey.[34]

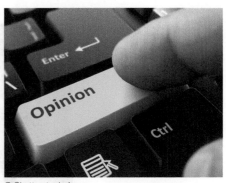
© Shutterstock, Inc.

Measurement Accuracy of Polls

Reputable polling organizations pick their samples randomly to reduce errors in approximating the true opinions of the country. We know this method works because we can test the outcomes through observation. As discussed previously, the accuracy of random sampling can be easily demonstrated by flipping coins, counting the number of heads and tails and comparing samples to much larger populations of coin flips. But, how do we know, however, if the opinions people selected by a small sample really reflect the political attitudes of an entire nation country? Indeed, when people were asked if this was possible, 68 percent of survey respondents said "no."[35] Because there is no census of opinions to verify opinions drawn from samples, there is no empirical reality check. Still, we know that some research methods are better than others. Polls conducted using live interviewers, for example, are more accurate than those using robotic messages. We also know that polls using larger samples are generally more accurate than those using smaller samples. Polling organizations that use these better methods will produce accurate results.

One way to increase confidence in the accuracy of opinion polls is to consult the pollster ratings. For example, the website fivethirtyeight.com uses a set of criteria to measure the quality of an organization's methods and its historical accuracy. The surveys are also rated for political bias (the degree that they lean toward the Democratic or Republican parties). They rate 374 survey organizations and, among other things, give each a letter grade ranging from "F" to "A+." Organizations receiving a grade of "F" are banned from use in their election forecasting models.[36] Ethics and standards for polling organizations are managed by the American Association for Public Opinion Research.[37]

6.3 Where Do Public Opinions Come From?

Public opinions are assumed to reflect the self-interest of the survey respondents. For example, when asking about taxes, researchers assume that people would prefer to pay as little as possible.

Indeed, most Americans (59 percent) say they pay too much federal income tax.[38] On the other hand, most people want the government to spend more in most areas (18 of 23 spending categories), especially when such spending benefits them. Such has been the case since these questions were first asked in the early 1970s.[39]

© Shutterstock, Inc.

ideology

A set of integrated ideas about the extent and purpose of government.

People generally understand that more spending leads to higher taxes, so pollsters also ask people if they would like more services if it meant higher taxes. When asked this way, a bare majority (53 percent) say they would prefer fewer services and lower taxes.[40] Of course, this question is not specific about which services would be cut or how much taxes would drop. Instead, this question requires the respondent to make broad assumptions about government and its purpose. A person who believes in social equity and that progressive taxes or spending for public services makes society more equal may support higher rates of taxation even if it is contrary to their personal economic self-interest. Political scientists refer to a connection such as these as an **ideology**, which helps people form opinions when their personal preferences in these matters are unclear. There are two major ideologies in American politics—liberal and conservative—and they are closely associated with the country's two political parties. The Democratic Party is linked to liberal ideology, while the Republican Party is connected to conservative ideology. We discuss ideology and its effects on voting in Chapter 7 and again in Chapter 8 on political parties. The question here is, where do political opinions come from and how do they develop into more complex sets of ideas?

Some political attitudes can be traced to personality traits. There are people more open to new experiences, while others prefer set routines. Some like spontaneity, while others tend to be self-disciplined and organized. Political liberals tend to have personality types that are more impulsive and open to new ideas, whereas conservatives tend to favor a more orderly society.[41] To the extent that genetics determines personality, some political behavior, such as openness to same-sex marriage, may be the result of liberal predispositions, whereas acquiescence to traditional social attitudes may stem from conservative propensities. Still, other than general tendencies, most political attitudes, including one's partisan identification, come from one's social environment.[42]

political socialization

The process through which people develop their political values and attitudes.

The process of forming political opinions is part of social development—a progression that begins early and continues throughout life. **Political socialization** is the process through which people develop political values and attitudes. It starts with their families, but also comes from the schools they attend, the community in which they live, their membership in social groups, the work they do, and what they read, hear, see, and do in the political system.

Two guiding principles are useful in thinking about how what one learns as a child profoundly affects one's later life. The **primacy principle** posits that lessons learned early in life are learned best; that is, our first understandings are the most likely to persist. Similarly, the **structuring principle** teaches that what one learns first structures subsequent or later learning. Together, the two principles help us understand how we learn about life and become functioning members of society. For example, from a very early age we learned that our parents are the source of sustenance, knowledge, and love. Because they are the basis of good in the world, we do not question the lessons we learned when we were first caught in the act of lying. Lying is bad, our parents told us, and to assume otherwise would be to doubt their goodness and wisdom. Still, later in life, when a salesman calls while your mother is preparing dinner, she says, "Tell him I'm not home," instructing you to lie. The mental contradiction you experience is resolved by the primacy and structuring principles. You don't seriously question your first lesson (mother's goodness), so the second lesson is structured by the first: maybe lying is not always bad.

When it comes to politics, we are made in our parents' image. There is a close association between one's party identification and the party preferences of one's parents. Where both parents identify with the same party, research shows that 76 percent of their children follow their lead. Where the parents disagree, a child is more likely to adopt the mother's preference.[43] The same goes for opinions relating to other political issues, especially if the issue is important to the adult members of the family.

Schools formally socialize their students by encouraging them to develop a sense of belonging to communities beyond the family and ultimately to develop a sense of national identity and loyalty. This identification begins with learning that there are authorities outside of the family, such as a crossing guard or a police officer. In school, such authorities are often personalized and understood as helpful and worthy of trust. Children soon develop attachments to the president or other symbols of government. When asked to pick out their favorite flag, elementary school students overwhelmingly choose the American or similar looking flag and agreed that "the government usually knows what is best for the people."[44] Of course, not all children idealize government equally; African American, Mexican American, Native American, and poor children show more cynicism toward political authority than do middle-class white children.[45]

As students age, they show more sophistication by accepting the "civics book" ideal of voting, saying that it is better to choose the "best" candidate rather than voting by party. By the time students are in middle or high school, most begin to think of themselves as citizens, with a core set of rights, such as free speech, the right to choose and practice their religious faith, and the right to a fair trial if accused of a crime.[46]

Adult socialization follows much the same pattern. Young adults will continue to develop their political views based on their experiences with the real world. What they learn in their 20s is likely to persist into late adulthood. Pollsters often characterize generations based on the shared experiences of their general birth cohort. For example, the Pew Research center currently divides "Millennials," (those aged 18-35) from "Generation X," (36-51), from "Baby Boomers" (52-70), and what they call "Silents" (71-88).[47] Presumably, Millennials share the experience of coming of age during a time of global economic and political uncertainty, but so do those in Generation X. That generation experienced an acceleration in globalization that came after the end of the Cold War. Most agree that the Baby Boom generation had distinctive experiences: the aftermath of World War II, the expansion of the middle class, the Civil Rights Movement, the Vietnam War, and the Watergate scandal. Similarly, the Silent generation experienced the Great Depression, the New Deal, World War II, and the Cold War. But as sociology professor Tom DiPrete says, "History isn't always so punctuated."[48]

Younger generations with fewer responsibilities tend to be more idealistic. On the other hand, raising a family and developing a career gradually makes one more conservative. Political learning continues, but reevaluation about what a person knows happens more often early in life rather than later, as one learns to resist experiences that contradict hard-learned life lessons.[49] Thus,

primacy principle

The concept that lessons learned early in life tend to be those learned best. Our first understandings are the most likely to persist.

structuring principle

The concept that what one learns first structures subsequent learning.

A father and daughter practice at a shooting range.

© Shutterstock, Inc.

gender gap

The difference between voting patterns of men and women.

young adults show weaker attachments to political parties than older adults. Indeed, the proportion of voters who consider themselves independents is twice as large among young adults than it is among senior citizens.[50] The persistence of early political lessons is the key to understanding public opinion. If you find yourself to be liberal Democrat today, you are likely to remain a liberal Democrat into your old age, even though some of your opinions on specific issues change. David Sears and Carolyn Funk conclude that, for most people, the process of political socialization is complete by their late 20s.[51] The exception to this rule may be marriage. People generally choose partners from the same class, race, and religion (partly because their political views are compatible), but over the course of a marriage, couples become more politically alike. It used to be that wives became more politically similar to their husbands, but these days the **gender gap** within married couples seems to close mutually.[52]

6.4 Effects of Social Background on Public Opinion

The fact that people often choose marriage partners with similar backgrounds reminds us that people think of themselves as belonging to groups, each of which can have a distinct political orientation. Major groups in U.S. society are based on race or ethnicity, gender, age, socioeconomic class, religion, and geography.

Political Attitudes Based in Race and Ethnicity

Researchers find that some of the widest differences in opinions lies between racial and ethnic groups, particularly between blacks and non-Hispanic whites. For example, in 1964, only 27 percent of whites expressed a desire for racial desegregation, while 73 percent of black respondents wanted desegregation.[53] Differences between the opinions of blacks and whites are especially wide regarding the treatment of blacks by the criminal justice system. Shortly after a jury found former football star O.J. Simpson not guilty of killing Nicole Brown and Ronald Goldman in 1995, about 70 percent of whites continued to believe O.J. was guilty while about 70 percent of blacks believed the jury made the right decision.[54] Similar attitudes were recorded after the Sanford, Florida, trial of George Zimmerman, who in 2012 was accused of murdering an unarmed black teenager, Trayvon Martin. Fifty-one percent of whites approved of the jury's not-guilty verdict for Zimmerman, while 87 percent of blacks disapproved. A majority of whites (58 percent) approved of a grand jury's decision not to charge police in the 2014 shooting death of Michael Brown in Ferguson, Missouri. A substantial minority (38 percent) of whites approved of a similar decision in New York City not to charge police in the choking death of Eric Garner. Over 90 percent of blacks disapproved of both grand jury decisions.[55]

Today, 84 percent of blacks believe they are treated unfairly by the police and 75 percent believe they receive unfair treatment in the courts. They also believe they receive unequal treatment in the workplace, in stores, when applying for loans, and when voting. Only a minority of whites agree. Many black Americans (43 percent) remain skeptical that the country will make changes needed to give blacks equal rights, while an almost equal number of whites (38 percent) believe that the country has already made such changes. In fact, more than 40 percent of whites (but only 22 percent of blacks) say that the country pays too much attention to race.[56]

FIGURE 6.1 Perceptions of How Blacks are Treated in the U.S. Vary Widely by Race
Note: Whites and blacks include only non-Hispanics. Source: Survey of U.S. adults conducted Feb. 29-May 8, 2016. Q19F2a-f. "On Views of Race and Inequality, Blacks and Whites Are Worlds Apart"

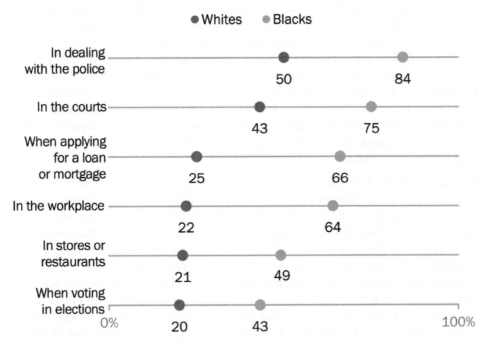

% saying blacks are treated less fairly than whites in the country

Adapted from "On Views of Race and Inequality, Blacks and Whites Are Worlds Apart." Pew Research Center, Washington, D.C. (June 27, 2016) http://www.pewsocialtrends.org/2016/06/27/on-views-of-race-and-inequality-blacks-and-whites-are-worlds-apart/.

Blacks also tend to more liberal than whites on matters other than civil rights and liberties. They are more inclined than whites to believe that government should do more to help the needy (72 to 55 percent) and are more likely to feel that the government should guarantee minimum food and shelter for all Americans (80 to 62 percent). Only about 17 percent of blacks believe that the poor have it easy because they get benefits from government without doing anything, but about twice as many whites (36 percent) believe this to be true. Blacks are also less likely than whites to deplore government waste. Among whites, liberal attitudes vary by income, with higher income whites showing more conservative attitudes. Among blacks, however, liberal positions are as likely to exist among upper-income as lower-income. Political scientist Michael Dawson argues that blacks tend to believe their economic well-being is tied to the overall progress of blacks as a group, whereas whites are more likely to identify with whites within their social class.[57] This alliance among blacks comes from a long history of racial discrimination and segregation that allowed black culture and feelings of solidarity to grow.

Latinas/os and Asians have also been the victims of discriminatory and segregationist policies and, like blacks, their social history has heightened awareness and feelings of group unity. Most Latinas/os in the United States trace their ancestry to Mexico, but substantial portions come from Puerto Rico, Cuba, and other Latin American countries. Among Mexican Americans, there are significant differences between American and Mexican-born immigrants. Given such diversity, Latinas/os are not as politically cohesive as black Americans. Still, Latinas/os have mobilized politically to end discrimination, promote bilingual education in schools, and improve labor conditions for migrant workers. Recently, fears that the languages and customs of immigrants in general are diluting American traditions and that immigrants are taking jobs from Americans have led to anti-immigrant rhetoric and policies aimed at Latinas/os. During the 2016 presidential campaign, candidate Donald Trump made disparaging comments about Mexican immigrants. He proposed to build a wall along the U.S.-Mexico border and deport millions who are in the country illegally. As a result, most Latinas/os, even those who are citizens or lawful permanent residents, say they worry about deportation. Thirty-eight percent of U.S.-born Latinas/os now say they have serious concerns about their place in America.[58]

Just more than half of Latinas/os in the United States (52 percent) say they have experienced discrimination or have been treated unfairly because of their race or ethnicity. Roughly one-fourth of Latinas/os identify as Afro-Latina/o. These individuals are more likely to say they have experienced discrimination or unfair treatment.[59] Like blacks, Latinas/os have less confidence than whites that they will be treated fairly by the criminal justice system.[60] Latinas/os generally favor increasing domestic spending and are more likely than whites to express support for a government-guaranteed job, a good standard of living, and affirmative action programs. By a factor of 2-to-1, Latinas/os identify with the Democratic over the Republican Party, although Latinas/os of Cuban origin are more likely than other Latinas/os to identify with the Republicans. Given the anti-immigrant rhetoric expressed in the 2016 campaign, the growing view among Latinas/os is that the Democratic Party is better attuned to the concerns of their community.[61] However, in 2020, Donald Trump was able to expand his support among Cuban Americans in southern Florida and Mexican Americans in southern Texas.

Although many Asian Americans describe themselves as typically American, most say they are very different and tend to identify themselves by their country of origin.[62] Nearly 40 percent of Asian Americans say they suffered a personal experience with discrimination, 19 percent within the past year. Among Asian Americans, racial discrimination is considered the third most important problem facing the United States, after jobs and terrorism. On other issues, the National Asian American Survey found that large majorities support greater government spending, even if it means paying higher taxes. They also support gun control and the Affordable Care Act, but oppose the Trump Administration's attempts to bar entry to the U.S. by those from several predominantly Muslim nations. Well over half (57 percent) of Asian Americans lean toward the Democratic party, while only 24 percent lean Republican.[63] It should be no surprise that 73 percent of Asian Americans voted for Barack Obama in 2012, but large majorities of Latinas/os (75 percent) and close to 95 percent of black Americans also voted for Obama.[64] In 2020, majorities in all three groups voted for the Democratic candidate, Joe Biden.

Political Attitudes Based in Gender

Most women (54 percent) voted for Hillary Clinton, the first female major-party candidate to run for the U.S. presidency, but slightly more (57 percent) women voted for Joe Biden in 2020. On the other hand, 53 percent of men voted for Republican Donald Trump. Overall, the gender gap, the difference between the number of men who voted for Biden and the number of women voting for him, was 13 points, the largest such gap recorded since exit polls began in 1972.[65]

john dory / Shutterstock.com

During the 2016 presidential campaign, Donald Trump crudely affronted a debate moderator, Megyn Kelly, for asking him about past misogynistic comments. He later suggested that women who seek abortions should be punished. Later in the campaign, a video surfaced showing Trump bragging about assaulting women, which prompted several allegations of sexual assault against him. Many were disturbed by these events, but some of Trump's male supporters had come to believe that society was becoming too soft and feminine. They saw the candidate as someone who would restore male dominance. Forty-one percent of Trump's supporters agreed with the assertion that today's society "seems to punish men just for acting like men." Forty percent of Republican men believed men now face discrimination of a moderate amount to a great deal. Among Republicans overall, 91 percent said the barriers that made it hard for women to be successful are mostly gone.[66]

Prior to 1968, gender differences in voting were hardly noticeable, but as men moved in the Republican direction, the gap became clear.[67] Still, there have always been differences between men and women on some issues. For example, a good deal of research confirms that men have a greater predisposition for the use of violence and aggression. This leads them to favor policies involving the use of force, such as war and capital punishment.[68] Men were 8 to 10 percent more enthusiastic in their support for the Korean and Vietnam wars.[69] In 1991, 60 percent of men but only 45 percent of women favored military action to force the Iraqis army out of Kuwait. After the September 11 terrorist attacks, men were more ready to invade Iraq than women by a margin of 80 to 68 percent.[70]

FIGURE 6.2 Percent Voting for Democratic Presidential Candidate: 1972-2008

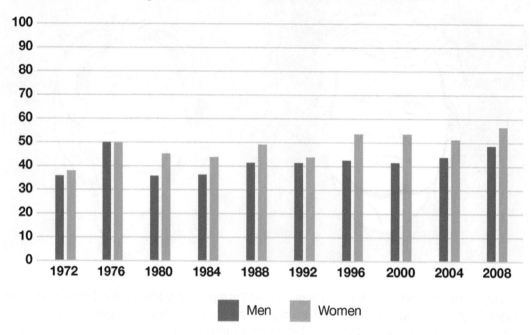

Men   Women

Data from "The Gender Gap: Three Decades Old, as Wide as Ever." Pew Research Center, Washington, D.C. (March 29, 2012) http://www.people-press.org/2012/03/29/the-gender-gap-three-decades-old-as-wide-as-ever/.

Support for war represents the largest gap in gender differences, but in general, women prefer a more compassionate approach to political issues. By large margins, women are more likely than men to say the government does not do enough to help older people (65 to 54 percent), children (62 to 52 percent), and poor people (61 to 52 percent). Correspondingly, women are more apt than men to list education and programs to help the poor and needy as top government priorities. Women are also more likely to say that the country should do whatever it takes to protect the environment (75 to 67 percent).[71]

However, the gender gap does not seem to explain opinions on the issue of abortion. About half of both women and men think abortion should be legal in all or most cases, a pattern that has remained consistent for more than a decade.[72] Still, about half of women (48 percent) said religiously affiliated institutions should be required to cover birth control as part of their health care benefits, but only 40 percent of men said they should. Most men (54 percent) but a minority of women (42 percent) said such institutions should be given an exception.

Political Attitudes Based in Religion

© Shutterstock, Inc.

Generally, the stronger one's religious convictions, the more that person agrees that abortion should be illegal in most cases. This opinion increases with church attendance, frequency of reading scripture, and the degree of certainty about the existence of God, heaven, and hell.[73] The most pro-life denominations are evangelical Protestants, such as Assemblies of God and Southern Baptists. Evangelicals emphasize the authority of the Bible and the centrality of the salvation experience—being "born again" through faith in Jesus Christ. The Church of Jesus Christ of Latter-day Saints (Mormons) is also opposed to abortion. Mormons happen to be the most conservative and Republican religious group. Evangelical Protestants lean Republican and conservative, but as a religious tradition, evangelicals are divided politically by race. White evangelical Protestants are more conservative and voted strongly Republican in 2012 (79 percent for Romney) and 2016 (81 percent for Trump). On the other hand, members of black evangelical churches such as the African Methodist Episcopal (AME) Church and the National Baptist Convention overwhelmingly identify with the Democratic Party (92 and 87 percent, respectively). Mainline Protestants like the Episcopal, Presbyterian, and Methodist churches tend to be conservative and Republican, but less pro-life and more moderate on other issues.

The Catholic Church, the country's largest denomination, opposes abortion in all circumstances, yet about half (48 percent) of its members say that abortion should be legal in all or most cases. This makes Catholics about as pro-life as most Americans, although Latina/o Catholics tend to be more pro-life than their fellow parishioners.[74] On most issues, Catholics tend to lean toward a liberal orientation and the Democratic Party, but not strongly. In 2016, a 50 percent of Catholics voted for Donald Trump, but in 2020, slightly more (52 percent) said they voted for Joe Biden, the fourth Catholic major-party nominee in U.S. history.[75]

Jews are generally pro-choice, liberal, and identify with the Democratic Party.[76] About 70 percent of Jews voted for Barack Obama in 2012, about the same number voted for Clinton in 2016, and about 75 percent of Jews voted for Biden in 2020.[77] The ordering of major religious traditions, with Jews being the most liberal and Democratic group followed by Catholics and then Protestants, has been stable over the half century of polling.[78] However, the most liberal, pro-choice, and Democratic leaning group are those who are unaffiliated with any religion.

TABLE 6.2 Religious Makeup of the Electorate
Note: "Protestant" refers to people who describe themselves as "Protestant," "Mormon," or "other Christian" in exit polls; this categorization most closely approximates the exit poll data reported immediately after the election by media sources. The "white, born-again/evangelical Christian" row includes both Protestants and non-Protestants (e.g., Catholics, Mormons, etc.) who self-identify as born-again or evangelical Christians. Source: Pew Research Center analysis of exit poll data. 2004 Hispanic Catholic estimates come from aggregated state exit polls conducted by the National Election Pool. Other estimates come from Voter News Service/National Election Pool national exit polls. 2012 data come from reports at NBCnews.com and National Public Radio. 2016 data come from reports at NBCnews.com and CNN.com.

	2000	2004	2008	2012	2016	Net Change '12-'16
	%	%	%	%	%	
Protestant/other Christian	54	54	54	53	52	-1
Catholic	26	27	27	25	23	-2
Jewish	4	3	2	2	3	+1
Other faiths	6	7	6	7	8	+1
Religiously unaffillitated	9	10	12	12	15	+3
White born-again/evangelical Christian	**n/a**	**23**	**26**	**26**	**26**	**–**
Attended worship services...						
Weekly or more	n/a	n/a	n/a	n/a	33	n/a
Monthly	n/a	n/a	n/a	n/a	16	n/a
Few times a year	n/a	n/a	n/a	n/a	29	n/a
Never	n/a	n/a	n/a	n/a	22	n/a

Adapted from "How the faithful voted: A preliminary 2016 analysis." Pew Research Center, Washington, D.C. (November 9, 2016) http://www.pewresearch.org/fact-tank/2016/11/09/how-the-faithful-voted-a-preliminary-2016-analysis/.

Political Attitudes Based on Geography

People with similar religious and ethnic backgrounds tend to cluster together. These settlement and migration patterns form distinct regional political cultures. For example, evangelical Christians tend to be concentrated in the South, which helps explain the region's conservative leanings. The

South's conservativism can also be traced to time-established traditions of social hierarchy based on racial, class, and gender divisions. Historically, much of government policy in this region has been aimed at preserving the social order. Many of these attitudes remain today.[79] For example, only 44 percent of people from the South support the expansion of same-sex marriage as opposed to 52 percent nationwide.[80] People in the South are also more likely than the rest of the country to believe that books containing dangerous ideas should be banned from public libraries (58 to 41 percent).[81]

By contrast, the Northeast is generally the most liberal region of the country. It was settled by reformers seeking religious freedom and to build a better society. To this day, small towns in the Northeast maintain a tradition of town meetings in which all citizens have an equal voice in matters of town policy. According to political scientist Daniel Elazar, the northeastern states tend to favor use of government policy as a means to address social problems.[82] For example, about 70 percent of the population believes that it is more important to control guns than to protect the right of Americans to own guns, as compared with 54 percent of the population in the South who support gun control.[83] About 70 percent of residents in the Northeast favor legal abortions in all or most cases, whereas support for legal abortion is only 40 percent in the southern central states.[84]

Others came to their region in search of individual opportunity. Atlantic states such as Maryland, New Jersey, Pennsylvania, and the midwestern states (including Illinois and Missouri) became home to large numbers of foreign-born residents and racial and ethnic minority populations. Elazar maintains that regions with populations like these believe in government as a means to achieve individual goals.[85] Western states with immigrants from Latin America and Asia favor providing illegal immigrants with a route to citizenship to pursue the American dream (78 percent), while many fewer people in the South favor this position (62 percent). In general, conservatives tend to be concentrated in the South, the Mountain West, and the Great Plains regions, while liberals are concentrated in New England and Middle Atlantic states as well as on the east and west coasts.[86]

FIGURE 6.3 Most and Least Conservative States

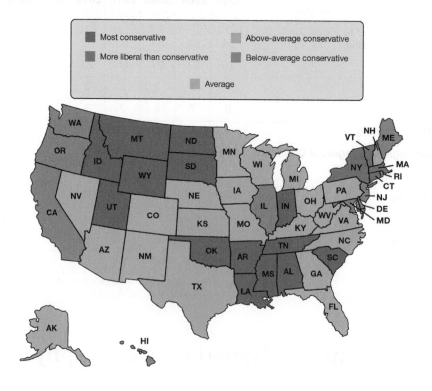

Based on Frank Newport. "Wyoming, North Dakota and Mississippi Most Conservative." Gallup. (January 31, 2017) https://news.gallup.com/poll/203204/wyoming-north-dakota-mississippi-conservative.aspx.

Within regions, researchers find contrasting opinions depending on whether one lives in a city, a suburb, or a rural area. About half of urban dwellers say that blacks in their community are treated less fairly by the police than whites, whereas only 44 percent of suburban residents and 30 percent of rural residents say blacks are treated less fairly. Similar urban/suburban/rural gaps become clear when referring to the treatment of blacks in the courts, at work, in stores and restaurants, in schools, and in voting.[87] Living in a large, dense, diverse community makes people more tolerant of social and political differences.[88] In urban areas, people are more likely to know more people who are gay, lesbian, bisexual, and transgender (32 percent) than those who live in suburban (27 percent) or rural (20 percent) communities.[89] Almost half of adults living in cities (45 percent) say that more people of different races marrying each other is a good thing for society, while only 38 percent of those living in suburban areas and 24 percent of people from rural areas agree.[90] Urban residents are supportive of protecting same-sex couples' rights to marriage, hospital visits, adoption, and housing choices. In 2020, their residents mostly voted for Democrat Joe Biden, including those in the largest cities in solidly Republican states like Alabama, Florida, Texas, Indiana, South Carolina, Tennessee, Kentucky, Arizona, Missouri, and Oklahoma.[91]

Political Attitudes Based in Socioeconomic Class

There are also differences between the political opinions of the rich, the poor, and those in the middle class. Generally, support for public policies designed to promote employment and living standards decrease as respondents become more affluent. Fifty percent of households with incomes less than $30,000 had favorable views of the Affordable Care Act (also known as Obamacare), while only 43 percent of families with incomes of more than $75,000 had favorable views.[92] When people were asked about cutting spending to reduce the deficit, 75 percent of those with lower incomes said it is more important to maintain spending at current levels for programs that help the poor, while those with higher incomes favored slashing such programs.[93]

This seemingly liberal pattern for lower-income people often reverses for social issues. For example, people with lower incomes were more likely than other Americans to agree that abortion should never be permitted. The poor were also more likely than the rich to feel that a woman's place is in the home. On the other hand, there is not much difference between opinions of the rich and the poor on spending for the military or on roads and bridges.[94]

As one moves down the income ladder from rich to poor, the frequency of Democratic Party identification increases. One's opinions about class differences are underlined by one's party identification. For example, Republicans were more likely than Democrats to describe the rich as hardworking (55 percent), while 65 percent of Democrats described them as greedy. By a large margin (61 to 24 percent), Democrats said that poverty was beyond one person's control, but most Republicans (57 percent) blamed the poor for lack of effort.

Party Identification and Ideology

Party affiliation serves to orient a wide range of political beliefs. At the beginning of this chapter, we noted that Democrats were more likely than Republicans to conclude that the war in Iraq was a mistake. Democrats were also much more likely to disapprove of George W. Bush's presidency overall.[95] On the other hand, Democrats were more likely than Republicans to approve of Obama's performance (83 to 17 percent).[96] Predictably, only about 6 percent of Democrats approve of the job Donald Trump is doing, while 85 percent of Republicans approve.[97] Much the same pattern is evident for policy issues. Violent crime decreased between 2000 and 2015, but during the time that

George W. Bush was president, Democrats were more likely than Republicans to believe that crime had increased. This pattern reversed when Barack Obama took office in 2009. This time, Republicans were more likely to say that crime had increased since Obama was elected.[98] Furthermore, well into Obama's presidency, almost one-third of Republicans continued to believe Obama was a Muslim, while about the same number (34 percent) believed he was born outside the United States and was thus ineligible to be president.[99]

While it seems to defy common sense for people to hold on to misinformation, keep in mind, as we have discussed, that political opinions are formed within social groups. Most of us live and work within relatively homogeneous communities demarcated by neighborhoods, regions, or urbanized areas, but also by social bonds defined by family, racial, ethnic, gender, religious, economic, and other ties. These groupings form like-minded clusters. The desire for Americans to segregate themselves along these lines is not new, but there is evidence that this sorting process is accelerating as people relocate.[100] As such, most political opinions result from convenience, in the sense that they are absorbed from our social environments without much effort. Further, such views are comforting in that they don't challenge our beliefs or those held by people around us. Americans have thus achieved a degree of ideological segregation, which entails isolation from those with whom they disagree.

© Shutterstock, Inc.

confirmation bias

A form of wishful thinking that causes individuals to interpret new information in a way that conforms to their preexisting beliefs.

False beliefs are also maintained by political leadership. As we will see in our chapter on Congress, the policy preferences of representatives usually align with those of their constituents because they share political and socio-economic characteristics and they come from the same place. Given that voters tend to support candidates who match their policy preferences, it is rational for elected officials to respond in kind. Because the sounds of political discourse often resemble those produced by an echo chamber, people are not likely to hear things from their representatives that contradict what they already know. However, if they do hear opposing information, individuals are likely to ignore it. Psychologists find that people employ **confirmation bias,** a form of wishful thinking that causes individuals to interpret new information in a way that conforms to their preexisting beliefs.[101] In other words, when people want something to be true, they make it true by ending their search for opposing information or selectively interpreting what they hear to confirm what they want to be true.

Of course, politicians often exaggerate their claims and sometimes spread outright falsehoods. For example, representatives seeking to replace Social Security with private accounts, and supporters of the program seeking funds to extend Social Security, claimed that the program was going bankrupt, which caused people to be overly pessimistic about the program's financial future.[102] It was candidate Trump who spread rumors that Obama was born outside of the United States, claimed that he saw thousands of Muslims cheering during the attack on September 11, and that Mexico was sending rapists and drug dealers to the United States. According to Politifact, 70 percent of Trump's claims made during his 2016 campaign were false or mostly false, while only 15 percent were shown to be true or mostly true.[103] The *Washington Post* catalogued all of President Trump's statements and found that he had made more than 50 false or misleading claims per day and was on track to exceed 25,000 false or misleading statements by election day 2020.[104] Trump's political rhetoric, whether by design or inclination, worked in his favor. The dark picture he painted of globalization causing factories to close and immigrants to take jobs and instigate terror was accepted by his supporters because research shows that individuals are better able to recall bad news and overestimate the probability of danger and loss.[105] Besides, the president had little incentive to dissuade his supporters from their misperceptions because they support his policy goals. Indeed, his spread of misinformation brings them psychological comfort by giving validity to their beliefs.[106] Still, the *New York Times* article that found Trump regularly spread falsehoods also showed growing public mistrust of the president. By June 2017, nearly 60 percent of Americans surveyed said the president was dishonest, up from the 53 percent who believed he was not honest when he took office.[107] According to a Gallup poll published in October 2020, only 40 percent of the American public believed Trump was honest and trustworthy.[108]

6.5 Does Public Opinion Matter?

The growing mistrust of President Trump shows that people are not only paying attention to what the president says, but also to what his critics say. The evidence also shows the public making reasonable judgments based on the information they receive. Of course, not everyone follows politics closely. On one side, some people are highly attentive. They follow public affairs regularly, develop nuanced views about public policy, and are not shy about sharing their opinions. At the other end of the scale are those who only notice alarming headlines, threats of war, or scandal. The rest of us fall between these extremes.

People vary not only in what engages their interest but in how much they know about politics. Given the amount of attention the press pays to the president, it is easy to know what he is doing, but pollsters find the public is less knowledgeable about facts not related to the president or candidates running for office. For example, in 2012 only 40 percent of the public knew that the Republican Party had a majority of the seats in the U.S. House of Representatives in 2016. Fewer (39 percent) knew that John Roberts was the chief justice of the U. S. Supreme Court.[109] However, the latest News IQ test conducted by the Pew Research Center found that 77 percent of the public could correctly answer 10 out of 12 questions about current events. Only 33 percent knew how many justices on the U.S. Supreme court were women, but 52 percent could identify the route of the proposed Keystone Pipeline on a map, while 72 percent recognized changes in the unemployment rate in graphic form. Political knowledge was higher among older Americans and those with more education. Men showed more political knowledge than women and white people scored higher than non-white.[110]

Still, while the public shows reasonable knowledge of major political events and personalities, it is much more difficult for them to follow the actions of their local congressional or state representatives. Less than half the public can recall the name of their district representative. The local media rarely covers congressional roll-call votes.[111] Even when policy debates are thoroughly covered, surveys show that few constituents knew on which side of the issue their representative stood.[112] It is also hard for representatives of legislative districts to know what their constituents are thinking. Polls may be available, but most are conducted nationally with sample sizes too small to accurately measure local sentiments. Further, the majority of polls cover controversial issues such as abortion, which represent a very small portion of the bills lawmakers must consider. Despite these difficulties, political science research does show that legislators seem to follow the policy preferences of the citizens in their districts. The evidence is circumstantial, however. When asked, representatives claim they act in the best interests of their constituents, but ultimately use their own judgment to decide what that may be. For their part, constituents claim to prefer their representative be guided by his or her own policy preferences rather than mindlessly following their dictates.[113]

When the policy preferences of district citizens are compared with the voting records of their representatives, research finds that the two are well matched. In general, the voting patterns of congressional representatives match the ideological leanings of their districts. Members from liberal districts vote for liberal policies, while those from conservative districts vote for conservative policies. The voting patterns of U.S. senators similarly match the liberal-conservative leanings found in state-wide opinion surveys.[114] At the state government level, political scientists Robert Erikson, Gerald Wright, and John McIver created a large sample in each state by combining 122 national CBS/New York Times surveys totaling 150,000 respondents. They found a high correlation between state voter ideology and policy, meaning that in states with liberal voters, state legislators produce liberal policies, while in conservative states, representatives adopt conservative policies.[115] Studies that have focused on specific policies such as abortion rights, capital punishment, environmental policy, and gay and lesbian rights also found substantial congruency between what the districts say they want and what they get.[116] Jeffery Lax and Justin Phillips found that constituent public opinion was a stronger predictor of policy adoption based on opinion than the partisanship of the representative.[117] Some studies show that the preferences of the most affluent Americans are more likely to become public policy than are those from poor and middle-income groups.[118]

The consistent finding is that voters generally get what they want from their representatives, even though little evidence exists that shows constituents are paying close attention. Political scientists assume that staying in office, especially in a prestigious institution like the U.S. Congress, is the dominant motivation for politicians.[119] For elections to motivate, however, representatives must believe their constituents are watching and willing to replace them if they support policies that are unpopular in their districts. In the 2018 congressional elections, 91 percent of the members of the House of Representatives and 84 percent of senators who sought reelection were successful. Such high retention rates have been common for more than a century. Good representation can explain why representatives nearly always get reelected, but so can incumbent advantages such as experience, name recognition, and success in securing federally funded projects for their districts. Incumbents also represent parties that are dominant in their districts and find it much easier than challengers to raise campaign funds.[120] Still, high reelection rates do not necessarily reduce reelection anxiety among members of Congress. It seems that they can afford to rely more on their unrepresentative personal preferences than they do. Instead, they act as if their constituents *are* paying attention. Why? The most common answer is that incumbent advantages do not mean that members of Congress are unbeatable. Rather, they are unbeatable if they continue to do the things they are doing.[121] Elected officials do not simply want to win the next election; they want to win several thereafter. Indeed, evidence shows that incumbents who vote according to the policy preferences of their constituencies stay in office longer. Research also shows that legislators become more responsive to public opinion as reelection time approaches and less responsive just before they retire.[122] In other words, public opinion matters because elections matter. The easiest way for voters to know if their representative is legislating contrary to their interests is for their election opponents to let them know. It is possible that voting records will be exploited by their opponents in the next election, which encourages legislators to pay attention to the polls and their constituents' letters, e-mails, and telephone calls.

Lawmakers can hear from voters when they visit their districts or hold "town" meetings to listen to their constituents' views on the issues. They also know personal contacts from voters or interest groups may not be particularly representative of overall opinion in their districts. Legislators also understand that those they encounter in their home districts are probably more active and informed, but also older, whiter, and more educated than their average voter. Still, even if the active constituents are only a small fraction of the total, their influence is larger than their numbers. As the influence of these active constituents diffuses, the rest of the district's residents respond to their opinions. It seems as if the whole district is more informed than it is.[123]

6.6 What Can I Do?

This is one instance in which you really don't need to do much. Just be willing to respond to opinion polls. We all have opinions in our heads and pollsters come to us to get them. As mentioned earlier, representatives who vote according to the wishes of their constituencies are more likely to keep their jobs, so we know that your opinion about the issues of the day matters to them a lot. Even the president cares about how well you believe he or she performs because it improves the president's influence with Congress. Of course, the president and other representatives don't care too much about the opinions of one person. Rather, it's the total that matters. But that's the beauty of public opinion. It is the aggregation of opinions that represents the public's judgment. Individuals can be uninformed, inconsistent, or misinformed, but they can also be knowledgeable and reliable in their opinions. The opinions of the whole public, however, are far more orderly than the individual responses of which they are composed. In the aggregate, random uninformed and inconsistent opinions cancel each other out. Informed opinions outweigh misinformed opinions simply because large, diverse groups are more likely to be correct than small, homogeneous groups, individuals, or even individual experts.[124] This takes the pressure off.

Public opinion is not formed in a vacuum. Rather, it is a process of citizens influencing each other through public and private conversation. Experts are involved too, which helps when dealing with complex issues. Of course, conservatives look to their experts while liberals look to theirs, but the experts themselves seek answers in part by engaging their counterparts with convincing arguments based on common rules of evidence. In time, on many issues, the experts come to agreement and the citizens usually follow along.[125] For example, we no longer debate whether the world is flat (at least not seriously), nor do most people maintain that the earth is the center of the universe. Most Americans no longer believe that blacks are genetically less intelligent than whites or that homosexuality is deviant social behavior, as they did a relatively short time ago. Although people don't change their opinions often or quickly, when they do, the shifts tend to be uniform. Over time, public opinion change becomes stable and coherent.[126]

Public opinion is also democratic because all views are considered equal. Scientific polling is fair and accurate because random sampling procedures assure that each American has the same chance of being in the sample as any other. Polling not only allows equal consideration, but permits average people to speak frankly. Among the many ways you can participate in governmental affairs, simply expressing an opinion is perhaps the most democratic. Still, most survey methods do not allow for serious debate and deliberation of issues. Thus, it remains the obligation of elected representatives to follow their conscience and use their best judgment, especially about new or involved issues on which the opinions of the public have yet to stabilize.

6.7 What's the Alternative?

The fact that random sample polling assures each American an equal chance of being selected suggests that perhaps representatives should be chosen by lotteries instead of elections. Each vote counts the same, but choosing representatives in elections produces other problems. Despite expanding the electorate beyond white property-owning males, elections still fall short of producing legislatures that resemble the diversity of the American population. In Congress, men outnumber women 80 percent to 20; senators are almost 30 years older on average than the average American; almost 90 percent of members are Christian, which underrepresents Jews, Mormons, Muslims, and other religions; the wealth of almost half of the members is over $1 million, whereas the median wealth of Americans is only about $45,000; managers and professionals are overrepresented while farmers, laborers, skilled workers, technicians, domestic service providers, retail workers, and small proprietors are underrepresented.[127] Such underrepresentation biases Congress' policy outcomes toward the interests of the groups that are well represented. Furthermore, members spend much of their time collecting campaign contributions to spend on advertisements designed to vilify their opponents rather than educate the voters.

Selecting representatives by lottery sounds like a crazy idea, but this is the method we use to select our juries, in which ordinary citizens face the complex task of sorting through evidence presented at trial (and the awesome responsibility of determining the guilt or innocence of the accused). Of course, the citizen legislature would be supported by professional staff and resources in much the same ways as lawyers, judges, and expert witnesses inform jury decisions. Further, members selected by lottery would owe nothing to special interests and party leaders.

However, the electoral connection between the representatives and those they represent would be severed. As we mentioned previously, public opinion matters because elections matter. Without recurring elections, representatives have little incentive to find out what the people they represent want (and to represent them faithfully). Legislative bodies are large, but not large enough to reflect the full diversity of many states and congressional districts. In this regard, picking representatives by lot runs into many of the same problems encountered by advocates of term limits. Such limits were placed on state governments to limit the influence of professional legislatures. Yet, term limits deplete the legislature of expertise. Thus, when it comes to complicated policy issues, it takes more time for the legislatures to become educated and slows down the legislative process. This applies to political as well as policy knowledge. For example, there are times when legislatures have resolved issues in the past, but new legislators have little knowledge of the new rules, forcing these issues to be re-negotiated and resulting in more lost time. The legislature would also take a back seat to the other parts of the political system, members of which would now have more knowledge of the programs and issues than the legislators would.

Endnotes

1. "Terrorist Attacks in the U.S. or Against Americans," Infoplease, accessed November 04, 2017, http://www.infoplease.com/ipa/A0001454.html.

2. "Presidential Approval Ratings—George W. Bush," Gallup, Inc., accessed November 04, 2017, http://www.gallup.com/poll/116500/presidential-approval-ratings-george-bush.aspx.

3. Brian Whitaker, "Bin Laden voice on video, says TV channel," *The Guardian*, September 9, 2002, accessed November 4, 2017, https://www.theguardian.com/media/2002/sep/10/alqaida.september112001.

4. "Eight of 10 Americans Support Ground War in Afghanistan," Gallup, Inc., November 1, 2001, accessed November 4, 2017, http://www.gallup.com/poll/5029/eight-americans-support-ground-war-afghanistan.aspx.

5. Joel Roberts, "Plans for Iraq Attack Began on 9/11," CBS News, September 4, 2002, accessed November 4, 2017, http://www.cbsnews.com/news/plans-for-iraq-attack-began-on-9-11/.

6. *Bill Moyers Journal*, season 4 episode 1, "Buying the War," performed by Bill Moyers, aired April 25, 2007, on PBS.

7. Nick Rivera, "Ten Years Later, Belief in Iraq Connection With 9/11 Attack Persists," The Moderate Voice, September 10, 2011, accessed November 4, 2017, http://themoderatevoice.com/ten-years-later-belief-in-iraq-connection-with-911-attack-persists/.

8. "Iraq," Gallup, Inc., accessed October 24, 2018, https://news.gallup.com/poll/1633/iraq.aspx.

9. Tom Rosentiel, "Public Attitudes Toward the War in Iraq: 2003-2008," Pew Research Center, March 19, 2008, accessed November 04, 2017, http://www.pewresearch.org/2008/03/19/public-attitudes-toward-the-war-in-iraq-20032008/.

10. "Presidential Approval Ratings -- George W. Bush," Gallup, Inc., accessed November 04, 2017, http://www.gallup.com/poll/116500/presidential-approval-ratings-george-bush.aspx.

11. See chapter 11 on Congress for a more detailed discussion on the institutional differences between the House of Representatives and the Senate.

12. "The Federalist Papers: No. 63," The Avalon Project, accessed November 4, 2017, http://avalon.law.yale.edu/18th_century/fed63.asp.

13. Benjamin Rush, "Of the Mode of Education Proper in a Republic," *The Selected Writings of Benjamin Rush*, ed. Dagobert D. Runes, (New York: Philosophical Library, 1947), http://press-pubs.uchicago.edu/founders/documents/v1ch18s30.html.

14. Philip E. Converse, "The Nature of Belief Systems in Mass Publics," *Ideology and Discontent*, ed. David E. Apter, (New York, NY: Free Press, 1964).

15. Christopher H. Achen, "Mass Political Attitudes and the Survey Response," *American Political Science Review* 69, no. 04 (1975): 1218-231, doi:10.2307/1955282.

16. Robert S. Erikson, Michael B. MacKuen, and James A. Stimson, *The Macro Polity* (New York: Cambridge University Press, 2006).

17. Tom Rosentiel, "Public Attitudes Toward the War in Iraq: 2003-2008," Pew Research Center, March 19, 2008, accessed November 4, 2017, http://www.pewresearch.org/2008/03/19/public-attitudes-toward-the-war-in-iraq-20032008/.

18. Tali Mendelberg, "The Deliberative Citizen: Theory and Evidence," *Political Decision Making, Deliberation and Participation*, Vol. 6 (2002).

19. S John Lawrence Sullivan, James Piereson, and George E. Marcus, *Political Tolerance and American Democracy* (Chicago: University of Chicago Press, 1993).

20. "General Social Survey 2012 Final Report," July 2013, accessed November 4, 2017, http://www.norc.org/PDFs/GSS Reports/Trends in Public Attitudes about Civil Liberties_FINAL.pdf.

21. Kate Zernike and Dalia Sussman, "For Pollsters, the Racial Effect That Wasn't," *The New York Times*, November 05, 2008, accessed November 4, 2017, https://www.nytimes.com/2008/11/06/us/politics/06poll.html.

22. Robert S. Erikson, and Kent L. Tedin, *American Public Opinion* (London: Routledge, Taylor & Francis Group, 2016).

23. Michael Suh, "Questionnaire design," Pew Research Center, January 29, 2015, accessed November 4, 2017a http://www.pewresearch.org/methodology/u-s-survey-research/questionnaire-design/.

24. Sigelman, (1981).

25. "Costing the Count." Accessed January 1, 2021. https://www.economist.com/international/2011/06/02/costing-the-count?story_id=18772674.

26. Giancarlo Sopo, "How much does it cost to commission a national opinion poll?" Quora, accessed November 4, 2017, https://www.quora.com/How-much-does-it-cost-to-commission-a-national-opinion-poll.

27. "Mobile Fact Sheet," Pew Research Center: Internet, Science & Tech, January 12, 2017, accessed November 4, 2017, http://www.pewinternet.org/fact-sheets/mobile-technology-fact-sheet/.

28. "Presidential Approval Ratings—George W. Bush," Gallup, Inc., accessed November 4, 2017, http://www.gallup.com/poll/116500/presidential-approval-ratings-george-bush.aspx.

29. Adam J. Berinsky, *In Time of War: Understanding American Public Opinion from World War II to Iraq* (Chicago: The University of Chicago Press, 2009).

30. Jack W. Brehm, "Control, Its Loss, and Psychological Reactance," *Control Motivation and Social Cognition* (1993): 3-30, doi:10.1007/978-1-4613-8309-3_1.

31. The offering of incentives has not been found to bias surveys. "Survey Refusals," AAPOR, accessed November 4, 2017, http://www.aapor.org/Education-Resources/Reports/Survey-Refusals.aspx.

32. Scott Keeter et al. Pew Research Center, 2000.

33. Monica Anderson and Andrew Perrin, "13% of Americans don't use the internet. Who are they?" Pew Research Center, September 7, 2016, accessed November 5, 2017, http://www.pewresearch.org/fact-tank/2016/09/07/some-americans-dont-use-the-internet-who-are-they/.

34. Brian Bailey, "Internet Surveys," Pew Research Center for the People and the Press, March 18, 2011, accessed November 4, 2017, http://www.people-press.org/methodology/collecting-survey-data/internet-surveys/.

35. M. W. Traugott and M. E. Kang, "Public Attention to Polls in an Election Year," *Election Polls, the News Media, and Democracy* (New York: Chatham House, 2000).

36. "Fivethyeight/data," GitHub, May 2, 2017, accessed November 4, 2017, https://github.com/fivethirtyeight/data/tree/master/pollster-ratings.

37. "AAPOR Code of Ethics," AAPOR, accessed November 4, 2017, http://www.aapor.org/Standards-Ethics/AAPOR-Code-of-Ethics.aspx.

38. "Government," Gallup, Inc., accessed November 4, 2017, http://www.gallup.com/poll/27286/government.aspx.

39. Tom Smith, "General Social Survey Final Report Trends in National Spending Priorities, 1973-2014," NORC at the University of Chicago, March 2015, accessed November 4, 2017, http://www.norc.org/PDFs/GSS Reports/GSS_Trends in Spending_1973-2014.pdf.

40. "Government," Gallup, Inc., accessed November 4, 2017, http://www.gallup.com/poll/27286/government.aspx.

41. D. R. Carney, J. T. Jost, S. D. Gosling, and J. Potter, "The Secret Lives of Liberals and Conservatives: Personality Profiles, Interaction Styles, and the Things They Leave Behind," *Political Psychology*, 29(6) (2008): 807-840, doi:10.1111/j.1467-9221.2008.00668.

42. John R. Alford, Carolyn L. Funk, and John R. Hibbing, "Are Political Orientations Genetically Transmitted?" *American Political Science Review* 99, no. 02 (2005): 153-67, doi:10.1017/s0003055405051579.

43. M. Kent Jennings and Kenneth P. Langton, "Mothers Versus Fathers: The Formation of Political Orientations Among Young Americans," *The Journal of Politics* 31, no. 2 (1969): 329-58, doi:10.2307/2128600.

44. M. Kent Jennings and Gregory B. Markus, "Partisan Orientations over the Long Haul: Results from the Three-Wave Political Socialization Panel Study," *American Political Science Review* 78, no. 04 (1984): 1000-018, doi:10.2307/1955804.

45. Robert S. Erikson and Kent L. Tedin, *American Public Opinion* (London: Routledge, Taylor & Francis Group, 2016), 128.

46. P.J. Conover and D.D. Searing, "A political socialization perspective," *Rediscovering the Democratic Purposes of Education*, eds. Lorraine M. McDonnell, P. Michael Timpane, and Roger W. Benjamin (Lawrence: University Press of Kansas, 2000).

47. David Kent, "The Generations Defined," Pew Research Center, May 8, 2015, accessed November 4, 2017, http://www.pewresearch.org/fact-tank/2015/05/11/millennials-surpass-gen-xers-as-the-largest-generation-in-u-s-labor-force/ft_15-05-11_millennialsdefined/.

48. Philip Bump, "Here Is When Each Generation Begins and Ends, According to Facts," *The Atlantic*, March 25, 2014, accessed November 4, 2017, https://www.theatlantic.com/national/archive/2014/03/here-is-when-each-generation-begins-and-ends-according-to-facts/359589/.

49. Virginia Sapiro, "Not Your Parents Political Socialization: Introduction for a New Generation," *Annual Review of Political Science* 7, no. 1 (2004): 1-23, doi:10.1146/annurev.polisci.7.012003.104840.

50. Robert S. Erikson and Kent L. Tedin, *American Public Opinion* (London: Routledge, Taylor & Francis Group, 2016).

51. David O. Sears and Carolyn L. Funk, "Evidence of the Long-Term Persistence of Adults Political Predispositions," *The Journal of Politics* 61, no. 1 (1999): 1-28, doi:10.2307/2647773.

52. Laura Stoker and M. Kent Jennings, "Political Similarity and Influence between Husbands and Wives," *The Social Logic of Politics: Personal Networks As Contexts for Political Behavior*, ed. Alan Zuckerman (Philadelphia, PA: Temple University Press, 2005).

53. "Favor Desegregation or Segregation," accessed November 5, 2017, http://www.electionstudies.org/nesguide/toptable/tab4b_3.htm.

54. Carl Bialik, "Most Black People Now Think O.J. Was Guilty," FiveThirtyEight, September 15, 2016, accessed November 4, 2017, http://fivethirtyeight.com/features/most-black-people-now-think-oj-simpson-was-guilty/.

55. "The Public, Race, and a Jury of Your Peers," Roper Center, September 16, 2015, accessed November 4, 2017, https://ropercenter.cornell.edu/public-race-jury-peers/.

56. "On Views of Race and Inequality, Blacks and Whites Are Worlds Apart," Pew Research Center's Social & Demographic Trends Project, June 27, 2016, accessed November 4, 2017, http://www.pewsocialtrends.org/2016/06/27/on-views-of-race-and-inequality-blacks-and-whites-are-worlds-apart/.

57. Michael C. Dawson, *Behind the Mule: Race and Class in African-American Politics* (Princeton, NJ: Princeton University Press, 1995).

58. Travis Mitchell, "State of Hispanics in the U.S. today," Pew Research Center's Hispanic Trends Project, February 23, 2017, accessed November 4, 2017, http://www.pewhispanic.org/2017/02/23/state-of-hispanics-in-the-u-s-today/.

59. Jens Manuel Krogstad and Gustavo López, "Roughly half of Hispanics have experienced discrimination," Pew Research Center, June 29, 2016, accessed November 4, 2017, http://www.pewresearch.org/fact-tank/2016/06/29/roughly-half-of-hispanics-have-experienced-discrimination/.

60. Mark Hugo Lopez and Gretchen Livingston, "Hispanics and the Criminal Justice System," Pew Research Center's Hispanic Trends Project, April 7, 2009, accessed November 4, 2017, http://www.pewhispanic.org/2009/04/07/hispanics-and-the-criminal-justice-system/.

61. Mark Hugo Lopez and Susan Minushkin, "2008 National Survey of Latinos: Hispanic Voter Attitudes," Pew Research Center's Hispanic Trends Project, July 24, 2008, accessed November 4, 2017, http://www.pewhispanic.org/2008/07/24/2008-national-survey-of-latinos-hispanic-voter-attitudes/.

62. Ibid.

63. Karthick Ramakrishnan, "Asian American Voices in the 2016 Election," National Asian American Survey, accessed November 4, 2017, http://naasurvey.com/wp-content/uploads/2016/10/NAAS2016-Oct5-report.pdf.

64. "Obama wins 75% of Latino vote, marks historic Latino influence in presidential election," Latino Decisions, accessed November 4, 2017, http://www.latinodecisions.com/blog/2012/11/07/obama-wins-75-of-latino-vote-marks-historic-latino-influence-in-presidential-election/.

65. "Hillary Clinton Had the Biggest Voter Gender Gap on Record," *Fortune*, accessed November 4, 2017, http://fortune.com/2016/11/09/hillary-clinton-election-gender-gap/.

66. Olga Khazan, "The Precarious Masculinity of 2016 Voters," *The Atlantic*, October 12, 2016, accessed November 4, 2017, https://www.theatlantic.com/politics/archive/2016/10/male-trump-voters-masculinity/503741/.

67. Robert S. Erikson, Michael B. MacKuen, and James A. Stimson, *The Macro Polity* (New York: Cambridge University Press, 2006), 219.

68. Adam J. Berinsky, *In Time of War: Understanding American Public Opinion from World War II to Iraq* (Chicago: The University of Chicago Press, 2009).

69. Robert S. Erikson and Kent L. Tedin, *American Public Opinion* (London: Routledge, Taylor & Francis Group, 2016), 222.

70. "Gender Gap Varies on Support for War." Gallup, Inc., November 19, 2002, accessed October 24, 2018, https://news.gallup.com/poll/7243/gender-gap-varies-support-war.aspx.

71. Mary Pat Clark, "The Gender Gap: Three Decades Old, as Wide as Ever," Pew Research Center for the People and the Press, March 29, 2012, accessed November 4, 2017, http://www.people-press.org/2012/03/29/the-gender-gap-three-decades-old-as-wide-as-ever/.

72. Ibid.

73. Benjamin Wormald, "Religious Landscape Study," Pew Research Center's Religion & Public Life Project, May 11, 2015, Accessed November 4, 2017, http://www.pewforum.org/religious-landscape-study/views-about-abortion/.

74. "Poll: 50 percent of all Catholics support abortion in 'all or most cases'," LifeSiteNews, accessed November 4, 2017, https://www.lifesitenews.com/news/poll-50-percent-of-all-catholics-support-abortion-in-all-or-most-cases.

75. Newport, Frank. "Religious Group Voting and the 2020 Election." Gallup.com. Gallup, December 3, 2020. https://news.gallup.com/opinion/polling-matters/324410/religious-group-voting-2020-election.aspx.

76. Benjamin Wormald, "Religious Landscape Study," Pew Research Center's Religion & Public Life Project, May 11, 2015, accessed November 4, 2017, http://www.pewforum.org/religious-landscape-study/views-about-abortion/.

77. "Jewish Voters Play a Role in Deciding the 2020 Election." Jewish Journal, November 25, 2020. https://jewishjournal.org/2020/11/12/jewish-voters-play-a-role-in-deciding-the-2020-election/.

78. Robert S. Erikson and Kent L. Tedin, *American Public Opinion* (London: Routledge, Taylor & Francis Group, 2016), 209.

79. Daniel Judah Elazar, *American Federalism: A View from the States* (New York: Harper & Row, 1984).

80. Michael Lipka, "Gay marriage arrives in the South, where the public is less enthused," Pew Research Center, October 15, 2014, accessed November 4, 2017, http://www.pewresearch.org/fact-tank/2014/10/15/gay-marriage-arrives-in-the-south-where-the-public-is-less-enthused/.

81. Robert S. Erikson and Kent L. Tedin, *American Public Opinion* (London: Routledge, Taylor & Francis Group, 2016), 214.

82. Daniel Judah Elazar, *American Federalism: A View from the States* (New York: Harper & Row, 1984).

83. Adam Nekola, "Public Views About Guns," Pew Research Center for the People and the Press, June 22, 2017, accessed November 4, 2017, http://www.people-press.org/2016/08/26/public-views-about-guns/#region.

84. Andrea Caumont, "North-South divide over abortion grows," Pew Research Center, September 2, 2013, accessed November 4, 2017, http://www.pewresearch.org/fact-tank/2013/09/03/north-south-divide-over-abortion-grows/.

85. Daniel Judah Elazar, *American Federalism: A View from the States* (New York: Harper & Row, 1984).

86. "Wyoming, North Dakota and Mississippi Most Conservative," Gallup, Inc., January 31 2017, www.gallup.com/poll/203204/wyoming-north-dakota-mississippi-conservative.aspx?g_source=IDEOL-OGY&g_medium=topic&g_campaign=tiles.

87. Eileen Patten, "The black-white and urban-rural divides in perceptions of racial fairness," Pew Research Center, August 28, 2013, accessed November 4, 2017, http://www.pewresearch.org/fact-tank/2013/08/28/the-black-white-and-urban-rural-divides-in-perceptions-of-racial-fairness/.

88. Wilson (1985).

89. Meredith Dost, "Section 1: Changing Views of Same-Sex Marriage," Pew Research Center for the People and the Press, June 8, 2015, accessed November 4, 2017, http://www.people-press.org/2015/06/08/section-1-changing-views-of-same-sex-marriage/.

90. Travis Mitchell, "Trends and patterns in intermarriage," Pew Research Center's Social & Demographic Trends Project, May 18, 2017, accessed November 4, 2017, http://www.pewsocialtrends.org/2017/05/18/1-trends-and-patterns-in-intermarriage/.

91. "The Largest City to Vote for Donald Trump," The Largest City to Vote for Donald Trump—Decision Desk HQ, accessed November 4, 2017, https://decisiondeskhq.com/data-dives/the-largest-city-to-vote-for-donald-trump/.

92. Kristen Bialik, "More Americans say government should ensure health care coverage," Pew Research Center, January 13, 2017, accessed November 4, 2017, http://www.pewresearch.org/fact-tank/2017/01/13/more-americans-say-government-should-ensure-health-care-coverage/.

93. Seth Motel, "In Deficit Debate, Public Resists Cuts in Entitlements and Aid to Poor," Pew Research Center for the People and the Press, December 19, 2013, accessed November 4, 2017, http://www.people-press.org/2013/12/19/in-deficit-debate-public-resists-cuts-in-entitlements-and-aid-to-poor/.

94. "The ANES Guide to Public Opinion and Electoral Behavior: Military Spending (2), 7-point scale 1980-2016," American National Election Studies, accessed November 4, 2017, https://electionstudies.org/resources/anes-guide/top-tables/?id=52.

95. "Americans Expect History to Judge Bush Worse Than Nixon," Gallup, Inc., January 16, 2009, Accessed November 4, 2017, http://www.gallup.com/poll/113806/Americans-Expect-History-Judge-Bush-Worse-Than-Nixon.aspx.

96. "Obama Weekly Job Approval by Demographic Groups," Gallup, Inc., Accessed November 4, 2017, http://www.gallup.com/poll/121199/obama-weekly-job-approval-demographic-groups.aspx.

97. "Presidential Approval Ratings -- Donald Trump, Gallup, Inc., accessed November 4, 2017, http://www.gallup.com/poll/203198/presidential-approval-ratings-donald-trump.aspx.

98. "More Americans Say Crime Is Rising in U.S.," Gallup, Inc., October 22, 2015, accessed November 4, 2017, http://www.gallup.com/poll/186308/americans-say-crime-rising.aspx.

99. Joseph Liu, "Growing Number of Americans Say Obama is a Muslim," Pew Research Center's Religion & Public Life Project, August 17, 2010, accessed November 4, 2017, http://www.pewforum.org/2010/08/18/growing-number-of-americans-say-obama-is-a-muslim/.

100. Bill Bishop, *The Big Sort: Why the Clustering of Like-Minded America Is Tearing Us Apart* (New York, Houghton Mifflin Harcourt, 2008).

101. Shahram Heshmat, "What Is Confirmation Bias?" *Psychology Today*, April 23, 2015, accessed November 4, 2017, https://www.psychologytoday.com/blog/science-choice/201504/what-is-confirmation-bias.

102. Jennifer Jerit and Jason Barabas, "Bankrupt Rhetoric: How Misleading Information Affects Knowledge About Social Security," *Public Opinion Quarterly*, Vol. 70, no. 3 (January 2006): 278–303.

103. "Donald Trump's file," @politifact, accessed November 4, 2017, http://www.politifact.com/personalities/donald-trump/.

104. "Analysis: Tracking All of President Trump's False or Misleading Claims." *The Washington Post*. WP Company, October 23, 2020. https://www.washingtonpost.com/graphics/politics/trump-claims-database/?itid=lk_inline_manual_4.

105. F. Pratto and O.P. John, "Automatic Vigilance: The Attention-Grabbing Power of Negative Social Information," *JPSP* 61 (1991): 380-391.

106. Anne Plute, "Trump Supporters Appear To Be Misinformed, Not Uninformed," FiveThirtyEight, January 07, 2016, accessed November 04, 2017, https://fivethirtyeight.com/features/trump-supporters-appear-to-be-misinformed-not-uninformed/.

107. David Leonhardt and Stuart A. Thompson, "President Trump's Lies, the Definitive List," The New York Times, June 23, 2017, accessed November 04, 2017, https://www.nytimes.com/interactive/2017/06/23/opinion/trumps-lies.html.

108. Jones, Jeffrey M. "Americans View Biden as Likable, Honest; Trump, as Strong." Gallup.com. Gallup, October 30, 2020. https://news.gallup.com/poll/321695/americans-view-biden-likable-honest-trump-strong.aspx.

109. Danielle Gewurz, "What Voters Know about Campaign 2012," Pew Research Center for the People and the Press, August 10, 2012, accessed November 4, 2017, http://www.people-press.org/2012/08/10/what-voters-know-about-campaign-2012/.

110. Benjamin Wormald, "The News IQ Quiz," Pew Research Center, April 28, 2015, accessed November 4, 2017, http://www.pewresearch.org/quiz/the-news-iq-quiz/results/.

111. Hutchings (2003).

112. Ansolabehere and Jones (2006).

113. Friesema and Hedlund (1981).

114. Tufte (from American Public Opinion Chapter 10, Table 10.4).

115. Robert S. Erikson, Gerald C. Wright, and John P. McIver, *Statehouse Democracy: Public Opinion and Policy in the American States* (Cambridge: Cambridge University Press, 1995).

116. Jeffrey R. Lax and Justin H. Phillips, "Gay Rights in the States: Public Opinion and Policy Responsiveness," *American Political Science Review* 103, no. 03 (2009): 367-86, doi:10.1017/s0003055409990050.

117. Jeffrey R. Lax and Justin H. Phillips, "The Democratic Deficit in the States," *American Journal of Political Science* 56, no. 1 (2011): 148-66, doi:10.1111/j.1540-5907.2011.00537.x.

118. Larry M. Bartels, *Unequal Democracy: The Political Economy of the New Gilded Age* (Princeton: Princeton University Press, 2016).

119. David R. Mayhew, *Congress: The Electoral Connection* (New Haven, CT: Yale University Press, 2006).

120. Roger H. Davidson, Walter J. Oleszek, Frances E. Lee, and Eric Schickler, *Congress and Its Members* (Thousand Oaks, CA: CQ Press, 2018).

121. David R. Mayhew, *Congress: The Electoral Connection* (New Haven, CT: Yale University Press, 2006).

122. James M. Snyder and Michael M. Ting, "An Informational Rationale for Political Parties," *American Journal of Political Science* 46, no. 1 (2002): 90, doi:10.2307/3088416.

123. Warren E. Miller, and Donald E. Stokes, "Constituency Influence in Congress," *The American Political Science Review* 57, no. 1 (March 1963): 45-56.

124. James Surowiecki, *The Wisdom of Crowds: Why the Many Are Smarter than the Few* (London: Abacus, 2014).

125. John R. Zaller, *The Nature and Origins of Mass Opinion* (New York: Cambridge University Press, 1992).

126. Benjamin I. Page and Robert Y. Shapiro, *The Rational Public: Fifty Years of Trends in Americans Policy Preferences* (Chicago: University of Chicago Press, 2003).

127. Refer to chapter on Congress.

CHAPTER 7
Citizen Participation and Voting: America Checks the Fluids

Chapter Objectives

1. Understand why everyone seems to be urging you to vote.
2. Explore why some people participate in politics more than others.
3. Learn how elections are regulated by government.
4. Reflect on whether voting is a rational act.
5. Discover why voters vote the way they do.
6. Learn about the last presidential election.

Introduction: Why the Fuss?

In an advertisement for Rock the Vote, actors Jake Gyllenhaal and Peter Sarsgaard sit in a coffee shop talking about their tennis game. They pause and stare when a tall blonde woman walks past the shop window. She smiles. Gyllenhaal: [bites his lower lip] "I wonder if she votes?" Sarsgaard: [sigh] "I hope so." In a similar ad in the same shop, Maggie Gyllenhaal puts down her cup and says: "We women often have to choose between two men; this time it really matters. So vote."

Rob Crandall / Shutterstock.com

collective action

Action resulting from the sharing of resources and coordination of efforts among individuals.

representative

A person who (or a group that) stands for and makes judgments on behalf of other people and groups.

policies

Formal acts, decisions, or plans made by government.

cost-effective

Something that is economical (a good value) in terms of the relationship between the cost needed to obtain something of value and its benefit.

Why the fuss? Millions of dollars are spent each election on such ads. Diverse groups from all areas of the political spectrum spend money to get people to vote. Some play on guilt by reminding you of how quick and easy it is to register online. Others will tell you about the stakes that are involved. Still others make appeals to your group or citizen identity. Note that such ads are not made on behalf of a particular candidate or issue, but simply to get people to exercise their right to vote. If voting is free, easy, and desirable, why do we need to be cajoled to do it?

This chapter is about the role of ordinary people directly and formally participating in democratic governance. Usually this happens during an election in which we as citizens decide between candidates and issues. There are many ways to participate, from writing to a government official to working for a political party to attending a meeting or party caucus. We focus this chapter on the political act of voting because it is the most common form of participation and, as we shall explain, because it is the most democratic.

Elections are decisive political acts. This means that the outcome or results are binding on all members of the society. Put differently, elections are the manner in which society as a whole makes its decisions. To understand the implications of this process, we will discuss what social scientists refer to as **collective action** problems—the dilemmas and paradoxes associated with producing shared outcomes.

In state and local elections, voters can sometimes, depending on location, determine actual laws or amendments to state constitutions or local government charters. In national elections, however, voters simply choose **representatives** to Congress or electors for the president. Thus, the product of a national election (what the people are producing) is representation. We send a group of representatives to Washington and they make binding decisions for us, as if we had made these decisions ourselves. In theory, we make judgments on how well our representatives have represented our interests in past elections. If we like the way they have acted on our behalf, we reelect them. If not, we can replace some or all of them with new ones. Thus, in elections, citizens determine who should temporarily control the government. Voters are much like the owners of a business who hire managers to run a company on their behalf. The owners can control the behavior of their agents with the threat of termination if they are not pleased with the agents' performance.

Indirectly, elections serve as an opportunity for the nation as a whole to make choices about its **policies**, programs, and directions of government. Like successful managers who want to keep their jobs, elected officials will do their best to keep the voters happy, ideally, by passing popular laws and policies that ensure the country will continue to run smoothly. To work as a means of democratic governance, voting requires that people pay attention to what is going on in the world, understand what their representatives are doing, and take the time and effort to vote.

The essence of this chapter concerns this understanding of representative democracy. Unfortunately, the ideal does not hold up very well when compared to the behavior of real people. As we learned from the previous chapter on public opinion, only a few people pay close attention to political affairs and many are confused by the issues and candidates. Only about half of those who are are eligible to vote actually do so in presidential elections. Fewer still vote in congressional, state, and local elections. Many Americans are dissatisfied, and perpetually so, with the performance of their representatives and the actions of their government. Yet, if we believe that our representatives are incompetent, shouldn't we look into a mirror to see who selected them and failed to hold them accountable in the first place?

When discussing elections and the power of the people, we will rely on what we call "the logic of participation" to explain who votes and who does not. This analysis gives us a good idea of whose interests are attended to and whose are not. More accurately, the logic of participation helps us to understand which groups find it easier to express their interests and have them satisfied. The analysis will also help us to see what we can do to increase the influence of ordinary people, or how we can rearrange institutions to make our collective voice heard and our wishes heeded more faithfully by our representatives.

We begin by discussing the importance of participation by ordinary Americans and showing the various ways that people participate in government. We also discuss why some groups participate more than others. Although voting is only one form of participation, once someone decides to participate in an election, we discuss the various ways that demonstrate how people decide to vote. The implications are that citizens need a set of institutions, such as political parties, that make voting more **cost-effective,** or more worth doing, if the ideal of democratic elections is to be fully realized.

7.1 The Logic of Political Participation

In *The Simpsons*™ episode titled "Mr. Spritz Goes to Washington," Krusty the Klown gets elected to Congress. Later, the Simpson family finds him drinking in a Washington tavern.

> *Marge: "There he is! Krusty, we've come to see how many campaign promises you've kept."*
>
> *Krusty: "Uh, let's see; did I promise to be a slave to Big Oil?"*
>
> *Marge: "No."*
>
> *Krusty: "Well, then none."*[1]

The Simpsons discover a truth about representative democracy: citizens are not done with their duties when they vote. If the people of Springfield want Krusty to keep the promises he made, they need to watch what he is doing. If they don't, he may well represent some other interest, in this case, that of "Big Oil." Social scientists refer to the connection between a representative and the people he or she represents as a **principal–agent relationship**, wherin one party, the agent, acts on behalf of another party, the principal. In the *Simpsons*™ example, the agent is Representative Krusty and the people of Springfield (whom Krusty represents) comprise the principal.

Economists see this as a potential problem because the agent is more likely to take risks if the agent knows he or she will not bear the **costs** of those risks. This problem is so common that it has its own ominous-sounding name: **moral hazard**. The problem is caused by the many actions the representative takes behind the scenes. Once elected to national office, the representative begins making decisions for constituents. In doing so, the representative has more information about his or her own actions and intentions than the people back home, who cannot easily monitor the representative's performance. It is also common for representatives to have incentives to act inappropriately from the viewpoint of the voters back home. Such incentives may include, but are not limited to, campaign contributions coming from lobbyists (such as the oil or pharmaceutical industries) and even threats to fund opponents in the next election.

Moral hazard is common. There are many things we could do ourselves, but lacking time and expertise, we instead hire someone to do them for us. Imagine you are ready to build a house. You have a set of plans that you and your architect have worked out and you have obtained a building permit from the city. Now, because of your job and other responsibilities, you don't have the time to find and supervise all the people to build the house, so you hire a general contractor. You could give the contractor $300,000 and say, "Build this house according to these plans; I'll be back in six months ready to move in." However, even if the contractor signs an agreement specifying how the work is to be done, he still could run off with your money. It is more likely, however, that the builder will cut corners and cover up mistakes that will be impossible to discover when you return. This problem is caused by **hidden action**. To minimize it, you need to monitor your contractor's work while also understanding that the contractor has more knowledge about building houses than you do. This is also why communities have building codes and require inspection of structures during construction to make sure they are built correctly. When hiring an agent (the contractor) to build your house, therefore, you need to monitor the progress and have a third party (like the city) inspect critical aspects of the project. The same goes for your elected legislators: you have to monitor your representatives' behavior or have someone do it for you.

---

principal–agent relationship

A relationship wherein one party (the agent) acts on behalf of another party (the principal).

costs

An outlay of time, effort, or money needed to obtain something of value.

moral hazard

A situation in which an individual is more likely to take risks because the person knows he or she will not bear the full costs of those risks.

hidden action

Action taken by the agent that is unknown to the principal.

7.2 The Framers' Understanding of the Problem of Moral Hazard

tyranny

Oppressive and unjust treatment by government.

self-interest

A focus on one's own wishes or needs.

republican form of government

A form of government in which the citizens govern indirectly, through representatives, and in which the power of the government is fragmented through a system of separation of powers as well as checks and balances.

The Framers of the Constitution understood the problem of moral hazard and designed the institutions of government to prevent or at least minimize its effects. Their understanding is best captured by James Madison in Federalist Papers 10 and 51, which can be understood in modern social scientific principles. Arguing for the necessity of a larger, more centralized national government, Madison saw the possibility of **tyranny** or oppression as the principle problem of government. He traced its cause to human behavior. According to Madison, with regard to public affairs, people are motivated by **self-interest**. These interests differ, conflict, and do not always conform to what is best for the country. In poorly constructed nations, Madison reasoned, it is likely that some powerful group will capture control of government, discard the public welfare, and produce policies designed to favor its own interests. He was convinced that most voters would consider their own interests, rather than that the common good, when voting. As he put it, "The latent causes of faction are thus sown in the nature of man ....On the other hand," Madison said, "the effect may be inverted. Men of factious tempers ... first obtain the suffrages, and then betray the interests, of the people." Madison worried that representatives would betray the interests of the people once elected.

Madison went on to argue that a "well constructed Union" would control the effects of human nature more or less automatically. By this he meant the **republican form of government** in which the people govern indirectly through representatives, rather than directly. As he put it, "Representatives would refine and enlarge the public views, by passing them through the medium of a chosen body of citizens, whose wisdom may best discern the true interest of their country."

In Federalist 51, Madison considered the problem of moral hazard more directly. He didn't use those words, but he was clearly concerned with the power given to the representatives and whether it would be used to serve the common good. His solution? Set self-interest against self-interest:

The interest of the man must be connected with the constitutional rights of the place. ... In framing a government which is to be administered by men over men, the great difficulty lies in this: you must first enable the government to control the governed; and in the next place oblige it to control itself. ...We see it particularly displayed in all the subordinate distributions of power, where the constant aim is to divide and arrange the several offices in such a manner as that each may be a check on the other—that the private interest of every individual may be a sentinel over the public rights.

Thus, the constitutional order (the institutions of government and their relationship to each other and to the people) is designed to minimize the problem of moral hazard by using human nature (self-interest) itself. The ambitions of those in the legislature are set against the ambitions of legislators from other districts. The interests of the legislature, in turn, are set against the interests of other institutions of government as well as "the private interest of every individual." Individual voters assess candidates and vote for those who best represent their interests. In seeking to maintain their interest in reelection, representatives are given an incentive to represent their constituents faithfully.

In theory, the scheme devised by the Framers seems to be brilliant. However, with regard to the idea that the conflicting interests of voters and elected officials provides a solution to the problem of moral hazard, we argue that the Framers based their assumptions on an incomplete understanding of self-interest. In short, they were too optimistic about the ability of the voters to be the "sentinel over the public rights."

Instrumental vs. Cost-Benefit Self-Interest

When citizens show up at the polls, they do attempt to choose representatives that will best embody their interests, as the Framers expected. The nice thing about this arrangement is the voters only have to think about themselves, which is natural and easy. More importantly, this system doesn't require anyone to sacrifice his or her interest for the greater good. This is very much like the way private markets work. When selecting products or services, all you need to do is think about your own needs and find the product that best satisfies your desires. On the other side, the manufacturer or service provider that best figures out what people want (and makes that product available) is going be the most successful. Similarly, the candidate who best understands the desires of the district's voters and convinces them that he or she is going to support those desires in office is likely to be the most successful. This is what it means to tie the self-interest of the voters to the self-interests of the office holders.

These are all examples of events caused by **instrumental self-interest**. Such actions produce outcomes consistent with an individual's goals. When people do things, it is common for social scientists to assume that those actions are instruments to achieving the people's goals. In this way, human behavior can be thought of as generally predictable, or at least explainable. For example, if you are a student reading this book, we can assume with considerable accuracy that you are not doing so because you love politics. Of course, some of you do want to know more about this fascinating subject, but it is more likely that you are reading this book as an act that is **instrumental** to another, more tangible, personal goal: to pass this class, to complete this requirement for your degree, and eventually to qualify for a job with good career prospects. Reading this book is a track to the good life just as participating in politics is one path people use to get what they want.

instrumental self-interest

Something that is done for the purpose of achieving an individual's goals.

instrumental

Something that serves as a means in pursuing a goal.

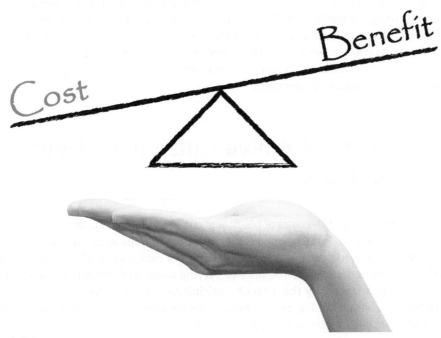

© Shutterstock, Inc.

cost-benefit self-interest

Something done with the purpose of achieving an individual's goals after comparing the costs of the action with its benefits.

Unfortunately, the concept of instrumental self-interest is too simple to fully predict human behavior. A better, more accurate way of thinking about how self-interest influences human behavior is the cost-benefit concept. That is, people tend to balance the costs of action with its benefits before they act. For example, one of the authors of this book has always wanted a Corvette. They are expensive but not completely beyond the means of a college professor. Even though it is in his interest to have one, the author does not have a Corvette. Why not? What's wrong with the theory of instrumental self-interest? The answer is that the theory is not by itself sufficient to cause the expected behavior. Just because the professor has decided that it is in his interest to have a Corvette doesn't mean that he will buy one. There are other things that place demands on his limited income: mortgage payments, utility bills, and food, to name a few. He spends his money for these things because they satisfy his needs for shelter, security, substance, and comfort better than a Corvette and thus deserve a higher priority for his money. Besides, he already has a car: a small pick-up truck. Why not a sports car to fill his need for transportation? The reason, provided by **cost-benefit self-interest**, is that the little truck provides more benefits (transportation, hauling, and serving nicely on occasional camping trips) for the money than would a Corvette. Note also that because he spent $20,000 instead of $60,000 for a vehicle, he can use the $40,000 that he would have spent on the sports car to buy other things.

The cost-benefit concept of self-interest is more complete and provides a better explanation of human behavior than instrumental self-interest because it recognizes that people have more than one goal and that they weigh benefits against costs in order to achieve their goals. More precisely, self-interested individuals make decisions in a way that maximizes benefits and minimizes costs. One's goals are prioritized and the costs and benefits of each are generally taken into consideration. This logic applies to many forms of human behavior and is very useful in understanding why some people participate in politics while others do not. It also helps explain why many otherwise eligible citizens do not bother to vote. Cost-benefit self-interest explains why some types of people find it easier to participate in politics and are more active, while others find it more difficult and are therefore less active.

cost

An outlay of time, effort, or money needed to obtain something of value.

poll taxes

A fee paid by an individual as a condition of voting in an election.

To understand how this concept applies to political participation, we first need to expand our idea about what constitutes a **cost**. Voting isn't really free. There is no fee to vote. **Poll taxes** were declared unconstitutional by the Supreme Court some time ago. Still, it takes some effort on your part to participate in voting. You are not automatically eligible to vote. In most states you first need to register by mailing in the National Voter Registration form about a month (the exact number of days varies by state) before the general election. If you live in North Dakota, you can skip this step. Wyoming doesn't recognize the National Voter Registration form, so you must register in person or obtain and mail in the state form. On the day of the election, you need to find your polling place, get there, and vote. As you can see, it takes time, effort, and some money (transportation isn't free) to participate. These are costs because you value your time, energy, and money. You would want more of each of these if you could have them.

How the Costs of Active Citizenship Determine Who Participates

An expanded understanding of the costs of political participation helps explain who is more active in politics and who is less so. As mentioned earlier, there are various ways one can participate in democratic politics, from voting in elections to working on a campaign. Each of these has associated costs that we can understand as the price of varying degrees of active citizenship. The first implication is that the more costly the form of participation, the lower the rate of participation. This relationship is illustrated in Figure 7.1, which shows some examples of the different types of participation arranged with actual rates of participation.

FIGURE 7.1 Civic and Political Involvement
The proportion of adults who did each of the following in the last 12 months.

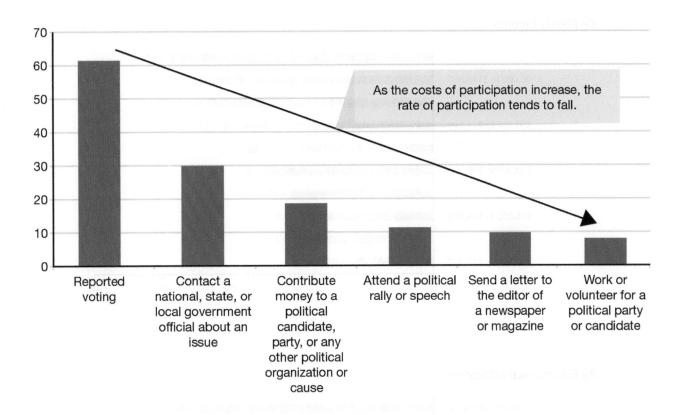

Data on reported voting from US Census, Election of November 2016. Pew Internet & American Life Project, August 2008. Survey margin of error is +/- 2% based on all adults (n-2551).

As Figure 7.1 shows, 61.4 percent of American citizens reported that they voted in the 2016 presidential election. The high percentage (relative to other forms of participation) suggests that voting is a relatively low-cost activity. On the other hand, the percentage of people who contribute money to a political candidate, organization, or cause is much lower at 18 percent, which suggests that doing so is a higher cost activity. Although this figure does not show the amount of individual contributions, obviously the cost of contributing to a candidate is low if a small amount is given; however, contributions that are sufficiently noteworthy to garner attention from a candidate for national office can be very expensive. If we examine the percentage of people who said they worked for a political party or a campaign, which takes even more time, effort, and opportunity costs (the cost of the time you could have used to do homework, for example), we find that only 8 percent are doing that.

The second implication of the costs of participation is that those with more political resources are better able to bear the costs of participation and therefore they participate at higher rates. Again, we can test this implication with data (shown in Figure 7.2), but first we need to explain what we mean by political resources. Obviously, money is a political resource. If you want to run for a statewide or national political office you will need plenty of money. Candidates for office often ask for cash contributions and their expressions of gratitude show that it is a valued resource. Political knowledge, contacts, and experience are also political resources, as is having a flexible work schedule that would allow you to attend a political rally, work for a candidate, or engage in social protest.

FIGURE 7.2 Reported Voting by Demographic Characteristics

By Family Income

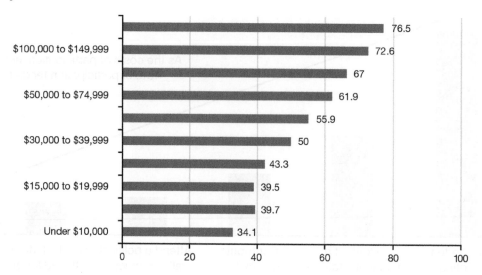

By Educational Attainment

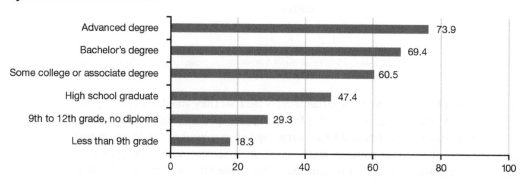

By Age

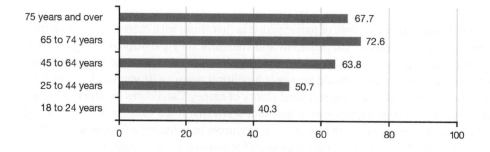

By Ethnic Group

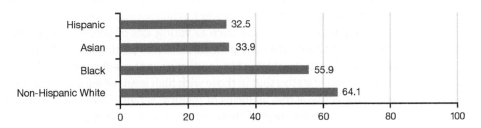

Data from U.S. Census Bureau, Current Population Survey, November 2016 election. Voting and Registration in the Election of November 2016. https://www.census.gov/data/tables/time-series/demo/voting-and-registration/p20-580.html.

If we examine the percentage of people who reported voting in the 2016 election and divide them according to their family income (see Figure 7.2), we find that those with higher incomes voted at higher rates than those with lower incomes. A similar relationship is present when we divide those who reported voting by different rates of education. Only about 20 percent of U.S. citizens who have less than a ninth-grade education reported voting, while about 70 percent of those with a bachelor's degree reported voting. How do we explain this pattern in terms of costs? The answer is education reduces the cost of voting, meaning people with more education find it easier to vote. Another way to explain it is that people with higher rates of education have already done some of the research needed to participate in voting. Those of you who are reading this book already know that registering is a requirement to vote and that states have varying laws and procedures for voting on Election Day. Maybe you attended a campus-sponsored forum or speech on some public policy issue. You really didn't spend a lot of extra time and effort doing this; it was just part of being a college student. Also, as a college graduate you will probably have a higher income and have a more flexible work schedule that will also make it easier to participate.

Age has a similar effect (see Figure 7.2). As people get older, they tend to vote at higher rates. Why would older people find it less costly to participate than younger people? The reason is found in the old saying, "With age comes experience." Over time, participating in elections takes less effort because older people are likely to be familiar with the issues, candidates, and local voting procedures. It is also likely that the polling place will be in the same location as past elections. Older people might also have more time to follow the issues and to vote since they are less likely to have children at home competing for their attention. There are limits, however; by about age 75 and older, voting starts to decline, simply because the physical effort of getting to the polls increases as seniors grow frail.

Voting by race or ethnic group tells a slightly different story (again, see Figure 7.2). In the case of black Americans, the data show that they voted at almost the same rate as white voters. Yet, the average levels of household income and education are higher for whites. Black Americans normally participate in politics at higher rates than other statistics would predict given their levels of income and education. The higher than normal black turnout in 2012 had something to do with the fact that Barack Obama was running for reelection, but black Americans, as a group, place a high value on political participation. The long history of discrimination and the relatively recent struggle for the right to vote produced a kind of social learning among those in the black community regarding the value of political power and participation. Conversely, if you look at voter turnout rates for Asian Americans, you find that they have much lower participation rates than whites. This is despite the fact that some 47 percent of Asian-American eligible voters in 2016 had a college education and a greater proportion had annual family incomes of $50,000 or more than did whites.[2] The much lower rates of voting that we see among Latinas/os are due to lower incomes, levels of education, and younger ages. These factors are mostly consistent with the notion that people of lower socio-economic status participate less in politics because it is more costly for them to do so.

The third implication stemming from the costs of participation follows from the first two: the greater the cost of a form of participation, the more biased that form of participation is in terms of its participants. In other words, people engaging in the costlier forms of participation are, on average, richer, and have higher levels of education than those participating in less costly forms. Like the first two implications, this one is fairly easy to understand if we look at data on the incomes of those participating in various ways. When we examined Figure 7.1, we noted that, where a form of participation was low cost, such as voting, lots of people participated. The data from Figure 7.2 showed that those with more political resources participated at higher rates than those with fewer resources. This suggests that the most important predictor of any form of political participation is socio-economic status; that is, those with high levels of education and income are more likely to be politically active across all forms of political activity than those with low economic status. Figure 7.3 shows the percentage of those active in various forms of participation divided between those with incomes under $15,000 and those with incomes $75,000 and above. About 55 percent of those surveyed with incomes under $15,000 reported voting, while more than 85 percent of those with incomes over $75,000 voted. This represents a significant difference between the rates of the two groups, with those in the higher-income group being 1.5 times more likely to vote. Perhaps most telling, the more affluent group was 8.6 times more likely to give a contribution to a candidate or organization supporting a candidate during a campaign. The point here is that people with higher socio-economic status tend to dominate all forms of political participation, but the more intensive, and often the more influential forms, show even greater degrees of bias toward higher-income groups.

FIGURE 7.3 Forms of Participation and Resource Bias

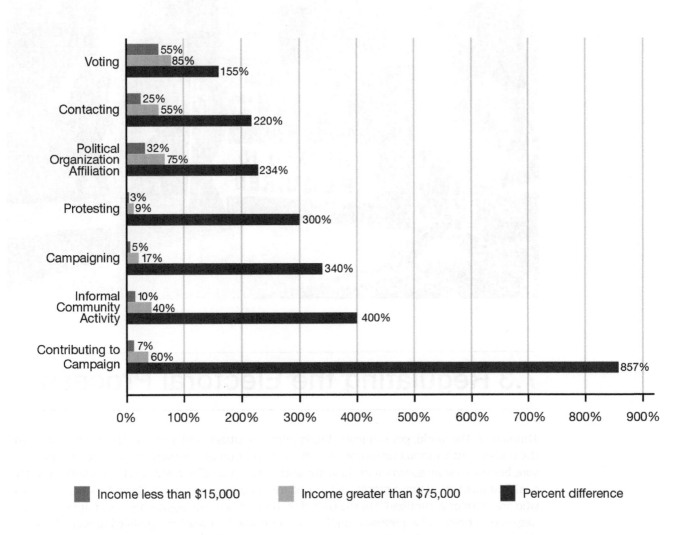

Based on Sidney Verba, Kay Lehman Schlozman, and Henry Brady. *Voice and Equality: Civic Voluntarism in American Politics*. Cambridge: Harvard University Press, 1995. P. 190.

Despite the fact that all forms of political participation are biased toward people with more resources, voting is more democratic, relative to other forms of participation, because the poor also vote (albeit at lower rates) due to the fact that it is relatively cheap and easy. We can make voting even more democratic by lowering its costs, say by removing onerous registration requirements or extending voting hours or days. This is what happened in 2020, when voting restrictions were reduced (by allowing no-excuse absentee and mail-in voting due to the COVID-19 pandemic) and voting turnout increased dramatically. The other democratic characteristic about voting is that every vote counts the same. The more people vote in numbers that are equal to their proportions in society, the more the outcome will reflect the true sentiments of the district or nation as a whole. The same cannot be said of contributing money to candidates, attending political meetings, or working for a party or candidate.

Rob Crandall / Shutterstock.com

7.3 Regulating the Electoral Process

Throughout the world, governments decide who is a citizen and who has the right to vote. In the United States, various amendments to the Constitution provide general guidance on who can vote, but the 50 state governments have the authority to establish their own laws governing voter qualifications, voting times, places, and procedures. According to the U.S. Constitution, all persons who are "born or naturalized"[3] in the United States and "who are eighteen years of age or older,"[4] "regardless of race, color, previous condition of servitude,"[5] or sex[6] are qualified to vote. However, the states have been allowed to deny the right to vote for other reasons. For example, state governments can deny voting rights to people who have been convicted of a felony or to those who fail to register. Most recently, some states have passed laws that would deny the right to vote to anyone failing to provide a government-issued photo identification as proof of citizenship.[7]

Determining Electoral Composition

The U.S. Constitution originally said little about who was eligible to vote, leaving authority to the states to set the requirements. Most states allowed only white males–and only those who owned enough property and who were free of debt sufficiently to make them "independent men"– to vote.[8] Women, free blacks, slaves, ex-slaves, and the property-less could not vote in most states, which left the vast majority of people out of the electorate. Property ownership as a requirement to vote was dropped by most states by 1850, but many states used poll taxes to deny the vote to the poor and used literacy and religious tests to prevent immigrants and others from voting.[9] Although the passage of the Fifteenth Amendment prevented states from using race to deny the right to vote, registration requirements, racially biased application of literacy tests, and poll taxes had the same discriminatory effect. Private groups such as the Ku Klux Klan used economic pressures, violence, and other forms of intimidation to fill in the gaps left by state law, effectively denying the vote to black Americans. Similar laws and practices were used across the states to prevent Asians, Mexican-Americans, and Native Americans from voting as well.

Poll taxes were prohibited in federal elections by the Twenty-fourth Amendment and declared unconstitutional by the U.S. Supreme Court for all elections in 1966.[10] The use of literacy tests and other means designed to prevent voting by black Americans and other racial minorities were prohibited by the Voting Rights Act of 1965. Still, states still manage to shape the composition of the electorate by making registering to vote (and therefore voting) less convenient. Those who have registered in the past can be denied the right to vote if they don't bring proper identification to the polls. This happened in Indiana when a group of Catholic nuns in their 80s and 90s from a retirement home were turned away because they didn't have the proper state-issued identification.[11] States can purge voters from voter rolls, making them ineligible to vote in the next election unless they register again. States can also restrict the hours or days that people can vote, making it difficult for college students or people with jobs to make it to the polls on Election Day. As we discussed earlier in the chapter, such laws raise the costs of participation and their effects fall disproportionately on people of lower socio-economic status.

Depressing the Vote

Voter turnout can be expanded by making registration and voting more convenient. On the other hand, turnout is depressed by long lags between voter registration deadlines and Election Day, winner-take-all, single member district election, and when the electoral college determines presidential elections.

stock_photo_world / Shutterstock.com

Long Lags between Elections and Voter Registration Deadlines

Restrictive registration laws affect more than convenience. Long periods of time between registration deadlines and elections can also depress voting. Some states require that voters register 30 days before an election. In other states, voters can register at the polls on Election Day. For example, Arizona and Colorado have similar registration procedures: both require the same documentation and both make registration available online. The major difference is that Arizona's registration deadline is 29 days before the election, while Colorado allows voters to register in person on Election Day. Colorado has more registered voters in part because people tend to procrastinate, but more importantly, because early registration deadlines reduce the mobilization effects of the campaign.[12] In the last days of the election, the candidates, parties, and other groups were highly active, putting ads on TV, handing out flyers, and knocking on doors to inform voters about the candidates and issues (while also reminding them to vote). Twenty-one days before the election, people in both states were thinking of other things and may not have taken the time to register. The campaigns created a great deal of interest and, by Election Day, people were ready to vote. For many in Arizona, however, it was too late because they didn't register 29 days earlier. The campaigns in Colorado, on the other hand, could register voters until the last minute. The shorter the time period between the registration deadline and the election, the more people register. The more people register, the higher the turnout. Registration requirements, more than any other law or regulation, have the greatest impact on the number of people who turn out to vote.[13]

Winner-Take All, Single Member District Elections

plurality

A decision rule in an election in which the candidate who receives the most votes cast (rather than a majority) wins.

single member district

An electoral district represented by only one person in the legislative body.

proportional representation

An election system in which each political party wins seats in the legislative body in proportion to the number of votes it received in the election.

Across the world, democratic nations have developed different forms of voting procedures that determine who wins elections and the way that representation is distributed in a given country's legislative body. In the United States, the national and state governments use a system called "**plurality** vote, **single member districts**."[14] In this electoral system (also known as "first past the post" or "winner-take-all"), one member is elected from each district and the winning candidate is the one who received the most votes among the candidates running for that office. Other nations use various forms of **proportional representation** in which voters vote for a particular political party that presents its candidates to the voters on a list. The parties are awarded seats in the legislative body in proportion to their share of the vote and the winning candidates (those who are elected and get to vote on the laws in the legislature) are taken from the list. For example, if there are 100 seats in the legislature and a party wins 20 percent of the vote, the first 20 people on that party's list win seats. There are several variants of this system, but the important point is that representation is determined by the proportion of votes received in the election.

In most countries, voting is considered a right of citizenship, but it is also considered optional. If you don't want to vote, for whatever reason, you don't have to. In a few countries, however, voting is considered a responsibility of citizenship and is compulsory (just like serving on a jury). In countries where there is a penalty in place for not voting, non-voters may be subject to a fine.

Figure 7.4 shows voter turnout and representation for a selection of industrialized countries.[15] Countries are ranked by their levels of voter turnout, which reflects the average percentage of registered voters casting a vote since 1945. It should be no surprise that the countries with the highest voter turnout are those with compulsory voting. These countries require voting because they believe every citizen has a duty to vote. They increase turnout by making it very costly not to vote. As you can imagine, the penalties are designed to be sufficiently high to ensure near-universal participation.

FIGURE 7.4 Voter Turnout by Voting System

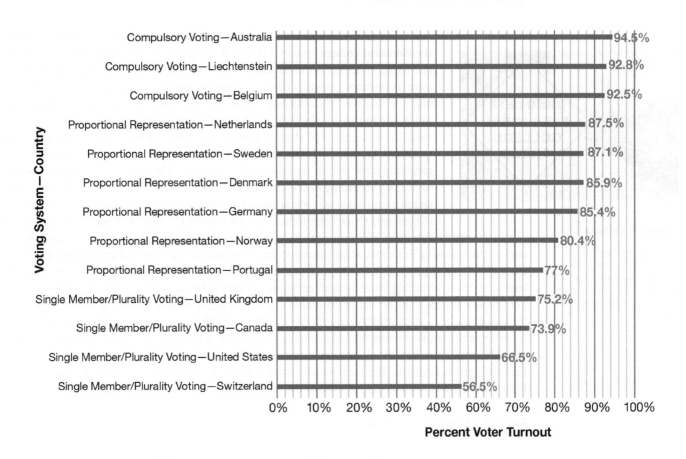

Data from Pintor, Rafael L., Maria Gratschew, and Kate Sullivan. "Voter turnout rates from a comparative perspective." Voter turnout since 1945: A global report. International Institute For Democracy And Electoral Assistance. International IDEA, 2002. Web. 7 Dec. 2014. http:// www.idea.int/publications/vt/upload/Voter turnout.pdf.

The countries in Figure 7.4 with proportional representation systems also have high rates of voter turnout, but for very different reasons compared to nations with compulsory voting. Remember, in a proportional representation system, if a political party gets 20 percent of the vote in the national election, they get 20 percent of the seats in the legislature. The major effect of this system is that the electoral rules encourage the development of multiple parties. Smaller political parties do not need to defeat a candidate from an established party in a specific district in order to win a seat in the legislature. The parties can start small, grow, and establish themselves over time. How does this lower costs for voters? Voters have more parties and candidates to choose from and thus more parties (and volunteers) trying to convince them to participate in elections and vote their way. With a higher number of political parties, voters have more free information, more people to help them register, more understanding of where their interests lie, and more help to find their polling places.

At the bottom of the figure are countries with the lowest rates of voter turnout, which have single member districts with plurality voting systems. In these countries, the voting system encourages the development of a two-party system. These countries have fewer parties because it takes a lot more votes (usually more than 50 percent) to win a district election outright in order to gain a single seat. If a party comes close but ultimately short of a win (say they get 49 percent of the vote in a two-way race), they get nothing (for a more detailed explanation for why this happens, read the discussion of Duverger's law in Chapter 8). In countries with single-member districts and plurality voting systems, there are fewer parties, less free information going to the voters, and fewer volunteers working to get voters to the polls. All this translates to higher costs for the voters and lower turnout at the polls.

The Electoral College

© Shutterstock, Inc.

electoral college

An institution made up of electors from each state that officially elects the president and vice president of the United States.

Every four years, Americans vote for the president and vice president using the **electoral college** system. When Americans vote for the president, they are not really choosing an individual. What they are actually doing is voting for a slate of electors, generally chosen by the candidate's political party, in each state and the District of Columbia. These electors then choose the president. Like much else in the U.S. electoral system, state laws differ on how to choose the electors. Some are selected at state party conventions, while other states allow the respective parties to choose the electors. It is important to note that the electors generally have strong loyalties to their parties. The electors are apportioned to each state according to the number of seats that state has in the House of Representative plus its two Senate seats. For example, Wyoming, with its population of 563,626, gets three votes (one for its member of the House of Representatives plus two for its senators) while California, with its population of 37,253,956, gets 55 votes (53 for its members in the House of Representatives plus two for its senators). The effect of giving each state two for its Senate seats gives states with small populations a disproportionate share of the electoral college vote. Thus, Wyoming ends up with one vote per 187,875 persons while California has one vote per 677,344 persons. The District of Columbia has three electoral college votes, based on its population, as if it were a state entitled to representation in the House of Representatives. The District, however, is not entitled to the two additional votes because it has no representation in the U.S. Senate. The total number of electoral votes equals the number of members of the House of Representatives (435) plus the number of senators (100) plus the three District of Columbia votes for a total of 538 votes. The distribution of the electoral college is shown in Figure 7.5.

FIGURE 7.5 Electoral College with Results of the 2016 Presidential Election

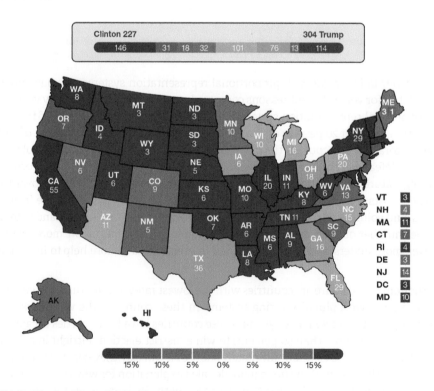

Based on "Historical Timeline: Margin of Victory View," 270towin.com, accessed January 10, 2019, https://www.270towin.com/historical-presidential-elections/timeline/margin-of-victory/.

The winner of the presidential election is not the candidate who wins the most votes cast in the general election. In theory, it is possible to collect enough electoral votes in the smaller states to win the presidency with only 22 percent of the total vote.[16] Rather, the winner garners an absolute majority of votes (270 or more) from the electors of the electoral college. With the exception of Maine and Nebraska, each state's electors are pledged to the candidate who wins the most votes in that state—another winner-take-all feature of the electoral system. However, there is no federal law or constitutional provision that electors must cast their votes according to the **popular vote**.[17] In practice, it is extremely rare that an elector does not vote for the candidate who won the popular vote in their state. After all, the electors are chosen for their partisan loyalty. To make sure that the state's electors remain faithful, 33 states and the District of Columbia bind their electors to vote for party's nominee, a practice that has been upheld by the Supreme Court.[18]

If you watch the election night returns, you will note that the news outlets reporting the election results keep track of both the popular vote and electoral votes each candidate wins on a state-by-state basis. When they calculate that a candidate has won more than 270 electoral votes, the network declares that candidate the winner. In practice, the winner of the electoral college is usually the candidate who wins the most votes in the general election, although five elections (1824, 1876, 1888, 2000, and 2016) produced winners that did not win the popular vote.

To win the presidency under the American system requires a strategy to win a majority of electoral votes. This tends to depress voter turnout. Because the votes are allocated on a winner-take-all basis, candidates for president tend to focus their campaign efforts on winning the most populous states with large blocks of electoral votes. But not every large state is winnable or even potentially winnable by each candidate. Most states are dominated by one of the two major parties. For exmaple, the Democratic Party candidate is likely to win all the electoral votes in California, Illinois, and New York, so the Republican Party candidate spends little time and money campaigning in those states. In turn, the Democratic candidate does not waste time and money in a state they are very likely to win. Similarly, states like Texas and Alabama are dominated by the Republican Party, so the Democratic Party candidate doesn't really try to win electoral votes from those states. This also means that states with small numbers of electoral votes aren't paid much attention. Instead, the entire presidential campaign is focused on the few, winnable, so-called "battleground" states that do not show an obvious advantage to either candidate. In the battleground states, enthusiasm is high, party activity is intense, and free information is plentiful, as is the turnout from these states in the general election. However, these aspects tend to be low in all the other states.

7.4 Is Voting Rational?

Another difficulty the Framers failed to fully consider is the collective action problem confronted by the average voter. The cost-benefit concept of self-interest accurately predicts political participation by assuming that people attempt to maximize the benefits of participation and minimize its costs. This concept explains nicely (together with the character of the U.S. voting system) why so few people vote despite the fact that, compared to other forms of political participation, it is relatively free and easy to do. Hardheaded social scientists take this logic a step further and ask whether voting is even a rational act. If you think of voter turnout in terms of its costs and benefits, it's not obvious why people vote. Ask yourself, what benefits do you get out of an election versus how much it will cost you to participate? To vote you need to register, figure out where to vote, take time out of your busy schedule, go there, and vote. Consider also that you have to bear these costs no matter what the outcome of the election. Calculating the benefits of voting is fundamentally different from the decision to purchase a personal product, such as a smartphone. To economists, these products belong in two separate categories. The smartphone is a **private good** while the election is a **public good**. A private good can be used and consumed exclusively by the purchaser. The more complex nature of a public good can be defined as a product that cannot be used exclusively

popular vote

The vote as expressed by the number of votes cast by the electorate.

private good

An item that can be used exclusively by an individual or group; use or consumption of the item prevents consumption by others.

public good

An item that cannot be used exclusively by an individual or group; use of the item does not prevent the item from being used by others.

after it is produced. After buying the smartphone, you can activate it and use it to store your contacts, music, and photos, and even program it to prevent anyone else from using it. If and when you ever sell, give, or loan it to someone, you lose the ability to use it for yourself.

free ride

Benefiting from resources, goods, or services without contributing to their cost of production.

To the economist, the product of an election is a public good. Public goods are associated with very different kinds of decision-making processes. They also connect to serious collective action problems. It is difficult to think about elections as producing products, but they do. As mentioned earlier, our national elections do not determine the laws and policies of government directly. When voters go to the polls, they decide who their representatives will be. The representatives then go and make laws and policies on behalf of the citizens. Thus, the product of an election is representation and, like all public goods, representation is a shared good. Representation cannot be divided among those who voted and helped produce it. After the election, everyone gets represented regardless of whether they voted. Also, one person's use of representation does not preclude or diminish another person's representation. Economists conclude that when it comes to producing public goods, it is rational to let others do the producing and enjoy the benefits for free, knowing that the product cannot be divided or consumed by just those who produced it. Why vote when you can **free ride** on the efforts of others? Why vote when you will get representation nevertheless? This is the collective action problem faced by average voters in elections.

Rob Crandall / Shutterstock.com

If you are not yet convinced that voting is an example of irrational behavior, consider the one thing you know, or at least suspect, about elections: your vote has only a tiny, almost immeasurably small probability of being the deciding vote that puts your candidate over the top. If you understand the American political system and are realistic, you know that most candidates win by thousands of extra votes. In the 2000 election, only 537 votes gave George W. Bush the presidency. He took Florida's 25 electoral college votes over Democratic challenger, Al Gore. Still, that means that the probability that any one voter influenced the election was 1/537 or about .002 percent. Across the country, the margins were much greater. In Texas, for example, George W. Bush won by 1,365,893 votes. The probability of one voter making a difference in that state was 1/1,365,893 or .0000007 percent. From the standpoint of cost-benefit self-interest, many of his supporters wasted their efforts. They could have stayed home and the outcome would have been the same. So why do people—Republicans, Democrats, and independents alike—vote in presidential elections in states like Texas despite knowing which candidate is likely to win? It is possible voters are delusional or that they become that way because their hopes are raised to unrealistic levels by campaign promises, but this is hardly rational behavior, at least in the strict cost-benefit sense.

The reality is that millions of American citizens do vote despite being tempted to free ride and knowing that their individual vote is unlikely to make a difference. In the 2020 presidential election, some 155.5 million Americans, or about 66.7 percent of eligible voters, showed up at the polls. So what explains this seemingly irrational behavior? The most accepted social scientific explanation of voter turnout is civic duty.[19] For most voters, the personal satisfaction derived from expressing themselves politically outweighs the relatively low cost of going to the polls. This explains why seemingly modest social pressures play a large part in stimulating voter turnout—from family and friends who note that by voting, they are performing their duty, to the deliberate efforts of celebrities (recall the Gyllenhal-Sarsgarrd dialogue at the beginning of this chapter), political activists, and institutions of all kinds to get people to vote. If participation were caused by self-interested behavior, why are these external motivations effective or even necessary?

Your teachers likely told you, starting in elementary school, that when you turned 18 you should be a good citizen, take your responsibility as a citizen in a representative democracy seriously, and vote. Many of your friends, family, neighbors, and co-workers have done the same. Unfortunately, this sense of citizenship is not distributed evenly across society. As we discussed earlier in the chapter, those of higher socio-economic status show higher levels of citizen duty than those of lower status.[20] This finding adds to the explanation of why some social groups participate more than others.

Elections are better understood as rituals or symbols that give citizens a chance to express general discontents and enthusiasms with the state of public affairs. In contrast to the assumptions of the Framers, most Americans are engaged in politics for symbolic reasons rather than from an innate love of politics or robust self-interest. This more accurate understanding of elections as symbolic rather than instrumental places only minimal expectations on the citizen to know and understand the consequences of his or her decisions. One can satisfy one's duty at low cost (or the cost of a little prodding), but the real problem is that most citizens vote with scant information. In truth, they have little reason to bear the information costs associated with discerning the candidates' true characteristics, where they stand on the issues, or how competent the incumbents may have been as political leaders.

7.5 Deciding How to Vote: The Problem of Adverse Selection

In an episode from the animated TV series *Futurama*™, Leela, Fry, and Bender are watching two candidates debate on TV.

> Candidate Jack Johnson: *"It's time someone had the courage to stand up and say, I'm against those things that everybody hates."*
>
> Candidate John Jackson: *"Now I respect my opponent, I think he's a good man, but quite frankly, I agree with everything he just said."*
>
> Fry: *"These are the candidates? They sound like clones."* After looking closer: *"Wait a minute, they are clones!"*
>
> Leela: *"Don't let their identical DNA fool you, they differ on some key issues."*
>
> Candidate Jack Johnson: *"I say your 3-cent titanium tax goes too far!"*
>
> Candidate John Jackson: *"And I say your 3-cent titanium tax doesn't go too far enough!"*[21]

You decided to do your duty and vote. In the voting booth you are faced with a long list of candidates for national, state, and local offices. How do you decide? Earlier we discussed the problem of moral hazard, but this is a different problem that voters must confront: the possibility of making the wrong choice. Like the problem of moral hazard, this one is also sufficiently common that social scientists have given it its own name: **adverse selection**. The source of this problem is the same as that of moral hazard: incomplete or hidden information. Do you have enough information to know which candidates for all these offices will best serve your interests?

adverse selection

Making a choice contrary to one's interest due to incomplete or hidden information.

third parties

A person or group that is independent of the two parties involved in a particular situation or dispute. Also, an alternative to the two major parties in a two-party system.

The problem is not unlike one we discussed earlier involving your decision to purchase a smartphone. You could go online and find information from the manufacturer, but you know that its website, which seems to be filled with objective information, is mostly a form of advertising. As a sophisticated consumer, you know that a seller has an incentive to tell you the good things about their product and hide the bad. You can do additional research by looking for reviews and opinions from **third parties**, but it will be impossible to find all the information given your busy life and limited time.

How Voters Decide

A good clue about how much time voters devote to following politics is provided by the U.S. Bureau of Labor Statistics' American Time Use Survey. On an average day in 2017, Americans slept for about 8.8 hours, worked for 3.6 hours, spent 1.8 hours doing household activities, and 5.2 hours doing leisure and sports activities. The remaining 4.6 hours were used for eating and drinking, attending school, and shopping. Those that spent time on organizational and civic activities did so for an average of .15 hours, or about 9 minutes per day.[22] It is safe to say that politics is remote among the concerns of most Americans most of the time.

That said, most American adults do watch network newscasts during the course of a month (65 percent). A substantial minority (38 percent) watches cable news.[23] News about government and politics accounted for 16.4 percent of the leading topics on network evening television news.[24] Still, there is little evidence that the political knowledge of the average American is detailed or sophisticated. In the 2017 Pew Research Center News IQ quiz, only 45 percent of Democrats and 52 percent of Republicans could correctly identify Justice Neil Gorsuch as a Supreme Court justice.[25] Given the reality that most Americans are engaged in politics for symbolic reasons (to express their citizenship), rather than from rational self-interest, this lack of sophistication is understandable. Besides, politics, policy, political institutions, and their procedures and relationships are confusing.

Because politics is remote and inherently unclear, deciding how to vote doesn't justify a lot of research. The reality is that most people vote rather casually by using simple decision rules or mental shortcuts that simplify the work of making rational choices. Such rules work well under most circumstances, but some work better than others.

Ideology

Many Americans rely on ideology to make political choices. An **ideology** is a group of related ideas about government and politics that help people understand and make decisions about political events. These include notions about the proper role of government and thus the nature and extent of public policies. The two major ideologies in the U.S. are **liberal** and **conservative**. With regard to public policies, liberals generally favor governmental intervention in the economy, the expansion of social services, and greater concern for consumers and the environment. They oppose government involvement in religious institutions and expression. Liberals also tend to identify with the Democratic Party. Conservatives, on the other hand, tend to believe that government policy poses a threat to citizen freedom, especially the freedom of employers to make contracts with their employees and sellers to make contracts with buyers without undue restrictions imposed by government regulations. Generally speaking, conservatives believe that most solutions to social problems should come from the private sector, but they do see a strong role for government in keeping the social order by, for example, restricting abortions, limiting marriage to those of the opposite sex, and supporting prayer in school and other public places. Conservatives also tend to identify with the Republican Party.

The use of ideology as a mental shortcut to voting works fairly well. During a campaign, the press often mentions which candidates are liberal or conservative and their policy stances are often labeled as such. Political advertisements from supporters, opponents, and the candidates themselves use ideology as a means to sway voters. In 2020, 89 percent of voters who considered themselves liberal voted for Joe Biden, while 85 percent of conservatives voted for Trump.

The problem is that most Americans are not particularly ideological and they do not develop or use ideology in a meaningful way. According to the Pew Research Center, in 2014, only 12 percent of Americans were consistently liberal, while 9 percent were consistently conservative (see Figure 7.6). This leaves 79 percent of the public in the "mixed" range: they were mostly consistent in their liberalism or conservatism, or they did not use an ideology.[26] In general, the ideological orientation of the American public is moderate. Political scientist Morris Fiorina and his colleagues wrote: "Americans are closely divided, but we are not deeply divided … because we instinctively seek the center while the parties and candidates hang out on the extremes."[27]

ideology

A set of integrated ideas about the extent and purpose of government.

liberal

An ideology in the United States associated with the Democratic Party that tolerates the use of government power to bring about equality and consumer/environmental protection, but which is hostile to the use of government power to impose religious criteria on individual behavior.

conservative

An ideology in the United States associated with the Republican Party that is hostile to the use of government power to bring about equality and consumer/environmental protection, but which tolerates the use of government power to ensure domestic and international order.

FIGURE 7.6 The Ideological Distribution of the American Public
Notes: Ideological consistency based on a scale of 10 political values questions. (See Appendix A for details on how the scale is constructed and how scores are grouped.) Source: 2014 Political Polarization in the American Public.

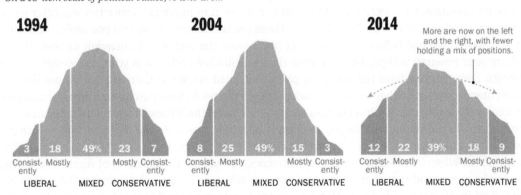

Adapted from "Political Polarization in the American Public." Pew Research Center, Washington, D.C. (June 12, 2014) http://www.people-press.org/2014/06/12/political-polarization-in-the-american-public/.

Partisan Identification and Loyalty

Americans are not particularly ideological, but they are somewhat partisan. The American National Elections Study reports that, currently, about 35 percent of Americans identify strongly or weakly with the Democratic Party, while 27 percent identify strongly or weakly with the Republican Party (see Figure 7.7). Only 14 percent of the American public describe themselves as completely independent of party affiliation. This distribution has been stable for nearly one-third of a century.[28]

FIGURE 7.7 Distribution of Partisan Identification from 1998-2012

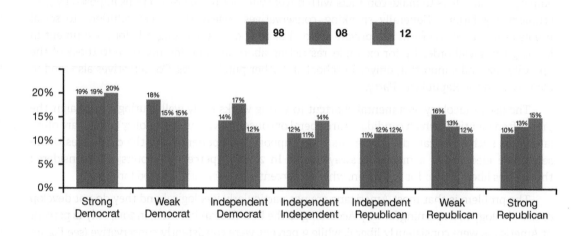

Data from Voting and Registration in the Election of November 2016. https://www.census.gov/data/tables/time-series/demo/voting-and-registration/p20-580.html

party identification

The political party with which an individual most closely identifies.

standing decision

A temporary decision.

Just because one identifies with a political party does not mean that one is wedded to it. **Party identification** simply represents the party that one supports most often. It represents a **standing decision**: you may consider yourself a Democrat, but that doesn't mean you won't vote for a Republican. For example, if during the next election you note that the Democrats are in control of government but the economy is poor, you might vote for the Republicans in hopes that they will improve the economy.

As a decision rule or mental shortcut, party identification works for voters like brand names work for consumers. For example, let's revisit the decision to purchase a smartphone. After some research you decide to buy an Apple iPhone. These phones are not cheap and you understand that it will take some time before the benefits of purchasing the phone will outweigh its cost. This is where your research will pay off. Still, your time was limited and so was your knowledge of electronics. Smartphones have thousands of parts that must work together and even more lines of computer code to make their software work properly. You could have purchased a smartphone produced by some other maker, but chances are you purchased the iPhone at least in part because you trusted the brand name. Your family or friends have iPhones and they told you that the phone worked well for them, or maybe you own an iPad or an Apple computer and that product satisfied your needs. When it comes to consumer electronics, you are a loyal customer of Apple. Executives at Apple understand that this is how products are selected. They work to protect the company's brand by making good products. This knowledge boosts your confidence that you made a good choice.

You do not need to be an electrical engineer or computer scientist to buy a good smartphone. Similarly, you do not have to be a political scientist to cast a reasonable vote. You can use a candidate's political party as a mental shortcut the same way you rely on a brand name to purchase a product or service. The candidate's party membership is listed on the ballot. It is possible for you to return home on Election Day after a year-long adventure in Antarctica out of the range of communication satellites and still make a reasonably informed vote. Party identification is the single most important shortcut that voters use. With it they can make fairly accurate predictions about how a candidate is going to act once in office. Unlike average Americans, professional politicians have and use well-developed ideologies. Before voting, you know that the Democrats will be reliably liberal while the Republicans will be reliably conservative. You will know this without doing research.

Evidence about the effect of party identification on voting for president, senators, and representatives is illustrated by Table 7.1. Across all offices, party identification is a highly accurate predictor of how someone will vote. From 1948 to 2012, 85 percent of Democrats voted for Democratic presidential candidates and 92 percent of Republicans voted for Republican candidates. In 2020, 94 percent of Democrats voted for Clinton while 88 percent of Republicans voted for Trump.[29] Party identification remains an accurate predictor as one moves down the ballot, from the candidates for Senate to those running for the House of Representatives.

TABLE 7.1 Voter Identification and Vote for President, Senate and House of Representatives (1948-2012)

Respondent's Party Identification	Party of Respondent's Vote for President	
	Democrat	Republican
Democrat	85%	15%
Independent	43%	57%
Republican	8%	92%

Respondent's Party Identification	Party of Respondent's Vote for Senate	
	Democrat	Republican
Democrat	86%	14%
Independent	53%	47%
Republican	16%	84%

Respondent's Party Identification	Party of Respondent's Vote for House of Representatives	
	Democrat	Republican
Democrat	86%	14%
Independent	53%	47%
Republican	17%	83%

Data from Center for Political Studies, University of Michigan, American National Election Study ANES Times Series Cumulative Data (1948-2012) Democrats: strong, weak & independent Democrats combined, Republicans: strong, weak, and independent Republicans combined. Independents: independent independents.

Issue and Policy Concerns

incumbent

An elected official currently holding office.

Besides ideology and party identification, many voters use their concerns about issues and policies to make their choices. This can be done generally, or a voter can make his or her choice contingent on a candidate's stance on one or several specific policies. For example, a voter can decide to vote for an **incumbent** because economic conditions have improved or, if the voter is avidly "pro-life," he or she can choose based on whether the candidate supports making abortions illegal.

Retrospective and Prospective Judgments

retrospective judgments

Judgments made by voters based on an incumbent's past behavior.

Voters often make **retrospective judgments** (conclusions regarding the past) by assigning responsibility for the general current political, social, or economic environment to an incumbent running for reelection. The approach is akin to doing what presidential candidate Ronald Reagan asked voters during a presidential debate in 1980: "Are you better off now than you were four years ago? Is it easier for you to go and buy things in the stores than it was four years ago? Is there more or less unemployment in the country than there was four years ago? Is America as respected throughout the world as it was? Do you feel that our security is as safe, that we're as strong as we were four years ago? And if you answer all of those questions 'yes', why then, I think your choice is very obvious as to whom you will vote for."[30] Reagan asked voters to think about the immediate past because he knew that voters would find an unhealthy economy, that Jimmy Carter had canceled America's participation in the Moscow Olympics over tensions with the Soviet Union, and that 53 Americans were being held hostage by Islamic militants in Iran.[31]

prospective judgments

Judgments made by voters based on assumptions about a candidate's promise of future behavior.

Retrospective judgments are fairly easy and accurate to make for groups of incumbent legislators or maybe for incumbents. One can know, or at least sense, the general state of social affairs and can, to a certain extent, assume that those in office had something to do with this. It is, however, difficult to conclude that an individual officeholder had much to do with the state of the economy or world peace. This is why incumbents running for reelection in bad times try to distance themselves from the immediate past by asking voters to think about the future. When voters make decisions based on their predictions about the future behavior of candidates, they are making **prospective judgments**. In 2020 two related issues were most important to the voters, the COVID-19 pandemic and rebuilding the economy. For those believing that containing the coronavirus even if it hurts the economy was important, 79 percent voted for Biden, for those who believed that rebuilding the economy was more important, 78 percent voted for Trump.[32]

Judgments Based on Specific Policies

Voters also make choices contingent on candidates' stances on specific issues or policy positions. An issue can be any source of conflict over the course of public policy. Many can be controversial. For example, laws restricting or loosening access to guns or abortions are frequently controversial. Debates over taxes or measures designed to reduce global warming can also be contentious. In order for a voter to make a decision, he or she must be able to compare positions to those of the candidates. However, even if issue voters have clear opinions on their issues of concern, the candidates may not. Differentiating the isue positions of one candidate from the others can be difficult. In the 2016 election, the issue of immigration was the important issue to about 13 percent of voters. Those voters voted 64 percent to 33 percent for Donald Trump.[33]

The Median Voter Theorem and Candidate Convergence

Even if the candidates are sincere, it will be hard to tell the differences between candidates' issue positions because public policies are complex and subtle answers to difficult questions are hard to comprehend. More importantly, the behavior of candidates on the campaign trail makes it difficult for voters to tell them apart. In a two candidate race, competition between the candidates has the effect of pushing candidates toward issue preferences taken by moderate voters in their district. Political scientists call this the **median voter theorem**.[34] Both candidates have a strong incentive to be moderates, or at least to sound like moderates, relative to the issues, in order to appeal to as many voters as possible (see Figure 7.8).

FIGURE 7.8 Candidate Issue Positions Often Converge on the Median Voter
Competition has the effect of pushing the candidate toward the middle of voter preferences.

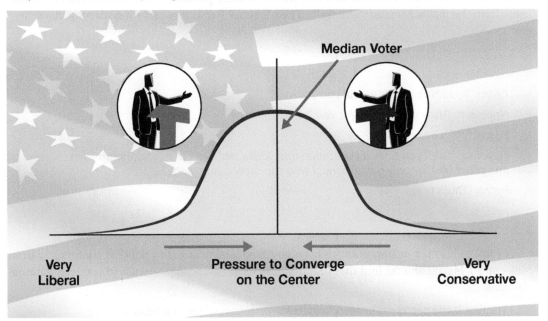

Images from © Shutterstock, Inc.

This difficulty can be shown if we consider a single issue in a single district. The incumbent in this district has decided to retire and two relatively unknown candidates are running for the **vacated seat**. One candidate is a liberal Democrat; the other is a conservative Republican. Both candidates have hired campaign consultants to advise them on how to attract a majority of voters. The consultants find that the district is evenly divided between Republican and Democratic voters. The ideological distribution in the district is unremarkable. About 10 percent of the district's residents are hard-core conservatives, while 10 percent are committed liberals. The consultants classify the remaining 80 percent of the voters in the "mixed" range, with moderates making up the largest group at about 40 percent. The big issue in the district is gun control. The consultants find that a local TV station has taken a poll asking the question: "In general, do you think laws covering the sale of guns should be made more strict, less strict, or kept as they are now?" The poll finds that that 25 percent of the district's voters want laws that are less strict, another 25 percent want laws that are stricter, while 50 percent want the laws kept the way they are. Before learning about the poll, the Democratic candidate favored stricter gun laws and the Republican candidate wanted the laws to be made less strict. Both candidates' consultants advised their clients to moderate their positions and adopt the position that the area's gun laws should be kept as they are.

median voter theorem

A theory that predicts that a candidate seeking a majority of votes will adopt a policy position preferred by those in the middle of the ideological spectrum.

vacated seat

A position within a representative institution of government that is no longer occupied.

Avivi Aharon / Shutterstock.com

This is exactly what the median voter theorem predicts: both candidates will moderate their positions and converge toward the issue position of the median voter in order to attract the most votes and avoid offending the majority of voters. From the perspective of democracy, this finding may be good for the district. If the winning candidate sticks to the policy positions taken during the campaign, he or she will maximize the policy preferences of the district's voters. The median voter theorem, however, goes a long way to explaining why candidates end up sounding the same during elections, why politics and policy is more confusing than it could be, and why it is difficult for voters to match their issue positions with the true positions of the candidates.

Candidate Characteristics

Some voters make their decisions based on the candidates' personal characteristics, as in this dialogue from the movie *Napoleon Dynamite*. The character Pedro is considering running in a school election.

> Pedro: *"You think people would vote for me?"*
>
> Napoleon: *"Heck yes! I'd vote for you."*
>
> Pedro: *"What are my skills?"*
>
> Napoleon: *"Well you have a sweet bike, and you're really good at hooking up with chicks, and you're like the only guy at school who can grow a mustache."*
>
> Pedro: *"That's true."*

Pedro's skills may be important to his high school classmates, but political scientists Warren Miller and J. Merrill Shanks find that four dimensions are especially relevant to voters in national elections:

1. The first is the perceived honesty and trustworthiness of the candidates.
2. Second is competence, usually involving the perceived knowledge and relevant experience of the candidate.
3. Third, voters look for leadership qualities, which they sometimes find in inspiring speakers.
4. Fourth, voters look for an element of compassion in their candidates.[35]

These four characteristics imply a common marketing strategy for campaign advertising. Candidates emphasize their empathy, experience, morality, and ability to lead. They attempt to define their opponents as corrupt, unqualified, unfeeling, and treasonous.

Surprisingly, exit polls taken during the 2016 presidential election found that less than 40 percent of voters said that Donald Trump was "honest and trustworthy" and only about the same number thought he was "qualified" to be president.[36] More voters believed that Hillary Clinton "cares more about me" (57 percent) and "has good judgment" (65 percent). Even more puzzling is the fact that 90 percent of voters believed that Clinton had the "right experience." But the quality that mattered most to voters was the perception that Trump was the candidate that could "bring change."[37]

These events suggest another decision rule that voters use to judge candidates: they find similarities between themselves and the candidates. In doing so, they presume that the candidate also has similar views about politics compared to their own. In 2012, for example, the fact that Mitt Romney's estimated net worth was more than $200 million didn't help the majority of Americans relate to him.

Beyond socio-economic status (usually based on income, wealth, and education), Americans classify themselves in terms of race, ethnicity, religion, and gender. They match these identities with those of the candidate when voting. For the candidate, this implies another balancing act as reflected in this exchange between *The Daily Show's™* former host Jon Stewart and its former Senior Black Correspondent, Larry Wilmore, before the 2008 presidential election:

> Wilmore: *"This isn't science fiction Jon, its politics. ... right now, only 20 percent of black voters support Obama. That's bad, but is it bad enough for him to win?"*
>
> Stewart: *"I'm sorry, bad enough to win?"*
>
> Wilmore: *"The last thing a black candidate wants is to be seen as the black candidate.... It works like this: for every three black votes you get, you scare away five white votes. Do the math: the black support is only worth about three-fifths as much as white support."*[38]

According to the exit polls from the 2020 presidential election, white Americans mostly voted for Donald Trump (58 percent) while 87 percent of black Americans, 65 percent of Latinas/os, and 61 percent of Asians voted for Joe Biden. Most of those earning under $100,000 voted for Biden, while those earning more than $100,000 favored Trump.[39] Most men (53 percent) favored Trump, while women tended to vote for Biden (57 percent). White born-again or evangelical Christians (about 28 percent of those polled) voted overwhelmingly for Trump (76 percent).

a katz / Shutterstock.com left; mark reinstein / Shutterstock.com right

Cognitive Dissonance Theory

There is reason to doubt that voters can be objective about the candidate's behavior based on his or her personal characteristics. One explanation for the impact of beliefs on voting behavior is cognitive dissonance theory, which postulates a human need for mental harmony or consistency in opinions, attitudes, knowledge, and values. The theory predicts that individuals who like a candidate, for whatever reason, will subconsciously bring their perceptions of the candidate's position on issues in line with their own preferences. In other words, if you like a candidate's smile, hair, personality, or other characteristics, you will strive subconsciously to believe that the candidate believes in the same things that you do. You may also discount information that does not fit your beliefs about the candidate. You will not want to deal with the fact that you like a candidate, but you don't like their politics, so you conveniently change your perception of the candidate's beliefs to match yours. This alleviates the discomfort of having inconsistent feelings.[40]

That is what happened when committed Democrats voted for Ronald Reagan. Reagan was personable, looked good on TV, and had the poise that came with his experience as an actor. When pollsters asked voters who liked Ronald Reagan and also believed in strong unions if they believed that Reagan also supported strong unions they said he did. As a conservative Republican, Reagan was suspicious of the power of unions. As president, he fired 11,000 federal air traffic controllers for going on strike, significantly weakening their union.[41] The voters in question were actually wrong about Reagan, but they predictably changed their perceptions of his position on unions to fit their own to avoid feelings of conflict. When voters like candidates, for whatever reason, it is hard for them to be objective about the candidate's true policy positions.

7.6 Does It Matter Who Participates?

In 1961, political scientist Robert Dahl posed the following question: "In a political system where nearly every adult may vote but where knowledge, wealth, social position, access to officials, and other resources are unequally distributed, who actually governs?"[42] In 1999, Molly Ivins answered Dahl's question: "We live in a state where a woman with two children on welfare gets $188 a month; that's not a week, that's a month for food, clothing, and shelter. It makes a lot of difference if there is somebody in the legislature saying they need a raise."[43]

Dahl's question and Ivins' answer are even more important to consider today. According to economist Thomas Piketty and his co-authors, inequality as measured by wealth and income in the United States is at its lowest point since Dahl posed his question.[44] Americans were more equal in the 1950s, '60s, and '70s than any time in U.S. history. Income inequality began to change in the 1980s and has skyrocketed since then. In 2012, the top 10 percent of Americans took home more than 50 percent of the nation's total available income (wages, salaries, dividends, interest payments, and capital gains).[45] The levels of inequality are worse when economists consider wealth (how much people own) or all forms of income, but even when confined to income generated by work (just wages and salaries), they find the United States to be a "hyperinegalitarian" society. This means it has levels of inequality "probably higher than in any other society at any time in the past, anywhere in the world."[46] Over the same time period, political campaigns have become more expensive and the lobbying activities of corporations, professional groups, and trade associations have grown relative to those of unions and public interest groups.[47] It is no accident that inequality and the political influence of the wealthy increased after tax rates for the top incomes were lowered in the 1980s. Those who benefited from the changes in tax laws then invested some of their windfall in more campaign contributions and more lobbyists to support further policies beneficial to them, becoming even richer (see Figure 7.9).

FIGURE 7.9 Share of Total U.S. Income (Top Earners)

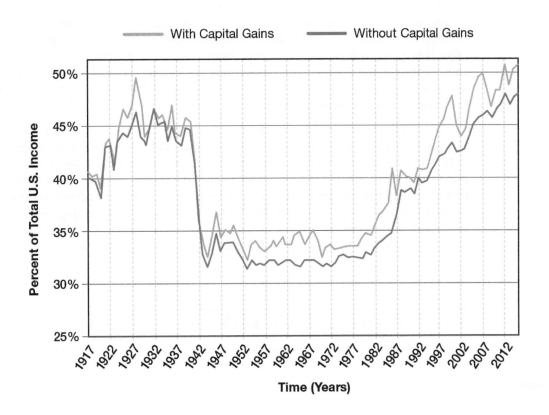

Data from Saez, Pikettey: https://eml.berkeley.edu/~saez/saez-UStopincomes-2015.pdf.

Political participation matters. As we have discussed, participation is unequal and systematically biased in favor of those who can better overcome its costs, meaning those with higher incomes, education, and other positions associated with high socio-economic status. Conversely, participation is biased against those who are less privileged. Unfortunately, as political scientist V. O. Key said 65 years ago, "The blunt truth is that politicians and officials are under no compulsion to pay much heed to classes and groups of citizens that do not vote."[48]

What about the fear that maximizing voter turnout will bring out citizens with little interest and knowledge in government, who will likely cast an uninformed vote? Such fears are misplaced, as those paying attention to this chapter should already know. Citizens with little interest and knowledge of government describes the vast majority of voters. Expectations about knowledgeable voters also ignore the effects of collective action problems faced by voters. Bringing more voters into the electorate will only make outcomes more equal and reflective of the true desires of the people. There is also good evidence that voting stimulates participation in other political activities.[49]

Much of the analysis in this chapter leads to conclusions that are somewhat troubling: most Americans are uninformed and inactive; many do not bother to vote; and those who do often vote casually by using mental shortcuts like ideology and party identification. Voters who try to use issues to make a decision are commonly confused by their complexity or the convergence of the candidates toward the median voter. They may also fall prey to cognitive dissonance. Perhaps most disturbing are the costs of participation and the biases that result.

Still, over time American society has moved closer to its democratic and egalitarian ideals. Property ownership, poll taxes, literacy, and religious tests have all been repealed as barriers to voting. Every adult over 18 has the right to vote, regardless of race or sex. In most states, thanks to the National Voter Registration Act, Americans can register to vote online or by mail. They can also register to vote when they renew their driver's licenses or conduct other routine business with state government. Additionally, the internet has made political information more readily available to voters interested in educating themselves.

If you are worried about uninformed non-voters suddenly voting and destabilizing the political system, researcher Ruy Teixeria found that even in the case of 100 percent voter participation, the outcome of most elections would not have been different. What is more, voters do seem to hold office holders accountable for their policy decisions. When researchers investigated the relationship between an incumbent's performance in the U.S. Congress using election data between 1956 and 1996, they found the incumbent receiving a lower vote share each time he or she strayed from the wishes of the local district voters.

There is also evidence that voters respond to political messages in fairly sophisticated ways. In their experiments, a team of political scientists did not find voters to be as ill-informed about candidates and issues as much of the literature suggests. Rather than immediately forgetting political information, most people appear to integrate immediately the critical parts of their assessments into a "running tally," which is stored in long term memory, while the details contributing to the evaluation are forgotten. When called on to make judgments in the voting booth, the summary impression of the candidate comes to mind. Voters may not be able to recall specific campaign events, but they seem to respond to political messages in a meaningful way.

7.7 What Can I Do?

name recognition

The extent to which a person's name on the ballot is familiar to the voters.

Vote and get others to do so. After trying to convince you that voting is an irrational act, why would we encourage you to vote? While voting may not do much for you personally, elections mean a great deal to society. The paradox of voting is that it provides large collective benefits but small individual ones. Yet, this does not mean that voting is not about you. There are some benefits. Doing your duty as a citizen may not be inconsequential for you. Cost-benefit analysis cannot be fully calculated for everyone because the benefit part of the equation is determined individually. Some people derive a good deal of satisfaction from doing their duty; some like being part of something larger than themselves. Voting reflects positively on our respective levels of self-esteem and that can have a positive effect on our future happiness. While we can't accurately calculate these intangible benefits, we do know that they don't have to be too substantial to provide positive benefits. This is because the costs of voting are low. It also makes the friends, family, and colleagues that are cajoling us to vote happy when we do. Getting others to vote also multiplies the benefits. Consider the following when weighing the costs and benefits of getting involved:

- How much time are you willing to devote to the act of voting? Do some research, locate your polling place, and calculate the time it will take you to get there. Will you drive, take the bus, or walk? Depending on the time of day you go to vote, estimate how much time you expect to wait in line to cast your ballot.

- Think about your friends and roommate(s) and their schedules. What do you think you could say or do to convince them to vote?

- Have no remorse about using mental shortcuts when voting. Voting doesn't have to require a lot of research on your part. Third parties, groups, or individuals independent of the candidates can help reduce the uncertainties associated with voting. This is why many people consult dining guides before trying new restaurants, or read reviews before going to the movies. Similarly, various groups—from the League of Women Voters to the Tea Party Patriots—will be happy to provide you with voting guides. Do some research and find a group that you trust. Let them educate you for free, or pick a party and make choices based on that party identification (as most voters do).

Act locally and run for political office. According to the Census of Governments, there were 493,830 state and local offices subject to election. These include governors; state legislators; and state-wide officials such as attorneys general, county supervisors, sheriffs, tax assessors, most judges, mayors, city councils, and school boards.[50] Chances are good that there is a political office in your area that you could run for and win. It will help if your party, race, or ethnic group matches that of the majority of the district's voters. Many of these offices are non-partisan, meaning that your party affiliation will not be listed on the ballot. If this is the case, you will have to campaign to develop **name recognition** or run for office a few times before you win. Campaigning door to door is not uncommon in small districts. Becoming known to regular participants by going to local political events and meetings helps a great deal.

All this seems like a lot of work. How can the benefits of being elected to political office possibly outweigh the costs? The answer is that the benefits of being an elected official are private. Unlike the benefits of voting, which are public, those associated with holding office—fame, prestige, privileges, salary, and per-diems—need not be shared. The costs of winning office may be high, but the benefits can be too. Because they will be all yours, the rational calculation may work in your favor even without considering intangibles (like the benefit of doing your citizen duty). If serving the public as an elected official is burdensome, why do so many compete so hard to be elected?

7.8 What's the Alternative?

The key to helping voters make better decisions is to make elections more competitive. Competition provides a solution to the problem of moral hazard because the people who want the incumbent's job have a strong incentive to monitor his or her behavior and tell voters all the things the incumbent did wrong before the next election. Thus, to be reelected, a representative must take care not to abuse his or her power, because those faults will be the subject of campaign advertisements funded by challengers. For the same reasons, competitive elections also provide a solution to the problem of adverse selection by reducing the likelihood that voters will choose a dishonest representative in the first place. We learned that most voters reduce the time and effort it takes to make voting decisions by using mental shortcuts such as party identification. Parties thus have a strong incentive to protect their brand names (by keeping their candidates in line) to help you make an easy and reliable choice in each election. How can political institutions be redesigned to help lower the costs of engagement in order to reduce biases that favor those segments of society with greater resources? Below are some suggestions.

Suggested Improvement	How It Works	How It Helps
Proportional Representation	Parties win seats in the legislative body in proportion to their share of the vote received in the election	• Encourages the development of multiple political parties • Stimulates voter participation by offering more choices* • Provides voters with more free information/ volunteers that can help them to register and understand where their interests lie • Gives voters a chance to vote sincerely
Make Voter Registration Less Restrictive	Increases turnout and makes the political system more democratic	• Historically, registration requirements were a method of preventing some people from voting; since the passage of the National Voter Registration Act of 1993, 141 million voters have used the registration services the Act provides[51] • States could increase voter turnout by 9.1 percent if reforms to make registration more convenient were adopted[52]

*Comparative politics research shows that moving to a proportional representation system would boost voter turnout between 9 and 12 percent. [53]

These are just two examples of reforms that can increase voter turnout, but there are many others, including:

- expanding early voting
- expanding voting hours
- expanding the number of voting days
- expanding the number of languages used on ballots
- expanding mail-in voting

Has your home state or school state implemented any of these reforms? What other types of voting reforms do you think would increase voter turnout? For more information, check out FairVote at www.fairvote.org or the Brennan Center for Justice at www.brennancenter.org/issues/voting-reform-agenda.

Endnotes

1. *The Simpsons*™. "Mr. Spritz Goes to Washington." Season 14 Episode 14. Directed by David Sliverman. Written by Dan Greaney. Fox, March 9, 2001.

2. K. L. Schlozman, S. Verba, and H. Brady, "The current state of civic engagement in America," September 1, 2009, http://www.pewinternet.org/2009/09/01/the-current-state-of-civic-engagement-in-america/.

3. U.S. Const. amend. 14.

4. U.S. Const. amend. 26.

5. U.S. Const. amend. 15.

6. U.S. Const. amend. 19.

7. A. Liptak, "Supreme Court Allows Texas to Use Strict Voter ID Law in Coming Election," *The New York Times*, October 18, 2014, http://www.nytimes.com/2014/10/19/us/supreme-court-upholds-texas-voter-id-law.html?_r=0.

8. "Shays' rebellion: America's First Civil War," *The History Channel*, April 13, 2006, https://images.history.com/images/media/pdf/ShaysRebellion.pdf.

9. B. Rowen, "U.S. Voting Rights," Infoplease, October 18, 2014, http://www.infoplease.com/timelines/voting.html.

10. *Harper v. Virginia Board of Elections* 383 U.S. 663 (U.S. 1966).

11. "Nuns with Dated ID Turned Away at Ind. Polls," NBCNews.com, May 07, 2008, accessed October 24, 2018, http://www.nbcnews.com/id/24490932/ns/politics-decision_08/t/nuns-dated-id-turned-away-ind-polls/#.W9C7q3tKiCg.

12. This is not to say that registration requirements alone explain registration, other factors such as the age of population and citizenship also need to be considered. Still, about 70 percent of Colorado's citizens were registered in 2012 versus 57 percent in Nevada. http://www.census.gov/hhes/www/socdemo/voting/publications/p20/2012/tables.html

13. S. J. Rosenstone and H. M. Hansen, *Mobilization, Participation, and Democracy in America* (New York: Macmillan, 1993), 230.

14. Two states, Louisiana and Georgia, hold run-off elections if no candidate receives more than 50 percent of the vote and technically the two U.S. Senators in every state share the entire state as a district so these might be considered multi-member.

15. Rafael L. Pintor, Maria Gratschew, and Kate Sullivan, "Voter turnout rates from a comparative perspective," *Voter Turnout Since 1945: A Global Report,* International Institute for Democracy and Electoral Assistance, April 2004, https://fortunedotcom.files.wordpress.com/2014/04/voter_turnout.pdf.

16. Cooper, Ryan. "Which States Got Screwed Worst by the Electoral College in 2016?" The Week - All you need to know about everything that matters. The Week, December 7, 2016. https://theweek.com/articles/665750/which-states-got-screwed-worst-by-electoral-college-2016.

17. "About the Electors," National Archives and Records Administration, 2012, http://www.archives.gov/federal-register/electoral-college/electors.html#selection.

18. "What Are Faithless Electors in the Electoral College? (2020)." Accessed January 1, 2021. https://ballotpedia.org/What_are_faithless_electors_in_the_Electoral_College?_(2020).

19. Raymond E. Wolfinger and Steven J. Rosenstone, Who Votes? (New Haven, CT.: Yale University Press, 1980).

20. Ibid.

21. Futurama™. "Decision 3012." Season 7 Episode 3. Directed by Dwayne Carey-Hill. Written by Patric M. Varrone. Fox, June 27, 2012.

22. "American Time Use Survey – 2017 Results," Bureau of Labor Statistics, U.S. Department of Labor, June 18, 2014, http://www.bls.gov/news.release/pdf/atus.pdf.

23. K. Olmstead, M. Jurkowitz, and J. Enda, "How Americans Get TV News at Home," Journalism.org, October 11, 2013, http://www.journalism.org/2013/10/11/how-americans-get-tv-news-at-home/.

24. "Leading Topics," Pew Research Center's Journalism & Media, July 16, 2012, http://www.journalism.org/2012/07/16/leading-topics/.

25. Samantha Smith, "From Brexit to Zika: What Do Americans Know?" Pew Research Center for the People and the Press, July 25, 2017, accessed June 05, 2018, http://www.people-press.org/2017/07/25/from-brexit-to-zika-what-do-americans-know/.

26. "Political Polarization in the American Public," Pew Research Center U.S. Politics & Policy, June 12, 2014, http://www.people-press.org/2014/06/12/political-polarization-in-the-american-public/.

27. M. P. Fiorina, S. J. Abrams, and J. C. Pope, Culture War? The Myth of a Polarized America (New York: Longman, 2005), xiii.

28. "The American National Election Studies Guide to Public Opinion and Electoral Behavior: Party Identification 7-Point Scale 1952-2016," November 7, 2014, https://electionstudies.org/resources/anes-guide/top-tables/?id=21.

29. "National Exit Polls: How Different Groups Voted." The New York Times. The New York Times, November 3, 2020. https://www.nytimes.com/interactive/2020/11/03/us/elections/exit-polls-president.html?action=click.

30. "October 28, 1980 Debate Transcript," Commission on Presidential Debates, October 28, 1980, accessed October 24, 2018, http://www.debates.org/index.php?page=october-28-1980-debate-transcript.

31. "The election of 1980," American Experience, November 7, 2014, http://www.pbs.org/wgbh/americanexperience/features/general-article/carter-election1980.

32. "National Exit Polls: How Different Groups Voted." The New York Times. The New York Times, November 3, 2020. https://www.nytimes.com/interactive/2020/11/03/us/elections/exit-polls-president.html?action=click.

33. Ibid.

34. A. Downs, (1957), An Economic Theory of Democracy (New York: Harper and Row, 1957).

35. W. E. Miller and M. J. Shanks, The New American Voter (Cambridge, MA: Harvard University Press, 1996).

36. Chris Cillizza, "The 13 most amazing findings in the 2016 exit poll," The Washington Post, November 10, 2016, accessed June 06, 2018, https://www.washingtonpost.com/news/the-fix/wp/2016/11/10/the-13-most-amazing-things-in-the-2016-exit-poll/?utm_term=.0878800cbed9.

37. "Exit polls," CNN Politics, 2016, accessed June 6, 2018, https://www.cnn.com/election/2016/results/exit-polls.

38. The Daily Show™. "Hybridization." Season 12 Episode 21. Directed by Chuck O'Niel. Written by Steve Bodow. Viacom, February 12, 2007.

39. Ibid.

40. Leon Festinger, A Theory of Cognitive Dissonance (Stanford, CA: Stanford University Press, 1957).

41. M. Murrmann, "33 Years Ago: Reagan Goes Union-Busting, Fires 11,000 Striking Air Traffic Controllers," Mother Jones, August 5, 2014, http://www.motherjones.com/mixed-media/2014/08/reagan-fires-patco-air-traffic-controllers.

42. R. A. Dahl, Who Governs? (New Haven, CT: Yale University Press, 1961), 1.

43. Last Man Standing: Politics Texas Style, directed by Paul Stekler (2004; PBS/POV).

44. T. Piketty and A. Goldhammer, Capital in the Twenty-First Century (Cambridge, MA: Belknap Press/Harvard University Press, 2014).

45. E. Saez, Striking it Richer: The Evolution of Top Incomes in the United States, UC Berkeley, June 30, 2016, https://eml.berkeley.edu/~saez/saez-UStopincomes-2015.pdf.

46. T. Piketty and A. Goldhammer, Capital in the Twenty-First Century (Cambridge, MA: Belknap Press/Harvard University Press, 2014), 244.

47. n.d., https://www.opensecrets.org/.

48. V. O. Key, Southern Politics in State and Nation (New York: Knopf 1949), 527.

49. G. A. Almond and S. Verba, The Civic Culture: Political Attitudes and Democracy in Five Nations (Thousand Oaks, CA: SAGE Publications, Inc., 1989).

50. "Popularly Elected Officials," 1992 Census of Governments, May 17, 1995, http://www.census.gov/prod/2/gov/gc/gc92_1_2.pdf.

51. Ari Berman, "How to Make Voting Easier," The Nation (blog), May 20, 2013, http://www.thenation.com/blog/174431/how-make-voting-easier#.

52. R. E. Wolfinger and S. J. Rosenstone, Who Votes? (New Haven, CT: Yale University Press, 1980), 73, 88.

53. A. Lijphart, "Unequal Participation: Democracy's Unresolved Dilemma," American Political Science Review 91, Vol. 1 (1995): 1-14.

CHAPTER 8
Political Parties: Making Politics Cost Effective

Chapter Objectives

1. Learn what parties are and how they encourage popular participation.
2. Identify how parties promote collective action and responsibility in a democratic society.
3. Understand how groups and individuals identify or associate with political parties.
4. Discover why there have been only two major parties throughout U.S. history.
5. Assess whether the parties are becoming more radical.
6. Explore how parties build and rebuild national majorities over time.
7. Reflect on the future of the Republican Party after the 2016 presidential election.

Introduction: Political Parties and Popular Participation

© Shutterstock, Inc.

"Hello? You play to win the game. You don't play to just play it."[1] Coach Herm Edwards said this about the National Football League, but winning is also central to political parties. Jim Nicholson, former chairman of the Republican National Committee, echoed Edwards' sentiments when he said winning is "the measure that should be used to gauge my effectiveness. Are we going to win more elections than we lose? And by winning elections, you're winning with the people who carry forward our Republican ideas and our Republican philosophy, and they carry it then into public office and then implement public policy that directly affects people and citizens; they make the laws that we all have to live by."[2] Nicholson's statement is one that is expected to come from the head of a political party, but people seem to want more from their political leaders. They want political leaders to represent the country's interests and govern accordingly, not just win elections and carry out one party's policies. A 2017 poll conducted by the Pew Research Center showed that only 40 percent of the American public had a favorable impression of the Republican Party. With a 44 percent rating, the Democrats didn't fare much better.[3]

separation of powers

A principle of the Constitution that declares that political power is to be shared among the three branches of government.

federalism

A political system in which authority is shared between a central government and state or regional governments.

divided government

Times when different parties control different branches of government.

party systems

A dynamic (changing) set of supportive coalitions assembled by the political parties for the purpose of governing at different points in history.

coalition

A collection of groups working together for a common political goal.

These sentiments have led to a new political movement called "No Labels." The group supports "political leaders who are willing to put country before party."[4] They strongly believe that partisan loyalty is the major barrier to progress in American politics because too often, partisans dismiss or ignore the ideas of others. It is likely your teachers in elementary, middle, and high school said something similar and advised that, when you are old enough to vote, you should vote for individuals who will best represent the concerns of the whole community, not those of a political party or group.[5] Interestingly, the No Labels group identifies elected officials who support their philosophy with a trademarked "problem solver" seal displayed on their campaign materials and website.[6] They also encourage and support groups and students to start their own chapters in their communities and schools. They want to create statewide organizations in every state ... just like a political party.

Still, the statement of the former chair of the Republican Party captures precisely what effective parties are *supposed* to do. The purpose of the party is to win elections, and not just some elections: the objective is to win enough elections so that its members end up with a majority of offices in an institution of government, such as the House of Representatives and/or Senate—or, even better, the presidency. Their ultimate goal is to unify the institutions of government to overcome gridlock caused by the **separation of powers**, **federalism**, and **divided government.** In this way, the party will have the authority to carry out its preferred laws and policies.

In stark contrast to most citizens, many political scientists like political parties. Respected political scientist E. E. Schattschneider wrote, "Political parties created democracy and ... democracy is unthinkable save in terms of parties."[7] If you think political life would be better without them, you would have an argument with another respected political scientist, V. O. Key, who said: "[O]rganized parties ... do better than a disorganized politics in producing candidates and public officials who are technically competent, personally stable and trustworthy, and capable of working with others to carry through long-term governmental programs."[8] Indeed, the one time political scientists tried to push for institutional reform of the American political system, they did not look for a way to place individuals over party. They saw the American parties as too weak to function properly and openly recommended changes to make them stronger.[9]

All of this raises a number of questions: Why do many Americans seem to hate the parties? Why is the "No Labels" movement trying to get people to shun labels while attempting to get voters to use *their* label? And why did political scientists think parties were so great that they once left their universities to lobby Congress to make those parties stronger?

The answers may surprise you, in part because parties are different compared to most institutions in our society. They are big, open, highly visible, and encompass the full range of political life. Competitive parties are important to the proper functioning of a democratic nation, just like business competition drives the effective operation of a market economy. The parties were created to meet the needs of professional politicians. These politicians, however, lost control over their parties' most important decision: nomination for office. The parties' most important resource—to control the personnel in government—is now in the hands of the voters in primary elections. Political parties are not formal parts of the government (they are not purely private institutions, either). The national and state governments heavily regulate political parties. These parties have been shaped profoundly by grassroots political movements in American history.

In this chapter, we will elaborate on these points and discuss **party systems**, times when the control of the government changed from one party to the other and the system remained stable, for a while. This may seem like a history lesson, except we will describe how political parties have formed majority **coalitions**, or different groupings of the American public large enough to govern the country, and how these coalitions have changed over time. The purpose of this lesson is to see how political parties adjust to changes in our society and how they help resolve crises and conflicts in a relatively peaceful manner. Parties continue to adapt; indeed, some of the most dramatic changes have taken place in the last 30 years and continue today.

8.1 Political Parties and Popular Participation

What Are Parties?

In the United States, political parties are completely open institutions. There are no requirements to meet, fees to pay, forms to sign, or cards to carry. One does not even need permission from the party to run for office under its name. For ordinary citizens, parties offer an effective way to participate in politics, in whatever way an individual finds most appropriate. For those with the time and energy, parties provide a means to increase one's political voice through active participation in party activities at the local, state, or national levels. With much less effort, one can be a loyal member by supporting a party, just as a devoted fan backs his or her favorite sports team. Unlike the sports fan, however, the ordinary citizen who supports a party is not a passive spectator. He or she helps determine whether the team wins by voting and getting others to do so. Lastly, one can stay aloof from party involvement by remaining independent. Like a picky customer, a person can show approval or disapproval of a party's choices by voting—offering or withdrawing support and even giving that support to the other party if that person chooses.

© Shutterstock, Inc.

Parties are not mentioned in the Constitution, yet they are very much part of the process of governing. James Madison and the other Framers were wary of any organized groups, or "factions," as Madison called them. They believed that factions were motivated by specific interests and thus contrary to the general interests of the community as a whole. This notion of interests organized as factions even applied to winning political parties that arguably represent a majority of the citizens.[10] George Washington captured this anti-party sentiment in his farewell address when he declared that "the spirit of party" in democratic form was society's "worst enemy."[11] Yet, the very same politicians who were suspicious of their existence created parties almost immediately after the formation of Congress. Parties formed to help like-minded politicians to agree over policy issues and create a working relationship among themselves. Parties expanded when they provided politicians with a means to organize a mass electorate during elections.

Parties also help with similar problems among ordinary citizens. They lower information costs for busy and distracted citizens by nominating candidates and focusing attention on a small number of would-be office seekers. Parties do much to overcome voter apathy by generating enthusiasm prior to elections and bringing voters to the polls. They educate individual citizens on the issues and the stakes involved in an election. They provide a brand name to make it easy to identify their candidates and an ideology to help voters know and predict the parties' positions on the issues. Using these tools, a voter can cast a reasonably informed vote. Parties also form majorities by drawing together groups of individuals working toward a common goal. Because parties use votes as their primary political resource, they offer the potential for the mass of regular people to make their voices heard above the few with extensive financial resources. In theory, parties provide perhaps the only means to join a fragmented government and move it in a single direction. Political parties do a lot to make our political system work better. We should probably appreciate their work more than we do.

People often think of a political party as a large interest group. It is true that both political parties and interest groups are collections of citizens who join together to influence the decisions of government. Both work to get their preferred candidates elected to office, and both remain involved after elections to influence public officials and citizens and get their preferred policies adopted by government. There is, however, an important difference between the two, beyond the party's larger size. The objective of the political party is to influence the decisions of government across a broad range of policies, not just within a particular area of policy. Parties do this by helping to elect enough of their members to an institution of government (like the House of Representatives) to potentially control that institution's votes. The Republicans achieved this objective in the House of Representatives after the 2010 midterm elections and in the Senate in 2012. They maintained their majorities after the midterm elections in 2014 and in 2016 gained control of both houses of Congress and the presidency. Democrats regained control over the House of representatives in 2018 and control of both houses of Congress and the presidency in 2020. If the Republicans vote together, as partisans often do, they control the legislative and executive branch of the federal government. The ultimate goal of a political party is to control all of the government's institutions to overcome barriers to majority rule imposed by the separation of powers and federalism. This potential to overcome the separation of powers helps to explain why the public is suspicious of political parties: people are understandably wary of the power of government, even when the party represents the interests of a majority of U.S. citizens.[12] Indeed, many Americans seem to like the idea that divided government (when different parties control different branches of government) serves as an additional check on power, even if the party in power is supported by a majority of voters.[13]

Parties and Popular Participation

Because political parties are open institutions designed to win elections, they function to expand the electorate. For parties in competitive contexts, larger is better and more is merrier. Close competition compels party leaders to enlarge their bases of support. Persuading more voters in new locations to vote with for the party results in more elections won. This means that building support by attracting voters from the lower socio-economic segments of society works about as well as building support from the top down. Indeed, the party as a means to power is a strategy traditionally used by working-class groups that must organize large numbers of individuals to counter their opponents' superior wealth.

Perhaps the best thing about political parties is that they provide a way for ordinary citizens to control the government. They do this by making it possible for the electorate to hold the party in power responsible for its actions. As political scientist E. E. Schattschneider pointed out, "The people are a sovereign whose vocabulary is limited to two words, 'yes' and 'no.'"[14] With these two words, the voting public can discipline a party that has failed to manage the government by saying "no" and voting the party out of office. Alternatively, if things have gone well the voters can say "yes" to the responsible party and reward it for good service by keeping it in office until the next election. With all due respect to the "No Labels" group and to your elementary, middle, and high school teachers, their faith in the electorate's ability to promote better representation by supporting candidates independent of parties is misplaced. It may be possible for voters in individual districts to communicate their preferences and hold their own members of Congress accountable, but is it fair to hold a single member responsible for the failures (or successes) of the entire government?

A democratic government puts the people in charge. If we are to take that idea seriously, there should be a way for citizens to hold the Congress as a whole accountable for the condition of the country, or at least to hold it responsible for the actions of government. After all, only the legislature can exercise the full powers of government—the power to compel action through legislation and to ensure compliance through taxing and spending. What the people need is the ability to promote collective responsibility. Political parties offer that possibility.

Advocates for more responsible parties want to fix the powers of government in the hands of the winning party. Ideally, the party that wins a majority of support among the voters would also win the presidency and a majority of seats in both branches of Congress. This way it would be clear to the voters which party is in control of policy and, consequently, who would be accountable to the voters. This would not give absolute power to the majority party; civil liberties and rights would still exist, as would the power of the Supreme Court to interpret and prevent the Congress or the executive from violating those rights. Most importantly, the party holding power would have control of government for only a limited time. In the next election, if the voters were displeased with the party's performance, they could vote it out and put the other party in charge.

In the time between elections, parties would continue to do what parties do: compete for attention. The party in power would have to govern under the watchful eyes of their opposition looking for evidence to convince the electorate to return that party to power in the next election. Remember that the minority party still sits on every congressional committee and is thus well placed to criticize what the government is doing while offering its alternative. This results in lots of free information for the public, relayed by the media. For the sake of ratings and readership, media outlets have an incentive to make known to their audiences all the bits of disagreement. Voters are admittedly uncomfortable with conflict, but can't help but watch when quarrels occur. Citizens benefit when the press monitors and broadcasts the actions of their representatives. High visibility expands knowledge of legislative conflict, mobilizes individuals and groups to engage in political action, and leads them to attract newcomers to politics to support their side. Party competition and conflict is inherently democratizing because, potentially, it puts the voters in charge.

Why Parties?

Under the right conditions, political parties provide a way for ordinary citizens to control the government. Citizens reward the party in power by retaining the party's members in office (if things go well) and by punishing the party's members through voting them out if (if things go badly). This raises an important political question: it may be reasonable to expect an elected official to be held accountable for his or her own actions, but why would individuals in office or running for office agree to be held accountable for the actions of their party?

When politicians work as a party and challenge the public to vote them out if they break their collective promises, they link their careers to their success as a group. From the perspective of the individual candidate, this seems to be an irrational act. The more rational strategy would seem to be neutral and campaign as someone who would put the interests of the district above those of the party. A compelling campaign promise would sound like this: "I generally agree with my party but, as a responsible representative, I should see the details of the actual bills after they come out of the committees and determine how they are going to affect my district before voting." This tactic is especially persuasive in districts where party competition is close and gaining the support of independents is vital to winning elections. Knowing that political parties are somewhat unpopular and that many voters want their representatives to stand for their district's interests over all others, this strategy seems less risky. Once in office, the representative could then wait to see if the proposed legislation remains popular. If so, the representative can vote for those items with substantial support and claim credit in the next election; if not, he or she could vote against them and avoid having to justify an unpopular stance. The interesting thing about this logic is that it applies to each member of Congress. All members have the incentive to wait and share in the benefits produced by successful collective action, but few are motivated to risk their jobs by stepping forward, putting forth the effort to bring the items to a vote, and then sharing the credit with everyone who eventually supports the legislation if it passes.

If candidates find it advantageous to run their own campaigns, downplay their party affiliations, and, once in office, to free ride on the efforts of others, why should they tie their careers to a political party? If parties are not mentioned in the Constitution and are not a part of government, why do they exist at all? They did not rise out of the public's desire to concentrate power, rather, political parties were created by the very politicians that kept them out of the Constitution. They did it almost immediately after the first Congress met, too.

To understand why parties formed, we need to more fully appreciate the problems and goals of elected officials. It should be no surprise that politicians generally want a stable career as well as the power and prestige that holding office brings. This necessarily puts their primary focus on not only election, but also re-election, which requires that they win and continue to win favor among the voters in their districts. However, in pursuing this goal, politicians face a dilemma: they are all motivated to play it safe and free ride on the efforts of others, but if they all pursue this strategy, nothing will happen. Thus, to keep their jobs they are compelled to find some way to cooperate and produce something they can claim has benefited their constituents in the next election. As such, they not only put their careers in the hands of the voters in their districts, but also link their futures to their fellow politicians and, in particular, to the leaders of their party. These leaders include party leadership in Congress or state legislatures, the president or their state's governor if he or she is a member of their party, and the members of their respective national and state party committees.

It should further come as no surprise, then, that political leaders have devised ways to harness the ambitions of their like-minded colleagues to form majorities around a common agenda and hold the group together long enough to formulate, pass, and implement legislation. Those that follow the leaders understand they can't do much alone, so they agree to work with the group and share the credit should their efforts lead to success. Over time, the need to produce steady results leads to the formation of durable groups coalesced around a general set of ideals and principles about the nature of government (otherwise known as an ideology).

8.2 Parties and Collective Action in Government

Political parties were created by politicians to make it possible for them to work together to produce the things they need to gain and hold office.[15] They are especially necessary in large political institutions like the House of Representatives, but they also perform similar functions within the smaller Senate. They link partisans in Congress to members in the executive branch and across the 50 state governments. Keep in mind that the party organizations across all these institutions are independent of each other. There is no commander-in-chief or central committee that creates a detailed agenda and issues orders about what, how, and when things should be done. Members of Congress are not selected by their party; rather, they are elected by winning primary and general elections in their home districts. Even if there happened to be a single leader or small committee in charge, they could not punish disloyal members by denying them the thing they want most: their jobs. Only the district voters can do that, which makes parties in the United States inherently weak. Across both state and federal government, parties are held together mostly by their ideologies (see Chapter 6 for a refresher on the conservative and liberal ideologies in the United States).

Still, within individual institutions, such as Congress, the parties are well organized. Each party's members meet in separate conferences (called a caucus by the House Democrats) to select their leaders. They then develop a strategy for transferring their ideas into legislation and moving it through the assembly. For the most part, the majority party in the respective chamber dominates this process. In each chamber, the majority party has the votes to elect its top leader to be the assembly's leading political officer: the Speaker of the House of Representatives and the Majority Leader in the Senate. The majority party also gets to have majorities on most of the committees and their choice of who will chair these committees. This gives party leaders significant control over the institution's operations, including control of the institution's agenda.

Ultimately, the party's success in getting its agenda passed through Congress will depend on the degree of unity among its members. In this regard, each party has resources that it uses to keep its members in line. In their respective conferences, the parties choose assistant leaders called **whips** who inform the members about the party's positon on each piece of legislation and persuade them to vote accordingly. They have campaign committees (headed by still more assistant leaders), which can provide financial support (or not) in the next election. Party leaders have the power to assign members to committees and they have influence over who becomes a committee chair. Committee assignments can be critical to individual members. For example, a representative from a corn-growing district in Illinois would want to be on the House Committee on Agriculture and someday be its chair. This member will have to show loyalty to the party to get what he or she wants.

whips

Assistant party leaders who inform members about the party's positon on each piece of legislation and persuade them to vote accordingly. Whips also keep count of how each member intends to vote and report the results to the rest of the party leadership.

jctabb / Shutterstock.com

Within their own party, the president is also an important leader. Soon after the development of the parties, the president came to be personally identified with the party. In recent years, presidents have also worked hard to help Congressional candidates get elected and re-elected. They draw big crowds on the campaign trail and large donations at fund-raising events. Even when President George W. Bush's ratings were at an all-time low, for example, he continued to raise millions for his fellow Republicans.[16] To the extent that the president is popular in a particular representative's state or district, the member will want to support their initiatives.

8.3 Party Identification Among the Voters

Still, the most important resource the party gives politicians lies outside of the institutions of government: a large group of voters who identify with a political party and stand ready to support its candidates. To gain and retain their jobs, office seekers must persuade voters by the thousands to vote for them. Presidential, senatorial, and candidates running for state-wide offices in most states need votes by the millions. This massive collective action problem is mostly solved when they run as members of a political party. In any given district across the country, most voters identify with one of the two major parties and usually vote for their party's candidates. Once an individual develops an attachment to a political party, he or she tends to remain loyal. This means that candidates for office don't have to start from scratch to build a following in every campaign. Given that one of the two major parties is usually dominant in any district, the majority needed to win an election may already reside in their area as self-identified partisans. The catch is that in most districts, would-be office seekers must first fend off other party candidates in primary elections (or caucuses) before they can run as the party's nominee in the general election.

Party identification is a psychological attachment, not formal membership. Many states do not require voters to specify which party (if any) they identify with. Those that do often don't update their lists. Most importantly, members do not have to vote for their party's candidates. Some people have strong attachments to their party and will vote for its candidates despite knowing almost nothing else about them. For others, party identification is more like a standing decision. They usually vote for their party's candidates but may vote for another party's candidate if they prefer that person. They may even consider joining another party, and perhaps will if their current party or another party gives them sufficient reason. Party identifiers make up the vast core of the political parties in the United States.

About one-third of all Americans admit to having a strong attachment to their party while another third believe their connection is moderate. Even those that classify themselves as being independents admit to leaning toward one of the parties.[17] It is helpful to think of party identification as similar to the loyalties that people develop for a sports team or a genre of music. Strong party affiliations can approximate the loyalties one feels for his or her community, ethnic group, or even religion.

Identification with a political party is often made early in life, well before one is eligible to vote. Children are strongly influenced by their families and tend to embrace their sentiments about most things, including politics. The sooner one adopts a partisan identification and the longer one holds it, the more stable it will become.[18] Because one party tends to dominate in a particular area, a community's political attitudes will reinforce those held by the bulk of the population. In local schools, students will learn about war, inequality, social relations, and history. These lessons will be associated with the actions of government and political actors, but most teachers avoid linking these ideas with the political parties. In general, schools do not challenge the prevailing political attitudes of their local communities.[19] Churches, on the other hand, differ in their association with the political parties. Some religious traditions steer clear of political issues, while others feel no reluctance to preach party politics. Party loyalties are often sustained after one leaves his or her home community because people tend to gravitate toward others like themselves. Thus, friends, relatives, and coworkers often share the same partisanship.[20]

FIGURE 8.1 Strong Groups for the Democratic and Republican Parties
Note: Whites and blacks include only those who are not Hispanic; Hispanics are of any race. Asians are non-Hispanic and English-speaking only. Source: All Pew Research Center political surveys from 2014. Based on the general public.

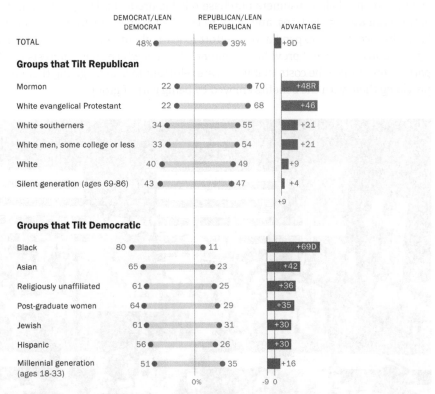

Adapted from "A Deep Dive Into Party Affiliation." Pew Research Center, Washington, D.C. (April 7, 2015) http://www.people-press.org/2015/04/07/a-deep-dive-into-party-affiliation/.

Like communities, social groups tend to associate with political parties (see Figure 8.1). Such affiliation is not official; rather, it is an empirical observation that most black Americans, for example, tend to align themselves with the Democratic Party. Latinas/os also lean toward the Democrats or rather lean against the Republican Party, with the exception of Cuban-Americans. Asians also lean toward the Democratic Party. On the other hand, the Republican Party has an advantage among non-Hispanic white voters. This advantage grows in the South where whites lean heavily toward the Republicans regardless of education or income. Men divide themselves more or less equally between the two parties, but many more women identify with the Democratic Party. Considering race makes a difference in how the men and women are divided between the two parties. While all men are about equally divided between the two parties, non-Hispanic white men are much more likely to identify as Republicans. On the other hand, non-Hispanic white women are more or less evenly divided between the two parties.[21]

Generally, the more college education one has received, the more one tends to identify with the Democrats. On the other hand, the older one gets, the more one tends to identify with the Republican Party, although this support declines among the oldest Americans. Younger people tend to be the least likely to identify with any party and often consider themselves to be independents. Some religious groups lean toward one party. For example, Mormons and white evangelical Protestants lean Republican, while Jews and those with no religious affiliation lean toward the Democrats.[22] In terms of income groups, the old stereotype still tends to apply: the more affluent groups tend to lean toward the Republican Party, other things being equal. Keep in mind that seldom are things equal. For example, Asians lean toward the Democratic Party despite having above average household incomes. Similarly, affluent people in states like New York and California lean Democratic, while their well-off counterparts in southern states tend to identify as Republicans.[23]

Identifying with a party places a person in the political world and, as such, party identification is enormously helpful to ordinary voters in dealing with politics. As we discussed in Chapter 6, voters face collective action problems. Political issues are not only ambiguous but also distant from the daily concerns of most people. Parties make voting choices easier by providing a name linked to a national organization, which helps voters make cost-effective decisions in much the same way as brand names help consumers purchase reliable products. The parties register voters, generate enthusiasm during elections, and work to get their people out to vote. While the average citizen lacks the incentive to expend a lot of effort to learn about political issues, the parties compensate by educating voters and providing a channel through which their interests can be expressed. The parties thus reduce the costs that voters are reluctant to bear by giving them free information and providing them with the benefits enjoyed by being part of group.

Joseph Sohm / Shutterstock.com

None of this happens by accident. The parties are an elaborate collection of organizations at town, city, county, state, and national levels. Some of these organizations are highly professional: they have full-time staff and permanent headquarters, particularly at the state and national levels. Other party organizations use unpaid or part-time staff and set up temporary quarters during elections. All party organizations work with volunteers and other groups interested in the party's issue priorities. The goal is to help the party's candidates (who usually have their own sources of campaign support) win elections, so these representatives can carry the party's issues into office and translate them into official government policy.

8.4 Parties as Service Institutions

Local Party Organizations

The organizational structure of parties roughly corresponds to electoral districts. The lowest level of the party would be at the precinct, ward, or township level, followed by the city, county (congressional district in some states), state, and national levels. Local committee leaders are normally elected or appointed by higher state party officials. At this level, most of the members are volunteers who work to recruit other volunteers to register, canvass, and get voters to the polls.

State Party Organizations

State level party organizations help local committees with voter mobilization, but they also recruit candidates for statewide offices and key state legislative seats. Since the 1980s, state parties have established permanent headquarters with professional staffs and healthy budgets. They have provided their candidates with money, training, and research to help them run more competitive campaigns. Fielding better candidates and linking them to corporate donors, organized groups, and local voter mobilization programs not only establishes statewide partnerships and builds the organization, but increases a party's chances of winning up and down the ballot.[24] State parties are responsible for organizing the state's conventions, drafting the **party's platform** (the policies the party intends to put into effect should its candidates win office), selecting representatives to serve on the party's national committee, and selecting many of the delegates and alternates for the party's national convention. The state parties also select those who will vote on behalf of the party in the Electoral College.

> **party platform**
>
> An officially adopted set of proposed actions, goals, or policies that the party intends to put into effect should its candidates win office.

In other nations, political parties are considered private institutions. In the United States, however, the parties are considered quasi-public agencies and are regulated by the state governments. This oversight began with the introduction of the Australian ballot in the 1890s, when most state governments took over the task of printing the election ballots. Prior to this time, the parties made their own ballots and gave them to their supporters who then dropped them into the ballot box. Naturally, these ballots only included the names of their party's candidates. Because the government now prints ballots with the names of candidates and their parties, it is an open question as to what constitutes an officially recognized political party and whose names should appear on the ballot. Most states resolve this issue by automatically putting a party's candidates on the ballot if they won a specified percentage of the vote in a statewide race in the previous election. This percentage varies from 20 percent in Alabama to less than 1 percent in Michigan and New Mexico. In Vermont, Mississippi, and Florida, an established party can stay on the ballot indefinitely.[25] Automatic ballot access helps the major parties protect their dominance. New parties seeking ballot access must first obtain signatures from a significant percentage of voters in the last election. The number of signatures required varies among the states, but the thresholds are determined by partisan legislators who have little incentive to encourage competition from additional parties.

© Shutterstock, Inc.

8.5 Why Are There Only Two Major Parties?

Leaders in the Democratic and Republican parties are not too worried about competition from another party even though the public holds them in low regard. A solid majority (59 percent) say a third party is needed.[26] From time to time, new parties do form and, despite state barriers, manage to make a difference. For example, Ralph Nader ran as a presidential candidate for the Green Party and made it on the ballot in 43 states, winning enough votes to swing the 2000 presidential election in favor of George W. Bush.[27] Still, for most of its history, the United States has had only two major political parties. Why?

The most common answer has to do with the way elections are organized and how the winners are determined. At the national level, each of the 435 members of the House of Representatives is elected from a single-member district. Similarly, about 85 percent of the representatives to the state legislatures are elected from single-member districts.[28] According to **Duverger's law**, the pervasive existence of such districts in Congress and across the states more or less determines that only two parties will exist.[29] This is simply the effect that comes with the fact that in these districts only one candidate can win, leaving those who come in second or third with nothing to show for their efforts.

Duverger's law suggests that parties and office seekers will see no point in running in districts where they do not have a shot at winning a **plurality** or majority of votes. If candidates try to beat the odds, voters would rather not waste their votes on candidates with little chance of winning. In other words, even if some voters are sympathetic to third-party candidates, they will instead vote insincerely for one of the two major party candidates rather than live with the possibility that their third and least favored candidate wins the election. If third-party candidates were to win a few districts, it is unlikely that they would gain enough seats to make an impact in a state legislature or even a city council. Without substantial numbers in such institutions, it would be almost impossible for the party to make good on the promises it made to supporters.

The election of state governors tends to reinforce this effect because the media pays scant attention to third parties, giving them little opportunity to make their issues known statewide. Running for president as a minor party candidate is even more daunting. Forty-eight states give the candidate who won the most votes all of their delegates to the Electoral College. The remaining two states apportion their delegates by congressional district but, once again, a candidate must come in first in the district to win anything. As a result, no third party candidate has won a single state in the Electoral College. The two parties have also been adept at absorbing issues raised by third parties, thereby preventing third parties from capitalizing on new political movements for long.

Still, even with only two parties, the political system has been remarkably competitive. Counting the 36 presidents by party since 1872, a little more than half have been Republicans, while the rest were Democrats. Some presidential elections have amounted to a popular vote landslide, such as when Democrat Lyndon Johnson won by more than 23 percent in 1964, but Ronald Reagan brought the Republican Party back in 1984 with an 18-point margin over Democrat Walter Mondale. This was only a few years after the party suffered significant losses related to the Watergate scandal. It appears the losing party is able to even the score in a relatively short time, even after a big loss. Overall, the average difference between the two-party vote in presidential elections since 1872 was only about 2 percent (see Table 8.1). In the last 20 years, the average difference between the two-party vote in presidential elections has been only 4 percent. The 2000 election between George W. Bush and Al Gore was a statistical tie and, four years later, Bush's popular vote margin was the smallest ever achieved by an incumbent president. Barack Obama's popular vote total was only about 3 percent larger than Mitt Romney's in 2012, and in 2016, Hillary Clinton received 3 million more popular votes than Donald Trump. In 2020 a record voter turnout during a pandemic pro-

Duverger's law

This political concept suggests that the pervasive existence of single-member districts structured by plurality rule essentially determines that only two political parties will exist.

plurality

A decision rule used to determine the winner of an election whereby the victor is the candidate with the most votes.

duced more votes than any election since 1900 yet the total vote difference between the Joe Biden and Donald Trump was less than 5 percent.

TABLE 8.1 Percentage of the Two-Party Vote for President by Party since 1872
1912 and 1924 election consolidated

Year	Party	Percent Vote	Party	Present Vote	Percent Difference
1872	Republican	56%	Dem., Liberal Rep.	44%	-12%
1876	Republican	48%	Democratic	52%	3%
1880	Republican	50%	Democratic	50%	0%
1884	Republican	50%	Democratic	50%	1%
1888	Republican	50%	Democratic	50%	1%
1892	Republican	48%	Democratic	52%	4%
1896	Republican	52%	Dem., People's	48%	-4%
1900	Republican	53%	Dem., People's	47%	-6%
1904	Republican	60%	Democratic	40%	-20%
1908	Republican	55%	Democratic	45%	-9%
1912	Republican + Progressive	55%	Democratic	45%	-10%
1916	Republican	48%	Democratic	52%	3%
1920	Republican	64%	Democratic	36%	-28%
1924	Republican	54%	Democratic + Progressive	46%	-9%
1928	Republican	59%	Democratic	41%	-18%
1932	Republican	41%	Democratic	59%	18%
1936	Republican	38%	Democratic	62%	25%
1940	Republican	45%	Democratic	55%	10%
1944	Republican	46%	Democratic	54%	8%
1948	Republican	48%	Democratic	52%	5%
1952	Republican	55%	Democratic	45%	-11%
1956	Republican	58%	Democratic	42%	-16%
1960	Republican	50%	Democratic	50%	0%
1964	Republican	39%	Democratic	61%	23%
1968	Republican	50%	Democratic	50%	-1%
1972	Republican	62%	Democratic	38%	-24%
1976	Republican	49%	Democratic	51%	2%
1980	Republican	55%	Democratic	45%	-9%
1984	Republican	59%	Democratic	41%	-18%
1988	Republican	54%	Democratic	46%	-8%
1992	Republican	47%	Democratic	53%	7%
1996	Republican	45%	Democratic	55%	9%
2000	Republican	50%	Democratic	50%	1%
2004	Republican	51%	Democratic	49%	-2%
2008	Republican	47%	Democratic	53%	7%

Year	Party	Percent Vote	Party	Present Vote	Percent Difference
2012	Republican	49%	Democratic	51%	3%
Average		51%		49%	-2%

infoplease, Presidential Elections, 1789–2012, http://www.infoplease.com/ipa/A0781450.html.

Similar close competition between the parties holds for elections to the House of Representatives as well. The percentage of votes gained by House Republicans in a two-party vote has averaged 47 percent. The difference between the Republican and Democratic votes across all districts has averaged less than 7 percent since 1940 (see Table 8.2). The parties also compete for control of state governments. For most of the twentieth century, the Democrats consistently controlled more state legislatures than Republicans due to their concentration in the South. Since the 1990s, however, party control in the southern states has been ceded to the Republican Party. Since that time, legislative control by the parties across the states has balanced. In some states, the Democrats control by a healthy majority; in others, the Republicans are securely in power. Yet, political scientists who study state governments classify the vast majority of states as competitive, two-party states and no state is currently classified as a one-party state.[30]

TABLE 8.2 Percentage of the Two-Party Vote Won by Republican Candidates for President, 1940 – 2012

	Percentage of Two-Party Vote Won by Republicans	Percentage Difference Between Republican and Democratic Vote
1940s	49.8	5.9
1950s	48.1	4.2
1960s	46.7	6.7
1970s	44.5	10.7
1980s	46.1	7.6
1990s	49.5	4.3
2000s	48.6	5.8
Average 1940 -2012	47.6	6.5

infoplease, Presidential Elections, 1789–2012, http://www.infoplease.com/ipa/A0781450.html.

8.6 Are the Parties Becoming More Radical?

The close competition between the parties can be seen as a consequence of a two-party system. As much as the parties care about their preferred policies, they cannot put them into effect until they win elections. Party leaders cannot (as they could during much of the 1800s) select their nominees in the back rooms of the state convention halls and command a small army of loyalists and patronage workers to vote the party's candidates. Today, individual office seekers raise most of their own money and run their own campaigns. Modern parties have adapted to this candidate-centered reality. Although state parties have grown into more professional organizations, their role is to supplement the activities of the candidates' personal campaign organizations.

The Case for Moderation

In an election featuring two candidates, the office seekers will find it in their self-interest to fit their policy positions to match those of the majority of a district's voters. Voters have different preferences, of course. No one candidate will match their preferences perfectly, but presumably each voter will be drawn to the candidate whose positions are closest to his or her own issue preferences. Within each district, then, is a policy positon that an ambitious office seeker could call a sweet spot, a place that shows which policies would potentially attract the most support. Most voters tend to be moderates on most issues; therefore, the strategic candidate will be tempted to take similarly moderate positions. In an election with two nominees from the major parties, both will be motivated to take the centrist policy positons. As political scientists like to say, in a two-way race, the candidates will tend to converge on the ideal policy position of the median voter.[31] Indeed, research shows that candidates do better the more moderate they become.[32]

At the state and national levels, the parties also devise a set of policies they intend to put into effect should their candidates win office. Because they want to win as many national, statewide, and district elections as possible, the same reasoning that affects individual candidates also applies to the parties. If most voters are moderate, the parties will be motivated to take moderate positions on any given issue. Given that both parties are tempted to converge on the median voter, then the platforms of the parties should be essentially the same. In 1968, American Independent Party candidate George Wallace captured this logic with his slogan: "There's not a dime's worth of difference between the Republicans and the Democrats."[33]

This represents a potential problem for voters. If the candidates and the parties stake out similar policy positions, then a voter looking to make a decision based on matching his or her issue preferences will have a difficult time making a choice. Such behavior on the part of candidates and parties will increase the inherent ambiguity of politics. Policy agreement is hardly the stuff that excites the media or generates enthusiasm. Turnout will be lower if voters see that the outcomes will be the same no matter which candidate wins.

The Case for Radicalization

Still, it is not hard to find fundamental differences between the Democrats and the Republicans. As liberals, Democrats are in favor of government regulation for protecting workers, consumers, and the environment. They want the nation's income, goods, and services to be redistributed more equally. Democrats also tend to oppose government involvement with religious institutions and are suspicious of restraints on individual expression. As conservatives, Republicans see government regulation as impinging on the freedom of employers to make contracts with their employees and sellers to do the same with their buyers (and vice versa). Such liberty, according to conservatives, will not make everyone equal but will use the society's resources more efficiently and maximize the accumulation of wealth. Thus, Republicans tend to look mostly to the private market or charities for solutions to social problems. However, they do see a role for government in keeping social order. Table 8.3 displays the official policy platforms on key issues adopted by the two parties in 2016. The comparison clearly shows that the parties take opposing stances on a wide variety of issues.

TABLE 8.3 Selected Comparison of Democratic and Republican Platforms 2016

Issue	Democratic Party Position	Republican Party Position
Abortion	Supports access to abortion regardless of ability to pay. Opposes Republican efforts to defund Planned Parenthood.	Supports a constitutional amendment to ban abortion and opposes the use of federal funds for abortion, embryonic stem cell research, and organizations that perform or promote abortion or organizations like Planned Parenthood.
Sex Education	Supports "evidence-based" sex education.	Supports education programs "that set abstinence until marriage as the responsible and respected standard of behavior."
Climate Change	Democrats believe that climate change poses an urgent threat to the economy, national security, and people's health. Supports meeting the goals of the Paris climate change agreement.	Cast doubts on whether the climate is changing, rejects the Paris Agreement, and argues that this agreement is not binding on the United States.
Same-Sex Marriage	"Applauds" the Supreme Court's ruling that the right to marry is guaranteed to same-sex couples by the U.S. Constitution. Rejects the "misuse of religion to discriminate against LGBT individuals."	"Condemns" the Supreme Court's ruling that the right to marry is guaranteed to same-sex couples by the U.S. Constitution. Seeks legislative protection for businesses and individuals discriminating against same-sex couples based on their religious beliefs.
Gun Control	Respects the rights of responsible gun owners but seeks to prevent gun violence by expanding background checks and outlawing the sale of assault weapons and large capacity ammunition magazines.	Opposes any effort to deprive individuals of their right to keep and bear arms. Supports the right to obtain and store ammunition without registration and opposes laws that would ban the sale of the assault rifles or restrict magazine capacity.
Minimum Wage	Raise the federal minimum wage to $15 per hour and index future raises to the rate of inflation.	No increase in federal minimum wage; changes "should be handled on the state and local level."
Health Care	Committed to supporting the Affordable Care Act	Committed to the repeal of the Affordable Care Act
Immigration	Supports immigration reform to "create a path to citizenship for law-abiding families." Rejects building a wall between Mexico and the U.S and rejects a religious test to bar immigrants.	Believes that "illegal immigration endangers everyone." Opposes "any form of amnesty." Supports building a wall between Mexico and the U.S., applying "special scrutiny" on immigrants from "regions associated with Islamic terrorism," and deportation for gang membership.
Voting	Opposes voter "identification laws, which disproportionately burden young voters, diverse communities, people of color, low-income families, people with disabilities, the elderly, and women."	Supports laws that require proof of citizenship to vote.

Based on 2016 Democratic and Republican Party Platforms. 2016 Democratic and Republican Party Platforms. https://democrats.org/wp-content/uploads/2018/10/2016_DNC_Platform.pdf. https://www.gop.com/the-2016-republican-party-platform/.

The contrasting party platforms raise an interesting question. If the parties are theorized to have moderate leaning motivations, why are they adopting policy positions that are starkly different? The median voter theory, which predicts that the issue positions of the parties will converge on the preferences of the median voter, does not seem to match the actual behavior of the parties. If anything, the parties seem to have moved away from the center. Rather than avoiding controversial issues that risk alienating moderates, they seem to be embracing them. Indeed, it is clear that the two-party organizations have diverged or perhaps even polarized. The official positions of the Democrats have become more liberal, while those of the Republicans have become more conservative.

FIGURE 8.2
Audience members at a Republican National Convention.

Joseph Sohm / Shutterstock.com

Party Activists to the Rescue

The reason the two parties have become more radical (or failed to converge) has to do with the behavior of a large group of people who are associated with each of the parties. Political scientists refer to these people as **party activists**. As the name implies, these are the most active members of the party. During the summer of every presidential election year, many of the most committed activists attend their party's national convention in non-pandemic years. They can be seen on television holding signs, wearing funny hats, and yelping and yahooing whenever a speaker says something they like. When the balloons and confetti drop at the end of their presidential nominee's acceptance speech, they erupt into a seemingly spontaneous celebration of dance and music. On election night, we see them on television mixed in among the campaign managers, advisors, and consultants for particular candidates, either celebrating victory or consoling each other after defeat.

Relative to those who work full time for the party, a particular candidate, or party members elected to office, the activists are a fairly large group, but they are small in number relative to the size of the voting public. They do not draw salaries like elected officials, political consultants, or the heads of the national and state party organizations and their staffs. Full-time, paid party members are considered professionals, while activists are thought of as amateurs.

Activists are not considered irrational by political scientists even though most are working for free. Indeed, their behavior is really not much different from most people. Usually the things we do without pay are activities from which we derive deep personal pleasure or satisfaction. In short, party activists get gratification from engaging in politics in the same way that other people enjoy rescuing abandoned pets from animal shelters or feeding the homeless. Party activists derive **solidarity benefits** from working face-to-face with like-minded people in the campaign offices or in the field. Others interact with comrades in public demonstrations for causes they also support through the party. Activists derive **purposive benefits** by helping the party achieve its policy goals, but they are mostly committed to their particular issues. For example, many activists in the Republican Party work to pass laws to restrict the availability of abortions, but they also work to pursue the same goal as members of anti-abortion groups. Similarly, some activists in the Democratic Party want to help produce legislation to reverse global warming, but they don't limit their efforts to helping just the party. The primary objectives for many activists are the policy goals and party success is one means to the end.

party activists

Individuals who are voluntarily, yet energetically, involved with a particular political party.

solidarity benefits

Intangible benefits that accrue to members of a group who derive positive feelings of camaraderie and purpose when working together towards a common goal.

purposive benefits

Shared political or policy benefits produced by a group that are related to the group's political or policy goals.

At first glance, it seems like the party professionals share the same objectives, but research shows that there is a big difference between the two groups.[34] The professionals are more pragmatic. They are mostly interested in doing what it takes to win elections. After all, if they don't win they don't get paid, or at least their futures will be diminished. They tend to be more strategic in their policy positons. This means they are more willing to take restrained policy positions needed to gain the support of moderate voters who make up the bulk of the electorate. On the other hand, most activists are primarily interested in their policy goals. They tend to be purists when it comes to these and are less willing to compromise. Strangely, they can "afford" to be more committed to policy causes because their means of financial support do not depend on winning elections. Research confirms that the activists support candidates for party nomination based on their policy positions.[35] Research also shows that activists in both parties are more ideological and more policy oriented than those involved in campaigns at lower levels. In turn, low-level party workers are more ideological than the rank-and-file, ordinary party identifiers.[36] As we separate activists by their level of involvement, those who are more active are not only more ideological, but more pure in their policy interests than their less active partisans (see Figure 8.3).

FIGURE 8.3 Ideology of Party Activists Relative to Party Identifiers and Independents

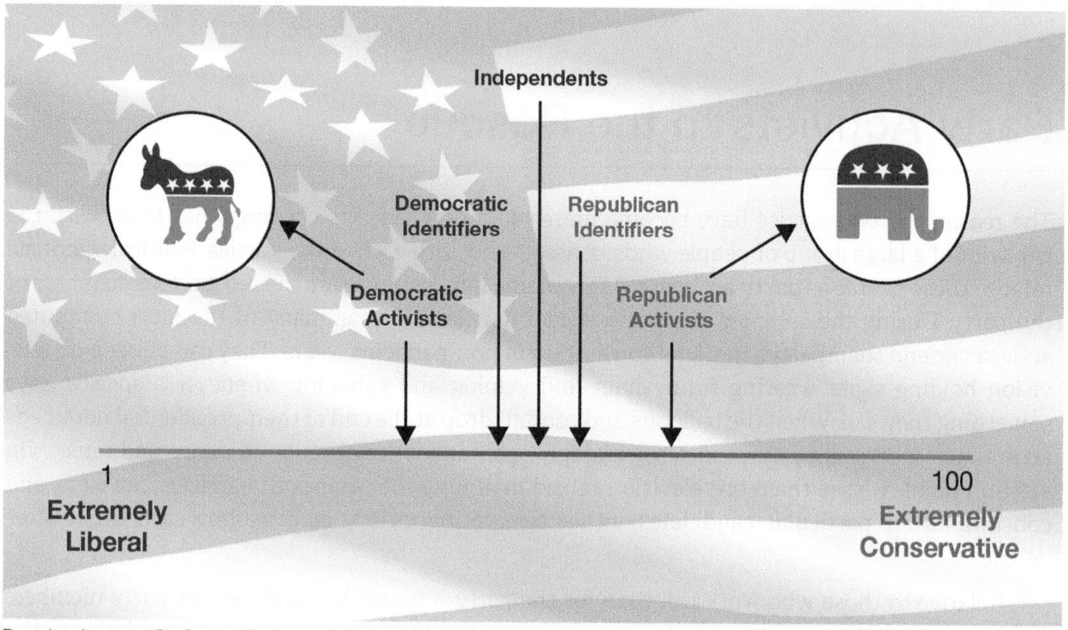

Based on Layman, G., Carsey, T., Green, J., Herrera, R., & Cooperman, R. (2010). Activists and conflict extension in American party politics. *American Political Science Review*, 104(2), 324-346. Images from © Shutterstock, Inc.

Not all activists are rabid ideologues or policy purists, but the proportion of those who are has increased. This helps explain why the parties stand farther apart ideologically today than when George Wallace saw no difference between the two major parties. One of the jobs of the delegates to the national party conventions is to approve the party's platform. It should be no surprise that the final document reflects their interests. The professionals tolerate the activists because energized supporters are a big help in winning elections. The candidates and office holders are free to ignore the party platforms, of course, but they won't because they need party support to win the nomination.

Thus, those seeking office are really vying for the support of two different groups at two different times. To win the nomination, would-be candidates must first appeal to the policy preferences of ideologically and policy oriented activists. These people are more likely to participate in the party's primaries, caucuses, and conventions and more likely to contribute money and other resources to their campaigns. On the other hand, to win the general election in the Fall, the candidates must maintain the support of the activists; win the support of the less-ideological party identifiers and voters within their own party; and attract as many centrist/independent voters as they can. If this sounds like a delicate balancing act, it is because the policy preferences of those supporting the candidate for nomination will be different from those who will be voting in the general elections. To ultimately win office, the candidate will be tempted to please both groups. Unfortunately, the best policy position to help win the primaries, caucuses, and conventions needed to gain the nomination is likely different from the best position to win in the Fall.

Thus, after considering the motivations of the party activists, we must modify our assumption that the policy positions of successful office seekers will end up matching those of a majority of the district's voters. In effect, the party activists are pulling the candidates away from the ideological center and toward the extremes, especially during the primaries. The Democrats pull their candidates to the left ideologically, while the Republicans pull theirs to the right. After the nomination is secured and during the general election campaign, the voters at large will draw the candidates from both parties to the middle. In political science terms, the candidates are pressured to diverge away from the center by the party activists (see Figure 8.4), then pressured to converge on the median voter. In effect, the parties constrain their nominees by keeping them from moving their policy positons too close to the center. They prevent their candidates from being too strategic and compel them to sincerely articulate their true policy positions.[37]

FIGURE 8.4 Party Activists Function to Keep Candidates from Converging on the Median Voter

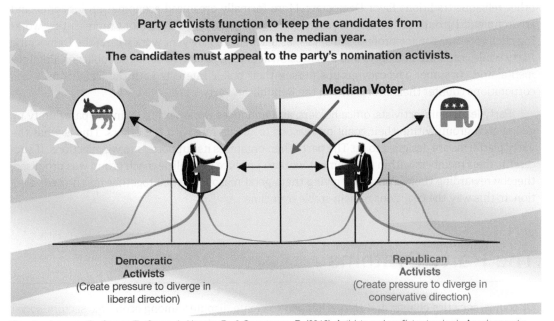

Based on Layman, G., Carsey, T., Green, J., Herrera, R., & Cooperman, R. (2010). Activists and conflict extension in American party politics. *American Political Science Review*, 104(2), 324-346. Images from © Shutterstock, Inc.

Strangely, all this benefits the voters and makes the political system more democratic than it would be without parties. As we mentioned, policy convergence creates a problem for the average voter seeking to make a decision based on the issues. When the candidates take similar policy positions, they increase the ambiguity of politics, raise information costs, and lower participation. Enthusiasm and turnout will be less because voters perceive that their votes will not matter. By keeping the candidates ideologically sincere, the parties function to offer the voters a clear choice. When the Democrats nominate a true liberal and the Republicans respond with a real conservative, the parties give tangible meaning to their brands. This makes it easy for busy voters to cast a reasonably informed vote by matching the candidates with their party's positions. It allows them to more reliably predict their behavior after the election. Candidates who take positions closer to that of the party's will also motivate the activists to do their jobs. Enthusiastic volunteers will work harder to educate citizens, make clear the stakes involved in an election, and bring more voters to the polls. All this helps overcome voter apathy, reduce free ridership, lessen the class and racial biases in voting, and ultimately makes office holders more responsive to the true wishes of people. It turns out that those policy-seeking purists are doing us all a big favor.

8.7 Building and Rebuilding National Majorities

Perhaps the biggest favor the parties do for the country happens every four years during a presidential election. Here the task of the party is no less than to get a majority of voters from across the nation to vote for its nominee for president. This undertaking is enormously difficult given an electorate divided by region, class, race, age, and religion. The chore has to be repeated every four years. Indeed, one of the reasons the parties formed in the first place was so politicians would not have to construct and reconstruct their own majorities from scratch.

Each party represents a giant coalition: a collection of disparate groupings within the population predisposed to vote for their party's candidates at a given time. As we mentioned earlier, certain social groups such as black Americans, Latinas/os, Asians, gays, lesbians, and most women lean toward the Democratic Party, while most non-Hispanic white men favor Republicans, especially in the South. Similarly, voters from particular religious traditions lean Republican while voters from other religious traditions favor Democrats. More formally organized economic, professional, and environmental groups divide their loyalties among the parties as well. Unions representing working-class voters and many professionals, such as teachers and lawyers, work within the Democratic Party, while corporate managers and business owners tend to side with the Republicans. Environmental and consumer advocacy groups pursue their policy interests with the Democrats, while corporations counter their efforts within the Republican Party.

Party leadership, activists, office holders, and nominees work hard to maintain party unity by giving each group within their coalition reasons to collaborate with the others. This is what the party platforms are designed to do. The party then organizes its supporters to win elections. If successful, their members within government work to produce the policies each group was promised, thereby rewarding their loyalty and giving them good reasons to stick together for the next election. In this way, the coalitions remain stable over time.

The Party Systems

Of course, societies change and things happen to create disputes among economic sectors, social groups, and regions of the country. Opposing parties, particularly the ones that lose elections, will look to increase their numbers by turning non-voters into voters. It can do this by generating enthusiasm, providing more information to potential supporters, or by taking sides on issues that will help mobilize groups that did not participate in the last election. Thus, losing parties have strong incentives to expand their electorate and bring up new issues for public debate. On the other hand, the winning party will be constrained by its need to maintain the support of its core constituencies. Sometimes, the very policies and programs the winning party produces to hold its coalition together cause some groups within the coalition to become disillusioned, which may prompt them to join the other party. At the same time, the losing party, ever vigilant for new supporters, stands ready to persuade the cynical to join their party. This happened when the Democratic Party embraced the Civil Rights Act and lost much of the South to the Republican Party.

This process of party growth and decline explains the shifting fortunes of the two parties over the span of American history. Political scientists have identified regularities in the history of elections and named them party systems. Each system is distinguished by the major issues of society at the time and the policies that the majority party puts into effect to respond to those issues.

The first party system emerged out of the same political divisions that existed at the time of the adoption of the Constitution and the Bill of Rights. Led by Alexander Hamilton, the Federalists wanted a strong federal government and, with the support of George Washington, moved to centralize the nation's banking system. This plan would benefit the country's developing manu-facturing sector and urban merchants concentrated in the northeastern states. On the other side were small farmers and southern planters organized by Thomas Jefferson and James Madison, who pressed for a weaker national government and state's rights. Jefferson and the Democratic-Repub-licans won big in the election of 1800 and became the dominant party, while the Federalists slipped into decline over the next 20 years. After about 1830, the parties would organize a mass electorate and control would shift regularly from one major party to the other following major developments in U.S. history.[38]

TABLE 8.4 Party Systems in U.S. History

Party Systems		
1788-1828	The First Party System: Federalists and Democratic-Republicans	Federalists dominate, then Democratic Republicans
1828-1860	The Second Party System: Democrats and Whigs	Democrats dominate, then balance between Democrats and Whigs
1860-1896	The Third Party System: Republicans and Democrats	Republicans dominate, then balance between the Democrats and Republicans
1896-1932	The Fourth Party System	Republicans dominate
1932-1968	The Fifth Party System: The New Deal–Coalition	Democrats dominate
1968-2012	The Sixth Party System	Divided government

In the second party system, the Democratic-Republicans represented workers, small farmers, and the less well-off. It held majority status by exploiting economic class divisions within society after most states allowed non-property owning white men to vote. A second party developed over questions of national expansion and slavery. One faction would continue the tradition of state's rights and slavery and would include small farmers in the west as well as urban workers. This party would be led by Andrew Jackson and shortened its name to the Democratic Party. The other party led by John Quincy Adams (originally called the National Republicans) would represent wealthier eastern voters and would eventually be absorbed into the Whig Party.

The third party system formed after the country divided into two factions over the issue of slavery. The Republican Party emerged from the break-up of the Whig Party in the North as an abolitionist party. After the Civil War, the process of industrialization created huge disparities in income and living conditions among Americans, but the Republicans maintained dominance because the Democrats were unable to unify their base of Catholic immigrants, industrial workers, western miners, poor farmers, and conservative southern Democrats against eastern business interests and professional and middle classes on both coasts.

It took the Great Depression in the 1930s for enough voters to finally shift their allegiance to the Democrats and create a new majority. The core of the Democratic coalition–blacks, Latinas/os, organized labor, poor farmers, urban liberals, and southern Democrats–was joined by Franklin Roosevelt's New Deal policies. Economic hardship was pervasive and the party capitalized on inequalities between the rich and the poor and on animosities between business and labor. The party won elections; its leaders reformed government and produced the benefits (jobs programs, farm subsidies, minimum wages, social security, etc.) that reinforced its coalition. Many of the core groups that made up the New Deal coalition remain loyal to the Democrats today.

Yet, over time, new social issues created divisions, and the Democratic Party was not able to maintain its majority. In 1963, civil rights activists led by the Reverend Martin Luther King, Jr. began a series of lunch counter sit-ins, marches, and boycotts to protest racial segregation in Birmingham, Alabama. When the peaceful demonstrations were met with police violence, public opinion began to turn in favor of the civil rights movement. Shortly after a bomb exploded outside of King's motel room, police began beating blacks who had gathered around the bomb site. In response, blacks rioted and the violence spread to other cities. On June 11, 1963, President John F. Kennedy appeared on television to quell racial tensions and committed to working with Congress to pass legislation to protect civil rights. After Kennedy was assassinated, his promise fell to Lyndon Johnson, who, after a landslide victory in 1964, managed to pass the Civil Rights and the Voting Rights Acts.

Republicans responded by the 1970s with a "southern strategy" that captured the loyalties of white voters in the South who became estranged from the Democrats after the passage of civil rights legislation. At the same time, Democrats sought to add new black voters in the South and to mobilize poor whites, blacks, and Latinas/os through its war-on-poverty programs.[39] Also at this time, the Democrats opened their party to a wide range of activists engaged in the civil rights, anti-Vietnam, counter-culture, women's, environmental, and consumer movements. Thus, the policies favored by these activists came to be tied with the existing economic concerns of the Democrats. On the other side, opposition to civil rights, welfare policy, affirmative action, and environmental and consumer protection became associated with the economic conservatism of the Republicans. A new Republican majority was fully formed when Ronald Reagan and his party's activists joined their issues with the moral and religious concerns of white evangelical Christians, who had been voting at low rates.

Today's Parties

Today, the typical Republican is likely to be male, white, older, less educated, rural, and intolerant of immigration at a time when the country has become more diverse, younger, better educated, and more urban. At the presidential level, the majority of voters began shifting back to the Democrats with the election of Bill Clinton because the Democrats developed policy positions on immigration, guns, abortion, the environment, gender equality, and race to appeal to the faster growing, younger, better-educated, and urbanized groups. Democratic candidates for president have won the popular vote in seven of the last eight presidential elections since 1992. This year their margin of victory in 2020 was more than 7 million votes.

After its loss in 2012, Republicans commissioned a study, known colloquially as the "autopsy" report. The study warned that by 2044, half of all Americans would consider themselves to be non-white. To remain competitive, the report warned the party would need to attract younger, more female, Latina/o, and black American voters. They would also need to adopt policy positions with greater appeal to these groups, such as comprehensive immigration reform. These efforts were stifled by the rise of the Tea Party, a faction within the Republican Party vehemently opposed to immigration reform, taxation, and the national debt. The group was also overwhelmingly white, male, and prone to raising Confederate flags at their rallies.[40]

By 2015, the group's supporters were ripe for mobilization by someone like Donald Trump, who was able to articulate their core grievances. For almost half a century this group has been overwhelmed by substantial declines in income and job opportunities, particularly for those lacking a college education. Policies devised by either party were unable to stop the losses of manufacturing jobs and the weakening of labor unions. Particularly hard hit was an area known as the "rust belt," the older Great Lakes regions of Ohio, Michigan, Indiana, and Wisconsin, where the core of Trump supporters live. As a group, they felt resentment toward minorities and women, but no single issue captured these grievances better than immigration.[41] It was logical for Trump to begin his campaign by characterizing Mexican immigrants as rapists, drug traffickers, and criminals.[42] The inflammatory rhetoric continued when he called for a "complete and total shutdown of Muslims entering the United States."[43] It was also easy to blame trade agreements negotiated by both parties, such as the North American Free Trade Agreement (NAFTA), for job losses and increased immigration.

During the 2016 campaign Trump mocked a reporter with a physical disability, accused a federal judge of being biased against him because of his Mexican descent, and insulted the parents of a Muslim soldier killed in Iraq.[44]

The Democrats had been making inroads since the 1990s among the fastest growing demographic groups in the country. Trump had already insulted the first black American president by questioning his birth status. Trump's daily insults aimed at immigrants, blacks, and other minority groups would only solidify their support for the Democrats. In the 2012 election, President Barack Obama won big among these groups. In addition, women voted in favor of Obama by a margin of almost 12 percent. With the first woman at the top of the Democratic ticket, that gap would only grow.

The gender gap between the parties exploded after a several recordings were released of Trump making what some termed misogynistic and sexually predatory comments. After Trump won a narrow victory in the Electoral College but lost the popular vote, thousands would protest across the U.S. rejecting the president proclaiming that he was "not my president."[45] President Trump came into office with Republicans in control of the House of Representative and the Senate, yet his party had trouble helping him his campaign promises. The president had vowed to end President Obama's Affordable Care Act, but team Republican was never able to agree on a replacement. Instead they worked to sabotage the act by ending the individual mandate which they hoped would render it unconstitutional. Republicans did manage to pass a promised tax bill to reduce corporate taxes permanently and cuts for individuals temporarily. Still, the president was never able to get Mexico or the U.S. Congress to fund the expansion of a wall between the U.S. and Mexico even after declaring a national emergency and shutting down the government for 35 days.

Congressional midterm elections are often a referendum on the President's party. The president campaigned for Republican congressional candidates touting a strong economy, the tax cuts, and confirming conservative judges to the federal courts. But Trump also returned to promoting fear of immigration warning of a so-called caravan of migrants from Central America seeking asylum in the U.S. "Democrats are openly encouraging millions of illegal aliens to break our laws, violate our sovereignty, overrun our borders and destroy our nation in so many ways," Trump said in Florida. "We can't let it happen."[46]

In the end, Trump's closing arguments backfired as 337 of the 435 congressional districts moved toward the Democrats, most of which were in the suburbs and among women and independents. After the so called "blue wave," the Republican Party lost control of the House of Representatives while Democrats vowed to use their powers of executive oversight to keep a close watch on the president. A year later President Trump became the third president to be impeached by members of House of Representatives along mostly party-lines for abuse of power and obstruction of Congress. Trump was accused of accused of soliciting investigations from the Ukrainian government of his would-be opponent in the next election, Joe Biden. Republicans in the Senate would acquit the president on an another mostly party-line vote setting the context for the 2020 presidential election.

By January 2020 it looked like the Republicans would win a second presidential election in November despite the first impeachment proceedings. Although President Trump's job approval was never high, the economy was flourishing, the nation was mostly at peace, and the president had several accomplishments to run on, including a crime bill popular among many Democratic voters. Unfortunately, the COVID-19 pandemic began to spiral across the country infecting millions, putting millions out of work, and killing more than 230,000 Americans by election day. After a limited shut-down in the spring Trump began to worry about the effects a worsening economy would have on his reelection prospects, so he began to pressure governors to reopen schools and businesses in their states. With no vaccine in sight, and as infections began to spike over the summer, people began to worry the country was reopening too soon. Trump's refusal to take advice from his public health advisors and to adhere to simple precautions against transmission politicized the pandemic. In the end, the Republican party lost control of the presidency by losing both the popular vote and the Electoral College. Exit polls would show that the party would lose voters in the suburbs, those with higher levels of education, and those who believe that presidents should show good judgement.[47]

It is easy to hate political parties. When they vigorously pursue their goal of winning elections, they seem indifferent to the good of all. Their real objective is to carry out the party's policies, but they can only do this by electing representatives who are committed to the party's platform. Given a Constitution that fragments power through federalism, separation of powers, and checks and balances, and given reforms designed to weaken their influence, today's parties have little choice but to foster intense loyalty up and down their ranks. Too often, partisanship becomes a blinder that causes followers to dismiss the ideas of others, to obfuscate rather than enlighten, and to appeal to the worst of human nature by fueling fear and suspicion rather than assurance and trust.

Recent polarization has made things worse. The evidence does not show that Americans are separating into extreme ideological camps, but that the Republicans successfully converted conservative southern whites to their party, resulting in a better overall match between ideology and party affiliation. This and other events lead to increased ideological polarization among elected officials and activists in both parties. The presence of fewer moderates among office holders has reduced possibilities for compromise within national and state legislatures and increased instances of partisan gridlock.

8.8 What Can I Do?

Strangely, the first step is to stop hating political parties or at least learn to appreciate the role they play in a modern democracy. Parties lower information costs for busy citizens by generating enthusiasm, nominating candidates, and providing free information and a brand name to make voting cost-effective. Under competitive conditions, they work to turn non-voters into voters, thereby reducing class bias and making the political system more democratic. In a presidential election, the candidate of the successful party often wins the support of a majority of voters across a very diverse nation. If their mandate is sufficiently strong, those elected under the winning party can overcome divided government and move the country in the direction preferred by most voters.

You can join the fray, or not, and either choice can bring benefits to you and to the political system as a whole. Staying independent will require more effort to decide how to vote, but the party label still provides a lot of useful information. Simply match the issues to the party of the candidate with your perceived need for change. In this way you can show approval of a party's/candidate's choices through your backing or lack of support. Doing the research may not be that difficult because in competitive districts, the parties and the candidates will spend a great deal of effort getting information to independent voters who often swing elections. To confirm your choices, fact-checking organizations abound on the internet to assess the sincerity/accuracy of their statements.

If you already identify with a party, you can stay loyal and vote for your party's candidates. You trust your choice, so it makes sense to stick with it. You can even vote a straight party-line ticket by voting for your party's candidates all the way down the ballot. If they all win they will find it easy to work together to bring about the policies that you and they prefer. Still, it is good idea to treat your association as tentative. There is no fee to pay for switching parties, so be fickle. Party identification helps ordinary voters satisfy their duty to vote, but after reading this book you know you can do better. Pay forward your education by making more sophisticated choices. This does not mean you need to become a political activist; just let the professionals do their jobs while you sit back in judgment like a CEO.

Remember, the goal of winning leads pragmatic professionals to take policy positions designed to gain the support of most voters. Thus, it is important to show approval of a party's/candidate's choices through your support or withdrawal of support. It is especially important to participate in the nominations process (the primaries and caucuses) to counter the influence of policy and ideological extremists and produce better matches between voters and candidates. In the general election you will have a second chance to judge your party's choices.

On the other hand, becoming an activist is a great way to increase your political voice. Volunteer for your favorite local party organization and multiply your influence by convincing voters to support your party's candidates. Recruiting family and friends to do the same makes your voice that much louder. Of course, volunteering means that you will be working for free, but you will gain solidarity benefits from working with like-minded people and by helping the party achieve goals that you share. You may even earn a trip to a state or national convention where you will be in a position to influence the party's policy platform. Recall also that party activists, even highly ideological ones, benefit democracy by providing distinct choices to the electorate.

8.9 What's the Alternative?

Advocates for more responsible parties want to put the powers of government into the hands of the winning party. This would make it clear to the voting public which party is in control of government and consequently who should be accountable for their actions. If things go badly, or even if the party in power raises expectations during an election but falls short of its promises, the voters can hold the party responsible by giving their support to another party. Theoretically, this would lead the parties to take more restrained policy positions needed to gain the support of moderate voters who make up the bulk of the electorate.

Institutionally, the surest way to put the parties in charge is to move to a parliamentary system of government in which executive and legislative authorities are combined. In our system, divided government undermines political responsibility because, when mistakes happen, the parties blame each other. Unfortunately for the citizens, these claims are legitimate because Congress has the authority to check the president (and vice versa) and each party has political incentives to undermine the other's policy program. Indeed, Senate Majority Leader Mitch McConnell, a Republican from Kentucky, recently said, "My number one priority is making sure President Obama's a one-term president."[48] In this case, separation of power undermines political responsibility and electoral democracy because citizens cannot tell who is responsible for what. Keep in mind that like other democracies that use parliamentary systems, the party holding power controls government only temporarily. Ultimately, it is the voters who decide who is in power. In the next election, if the voters are displeased with the majority party's performance, they can reduce that party's status to the minority party, thus taking away its power. By choosing between parties in parliamentary systems, citizens determine the direction for the ship of state, while the politicians and bureaucrats do the rowing.

Less fundamental change would reform the party nominations process. Since parties are not mentioned in the Constitution, amending the Constitution would not be required. The system in place now has essentially only been there since the 1970s, so returning the task of selecting nominees to party insiders is not terribly radical. This would produce a greater distance between the party insiders and the identifiers, who would likely act more neutrally as judges of the candidates and their platforms in the general election. The parties are subject to government regulation and press scrutiny, so there is good reason to expect a relatively transparent process. This change would also return the nuances of policy formation to the party and make the conventions more interesting. Recall that the incentive to win creates pressures for the parties to devise platforms to attract a majority of voters. The party also has strong incentives to protect its brand name, so it is unlikely that its nominee will be a racist demagogue. The party professionals tend to be more pragmatic than the policy activists who dominate primary elections. Controlling nominations would also give leadership more control over elected officials after the election. This would help them move the government's agenda in a single, coherent direction.

Instead of returning control of the nominations to the party establishment, the process could be opened more widely. As we mentioned in this chapter, the most committed partisans and activists vote in the primary elections and show up to the caucuses. Those with weaker attachments, who also happen to be moderates, participate less, which gives ideologues undue influence on the nominees. Part of the problem is that the nominations process is a mishmash of caucuses, primaries, and conventions with different rules and procedures offered at different times depending on the state. A single, national primary would boost participation by reducing information costs to the average voter.

Endnotes

1. Herm Edwards and Shelley Smith, *You Play to Win the Game: Leadership Lessons for Success On and Off the Field* (New York: McGraw-Hill, 2005).

2. *Voices in Democracy*, (2005; Dallas, TX: TeleLearning/Harcourt Brace & Company), DVD.

3. "Both Democrats, Republicans Face Public Criticism." Pew Research Center - U.S. Politics & Policy. Pew Research Center, May 30, 2020. https://www.pewresearch.org/politics/2017/06/20/public-has-criticisms-of-both-parties-but-democrats-lead-on-empathy-for-middle-class/.

4. "No Labels," No Labels, December 11, 2015, http://www.nolabels.org/.

5. "How to Vote," wikiHow, accessed December 11, 2015, http://www.wiki-how.com/Vote.

6. "Problem Solvers - No Labels," No Labels, accessed May 2, 2016, https://www.nolabels.org/problem-solvers/.

7. E. E. Schattschneider, *Party Government* (New York: Holt, Reinhart and Winston,1942), 1.

8. David Mayhew, *Parties and Policies* (New Haven: Yale University Press, 2008) 79.

9. "The Need for Greater Party Responsibility: Toward a More Responsible Two Party System: A Report of the Committee on Political Parties," *American Political Science Review* 44 no. 3(1950): 15-36.

10. James Madison, "The Federalist No. 10: The Utility of the Union as a Safeguard Against Domestic Faction and Insurrection (continued)," *Daily Advertiser*, November 22, 1787, accessed May 2, 2016, http://www.con-stitution.org/fed/federa10.htm.

11. "Washington's Farewell Address 1796," Avalon Project, accessed May 2, 2016, http://avalon.law.yale.edu/18th_century/washing.asp.

12. "Values About Government and the Social Safety Net," Pew Research Center, June 4, 2012, http://www.people-press.org/2012/06/04/sec-tion-4-values-about-government-and-the-social-safety-net/.

13. David Mayhew, *Divided We Govern* (New Haven: Yale University Press. 2002).

14. E. E. Schattschneider, *Party Government* (New York: Holt, Reinhart and Winston, 1942), 52.

15. John Aldrich, *Why Parties?* (Chicago: University of Chicago Press, 1995).

16. Marjorie Randon Hershey, *Party Politics in America, 14th Edition* (New York: Pearson, 2011), 250.

17. Amy Walter, "The Myth of the independent Voter," The Cook Political Report, January 15, 2014, http://cookpolitical.com/story/6608.

18. Duane F. Alwin and Jon A. Krosnick, "Aging, Cohorts, and the Stability of Sociopolitical Orientations Over the Life Cycle," *American Journal of Sociology* 97 (1991): 185-87.

19. Marjorie Randon Hershey, *Party Politics in America, 14th Edition* (New York: Pearson, 2011), 102.

20. Paul Allen Beck, Russell J. Dalton, Steven Greene, and Robert Huckfeldt, "The Social Calculus of Voting," *American Political Science Review* 96 (2002): 57-73.

21. "Section 9: Trends in Party Affiliation," Pew Research Center U.S. Politics & Policy, June 4, 2012, http://www.people-press.org/2012/06/04/sec-tion-9-trends-in-party-affiliation/.

22. "A Deep Dive into Party Affiliation," Pew Research Center, April 7, 2015, http://www.people-press.org/2015/04/07/a-deep-dive-into-party-affilia-tion/.

23. Derek Thompson, "Does Your Wage Predict Your Vote?" *The Atlantic*, November 5, 2012, http://www.theatlantic.com/business/archive/2012/11/does-your-wage-predict-your-vote/264541/.

24. Thomas M. Holbrook and Raymond J. La Raja, "Parties and Elections," *Politics in the American States: A Comparative Analysis, Seventh Edition*, eds. Virginia Gray, Russell L. Hanson, and Thad Kousser (Washington, D.C., CQ Press, 2013).

25. Ibid.

26. Jeffery M. Jones, "Americans Continue to Say a Third Political Party Is Needed," Gallup, Inc., September 24, 2014, http://www.gallup.com/poll/177284/americans-continue-say-third-political-party-needed.aspx.

27. John F. Bibby and Sandy Maisel, *Two Parties – Or More? 2nd Edition* (Bounder, CO: Westview, 2003), 46.

28. "State legislative chambers that use multi-member districts," Ballotpedia, assessed December 15, 2015, http://ballotpedia.org/State_legisla-tive_chambers_that_use_multi-member_districts.

29. Maurice Duverger, *Political Parties* (New York: Wiley, 1954).

30. Thomas M. Holbrook and Raymond J. La Raja "Parties and Elections," *Politics in the American States: A Comparative Analysis, Seventh Edition*, eds. Virginia Gray, Russell L. Hanson, and Thad Kousser (Washington, D.C., CQ Press, 2013).

31. Anthony Downs, *An Economic Theory of Democracy* (New York: Harper, 1957).

32. Brandice Canes-Wrone, David W. Brady, and John F.Cogan, "Out of Step, Out of Office: Electoral Accountably and House Members' Voting," *American Political Science Review* 96 (2002): 127-140.

33. Joshua C. Yesnowitz, "American Independent Party," *Encyclopedia of U.S. Campaigns, Elections, and Electoral Behavior: A-M*, Volume 1 ed. Kenneth F. Warren (New York: Sage, 2008): 30.

34. Peter B. Clark and James Q. Wilson, "Incentive Systems," *Administrative Science Quarterly* 6 (1961):129-166.

35. Alan I. Abramowitz and Walter J. Stone, *Nomination Politics: Party Activists and Presidential Choice* (New York: Praeger, 1984).

36. John Aldrich, *Why Parties?* (Chicago: University of Chicago Press, 1995),188.

37. Gerald C. Wright and Brian Schaffner, "The Influence of Party: Evidence from the State Legislatures," *American Political Science Review* 96 (2002): 367-380.

38. The Republican Party did not form until the 1860s but the mass-based party system did begin with Democratic Party dominance.

39. Edward G. Carmines and James A. Stimson, *Issue Evolution: Race and the Transformation of American Politics* (Princeton, NJ., Princeton University Press, 1989).

40. "Hundreds Rally for 'Confederate Pride' Parade Displaying Rebel Battle Flag," Tea Party, July 27, 2015, accessed October 22, 2016, http://www.teaparty.org/hundreds-rally-confederate-pride-parade-dis-playing-rebel-battle-flag-104974/.http://www.teaparty.org/hundreds-rally-confederate-pride-parade-displaying-rebel-battle-flag-104974/.

41. Michael Pollard and Joshua Mendelsohn, "RAND Kicks Off 2016 Presidential Election Panel Survey," The Rand Corporation blog, January 27, 2016, accessed October 22, 2016, http://www.rand.org/blog/2016/01/rand-kicks-off-2016-presidential-election-panel-survey.html.

42. Michelle Ye Hee Lee, "Donald Trump's False Comments Connecting Mexican Immigrants and Crime," *The Washington Post*, July 9, 2015, accessed October 22, 2016, https://www.washingtonpost.com/news/fact-checker/wp/2015/07/08/donald-trumps-false-comments-connecting-mexican-immigrants-and-crime/.

43. "Donald J. Trump Statement on Preventing Muslim Immigration," Trump/Pence, December 7, 2015, accessed October 22, 2016, https://www.donaldjtrump.com/press-releases/donald-j.-trump-state-ment-on-preventing-muslim-immigration.

44. Keith Olbermann, "176 Reasons Donald Trump Shouldn't Be President," *GQ*, September 13, 2016, accessed October 22, 2016, http://www.gq.com/story/176-reasons-donald-trump-shouldnt-be-presi-dent-olbermann.

45. Matea Gold, Mark Berman. "'Not My President': Thousands Protest Trump in Rallies across the U.S." The Washington Post. WP Company, April 28, 2019. https://www.washingtonpost.com/news/post-politics/wp/2016/11/10/not-my-president-thousand-protest-trump-in-rallies-across-the-u-s/.

46. Watkins, Derek, and K. K. Rebecca. "Sizing Up the 2018 Blue Wave," November 7, 2018. https://www.nytimes.com/interactive/2018/11/07/us/politics/how-democrats-took-the-house.html.

47. National Exit Polls: How Different Groups Voted. (2020, November 03). Retrieved January 01, 2021, from https://www.nytimes.com/interactive/2020/11/03/us/elections/exit-polls-president.html

48. David Weigel, "Mitch McConnell and the One-Term President," *Slate Magazine*, September 25, 2012, accessed November 14, 2018, http://www.slate.com/blogs/weigel/2012/09/25/mitch_mcconnell_and_the_one_term_president.html.

CHAPTER 9
Interest Groups: Effective Participation with an Upper-Class Bias

Chapter Objectives

1. Explore Madison's Federalist 10 and the rise of interest groups.
2. Understand the relationship between democracy and interest group participation.
3. Discover the upper class and business-oriented biases of the interest group system.
4. Investigate interest group formation, mobilization, and maintenance.
5. Consider changes in the interest group system.
6. Assess how interest groups influence policy.

Introduction: Marjory Stoneman Douglas High School Students Organize for Gun Control

Emma Gonzalez, Parkland gun violence survivor.

lev radin / Shutterstock.com

On February 14, 2018, 19-year-old Nikolas Cruz opened fire on his schoolmates at Marjory Stoneman Douglas High School in Parkland, Florida, with a Smith and Wesson AR-style rifle originally designed for modern, close quarters military combat. He killed 17 and injured 17 others, including three staff members. Cruz had a history of disciplinary problems. He had made threats against other students and he had been transferred between six schools in three years. Although only 18, he purchased his gun legally at Sunrise Tactical Supply in Coral Springs, Florida. Three months earlier, Devin Kelley, 26, opened fire on the congregation at the First Baptist Church in Sutherland Springs, Texas, killing 26 and injuring 20 others, including whole families with children. Kelley had a history of domestic violence, stalking underage girls, and cruelty to animals. He spent time in a mental health facility after threatening to kill his superiors. He purchased his rifle from a sporting goods store in San Antonio. One month earlier, Stephen Paddock, 64, rained gun fire on country music fans gathered in an outdoor amphitheater below his suite on the thirty-second floor of the Mandalay Bay Resort and Casino in Las Vegas, Nevada. Paddock killed 58 and injured 546 using multiple AR- and AK-style rifles, two of which were fitted with legal "bump stocks," effectively converting them into machine guns. Paddock had 23 firearms and a sizeable stockpile of ammunition in his room. Investigators found another 1,600 rounds of ammunition in his car, most of which he purchased at gun shops in Nevada. A year earlier, Omar Mateen, 29, killed 49 people and injured 53 in the Pulse nightclub in Orlando, Florida, using a Sig Sauer MCX with high-capacity magazines originally designed for U.S. Special Operations forces. The gun was purchased at a shooting center in nearby Port St Lucie, Florida.The

Since the April 1999 Columbine High School Massacre in which two students killed 12 of their schoolmates, a teacher, and wounded 21 others with firearms purchased at a local gun show, there have been 74 indiscriminate shootings in public places resulting in four or more victims killed for a total of 637 deaths and 1,075 persons wounded in the United States. Twenty-two of these incidents took place in schools or churches, claiming 379 victims. In 23 cases, 286 people were killed by shooters using assault rifles. In most cases (45), the shooters had multiple firearms, including semi-automatic pistols. In about half of the instances (39), the shooters showed prior signs of mental health issues.[1]

Fortunately, mass shootings are not indications of increasing violent crime in the United States. Violent crime rates (including murder, rape, robbery, and aggravated assault) peaked in 1991, then declined by almost 50 percent by 2016. However, the rate of death by fire arms increased to about 33,000 or 12 deaths per 100,000 persons over the last decade, reaching about the same rate as motor vehicle deaths. It has been nearly two decades since there has been any substantial improvement in the rate of gun deaths.[2] According to the Centers for Disease Control and Prevention (CDC), 93 Americans are killed with guns every day, seven of whom are under the age of 19. Most of these deaths, about 62 percent, are the result of suicides, but 12,000 per year are from gun homicides, making the U.S. homicide rate more than 25 times higher than countries with comparable incomes.[3] A broad array of research shows that mere availability of guns is a risk factor in homicide. In other words, more guns equate to more homicides whether the places are countries, cities, regions, or U.S. states.[4] It should be no surprise that U.S. citizens own more guns per capita than any other country in the world, or that Americans own almost half the world's guns in private hands.[5]

The U.S. government has tried to prevent deaths by limiting the accessibility of the most dangerous firearms. In 1934, Congress passed the National Firearms Act, restricting the ownership of machine guns and short-barreled rifles and shotguns.[6] After the assassinations of President John F. Kennedy, Senator Robert Kennedy, and Dr. Martin Luther King Jr., the Gun Control Act of 1968 limited commerce in firearms to licensed manufactures, dealers, and importers, and prohibited selling firearms to certain individuals. The assassination attempt on President Ronald Reagan led to the enactment of the Brady Handgun Violence Prevention Act of 1993, which established a national background check system to prevent dealers from selling guns to people convicted of certain crimes or who have been found to be "mentally defective."[7] The Stockton, California, schoolyard shooting led to the Federal Assault Weapons ban of 1994, which restricted the manufacture, sale, and ownership of semiautomatic assault weapons and large capacity ammunition feeding devices.[8]

However, under the U.S. Constitution, Americans have the right to keep and bear arms, a right vigorously protected by an **interest group** organized to influence government decisions: The National Rifle Association (NRA). Since the 1999 shootings in Columbine, Colorado, the NRA has evolved into a high-profile advocate for the rights of gun owners and makers, opposing many attempt to limit what the organization argues is an unrestricted right to bear arms. Over the same time, public opinion has consistently supported stricter gun regulation.[9]After Columbine, the NRA supported gun-free, safe zones around schools but opposed Congressional action to eliminate a loophole that would have subjected hand gun purchases at gun shows to background checks. In 2003, the interest group supported the passage of a law that forbids the U.S. Bureau of Alcohol, Tobacco, Firearms, and Explosives from sharing data it collects regarding the types of guns used in crimes with the public or even with Congress. In 2004, the NRA pushed Congress to allow the Assault Weapons Ban to expire, which reinstated the right of gun manufactures to make and sell assault rifles and high-capacity magazines. The following year, **lobbyists** from the NRA engineered the passage of the Protection of Lawful Commerce in Arms Act, which protected gun manufacturers, importers, distributors, and dealers from being held liable for crimes committed with their products.[10] Shortly after a 20-year-old with a history of serious mental health problems killed 20 first-graders and six adults with his mother's assault rifle at Sandy Hook Elementary School, the NRA reversed its support for gun-free schools. Declaring that "The only thing that stops a bad guy with a gun is a good guy with a gun," the group's leader proposed that each of the nation's 100,000 schools be patrolled by armed guards.[11] Since then, NRA lobbyists have been encouraging states to pass laws giving citizens the right to wear concealed guns in public. They have also supported "stand your ground laws" which allow individuals to kill in the name of self-defense even if deadly force can be safely avoided. In 2013, George Zimmerman was acquitted in the shooting death of Trayvon Martin in Sanford, Florida, because of the existence of such a law in that state.[12]

© Shutterstock, Inc.

The NRA is typical of many interest groups in America. It hires professional advocates to lobby national and state government lawmakers to achieve the group's goals. It provides campaign contributions to candidates for elected office who are supportive of the groups' policy preferences and it works to defeat those who are not. It monitors government programs and educates its members about pending legislation. It mobilizes its members for elections and grass roots lobbying efforts. In other ways, the NRA is unusual because of its size, complexity, and success. Indeed, *Forbes* magazine once named the NRA the most powerful lobby in America. The NRA claims more than 5 million members, making it one of the largest membership groups in Washington.[13] In 2015, the organization had 852 full-time employees, claimed 150,000 volunteers, and generated revenues of $336.7 million, more than half of which came from program service (firearms safety, education, and training) and other revenues.[14] It has a well-funded legal foundation and a political action committee. Its chief executive officer, Wayne LaPierre, earns more than $1 million per year.[15]

As a self-described protector of the Second Amendment, the organization claims to be America's longest-standing civil rights organization.[16] Yet, the group's insistence on an unrestricted right to keep and bear arms does not accurately reflect the views of the nation's gun owners. According to the PEW Research Center, 77 percent of gun owners believe the federal government should require background checks for private sales and at gun shows. Most believe in creating a federal database to track gun sales and almost half of gun owners think the government should ban assault-style weapons and high-capacity magazines. Only one-third believe local governments should allow individuals to carry concealed guns in more places even with permits, or to allow teachers and others to carry guns in schools.[17] The country's majority of non-gun owners feel more strongly about regulating firearms than gun owners do.

Like other groups, the NRA struggles to balance differing interests within its own organization as it tries to generate enthusiasm for its cause and enlarge its membership base without alienating its moderate members and the public. Some people are members because they want the organization to oppose any attempts to regulate firearms, but others do not oppose reasonable regulation. Republican pollster Frank Luntz found that 82 percent of NRA members supported background checks for every gun purchase, 71 percent think the government should prohibit people on the terrorist watch list from purchasing guns, 74 percent believe that concealed carry permits should only be granted to applicants who have completed gun safety training, and 64 percent believed that gun owners should alert police when their firearms are lost or stolen. The group must also reconcile differences between regular members and the much smaller group entitled to elect its board of directors, the board itself, which is dominated by representatives of sellers and manufacturers of guns, and its permanent staff charged with keeping the organization healthy and contributions flowing.[18] The fact that gun sales increase after each shooting, and rise dramatically after each mass shooting, is not lost on the organization's leadership.[19]

In fulfilling its role as an interest group, the NRA's actions raise several questions about the nature of interest groups in a democratic government. Is the group representative of gun owners in general and its members in particular, or does it bias its actions toward those of its leaders, large contributors, and management? Is this group moving the country toward a safer, healthier society, or is it promoting the sale of guns by spreading fear and enabling potential criminals or the mentally unstable to stockpile weapons and ammunition designed for military use?

9.1 Federalist 10 and the Rise of Interest Groups

Americans have always been suspicious of the power of groups organized to assert political power. Prior to the adoption of the Constitution, James Madison warned in Federalist Paper #10 of the tendency of nations to suffer the "violence of faction." Madison was concerned about society's natural predisposition to form different opinions and interests about nearly everything. Madison also noted the tendency of leaders contending for reputation and power to exploit "the most frivolous and fanciful distinctions ... to kindle their unfriendly passions and excite their most violent conflicts." Such leaders, he warned, have "divided mankind into parties, inflamed them with mutual animosity, and rendered them much more disposed to vex and oppress each other than to co-operate for their common good ... The causes of faction," Madison observed, "are thus sown in the nature of man."[20]

Madison also argued that government efforts to control groups would destroy liberty. He proposed to limit the negative effects of factions by suggesting only a large society that promotes competition among groups within an elaborate system of checks and balances would reduce the potential of any alliance to form and monopolize political power. At the same time, the division of power among branches and levels of government would allow a large variety of groups to have some power via multiple points of access. The inevitable conflict among the competing interests in a free society would lead to compromise and the expression of the common good.

At the urging of the anti-federalists and as a condition of their support for the ratification of the Constitution, the right of individuals and groups to petition government would be enshrined in the Constitution in the Bill of Rights. It was Madison himself who wrote the words of the First Amendment that would establish the right to freely assemble and petition government, ensuring that government attempts to suppress groups would be deemed unconstitutional.[21]

Agents representing various interests would petition members of Congress and the executive branch almost from the beginning. Banking interests worked with Treasury Secretary Alexander Hamilton to consolidate and assume national and state debts incurred during the Revolution by the newly established Bank of the United States.[22] Later, individuals representing boat owners would seek rights to control trade on rivers and canals, railroad companies would pursue rights-of-way and cash subsidies to build the nation's rail infrastructure, and weapons manufacturers would seek military contracts. Others would lobby elected officials for patronage jobs or other favors.[23] By the turn of the twentieth century, businesses formed trade associations to deal with anti-monopoly laws and workplace safety regulations coming out of Washington.[24] At the same time, professional associations such as the American Medical and the American Bar associations formed to represent the interests of doctors and lawyers. Their lead would be followed by other professional associations, from butchers to bakers to candlestick makers.

By the 1920s, virtually all businesses or professions were represented in Washington. The National Grange and the National Farmers Alliance would represent farmers and lobby for price supports for most crops. Women's rights and social activist groups would lobby Congress and the state governments to pass constitutional amendments to ban alcohol and to give women the right to vote. Other groups would press lawmakers for child labor restrictions, safer working conditions, immigration reform, and assistance for the elderly and unemployed.[25] The number and variety of interest groups would explode following the federal government's efforts to regulate the economy and influence President Roosevelt's New Deal policies during the Great Depression. Labor unions, which had largely avoided politics in favor of strikes, mobilized to support the National Industrial Recovery and Labor Relations acts, which protected the right to organize and bargain collectively for higher wages, increased job security, better benefits, and safer working conditions. Unions also worked to establish basic labor standards for all workers including minimum wages, overtime protections, unemployment insurance, and financial support for poor families with children and the elderly.[26] In turn, new business and other associations formed to resist such legislation.[27] Still other associations would be encouraged by government to ease the operation of federal programs.

Interest group formation expanded again in the 1960s and 1970s with another round of activist groups pushing for social rather than economic change. Political entrepreneurs like Ralph Nader would form Public Citizen groups to advocate for consumer and environmental protection policies. Nader also helped to establish state-based public interest research groups on college campuses to lobby for consumer and environmental protection laws in state legislatures. John Gardner would established Common Cause to promote governmental reforms to promote greater transparency in government and politics. Today, there are thousands of interest groups in Washington lobbying on nearly every issue before the federal government.

9.2 Democracy and Group Participation

The plethora of interest groups means that citizens need not wait for the next election for their interests to be represented in government. If your college is anything like ours, a trip across campus involves running the gauntlet of fellow students prodding you to read their brochures, come to a meeting, sign petitions, engage in debate, or join their marches for justice. Your campus encourages students to form groups and lobby government around seemingly every issue, from student debt to sexual violence. Students form local segments of nationally organized groups like the College Republicans, People for the Ethical Treatment of Animals, Black Lives Matter, and Students for Life. You may think of yourself as a free rider on most issues, satisfied to let your more passionate colleagues deal with political issues while you go about your business of getting an education and preparing for a professional career. You may tactfully avoid these groups, but if you believe you are not involved in interest group politics, think again.

a katz / Shutterstock.com

Almost every group, business, or institution you associate with represents your interests in government even though you may not know it. If you belong to a pre-professional association like the student chapter of American Society of Engineers or the Society of Professional Journalists, these groups do more than network with local professionals or help you find an internship. They speak on your behalf. If you attend a local church or belong to a labor union because of your job, these groups represent you. Even if you just rent a house or an apartment, there is a neighborhood association in your area that actively monitors local development issues and represents your interests to the city council regarding zoning changes, crime control, or even when they lobby sweeping the streets more often. When you were in elementary, middle, and high school, a parent-teacher association helped your school raise funds for field trips and supported the school district efforts to pass bond issues to upgrade school facilities. If your grandparents are retired, they are likely to be members of the American Association of Retired Persons (AARP) if only for their travel discounts or supplemental medical insurance. The AARP also sends its members a monthly magazine that helps them to monitor the federal government's efforts to modify Medicare and Social Security while the organization lobbies government on their behalf. You may even own a gun and took advantage of the free membership to the NRA that came with your purchase. Even if you are not formally a member, the NRA is happy to lobby government on your behalf as a gun owner.

Far from the contemporary image of Americans as passive spectators, French historian Alexis de Tocqueville's early nineteenth century observation about Americans as a nation of joiners is still true today. Between 70 and 80 percent of Americans are members of at least one group, most of which (61 percent) take stands on political issues.[28] Americans are also more likely to join groups at higher rates than citizens of other countries.[29] That said, most Americans are only loosely attached to the group system. Many are members in name only. They pay their membership dues but do little else with the group, while a small fraction can be described as very active. On the other hand, about 5 percent of the population is a member of six or more organizations, which gives these citizens much more representation than average.[30]

The beauty of the interest group system is that those associated with groups need not become textbook versions of active citizens, keeping up with the news, making their views known to their representatives, or monitoring government activity. All you need to do is live your life and pursue your interests. Most likely, the groups and institutions linked to you are doing these things for you. Theoretically, the variety of groups you associate with reflect your varied interests. They may even represent your personal conflicts. For example, you may be a member of the American Automobile Association (AAA) because you want their emergency road service and the Sierra Club because you support their efforts to protect the natural environment. The two organizations often clash over providing roads in national and state parks, but that's okay with you because you want the parks *and* convenient access. The same applies to your family, friends, and associates. Since individuals are free to join or form groups that reflect their interests and groups are easy to form, a wide variety of associations materialize as a natural consequence of social living and the diversity of interests.

Indeed, the fragmented nature of government in the United States seems to be designed specifically to accommodate interest groups. For example, if the peace and quiet of a neighborhood is threatened by a freeway expansion, those living in the area can organize and petition their city council representative for redress. If the group isn't satisfied, it can appeal to the mayor, or their representatives in the state legislature or in Congress, or sue the highway department in state or federal courts. In a decentralized political system, there always seems to be a door or two to knock on. Public officials are willing to listen because they need support from broad-based coalitions and responding to groups is more efficient than dealing with constituents individually. Unlike voting, where everyone—regardless of how much they care about an issue—gets one vote, groups reflect the intensity of their members' interests. The neighborhood threatened by the freeway is more likely to to organize to express opposition than the much larger group of supportive commuters who are mildly pleased about the few seconds they will save on their daily commutes.

Rena Schild / Shutterstock.com

Traditional groups, such as the neighborhood organization, are made up of individual citizens promoting economic, social, or political concerns. Examples include the Sierra Club, Americans for Tax Reform, the National Organization for Women, and the John Birch Society. But these are examples of just one of many types of associations that attempt to influence government. Groups include labor unions such as the United Auto Workers, or professionals such as doctors, lawyers, librarians, and political consultants. Other groups are made up of organizations rather than individuals such as the U.S. Chamber of Commerce, the American Petroleum Institute, or the American Federation of Labor and Congress of Industrial Organizations (AFL-CIO). There are also groups that represent institutions without traditional memberships, such as individual businesses, hospitals, local and state governments, universities and colleges, and federal agencies.

Groups play an important role in representing various interests before government. They lower the costs of gathering information by educating members about policy debates relevant to the group. They facilitate political action by organizing like-minded citizens and moving them in a common direction. Like political parties, they help link citizens to government and enable citizens to participate in governmental policy-making while they live their normal lives. In many ways, interest groups are at the heart of American politics. In theory, the vast diversity of groups, the multiplicity of access points to government, and the competition among countervailing groups assures that policies will be responsive to many interests rather than to a single set of interests.

However, political scientists have studied interest groups since the 1960s and found a number of less-than-democratic features in the system. Foremost is the long-standing observation that interests with access to more resources (money, people, information, etc.) usually get better results than interests with fewer assets. There are no participation fees in politics, but time and effort are valuable. Resources are the core of any system of cooperation. They provide the capacity to act purposefully and can be used to prevent other actions or counter the actions of rival groups. Anything that can be converted into political influence may be considered a resource. Many groups use money to pay staff to manage and recruit their membership, write and distribute their newsletter, and retain lobbyists at the capitol. All groups have some resources. Even the poor can organize through volunteers.

It is not just the amount of resources that underlies groups' power: there is also the range of resources that can be brought to bear. Group size is important. It adds to the ability to influence elections (as does geographical dispersion) and increases potential for dues-paying members. But without good organization, the group's resources cannot be easily mobilized. Often the durability of resources is more important than the amount. Influence is not normally based on a single show of strength, but on the capacity to sustain an effort. For example, the neighborhood fighting the freeway expansion may have to rally residents to show up at meetings and protests on multiple occasions and across a number of years. An institution such as a corporation, on the other hand, usually has an established, ongoing stream of resources that it can use to engage in politics. Eighty percent of groups representing corporations, trade and other business associations, professional associations, and unions in Washington, D.C., in 1960 were still active 20 years later. Only 45 percent of comparable public interest groups were still operational.[31]

A group must also be unified. Internal divisions can undermine the organization's efforts and bargaining power. Group cohesion often enables smaller associations to win policy concessions over larger groups with diffuse interests. Similarly, intensity matters. Groups often face significant opposition and highly committed members help overcome such barriers. Intensely concerned members are also more likely to contribute time and money, which increases the scope and range of what the group can do. Social status or the wealth of the membership and the occupations they represent matter as well. Wealth can be put to many uses, but so can expertise. Doctors testifying about the effects of noise and air pollution on children are more credible than testimony given by cashiers and office clerks.

9.3 The Upper Class and Business Biases of the Interest Group System

If resources are critical to group success, it should be no surprise that the interest group system shows a strong social class bias. One of the most famous quotes in the American political science literature comes from E.E. Schattschneider, who wrote in 1960 that the "flaw in the pluralist heaven is that the heavenly chorus sings with an upper-class accent."[32] Since then, scholars have repeatedly found evidence for an upper-class bias in participation in interest groups. Much of this is because many Americans are active through their managerial or professional occupations, which pull members into the interest-group system automatically. Indeed, political scientist Jack Walker found that three-quarters of all Washington-based membership groups had their origins in the occupational structure of the American economy.[33] For many occupations, such as doctors and lawyers, membership in the professional association is required to work in the profession. Membership also provides personal contacts and networking opportunities. Members of professional occupations tend to have higher incomes and higher levels of education than other workers. On the other hand, those who are unemployed, employed outside of the labor force, or those with low status jobs (such as clerks and cashiers) are much less likely to be represented by interest groups.

Taken as a whole, the groups organized for representation in Washington, D.C., heavily favor business organizations. Using a directory listing nearly 7,000 organizations that either maintain an office or hire counsel to represent them, political scientists Kay Scholzman and John Tierney found that 72 percent of those organizations in 1980 were either corporations or trade and business associations. Further, they show that the dominance of business interests grew even after the arrival of new citizen groups that flooded Washington in the previous two decades. Had Scholzman and Tierney counted only those organizations with economic interests, such as firms, unions, and professionals, business organizations would have accounted for 86 percent of the total.[34] However, it is not just the number of groups that matter. Workers, for example, are represented by a few large unions or associations of unions (like the AFL-CIO) while businesses are represented by a larger number of smaller organizations. The situation is further complicated by the fact that organizations frequently share members and are often allied, resulting in multiple representation. For example, businesses and stockholders might be represented by their own firm, by other firms in the industry, and by one or more trade associations.[35] The same is true for business managers, who might also be represented by their professional associations.

TABLE 9.1 Groups Organized for Representation in Washington

Economic Role of the Individual	U.S. Adults (%)	Orgs. (%)	Type of Org. in Washington	Ratio of Orgs. to Adults
Managerial/Administrative	7	71.0	Business Association	10.10
Professional/Technical	9	17.0	Professional Association	1.90
Student/Teacher	4	4.0	Educational Organization	1.00
Farmworker	2	1.5	Agricultural Workers' Organization	0.75
Unable to Work	2	0.6	Organization for the Handicapped	0.30
Other Non-Farm Workers	41	4.0	Union	0.10
Homemaker	19	1.8	Women's Organization	0.09
Retired	12	0.8	Senior Citizens' Organization	0.07
Looking for Work	4	0.1	Unemployment Organization	0.03

Schlozman, Kay Lehman., and John T. Tierney. *Organized Interests and American Democracy*. New York: Harper & Row, 1986.

The economic basis of most interest groups ensures that business owners and professionals are overrepresented in Washington, while citizen groups, civil rights, social welfare, and ideological organizations only represent about 20 percent of the total.[36] But the dominance of the number of groups represented in Washington is not the end of business advantage. Above, we noted that the durability of organizations with stable revenue sources ensures that business and professional groups will remain active over time. The same can be said for mobilization. We also noted that the neighborhood organization fighting the freeway expansion regularly nudges its people out of their usual political apathy to attend meetings and protests. Professional and business organizations often have existing lines of communication and dedicated personnel that enable them to respond to new threats quickly and efficiently. In addition, wealth is a political resource that is not only durable but also flexible. As Virginia Gray and David Lowery note, business associations sometimes go into "hibernation" during periods when there is little legislative activity of concern to them, but the on-going presence of business groups in the capitol is helpful when they need to act quickly.[37]

Perhaps more fundamentally, we need to acknowledge that in a capitalist economy, the consequences of business regulation frequently fall broadly on the population. Economic reforms and regulation often trigger penalties in the form of unemployment or a sluggish economy. If we want businesses to provide their employees with healthy working conditions, living wages, health care benefits, or to carry a larger share of the nation's tax burden, we must acknowledge that such reforms may discourage business investment and increase unemployment. In a capitalist economy, the combined decisions of businesses direct the distribution of labor, wealth and income, the extraction and use of natural resources, and the accumulation of capital and investment. Private business also organizes the production of food, materials, transportation, housing, and most other commodities. If we want automobile manufactures to build safer, more environmentally sustainable cars, we must consider the costs to them and the resultant declines in investment and jobs. Such economic punishment is not a conspiracy on the part of the business community. Instead, in anticipation of new regulations, managers simply decide to forgo a planned expansion, in effect curtailing investment and slowing the economy without intending to do so. Unfortunately, government cannot command business to provide jobs and perform these functions; businesses must be induced to do so. Thus, business cannot be thought of as another group. As Charles Lindblom says, "Business is in a position of privilege in the political system of all market oriented societies."[38]

The power and influence of business is felt throughout the political system. Political scientists Clive Thomas and Ronald Hrebenar organized comprehensive assessments of interest group power in the 50 states for nearly 20 years. They found that general business interests are the "most powerful types of groups, followed by teachers' organizations, utilities, manufacturers, hospitals, insurance-related interests, physicians, contractors, local governments, and lawyers."[39] A survey of state legislators showed that state politicians felt even more constrained by business than did national leaders, given the constant threat to exit from their states should they pass legislation that threatens business interests.[40] Lastly, the urban politics literature is replete with similar references to cities competing for jobs, industry, and professional sports with offers of cash, tax breaks, and land. Urban scholars commonly explain such behavior by referring to the "systemic power of business."[41]

9.4 Interest Group Formation, Mobilization, and Maintenance

More biases are discovered when we attempt to understand why people form groups and keep them active. In 1965, economist Mancur Olson published a ground-breaking book titled, *The Logic of Collective Action*. In it he argues that small groups, whether businesses or non-business, had organizational advantages over larger groups.[42] Further, groups that seek private goods or benefits from government (those seeking special tax breaks, procurement contracts, or permission to extract natural resources on federal lands) were at a considerable advantage over groups seeking public goods or benefits (those asking for policies to protect the natural environment or lower the rate of crime) and were unlikely to mobilize even to a fraction of their potential.

Olson's logic assumes that rational individuals will join others for collective action if the benefits of working with a group outweigh the costs of participation. The costs of participation can be large or small and range from simply paying dues to the time it takes to run the organization as a volunteer. The benefits include a share in the outcome of the organization's efforts—the tax breaks, government contracts, a pristine environment, or reduction in crime, for example. The smaller the association, the larger the share for each member, which makes it more likely that the benefits or outcomes will end up on the positive side of each member's cost/benefit calculation. In large groups, every member will reason that their individual contribution will make little difference and decide to free ride on the efforts of others. If many participate, would the efforts of one make much difference? Probably not. If no one participates, the outcome is unlikely to be successful, but with little or nothing invested, there is scant loss to the individual member. Large groups also have difficulty preventing slackers from receiving the benefits should the group be successful. Small groups, on the other hand, are more personal. Members can easily observe the free riders and are likely to pressure the slackers into action, deny them their share of the benefits, or toss them out of the group.

The members of a group seeking private benefits (such as tax breaks for their organization) need not share what they have won from government with those outside the group. All groups, however, whether large or small, share with everybody the benefits of a successful lobbying campaign for a public good. The environmental group lobbying for regulation to reduce air pollution will share the benefits of clean air with all that breathe. Thus, groups working for public benefits face the same free rider problem as large groups because, according to Olson's logic, rational individuals choose not to bear the participation costs of group membership because they can enjoy the benefits produced without helping. Why join and contribute to an environmental group when you can get cleaner air for no cost if the group is successful? This explains why issues promoted by groups seeking public benefits, from climate change to public radio, tend to be under-supported and their benefits under-produced.

This is unfortunate because groups looking for public benefits from government often tend to be more democratic than groups seeking private benefits. For example, you may be a contributor to the Environmental Defense Fund because of its work to prevent global warming, but disagree with the group's stance on a pending carbon tax because it will increase the cost of gasoline. You can easily express your dissatisfaction with the EDF's policy position by quitting the group. This ability to exit applies to all members, so we can assume that the remaining members approve of the EDF's stance on the carbon tax (as well as its other goals). In another part of your life you belong to a union because it's a requirement of the job. You enjoy the private benefits you get from the group's collective bargaining with your employer. But, being politically conservative, you dislike your union's political stance on affirmative action. Do you quit your job? Probably not, because the private benefits your union helps provide, your good wages and health insurance, easily outweigh the costs of being unemployed. Instead, you and your fellow conservative union members learn to live with the union's policy positions even though you don't agree with them.

selective benefits

Goods or benefits offered exclusively to group members.

If Olson's logic is correct, and rationally self-interested people will free ride on the efforts of others, groups seeking purely public goods would not occur—but they do. Indeed, the National Rifle Association, mentioned at the beginning of this chapter, exists to protect a public good, the right of individuals to own guns—a right we all share. For Olson, a key to the formation and survival for a group like the NRA is **selective benefits**, benefits that need not be shared with nonmembers. Organizations like the union and businesses that were initially formed for nonpolitical purposes are in the best position to offer selective benefits, but political groups have learned to offer them as well.

material incentives

Tangible rewards that come with group membership.

solidary incentives

Intangible benefits that come with social association with a group.

informational incentives

Group benefits that provide valued facts or information.

purposive incentives

Intangible rewards that come with group membership.

The NRA, which has always done more than lobby for public polices, has developed into a full-service interest group. The benefits it provides to its members, like the benefits provided by other groups seeking public goods, can be classified into four types: material, solidary, informational, and purposive.[43] **Material incentives** are tangible benefits such as discount purchasing or the wage and other forms of compensation given to union members. In the NRA's case, the group offers its members gun loss and accidental death insurance, car rental, hotel, and airline discounts. Members also receive **solidary incentives**, which come from the act of associating with like-minded individuals, including intangibles like friendship and fun. The NRA offers numerous opportunities to enjoy the community of individuals from its over 10,000 state and local clubs.[44] Their national convention allows members the chance to mingle, attend seminars and workshops, listen to live music and lectures, and view exhibits featuring the latest in guns and gun accessories. The group's 2017 convention attracted some 80,000 members and 800 exhibitors to Atlanta, Georgia. The group also sponsors more than 12,000 local shooting tournaments and over 50 national shooting championships each year. Specialized benefits include general firearm safety, instructor certification, gunsmithing, and "Eddie Eagle" gun safety courses for children. **Informational incentives**, such as those offered at the convention and training classes, are supplemented by the NRA's magazines. These are published for its various membership groups and include the *American Hunter, American Rifleman, America's 1st Freedom, Woman's Outlook, Shooting Sports USA, and NRA Insights*. Lastly, what we think of as the core rationale of the group are **purposive incentives**. These include the satisfaction people get from contributing to and accomplishing a common cause. In the NRA's case, its members expect the organization to protect their right to own guns. They remain members as long as they believe the group is successful in achieving this goal.

TABLE 9.2 Selective Incentives

Category	Benefits
Informational Benefits	• Conferences • Professional contacts • Training programs • Publications • Coordination among organizations • Research • Legal help • Professional codes • Collective bargaining
Material Benefits	• Travel packages • Insurance • Discounts on consumer goods
Solidary Benefits	• Friendship • Networking opportunities
Purposive Benefits	• Advocacy • Representation before government • Participation in public affairs

Most groups offer solidary and purposive benefits, while personal material benefits like insurance and merchandise discounts are less common.[45] Many people remain members of a group because they believe they can make a difference even if they overestimate the importance of their own contribution. Such miscalculations are not uncommon since the investment most members make is normally small.[46] As political scientist Michael McCann notes, "There seems to be a general threshold level of involvement below which free rider calculation poses few inhibitions for ... commitment from moderately affluent citizen supporters."[47] Thus, groups that cannot afford much in the way of material incentives work hard to create an atmosphere of community and social inclusion and emphasize to their members that they are "making a difference" toward their policy goals. Leadership is also important. Many groups are started by individual entrepreneurs who offer others individual incentives to join. The group's leaders benefit by having jobs and controlling the group's resources to further their political agendas.[48]

Research testing Olson's hypotheses generally found support for the idea that groups seeking public benefits do not organize to their full potential. Studies also confirmed Olson's predictions that associations with intense preferences have organizational advantages over groups with diffuse interests. There is also considerable support for the numerical dominance of professional and business groups.[49] These findings support Olson's assumptions that the dilemmas of collective action reinforce the overrepresentation of groups already powerful in society. However, research also shows that motivations other than material benefits can make a difference. For example, the civil rights movement showed that collective action occurred within a large community with few resources and little traditional power. The movement had success even though it offered few selective benefits other than high levels of solidarity. It mobilized far fewer people than the number who stood to benefit from the movement's goals. Indeed, participants in civil rights marches often suffered disincentives such as insults, arrests, and beatings. Others in the movement were subjected to shootings and bombings. Less dramatic cases show that the civil rights movement was not aberrant. For example, after the nuclear accident at Three Mile Island, researchers found that organized opposition to nuclear power grew and eventually put an end to the growth of the nuclear power industry in the United States, even though most people who opposed nuclear power never participated in any collective action.[50]

Still other groups are formed and maintained with the help of charitable foundations, wealthy individuals, professional associations, or the government. For example, the neighborhood group fighting the freeway expansion got help from other neighborhood organizations originally organized by the federal government as part of President Lyndon Johnson's Community Action Programs. These policies required federal agencies to foster "maximum feasible participation" from low-income area residents and to subsidize the formation of community organizations to help deliver services. Years later, the established neighborhood development organizations could offer their neighbors fighting the freeway some of their organizational resources, including expertise, staff, office space, and other assets to sustain their cause. A local philanthropic foundation established by an oil company executive granted the group funds to hire an independent traffic engineer to break the highway department's monopoly on information allowing the group to offer its own technically plausible alternatives. In addition, the neighborhood group received pro-bono legal services from a downtown law firm willing to challenge the government's environmental impact study.[51] One study found that one-third of public interest organizations based in Washington received more than half of their funds from private foundations. Another 10 percent received more than 90 percent of their funding from foundations.[52]

Some interests, such as children or those with intellectual disabilities, cannot easily mobilize on their own. For these interests, social service professionals or other political entrepreneurs sometimes form clientele organizations to lobby government on their behalf.[53] Many of these surrogate groups come from state and local governments and have accounted for a growing share of total group growth formation since the 1960s.[54]

9.5 Change in the Interest Group System

Groups other than those representing business and professionals are becoming increasingly important. Growing in numbers are organizations from the nonprofit sector: health, social welfare, cultural, educational, public affairs, governmental, and religious groups. Health care groups in particular have expanded beyond a small number of professional, hospital, and insurance associations. Similar growth has occurred among organizations based on social movements that have traditionally found it difficult to overcome collective action problems, such as civil rights, women's rights, and other organizations.

Many of the changes are the result of increasing economic specialization, social diversity, technological change, and the growth of government. These fluctuations often create new interests or cause existing groups to fragment, as some members leave their umbrella association to lobby on their own with a more specialized focus. The expansion of the interest group universe, in other words, is a natural consequence of growing societal complexity. When the existing order is stable, the number and activities of interest groups remains steady, but when things become disturbed and certain interests are helped or hurt, interest groups proliferate. Any time governments consider new legislation or modify existing policies, they provide energy to the groups dealing with the issue.[55] For instance, if Congress or a state legislature reconsiders is policy on abortion, it provides energy to pro- and anti-abortion groups and spurs them to mobilize their existing assets or seek additional allies and resources.

Economic, Social, and Technological Change

Changes in the economy spurred economic interests to improve their political position relative to rival groups. Industrialization concentrated workers in factories and gave rise to the formation of unions. In turn, trade associations such the National Association of Manufacturers increased their memberships and resources in response to the rise of organized labor.[56] Business interests mobilized again in the 1970s in answer to threats posed by the federal government and by consumer advocates and environmentalists seeking protective policies (such as new safety and air pollution standards). Later, the rise of a post-industrial society, based on the increased importance of knowledge, created new technically oriented occupations and, with them, increased affluence, new lifestyles, and political expectations.[57] Increased affluence created a larger potential for "checkbook" membership.

In the 1960s, college enrollment increased and added force to the civil rights and antiwar movements. The spread of higher education also gave rise to a new set of groups in which ideas became more important than the distribution of wealth.[58] In this new environment, issue-based groups, such as the National Abortion Rights Action League (NARAL Pro-Choice America), Common Cause (a "good government" group), and People for the Ethical Treatment of Animals (PETA), have done especially well. Common Cause, for example, found that 43 percent of its members had an advanced degree and household incomes well above the national average.[59] Similarly, animal rights groups such as PETA are disproportionately composed of college-educated, professional women.[60] These growing groups tend to be more urban and socially permissive than the rest of society. At the same time, more traditional elements in society began to feel alienated from college-educated professionals on the one hand and resentful of government attempts to favor minorities (as they saw it) on the other. In the 1990s, the Christian Coalition and the Moral Majority organized nationally and locally. They began influencing electoral and legislative politics. Conservative groups reacted to the Supreme Court decision in *Roe v. Wade*, which legalized abortion nationally, but they also felt threatened by various technological advances, such as use of fetal tissue for medical research.

What interest groups do and how they accomplish their goals can also be traced to technological change. Along with the proliferation of computers, satellites, and cable television are new industry groups organized to foster and protect their interests. More fundamentally, however, communications breakthroughs make group politics much more visible and powerful. Networked computers and other "smart" devices revolutionized recruitment, fund-raising, and communication with members, but also enabled more organizations to exert pressure on elected officials.

Growth of Government

Government officials are the targets of lobbying from pressure groups, but they are also responsible for the formation of many groups in the first place. Whenever the government enters a new policy area, interest groups form. For example, in the 1930s the federal government encouraged the growth of labor unions by protecting collective bargaining rights for workers and prohibiting injunctions in labor disputes. At the same time, the Social Security Act was passed by Congress to provide retirement and other benefits to working Americans. Over time, organizations formed to protect and expand such benefits, such as the American Association of Retired Persons. Similar rounds of group formation followed initiatives in education, civil rights, housing, urban affairs, and health care. Anti-abortion groups formed after the 1973 Supreme Court decision in *Roe v. Wade*, while pro-abortion groups rallied after the 1992 *Planned Parenthood v. Casey* decision.

It is also common for the government to form groups directly. At the turn of the twentieth century, local farm bureaus were formed by the Department of Agriculture to help its agricultural agents provide educational services to the country's farmers. The local bureaus soon affiliated and formed the American Farm Bureau Federation.[61] The Commerce Department did the same when it encouraged the formation of the U.S. Chamber of Commerce. Since the 1960s, much federal legislation included a provision requiring participation from various citizen groups, including environmental action councils, health care organizations, and senior citizens groups. The reasons are straightforward. Government agencies use interest group input to improve, justify, and develop support for their decisions.[62] Public participation is also required during the process of administrative rule-making before final regulations are adopted.

Much of interest group politics is characterized by waves of mobilization and countermobilization. As one group gains an upper hand, it gives incentives to rivals to increase their efforts to get more people and resources on their side. As E. E. Schattschneider says, "It is the loser who calls for outside help."[63] Still, this does not mean imbalances in the interest group system are self-correcting or eventually lead to an equilibrium among groups. History is filled with circumstances of injustice, poverty, and discrimination that, in retrospect, should have prompted groups to emerge but did not. Resources needed to participate effectively are not evenly distributed. Businesses, professionals, and the better-off are greatly advantaged, while social welfare, civil rights, and handicapped groups are still too few. According to Kay Schlozman, of the 39 women's associations in Washington, none are organized to represent homemakers and no organization represents the interests of men. Of the 92 educational associations, only the American Student Association represents the interests of the country's estimated 70 million students.[64]

9.6 Lobbying: How Interest Groups Influence Policy

Interest groups should be understood in terms of their public policy objectives. They attempt to influence the decisions of government officials by using lobbyists to talk with them directly or by communicating indirectly through their constituents. Interest groups also try to reach their goals by giving campaign contributions to politicians. Stereotypically, lobbyists are viewed as hosting fancy parties or outings to exclusive golf resorts where they sweet-talk legislators and offer them bribes in the form of campaign contributions. The reality is more mundane. Lobbyists do meet face to face with decision makers, contribute to campaigns, and attempt to talk them into supporting their client's policy preferences. They also conduct and distribute policy research, design grassroots programs to mobilize citizens to contact their representatives, and conduct public opinion polls to gather information about constituency opinion. The most influential lobbyists are a small group with addresses on K Street in Washington, D.C., but political scientist James Thurber estimates there are well over 100,000 lobbyists active in Washington.[65] More than $2 billion is spent annually on lobbying activities. More money is spent by interest groups on lobbying than on campaign contributions.[66]

bakdc / Shutterstock.com

Legislatures are seemingly tailor-made for interest group influence. Much of their work is done in the somewhat isolated world of committees, where they attract clusters of organized group and bureaucratic interests and where members, staffers, and lobbyists are content to restrict controversies to the people who show up. Often, self-serving alliances called **iron triangles** or **sub-governments** form between committee members, interest group lobbyists, and executive branch officials around the policy area dealt with by the committee.[67] Committee discussion is open to the public, but obscured from the press and the intrusion of other interests that might become involved. Because the committee system fragments and complicates the legislative process, it is necessary to monitor what committees and subcommittees are doing in order to influence the actions of Congress. Such monitoring is cumbersome for the press and impractical for the average citizen, but lobbyists are paid to sit though hours of testimony and listen to questions posed by members. As one lobbyist put it, "I'll be on the scene; I'm my clients' eyes and ears."[68]

Contract lobbyists do not work for a single organization. Rather, they have many clients. These are the "hired guns" with the high salaries, select contacts, and ample expense accounts you often read about. Some are independent, but most operate out of public relations, consulting, or law firms.[69] In-house lobbyists work for a wide range of organizations including businesses, chambers of commerce, trade associations, state bar associations, environmental groups, and others. They often serve as executive directors, presidents, and public relations directors for their organizations.[70] Government lobbyists, as the name implies, work for state, local, or federal agencies who, as part of or all of their jobs, represent their agency. Lastly, volunteer lobbyists are ordinary citizens who normally represent a wide variety of groups including charitable, social welfare, or single-issue organizations. Often, citizen lobbyists are part of an effort to use constituent groups to their advantage. Such organizations may also encourage the group's members to send e-mails or letters to legislators supporting their groups' policy positions.

iron triangles

A mutually beneficial relationship between congressional committee members and their staffs, interest group lobbyists, and executive branch officials.

sub-governments

A mutually beneficial relationship between interest groups and government officials surrounding a particular policy area.

Direct Lobbying

At the national level, lobbying takes two forms. Direct techniques are the most common. It involves contact with government officials, usually involving meeting and talking with the targeted official or testifying during committee hearings. Indirect techniques target citizens through media or direct mail campaigns. At the end of the appeal, citizens are encouraged to make their voices heard to public officials, hopefully in accordance with the group's wishes.

Over the past decade or so, indirect or media lobbying has become more common, but lobbyists believe that meeting personally with government officials is still the most effective way to influence government decisions.[71] Thus, much lobbying remains direct and personal. Lobbyists develop their relationships with public officials over many years, building trust and friendships. Legislators, their staffs, executive branch officials, and regulators value high-quality information and lobbyists rely on information to make their cases. Public officials exist in an uncertain and constantly changing environment, so the information that lobbyists provide is designed to reduce uncertainty. The kinds of information they find valuable gives details about the implications of a course of action for the targeted official's political career, information about the status of a proposed government decision, or policy-analytic information about the consequences of a particular course of action.[72] Consequently, the information that lobbyists provide is designed to help public officials reach their professional goals, which for legislators is to win reelection, make public policy that benefits their constituents, or gain influence among their colleagues in the legislature.[73]

The picture of lobbyists painted by the political science literature is one of influence-peddlers helping to draft legislation and delivering testimony, but also one of information brokers essential to maintaining the flow of ideas and findings that fuel the process of policy making. Lobbyists often provide a service to legislators and their staffs by synthesizing into concise documents disparate studies written by academics, think-tank analysts, or government officials.[74] Legislators and their staffs share information, so their standing in the political community would be damaged by promoting shoddy or false information. Lobbyists also work together by sharing information they gather or by dividing their efforts to cover committee hearings scheduled simultaneously. It often takes a long time to build trust in politics. Lobbyists know they can be shut out of the legislative process if their information is questionable. As lobbyist Rogan Kersch observes, "I double-deal one time, and my credibility in this town is gone."[75]

Lobbyists also inform their clients. They often send weekly or bimonthly reports on pending legislative and regulatory issues. Lobbyists offer observations about the political landscape and its consequences and give guidance about what to do.[76] They also give reassurance to their clients that their interests are being protected. Again, as lobbyist Robert Kersh writes, "Monitor, observe, question, report: these are the verbs that describe a lobbyist's professional life.[77]

Indirect Lobbying: Mobilizing Public Opinion

It is also common for interest groups to influence public policy indirectly by trying to move public opinion in their direction in the hope that elected officials will respond to their constituents. Techniques that involve television advertising are common but expensive, so they tend to be used by larger, wealthier groups. In 1994, for example, groups opposed to President Bill Clinton's health care plan mobilized key votes in Congress to defeat it. The ads featured Harry and Louise, a fictional well-read wife and her husband, sitting in their kitchen worried about the effects of the Clinton plan. The campaign was orchestrated by congressman turned lobbyist Bill Graidson, who was working for the Health Insurance Association of America. The association spent some $17 million on the ads focused in key congressional districts. The novelty of the campaign gained national attention when ads were broadcast on regular news programs across the country. Over 500,000 people called the 800 number and 250,000 contacts were made with members of Congress. All this attention promptly killed the proposal.[78]

Most groups maintain internet sites that present their messages along with information on how to help, join the group, or contribute financially. Interest groups also use grassroots techniques involving rank-and-file members to influence legislators. Among these are efforts to inspire members to write letters to, call, or email legislators or agency officials to show their support (or opposition) to an upcoming bill or regulation. However, these tactics have become so common that they are sometimes discounted as routine or perceived as "manufactured" by lobbyists.[79] Journalists and scholars sometimes refer to such efforts as **astroturfing**, implying that the campaign only has the appearance of a spontaneous campaign by average citizens. Indirect techniques are common in the states as well. Studies suggest that well over half of state lobbyists engage in some form of media lobbying.[80]

> **astroturfing**
>
> An artificial grassroots lobbying campaign using deceptive tactics to make it appear that support (or opposition) comes from average citizens.

Does Lobbying Affect Public Policy?

Is lobbying effective? Can lobbyists make a public official change his or her mind or move in a policy direction he or she would not otherwise have gone? For their part, the public and the press generally believe that lobbying is effective. What else explains why the practice has become prevalent or why interest groups are willing to spend so much money on lobbying? Reports from newspaper accounts often show an exchange of favors between lobbyists and public officials, but does this behavior indicate bribery or corruption? After President Barack Obama promised legislation to restrict federal funding to for-profit colleges that lure students with false advertising, a consortium of colleges spent more than $61 million on well-connected lobbyists to plead their case. The campaign successfully weakened the proposed regulation, but did the administration cave to the group's influence? According to Cass Sunstein, the White House official who negotiated the proposal, the lobbying effort had "zero effect." The administration concluded that the industry had reasonable arguments and decided on its own to narrow the scope of the legislation.[81]

Political scientists have found it difficult to show the direct effects of lobbying on policy outcomes because it is hard to separate the many other influences on congressional decision making. For example, defense contractors who sell boots, ammunition, and expensive weapons systems are often accused of successful lobbying because the Department of Defense sometimes tells Congress to stop buying equipment it doesn't need.[82] But scholars also note that military contracts bring jobs to local districts and it is the Congress member's duty to bring the benefits of government home. Is the member bending to the will of military contractors, or making his or her constituents happy? It's probably both. Contracts for parts of the B2 bomber are placed in all of the continental states to ensure that members of Congress have jobs to protect.[83]

Political scientists often focus on lobbyists' access to decision-makers as a measure of influence. Access is vital in lobbying. As notorious lobbyist Jack Abramoff explained, "If you can't get in your door, you can't make your case....So that's the lobbyist safe-cracker method: throw fundraisers, raise money, and become a big donor."[84] This creates unequal access among groups, especially for those who are unorganized or resource-poor. Some studies conclude that lobbies are less influential than press accounts suggest, but most conclude that the results are sufficient to justify their expenditures.[85] A review of 78 studies published from 1976 to 2010 found a positive correlation between corporate political activity and firm performance.[86] Similarly, a study of the 50 companies that spend the most on lobbying determined that these companies gained a substantial return on their investments.[87] More disturbing is the conclusion drawn by Martin Gilens in his 2014 book, *Affluence and Influence*. Gilens and a small army of research assistants gathered data on 1,778 policy cases between 1981 and 2002. They found that America's policymakers respond almost exclusively to the preferences of the economically advantaged. In contrast, they found almost no relationship between policy outcomes and the desires of less advantaged groups, including the middle class.

9.7 What Can I Do?

Follow your interests and join a group, or start one of your own. There are lots of things you can do to make your community a better place. We are not talking about recycling or becoming an organ donor. We are talking about increasing your voice in politics through actions designed to change public policies—the things interest groups do.

Joining an interest group is one of the easiest ways to participate in American politics. If you are passionate about a particular issue, it is likely there is a group of like-minded individuals whose efforts you can join. Are you passionate about animals? The Humane Society of the United States works to create a humane world for animals and people. They work to rescue homeless or mistreated pets but also to prevent larger-scale cruelties such as animal fighting, factory farming, and puppy mills. They have local organizations in all 50 states and most cities and towns that offer volunteer and internship opportunities (and even jobs as public policy specialists). On the other side, the Center for Consumer Freedom works to protect consumer choice and responsibility. They believe consumers, not governments, should decide whether to boycott puppy mills, animal fights, or hunting endangered species. Like guns? The NRA works to preserve your right to own one. On the other hand, if you are concerned about the dangers of guns, the Coalition to Stop Gun Violence works to counter the efforts of the NRA by working with state, local and the national government to regulate gun ownership.

If your political interests are more general, the non-partisan group Common Cause works to create an open, honest, and accountable government that promotes the common interest. They are a national network with offices in 35 states and Washington, D.C., with more than a million members and supporters. They work to promote voting and organize communities to petition governments to limit the influence of money in politics. The League of Women Voters does much the same by focusing on providing education on election issues and encouraging citizens to vote. If you are unsure about your interests, contact your local volunteer center for opportunities to help. Most groups encourage participation through social media. You can also join a protest and march for justice. Show up and lend yourself to the cause for a morning or afternoon.

You can also start your own group and lobby government like the students at Marjory Stoneman Douglas High School in Parkland, Florida. Paul Preston recently made national news by starting a movement to split the state of California into two states. The group claims that California's current domination by the Democratic Party is unfair to conservatives living in the state. They propose to separate the Republican leaning inland areas of the state from the more liberal coastal communities. Will they succeed? Probably not, but Preston and his small group are being heard and making people think. States like California allow citizens to bypass the legislature and pass laws via the initiative process. All one needs to do is draft a legislative bill or an amendment to the state's constitution and collect signatures on a petition supporting the measure. If they collect a enough signatures, usually a small proportion of the votes cast in the last election, the measure is placed on the ballot and enacted into law if supported by a majority of voters. Small groups in states that use the initiative process can have a major impact if they can get a majority of voters to agree with them.

Most of the groups mentioned previously produce public or shared benefits, but that doesn't mean your efforts will go unrewarded. Many groups have staffs and therefore jobs to offer, but as a student, your college or university can offer you internship credit toward your degree if you don't get paid. Less tangible benefits include the friendships you make working with like-minded individuals or simply the fun and camaraderie of working for a common cause. You will also receive increased knowledge about an issue you care about and gain valuable experience from working with the group. Experience is something you can include on your resume. The pleasure you receive from working for a cause in which you believe, on the other hand, is its own reward.

9.8 What's the Alternative?

The previous discussion about the Center for Consumer Freedom countering the efforts of the Humane Society should remind us of the virtues of the interest group system in American politics. In a large and diverse society, the many different interests serve to check one another. Groups are easy to form. The right to petition government and speak freely is guaranteed by the Constitution. The Constitution also disperses power by separating institutions, allowing one institution to check the actions of another. It gives the states significant authority to act independently of the federal government. All this creates multiple points of access for groups to be heard and counter each other's efforts. The result is a competitive system in which multiple groups prevent one or a coalition of groups from controlling government and perpetuating a tyranny.

We also learned in this chapter about how the interest group system is clearly biased in favor of business and upper-class interests. Looking more broadly, political scientists Martin Gilens and Benjamin Page comprehensively tested four theoretical traditions of American politics: majoritarian democracy based on elections, economic-elite domination of politics, majoritarian politics, and biased group politics. They used a large data set derived from 1,779 policy cases between 1981 and 2002. Their analysis suggests "that majorities of the American public actually have little influence over the policies our government adopts, as policymaking is dominated by powerful business organizations and a small number of affluent Americans."[88] Interestingly, Gilens found the policy opinions of average Americans counts only every four years, during presidential elections.

Critics of interest group politics conclude that elections are the only time that the poor and middle class have the same influence as the affluent because everyone has one and only one vote. Elections should be emphasized because of this fundamental equality among citizens and because evidence shows that elected officials can be depended on to be responsive to their constituents as a way of increasing their chances of holding onto power. As we pointed out in Chapter 7 on elections, all forms of political participation favor more affluent segments of society, but the more costly forms of participation are more biased than low-cost forms of participation. Voting is more democratic because it is less costly than participation in groups. Critics of interest groups also argue that the dispersal of governmental power is not a solution to the problem of tyranny. Rather, it contributes to the problem because it raises information costs for average citizens and undermines political responsibility. This is because citizens have a great difficulty determining who is responsible for what results.

Endnotes

1. Sarah Almukhtar and K. K. Rebecca, "What Happened in the Parkland School Shooting," *The New York Times*, February 15, 2018, accessed June 02, 2018, https://www.nytimes.com/interactive/2018/02/15/us/florida-school-shooting-map.html. Eli Rosenberg, Derek Hawkins, and Julie Tate, "Who is Devin Patrick Kelley, the gunman officials say killed churchgoers in Sutherland Springs, Tex.?" *The Washington Post*, November 06, 2017, accessed January 19, 2018, https://www.washingtonpost.com/news/morning-mix/wp/2017/11/06/who-is-devin-patrick-kelley-gunman-who-officials-say-killed-churchgoers-in-sutherland-springs/. Jose A. Del, "Stephen Paddock, Las Vegas Suspect, Was a Gambler Who Drew Little Attention," *The New York Times*, October 02, 2017, accessed January 19, 2018, https://www.nytimes.com/2017/10/02/us/stephen-paddock-vegas-shooter.html. Alex Yablon, "To Limit Mass Shooting Carnage, Start by Banning High-Capacity Magazines," *Slate Magazine*, June 14, 2016, accessed January 19, 2018, http://www.slate.com/articles/news_and_politics/crime/2016/06/the_ar_15_and_other_assault_rifles_are_bad_high_capacity_magazines_are_worse.html.

2. Christine Hauser, "Gun Death Rate Rose Again in 2016, C.D.C. Says," *The New York Times*, November 04, 2017, accessed January 19, 2018, https://www.nytimes.com/2017/11/04/us/gun-death-rates.html.

3. "Gun Violence by the Numbers," EverytownResearch.org, January 18, 2018, accessed January 19, 2018, https://everytownresearch.org/gun-violence-by-the-numbers/.

4. Lisa M. Hepburn and David Hemenway, "Firearm Availability and Homicide: A Review of the Literature," *Aggression and Violent Behavior* 9, no. 4 (2004): 417-40, doi:10.1016/s1359-1789(03)00044-2.

5. Youyou Zhou, "Three percent of the population own half of the civilian guns in the US," Quartz, October 06, 2017, accessed January 19, 2018, https://qz.com/1095899/gun-ownership-in-america-in-three-charts/.

6. "Bureau of Alcohol, Tobacco, Firearms and Explosives," National Firearms Act | Bureau of Alcohol, Tobacco, Firearms and Explosives, accessed January 19, 2018, https://www.atf.gov/rules-and-regulations/national-firearms-act.

7. *Brady Handgun Violence Prevention Act*, HR 1025, 103rd Cong., 1st sess., *Congressional Record*, https://www.congress.gov/103/bills/hr1025/BILLS-103hr1025enr.pdf.

8. Mark Emmons and Josh Richman, "Stockton shooting: 25 years later, city can't forget its worst day," *The Mercury News*, August 12, 2016, accessed January 19, 2018, http://www.mercurynews.com/2014/01/16/stockton-shooting-25-years-later-city-cant-forget-its-worst-day/.

9. "Support for Stricter Gun Laws Edges Up in U.S." Gallup, Inc., October 16, 2017, accessed January 19, 2018, http://news.gallup.com/poll/220595/support-stricter-gun-laws-edges.aspx.

10. David Kopel, "Opinion | The Protection of Lawful Commerce in Arms Act: Facts and policy," *The Washington Post*, WP Company, 24 May 2016, www.washingtonpost.com/news/volokh-conspiracy/wp/2016/05/24/the-protection-of-lawful-commerce-in-arms-act-facts-and-policy/?utm_term=.b5ec7f4f8063.

11. Peter Overby, "NRA: 'Only Thing That Stops A Bad Guy With A Gun Is A Good Guy With A Gun'," NPR, December 21, 2012, accessed January 19, 2018, https://www.npr.org/2012/12/21/167824766/nra-only-thing-that-stops-a-bad-guy-with-a-gun-is-a-good-guy-with-a-gun.

12. Susan Ferrissemail, "NRA pushed 'stand your ground' laws across the nation," Center for Public Integrity, May 19, 2014, accessed January 19, 2018, https://www.publicintegrity.org/2012/03/26/8508/nra-pushed-stand-your-ground-laws-across-nation.

13. "Home," NRA.ORG, accessed January 19, 2018, https://home.nra.org/.

14. U.S. Department of the Treasury, Internal Revenue Service, Form 990, (Washington, DC: 2015), http://990s.foundationcenter.org/990_pdf_archive/530/530116130/530116130_201512_990O.pdf.

15. Dan Bigman, "What The NRA's Wayne Lapierre Gets Paid To Defend Guns," Forbes, December 22, 2012, accessed January 19, 2018, https://www.forbes.com/sites/danbigman/2012/12/21/what-the-nras-wayne-lapierre-gets-paid-to-defend-guns/#7346856d16d6.

16. "Home," NRA.Org, accessed January 19, 2018, https://home.nra.org/.

17. Ruth Igielnik and Anna Brown, "Key takeaways on Americans' views of guns and gun ownership," Pew Research Center, June 22, 2017, accessed January 19, 2018, http://www.pewresearch.org/fact-tank/2017/06/22/key-takeaways-on-americans-views-of-guns-and-gun-ownership/.

18. Tim Dickinson, "The NRA vs. America," Rolling Stone, January 31, 2013, accessed January 19, 2018, http://www.rollingstone.com/politics/news/the-nra-vs-america-20130131.

19. Corky Siemaszko, "Fear—and big sales—propelled record-breaking Black Friday gun checks," NBCNews.com, November 27, 2017, accessed January 19, 2018, https://www.nbcnews.com/news/us-news/fear-big-sales-propelled-record-breaking-black-friday-gun-checks-n824216.

20. James Madison, "The Federalist #10," Constitution Society, accessed January 19, 2018, http://www.constitution.org/fed/federa10.htm.

21. First Amendment Center, accessed January 19, 2018, http://www.firstamendmentcenter.org/petition-overview/.

22. Pendleton Herring, Group Representation Before Congress (New York: Russell & Russell, 1967).

23. Margaret Susan Thompson, The "Spider Web": Congress and Lobbying in the Age of Grant (Ithaca, New York: Cornell University Press, 1986).

24. Howard E. Aldrich, Catherine A. Aimmer, Udo H. Staber, and John J. Beggs, "Minimalism, Mutualism, and Maturity: The Evolution of the American Trade Association Population in the 20th Century," Evolutionary Dynamics of Organizations (1994).

25. Gerald Gamm and Robert D. Putnam, "The Growth of Voluntary Associations in America, 1840–1940," The Journal of Interdisciplinary History 29, no. 4 (1999), 511-557.

26. J. David Greenstone, Labor in American Politics (Chicago: University of Chicago Press, 1977).

27. Howard E. Aldrich, Catherine A. Aimmer, Udo H. Staber, and John J. Beggs, "Minimalism, Mutualism, and Maturity: The Evolution of the American Trade Association Population in the 20th Century," Evolutionary Dynamics of Organizations (1994).

28. Sidney Verba, Henry E. Brady, and Kay Lehman Schlozman, Voice and Equality: Civic Voluntarism in American Politics (Cambridge, Massachusetts: Harvard Univ. Press, 2002).

29. James E. Curtis, Douglas E. Baer, and Edward G. Grabb, "Nations of Joiners: Explaining Voluntary Association Membership in Democratic Societies," American Sociological Review 66, no. 6 (2001): 783, doi:10.2307/3088873.

30. Baumgartner and Walker (1988), 919.

31. Kay Lehman Schlozman, "What Accent the Heavenly Chorus? Political Equality and the American Pressure System," The Journal of Politics 46, no. 4 (1984): 1006-032, doi:10.2307/2131240.

32. Elmer E. Schattschneider, The Semisovereign People: A Realist's View of Democracy in America (Boston, MA: Wadsworth, 2013).

33. Jack L. Walker, Mobilizing Interest Groups in America: Patrons, Professions, and Social Movements (Ann Arbor: Univ. of Michigan Press, 2003).

34. Kay Lehman Schlozman and John T. Tierney, Organized Interests and American Democracy (New York: Harper & Row, 1986).

35. Ibid.

36. Ibid.

37. Gray and Lowery, (1976) from Baumgartner and Leech.

38. Charles Edward Lindblom, Politics and Markets: The World's Political-economic Systems (New York, NY: Basic Books, 1995).

39. Anthony J. Nownes and Adam J. Newmark, "Interest Groups in the States," Politics in the American States: A Comparative Analysis, Seventh Edition ed. Virginia Gray, Russell L. Hanson, and Thad Kousser (Washington, D.C., CQ Press, 2013).

40. Margery M. Ambrosius and Susan Welch, "State Legislators Perceptions of Business and Labor Interests," Legislative Studies Quarterly 13, no. 2 (1988): 199, doi:10.2307/439821.

41. Clarence Nathan Stone, Regime Politics: Governing Atlanta, 1946-1988 (Lawrence, Kansas: University Press of Kansas, 1989).

42. Mancur Olson Jr., The Logic of Collective Action: Public Goods and the Theory of Groups (Cambridge, Massachusetts: Harvard University Press, 1965).

43. Peter B. Clark and James Q. Wilson, "Incentive Systems: A Theory of Organizations," Administrative Science Quarterly 6, no. 2 (1961): 129, doi:10.2307/2390752.

44. "General Information," Institute for Legislative Action, 2001, http://www.nraila.org/research/19991123-generalinfo-OO1.shtml.

45. Jack L. Walker, Mobilizing Interest Groups in America: Patrons, Professions, and Social Movements (Ann Arbor: University of Michigan Press, 2003).

46. Lawrence S. Rothenberg, "Organizational Maintenance and the Retention Decision in Groups," The American Political Science Review 82, no. 4 (1988): 1129, doi:10.2307/1961753.

47. Public Interest Liberalism & the Modern Regulatory State. Polity Vol. 21, No. 2 (Winter, 1988), pp. 373-400. University of Chicago Press Journals

48. Robert H. Salisbury, "An Exchange Theory of Interest Groups," Midwest Journal of Political Science 13, no. 1 (1969): 1, doi:10.2307/2110212.

49. Frank R. Baumgartner and Beth L. Leech, Basic Interests: The Importance of Groups in Politics and in Political Science (Princeton, NJ: Princeton University Press, 1998).

50. Frank R. Baumgartner and Bryan D. Jones, "Agenda Dynamics and Policy Subsystems," The Journal of Politics 53, no. 4 (November, 1991): 1044-1074, doi:10.2307/2131866.

51. Martin R. Saiz, "Transforming Growth Politics: Denver During the Peña Administration" (Prepared for delivery at the 1993 Annual Meeting of the Western Political Science Association, Pasadena, California, March 18-20, 1993).

52. Philip A. Mundo, Interest Groups: Cases and Characteristics (Chicago: Nelson-Hall, 1992).

53. Frank R. Baumgartner and Beth L. Leech, Basic Interests: The Importance of Groups in Politics and in Political Science (Princeton, NJ: Princeton University Press, 1998).

54. Allan J. Cigler, Burdett A. Loomis, and Anthony J. Nownes, Interest Group Politics (Thousand Oaks, CA: CQ Press, 2016).

55. David Lowery and Virginia Gray, "The Population Ecology of Gucci Gulch, or the Natural Regulation of Interest Group Numbers in the American States," American Journal of Political Science 39, no. 1 (1995): 1, doi:10.2307/2111755.

56. James Q. Wilson, Political Organizations (Princeton, New Jersey: Princeton University Press, 1995).

57. Everett Carll Ladd and Charles D. Hadley, Transformations of the American Party System: Political Coalitions from the New Deal to the 1970s (New York: Norton, 1978).

58. James Q. Wilson, Political Organizations, (Princeton, New Jersey: Princeton University Press, 1995).

59. Andrew S. McFarland, Common Cause: Lobbying in the Public Interest (New Delhi: Asian Books, 1987).

60. Lauristan R. King and Kimberly Stephens, "Politics and the Animal Rights Movement" (paper presented at the annual meeting of the Southern Political Science Association, Tampa, FL, November 7–9, 1991).

61. James Q. Wilson, Political Organizations (Princeton, New Jersey: Princeton University Press, 1995).

62. Stuart Langton, Citizen Participation in America: Essays on the State of the Art (Lexington, MA: Heath, 1979).

63. Elmer E. Schattschneider, The Semisovereign People: A Realist's View of Democracy in America (Boston, MA: Wadsworth, 2013), 16.

64. Kay Lehman Schlozman, "What Accent the Heavenly Chorus? Political Equality and the American Pressure System," Journal of Politics 46 no. 4 (1983): 1006-32.

65. "What is shadow lobbying? How influence peddlers shape policy in the dark," Sunlight Foundation, October 26, 2016, accessed January 19, 2018, https://sunlightfoundation.com/2016/04/19/what-is-shadow-lobbying-how-influence-peddlers-shape-policy-in-the-dark/.

66. "Data on Campaign Finance, Super PACs, Industries, and Lobbying," OpenSecrets, accessed January 19, 2018, https://www.opensecrets.org/.

67. Theodore J. Lowi, The End of Liberalism: The Second Republic of the United States, (New York: W.W. Norton & Co., 2010).

68. Rogan Kersh, "The Well-Informed Lobbyist," Interest Group Politics, eds. Allan J. Cigler and Burdett A. Loomis (Washington, DC: CQ Press, 2007).

69. Anthony J. Nownes and Adam J. Newmark, "Interest Groups in the States," Politics in the American States: A Comparative Analysis, Seventh Edition, eds. Virginia Gray, Russell L. Hanson, and Thad Kousser (Washington, D.C., CQ Press, 2013).

70. Clive S. Thomas, "Lobbyists: Definitions, Types, and Varying Designations," Research Guide to U.S. and International Interest Groups (Westport, CT: Praeger, 2004).

71. Alan Rosenthal, The Third House: Lobbyists and Lobbying in the States (Washington DC: SAGE Publications, 2015).

72. John R. Wright and Bruce Ian Oppenheimer, Interest Groups and Congress: Lobbying, Contributions, and Influence (New York: Longman, 2003).

73. Ibid.

74. Rogan Kersh, "The Well-Informed Lobbyist," Interest Group Politics, eds. Allan J. Cigler and Burdett A. Loomis (Washington, D.C: CQ Press, 2007).

75. Ibid, 406.

76. Ibid, 402.

77. Ibid, 398.

78. "The People & The Power Game: Transcript of The Unelected: The Media & The Lobbies," Hendrick Smith Productions, accessed January 19, 2018, http://www.hedricksmith.com/site_powergame/files/uneltrans.html.

79. Allan J. Cigler, Burdett A. Loomis, and Anthony J. Nownes, *Interest Group Politics* (Thousand Oaks, CA: CQ Press, 2016).

80. Anthony J. Nownes and Patricia Freeman, "Interest Group Activity in the States," *The Journal of Politics* 60, no. 1 (Feb.,1998): 86-112,doi:10.2307/2648002.

81. Eric Lichblau, "With Lobbying Blitz, For-Profit Colleges Diluted New Rules," *The New York Times*, December 09, 2011, accessed January 19, 2018, http://www.nytimes.com/2011/12/10/us/politics/for-profit-college-rules-scaled-back-after-lobbying.html.

82. Matthew Cox, "Pentagon Tells Congress to Stop Buying Equipment it Doesn't Need," Military.com, accessed January 19, 2018, https://www.military.com/daily-news/2015/01/28/pentagon-tells-congress-to-stop-buying-equipment-it-doesnt-need.html.

83. Chalmers Johnson, "Tomgram: Chalmers Johnson on electing the Pentagon's man," TomDispatch.com, September 14, 2004, accessed January 19, 2018, http://www.tomdispatch.com/post/1818/chalmers_johnson_the_military-industrial_man.

84. "Jack Abramoff On Lobbying," NPR, December 20, 2011, https://www.npr.org/sections/money/2011/12/20/144028899/the-tuesday-podcast-jack-abramoff-on-lobbying.

85. Ken Kollman, *Outside Lobbying: Public Opinion and Interest Group Strategies* (Princeton: Princeton University Press, 1998).

86. S. Lux and D. Woehr, "Mixing Business With Politics: A Meta-Analysis of the Antecedents and Outcomes of Corporate Political Activity," *Journal of Management* 37 no. 1 (2011): 223-247.

87. "Money and politics," *The Economist*, October 01, 2011, accessed January 19, 2018, http://www.economist.com/node/21531014.

88. Martin Gilens and Benjamin I. Page, "Testing Theories of American Politics: Elites, Interest Groups, and Average Citizens," *Perspectives on Politics* 12, no. 03 (2014): 564-81, doi:10.1017/s1537592714001595.

CHAPTER 10
Media: Biased or a Business?

Chapter Objectives

1. Understand the role the media play in the era of high-tech politics.
2. Trace the evolution of the mass media.
3. Explain the agenda-setting power of the media.
4. Clarify how the media act as key linkage institutions between the public and political officials.
5. Think critically about the relationship among the media, government, and democracy.

Introduction: Lights, Camera, Action

In 1991, the government of Somalia, a country in the Horn of Africa, collapsed and fell into the hands of warlords competing for power. The warlords used food and resources as weapons of war, resulting in mass looting and widespread starvation. In response to the growing humanitarian crisis in Somalia, U.S. President George H.W. Bush committed 28,000 troops to "save innocent lives."[1] His decision to intervene in Somalia marked a departure from traditional foreign policy. Such policy typically dictates that, in order to send American troops overseas, there must be a pressing national security concern. The rhetoric that Bush and his administration used to justify the commitment of troops to Somalia suggested that the decision was not based on geostrategic national security calculations, but instead on the desire to protect civilians. Humanitarian crises are not new, nor are they rare. What was unusual about the Somalia situation is that the United States became involved. In fact, the last true humanitarian mission that the United States led prior to 1991 was the Berlin Airlift from 1948-49. Why, then, did Bush decide to intervene in Somalia?

The story goes that one evening, President Bush and First Lady Barbara Bush were watching the nightly news when a piece about starving children and women in Somalia aired. The president was so disturbed by the images that he told Barbara he wanted to do something about the situation. Soon after, he consulted with advisers and the decision to deploy troops was made. Some have argued there were in fact national security concerns in Somalia (and the United States' previous engagements with the country certainly suggest this could be the case), but if we listen to Bush's own words about why he chose to intervene in 1992, humanitarian issues seemed to be the policy priority. He said at the time that the forces he was sending to Somalia to lead an international humanitarian coalition had orders to use "whatever military force is necessary to safeguard the lives of our troops and the lives of the Somali people."[2] The question, then, is do the nightly news shows really have that much influence on the President of the United States? Does the media really have the power to shape policy and, in the case of Somalia, send us into war for purely humanitarian reasons?

The mission of the Newseum in Washington, D.C., is to increase understanding of the importance of free press and the First Amendment. Through interactive exhibits, the museum tells the history of the news media and includes a 9/11 Gallery that displays the broadcast antennae from the top of the World Trade Center.

AgnosticPreachersKid [CC BY-SA 3.0 (https://creativecommons.org/licenses/by-sa/3.0)], from Wikimedia Commons. https://commons.wikimedia.org/wiki/File:Newseum_-_WTC_radio_mast.JPG.

Television could have the power to determine how we think about politics and what we believe to be important political issues largely by paying attention to some problems and ignoring or paying minimal attention to others.[3] The Somalia case suggests this is true: it was perhaps the media that focused Bush's attention on Somalia and played an important role in putting the crisis on the political agenda. Former U.S. Secretary-General Boutros Boutros-Ghali once said, "CNN is the sixteenth member of the Security Council."[4] This statement reflects the increasing power of cable news networks and the mass media to more broadly set the policy agenda while shaping the development of major events.

The relationship between the media and the government has evolved over time. While the media depends heavily on the government for sources and information, technological developments and a network of worldwide correspondents have transformed the media's role in politics. Because the media now has the capacity to report events as they unfold, the time between the public learning about what has happened and the government being able to develop a response has shrunk considerably. The media also has the increasing capacity to bypass the government altogether in reaching out to the public and generating concern for an issue. The public can then agitate and pressure political officials to put the issue on the policy agenda.

In this chapter, we address the development of the mass media in an effort to understand how their political power has increased. We also discuss the role played by the media and by journalists. We consider two ideas, the CNN Effect and Manufactured Consent, to better understand the agenda-setting power of the media. We conclude by examining the relationship between the media and democracy.

10.1 Mass Media Today

We are living in an era of high-tech politics, and it is difficult to ignore the increasing influence of the mass media on political decision-making. Television, radio, newspapers, magazines, online sources, and other means of popular communication are called the **mass media**, or "the press," because they reach a large audience through channels of mass communication.

The news media has become a critical linkage institution between the public and the government. Like other such institutions in U.S. politics, including elections, political parties, and interest groups, the media is an access point through which issues and policy preferences are communicated between the government and the public. That relationship affects the political policy agenda. We depend on the media to connect us to the government and to provide a space for discussion of political issues. But as the media has evolved, the effect it has on American political culture has changed. The rise of cable news and the internet and the ability to share information in real time have meant that the media is now encroaching on functions once dominated by political leaders and institutions. The media is revolutionizing the relationship between citizens and politics and altering our very understanding of democracy as possibilities open up for more direct participation.

In his book *The Making of the President*, political journalist Theodore White notes that the "power of the press in America is a primordial one. It sets the agenda of public discussion; .... It determines what people will talk and think about—an authority that in other nations is reserved for tyrants, priests, parties, and mandarins."[5] His observation is echoed by media critic Robert McChesney, who cautions, "A specter now haunts the world: a global commercial media system dominated by a small number of super powerful, mostly U.S.-based transnational media corporations ... that works as to advance the cause of the global market and promote commercial values."[6] Both of these quotes paint a picture of the media as an almost uncontrollable force in society that has the power to tell us what issues are important and to determine our ideas about them.

The media's influence on politics has increased so significantly that in order to be successful in politics, one must be able to control the mass media. The media plays a critical role in elections as candidates rely on news outlets to communicate their messages to the public and to shape their images. The media can determine whether that image is positive or negative and, knowing this, candidates work to limit what the media reports to carefully **scripted events** that are staged primarily for the purpose of being covered. Of course, the media is free to report on what it determines to be the most interesting angle of a story. Since one of the main goals of the media is to increase revenue from advertisers, newspapers, radio, television, and the internet, all have the incentive to highlight stories that will attract readers, viewers, and listeners and hold their attention. Journalists can have an enormous influence on the outcome of elections by choosing which stories are newsworthy and, in doing so, aid one candidate while ruining another. The First Amendment's guarantee of freedom of the press provides legal protections to the media in the United States that are unavailable in most other countries, including other democracies like Japan and Great Britain, where there is much tighter government regulation of media content. The American media can therefore operate almost completely unchecked. In addition to shaping public opinion about elections, the increasing power of the media has raised the cost of campaigns, as candidates must buy costly media space to get their messages out and be competitive.

mass media

Television, radio, newspapers, magazines, online sources, and other means of popular communication that reach a large audience through channels of mass communication.

scripted events

Events that are staged primarily for the purpose of being covered.

investigative journalism

The use of detective-like reporting methods to unearth scandals.

muckraking

A popular form of investigative journalism that seeks to expose societal ills such as corruption in politics and business.

Once the campaign is over, politicians must continue to work closely with the media to try to control the image that is presented to the public. While the media has historically been an important tool for presidents to communicate with the public, the nature of the relationship between the Oval Office and reporters has changed. The media and U.S. presidents were once allies. Consider, for example, the fact that even though he was in wheelchair for his entire presidency, the media never showed images of President Franklin D. Roosevelt in his wheelchair. The majority of Americans had no idea that FDR was disabled as the result of a childhood polio infection because the media was careful to direct cameras to cut away when the president was helped out his chair or used braces to reach the podium. Over time and as the result of events such as Vietnam and Watergate, the media transformed from an ally into a potential enemy of the Chief Executive who had to be closely watched. Gone is any respect for a politician's private life. Everything is fair game for coverage and criticism, including a president's children and extended family members. Presidents can no longer rely on the media as a partner in shaping the political landscape. This shift in interactions has complicated the ability of political leaders to control the flow of information to the public. This not only has implications for communicating with the public, but for safeguarding national security. Today's media tends to be very cynical and suspicious of politicians. Journalists have therefore become detectives and their style of reporting—**investigative journalism**—tries to uncover the truth and unearth scandals. Around 1900, a popular form of investigative journalism emerged called **muckraking**. This was a term coined by Theodore Roosevelt to describe journalists who were primarily interested in investigating and exposing societal ills such as corruption in politics and business. The shift in what stories journalists chose to cover has meant that the media's loyalty is no longer first and foremost with the president and other political leaders. That loyalty might not, however, be with the American public, either. Instead, the media may be most loyal, as McChesney warned, to the multinational corporations that own them. The question that then arises is, who is really setting the political agenda: our leaders, the media, or the companies that own the media?

10.2 The Evolution of the Mass Media

Before answering questions about the role of the media as an agenda setter, it is important to first understand the historical development of the mass media and how its consumption has changed over time. We distinguish between two kinds of media: the print media, which include newspapers and magazines, and the broadcast media, which is comprised of radio and television. Each type of media has had a profound impact on political communication at different moments in history.

FIGURE 10.1 Main Source for News
Source: Survey conducted July 30-Aug. 12, 2018. "Americans Still Prefer Watching to Reading the News – and Mostly Still Through Television"

% of U.S. adults who answered each way to the following question: "Which of the following would you say you prefer for getting news?"

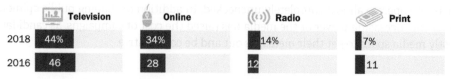

	Television	Online	Radio	Print
2018	44%	34%	14%	7%
2016	46	28	12	11

Adapted from "Americans Still Prefer Watching to Reading the News – and Mostly Still Through Television." Pew Research Center, Washington D.C. (December 3, 2018) http://www.journalism.org/2018/12/03/americans-still-prefer-watching-to-reading-the-news-and-mostly-still-through-television/.

Print Media

Newspapers were the earliest form of communication between the government and the public. The *Federalist Papers* were originally published as newspaper articles in the *New York Independent Journal*. While there were numerous newspapers in circulation, the daily paper did not become common until rapid printing and cheap paper led to the advent of the **penny press** (which meant papers could be bought for one penny and read at home). The influence of newspapers grew throughout the nineteenth century, thanks in large part to the telegraph, which allowed for a primitive wire service that carried news stories from city to city faster than ever before.

The twentieth century ushered in the era of **yellow journalism**, a style of reporting that focuses on sensationalized accounts of violence, scandals, corruption, and gossip. The newspaper magnates Joseph Pulitzer and William Randolph Hearst were largely responsible for this shift toward sensational news reporting as they competed with each other for readers.

Pulitzer and Hearst also led the way for newspapers to consolidate into chains. Massive media chains control newspapers with 78 percent of the nation's daily circulation. These conglomerates frequently own television and radio stations as well.[7] The *Wall Street Journal* is the most widely read newspaper is the United States, followed by *The New York Times* and *USA Today*.

penny press

Rapid printing and cheap paper meant that papers could be bought for one penny and read at home.

yellow journalism

A style of reporting that focuses on sensationalized accounts of violence, scandals, corruption, and gossip.

Fake or misleading news is not a new phenomenon. This image shows part of the front page of *The New York Journal* in 1898 when unsubstantiated news helped start a war. In 1898, more than 250 Americans were killed when the USS Maine, a US Navy battleship, exploded off the coast of Cuba. The cause of the explosion was unknown, but the yellow press published that the Spanish had intentionally blown up the ship. With the slogan "Remember the Maine," the yellow press helped rally public opinion in support of what would become the Spanish-American war.

New York Journal [Public domain], via Wikimedia Commons. https://commons.wikimedia.org/wiki/File:Journal98.gif

Magazines were once an important part of print media. Political magazines such as *Time* and *Newsweek*, which previously dominated the market, have given way to *The Atlantic* and *The New Yorker*, which mix news coverage with human-interest stories and fiction. The most widely read magazines (such as *Reader's Digest* and *Better Homes and Gardens*) have nothing to do with politics. Serious magazines of political news and opinion are primarily read by the educated elite.

The Death of the Newspaper

Newspapers were once the main medium through which Americans got their news, but there has been a sharp decline in readership. While newspapers have lost popularity across the board (only 29 percent of the U.S. population regularly read a newspaper in 2012, down from 56 percent in 1991), it is young people who are the least likely to get their news from a paper. In fact, according to a Pew Research poll, 6 percent of people under the age of 30 reported they had read a newspaper the previous day, compared to 50 percent of adults over 65 who had done so. More than three quarters of those who read newspapers are over the age of 45, even though that age demographic group represents only 39 percent of the population.[8] This suggests that newspaper readers are an aging and dying breed.

FIGURE 10.2 Main Source of News by Age
Main news source by user age. The younger the group, the more likely it is to use online and social media sources.

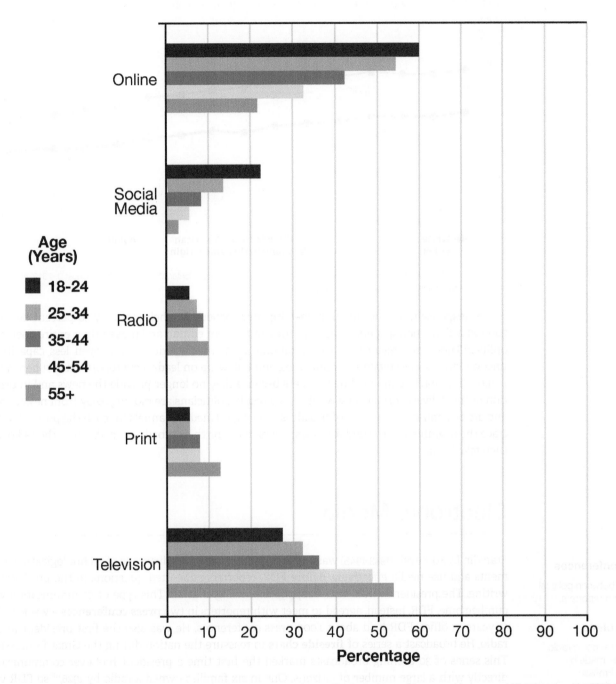

Data from Reuters Institute for the study of journalism: "Digital News Report 2015", https://reutersinstitute.politics.ox.ac.uk/our-research/digital-news-report-2015-0.

When we look at newspaper readership by ethnic group, we see that whites have the highest levels of daily newspaper readership, followed by blacks. The most significant decline in readership is among Asian and Latina/o groups, which suggests that language may be a barrier.

FIGURE 10.3 Newspapers: Daily Readership by Ethnic Group
Source: Nielsen Scarborough USA+ 1999–2014, Release 1.

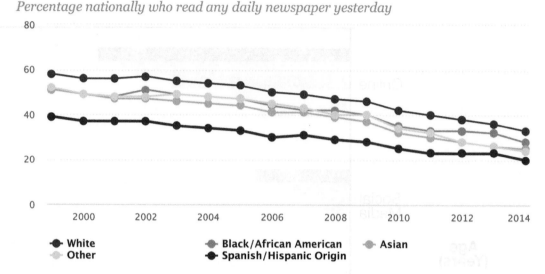

Percentage nationally who read any daily newspaper yesterday

Adapted from "Newspapers: Daily Readership by Ethnic Group." Pew Research Center, Washington D.C. (August 3, 2015) http://www.journalism.org/chart/newspapers-daily-readership-by-ethnic-group/.

In response to the decline in readership, newspapers cut their staffs by 30 percent between 2000-2012. Some newspapers stopped putting out a print edition and moved their entire operation online.[9] These cuts mean that the traditional print media industry has even less capacity to uncover stories, investigate emerging ones, and follow up on leads. Pew reports that 31 percent of respondents have abandoned newspapers because they no longer provide the news and information or the delivery format they want.[10] As a result, politicians are moving away from newspapers and are becoming skilled users of broadcast and digital media channels to reach the public. We can trace the beginning of the end for newspapers to the birth of broadcast media, first the radio and then television.

Electronic Media

press conferences

Meetings between political officials and reporters.

fireside chats

A series of evening radio broadcasts made by President Franklin Roosevelt during the Great Depression.

Franklin D. Roosevelt (1933-1945) was the first president to take advantage of technological developments and use media effectively. Before FDR, reporters submitted questions to the president in writing. The president would then respond in writing, if at all. This type of communication was cumbersome. FDR, instead, agreed to meet with reporters in two **press conferences** a week. In his 12 years in office, FDR held about 1,000 press conferences. He was also the first president to use radio. He broadcast a series of **fireside chats** to reassure the nation during the Great Depression. This series of 30 evening broadcasts marked the first time a president had ever communicated directly with a large number of citizens. One in six families owned a radio by 1926,[11] so FDR was able to reach a broad audience and connect with them in a much more personal way. He delivered his first chat eight days after taking office. His voice on the radio was calm and measured as he explained his policies and reassured the public during a time of desperation and uncertainty. Radio as a technology had been around since 1903, but it was FDR who transformed it into a political tool. His popularity was due in large part to the success of the fireside chats. Radio remains a part of the political landscape, with stations like National Public Radio affiliates delivering news and providing commentary. Political talk shows have also created a space for discussion and remain popular to this day.

Statue by George Segal of a citizen listening to one of President Roosevelt's "fireside chats" at the Franklin Delano Roosevelt Memorial, Washington, D.C. Roosevelt said, at the time, that he hoped "these conferences are going to be merely enlarged editions of the kind of very delightful family conferences I have been holding in Albany for the last four years. I am told that what I am about to do will become impossible, but I am going to try it." These chats were in fact effective to calm fears during the Great Depression and World War II.

Orhan Cam / Shutterstock.com

The Power of Television

Television as a technology is almost as old as radio, but its impact has been far more significant. The first TV station began broadcasting in 1931. While only 9 percent of American homes had a television set in 1950, by 1975, 97 percent owned one. The majority of households today have more than one TV set, with most homes owning three or more. Televisions are turned on for an average of eight hours and 14 minutes a day,[12] which comprises a major part of how Americans spend their leisure time. TV is watched primarily for entertainment content, but more Americans get their news from TV than from any other medium. CBS, NBC, and ABC still dominate the industry, but the rise of cable and stations like CNN and Fox News have changed the way that news is delivered and consumed. The lines between news and entertainment are now being blurred as a new type of political commentary has been introduced in the form of **infotainment**. Programs like *The Daily Show with Trevor Noah*, *The Late Show with Stephen Colbert*, Weekend Update on *Saturday Night Live*, and *Jimmy Kimmel Live!* mix satire with news coverage. All have become outlets for political discussion and analysis. A Pew poll reported that young people (ages 19 to 29) were as likely to get their news from *The Daily Show* as they were from one of the major networks.[13]

    Television plays an important role in politics. Not only is it the primary medium through which the public learns about what is happening in the world, but it also has the power to shape political debates and alter opinions about our leaders. The 1960 Kennedy/Nixon debate was the first televised presidential debate. Poll results illustrate the visual power of television in American politics. People listening to the debate on the radio believed that Nixon had outperformed Kennedy. He sounded like he was more experienced and had a greater command of what the office of president entailed. Those who watched the debate on TV, instead, gave the advantage to Kennedy. Kennedy stared directly into the camera as he answered each question. His suntanned, youthful good looks gave him an appealing charm. Nixon, on the other hand, appeared tired and his fast-growing stub-

infotainment

A new type of political commentary that blurs the lines between news and entertainment.

ble gave him a grayish hue. The makeup he put on to cover his stubble melted under the hot TV lights, making him seem sweaty and nervous. He also looked off to the side to address reporters, which came across as avoiding eye contact with the viewers at home. When election time came, more than half of all voters said they had been influenced by the debate, and 6 percent claimed that the debates alone decided their vote. While the debate ultimately may not have been what cost Nixon the presidency, it was a significant turning point in the 1960 campaign and in the relationship between television and politics. We were now in an era in which manufacturing a public image and capitalizing on media exposure is essential to succeed in politics. Today, televised debates are an important part of the campaign season. They have the power not only to communicate the candidates' messages, but also to sway public opinion. Television plays a critical role in the democratic process and politicians would do well to remember that. As Nixon wrote in his memoir, *Six Crises*, "A picture is worth a thousand words."[14]

While television remains a top news source for Americans, the percentage of viewers is dropping, especially among younger generations. The average age of a regular nightly news viewer is 53. Adults under 30 who watch TV news fell from 42 percent in 2006 to just 28 percent in 2012.[15]

The Rise of Social Media

The internet has changed how we produce and consume news. The instantaneous nature of the internet means that users have access to stories long before they appear in print media or even on television. This has a profound effect on the ways in which people get their news. It has also turned average citizens into pundits who share their opinions and ideas about politics with a wide and transnational audience. We all have the capability to act as reporters. We can observe an event, record it on our smartphones, post it to the internet, and watch it go viral. Because online profiles can be anonymous, citizens may feel more comfortable expressing themselves freely on social media than they would in face-to-face conversations. As a result, the internet is replacing the traditional office water cooler discussions about elections, the economy, and world politics.

Donald J. Trump ✔
@realDonaldTrump

Follow ⌄

North Korean Leader Kim Jong Un just stated that the "Nuclear Button is on his desk at all times." Will someone from his depleted and food starved regime please inform him that I too have a Nuclear Button, but it is a much bigger & more powerful one than his, and my Button works!

4:49 PM - 2 Jan 2018

Twitter: https://bit.ly/2rUCMj7.

Digital media is also changing the way politicians interact with citizens. Barack Obama announced his decision to seek reelection in 2012 in a YouTube video. Social media platforms allow for even greater direct access to a wide audience. By using resources like Facebook, Twitter, and

Instagram, political leaders and candidates can communicate their messages and shape opinions quickly, directly, and without the filters of traditional media. President Donald Trump, for example, has departed from conventional channels of political communication and frequently uses Twitter to announce policy decisions, engage with the public, and conduct (sometimes hostile) relations with foreign countries. This style of communication makes the president more accessible because it allows users to reply and express their own ideas, but it is also unsettling because it is a new political forum. When Trump's tweets contradict long-standing U.S. positions, they can also send mixed messages to the nation's allies, who are unsure how much to read into the president's social media posts. Countries are unsure whether the president's tweets should be taken as policy announcements or whether they can be ignored. Whether they are intended to be policy pronouncements or efforts to secure his political base, because he often tweets early in the morning, what President Trump communicates can set the media's agenda for the day.[16] These tweets, arguably, should be treated as important because they are statements of the president and of the White House. Because users can reply to the president's tweets and express their own opinions in their responses, the president had been blocking those who contradict him from being able to access his account. In May 2018, a federal district court judge ruled that President Trump could not block users from viewing his Twitter feed because of their political views. Because the president's Twitter account is public, the judge held that blocking people who reply to his tweets with different views violates the Constitution's First Amendment right to free speech.[17]

Donald J. Trump ✔
@realDonaldTrump

(Follow) ⌄

Military solutions are now fully in place,locked and loaded,should North Korea act unwisely. Hopefully Kim Jong Un will find another path!

4:29 AM - 11 Aug 2017

Twitter: https://bit.ly/2CUMmI7.

In addition to providing a new channel for political communication, the internet is slowly replacing print and broadcast media outlets as the main source for news, particularly among younger Americans. In fact, the only outlet to witness new audience growth in recent years is digital media. The proliferation of digital devices is part of the reason why people are more likely to turn to the internet for news rather than to another source. We can now stream the president's speeches on our smartphones and watch White House press briefings on our tablets in real-time. According to Pew Research data from 2013, 39 percent of survey respondents said they get their news online or from a mobile device. That number is up from 34 percent in 2010, when the survey was last conducted. Pew also reported that as of 2013, 31 percent of adults owned a tablet computer, almost four times the number recorded in May 2011. In addition, about 45 percent of adults owned a smartphone in 2013, an increase of 10 percent from May 2011. One of the most popular uses for the devices is accessing news "on the go." Researchers found that 64 percent of tablet owners report they get news on their devices weekly, while 37 percent say they do so daily. The trend is similar for smartphone users—62 percent said they get news on their device weekly and 36 percent do so daily.[18] Social media is playing an increasingly important role when it comes to news people hear from friends and family. While nearly three-quarters of people report they hear about news events by talking in person or over the phone to friends and family, 15 percent get most news from family and friends through social media sites. This number rises to about 25 percent among 18-to-25-year-olds.[19]

One of the implications of the rise of social media as a news source is that we must work to be informed consumers. Anyone with basic computing skills can create a webpage or host a blog, which means that not all information that is posted online is reliable. Some of it may be biased, imprecise, or completely untrue. We need to learn to navigate various online sources in an effort to distinguish between information that is reliable and accurate and information that is irrelevant, biased, or intentionally manipulative.

10.3 The Role of Media

The media is an important linkage institution between the public and the government. As such, it plays several important roles. Journalists are responsible for reporting the news, but they can also define what is newsworthy. They help set the policy agenda and shape public opinions about politics. The media can also draw attention to corruption, scandal, and instances of poor governance.

The Informant Role

It is the media's responsibility to alert and inform the public of events and developments as soon as possible. But the media can help define, or signal, what is newsworthy. News reporting has become a business in America and profits often dictate what journalists cover. The more advertising dollars that a media outlet can attract, the more successful that outlet is. Journalists often look for stories that will draw the most eyeballs, even if they are not the most critical stories from a political perspective. We frequently describe the news as a mirror held up to reality, but the truth is that the news is a highly selective representation of reality. Human-interest stories, for example, are frequently prioritized over stories about poverty or war in foreign countries. We often joke about the attention the nightly news programs will pay to stories about cats being stuck in trees. It is obviously the media outlet's decision to cover the cat-in-the-tree stories, but that decision reflects audience interest and what is going to hold people's attention. News is then defined as that which is timely, dramatic, and compelling. The media favors stories with high drama that will attract people's interest and provide good pictures. Audiences complain that there is so much stress in their everyday lives that they do not want to turn on the news and be further depressed. Journalists are responsive to this sentiment and tailor their reporting to a fairly low level of audience sophistication.

beats

Locations from which news emanates.

Part of their success in defining news comes from the media's ability to find the news. Most news comes from well-established sources and specific **beats** or locations from which news emanates, such as Capitol Hill and the White House. These sources depend on the media to spread information and communicate ideas to the public. Though much less common, journalists do work with anonymous sources in their attempts to provide complete information. One of the most famous examples of this occurred when *Washington Post* reporters Carl Bernstein and Bob Woodward relied on a source named "Deep Throat" to uncover important evidence in the Watergate case. The evidence that Woodward and Bernstein gathered from their anonymous source proved that President Nixon had lied about the role his administration played in the burglary of the Democratic National Committee's headquarters–and that he had subsequently tried to cover it up. As a result of their investigative reporting, Woodward and Bernstein blew open the scandal that ultimately led to Nixon's resignation in 1974. In the aftermath of the Watergate scandal, journalists became much more critical of traditional sources and more convinced that politicians had something to hide. Politicians in turn became less trusting of journalists and more concerned about controlling the flow of information to them.

The Disseminator Role

The media is a critical channel of communication between political leaders and the public. Leaders rely on the media to convey information about proposed policies and plans. The public in turn uses this information to decide whether to support or oppose the actions. As a linkage institution, the media offers a means for government to speak directly to the people, which is an essential component of effective democracy. In communicating with the public, political leaders try to get the most favorable coverage they can. They work to impose their own **spin** or interpretation on the media's reporting of events. The media can also put its own spin on stories and, because of increasing mistrust of the government after Vietnam and Watergate, the public now looks to journalists to provide analysis and commentary on political decision-making.

> **spin**
>
> An interpretation imposed on the media's reporting of events.

The Watchdog Role

We have come to rely increasingly on the media as a check on government behavior and to alert us when our political leaders have done something wrong. As a watchdog, the media looks for evidence of unethical or illegal behavior. When it occurs, they are ready to report it to the public. The media is protected by the First Amendment. As long as reporting does not threaten national security, journalists can report on events even if these are unfavorable to elected officials. The public learned about the mistreatment and human rights violations of Iraqi prisoners by U.S. soldiers in 2004 in Abu Ghraib prison because of journalists who were willing to break the story. The media acquired and published graphic pictures of Iraqi prisoners being sexually humiliated and abused. U.S. officials, including then Secretary of Defense Donald Rumsfeld, knew about the abuse occurring in Abu Ghraib, but kept the story from the president, Congress, and the American public. When the photos were released by the media, Congress began an investigation to determine who was responsible for allowing U.S. troops to violate laws governing the treatment of prisoners. The media also exercised its watchdog role in exposing presidential misconduct during the Watergate scandal and the Bill Clinton-Monica Lewinsky affair.

There are times when the media's watchdog role comes into conflict with national security concerns. This occurred in 1970 when *The New York Times* published the Pentagon Papers, which were classified documents that revealed the government was lying to the public by claiming that the Vietnam War was going well for America. In fact, the government knew the mission was not succeeding. The Nixon administration had its reasons for wanting to put a positive spin on news about the Vietnam War, but, acting as a watchdog, the media felt an obligation to reveal the truth to the American public. A similar case came about in 2005 when *The New York Times* reported that President George W. Bush had put National Security Agency wiretaps on communications between people suspected of having links to terrorist groups. The media was eager to alert the public about this violation of the right to privacy, while the White House claimed that, by reporting the story, the media had damaged the government's ability to monitor suspected terrorists and prevent future attacks against the United States.

The Public-Representative Role

The media communicates information from the government to the public. It also speaks or advocates for the public and reports opinions and attitudes about political actions and behavior back to the government. While this type of two-way representation is an important component of the media's role as a linkage institution, it also suggests that the media may not be as well suited to act as public representatives as political leaders are. First of all, the media is not accountable to the public in the same way as elected officials. We do not vote for members of the media, so there is no system of checks and balances that applies. Because ownership of the media is in the hands of big businesses, it is not always clear where the media's loyalties lie. The second problem with relying on the media as public representatives is that they may be biased.

A growing number of Americans believe that political bias in the media has risen to a new high. As Figure 10.4 suggests, 37 percent of public say there is a great deal of bias in news coverage. This percentage increased by six points between 2008 and 2012. The majority of reporters are Democrats and they are more likely to identify themselves as liberal than the general public. There are some news shows that are openly biased. For example, Fox News caters to a conservative audience, while MSNBC appeals to liberals. Despite the presence of some biased news outlets, **journalistic objectivity** dictates that personal attitudes be left out of news reporting. Journalistic objectivity became an important principle in American journalism in the wake of the increasing popularity of sensational news reporting at the turn of the twentieth century. Objectivity requires that each news item be attributed to a credible source. This requirement improved the quality of the news and created a standard for ethics in journalism. Critics of journalistic objectivity argue it is a biased principle that favors the status quo and does not encourage independent thinking. By striving to be objective, news has become something journalists are compelled to report and not something they are responsible for creating. As such, journalistic objectivity has resulted in a disregard for the consequences of newsmaking, these critics argue.[20]

journalistic objectivity

The notion that personal attitudes should be left out of news reporting and that each news item should be attributed to a credible source.

While there is room for debate about political bias in the news, there is undoubtedly a **commercial bias** toward stories that will hold the attention of audiences and increase revenue from advertisers. Today, just six companies—Time-Warner, Disney, CBS Corporation, General Electric, News Corporation Limited, and Viacom—own the majority of the country's newspapers, networks, publishing houses, film studios, telephone companies, and other multimedia businesses. They have created multimedia empires, which led media critic Ben Bagdikian to describe them as a "new communications cartel within the United States [with the] power to surround every man, woman, and child in the country with controlled images and words, to socialize each new generation of Americans, to alter the political agenda of the country."[21] Because just a handful of companies own most of the news and entertainment sources, one could argue that there is not a lot of space for independent thought and analysis, for stories that challenge the mainstream, or for pieces that might not generate as much advertising revenue. Less popular political news receives less coverage than hot topics like the weather, sports, scandals, or human-interest stories.[22] Corporate ownership of the media can also create conflicts of interest about what news to report. Many outlets are reluctant to cover stories that may cast a negative light on their parent company.[23] Despite the extensive corporate control of the media, there are independent sources for news coverage, such as PBS, National Public Radio, and *Mother Jones*. Being independently owned, however, does not mean the same thing as being unbiased. Some independent media outlets have an implicit bias toward the left (*Mother Jones*) or the right (*The Daily Wire*). Social media is another possible source for coverage of the news that is free of corporate oversight. As discussed earlier in the chapter, identifying reliable sources on the internet and social media can take effort and requires thoughtful research.

FIGURE 10.4 Percent of People that Believe There Is a Great Deal of Bias in the News
Source: Pew Research Center, Jan. 4-8, 2012. Q60.

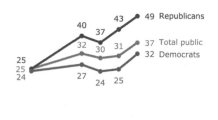

Adapted from "Twitter, Facebook Play Very Modest Roles: Cable Leads the Pack as Campaign News Source." Pew Research Center, Washington D.C. (February 7, 2012) http://www.people-press.org/2012/02/07/cable-leads-the-pack-as-campaign-news-source/.

commercial bias

The idea that the media is biased toward stories that will hold the attention of audiences and increase revenue from advertisers.

10.4 Media as the Fourth Branch of Government

The media is sometimes referred to as the fourth branch of government, suggesting that it has the capacity to check and balance the political agenda in the same way as the executive, legislative, and judicial branches. The notion comes from the idea of the Fourth Estate in reference to the ancient European division of society into aristocrats, clergy, and townspeople, with the Fourth Estate serving the interests of outsiders and the unrepresented. Media as the fourth branch of government takes the Fourth Estate and adapts it to American democracy, pitting the media against the other branches defined in the Constitution. The media plays a critical role in investigating and considering the actions undertaken by the three branches of government and, in doing so, demands transparency and asks questions on behalf of the public.[24] Malcolm X characterized the media as "one of the most powerful entities on Earth that could make the innocent guilty and the guilty innocent."[25] Supporters of this idea argue that the media not only shapes our opinions about issues, but it has also the power to determine political action. Critics argue instead that the media is a tool used by the government to garner support for its policies. In this section, we explore the agenda setting role that the media plays.

One way the media can influence readers and audiences is through **priming**, which is emphasizing certain features or characteristics of people, events, and issues in such a way that it influences the public's perception of those people, events, and issues. For example, if the media covers a story about self-driving cars, emphasizing the safety and "green" features of the cars while contrasting them with pictures of human-caused tragic accidents, traffic, and pollution, the media is priming the audience to have a positive perception of self-driving cars. If instead the media were to show images of the cars driving off the road in crash-tests, the public's attitude toward self-driving vehicles would likely be negative.

When the media chooses a particular slant on an issue, we characterize it as **framing**. For example, North Carolina passed House Bill 2 in 2016, which placed limits on transgendered access to public bathrooms by requiring people to use the restroom that corresponds to the sex on their birth certificate—not their identified gender. North Carolina's governor filed a lawsuit asking federal courts to uphold the law. The U.S. Justice Department responded by suing the state of North Carolina for gender discrimination. These lawsuits sparked a race between rivals about how to frame the issue. For North Carolina, this was a question about national government interference and overreach in affairs that should be left to the states. For the Obama Administration, the question at hand was about a single national standard regarding fundamental civil rights. Various media outlets also had their own framing of the issue. FOX News, for instance, focused on the idea that straight sexual predators might exploit the law and present a public safety risk while posing a challenge to law enforcement.[26] MSNBC, on the other hand, pointed out that there is no evidence of an increase in assaults in public bathrooms in states where people can use the restroom that corresponds with their gender identity. What we should be considering, according to MSNBC, is the safety of the LGBTQ community and what the law says on the issue. In this case, the cable news channel argued that Title IX protects people from discrimination based on sex in education initiatives that receive federal financial assistance.[27] How the media choses to frame and describe the issue proved critical for gathering public support and ultimately having the lawsuits resolved in a particular side's favor.

Media outlets increasingly tailor their reporting for specific audiences in what is known as **narrowcasting**. Instead of trying to reach a mass audience, some internet and television news providers are working to appeal to narrower audiences. This trend is evident in changes in print media and in programming for Spanish speakers. Both Univision, the leading media outlet serving Latinas/os, and Telemundo have nightly news programs tailored to Latina/o viewers. These programs focus on issues and provide analysis of politics through a Latina/o lens. Because Latinas/os

priming

The media's emphasis on certain features or characteristics of people, events, and issues in such as way so as to influence the public's perception of those people, events, and issues.

framing

The media's particular slant on an issue.

narrowcasting

The practice adopted by media outlets to tailor their reporting for specific audiences.

can get their news from sources that cater to their interests, many do not watch English language news programs on the major national networks. This means that there is less pressure on the networks to cover topics that are relevant to the Latina/o community. As a result, many non-Latinas/os are not sufficiently exposed to issues such as challenges facing migrant farm workers or inequalities in pay for Latina women that are of concern primarily to Latinas/os. Some observers worry that narrowcasting and tailoring news reporting to specific groups will further fragment American society and make it more difficult to mobilize support for important issues.

CNN Effect vs. Manufactured Consent

CNN effect

An idea that it is the cameras that lead the politicians and dictate what stories are important and what should be done about them.

manufactured consent

The idea that government leads the cameras by identifying an issue or event as important, seeking public support, and using the media as tools to gather that support.

Priming, framing, and narrowcasting are ways that the media can set the policy agenda, determining what stories get covered, how they are covered, and potentially shaping what political actions are taken as a result of the coverage. How much agenda-setting power the media has is captured by the **CNN effect** and **manufactured consent**. The CNN effect holds that it is the cameras and pictures that lead politicians and dictate what stories are important and what should be done about them. In other words, it is the media that first draws attention to an issue or an event and then raises public awareness and support to bring the government on board. Because those in the news media (and television in particular) choose the pictures and how the story is presented, they have the capability to shape the policy agenda and move government. Through repeated exposure to information, audiences believe that what they hear or see through media outlets is an accurate depiction of reality.[28] What is reported through the media often creates stable yet unrealistic expectations about the probability of events occurring. This can help explain why certain beliefs, such as the notion that crime is rampant and growing in the United States, is taken as fact despite evidence demonstrating that crime rates are in fact decreasing. Daily exposure to violent crime on local TV news makes these events easy to recall and creates the impression that such crimes are more common than they actually are.[29] By exposing audiences to certain topics, the media encourages discussion and debate about those issues. In addition, because the media can be our first source of information about an issue or event, it can shape our initial opinions of the issue or event. The media often presents itself as working on behalf of the public and positions itself as an ally of the American people. This can induce policy action and change by portraying angry voters as a threat to guide the hands of politicians. The Watergate scandal is an example of this. More recently, after the government's failure to adequately respond when Hurricane Katrina hit New Orleans in 2004, the press was relentless in trying to determine the cause of the insufficient response. This led, ultimately, to the reorganization of several government agencies.[30]

Social media is contributing to the role that media plays in changing the course and focus of public debate. Social media has changed how individuals produce and consume news and how quickly information is disseminated, even before it has been verified for accuracy. For example, the media prioritized coverage of the Boston Marathon bombing in 2013, which claimed the lives of three people and injured dozens. When the national manhunt was underway to find the perpetrators of the bombings, the media played a critical role in mobilizing the public to help locate the suspects. The Boston Marathon bombing was the first event in history to rely so heavily on the public to track down the perpetrators.[31] Leads were flowing into media outlets and journalists had to sift through the information to make quick judgments about what was real and what were just speculations. Social media servers such as Reddit and Twitter participated in the news-gathering process and were publishing stories in tandem, sometimes even before traditional news outlets. The problem was that these online sources were not always taking the necessary steps to verify information, which resulted in people being wrongly accused of perpetrating the attacks. The website Reddit, for example, falsely identified Brown University student Sunil Tripathi as a suspect. The names of the real suspects, brothers Dzhokhar and Tamerlan Tsarnaev, were soon released and Tripathi's name was cleared, but the damage to his reputation had already been done by what has been called "'vigilante justice' perpetuated by social media."[32]

The CNN effect is taking on new meaning in the era of social media. The power of both official journalists and would-be reporters to shape our opinions and influence government action seems to be increasing. The rise of social media has become so prominent that some are referring to the formation of a "Fifth Estate," which exists separate from the traditional media.[33] While social media provides unprecedented access to information, its power can also be corrosive. Minor events can receive unwarranted attention from social media outlets and non-stories can rise in prominence and distract the public from more important issues. There is a movement back to the muckraking days of the nineteenth century, when competition for readers made newspapers publish every salacious story they could find to the detriment of hard news. Social media is transforming the landscape of news reporting and is altering the relationship among the media, the public, and the government.

Scholars on the other side of the argument suggest it is the government that leads the cameras and manufactures consent. The government identifies an issue or event as important, seeks public support, and uses the media as a tool to gather that support. The media does not create policy, but instead is mobilized by the government and is a puppet in the hands of the political leaders, who retain control of the policy agenda. Journalist and political writer Walter Karp observed, "The press does not act, it is acted upon. ... So passive is the press that even seemingly bold 'adversarial' stories often have the sanction of the highest officials."[34] People who argue that the government manufactures consent describe the media as playing a **propaganda** role for the government.[35] This role is comprised of five filters through which information passes from the media to the public. The filters are: ownership; advertising; official sources; flak; and marginalizing dissent. As discussed earlier, whoever owns the media can determine which stories are covered and how they are framed. Because advertising is an essential revenue source for the media, stories that are going to attract the biggest audiences and secure advertising commitments are more likely to be covered. Most of the news reported comes from official government sources, which affects the information available. When the media covers wars, for example, it is frequently organized into press pools, and reporters are selected to cover stories chosen by the military. The official sources can also spread misinformation, as was the case during the Panama invasion in 1989, when the designated Pentagon spokesperson Pete Williams lied about mass graves, executions, and the burning of entire neighborhoods (all of which were then reported in the mainstream media). This reliance on officially provided information is so problematic that the prominent *New York Times* columnist Tom Wicker described it as the "biggest weakness" of the American press. Flak refers to the fear of retribution if reporters cover stories that those in power do not want. The consequences for reporters in these cases can be serious. For example, Joseph Wilson wrote a story for *The New York Times* that called out President George W. Bush for sticking to the claim that Iraq had acquired uranium from Niger even after Wilson had reported the transaction to be false. In reaction to his criticism of Bush, a member of the Bush administration leaked the fact that Wilson's wife was a CIA agent. Reporters can also be reprimanded and kept in line through the strategy of marginalizing dissent, whereby personal attacks are used to discredit them and the stories they cover.

Given their ability to influence perceptions, the media is also used by **political entrepreneurs**, who invest capital in an issue and depend heavily on the media to get their ideas placed high on the policy agenda. These entrepreneurs rely on press releases, press conferences, letter writing campaigns, buttonholing reporters and columnists, trading on personal contacts, and carefully leaking information. They also stage political events to attract media attention. Policy entrepreneurs can work on behalf of political candidates or other officials. In addition, they can be employed by interest groups and transnational advocacy networks to place stories in the media. In *Media Power Politics*, David Paletz and Robert Entman argue that "by granting elites substantial control over the content, emphases, and flow of public opinion, media practices diminish the public's power." In this analysis, the media is regarded as the "unwitting handmaidens of the powerful."[36]

propaganda

The passing of information through five filters (ownership, advertising, official sources, flak, and marginalizing dissent) from the media to the public as that information is managed and manipulated by government.

political entrepreneurs

Those who invest capital in an issue and depend heavily on the media to get their ideas placed high on the policy agenda.

salience transfer

The media's ability to focus the public's attention and influence its perceptions of what are the most critical issues of the day.

Whether we believe the media has the capacity to set the political agenda or see them as strategic tools in the hands of the government and policy entrepreneurs, what is clear is that the media provide information. How it provides that information affects the public's perceptions and attitudes. What the media does when it works to set the agenda is called **salience transfer**, the ability to focus the public's attention and influence its perceptions of what are the most critical issues of the day. The most significant effect of the mass media may be "its ability to mentally order and organize our world for us. [The news media] may not be successful in telling us what to think, but they are stunningly successful in telling us what to think about."[37]

While there is evidence that the news and how it is presented shapes public opinion and behavior, it is difficult to isolate the impact of the media and separate it from other influences. Moreover, the impact of any one news story may be negligible, but the cumulative effect of several stories may be significant. The media can influence the criteria by which we evaluate our leaders and prioritize issues requiring political action. The impact of social media on public opinion is an emerging area of research. Social scientists are looking at how engagement with stories on the internet affects our voting behaviors and policy preferences.

Government Regulation of the Media

When media outlets play their watchdog role, they are performing a sort of check on government behavior and actions. The government, however, also has its own checks on the media. The press is protected by the First Amendment, which declares, "Congress shall make no law … abridging the freedom of speech or of the press." The Supreme Court has tended to protect the rights of the press, except when national security is in question. There is, however, some government control of the media, especially of broadcast media. When radio first emerged, there were so many stations that signal interference became a major problem. In response, the government passed the Federal Communications Act, which created the Federal Communications Commission (FCC) in 1934. The goal of the bill was to promote fairness in broadcasting. In doing so, it contained three provisions: 1) the equal time rule, which required stations that allowed candidates for office to buy or use airtime outside of a regular news broadcast to provide the same opportunity to all candidates; 2) the fairness doctrine, which required stations to devote equal time to opposing points of view; and 3) the right of rebuttal, which required that individuals whose reputations had been damaged on the air be given the chance to respond. The fairness doctrine was repealed in 1983, which means that stations no longer have to offer equal airtime to opposing perspectives. In the absence of the rule, broadcasters like Rush Limbaugh and Rachel Maddow are allowed to engage in their respective conservative and liberal political commentary without their stations being required to present the other side.

10.5 Understanding the Relationship Between Media, Government, and the American Public

As a linkage institution, the media occupies a unique place in American politics. Media outlets are not elected by citizens, but they often act as their representatives. They are not appointed by the government, but they can serve as its mouthpiece. They have the power to determine what we talk about and what we believe reality to be. That means whatever our opinions about the media's agenda-setting capability, they are an essential component of the political system. In this section, we look more closely at the relationship among media, the government, and the public to better understand the impact the media has on American democracy.

The Media and Political Behavior

Politicians acknowledge the power of the media to sway people's opinions. They therefore may alter their behavior based on how they might be portrayed by the media and perceived by the public. The watchdog function of the media keeps the government in check. It shines a spotlight on political decision-making and can impact the scope of government. When the government makes a new proposal, the media can focus attention on it and encourage debate. The discussions and debates can put restraints on the growth of government and keep the government from being able to implement new programs and policies. The media can also encourage the growth of government. When the media turns its attention to injustices in society, it can put pressure on the government to develop new programs and services to address that injustice. In identifying problems in society, reporters ask what the government is doing about the problem. The media points to the government as being responsible for almost every major problem. In doing so, they put a strong check on our leaders' actions.

Media and Elections

One area where the media seems to have a lot of influence is campaigns. Some people believe the media can actually determine the outcomes of elections. This certainly overstates the media's power, but what is true is that by focusing on specific candidates and issues, media outlets draw the public's attention to those candidates and issues. This elevates them in importance. When the media gives more print space and airtime to certain candidates, this makes it easier for them to remain in the public eye and raise money. If candidates are able to raise more money, they can spend more on advertising, which then ensures that the candidates hold the public's attention. The media can also narrow the field of candidates by focusing on front-runners, particularly in the early nomination process. In the 2016 presidential elections, for example, Democratic candidates Hillary Clinton and Bernie Sanders were labeled early front-runners by the media and, when the Democratic debates were held, the public knew very little about their competitors Martin O'Malley and Lincoln Chafee. By focusing on the front-runners in polls and news coverage, the media makes it hard for the lesser-known candidates to raise the funds necessary to stay in the race. Media coverage tends to privilege the "horse race" aspect of elections. The media highlights competition between individuals and, instead of concentrating on policy differences or the impact their proposals will have on the public, the media often reports on candidates as if they were competing in a game where they are more concerned with their relative gains against each other and not with the concerns of citizens. The media, always attuned to what will hold the attention of readers and viewers, focus more on strategy than on substance. This makes election coverage more entertaining, but much less informative and educational for voters.

Part of Breitbart's popularity comes from the structure of its website. The homepage, which looks similar to mainstream traditional news outlets, shows a running banner with entertainment, technology, and sports sections, but the stories on the site are all written from Breitbart's populist perspective.

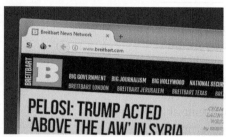

Sharaf Maksumov / Shutterstock.com

sound bite

A short clip made from a longer speech.

In addition, the media today devotes much more time to its own analysis and commentary of candidates' positions rather than on covering candidate speeches. In 1968, the average clip of a candidate speaking, known as a **sound bite**, ran over 40 seconds. The average clip today is less than eight seconds. While the candidate may still appear on screen, his or her voice is covered by the reporter's own commentary. In this way, the media has become the filter through which we hear and understand the positions of candidates. The media also creates profiles of candidates that may be only loosely rooted in reality. These profiles are often exaggerated as the media tries to make coverage of the candidates as attention-grabbing as possible. During the 2016 campaign, Hillary Clinton was depicted as an emasculating, deceitful shrew. Donald Trump was characterized as a racist misogynist. The media sought out clips and statements that reinforced these profiles, thereby perpetuating the narratives they manufactured. These profiles can become powerful images in voters' minds and may become more persuasive than the candidates' own statements and projections about their political ideas and values.

To counter the media's increasing power of persuasion in campaigns, candidates spend a lot of money on advertising. These advertisements are intended to paint the candidate in the best possible light, but to do so, they often attack their opponents. In 2008, the Hillary Clinton campaign aired an ad that showed images of children sleeping in bed at 3 a.m. while a phone rings in the background. The voiceover tells us that the phone is ringing in the White House, alerting the president there is something happening in the world. The narrator says: "It's 3 a.m. and your children are safe and asleep. Who do you want answering the phone?" The camera then cuts to an image of Hillary Clinton on the phone. The ad is intended to suggest that Hillary Clinton has more experience with international affairs and is the one voters should want answering that 3 a.m. call, rather than her opponent Barack Obama. Ads like these get picked up by the media and the campaign's message is amplified. Media has increased the role of the individual in American politics. Candidates have learned to use this to their advantage as they appeal directly to the people through television. Candidates are also using social media more effectively, including Facebook, Twitter, and email campaigns to bypass traditional media outlets and target voters directly. The use of social media was important for Obama's success and helps explain why 2016 Democratic candidate Bernie Sanders was so popular with young voters. The rise of nontraditional news outlets was also critical to Donald Trump's presidential victory in 2016. Many Americans who were disillusioned with and frustrated by what they perceived to be a liberal bias in mainstream media turned, for example, to Breitbart News, a news organization backed by Trump advisor Steve Bannon. Breitbart promotes a populist, anti-establishment political platform. The website became a critical outlet for formalizing Trump's message, garnering support for him among voters by disrupting mainstream media. For its part, the mainstream media also covered everything Trump said and did, giving him a lot of free publicity.

Democracy and the Media

Establishing casual relationships between democracy and the media is hard. Does the media encourage civic participation by linking the government and the public? Does the media alienate the public from politics by fomenting cynicism and disillusionment with politicians? Does an increase in public participation in politics create a greater demand and an expanded role for the media? With average citizens being able to produce and consume information in new ways thanks to social media, how much power does the media have to shape the political agenda? Does the media set the agenda or is it a tool of the government? These are important questions that guide current and future research about the effect that the media have on democracy.

One thing that does seem apparent is that the rise of the internet and the unprecedented access to information it provides has not resulted in the rise of an informed society. That is to say that even though we have more information at our fingertips than ever before, we are not using that information to make us better informed about domestic politics or world affairs. As we discussed in this chapter, the media's coverage of the "horse race" aspects of elections often happens at the expense of considering more substantive issues. The media tends to treat important policy issues superficially. Even when the media does provide detailed and thoughtful analysis, it may still not offer the public information about their choices and how to engage with politics. Journalists do not view themselves as facilitators of communication or public dialogue. They serve news consumers and often ignore the public's role as citizens. We should perhaps not be surprised, then, when citizens do not take the large amount of information available to them and translate it into increased civic awareness and participation. A healthy democracy requires a media that provides information and acts as a conduit between the public and government officials. But it is not the information itself that is crucial; it is the ability to debate and engage in political discourse that comes from having information that is essential for democracy to thrive. As one critic describes it: "What democracy requires is public debate, not information. . . . Unless information is generated by sustained public debate, most of it will be irrelevant at best, misleading and manipulative at worst. ... Much of the press, in its eagerness to inform the public, has become a conduit for the equivalent of junk mail."[38]

10.6 What Can I Do?

When it comes to the media, we can be more responsible consumers and producers. As media consumers, there is a constant flow of information coming at us and not all of it is accurate. We must develop the ability to sift through the information and determine what is true and what we can ignore. Being able to do that requires effort on our part as we research sources and stories more carefully. If you can read another language, it is a good idea to try to access media reports in that language so that you can get a different perspective. Even if you cannot read another language, it is still a good idea to follow foreign news sources to broaden your understanding of an issue. The internet provides easy access to the news, but try to balance your consumption of stories that you read through social media and those that you find in newspapers. For coverage of world events, *The New York Times* remains an excellent source. For news about politics, *The Washington Post* provides excellent coverage. *The Chicago Tribune*, *The San Francisco Chronicle*, and *The Los Angeles Times* also offer balanced reporting on domestic and international issues. The most important thing you can do as a media consumer is know where your information is coming from and be careful about what you repost. Not everything published is fact. It is good practice to check and double-check before repeating anything we read or hear.

If you are interested in producing media, it is easier than ever before to get involved. Traditional print and broadcast journalism positions remain. The internet has opened up even more opportunities to try to your hand at reporting, writing, and producing stories. For many, journalism is an attractive career. It is fast-paced, exciting, and high-profile. But it is also very competitive. It can be hard to get your foot in the door without knowing someone who works in the industry. Internships at your local newspaper and TV stations can be a way to build up your list of contacts and get some experience. Writing for your college paper or reporting for your university's news station can also expose you to the rewards and challenges of a career in media. Of course, you do not need to be employed by a media outlet to produce media. With blogs and social media sites, anyone can share information and be a reporter. As is the case with consuming media, it is important to be responsible with the information that you put out there by fact-checking and confirming your sources.

10.7 What's the Alternative?

The media has the power to shape the political discourse. Ensuring that the media is free and open is essential to democracy. Reforms to the media could improve the institution and make it more democratic. Specifically, slowing media consolidation, advocating for responsible reporting and advertising, and making the internet free and accessible to all could promote a more democratic media in the United States.

Media ownership has become increasingly consolidated. When the media is in the hands of a few owners, the lack of competition can lead to a decline in the quality of how, and even whether, issues are reported. Because the media is responsible for framing the debate over issues, what it chooses to cover and how it portrays events is critical to the national conversation. Media monopolization can have harmful effects, so to be more democratic, we should promote a more diverse media landscape. The Federal Communications Commission (FCC) can play a role in upholding rules that limit newspaper-broadcast cross-ownership, limit the number of media mergers, and allow media ownership rules that promote local and diverse ownership of radio and television. For example, in an effort to mitigate the negative effects of media conglomerations, the FCC in 2015 passed net neutrality laws which upheld the principle that all traffic on the internet should be treated equally. Internet service providers could not block or slow down services or applications accessed over the Web. In addition, net neutrality regulations prevented service providers from censoring content, throttling traffic to their competitors' products, or creating "fast lanes" that require companies like Netflix to pay additional fees to deliver their content faster. In December 2017, the FCC voted to roll back net neutrality rules, contending that they deter innovation and depress investment in building and expanding broadband networks. Net neutrality remains a divisive issue in the United States as concerns about fair access to the internet compete with concerns about government intervention.

Reforms could be implemented to ensure that the media is reporting the news responsibly. Harper's Magazine warned in 1925 that the spread of fake news via new technologies would be "a source of unprecedented danger." That danger seems to be ever threatening as some of the most shared news stories from the election in 2016 were Hillary Clinton's links to a pedophile ring at a pizza parlor in Washington, D.C. and Pope Francis endorsing Donald Trump for president. These stories were fabricated and yet the public shared them again and again. We know that something does not need to be true in order for people to believe it. Recent research from political scientist Adam Berinsky, psychologist Gordon Pennycook, and others suggests that if we are exposed to a story—even a false one—enough times, we will end up accepting it as true. We tend to forget where or how we found out about a news story; all that matters in making us believe it is prior exposure. Repetition—and not truth—is what matters. The media can play a role in reducing the acceptance of fake news by not repeating these stories, especially in their headlines. The public is much more likely to remember a news headline rather than any fact-checking or conclusions in a report. The media, in its fact-checking stories, must therefore open by debunking myths and not restating them to grab attention. Internet platforms such as Google and Facebook can also play a critical part in combatting fake news by altering their algorithms and moving suspect new stories further down the list of social media feeds and search engine returns. As we learn more about why the public believes what it does and what makes certain stories stick, we can also become more informed and aware consumers of media. Not everything that we read is true, even if it has been shared multiple times.

Protesters participating in a rally to protect net neutrality in San Francisco in 2017 argue that everyone should have fair access to websites and apps and that internet providers like Comcast, Verizon, and AT&T should be prevented from creating "fast lanes," censoring content, or throttling traffic to competitors' products.

Credo Action (Protect Net Neutrality rally, San Francisco) [CC BY 2.0 (https://creativecommons.org/licenses/by/2.0)], via Wikimedia Commons. https://commons.wikimedia.org/wiki/File:Protect_Net_Neutrality_rally,_San_Francisco_(23909304618).jpg.

The media could also be made more democratic by being more careful about how it uses advertising. Political ads are important for educating citizens about candidates' positions. Candidates are required to identify themselves and state their support of the claims made in ads. The groups paying for the ads are not always transparent, however. These secret money advertisers hide behind generic names and air misinformation about candidates and issues. According to the Center for Responsive Politics, the rate of spending by these groups is increasing. The FCC has the authority to reform this practice by requiring in-ad disclosure of the top sponsors behind an ad.

One of the most important reforms that could make the media more democratic is providing free and accessible internet to all. For many Americans, accessing the internet still requires going to a public library or using the WiFi at local restaurants and cafes. The United States lags behind much of the world in providing affordable internet access. Being able to use the internet can help citizens find jobs, move out of poverty, and access health care and social services. Free and open internet access would also promote a better-informed electorate, a more responsive government, and greater civic engagement.

As U.S. Supreme Court Justice Hugo Black reminded us in the 1971 ruling in *New York Times Co. v. United States*, "The press was to serve the governed, not the governors." The First Amendment to the Constitution protects the freedom of the press, a critical linchpin of a democracy in which the government is accountable to the people. U.S. courts have affirmed that the First Amendment prohibits government censorship and offers protection against defamation lawsuits. The media can also rely on nonlegal safeguards such as political norms and traditions, the good will of the public, and a mutually dependent relationship with government officials. These protections mean that even if access to government sources and documents is not guaranteed by the Constitution, the media can rely on norms to function as a watchdog, meaning to investigate and report back to the public. The media has the freedom to be a source of information, a forum for discussion, and an outlet for the expression of ideas and opinions.

Endnotes

1. Michael Wines, "Mission to Somalia: Bush Declares Goals in Somalia to 'Save Thousands," *The New York Times* (New York City, NY), December 5, 1992.

2. Martin Walker, "US Troops in Somalia Will Do God's Work, Says Bush," *The Guardian* (New York City, NY) December 5, 1992.

3. Shanto Iyengar and Donald Kinder, *News That Matters: Television and American Opinion* (Chicago, Illinois: University of Chicago Press, 1987).

4. Larry Minear, Colin Scott, and Thomas G. Weiss, *The News Media, Civil War, and Humanitarian Action* (Boulder, Colorado: Lynne Rienner Publishers Inc., 1996), 4.

5. Theodore White, *The Making of the President, 1960* (New York City, New York: Atheneum Publishers, 1961).

6. Robert McChesney, "The Global Media Giants," November 1, 1997, http://fair.org/media_criticism/the-global-media-giants/.

7. "Who Owns the Media?" Pew Research Center's Project for Excellence in Journalism, http://www.stateofthemedia.org/media-ownership/.

8. "In Changing News Landscape, Even Television is Vulnerable: Trends in News Consumption: 1991-2012," Pew Research Center, September 27, 2012, http://www.people-press.org/2012/09/27/in-changing-news-landscape-even-television-is-vulnerable/.

9. Mark Jurkowitz, "The Losses in Legacy: The Growth in Digital Reporting," Pew Research Center, March 26, 2014, http://www.journalism.org/2014/03/26/the-losses-in-legacy/.

10. "The State of the News Media," Pew Research Center's Project for Excellence in Journalism, 2013, http://www.stateofthemedia.org/files/2013/08/SOTNM-low-rez-pdf.pdf.

11. Richard Davis, *The Press and American Politics: The New Mediator* (Upper Saddle River, New Jersey: Prentice Hall, 1996).

12. "Nielsen Reports Television Tuning Remains at Record Levels," The Nielson Company, October 17, 2007, https://www.nielsen.com/content/dam/nielsen/en_us/documents/pdf/Press Releases/2007/October/Nielsen Reports Television Tuning Remains at Record Levels.pdf.

13. Jeffrey Gottfried, Katerina Eva Matsa, and Michael Barthel, "As Jon Stewart Steps Down, 5 Facts about *The Daily Show*," Pew Research Center, August 6, 2015, http://www.pewresearch.org/fact-tank/2015/08/06/5-facts-daily-show/.

14. Richard M. Nixon, *Six Crises* (New York: Doubleday, 1962).

15. "The State of the News Media, 2013," Pew Research Center's Project for Excellence in Journalism, 2013, http://www.stateofthemedia.org/files/2013/08/SOTNM-low-rez-pdf.pdf.

16. Stephen Erlanger, "Trump's Twitter Threats Put American Credibility on the Line," *The New York Times*, January 7, 2018, https://www.nytimes.com/2018/01/07/world/europe/trump-tweets-american-credibility.html.

17. "Trump Blocking Critics on Twitter Violates Constitution: Judge," *The New York Times*, May 23, 2018, https://www.nytimes.com/reuters/2018/05/23/us/politics/23reuters-usa-trump-twitter.html.

18. "The State of the News Media, 2013," Pew Research Center's Project for Excellence in Journalism, 2013, http://www.stateofthemedia.org/files/2013/08/SOTNM-low-rez-pdf.pdf.

19. Ibid.

20. Theodore J. Glasser, "Objectivity Precludes Responsibility," *Quill*, February 1984.

21. Ben H. Bagdikian, *The Media Monopoly, 5th Edition* (Boston: Beacon Press, 1997), ix.

22. Robert Entman, *Democracy Without Citizens* (New York: Oxford University Press, 1989), 110-11.

23. Bagdikian, 217.

24. John Buescher, "The Fourth Estate as the Fourth Branch," http://teachinghistory.org/history-content/ask-a-historian/23821.

25. LaGarrett King, "The Media and Black Masculinity: Looking at the Media Through Race(d) Lens," *Critical Education* 8:2 (February 1, 2017).

26. "Should NC Lawmakers Repeal HB2 'Bathroom Bill'?" FOX News, December 21, 2016, http://video.foxnews.com/v/5257150034001/?#sp=show-clips.

27. Jeff Mason and Reuters, "Obama says transgender bathroom bill based on law," MSNBC, June 2, 2016, http://www.msnbc.com/msnbc/obama-says-transgender-bathroom-directive-based-law. Emma Margolin, "What Do Trans People Really Do in the Bathrooms? Web Series Flushes Fears," MSNBC, May 19, 2016, http://www.msnbc.com/msnbc/what-do-trans-people-really-do-bathrooms-web-series-flushes-fear.

28. Daniel Romer, Kathleen Hall Jamieson, and Sean Aday, "Television News and the Cultivation of Fear of Crime," *Journal of Communication* (March 2003): 8-104.

29. Amos Yversky and Daniel Kahneman, "Availability: A Heuristic For Judging Frequency And Probability," *Cognitive Psychology* 4 (1973): 207-232.

30. Michael Dean Barnes et al. "Analysis of Media Agenda Setting During and After Hurricane Katrina: Implications for Emergency Preparedness, Disaster Response, and Disaster Policy," *Am Journal of Public Health* 98 no. 4 (April 2008): 604–610.

31. Stav Ziv, "How Social Media Changed News Coverage After the Boston Marathon Attack," *Newsweek*, April 15, 2015.

32. Ibid.

33. Stephen D. Cooper, *Watching the Watchdog: Bloggers as the Fifth Estate* (Spokane, WA: Marquette Books, 2006).

34. Walter Karp, "All the Congressman's Men," *Harper's*, July 1989, 55-63.

35. Edward Herman and Noam Chomsky, *Manufacturing Consent: The Political Economy of the Mass Media* (New York: Pantheon. 2002).

36. David L. Paletz and Robert M. Entman, *Media Power Politics* (New York: Free Press, 1981).

37. Donald Shaw and Maxwell McCombs, *The Emergence of American Political Issues: The Agenda Setting Function of the Press* (St. Paul, MN: West Group, 1977).

38. Christopher Lasch, "Journalism, Publicity, and The Lost Art of Political Argument," *Gannett Center Journal*, Spring 1990, http://j647commethics.weebly.com/uploads/6/4/2/2/6422481/lasche_article.pdf.

CHAPTER 11
The US Congress: We Love Our Representative, but Not the Institution

Chapter Objectives

1. Understand why Americans love their own representatives but not Congress.
2. Learn how members of Congress are tightly secured to local interests but loosely tied to national interests.
3. Examine what the Constitution says about the powers of Congress and how it is structured.
4. Analyze how members of Congress get elected and reelected.
5. Assess how Congress does its work in committees and subcommittees.
6. Explore how party leaders help keep members from completely pandering to local interests.

Introduction: California's 30th Congressional District Loves Brad Sherman

© Shutterstock, Inc.

In one of his 535-part series, "Better Know a District," comedian Stephen Colbert asked Congressman Brad Sherman the following question: "Are people shocked when they learn that bald, bespectacled, Brad Sherman is in fact a certified public accountant?" Sherman answered, "No, not at all." Although a seemingly regular guy to his constituents, Sherman is by most measures an extraordinary person. He graduated magna cum laude from Harvard Law School and taught at the school's International Tax Program. He worked his way to the U.S. House of Representatives after winning a seat on California's Board of Equalization. Once in Congress, he authored the "Sherman Amendment" to purchase environmentally sensitive lands. He helped produce legislation to end Wall Street bailouts, shield family retirement and college savings, and protect bank consumers from exorbitant fees. He fought for legislation to keep corporations from giving their poorly performing CEOs million-dollar bonuses and he championed the Consumer Financial Protection Bureau. For his district, Sherman secured $20 million to complete the Backbone Trail through the Santa Monica Mountains, $190 million for carpool and ramp improvements to the 405 and 5 freeways, and federal funding for Topanga State Park and the Valley Performing Arts Center, among many other projects. Since 1996, he has been elected to Congress eleven times, often with at least 60 percent of the vote.

Sherman's background is characteristic of many members of Congress. Using reelection rates as a measure of constituent satisfaction, the members seem to be doing their jobs well. In the 2018 Congressional election, 93 percent of the members of the House of Representatives and 86 percent of senators who sought reelection were successful even though public approval of Congress was generally low.[1]

Like most members of Congress, Sherman wins office consistently and decisively because he understands and nurtures his connection with the people in his district. Since 1997, he has hosted over 200 "town hall" meetings to discuss issues that concern his constituents. At such events, the balding representative gives out plastic combs stamped with his name and phone number and introduces himself as the guy from "America's best named community, Sherman Oaks." In his interview with Colbert, he defended his district's reputation against suggestions that the San Fernando Valley was home to the nation's largest porn industry. In contrast, the representative praised the area as America's first suburb, calling it the best place to live and raise a family.

FIGURE 11.1 Congressional Job Approval Ratings: 2001-2015

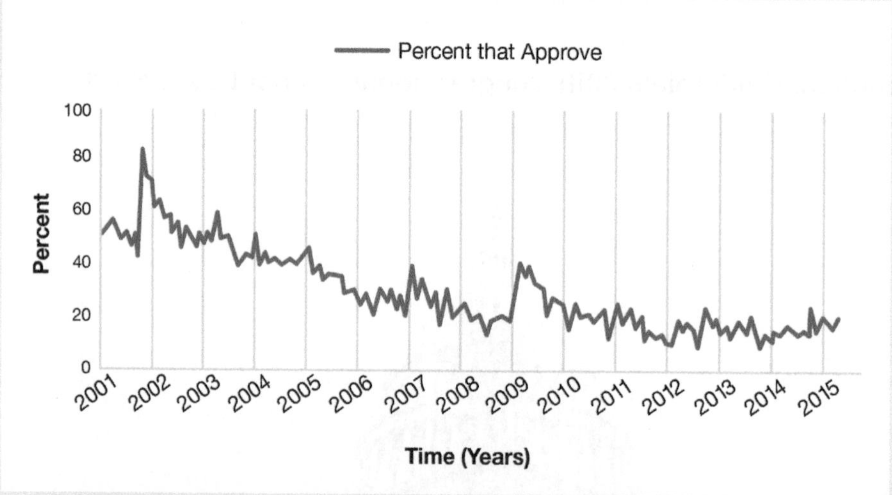

Data from "Five Months Into GOP Congress, Approval Remains Low at 19%." Gallup.com. Accessed June 17, 2016. http://www.gallup.com/poll/183128/five-months-gop-congress-approval-remains-low.aspx.

In the 2012 general election, Sherman faced fellow long-time House incumbent Howard Berman. California's new redistricting process and primary rules matched the two incumbents from formerly neighboring districts against each other. Being liberal Democrats from the Los Angeles area, both candidates had similar issue positions. They were staunchly pro-consumer, pro-environment, and pro-choice on abortion. Still, it was Berman who received the endorsements from nearly the entire California Democratic Party establishment, including the governor, both U.S. senators, and most of its congressional delegation. Berman had spent years focusing on national and international issues like immigration reform and intellectual property law. Sherman had also championed national issues, but dedicated more time to being present in the district and working to bring benefits from the federal government back home. Sherman's stronger reputation for local service paid off with a November win. In the end, the representative most closely in touch with his constituents returned to Congress, while the one more focused on national issues and favored by the party lost his job.

In this chapter, we will address a central paradox of American politics: How is it that citizens love their members of Congress yet dislike the institution they represent? We will learn that Congress is the most powerful branch of the federal government, yet its institutional structure and large membership make it difficult to work efficiently. Congress's solution for dealing with its complexity—dividing tasks among various committees—gives members advantages over their challengers for reelection and insulates them from Congress's unpopularity. Lastly, we will see how Congress is organized by the political parties and how their leaders get members to work toward partisan goals.

11.1 District Representation, National Representation, and the Electoral Connection

Sherman's victory should be no surprise. Like most voters, those in California's 27th Congressional District chose the representative who they believed most closely shared their interests and who they assumed would best satisfy their needs. For his part, Sherman understands that it was in his best interest to foster these beliefs and reinforce them with his actions. Like Sherman, members of Congress know that their first allegiance must be to the people of their districts and not the leadership in Congress, the president, or their political party, ideology, or even the country as a whole. They know the citizens in their districts determine whether they get and keep their jobs. Some time ago, political scientist David Mayhew called this relationship the **electoral connection**, a simple formulation based on self-interest. Citizens choose representatives who will get their desires satisfied by government. Because representatives are also self-interested, they do their best to give their constituencies what they want in order to keep their jobs. Mayhew referred to members of Congress as "single-minded seekers of reelection" and Brad Sherman is a good representation of the ideal prototype.[2]

Still, Mayhew's observations about the motivations of Congress are a rough simplification. Members have goals and allegiances that lie beyond their districts. They genuinely want to produce effective public policies that will benefit the nation as a whole. They also care a great deal about the success of their party and its leaders. However, they cannot accomplish their goals unless they win office and learn how to stay there. Thus, we can understand much of how Congress is organized and goes about its business through this connection of individual members to their districts or states. The Constitution outlines the basic features of Congress in Article 1 and other places. This document shapes the behavior of Congress members, as it does for the president, the parties, and other leaders and institutions. However, the members of Congress invented and modified most of the organizational details of their institution. As Congress matured and became more professional, its rules and traditions evolved to ease the members' anxieties over job security.

Congressman Brad Sherman

Jose Gil / Shutterstock.com

electoral connection

A relationship between an elected official and his or her constituents whereby the self-interest of the elected official is tied to the self-interest of the constituents.

A joint session of the 115th Congress.

The connection between most members of Congress and their districts is healthy and strong. Across the country, representatives seem to be working hard, satisfying their constituents, and returning to Congress. Yet, when pollsters ask the public about the performance of the Congress, they regularly give it low marks. In November 2020, the Gallup polling organization found that only 23 percent of the people they asked approved of the way Congress is handling its job.[3] Congress's ratings have been dreadfully low (below 20 percent approval) since 2010, but ratings have never been consistently high. Congressional approval has fluctuated over time, but on average, only about one-third of the public has liked Congress's performance since Gallup began measuring its job performance in the 1970s.[4] Something must be wrong. How can Americans overwhelmingly disapprove of the job that Congress is doing, yet retain more than 90 percent of its members?

FIGURE 11.2 Record High Anti-Incumbent Sentiment Toward Congress

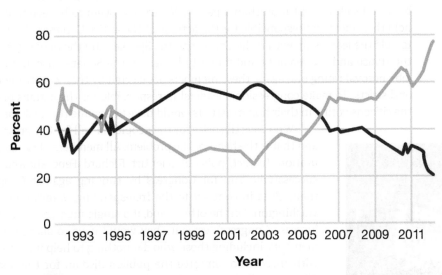

■ % of registered voters that believe most members of Congress deserve to be re-elected

▨ % of registered voters that believe most members of Congress do not deserve to be re-elected

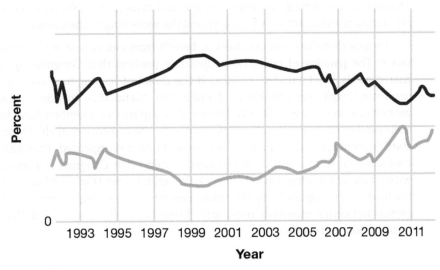

■ % of registered voters that believe most U.S. representatives in their congressional districts deserve to be re-elected

▨ % of registered voters that believe most U.S. representatives in their congressional districts do not deserve to be re-elected

There is evidence that disapproval of one's own representative is linked with Congress's performance ratings, but opinion of one's representative is always much higher than that of the institution.[5] People today have better information about their representatives and it is easier to blame a faceless institution than a person. Voters also seem to believe that it would be unfair to hold their members responsible for the actions of the entire Congress. It would make more sense to hold the leadership within the Congress—the Speaker and the majority and minority leaders in the House and the majority and minority leaders in the Senate—accountable for Congress's low job-approval rating but, again, these members are elected by their constituents in individual states or districts. To make congressional leadership responsible for the actions of Congress as a whole, the citizens voting in their home districts would have to assume this task for the entire country.

© Shutterstock, Inc.

paradox of collective action

A situation in which individual rational behavior and the ability to free-ride on the efforts of others leads to an outcome in which persons end up worse off than if they had cooperated.

Who pays the price for the people's ill will for Congress? No one in particular, and that is the heart of the problem. All members of Congress share its poor reputation. In fact, political scientist Richard Feno showed that some members successfully "run for Congress by running against Congress."[6] They portray themselves in contrast to the free-spending, vote-trading, career politicians in Washington. On the other hand, if a single member or the leaders work hard to increase Congress's esteem, they would have to share this outcome will all its members, including those who did nothing to help increase its ratings (and even with those who reinforce the public's disdain for the institution). We see this dilemma, called the **paradox of collective action**, at work in the chapters on federalism, voting, and interest groups. Since the reputation of Congress is shared, individual members of Congress know that they can free ride on the efforts of those working to raise the approval ratings of Congress. Still, most benefits of office are not shared; they are exclusive to the member. The power, the salary, the press coverage, and that parking spot in front of the national airport in Washington are private benefits that belong to the member alone. This logic creates strong incentives to work hard to keep one's job and to let others worry about the reputation of the institution, the party, and the well-being of the country.

Despite that, Congress members do benefit from and care about increases in Congress's reputation. The paradox of collective action only predicts that Congress's good reputation, like all shared goods, will be under-produced if the choice of helping to make it is left to the individual members. Coupled with the electoral connection, this not only provides a good explanation for why we love our member yet hate Congress; it also implies that members have found ways to insulate their careers from popular dissatisfaction with the institution itself. These ideas give us a good starting point for understanding Congress and how it is organized. They also provide insights into congressional rules and procedures. Keep in mind that Congress is a complex, living institution with a long and distinguished history. Although it is true that members shield their careers from the institution's unpopularity, they must nevertheless pass legislation, collect taxes, and fund programs. Individual members must still "bring home the bacon" and that involves leadership, organization, and cooperation.

11.2 Congress and the Constitution

The Constitution lists the official powers of Congress. The framers designed the Congress, borrowing from a rich history of government in England and governmental experience in the colonies and the newly formed state governments. The British experience produced lessons from the struggle between monarchs and the landed gentry as well as a body of political and philosophical writings about the proper way to organize government. The result was the influence of Parliament over the crown. During the colonial experience, representation was expanded to propertied adult white men in the colonial assemblies. This fostered autonomy in governing. Colonial experience not only nurtured a tradition of self-governance but a distrust of centralized authority. Much is made of the proclamations of King George III as causes of the Revolutionary War, but the colonial governors were administrative agents of the king, complete with royal veto powers over the colonial assemblies. The framers of the Constitution looked at such powers with suspicion. When the states wrote their constitutions, their framers were mindful of the need to separate the powers and functions of government, but they were especially alert to place checks on the powers of executive authority. Nearly all the state constitutions and the national Constitution give the most important powers of government to the legislative branch.

Constitutional Powers

The Constitution gives the members of Congress sole authority to organize the institution. To ensure independence from other branches of government and from state governments, the Constitution gives lawmakers immunity from liability for what they say and from arrest (except for major crimes) while in session.

Section 8 of Article 1 enumerates Congress's many powers. At the top is the authority to levy and collect taxes to provide for the safety and general welfare of the country. All tax legislation must originate in the House of Representatives. Congress can also borrow money and regulate commerce among the states, Native American tribes, and other nations. Congress establishes the rules for the government, its land, immigration and naturalization; the courts to deliver justice; and post offices and roads to deliver the mail. It protects patents and copyrights, prints, safeguards and determines the value of the country's money, and fixes the official weights and measures for just about everything else. Congress also creates and maintains the Navy and Army and can call the military to action to enforce its laws or to protect the country from invasion, piracy, or domestic insurrections. Congress is the only branch of government that can declare war and appropriate money. At the end of the list, the framers added the elastic or necessary and proper clause, which gives Congress the power: to "make all laws which shall be necessary and proper for carrying into execution the foregoing powers, and all other powers vested by this Constitution in the Government of the United States..."

Outside of the limitations on governmental power guaranteed by the Bill of Rights, it is difficult to think of a power that the Congress does not have. As the fictional character Tony Montana said in the movie *Scarface*, "First you get the money, then you get the power." The authority to tax and spend to enforce a law or policy created by Congress is almost complete. It is important to note that neither the executive nor the courts can tax or appropriate money, nor do they have the power to pass legislation. Both these branches have significant powers, but they are formally weak by comparison.

Moreover, some of Congress's powers have been expanded, particularly those emanating from its power to regulate business. The Supreme Court has broadly interpreted the commerce clause to give Congress the ability to regulate business both within and between states, and to regulate transportation and communications, as well as things only tangentially related to commerce (such as civil rights and crime). Congress expanded the power to tax and spend to include offering grants (or the threat to reduce existing grants) to induce state and local governments to comply with federal wishes. They use the same sorts of inducements to influence individual behavior, from encouraging folks to buy homes with tax breaks and low-interest mortgages to enacting tax penalties to encourage citizens to buy health insurance.

There are no term limits for Congressional members, but Congress is not almighty. The most basic restraints come from the power of the people to remove its members from office. Those in the House of Representatives must face the consequences of their decisions every two years; senators, every six years. Congress must share its powers with the other branches of government. The institution depends on the executive branch to carry out its orders, although the Senate has the power to approve a long list of important government officers and oversee their activities. Indeed, the Congressional Research Service estimates the senators approve between 1,200 and 1,400 positions in the executive branch alone.[7] Still, the president's ability to veto legislation makes him or her a significant partner in the law-making process, because canceling or overriding a veto requires a vote of two-thirds of the members in both the House and the Senate. The judicial branch interprets and applies the laws passed by Congress and—as part of the system of checks and balances—can terminate a law that justices decide is incompatible with the Constitution. Congress's check on such court actions would be to pass a new law or seek a constitutional amendment, which would require approval by three-fourths of the states.

Bicameralism: Congress Has Two Bodies

Congress must also contend with its divided structure. The Constitution separates Congress into two differently ordered and independent bodies. Each chamber must agree within itself and then with the other body before legislation is finalized. Such differences did not come about by accident. The framers borrowed bicameral design from Great Britain. British Parliament separates itself between the House of Lords and the House of Commons. The framers modeled the Senate or "upper house" on the House of Lords. Originally, the people did not elect the members of the Senate; rather, they were selected by various state legislatures to contain the effects of popular democracy. James Madison and many of the framers equated direct democracy with mob rule. They believed that senators, given their method of election and longer terms of office, would proceed with less emotion than the popularly elected members of the House. The calmer heads in the Senate, they thought, should have the power to block popular initiatives coming from the House, or at least slow things down. The Senate's own website quotes George Washington as saying, "The framers had created the Senate to 'cool' House legislation just as a saucer was used to cool hot tea."[8]

Representation in the House and Senate

The Great Compromise

The result of a debate among the delegates to the Constitutional Convention of 1787 that decided the number of representatives in the House of Representatives would be proportional to the number of people in the states and the states would have equal representation in the Senate.

This bicameral structure also provided solutions to conflicting demands for representation. States with smaller populations, like Rhode Island, knew they would be dominated by the larger states if representation were determined by the number of people in each state. On the other hand, the larger states argued that it would be unfair if the smaller states had the same number of votes as the more populous states. **The Great Compromise** ensured that the House would represent the people proportionally by allocating representation by population. The Senate would represent the states equally by giving each state two representatives regardless of the number of people living in the state.

With 435 voting members, the House is the larger of the two chambers. Its members mostly represent areas much smaller than states and reflect more precisely the diversity of interests residing in the country. Currently, the smallest congressional district (New York's 13th) is roughly the size of the island of Manhattan, about 20 square miles (the smallest state—Rhode Island—is more than 1,500 square miles). Still, some very sparsely populated areas have House districts that are bigger than most states.[9] By contrast, both Senate members from each state represent the interests of their state as a whole.

It is important to note that the formula that gives each state the same number of representatives in the Senate violates the democratic principle of "one person, one vote." Although it takes the combined population of the smallest twenty-two states to equal California's population, they get forty-four votes in the Senate to California's two. Thus, in terms of numerical representation, the people in states with small populations have much more influence in the Senate than people living in the populous states. If the smallest twenty-six states, which represent only about 18 percent of the U.S. population, decided to vote as a block, they would control the majority of the votes in the Senate and all of its legislation. On the other hand, the eight most populous states have only 16 percent of the votes in the Senate. If these states voted together, nothing would happen even though they represent most of the American public.

Such disproportionate representation in the Senate matters. Only the Senate has the power to approve treaties, ambassadors, and other government officials appointed by the president. When it comes to federal funding, political scientist Sarah Binder concluded that, "Small states make out like bandits."[10] Lower population states receive more federal dollars than their residents pay in taxes, whereas the residents of higher population states tend to give more to the federal government than they receive.[11] The host of *The Daily Show*, Jon Stewart, complained after the Senate voted to distribute Homeland Security funds equally among the states rather than by likelihood of attack. While this was bad news for New York, he said it was good news for Wyoming, which only had "one high-risk target, the world's largest pile of Homeland Security money." The Senate overrepresents rural populations, which undervalues the preferences of liberals, Democrats, African Americans, and Latinas/os.[12] Overrepresentation in the Senate also matters in presidential elections. The formula for the distribution of electoral college votes gives small states an advantage by giving each state an additional vote for each of its senators. For example, Ryan Cooper calculates that residents of Wyoming voting for president count 3.5 times more than people voting in Florida.[13] This overrepresentation of some states in the electoral college helped George W. Bush win the presidency in 2000 and Donald Trump in 2016, despite winning only a minority of votes nationwide.

Implications of the Size of the Chamber

The institutional differences between the House and the Senate also affect the behavior of the representatives in each chamber. The average state contains more than 6 million people, whereas each House district averages less than three-fourths of a million constituents. Because states encompass the Congressional districts, the constituencies of most senators are not only larger but they are generally more diverse than those of their counterparts in the House. Even midwestern farm states such as Indiana, Illinois, and Minnesota have cities and significant industrial areas. With diverse interests to manage, senators tend to take moderate positions on issues and are more likely to seek compromise to reduce conflict among their diverse constituencies. In general, senators, except those from very small states, live at a greater distance from their constituents. This prompts citizens to go to their representatives in the House to express their views on pending legislation or to get help with government services.

Socially, House districts are much more homogeneous than entire states, even in diverse urban areas. Our prototypical House member from Los Angeles, Brad Sherman, represents a district that is socially varied but uniformly urban, moderately liberal, and mostly Democrat. He has little incentive to care much about the interests of ranchers, miners, or conservative Republicans—and the people of his district would not be terribly pleased if he did. While California's two U.S. senators are attuned to statewide issues, including those that concern ranch and mining interests, Sherman focuses on issues that affect his area, like mass transportation, air quality, and affordable housing.

The large number of small, homogeneous districts makes the House a place where members develop specialties in certain policy areas, particularly those that affect their districts. As Mayhew wrote, "the quest for specialization in Congress is a quest for credit."[14] Members tend to gravitate to committees that deal with policy issues that help their districts and careers. The House of Representatives has a greater division of labor than the Senate. The House spreads its 435 members among 20 committees and 104 subcommittees, whereas the Senate disperses its 100 members among 16 committees and 72 subcommittees. More subcommittees in the House means that its members can influence specific policy domains, making it easier to claim personal responsibility for the things that happen within their realm. Further, House rules prevent members from serving on more than four subcommittees, forcing members to have a narrow focus. Specialization develops policy expertise among committee members, but such awareness comes at a price. Members typically know little about policies that fall outside of their areas of proficiency.

It is a happy consequence that House members' policy preferences most often align with those of their constituents because they normally share socio-economic characteristics and come from the same place. Thus, Congress becomes a reflection of the nation's diversity and a forum for managing disparate policy opinions. This feature should not be undervalued. No single party or individual can truly represent the views of a large nation.

The House members' short, two-year term means they must work fast to produce legislation before the next election. At the same time, the House's larger size brings difficulties of agenda control and time management. Over the years, the leadership in the House has accumulated authority to channel the flow of business and restrict the behavior of members to move business efficiently through the chamber. For example, the Speaker of the House (in consultation with other party leaders) more or less determines how and in what order bills are considered, if at all. The Rules Committee decides the conditions for debate or amendment. With more members to organize, the House's rules and procedures are more numerous. With more committees and subcommittees, there are more leadership positions. "Whip teams" broaden involvement in leadership, but also help move legislation. For their part, ordinary members are expected to work in committees, know the rules and procedures of the chamber, and not to criticize their colleagues on the House floor.[15] Faithful following of the principle of majority rule also helps push legislation through the larger body.

A Senate Armed Services Committee budget hearing.

mark reinstein / Shutterstock.com

filibuster

A tactic used in the U.S. Senate to delay or prevent voting on a measure by holding the floor (refusing to yield the right to speak) indefinitely. The procedure is derived from the Senate's custom of unlimited debate and is traditionally, but not necessarily, associated with long, uninterrupted speeches.

In the Senate, fewer members mean they spread their work more thinly as each sits on more committees and subcommittees. This feature tends to create more generalists than experts in specific areas of public policy. With fewer members, they are able to discuss the issues at greater length. Their terms are staggered over six years such that normally, only one-third of the senators face the electorate every two years. Most are not running for reelection during non-presidential or mid-term elections, which often serve as a referendum on the president's performance during the previous two years.[16] The Senate's longer, staggered terms provide continuity and some distance from the voters. They can relax a bit between elections and perhaps focus further on national or international issues. They not only have the luxury to consider new ideas, but they can bring together varied groups to support their initiatives. Such efforts are not only time-consuming but politically difficult and risky. At the same time, groups that form around long-term international, national, or statewide issues are more likely to look for support in the Senate.

Relative to the House of Representatives, the Senate is less formal to the point of being almost folksy. Limits on debate are rare and require a supermajority to enact. Indeed, senators cherish and safeguard the **filibuster**, their right to talk forever. This gives individual senators a great deal of influence because each can use the rule to block a vote on any matter, forcing the entire chamber to consider that Senator's wishes. This institutional feature makes the Senate's leaders weaker than their counterparts in the House. They depend more on personal relationships than formal procedures. With freedom to debate and offer amendments, leadership has difficulty managing the chamber's agenda or controlling the pace of legislation. Indeed, the Senate often dispenses with the rules altogether in favor of negotiated agreements that require unanimous consent to move business though the chamber. Such agreements determine the order of bills to be considered and the conditions for debate and amendment. In the House, the Speaker and the majority-controlled Rules Committee decide these matters.

11.3 Getting to Congress and Staying There

Getting into Congress requires winning a district election. For most politicians, this represents the pinnacle of their professional careers, much like getting a contract to play Major League Baseball is to an aspiring baseball player. The athlete's journey usually starts in Little League, then high school, then college and up through the various levels of the minor leagues. Ability is important, but so is catching the eye of scouts. Similarly, politicians often start by winning election to local offices, such as school boards and city councils, and then perhaps to statewide office before winning a seat in Congress. Along the way, they learn what is expected of them and find friends and supporters who help with their careers. Like becoming a professional athlete, it takes more than ambition and ability to make it to "the show." It also takes expertise, timing, and help.

Getting to Congress

At the beginning of the county's history, office holding was considered honorific, a duty, not a career. Early public officials gained public office based on their reputations but also on personal relationships built from obligations among individuals, families, and communities. As the political parties developed in the early 1800s, local organizations began to recruit candidates but, while the actors changed, the relationships involved remained personal. Political power and office holding began to revolve around the awarding of jobs and contracts and giving favors in the administration of the law. The parties used this special treatment to maintain their power. Still, sustaining the party was much like running a family business, albeit a very large one with a national scope.

The party's army of workers, favor seekers, and office holders were held together through the years by personal bonds, loyalty, ethnic solidarity, and community. Entry into politics was a matter of who knew you. Political scientist Milton Rakove repeats a story about an ambitious young man who showed up to help Chicago's Democratic Party get Adlai Stevenson elected as president. The party's local ward committeeman turned him away, saying, "We don't want nobody nobody sent."[17] The young man was unwanted—even as a volunteer—because he was not acquainted with his local precinct captain. The local, state, and national party organizations had to enlist and sponsor candidates for political office.

Since the 1960s, individual ambition has become more important in determining who runs for political office. Today, politicians more or less nominate themselves. Our prototypical member of Congress, Brad Sherman, decided to run for Congress due to his personal experience as a tax attorney and concern for tax fairness. He set out on his own to raise money and run his campaign in much the same way that an entrepreneur starts his or her own business. He won the local democratic primary and then the general election. Nominations, campaigns, and fund raising now center on the candidates.

Beto O'Rourke represented Texas's 16th Congressional District from 2012-2018.

michelmond / Shutterstock.com

Much of this change has to do with the passage of regulations that drastically reduced the power of the political parties at the close of the 19th century. Working state by state, the Progressive Movement managed to institute the direct primary system as a way to take the nominations process away from the party organizations. The movement also weakened the parties when they took control of government jobs and placed distribution in the hands of civil service systems. Public sector unions moved the control of government jobs even farther away from party politicians.

Today, nominees appearing on the party label are mostly chosen by ordinary voters in local primary elections rather than selected by party leaders. In turn, the party's efforts to find loyal candidates is hampered because it can no longer guarantee that its choice will even be on the November ballot. An ambitious would-be nominee can now directly challenge the party establishment's choice in an area where the party is dominant. If the candidate is successful in the primary, he or she will be the party's nominee and have an excellent chance of winning the office in the general election.

Self-Recruitment: Newcomers vs. Experienced Professionals

Only a few political newcomers manage to make it to the U.S. Congress. Economics Professor Dave Brat shocked the party establishment when he upset House Majority Leader Eric Cantor in Virginia's 2014 Republican primary. Brat's victory marked the first time a challenger had ousted a sitting House Majority Leader in a primary since 1899. The voters in the district had reportedly come to believe that the Congressional leader was spending too much time in Washington working on national issues and too little time at home. Still, Brat had help. Conservative talk-radio hosts unsatisfied with the efforts of congressional Republicans to challenge the Democratic president boosted his primary bid.[18]

There are a few requirements for serving in Congress listed in the Constitution. Senators need to be at least thirty years old and have been a U.S. citizen for nine years. Members of the House of Representatives can be younger—at least twenty-five years old—and need only have been a U.S. citizen for seven years. Both chambers require that the member be a resident of the state they are representing. Nevertheless, the newcomer that makes it to Congress is usually someone with a name easily recognized by the voters. When John F. Kennedy ran for the U.S. Senate, his family was already known in Boston politics. His status as a war hero only enhanced his reputation. Similarly, Senator John Glenn was already a famous astronaut and Senator Bill Bradley was an Olympic gold medalist and professional basketball player for the New York Knicks.

Still, more than half of the current senators made it to the Senate after serving in the House of Representatives. When a senator decides to retire, or becomes vulnerable to losing an election, openings in the Senate become available. Similarly, ambitious local office holders wait for an incumbent to retire or become vulnerable before running for a seat in the House of Representatives. Voters are more likely to elect experienced politicians to Congress than newcomers because experienced politicians have worked their way up the ladder of political opportunity in their local communities. They often have experience with grass-roots organizations and political movements but, more typically, have held local elected offices as mayors or state legislators. As such, they are familiar with their political and economic environments. They know the voters, the issues, and the election laws, and they have experience as campaigners and fundraisers. They hire their own advisers and managers and decide which issues to emphasize.

Recruitment by the Parties

Would-be members of Congress do not need to seek election as a nominee for one of the two major parties, but most advance within the party system. Attachment to a political party allows candidates to take advantage of the partisan loyalties felt by the voters. They also benefit when the parties mobilize their activists and energize citizens to get them to the polls to vote for their candidates. Thus, most candidates running for Congress have long been active in their state and local parties before running for Congress.

For their part, the political parties are on the lookout for good candidates. When vacancies appear in local political offices, the local political parties attempt to recruit a candidate to run for that office. Similarly, when vacancies appear on state ballots, the state party committees look for candidates to fill them. Party organizations urge potentially strong candidates to run for Congress. Those called report that such contact made them more likely to run.[19] In a few states, the parties nominate or endorse candidates at party conventions held before the primary elections.

Attractive recruits are those with good looks, a likeable personality, and talents for public speaking, organizing, and fundraising. One also needs to endure a long campaign filled with rallies, debates, and hostile questions. The candidate must smile, shake hands, and eat with relish whatever dish they are served. Previous involvement with public office helps, along with the visibility and credibility that experience brings. Beyond recruitment, the parties provide financial and other resources and services to their candidates. They do much more than call voters, distribute campaign material, and plant yard signs. Most state parties are multimillion-dollar organizations.[20] With healthy budgets, they have experienced directors and talented staff. They have become effective fundraisers, so they pass money to their candidates or organize fund-raising events. They offer training to candidates and their staffs, and they provide the latest public opinion research. They give their candidates lists of voters to contact and advice on which consultants to hire. Most states have relaxed their requirements for early, absentee, and mail-in balloting, and the parties help their candidates by identifying and delivering ballot requests to potential early voters who are members of their party.

Alexandria Ocasio-Cortez was sworn in as a Member of the United States House of Representatives on January 3rd, 2019.

Rachael Warriner / Shutterstock.com

Further, working with parties matches the candidate with the party's allies. Each party is associated with large groups that support their candidates. On the Democratic side, the major groups include labor, teacher, and other government unions, professional associations, environmental groups, women's organizations, and those working to protect choice in abortion. The Republicans offer support through small business and trade associations, pro-life groups, and conservative Christian congregations. These groups not only help the established party candidate fend off potential primary challenges, but they offer more support in the general election. Beyond votes, groups provide candidates with their lists of people to contact, money, volunteers, and other resources.

All this shows that although the decision to run for Congress remains a personal decision and the candidates themselves come up with the bulk of what they need to run for office, the political parties, interest groups, and others remain important agents in this process. Their support leads to more support and a greater likelihood of success. Since attaining a seat in Congress usually requires a progression up a political career ladder, lawmakers need such recognition early and often. Like most institutions, the people within parties and their allied groups have preconceived notions about who is likely to be a successful candidate and who is not. Women and minorities may thus be less likely to gain their support and less likely to seek office in the first place.[21] Popular attitudes, social preferences, and prejudices also influence which candidates the public is likely to support or reject. The ambitions, skills, and resources that advantage certain candidates over others are not equally distributed.

Congress does not display an accurately descriptive selection of the American public. Former Representative Loretta Sanchez described her first experience in the House with all 435 members present. As a financial analyst, she had known work at a place with mostly men. Still, calling to mind Abraham Lincoln's phrase describing democracy as "of the people," she thought Congress would be more reflective of a diverse society. She said, "I remember walking in the first day in the chamber and thinking: Oh my god, it's a bunch of old guys!"[22] In fact, the average age of members of the House of Representatives is about 57, much older that the age of the average American, which is about 38. Senators, on average, are even older at about 63, which makes the 116th Congress one of the oldest of any in recent U.S. history.[23]

FIGURE 11.3 Number of Men and Women in Congress, 2018

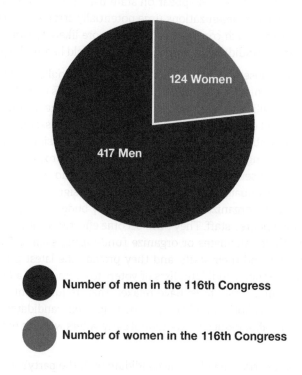

● **Number of men in the 116th Congress**

● **Number of women in the 116th Congress**

Judy M., "The 116th Congress Reveals a Major Diversity Gap Between Democrats and Republicans," November 20, 2018, https://www.care2.com/causes/the-116th-congress-reveals-a-major-diversity-gap-between-democrats-and-republicans.html.

Fifty-nine members of the 117th Congress are black Americans. They represent about 13 percent of the membership of Congress but account for more than 13 percent of the U.S. population. Latinas/os are more underrepresented. In the 117th Congress, they total 46 members or about 9 percent of Congress, but make up about 17.5 percent of the U.S. population. Still, while most groups remain underrepresented, Congress has never been more diverse.[24]

FIGURE 11.4 Race and Ethnicity of Representatives and Senators

Note: Data for the House and Senate, 112th Congress, and the U.S. Population, 2010. Source: CQ Press Electronic Library, CQ Congress Collection; CQ Roll Call, *Guide to the New Congress, 112th Congress*; U.S. Census Bureau; and CRS calculations.

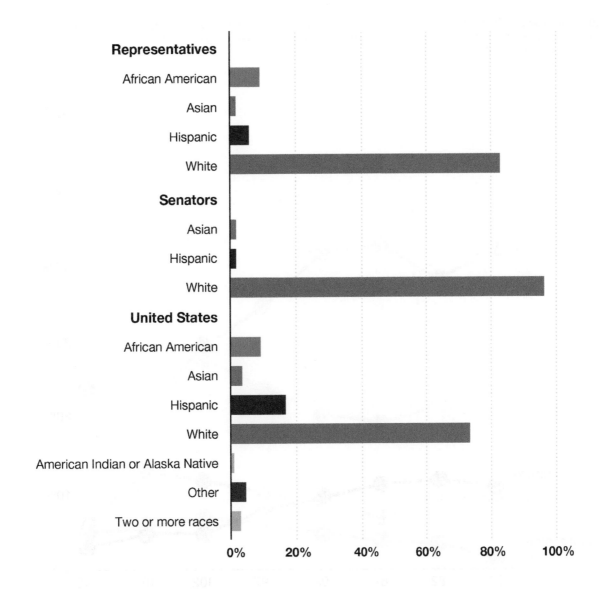

Almost 90 percent of Congress members are Christian, with more than half of these being Protestant and about one-third Catholic. Both these denominations are overrepresented in the institution, as are Jews, who account for 6.4 percent of Congress but only 2 percent of American adults. In addition, in the 116th Congress, there are 10 Mormons, 3 Muslims, 2 Buddhists, and 3 Hindus. The most underrepresented group in this category are Americans who say they do not identify with any particular faith. They make up 23 percent of the public but only Arizona Senator Kyrsten Sinema describes herself as religiously unaffiliated.[25]

The members of Congress are also a highly educated group, with 95 percent of the members of the House of Representatives having university degrees; 295 of these are advanced degrees and twenty-one are doctorates. The legal profession has always been well represented. The 116th Congress was no exception, with 161 members of the House and fifty-three members of the Senate holding law degrees, a common springboard profession into politics. There are fifteen former judges and forty-seven former prosecutors. Education was well represented in the 116th Congress, with 95 members who are teachers, professors, counselors, coaches, or school administrators. Eight members, all in the House, are ordained ministers. Overall, 231 members of Congress come from public service occupations, while 212 come from private business.

FIGURE 11.5 Most Frequently Reported Occupations of Representatives, Selected Congresses Since 1945

Source: CQ Press Electronic Library, CQ Congress Collection, CQ Roll Call, *Guide to the New Congress, 112th Congress*, http://innovation.cq.com/ newmember/ 2010elexnguide.pdf, CRS calculations.

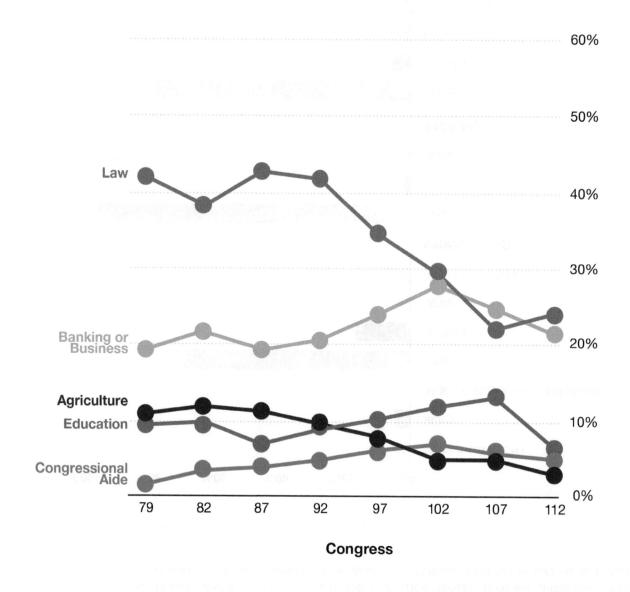

Based on Petersen, R. Eric. U.S. Representatives and Senators: Trends in Member Characteristics Since 1945. Rept. Washington, DC: Congressional Research Service, 2012.

As professional legislators, members of the House and Senate earn salaries of $174,000 per year plus health and life insurance and retirement benefits. The Speaker of the House earns $223,500. The majority and minority leaders in both houses are paid $193,400. In addition, members are entitled to an allowance to support staff, travel, mail, and office expenses. Such allowances amounted to an average of about $1.2 million per member.[26] Their salaries alone place them among the top 10 percent of American wage earners, but the wealth of the top half of members is over $1 million and the richest 53 own 80 percent of the total personal wealth of the membership.[27]

Congress woefully underrepresents some occupational groups, particularly from areas that Americans consider low-prestige, such as farm workers and other laborers. Skilled workers and technicians, domestic service providers, retail workers, and small proprietors are also underrepresented. More than half of all U.S. citizens have such jobs and, when people from some vocations are missing, their perspectives will be absent and their preferences are likely to be overlooked. Political scientist Nicholas Carnes shows that the overrepresentation of managers and professionals in Congress biases national policies in a conservative direction toward the interests of business and the upper classes.[28] Electing more members to Congress with working-class backgrounds would presumably move legislation concerning taxation, social spending, and workplace regulation in a liberal direction. The evidence shows that Congress took issues concerning family, workplace, gender discrimination, and women's health more seriously after more women became lawmakers. Women are simply more likely to introduce, sponsor, and vote for issues that affect them and children.[29] Similarly, black and Latina/o legislators are more likely to be active on issues of interest to communities of color.[30] It matters who runs for Congress and who ends up there.

The 117th Congress, elected in November 2020, brings a record number of women to Congress, (105 Democrats and 36 Republicans), bringing the total to 141, an increase from 24 to 27 percent over the 116th Congress. Sharice Davids became the first Native American woman elected to Congress; Rashida Tlaib and Ilhan Omar became first Muslim-American women in Congress; and Alexandria Ocasio-Cortez is the youngest woman ever elected to Congress in 2018. This year saw a record fifty-one women of color elected to Congress including the first Black congresswoman from Missouri and the state of Washington. Michelle Steek became the first Korean American in Congress. Overall, about 28 percent of the members of the new Congress will be non-white.[31]

Still, the framers of the Constitution made no provision that the representatives should match the social characteristics of the population in terms of race, gender, or class. Rather, they depended on the idea that individual self-interest on the part of both the citizens and their legislators would guarantee faithful representation. In addition, the framers believed that the people's views would be refined and enlarged through representation by experienced lawmakers.[32] The logic of this formulation is complete when members of Congress run for reelection. It is here that citizens have the opportunity to judge how well their members have represented them.

Sharice Davids was sworn in as a Member of the United States House of Representatives on January 3rd, 2019.

Sandeep.Mishra / Shutterstock.com

Getting Reelected to Congress: The Incumbency Advantage

If reelection rates show how well Congress represents the country, the framer's scheme seems to be working. In the November elections, only 11 incumbent members of the House of Representatives and 2 of the incumbent senators that ran for reelection were defeated. From the late 19th through the 20th centuries, the average years of service for senators increased, from less than five years to about 13 years. The tenure for members of the House also increased from just over four years to an average of about 10 years over the same period.[33] One hundred years ago, turnover in Congress was more frequent and resignations were common. Today, not many members are defeated, some die in office, and a few are forced to leave due to arrest, indictment, or allegations fo unethical behavior. Rarely do members leave voluntarily. Turnover has decreased and careers have lengthened as Congress changed from a citizen to a professional legislature.

It may be that the American people want a professional legislature with long and stable careers, but survey research seems to suggest otherwise. The public consistently gives Congress low approval ratings and overwhelming majorities would vote to limit the terms of members if they could.[34] Polls also show that most voters know little about what their representative did during the last session and most relied on mental shortcuts like name recognition and party identification when they voted in the last election.[35] A likely answer to this contradiction concerns the advantages that incumbency brings to a member of Congress when he or she faces reelection.

The Professionalization of the Modern Congress

When turnover in Congress was high throughout the 1800s, few politicians had a strong desire to be in Washington. It is not easy to live far from home. Summers are hot and muggy in the nation's capital and temporary housing has always been expensive and in short supply. Most of the political action was in the states, and it was there that the country's most important legislation—from property and family law to criminal codes—was developed. Ambitious individuals did their time in Washington out of duty to their parties and gained political experience to return to careers in their state legislatures or other professions.[36] Beginning with industrialization in the middle of the 19th century, the big issues, such as those associated with building and protecting domestic industries, became national issues. Along with national focus came more revenue, higher pay, more prestige, better staffing, and amenities that made Washington and Congress a more attractive place to build a political career. At the same time, institutional changes, particularly longer sessions and specialized work in committees, made Washington less attractive for citizen, or part-time, legislators.

FIGURE 11.6 Percentage of Representatives Who Did Not Seek Re-Election (1789-2017)

Note: Data for 1st through 115th Congresses. Opening year of each Congress is noted in parentheses. Source: CRS analysis of *Biographical Directory of the United States Congress*, ICPSR, and proprietary data. Interuniversity Consortium for Political and Social Research, and Carroll McKibbin, *Roster of United States Congressional Officeholders and Biographical Characteristics of Members of the United States Congress, 1789-1996: Merged Data* [computer file] 10th ICPSR ed. (Ann Arbor: MI: Inter-university for Political and Social Research [producer and distributor], 1997).

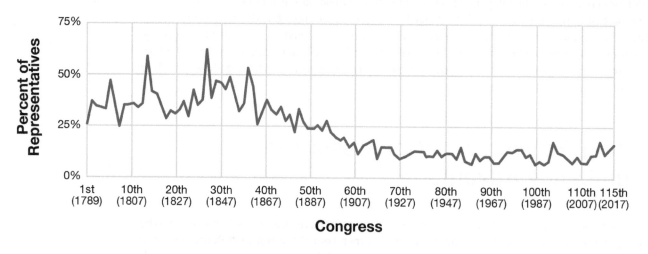

Data from Congressional Careers: Service Tenure and Patterns of Member Service, 1789-2019. Rept. Washington, DC: Congressional Research Service, 2019.

Weaker Parties and Candidate-Centered Politics

Australian ballot

A ballot printed by government which lists the names of all candidates running for public office and which the voter fills out in private.

At the end of the 19th century, state governments began to change their voting systems by adopting the **Australian ballot,** a voting system in which the local governments printed the ballot and voting took place in a private booth. Today this seems like the only way to properly vote but, prior to the adoption of the Australian ballot, the political parties supplied voters with pre-printed ballots, which the voters dropped in boxes. In other states, the citizens voted orally. Both these methods helped the parties influence the outcome of elections because, as you can imagine, the party's ballots had only their candidates' names on them, or they used subtle pressure or outright intimidation during the voting process. In contrast, the Australian ballot listed the names of all the nominees and helped the voters to choose individuals of different parties for the various offices.

Private voting booths limited a party's ability to apply pressure or intimidate voters. After 1900, straight ticket voting (voting for the same party for all offices) declined and congressional candidates became less dependent on the volatility of presidential elections. Weaker parties also meant that candidates became less dependent on their party's resources and more responsible for their own campaigns.

As more incumbents returned to Washington, professionals gradually replaced amateurs and Congress filled with careerists. Over time, members changed the institutional rules and procedures to more closely fit their need for job security. Just before the end of the 19th century, the members began ranking themselves according to how long they served in the House or Senate and using seniority to determine who would be assigned to what committees. In turn, the chair of each committee would be the longest serving member on the committee from the majority party. Shortly after, power moved downward from the party's leadership in Congress, the Speaker and the majority leaders in the House, and the majority leaders in the Senate, to the chairs of the individual committees, sometimes referred to as "dukes" or "barons" of Capitol Hill.[37]

The Rise of Committees, Seniority, and Specialization

The longer members stayed in Congress, the more they could write or sponsor bills or offer amendments to bills, and the more they could claim credit for such actions when they ran for reelection. Gaining seniority meant that members would eventually get on the committees of interest to their constituents back home. For example, a representative from a farm state could get on the House Agriculture committee, where he or she could help local growers by shaping farm policy when the committee considered and amended its bills. If the representative remained on the committee long enough, he or she could qualify to become its chair and have even more influence on agriculture policy. Although not as rigidly followed as in the past, the rules that assign members to committees and determine who becomes chair still consider seniority. Seniority rules also help determine who sits on committees designed to resolve differences between House and Senate versions of bills, another opportunity to influence legislation.[38]

Incumbency builds experience. As the Danish proverb says, he or she "knows the water best who has waded through it." It takes time to learn the intricate rules, culture, and procedures of Congress. Beginners may have enthusiasm and new ideas, but they may also lack patience, bargaining skills, or even respect for their peers and the lawmaking process. Research confirms that "effectiveness rises sharply with tenure."[39] Successful negotiation and compromise often requires in-depth knowledge about the other players and the development of trust. The more time one spends in the institution, the more skilled one becomes at striking deals.[40] Unlike most professions, legislating is not a branch of formal knowledge taught in college and few universities have a program in political campaigning. Most politicians learn their trade on the job. While seniority is no longer a hard rule when making committee and chair assignments, it is reasonable for leadership to consider experience when making these decisions.

Policy expertise also comes with incumbency. After power diffused to the committees at the beginning of the 20th century, the job of members became increasingly specialized. Not only did the breadth and scope of government increase, but also the details of national programs became increasingly complex. Today, bills are frequently long and written in precise language often using specialized syntax and scientific terms. Committee hearings involve the testimony from the heads of bureaucratic agencies and experts from science and industry. Asking the right questions requires knowledge and forethought. Because members gravitate to the committees that interest their districts, specialized knowledge is helpful to their political careers. Members become proficient at dealing with the agencies that serve their districts. Come election time, they not only have an established record of accomplishment, but in-depth familiarity of the people and policies that most directly affect their districts. This is expertise that few challengers can match.

During the 1800s, it was common practice for senators and representatives to write their own speeches and respond to their own correspondence. Today, members have professional staffs to deal with such traditional forms of communication as well as newer forms of communication, including emails, text messages, and social media. To supplement their staffs each member recruits a number of interns from local colleges and universities for their district and Washington offices. The newer forms of electronic communication are becoming increasingly important. Political scientist Colleen Shogan found that before email came into widespread use in the late 1990s, members received about 30 million pieces of posted mail. By 2007, regular mail had dropped to less than 19 million pieces, but email surged to 491 million messages.[41]

Bringing Home and Claiming Credit for Particular Benefits

franking privilege

A benefit given to members of Congress to send mail to their constituents by using their signature instead of a postage stamp.

The ability for members to communicate with their constituencies through regular mail remains an important benefit of incumbency. The **franking privilege** allows members to send unsolicited mail to their constituents by simply writing their signature (or frank) instead of using a postage stamp. This allows members to send mass mailings for free. Home delivery helps the member's correspondence cut through the clutter of other advertising by targeting specific messages to specific groups within their districts. Although the total number and cost of franked mail has declined in recent years, the Congressional Research Service shows that volume and expenditures predictably increases during election years and declines in non-election years.[42] All these forms of communication provide the member with multiple forums to publicize more popular issue positions, to claim credit for actions, and to increase name recognition.

FIGURE 11.7 The Franking Privilege

Example of Franked Mail Sent by House of Representatives Member Brad Sherman

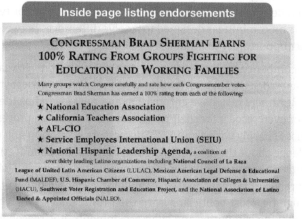

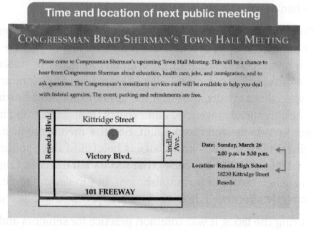

Another advantage of holding legislative office includes money for staff to respond to requests for help with government services or problems. Responding to constituency requests for service has always been a part of the job, but in the past, the federal government was much smaller than today and the scope of what it did was narrow. For about the first century and a half, the national government mostly managed international trade, delivered the mail, and subdued the Native American tribes. The country had no standing army and no prolonged international military conflicts that characterized 20th-century history and continue today. With a smaller government, the member's constituency service was limited to awarding mail routes and helping with survivor benefits for Civil and Mexican war veterans.[43] Since the 1930s, citizens have come to expect a broad range of services from the federal government. Some of the bigger programs include Medicare, Social Security, and Veteran's Affairs, but the federal government offers many other benefits. State and local governments are eligible for federal grants to help build transportation and public facilities. Students are eligible for financial aid and universities for research grants. Similarly, private industry is eligible for federal subsidies but is also subject to a wide range of federal regulations. Regular citizens and institutions often need help in dealing with the federal government, and the local congressional office is usually happy to lend a hand.

When representatives or their staffs help constituents with their personal problems or services with government, they call such assistance **casework**. Help may include finding a lost social security check or a government job. A promising young student may get a nomination to attend one of the military academies or assistance in finding financial aid. Developing a reputation for constituent service is an important component of a long and stable career because the public looks favorably on members who work hard for their districts. They are more likely to vote for incumbents who provide such services.[44] A field experiment involving 500 federal and state legislative offices showed that representatives were more responsive to service than policy requests. Those members who favored service over policy won reelection by larger margins.[45]

Helping constituents acts as a powerful form of advertising when grateful recipients spread the word among family and friends. Members multiply this effect when they secure federal funds that bring jobs and contracts to their districts. These are informally referred to as **pork-barrel projects**, a historical reference to the storage of salt-cured pork and the manner by which the representative was to "bring home the bacon." Such projects normally include funds to build local infrastructure such as highway, mass transit, airport, or water projects, but also anything that the federal government might purchase locally from ships to satellites. Securing the district's share of federal spending can bring positive publicity, especially for the brick-and-mortar type projects that bring media attention when the project is funded, when construction begins, and when the project is opened to the public. Each time, the representative has an opportunity to claim credit for getting the project. Such exposure improves the member's name recognition among the district's voters.[46] Those who are aware of the project are likely to view the incumbent more favorably.[47]

Favorable publicity leads to a practice within Congress called "earmarking" when the federal budget is prepared. An **earmark** mandates that a specific amount of money be spent for a project in a particular district. In the past, it was not unusual for a highway bill to contain a number of projects earmarked for each member of Congress. This practice became controversial, however, when legislation funded the Gravina Island Bridge, often referred to as the "Bridge to Nowhere." The bridge was to link an island with only 50 residents to mainland Alaska at a cost of $320 million in three separate earmarks.[48] It was never constructed. While earmarks were never a major portion of the federal budget, they became subject to a number of restrictions in 2009.[49] Nevertheless, such projects provide the incumbent with clear evidence to show he or she is serving the district.

casework

Efforts by members of Congress and their staffs to help their constituents with personal problems or services with government.

pork-barrel projects

Legislation usually funding brick-and-mortar type projects such as highways and bridges that allow representatives to claim credit for bringing benefits to their home districts.

earmark

A special provision, usually within legislation funding public infrastructure projects like highways and bridges, that directs spending within specific districts.

Advantages in Fundraising

lobby

Attempting to influence a public official through persuasion as an individual or group. The name comes from lobbyists (those attempting to persuade) waiting in or near the entrance of a building for a chance to speak with public officials.

At election time, incumbents can take advantage of publicity that comes from the provision of benefits to their districts. They also find it much easier than challengers to raise campaign funds. In 2020, the average House incumbent raised more than $2.7 million, nearly three times more than their challengers did. The thirty-one incumbent senators running for reelection in 2020 averaged more than $28 million, or about five times more than their 206 challengers did.[50] Unfortunately, challengers need more money than incumbents to build name recognition among the voters. The incumbent's advantage should come as no surprise given the source of most campaign funds. Fewer than 10 percent of Americans contribute to political campaigns at all. On the other hand, 67.8 percent of all such funds come from donors contributing more than $200, but these amount to only .25 percent of the U.S. population. For the large contributor, money given to an incumbent is simply a better investment than giving to a challenger.[51] Funders are not really buying votes; rather they are attempting to develop a responsive relationship, so they will have the opportunity to **lobby** the member when necessary. Legislation takes time. No one knows for sure when an issue affecting you, your group, institution, or business will come up, so most big donors will give year after year. Given that the incumbent has a greater chance of actually winning and may not appreciate money going to his or her challenger, backing the person already in office is the safe bet. Regular contributions also help donors maximize their contributions given yearly spending limits.

FIGURE 11.8 The Cost of Winning Congressional Elections
Note: Graph shows the average cost of winning elections in the House and Senate since 1986 (in 2012 dollars).

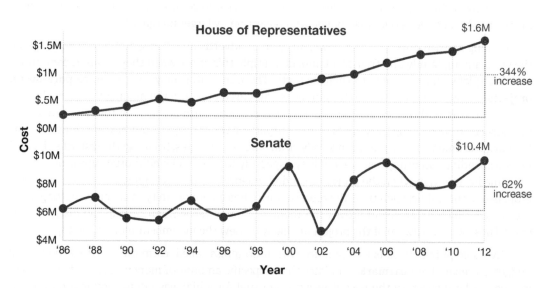

Data from CNN. Accessed June 17, 2016. http://www.cnn.com/2013/07/11/politics/congress-election-costs/.

Incumbents also face uncertainty. They never know when a strong challenger might surface in their district, so they adopt the Boy Scout motto, "Be prepared." To illustrate the point, a presentation as part of an orientation to new members of Congress given by the House Democratic Congressional Campaign Committee recommends that lawmakers spend four hours each day on "call time" to contact donors asking for campaign contributions. The committee recommends members spend another hour on "strategic outreach," set aside time for breakfast or lunch meetings, and set aside more time to attend fundraisers or to deal with the press. This is in addition to the one to two hours set aside for meeting with constituents. Interestingly, the committee anticipates that only two hours per day need to be spent in committee or on the floor.[52] It is reasonable to conclude that most incumbents end up with far more money than they need to win reelection. Indeed, evidence suggests that members engage in early fundraising and amass large campaign war chests to scare away potential challengers.[53]

Shaping the Districts

The process of drawing election district boundaries also favors incumbents in the House of Representatives. Senators represent entire states, but seats in the House are **apportioned** by population such that they represent districts averaging about 700,000 people each. Because some people move, the districts need to be **reapportioned** periodically to make sure they contain the same number of people, more or less.[54] This is why (among other reasons) the Constitution mandates a census of the population every ten years and that the states redraw their congressional district lines. The states, not the federal government, draw the district lines. The federal courts oversee the process to make sure that all districts elect only one representative and that the states do not draw boundaries in such a way as to dilute the influence of minority voters.

Of course, if the states can draw district boundaries to reduce the influence of minority voters, they can just as easily draw them to increase minority influence. In fact, demographic groups tend to cluster geographically. The states can draw district lines to increase or decrease the voting power of many groups. For example, if you want to reduce the influence of your rivals, all you need to do is to divide an adversary's supporters among several districts, making sure they constitute a minority of voters in each district. Alternatively, you can pack your rivals into as few districts as possible. This would create large majorities in these districts but would also cause your adversaries to waste votes, because only a small majority is needed to win the seat and the surrounding districts now have fewer opponents with which to contend. To maximize your group's legislative seats, just reverse the logic and draw the lines to make sure your people are bare majorities in as many districts as possible. In practice, both of these strategies are used to maximize safe districts with reasonable margins to account for the occasional anti-incumbent movements. Drawing lines in this way can be difficult but, with computers, special software, census data, and information that matches this data with how people vote and where they live, redistricting can have a considerable impact on elections.[55]

Since changing district lines affects the fortunes of House members, state legislators, and just about everyone in politics, redistricting is and has always been a high-stakes political process. A few states have attempted to reduce the politics of it by creating independent commissions to fashion the districts, but most state legislatures draw the lines with the approval of their governor.[56] This means that the party in control of the state legislature hires a consultant to draw the lines to maximize the number of seats it controls in the state and Congress. This age-old process dates back to when supporters of Elbridge Gerry of Massachusetts drew a district on a map that looked like a salamander, hence the name "**gerrymander**." While this practice is clearly unfair to the minority party, thus far the federal courts have taken a hands-off policy toward political gerrymandering, even if done for the purpose of solidifying a majority.[57] What this means for incumbents in Congress is that when their party gains majorities in the state legislatures, they have another tool to protect their seats.

apportioned

Territory that is divided or allocated for the purpose of determining representation in a legislative body.

reapportioned

Re-dividing or re-allocating districts for the purpose of determining representation in a legislative body.

FIGURE 11.9 Gerrymander

"Gerrymandering." Wikipedia. Accessed June 17, 2016. https://en.wikipedia.org/wiki/Gerrymandering.

gerrymander

Drawing electoral district lines to give an advantage to a particular party, group, or individual.

FIGURE 11.10 Gerrymandered Districts

Note: Graphics from 1990 Supreme Court Redistricting Decisions, Peter S. Wattson www.senate.leg.state.mn.us/departments/scr/REDIST/red907.htm

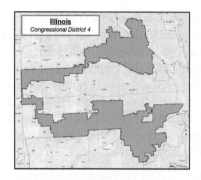

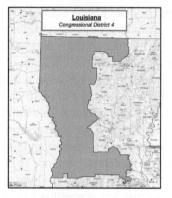

Based on "1990s Supreme Court Redistricting Decisions." http://www.senate.leg.state.mn.us/departments/scr/REDIST/red907.htm.

Political gerrymandering became evident after the 2010 elections when the Republicans gained control of the state legislatures and the governors' offices in seventeen states. In winning these states, they gained the once-in-a-decade opportunity to reapportion four times as many districts as the Democrats and influence nearly half of all seats in the House of Representatives.[58] Did they use the new census data to redraw the districts to protect their party's incumbents? The evidence shows that they did. The Center for American Progress calculates that gerrymandered districts shifted 59 seats (20 for Democrats and 39 for Republicans) in the House of Representative seats in 2012, 2014, and 2016, more than the total number of seats in 22 states or changing the preferences of 42 million Americans. [59] Still, there was nothing special about what the Republicans did in 2010. Both parties see gerrymandering as part of the spoils that come with winning elections.[60] There is also evidence of "sweetheart" gerrymandering whereby incumbents of both parties work together to draw the lines to make sure they have the best chance of staying in office. In this case, they intend to reduce competition from challengers of either party.[61]

FIGURE 11.11 Gerrmandering, Explained

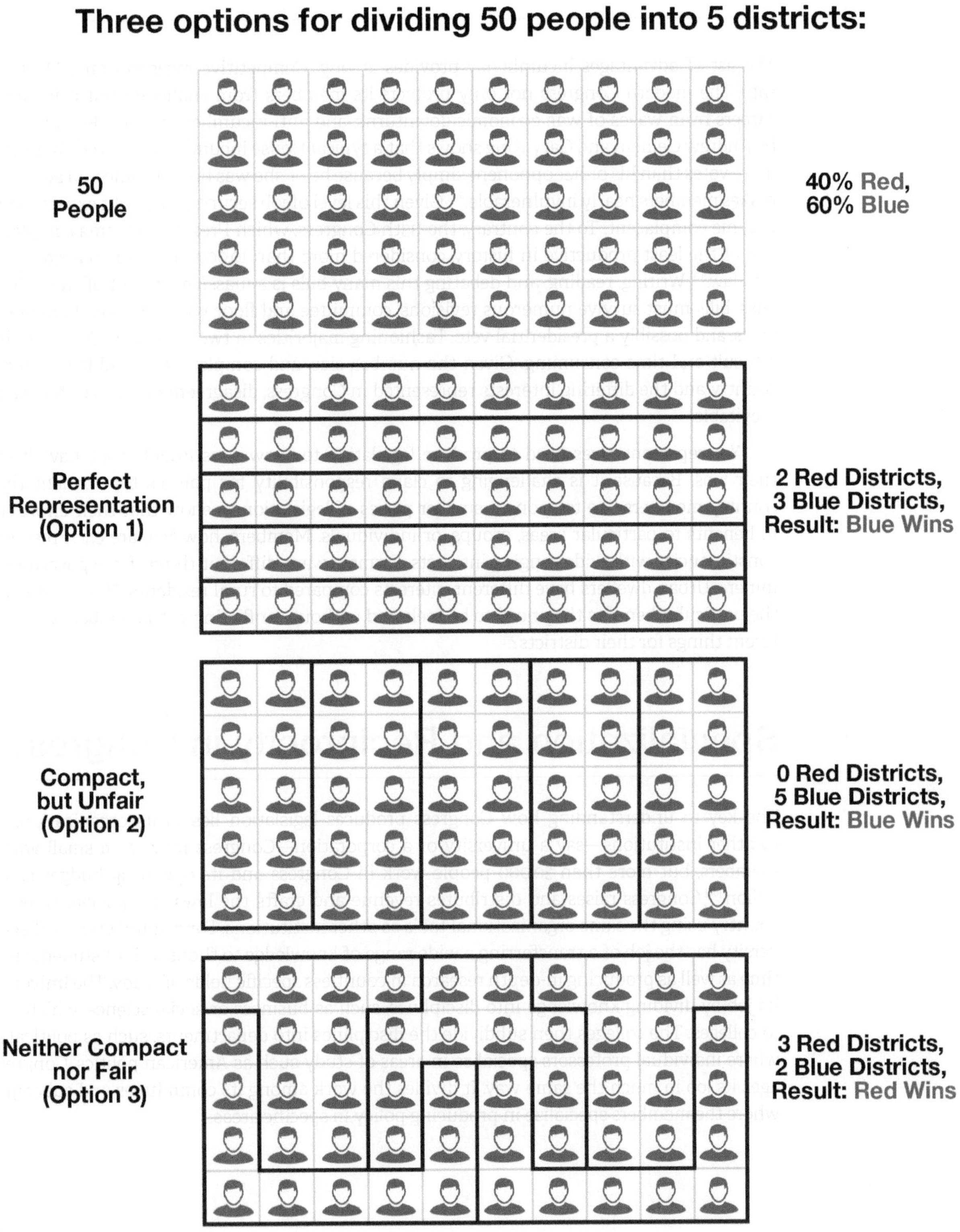

Three options for dividing 50 people into 5 districts:

50 People — 40% Red, 60% Blue

Perfect Representation (Option 1) — 2 Red Districts, 3 Blue Districts, Result: Blue Wins

Compact, but Unfair (Option 2) — 0 Red Districts, 5 Blue Districts, Result: Blue Wins

Neither Compact nor Fair (Option 3) — 3 Red Districts, 2 Blue Districts, Result: Red Wins

Washington Post. Accessed June 17, 2016. https://www.washingtonpost.com/news/wonk/wp/2015/03/01/this-is-the-best-explanation-of-gerrymandering-you-will-ever-see/.

11.4 Congress Works in Committees

The list of advantages incumbency provides is long. Competitive races are rare. Most seats are safe. The modern Congress not only protects its members from challenge, but it insulates their careers from waves of war, economic downturns, and anti-incumbent moods. Research produced by Andrew Gelman and Gary King shows that a typical House incumbent received about 12 percent more votes than his or her opponent simply because he or she was holding office, an advantage that makes members nearly invulnerable.[62] Given this level of job security, we might expect members to become complacent. To the contrary, the 113th Congress, which President Obama complained was one of the least productive in history, considered more than 10,000 bills and enacted 224 of them into law.[63] Writing, reading, and debating this many bills is a massive amount of work. To become laws, bills must survive numerous revisions, committee and floor votes in both chambers of Congress, and possibly a presidential veto. Fashioning majorities in two houses of Congress should be difficult and time-consuming. Given the number, size, and complexity of problems affecting the country and the differing interests represented in Congress, disagreement and conflict seem to be inevitable.

Yet, representatives need to produce legislation to show constituents they have been doing their jobs. Because it is challenging to claim responsibility for policies that benefit the whole country, members like to sponsor smaller pieces of legislation to show that their efforts resulted in benefits to particular areas, groups, or individuals. Members, however, are each responsible to constituencies with wide-ranging interests. Farmers want different things from government than miners. Urban dwellers have different interests compared to rural residents. How do members get the particular benefits they need to be reelected without conflicting with members who want different things for their districts?

Specialization and Reciprocity in Congress

The key to understanding how Congress produces legislation lies in its organization. Relative to other institutions—say a university or a corporation—Congress may seem small with its 535 members, but more than 30,000 people work in Congress and its operating budget is above $3 billion.[64] Congress raises and distributes revenue and crafts the laws and policies to govern the country using the same organizational tools as other institutions. For example, your college or university has the job of a transferring a wide range of knowledge to thousands of students in a short time as well as producing in-depth research in countless specific fields of study. The university does its job by dividing knowledge into disciplines, such as business or social science, which it assigns to colleges. The colleges then subdivide the disciplines into departments, such as political science, where individual professors specialize in areas of study such as American politics. Congress manages its job in much the same way. It divides the work among its committees and subcommittees, where the members specialize in producing policy in specific areas.

FIGURE 11.12 How a Bill Becomes a Law

How a Bill Becomes a Law

A bill is introduced in the House of Representatives.

The bill is referred to a House committee and subcommittee.

A full committee votes on the bill.

The House of Representatives debates the bill and votes on its passage.

A bill is introduced into the Senate.

The bill is referred to a Senate committee and subcommittee.

A full committee votes on the bill.

The Senate debates the bill and votes on its passage.

A House-Senate conference committee writes a compromise bill. The compromise bill then goes back to both houses.

The House of Representatives and the Senate vote on the final passage of the bill. The approved bill is sent to the President.

The president can either veto the bill or sign it into law.

Images from © Shutterstock, Inc.

The division of labor in Congress is varied and complex. There are twenty **standing committees** in the House of Representatives and sixteen in the Senate. These permanent committees process the bulk of the work. The appropriate committee must first approve any item before it can be considered for a vote. Measures that do not make it beyond this stage "die" in committee. Congress subdivides the standing committees into **subcommittees** where they do most of the day-to-day work. In all, there are 104 subcommittees in the House and 70 in the senate.[65] Congress also creates **select or special committees** for such work as overseeing or investigating a matter of concern to individual members, groups, or issues that overlap the areas of two or more committees. **Joint committees** contain members from both the House and the Senate. Some of these deal with a special issue; others have routine investigative or oversight duties. Lastly, **conference committees** are formed to resolve differences in similar bills passed by the House and the Senate so that they send one bill to the president for his signature.

TABLE 11.1 Standing Committees of the U.S. Congress

House	Senate
Agriculture	Agriculture, Nutrition, and Forestry
Appropriations	Appropriations
Armed Services	Armed Services
Budget	Banking, Housing, and Urban Affairs
Education and the Workforce	Budget
Energy and Commerce	Commerce, Science, and Transportation
Ethics	Energy and Natural Resources
Financial Services	Environment and Public Works
Foreign Affairs	Finance
Homeland Security	Foreign Relations
House Administration	Health, Education, Labor, and Pensions
Judiciary	Homeland Security and Governmental Affairs
Natural Resources	Judiciary
Oversight and Government Reform	Rules and Administration
Rules	Small Business and Entrepreneurship
Science, Space, and Technology	Veterans' Affairs
Small Business	
Transportation and Infrastructure	
Ways and Means	

"Committees of the U.S. Congress." Congress.gov. Accessed June 17, 2016. https://www.congress.gov/committees.

Congress employs about 2,000 professionals to help the committees. These are permanent employees responsible for administering and organizing the committees' work. Congress also has three **staff agencies** to provide information and research. The Congressional Research Service is a branch of the Library of Congress and consists of about 600 lawyers, economists, and reference librarians, as well as social, natural, and physical scientists. The Government Accountability Office is the investigative arm of Congress that performs audits on executive agencies and policy analysis to evaluate the effects of legislation. Lastly, the Congressional Budget Office provides information on government revenues and expenditures. It provides projections that determine how much money the government will have and how much proposed federal programs are likely to cost.

Dividing the work among the committees is key to understanding how Congress does its work efficiently. Each committee deals with a general policy area that is broken down into more specific policy areas. For example, the House Committee on Agriculture deals with policies surrounding the production and trade of food and its safety, quality, and affordability. The use and conservation of the nation's land, water, forests, and wildlife habitats is also the committee's responsibility. This committee is separated into six subcommittees, one of which, the General Farm Commodities and Risk Management Committee, specializes in laws and policies relating to major farm commodities such as corn, rice, and sugar. It also sets policy for the government's crop insurance and loan programs. The members sitting on this committee specialize in farm commodities and the related loan and insurance programs. Over time, they become experts and can easily handle what seems like an enormous and complex workload.

Within the subcommittee, the members know which bills to consider and which they can safely ignore. They conduct hearings regarding a particular bill in which they listen to and question officials from the Department of Agriculture or other federal agencies, representatives from the various industries, other businesses, consumer groups, and private citizens. After the hearings, the members work to **markup** or decide on the exact wording of the bill.

markup

To edit or decide on the wording of a measure before it is voted on.

At this time, amendments to the bill are proposed; modifications are publicized, debated, and voted upon. Each subcommittee follows a slightly different amendment process. Some take formal votes on each one while others operate by consensus or use "conceptual markups" to establish the general areas of agreement while adding the legislative language later.[66] The goal of the committees is to create a bill that can be agreed on by their colleagues in the full committee and by the rest of the House, the Senate, and the president.

After all this is done, the subcommittee sends the bill to the full committee where more hearings and amendments may occur, the bill is ratified, or the bill is returned to the subcommittee for more work. It is also possible for a bill to be ignored by the full committee, in which case it can languish and die. If the full committee approves the bill, it sends it to the floor of the House for a vote along with a report describing its provisions and merits, and a summary of the results of the committee's research and hearings. The reports are used to guide executive agencies and the federal courts when they interpret whether the bill's language should become law. A similar process is followed in the Senate.

Committee work helps Congress manage conflict among its members. Most of the bills that go to the floor for a vote are the ones preferred by the specialists on the committee and its subcommittees. Unfortunately, no member can be an expert in all matters before Congress. For individual members, the cost of policy expertise is relative ignorance of policies in other areas. This is a common problem in complex institutions and is usually resolved by some form of reciprocity. At your college or university, for example, the professors of business administration develop the curriculum for their discipline, while the professors of political science develop theirs. The two groups defer to each other's knowledge and reciprocate by not becoming involved in areas outside their areas of expertise. Curriculum is developed with a maximum of expertise and a minimum of conflict. In Congress, the peace is preserved in the same manner when the non-specialists remove themselves from the focused policy debates and let the experts do their work in the confines of their committees.

The committee system serves the needs of the members well. They get the benefits of efficiency and harmony, but also the policies they need to for reelection. Across Congress, individual members gravitate to committees that fit their interests. It should be no surprise that the current members of the General Farm Commodities and Risk Management Committee mostly represent rural districts where growing market goods is a major part of life. The largest cities within the districts represented by the Republicans on the committee are Modesto, California, and South Bend, Indiana. Ranches or farms dominate the areas of both districts. Democrats on the subcommittee represent similar districts. Most of these members are on the committee because they know that only the bills that survive their review have a chance to become law. They are the gatekeepers for Congress when it comes to agricultural commodities and insurance.

Party leaders make the committee assignments at the beginning of each session after the members formally make their preferences known. Lawmakers are attracted to committees on which they can influence policy important to their districts, but some committees matter more than others do. For example, in the House, the Ways and Means committee decides on issues that affect all Americans, such as taxes, trade policy, Social Security, and Medicare. The Finance Committee decides on these issues in the Senate.

There are a few formal rules used to assign members to committees. Democrats in the Senate follow the "Johnson Rule," which says all Democrats get one major committee assignment before any other Democrat gets a second major assignment. Similarly, Senate Republicans rank their committees and limit the number of top-ranked committees on which any party member can sit. However, most of the rules are informal. Geography and gender are considered to balance a committee's membership, but the member's preferences, substantive expertise, electoral vulnerability, and party loyalty are considered for political reasons.

By tradition, members with the longest continuous membership on a committee are given top priority. Generally, the leaders in the Senate more strictly adhere to seniority than their counterparts in the House, but even there, longevity is deeply rooted. Senior members who have "paid their dues" understandably want to keep their positions, but longevity on a committee usually adds to the member's expertise and correlates with his or her preferences. Senior members also tend to amass influence among their colleagues over time, including those in the leadership. This respect for power and seniority leads to the "property norm" that generally allows incumbent members to retain their seats on committees before considering new members.[67] The interests of party leaders and members also coincide when vulnerable members are assigned to committees to increase their chances for reelection. Both the party and the member lose when the member's incumbency advantage is weakened and he or she fails to retain the seat. Therefore, politically exposed members are likely to get their preferred committee assignments. In sum, although the committee assignment criteria do not require accommodation of the members' preferences, in practice the interests of the members and their leaders overlap considerably.

The Win-Win Congress

norm of universalism

When members pursue activities to get themselves reelected, they do so in ways that do not hinder other members' attempts to be reelected.

Given the diversity of interests represented in Congress, one would think some members would gain at the expense of others as they fight to capture the benefits of government for their districts. Conflict over policy happens, but much less than we would expect. To understand how cooperation overcomes conflict in Congress, keep in mind that the preoccupation among members is job security. Consider also, however, that each member is elected from a different district. Therefore, the principle competition for what the members want most is not within the chamber but back home. Indeed, this shared concern makes members of Congress allies in defending their jobs from outside rivals. David Mayhew, the same political scientist who characterized Congress members as persistent reelection seekers, referred to the behavior this union produces as the **norm of universalism**. In practice, when members pursue activities to get themselves reelected, they do so in ways that do not hinder other members' attempts to be reelected. Recall that members acted together when they diffused power to committees and when they adopted the traditions of seniority and the criteria for distributing committee assignments that match the interests of the members with their constituents. They also gave themselves resources for travel, staffs, and district offices to serve their districts, as well as franking privileges to claim credit for doing so. All this behavior is consistent with the norm of universalism because every member gets resources he or she needs to be reelected.

logrolling

A practice in legislatures whereby votes are reciprocally exchanged.

Reciprocity comes into play when the specialist members of one committee defer to experts on other committees. This behavior maximizes expertise but minimizes conflict among the committees. The norm of universalism triumphs during floor votes when members engage in **logrolling** or vote trading, whereby each member votes for bills he or she knows or cares little about in exchange for votes on bills that are personally important to the member. Of course, this pattern is not perfect, but the practice is common in legislative assemblies, especially when it comes to pork-barrel or distributive policies. The tendency for committees to reciprocate by voting for each other's bills results in everyone generally getting what they need to take home. The members respect each other's territory as they divide the legislative pie.

11.5 Party Leadership in the House and the Senate: The Forces of Centralization

If the electoral connection and the norm of universalism were the only factors that explained the behavior of members of Congress, federal spending for Social Security and Medicare would outpace contributions, and military spending would balloon as Congress bought tanks and other equipment the military said it did not need.[68] Because raising taxes is unpopular, revenues would fall behind spending, deficits would be common, and the national debt would grow. Of course, all this happens, but things would be worse if it were not for leaders in Congress who keep the members from completely pandering to local interests.

The leaders of Congress are regular members elected by the membership in their respective parties. In the House of Representatives, the full membership elects the **Speaker of the House**. The members always cast straight party line votes, so the Speaker is chosen, in effect, by the majority party. The remaining leaders are elected by each party, called **caucuses** by the Democrats and **conferences** by the Republicans. The majority party elects the **majority leader**, while the minority party elects the minority leader. The parties also elect majority and minority assistant leaders. The Senate follows a similar pattern of leadership elections. The majority party elects the majority leader and the minority party elects the minority leader. Technically, the vice president is the chief presiding officer in the Senate, but mostly for ceremonial occasions and to cast tie-breaking votes.

The important detail to keep in mind is that the membership in the House and Senate elect their leaders. These leaders serve at the membership's pleasure. The authority given to them by their peers, in other words, can be taken away. The question is, why do members of Congress follow their leaders at all? If they run their own reelection campaigns, raise most of their funds, do not need the party to get on the ballot, and keep their jobs by serving their districts and trading votes, why do they put their careers in the hands of leadership? The answer is that most members want more than just job security. They also sincerely believe in the goals of public policy and to help the country prosper. Members of Congress are also enormously ambitious. They have achieved national office and most want to be leaders among their colleagues so they can better shape national policy or move to higher positions of power and prestige.[69] For the ambitious members of Congress—and even those who are content with simply serving their districts—to control legislation, they need to win consistently, not merely trade votes issue by issue. To do this they need to team up with like-minded members to control the majority of votes in their chamber as well as to determine leadership positions and the chairs of the committees. To have a chance to control policy in Congress as a whole, they need to do this in both chambers. This is why political parties formed in Congress in the first place.

Speaker of the House

The chief presiding officer of the House of Representatives.

caucuses

Any group of members in Congress that meet to pursue common interests, typically formed by each of the major parties. Republicans call these "conferences."

conferences

A group formed by Republican members in Congress that meets to pursue partisan interests. The term includes other groups formed to pursue common legislative objectives. Democrats call these "caucuses."

majority leader

The elected leader of the party with the majority of seats in the House of Representatives or Senate.

Once the party system formed, those in the majority coalition found that if they continued to vote together, they could control policy. For members seeking particular benefits, party voting provides more opportunities to win across a broader range of issues with less effort and uncertainty than alternative methods of forming a majority.[70] In both chambers, the winning party not only picks the chairs of the committees and subcommittees, but gets the majority of votes on each. This gives them considerable power to control the institution's agenda and its outcomes.

Electing the Speaker in the House gives the controlling party significant authority to direct legislation to committees and to schedule floor votes. The Speaker picks the majority of members of the House Rules Committee that determines the order in which bills are considered. With a crowded agenda, this means that their party's priorities come first, while other bills may not reach the floor before Congress adjourns. The Rules Committee also sets the conditions for debate and amendment, including authority to prohibit amendments. The Speaker also has influence over the committee assignment process and can decide who gets to serve on select and conference committees. In the Senate, the majority leader has less power. Like the Speaker in the House, the Senate majority leader sets legislative priorities through scheduling, but the ability of each senator to speak without limitation weakens this authority.[71] The threat of a filibuster—the ability of members to talk indefinitely—allows any member to hold, delay, or even prevent a vote. To overcome this threat, the majority leader must

Nancy Pelosi currently serves as the Speaker of the U.S. House of Representatives for the 116th Congress.

Albert H. Teich / Shutterstock.com

invoke cloture

To arrange at least sixty votes in the Senate to close debate and end a filibuster.

political action committees (PACs)

Groups formed to raise and distribute campaign funds.

invoke cloture or arrange a supermajority of sixty votes to close debate. In practice, the majority leader negotiates unanimous consent agreements with the minority party leaders to impose limits on debate and amendment.

In both chambers, the party leaders develop a strategy to implement their party's overall agenda. They choose assistant leaders called whips to communicate the party's positions and mobilize its members on important votes. The whips keep track of each member's loyalty on these matters and the results are used when the party leaders make committee assignments. They distribute policy papers, assist with research, provide members with talking points before they meet with the press, and devise arguments to neutralize the opposition's positions.[72] Leaders also form their own **political action committees (PACs)** to gather funds from contributors to help their party's vulnerable incumbents win reelection. The leaders use these tools to shape legislation and serve broader interests.

Perhaps most fundamentally, the partisans in Congress tie themselves together ideologically. Conservative legislators are predisposed to follow Republican leaders, while liberal members generally want to follow Democratic ones (see Chapter 6 for a refresher on these two major ideologies in the United States). When the whips lobby for votes on important issues, they need only show their members how the legislation promotes what they already believe. Evidence shows that the party leaders are doing their jobs. In 2018, House Republicans voted with their party about 91 percent of the time on average, while Democrats voted with their party 89 percent of the time. In the Senate, Republicans voted together 79.4 percent of the time, while Democrats voted together a record 94 percent of the time.[73] Party voting among members of Congress has increased over the last fifty years.[74]

FIGURE 11.13 Average Party Unity Scores in the House and Senate

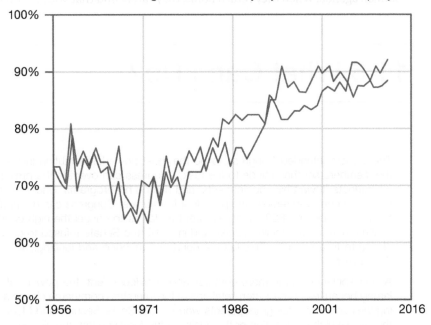

Average Party Unity Scores in the House of Representatives

The percentage of House of Representatives party unity votes for which a membervoted in agreement with a majority of his or her own party.

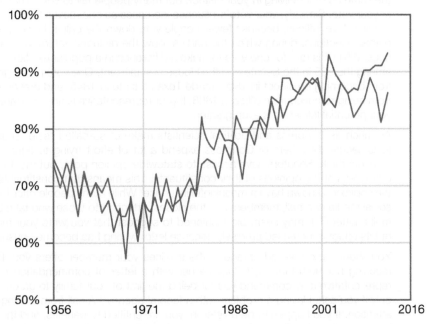

Average Party Unity Scores in the Senate

The percentage of Senate party unity votes for which a member voted in agreement with a majority of his or her own party.

Data from "CQ.com - Vote Studies." CQ.com - Vote Studies. Accessed June 18, 2016. http://media.cq.com/votestudies/.

Giving party leaders in Congress the power to organize votes in this way is easy because it is in harmony with the members' general policy goals. Such behavior is also consistent with the members' need to be reelected. Most Republican lawmakers are elected from conservative districts where the majority of voters identify with the Republican Party. The Democrats find themselves in similar situations, except that the majority of their constituents are liberal Democrats. Once elected, officeholders remain partisans; they sit together and organize their work according to a common agenda. When they return home, they rarely find that voting with the party is a problem.

11.6 What Can I Do?

The framers intended Congress to be the most powerful institution in the U.S. government. If the members set their minds to the task, Congress can override the president's vetoes, ignore his budgets, thwart his appointments, and defund his programs. Under the right circumstances, Congress can even remove the president from office. Congress can do much the same with the Supreme Court. In 1802, Congress went as far as to cancel the high court's entire term, preventing them from deciding cases, and in 2016, the Senate refused to consider the president's choice to fill a vacancy. This left the court shorthanded and ideologically deadlocked for more than a year.

As our society became more complex and interdependent, the powers of Congress increased largely because of broad interpretations of the interstate commerce clause and its role in regulating the economy. Your grandparents worry about Social Security and Medicare. You care about the cost of higher education or the quality of the food you eat, the air you breathe, and the water you drink. The actions of Congress affect these and other policies that shape your daily life, so pay attention to what the assembly is doing.

In this chapter, you learned that members do in fact pay close attention to their constituents. This means you have influence over who represents your district or state. Of course, your vote counts the same as others living in your district, but many people fail to vote. That increases the impact of your vote. Similarly, your vote's influence increases as one moves from voting for the president to lower-level offices, because fewer people vote down the ballot. Fewer people still vote in the primary elections, during which the parties allow the districts' voters to select the party's nominees. While it is rare for one vote to make a difference in a popular election, each member's vote among the 535 in the Senate and the House is significant. One vote in Congress kept Aaron Burr from becoming president in 1800, made Texas a state in 1845, and prevented Andrew Johnson from being removed from office in 1868. If your representative is an important leader in Congress, your potential influence is even greater.

As much as the press and political scientists make of so-called "safe" seats, no member truly feels secure. Members of Congress expend a lot of effort trying to figure out what their constituents think. Senators have access to statewide opinion polls, but most House members can only guess at the opinions of their constituents. This means that constituents motivated to make their opinions known have a meaningful influence. While many people offer their opinions through social media or email, members pay the closest attention to those who take the time to write and mail a letter.[75] It may seem old-fashioned to suggest that you write your member of Congress, but its effect is increased precisely because letter writing has become unusual.

You should also take advantage of the services your member offers you. Is your grandmother reaching her 90th birthday? Surprise her with a letter of commendation from Congress. Your representative may commend you for being the first of your family to graduate from college, but only if you ask. Having a problem with a federal agency? A call from a congressional office gets attention. If you happen to be a veteran, you are entitled to benefits, and the federal agency that handles veteran's affairs is large and complex. Members of Congress have staff members who routinely deal with the agency and can help solve problems. If you are visiting Washington, give your representative a visit. Members attest that the most effective lobbyists come from home.

Representatives don't have many jobs to distribute, but if you are looking to establish a career in the military, your member can have up to five cadets at each military academy and can nominate you for admission. Closer to home, your representative is always on the lookout for bright, energetic interns to staff their office to help with all the casework. At the end of your internship, you will have gained valuable experience and perhaps a glowing letter of recommendation from a U.S. senator or member of the House of Representatives.

11.7 What's the Alternative?

Ending the Small State Advantage in the Senate:

The most undemocratic feature of Congress is the advantage that small population states have in the Senate. As previously noted, the allocation of representation that gives each state two senators regardless of the state's population violates the democratic principle of "one person, one vote." We also mentioned that the greater influence of small states in the Senate results in their receiving disproportionate federal funding than their population warrants. This systematically underrepresents liberals, Democrats, African Americans, Asians, and Latinas/os who live in large, urbanized states like New York and California. In Reynolds v. Simms (1964), the Supreme Court ruled that state governments could no longer apportion any of their legislative chambers by geographic area regardless of population. This, they determined, was a violation of the equal protection clause of the Fourteenth Amendment. The mandated changes, together with an earlier order that state election districts be reapportioned to reflect population on a regular basis, significantly increased the number of representatives from urban and suburban districts and the number of women and minorities serving in state legislatures. Such changes in the U.S. Senate would have a similar effect.

Changing the basis of representation in the Senate to population would probably require consolidating some smaller population states into single regions and giving more seats to larger states. The Senate's features of smaller numbers, unlimited debate, and staggered and longer terms could be preserved. The chamber would still provide a place for the representation of regional interests, the luxury of time to fully debate issues, focus on national and international issues, consider new ideas, and form broad-based coalitions. The Senate could still function as the saucer that cools the hot tea of democratic passions coming from the House. This change would also fix the electoral college by making it more likely that the president is elected by a majority of votes cast.

Unfortunately, the Supreme Court has no power to compel the Senate to change its basis of representation. Such a change would necessitate a Constitutional amendment, which would require a two-thirds majority vote in the Senate and the House and ratification by three-fourths of the states. An amendment like this is unlikely to pass because small states would have to voluntary give up their advantage.

Reforming the Filibuster in the Senate:

The tradition of the filibuster in the Senate also favors conservative rural populations since these areas, and the people who live in them, are overrepresented. The filibuster is often celebrated as a hallmark of democracy largely because of the heroic depiction of naive Senator Smith standing alone against his colleagues to inform the nation of corruption in the movie, "Mr. Smith Goes to Washington."

Changing the filibuster would alter the Senate's rules of debate. This would be a serious deviation for a chamber that holds its traditions dearly and refers to alterations in the filibuster as the "nuclear option." But back in fictional Senator Smith's day, senators had to risk the well-being of their bladders to hold the floor long enough to make an impact. Today the filibuster is used routinely to keep legislation from receiving consideration unless those in favor can arrange for a supermajority to bring the matter up for a vote. Don't read this as something better than a majority. In effect, supermajority means that control of that legislation ends up in the hands of the minority. The filibuster may be necessary at times to prevent the majority from violating the civil rights or liberties of the minority, but such instances are rare. Since the filibuster was first allowed in 1806, it has been used sparingly. In the last decade, however, it was used more than 600 times.[76] In 2010, Senator Richard Shelby alone blocked seventy nominations and held the business of the country hostage as a tactic to increase spending for his state.[77]

Still, there has been some movement in the Senate to curtail the use of the filibuster. In 2015, Majority Leader Harry Reid changed the rules to prevent a minority of senators from blocking judicial appointments, except for the Supreme Court. More recently, after Senate Democrats filibustered Donald Trump's nominee for the Supreme Court, Senate Majority Leader Mitch McConnell pulled the trigger on the nuclear option to allow a majority vote.

The rule should be extended to end the de facto supermajority requirement for other Senate business except when the rights of the minority are truly threatened. The framers of our Constitution did not intend to require sixty votes to advance ordinary matters. Ending the routine use of the filibuster not only returns control to the majority, it increases legislative transparency. If a minority can thwart the preferences of the majority from behind the cover of parliamentary procedures, it increases the ambiguity of politics. No matter which party voters put in control of Congress, they deserve a clear view of what the party is doing so they can hold the majority party accountable in elections.

Increased Polarization:

Trends in party politics that point to increased polarization may help Congress become more attuned to national issues. In the last few decades, the parties have become more ideologically uniform. The movement of voters in the southern states toward the Republican party made the party not only more competitive but more homogeneously conservative. At the same time, the loss of southern conservatives from the Democratic party has made it more consistently liberal. Most political pundits seem to view polarization with alarm but, as the public has sorted itself into more consistent parties, it has reduced the cross-pressures that members face as they attempt to balance their roles as constituency representatives and national policy makers.[78] In other words, the members feel less backlash from local voters when they vote in accordance with their party leaders in Congress.

Endnotes

1. "Reelection Rates Over the Years," The Center for Responsive Politics, accessed April 07, 2017, https://www.opensecrets.org/overview/reelect.php. J. McCarthy, "Ahead of Elections, U.S. Congress Approval at 18%," October 12, 2016, accessed April 07, 2017, http://www.gallup.com/poll/196268/ahead-elections-congress-approval.aspx.

2. David R. Mayhew, *Congress: The Electoral Connection* (New Haven: Yale University Press, 1974), 5.

3. Gallup. (2020, December 22). Congress and the Public. Retrieved January 01, 2021, from https://news.gallup.com/poll/1600/congress-public.aspx

4. Ibid.

5. Harry Enten, "Disliking Congress, as a Whole And as Individuals," DataLab, July 01, 2014, accessed June 16, 2016, http://fivethirtyeight.com/datalab/disliking-congress-as-a-whole-and-as-individuals/.

6. Richard F. Fenno Jr., *Home Style: House Members in Their Districts* (Longman, 2008), 168.

7. Maeve P. Carey, "Presidential Appointments, the Senate's Confirmation Process, and Changes Made in the 112th Congress," Congressional Research Service, October 9, 2012, http://www.fas.org/sgp/crs/misc/R41872.pdf.

8. "Senate Created," United States Senate, accessed June 16, 2016, http://www.senate.gov/artandhistory/history/minute/Senate_Created.htm.

9. The states of Alaska, Montana, North Dakota, South Dakota, and Wyoming are large states with only one, at-large congressional district.

10. Adam Liptak, "Smaller States Find Outsize Clout Growing in Senate," *The New York Times*, March 11, 2013, accessed June 16, 2016, http://www.nytimes.com/interactive/2013/03/11/us/politics/democracy-tested.html.

11. Russell L Hanson, "Intergovernmental Relations," *Politics in the American States: A Comparative Analysis*, eds. Virginia Gray, Russell L. Hanson, and Thad Kousser (Washington. DC: CQ Press 2013), 41.

12. John D. Griffin, "Senate Apportionment as a Source of Political Inequality," *Legislative Studies Quarterly* 31, no. 3 (2006): 425.

13. Cooper, R. (2016, December 07). Which states got screwed worst by the Electoral College in 2016? Retrieved January 01, 2021, from https://theweek.com/articles/665750/which-states-got-screwed-worst-by-electoral-college-2016

14. David R. Mayhew, *Congress: The Electoral Connection* (New Haven: Yale University Press, 1974), 95.

15. Roger H. Davidson, Walter J. Oleszek, Frances E. Lee, and Eric Schckler, *Congress and Its Members* (Washington: CQ Press, 2014), 111.

16. Samuel Kernell, "Presidential Popularity and Negative Voting: An Alternative Explanation of the Midterm Congressional Decline of the President's Party," *The American Political Science Review* 71, no. 1 (1977): 44.

17. Milton L. Rakove, *We Don't Want Nobody Nobody Sent: An Oral History of the Daley Years* (Bloomington: Indiana University Press, 1979).

18. Robert Costa, Laura Vozzella, and David A. Farenthold, "Eric Cantor Succumbs to Tea Party Challenger Tuesday," *Washington Post*, June 11, 2014, accessed June 16, 2016, https://www.washingtonpost.com/local/virginia-politics/eric-cantor-faces-tea-party-challenge-tuesday/2014/06/10/17da5d20-f092-11e3-bf76-447a5df6411f_story.html.

19. L. Sandy Maisel, "American Political Parties: Still Central to a Functioning Democracy?" *American Political Parties: Decline or Resurgence?* eds. Jeffery E. Cohen, Richard Fleisher, and Paul Kantor (Washington, DC: CQ Press, 2001), 112-14.

20. Sarah M. Morehouse, Malcolm E. Jewell, and Rick Farmer, "State Parties," *The State of the Parties, 4th Edition*, ed. John C. Green (Lanham, MD: Rowman & Littlefield, 2003), 151.

21. Margaret M. Conway, "Women and Political Participation," *PS: Political Science and Politics* 34, no. 2 (June, 2001): 231–33.

22. "Congress," *Voices in Democracy*, PBS, March 9, 2002.

23. "Congress By the Numbers," Legistorm, accessed February 15, 2019, https://www.legistorm.com/congress_by_numbers/index/by/house.html.

24. "Congress By the Numbers," Legistorm, accessed February 15, 2019, https://www.legistorm.com/congress_by_numbers/index/by/house.html.

25. "Faith on the Hill," Pew Research Center, accessed February 15, 2019, http://www.pewforum.org/2019/01/03/faith-on-the-hill-116/.

26. Ida A. Brudnick, "Salaries of Members of Congress: Recent Actions and Historical Tables," Congressional Research Service, February 23, 2016, http://library.clerk.house.gov/reference-files/114_20150106_Salary.pdf.

27. Will Tucker, "Personal Wealth: A Nation of Extremes, and a Congress, Too," Opensecrets News, November 17, 2015, accessed June 16, 2016, http://www.opensecrets.org/news/2015/11/personal-wealth-a-nation-of-extremes-and-a-congress-too/.

28. Nicholas Carnes, *White-Collar Government: The Hidden Role of Class in Economic Policy Making* (Chicago: University of Chicago Press, 2013).

29. Arturo Vega and Juanita M. Firestone, "The Effects of Gender on Congressional Behavior and the Substantive Representation of Women," *Legislative Studies Quarterly* 20, no. 2 (May 1995): 213-22.

30. Kerry I. Haynie, *African American Legislators in the American States* (New York, NY: Columbia University Press, 2001).

31. Judy M., "The 116th Congress Reveals a Major Diversity Gap Between Democrats and Republicans," November 20, 2018, https://www.care2.com/causes/the-116th-congress-reveals-a-major-diversity-gap-between-democrats-and-republicans.html.

32. All this is in Madison's Federalist paper #10 and elaborated on in the chapter on elections.

33. Matthew E. Glassman and Amber H. Wilhelm, "Congressional Careers: Service Tenure and Patterns of Member Service, 1789-2015," Congressional Research Service, January 3, 2017, https://www.fas.org/sgp/crs/misc/R41545.pdf.

34. Jeffrey M. Jones, "Congressional Job Approval Averages Meager 16% in 2015," Gallup, Inc., December 17, 2015, accessed June 16, 2016, https://news.gallup.com/poll/187844/congressional-job-approval-averages-meager-2015.aspx?g_source=support for congress. Lydia Saad, "Americans Call for Term Limits, End to Electoral College," Gallup, Inc., January 18, 2013, accessed June 16, 2016, https://news.gallup.com/poll/159881/americans-call-term-limits-end-electoral-college.aspx?g_source=support for term limits.

35. "The Annenberg Public Policy Center of the University of Pennsylvania – Americans Know Surprisingly Little about Their Government, Survey Finds," The Annenberg Public Policy Center of the University of Pennsylvania, September 14, 2014, accessed June 16, 2016, http://www.annenbergpublicpolicycenter.org/americans-know-surprisingly-little-about-their-government-survey-finds/.

36. Samuel Kernell, "Toward Understanding 19th Century Congressional Careers: Ambition, Competition, and Rotation," *American Journal of Political Science* 21, no. 4 (November 1977): 669-93.

37. Roger H. Davidson, Walter J. Oleszek, Frances E. Lee, and Eric Schckler, *Congress and Its Members* (Washington: CQ Press, 2014), 136.

38. Ibid, 242.

39. Gerard Padró I. Miquel and James M. Snyder. "Legislative Effectiveness and Legislative Careers," *Legislative Studies Quarterly* 31, no. 3 (2006): 347-81.

40. Gary W. Cox and William C. Terry, "Legislative Productivity in the 93d-105th Congresses," *Legislative Studies Quarterly* 33, no. 4 (2008): 603-18.

41. Colleen J. Shogan, "Blackberries, Tweets, and YouTube: Technology and the Future of Communicating with Congress," *PS: Political Science & Politics* 43, no. 02 (2010): 231.

42. Matthew E. Glassman, "Franking Privilege: Mass Mailings and Mass Communications in the House, 1997-2014," Congressional Research Service, May 6, 2015, https://www.fas.org/sgp/crs/misc/RL34458.pdf.

43. Roger H. Davidson, Walter J. Oleszek, Frances E. Lee, and Eric Schckler, *Congress and Its Members* (Washington: CQ Press, 2014), 38.

44. Bruce E. Cain, John A. Ferejohn, and Morris P. Fiorina, *The Personal Vote: Constituency Service and Electoral Independence* (Cambridge, MA: Harvard University Press, 1987).

45. Daniel M. Butler, Christopher F. Karpowitz, and Jeremy C. Pope, "A Field Experiment on Legislators' Home Styles: Service versus Policy," *The Journal of Politics* 74, no. 2 (2012): 474-86.

46. J. M. Box-Steffensmeier, D. C. Kimball, S. R. Meinke, and K. Tate, "The Effects of Political Representation on the Electoral Advantages of House Incumbents," *Political Research Quarterly* 56, no. 3 (2003): 259-70.

47. Robert M. Stein, and Kenneth N. Bickers, "Congressional Elections and the Pork Barrel," *The Journal of Politics* 56, no. 2 (1994): 377-99.

48. Ronald Utt, "The Bridge to Nowhere: A National Embarrassment," The Heritage Foundation, October 20, 2005, http://www.heritage.org/research/reports/2005/10/the-bridge-to-nowhere-a-national-embarrassment.

49. Scott A. Frisch and Sean Q. Kelly, *Cheese Factories on the Moon: Why Earmarks Are Good for American Democracy* (Boulder, CO: Paradigm Publishers, 2011).

50. "Incumbent Advantage," OpenSecrets.org, accessed November 26, 2018, https://www.opensecrets.org/overview/incumbs.php.

51. "Donor Demographics," OpenSecrets.org, accessed April 7, 2017, https://www.opensecrets.org/overview/donordemographics.php.

52. Ryan Grim and Sabrina Siddiqui, "Call Time For Congress Shows How Fundraising Dominates Bleak Work Life," *The Huffington Post*, January 9, 2013, accessed June 16, 2016, http://www.huffingtonpost.com/2013/01/08/call-time-congressional-fundraising_n_2427291.html.

53. Peverill Squire, "Preemptive Fund-Raising and Challenger Profile in Senate Elections," Iowa Research Online, November 1, 1991, accessed June 16, 2016, http://ir.uiowa.edu/cgi/viewcontent.cgi?article=1091&context=polisci_pubs.

54. The districts do not contain the exact same number of people because each state must have at least one House member and districts cannot cross state lines. The remaining seats are assigned to each state using the Method of Equal Proportions as applied by the U.S. Census Bureau. "Congressional Appointment," United States Census Bureau, http://www.census.gov/population/apportionment/about/computing.html

55. Micah Altman and Michael McDonald, "Technology for Public Participation in Redistricting," *Reapportionment and Redistricting in the West* (Lanham, MD: Lexington Books, 2012).

56. "State-by-state Redistricting Procedures," Ballotpedia, accessed June 16, 2016, https://ballotpedia.org/State-by-state_redistricting_procedures.

57. *League of United Latin American Citizens v. Perry*, 548 U.S. 399 (U.S. 2006).

58. Aaron Blake, "GOP Can Draw Nearly Half of New House Districts," *The Washington Post*, November 4, 2010, accessed June 16, 2016. http://voices.washingtonpost.com/thefix/redistricting/gop-can-draw-nearly-half-of-ne.html.

59. Tausanovitch, A. (2019, October 01). The Impact of Partisan Gerrymandering. Retrieved January 01, 2021, from https://www.americanprogress.org/issues/democracy/news/2019/10/01/475166/impact-partisan-gerrymandering/

60. Charles Backstrom, Samuel Krislov, and Leonard Robins, "Desperately Seeking Standards: The Court's Frustrating Attempts to Limit Political Gerrymandering," *PS: Political Science & Politics* 39, no. 03 (2006): 409-15.

61. Keith E. Whittington, R. Daniel. Kelemen, and Gregory A. Caldeira, *The Oxford Handbook of Law and Politics* (Oxford: Oxford University Press, 2008).

62. Andrew Gelman and Gary King, "Estimating Incumbency Advantage without Bias," *American Journal of Political Science* 34, no. 4 (1990): 1142.

63. "Statistics and Historical Comparison," GovTrack.us, accessed June 16, 2016, https://www.govtrack.us/congress/bills/statistics.

64. Curtis W. Copeland, "The Federal Workforce: Characteristics and Trends," Congressional Research Service, April 19, 2011, www.dtic.mil/cgi-bin/GetTRDoc?AD=ADA543409.

65. "The Legislative Branch," The White House, accessed June 16, 2016, https://www.whitehouse.gov/1600/legislative-branch.

66. Roger H. Davidson, Walter J. Oleszek, Frances E. Lee, and Eric Schckler, *Congress and Its Members* (Washington: CQ Press, 2014), 190.

67. Judy Schneider, "House Committees: Assignment Process," Congressional Research Service, May, 2007, http://archives.democrats.rules.house.gov/archives/98-367.pdf.

68. Matthew Cox, "Pentagon Tells Congress to Stop Buying Equipment It Doesn't Need," Military.com, January 28, 2015, accessed June 16, 2016, http://www.military.com/daily-news/2015/01/28/pentagon-tells-congress-to-stop-buying-equipment-it-doesnt-need.html.

69. Richard F. Fenno, *Congressmen in Committees* (Boston: Little, Brown, & Co., 1973).

70. John H. Aldrich, *Why Parties?: The Origin and Transformation of Political Parties in America* (Chicago: University of Chicago Press, 1995), 26.

71. Roger H. Davidson, Walter J. Oleszek, Frances E. Lee, and Eric Schckler, *Congress and Its Members* (Washington: CQ Press, 2014), 229.

72. Jonathan Allan and John Cochran, "The Might of the Right," *CQ Weekly*, November 8, 2003, 2762.

73. Party unity on congressional votes takes a dive: CQ Vote Studies. (n.d.). Retrieved January 01, 2021, from https://www.rollcall.com/2019/02/28/party-unity-on-congressional-votes-takes-a-dive-cq-vote-studies/

74. "Vote Studies," CQ.com - Vote Studies, February 3, 2014, accessed June 16, 2016, http://media.cq.com/votestudies/.

75. Kevin B. Smith and Alan Greenblatt, *Governing States and Localities* (Los Angeles: SAGE | CQ PRESS, 2019), 417.

76. Understanding the Filibuster," No Labels, accessed April 14, 2017, https://www.nolabels.org/understanding-the-filibuster/.

77. John Avlon, "Three simple ways to make Congress work," CNN, March 15, 2012, accessed April 14, 2017, http://www.cnn.com/2012/03/15/opinion/avlon-fix-congress/.

78. Roger H. Davidson, Walter J. Oleszek, Frances E. Lee, and Eric Schickler, *Congress and Its Members* (Los Angeles, CA: CQ Press, an Imprint of SAGE Publications, Inc., 2014).

CHAPTER 12

The President: Hoping for a Hero

Chapter Objectives

1. Discover what powers the Constitution gives the presidency.
2. Differentiate between the president's powers in foreign and domestic policy.
3. Learn about the president as negotiator.
4. Understand why presidents go public.
5. Explore what makes a president popular.
6. Assess presidential popularity.

The 2020 presidential election showed that most Americans were ready for a return to normalcy after four years of experience with Donald Trump, a political outsider who never held an elected office and promised to radically change Washington politics. This time, the majority chose the quintessential example of political professional for president: 78-year-old Joe Biden, who was Barack Obama's vice president and served for 37 years as a U.S. Senator from Delaware. Biden was elected to the U. S. Senate for the first time at age 30, one of only six U.S. senators to be elected at the minimum age. He was reelected six times during his long career in the Senate and elected twice as vice president.

Over the four years of his presidency, President Trump refused to conform to behaviors set by past presidents. For example, presidents are expected not to profit from their personal businesses while in office. But Trump, the real estate developer, insisted on using his own hotels for official government business, charging the Secret Service and other government agencies for rooms and other expenses and did the same for foreign and domestic interests. His refusal to release his tax returns broke a fifty-year old tradition followed by every president since Richard Nixon. *The New York Times* eventually found the documents and discovered years of losses and tax avoidance.[1] Trump broke with presidential norms when he refused to submit to oversight by removing the independent inspectors general who watch over the Defense, Health and Human Services, Transportation, and State Departments. He regularly intervened in Department of Justice affairs/matters when he called for investigations of his political rivals, when he tried to fire the special counsel investigating his involvement with Russian inference in the 2016 election, and when he dodged the Department's review process before granting pardons. He diverged from past practice by avoiding Senate confirmation of his presidential appointments thereby evading public scrutiny of his choices and relying on temporary staff to run government agencies. He parted from tradition when he attacked judges that ruled against him, when he slighted allies by withdrawing from 13 treaties and international organizations while indulging America's adversaries, and when he undermined U.S. intelligence agencies.[2]

Trump also departed from accepted behavior by becoming a chief purveyor of disinformation. According to the *Washington Post*, Trump made more than 25,000 false or misleading claims since assuming office, including assertions that the COVID-19 virus was less severe than the seasonal flu, that 85 percent of mask-wearers catch the virus, that no president has done more for Black Americans since Abraham Lincoln, that he would have won the popular vote in 2016 but for millions of votes cast by illegal immigrants in California, and that he won 2020 elections "by a lot."[3] He swore that the mainstream press was inventing news and characterized the reporters and editors that criticized him as "enemies of the people."[4] Trump's false or misleading statements increased during his time in office accumulating to more than 600 per week, seeming to cause his believers to question the nature of reality itself.[5] But to his most ardent supporters, "Trump is not a liar, he is a bullshitter," a plain-spoken man of the people, an anti-politician who would save the nation from decline by putting the historically dominant, racial, religious and numerical core of America first.[6] They were weary of hearing from politicians afraid to offend anyone, including America's adversaries. In contrast, they believed Trump's words were unfiltered by "political correctness," showing the courage to say what others would not, sharing his true feelings toward immigrants, racial and religious minorities, women, and American soldiers killed or captured in war who he said were "losers" and "suckers."[7]

Halfway through Trump's presidency, the Democratic Party won control of the House of Representatives after gaining a net 41 seats in the 2018 midterm congressional elections. By April 2019, Special Counsel Robert Mueller completed his investigation into Trump's involvement in Russia's involvement in the 2016 presidential election. Although Muller concluded that the Russian government illegally interfered with the election, he did not find enough evidence that Trump had conspired with the effort. Muller also declined to charge Trump with obstructing his investigation, citing a Department of Justice opinion that the president is immune from criminal prosecution while in office.[8] In September 2019, another scandal surfaced after official transcripts showed that Trump sought to force the government of Ukraine to initiate a criminal investigation of his would-be opponent in the coming 2020 election, making U.S. aid contingent on the announcement. The House of Representatives opened a formal impeachment inquiry for the first impeachment, but the president departed from accepted norms again by ignoring congressional subpoenas and refusing to allow witnesses to testify. After a series of televised hearings, House members approved articles of impeachment mostly along party lines, leaving the Republican controlled Senate to determine whether Trump should be removed from office. In the end, all but one of the Republican senators voted to acquit the president, many arguing that his transgressions were not serious enough to justify removal from office while others said the voters would render a verdict in the upcoming election.[9]

Such was the political context prior to the 2020 presidential election year. By February 2020, the COVID-19 pandemic would move many states to adopt early and no-excuse absentee mail-in voting and establish convenient drop-boxes to allow voters to cast their ballots safely. After a spring stay-at-home advisory designed to curb the spread of the virus, Trump would attempt to repeat the campaign strategy that proved successful in 2016 by holding large, in-person rallies despite the raging pandemic. Meanwhile, the death of George Floyd, Breonna Taylor, and others at the hands of municipal police would give rise to mass protests sponsored by the Black Lives Matter movement in 500 communities involving tens of millions from all races and nationalities in marches during the summer peak of the pandemic.[10] Riots would break out across the country but particularly in the Pacific Northwest cities of Portland and Seattle where the president threatened to send federal troops. President Trump broke with tradition by using troops armed with teargas to clear protesters gathered outside the White House for a 17-minute photo session.[11]

In early September 2020, Trump nominated and the Republican majority in the Senate rapidly confirmed Amy Coney Barrett to fill a vacancy caused by the death of Ruth Bader Ginsburg, Just five weeks before the general election, the White House sponsored a mask-free celebration for Trump's newly confirmed justice. The event would be labeled a COVID-19 "super spreader" event by Dr. Anthony Fauci, the director of the National Institute of Allergy and Infectious Diseases after a dozen guests including senators Thom Tillis and Mike Lee, former New Jersey governor Chris Christie, the president of the University of Notre Dame, and several members of the White House press corps became infected.[12] Three days later, during the first presidential debate Trump initiated a display of constant interruptions and bullying, causing Biden to call the president a clown, a liar, and a racist. The second debate never happened because Trump had to be hospitalized after contracting the virus. After recovery, Trump continued to hold mass rallies in midwestern battle ground states during the last week before the election despite their surging infection and death rates. Meanwhile Biden continued to play the anti-Trump by running a low-key, mostly online campaign from the basement of his home, with some drive-in public events.

In a year with the two political parties spending over $14 billion on campaign activities, a summer of police shootings and social protests followed by the death of an old and the confirmation of a new supreme court justice and after nearly 10 million confirmed infections and more than 230,000 COVID deaths, the people were ready to vote. The reelection of President Donald Trump, party control of both houses of Congress and control of the 50 state legislatures was at stake.

On the eve of the election, public opinion polls showed Biden with a substantial (8.2 percent) lead in the popular vote fueling hopes among Democrats for a clear repudiation of Trump.[13] The president's supporters, on the other hand, were confident that passion for their hero would translate into an easy victory. The intense partisan drama together with increased voting convenience would produce a turnout of 66.2 percent of eligible voters, the highest percentage in 112 years of American elections. Even those who rarely vote came out to express their choice.[2] Biden's votes totaled 81.2 million, the largest in U.S. history while President Trump's total was the second highest. Biden's 4.5 percent margin of victory was the second largest since 2000 and twice as large as Hillary Clinton's vote total over Trump in 2016. Trump's 47 percent of the vote share seems large, but it was smaller than Gerald Ford's, the last incumbent president to lose in a two-way race.[14]

Still, on election night the network vote counters would remind audiences that the popular vote does not determine the winner of presidential elections. To become president, a candidate must receive a majority of votes cast by electors in the Electoral College. It wouldn't be until the Saturday after Election Day that the Associated Press counted more than the 270 electoral votes needed to declare Biden the winner. The long wait made it seem like the election was closer than it was, but in the end, Biden's 306 electoral votes to Trump's 233, was exactly the margin that Trump claimed was a landslide victory in 2016. The win was notably high in an era of close presidential elections and because sitting presidents running for re-election seldom lose.

Exit polls showed that most people voted according to their party identification. According to the New York Times, 94 percent of Democrats voted for Biden while 93 percent of Republicans voted for Trump. Democrats have a slight (37-35%) advantage in the general electorate. For a reminder on how voters divide themselves among the Democratic and Republican parties see Chapter 8, but briefly, this meant that the mostly white Republican Party was pitted against the Democratic coalition of liberal whites, Latino/as, Asian Americans, Black Americans, Native Americans, and members of the LGBTQ+ community. The "density divide" which had been developing since the turn of the century would be starkly evident with Republicans mostly voting in predominately rural, small town and outlying suburban areas versus Democrats who mostly live in cities and close-in suburbs.[15] The parties were also divided by religion, education, race, ethnic identity and social class (for the distribution of these groups among the two political parties see Chapter 8). 92 percent of Biden supporters firmly believed that he would handle the pandemic better, but 93 percent of Trump's voters felt the opposite. Of course, there is a trade-off between handling the pandemic and rebuilding the economy. Again, nearly all (80 percent) of Biden's voters approved the strategy of using science to blunt the effects of the pandemic before re-opening restaurants, bars, theaters, and stadiums. Most of Trump's (76 percent) voters thought Trump's path of minimizing the dangers of the virus and re-opening the economy was best. The two candidates evenly split the voters who said they wanted a candidate who "cares about people like me." Partisan polarization was so pervasive that even the act of wearing masks to reduce the spread of the virus became a sign of party allegiance. The tide of the election, it seemed, would turn on the people who claim independence from a political party. They voted for Biden 54 to 40 percent, in 2016 independents had favored Trump 48 to 42 percent.[16]

In January, President Trump seemed to have an advantage given the U. S. economy's fairly robust growth and low unemployment. The pandemic slowed the economy, but stimulus bills passed by Congress staved off more serious declines. By election time, 41 percent of voters believed they were better off financially since 2016 and voted for Trump versus the 20 percent who thought they were worse off and voted for Biden. In most years, this would have ensured Trump's reelection but among the 39 percent who that believed their financial situation was about the same, most (64 percent), voted for Biden. Biden won voters who wanted someone to unite the country while Trump was the choice among those who wanted a strong leader. The voters, however, are not split evenly on these two features as those who want a strong leader outnumber those who prefer someone who can unite the country. The two candidates evenly split the votes of those with no college degree, but among those with college degrees, Biden won decisively 55 to 42 percent. Another edge that seemed significant was the 23 percent of voters who wanted a president that showed good judgement: two-thirds of these said they voted for Biden.[17]

After the Associated Press called the election for president-elect Biden, Trump would break tradition again by refusing to concede defeat. Despite the court challenges and drama that resulted when Trump and his allies challenged the votes in 5 states by filing 55 lawsuits, including two filed with the U.S. Supreme Court, the process of counting, auditing, recounting and certifying the vote went fairly smoothly although the state of Georgia had to count their votes three times, including once by hand.[18] No court found any perceptible evidence of significant voter fraud, some judges even scolded the plaintiffs for lacking credibility, standing, or evidence, and asking to disenfranchise millions of voters. Before the so-called "safe harbor" date of December 6, all 50 states certified their votes and chose their respective slates of electors. Members of the Election Infrastructure Government Coordinating Council, the National Secretaries of State, and others issued a report saying election was the "most secure in American history" after finding "no evidence that any voting system deleted or lost votes, changed votes, or was in any way compromised."[19] Attorney General William P. Barr did not see "fraud on a scale that could have effected a different outcome in the election" contradicting the claims of the president.[20] On December 14, electors chosen by their state legislators met in their respective states and voted according the popular vote in their states. Still, President Trump refused to concede, insisting that he was the victim of a stolen election and leading most of his fellow Republicans to believe the same.

The President continued his efforts to overturn the election by inviting his followers to gather across from the White House on January 6th, the day Congress was to meet and count the Electoral College votes certified by the states. "Be there, will be wild!" the President said. At the rally, he repeated his claims that the election was stolen and implored the crowd to march to the Capitol complex where the certification was in progress saying they had to "fight much harder" and "show strength" and if they did not, "you're not going to have a country anymore." Thus provoked, the protestors turned mob, breached then vandalized the Capitol, menaced Members of Congress, the Vice President, and congressional personnel, obstructed the certification of the 2020 presidential election and for the first time in US history, disrupted the peaceful transfer of power. Five individuals died in the riot including a Capitol Police officer.[21] The following Wednesday, Members of the House of Representatives passed an article of impeachment against Donald Trump for incitement of insurrection against the Government of the United States, making him the first president to be impeached a second time.

12.1 The Constitution and The Presidency: An Invitation to Struggle

The executive serves a fixed term of four years, but unlike members of Congress, the president is limited to two terms. The U.S. Constitution also decrees that power is to be shared among the executive, legislative, and judicial branches of government. In addition, a system of checks and balances promises that no single branch of government completely overwhelms another. For example, the president can check the power of Congress by vetoing legislation. However, when the president rejects legislation, he is simply returning it to Congress, much like when a professor returns an unacceptable paper to a student. But, unlike the student who must change the paper to suit the professor, Congress can refuse to compromise and instead pass the legislation unchanged with a two-thirds majority vote. If they do the latter, the bill becomes law and Congress, not the president, gets its way. Thus, the phrase "checks and balances" does not imply that the powers of the three branches of government are equally balanced; in many ways, the Framers designed the Constitution to give Congress the upper hand.

When the Constitution was written, the Framers looked on the powers of the executive with great suspicion. They feared concentrated power and hated the fact that the colonial governors had royal authority to approve or veto the acts of the colonial assemblies. America's first constitution, the Articles of Confederation, didn't even include an executive office as a separate branch of government. When they wrote the Constitution, the Framers recognized a need for a stronger executive. Still, they were eager to limit the powers of the president.

Article 2, Section 1 of the Constitution says "The executive Power shall be vested in the President of the United States of America." But the document is not clear about the meaning of "executive power." In contrast, Article 1 specifies the powers of Congress by listing 18 enumerated powers. We know, for example, that Congress has the power to make laws, collect taxes, declare war, and regulate commerce, because these are clearly listed in Article 1, Section 8. Because Article 2 lacks such specificity, executive power becomes subject to interpretation and debate. This has allowed presidents to read the article as they wish, but the ambiguity of the article also creates conflict over the interpretation of the president's powers with Congress and the courts. Some presidents have interpreted executive power to mean they only have those powers precisely listed in the Constitution, while others have taken it to mean anything that is not unconstitutional. Article 2 is vague. Constitutional scholar Edward Corwin referred to it as "the most loosely drawn chapter of the Constitution."[22]

Still, the Constitution commands that the president "shall take Care that the Laws be faithfully executed" and swear an oath to do so.[23] The laws are made by Congress and it is the president's duty to implement them. As comedian Jon Stewart says, the president can observe a problem, "shake his head and say out loud, 'there ought to be a law,' but the president cannot make that law. The president cannot write up that law and submit it with his name on it. The president needs someone in Congress to submit it for him. ... Sometimes this makes the president feel like a total wuss."[24]

Congress traditionally gives the president considerable freedom to make decisions about foreign policy. There is constitutional justification for this. Political scientist Aaron Wildavsky argues there are two dimensions of the presidency: as head of state and head of government. The president's constitutional powers can be understood as a combination of these two dimensions. As head of state, the president represents the country in its affairs with other nations. This happens when the president accepts ambassadors or orders the armed forces into combat as the commander in chief. Congress also has foreign policy powers, including the power to declare war and approve treaties. Depending on the situation, however, the president often has the advantage when it comes to dealing with other nations. On the other hand, the president as head of government manages the bureaucracy. In this case, the president's power is closely shared with Congress given its authority to create, fund, and oversee bureaucratic actions. The fact that members of Congress generally care more about domestic than foreign policy also contributes to Congress' direct involvement.

The Foreign Affairs Presidency

Section two of Article 2 makes the president the "commander in chief of the Army and Navy of the United States, and of the militia of the several states."[25] This makes the president the highest military authority in the Unites States, even if he or she has never served in the military. The president is not only the chief of the military but also head of the other security agencies, including the Central Intelligence Agency, the National Security Agency, and the Federal Bureau of Investigation.

Only Congress has the power to declare war and, in 1973, it passed the War Powers Resolution over President Richard Nixon's veto. The legislation attempted to correct actions made during the Vietnam War in which Presidents Johnson and Nixon committed the United States to the Vietnam War and directed secret military operations in Cambodia and Laos without asking Congress to declare war. The **War Powers Act** allows the president to send troops abroad in the event of a declaration of war or if U.S. troops are attacked. The president can mobilize troops without declaring war, but the president must report that commitment promptly to Congress. Further, the troop deployment must be limited to 60 or 90 days–unless Congress extends the deadline. When the war powers act was put forward, there was concern that it would hinder a president's ability to act in an emergency. Yet, since Vietnam, the president has authorized military operations in Grenada, Libya, the Persian Gulf, Honduras, Panama, Iraq, Kuwait, Bosnia and Herzegovina, Somalia, Macedonia, Afghanistan, Sudan, Yemen, and Syria without asking Congress to declare war. But the president usually requests Congress to pass a resolution supporting troop deployment. For example, when President George H. W. Bush ordered more than half a million troops into the Persian Gulf after Iraq invaded Kuwait, he notified Congress and it gave permission to engage in combat. However, when President Trump sent 59 cruise missiles to destroy an airfield in Syria, he did not

War Powers Act

A law passed by Congress designed to limit the president's ability to commit troops or make war with foreign nations.

notify Congress, nor did president Bill Clinton ask permission to send troops to Kosovo, nor did Obama ask permission to authorize airstrikes against the Islamic State.[26] Clinton's decision was eventually ratified by Congress, but Obama determined that his actions were simply consistent with the Constitution because his actions were limited and served the "national interest."[27] When it comes to deploying troops, practically speaking, once they are in harm's way, Congress has little choice but to support deployment. To do otherwise would increase the danger and weaken support for their efforts. The president also has access to more and better information regarding security issues than most members of Congress.

Cold War

A state of hostility short of warfare between the Soviet Union and the United States, which took place from the end of World War II in 1945 until 1990.

Given the high stakes states of war, including the **Cold War**, foreign policy often requires speedy and decisive action. Under these circumstances, it makes sense for the president to set and carry out national foreign policy. However, as fighting terrorism has become a major policy area, the lines between domestic and foreign policy have become blurred. Following the attacks on 9/11, President George W. Bush opened a detention facility at the U.S. Naval Station at Guantanamo Bay, Cuba. Its purpose was to hold suspects in the war on terror for interrogation. During its use, many prisoners were detained indefinitely without charges or trials, while others were physically and psychologically abused, causing the facility to become an international symbol of injustice and human rights abuse. During his 2008 campaign, Barack Obama promised to close the controversial camp, but even though he ordered the facility closed and had substantial support from his own party in Congress, the prison remains open and its detainees locked up.

bipartisan

A policy or position that involves the cooperation or agreement of members of both Republican and Democratic party members.

executive agreements

International agreements between the United States and other countries made by the president without ratification by the Senate.

As head of state, the president also has the power to receive ambassadors from other countries, to appoint those representing the United States, and to make treaties. In effect, this makes the president the country's chief negotiator with other nations. Still, appointing ambassadors and making treaties requires the advice and consent of the Senate. In recent years, this function has also been subject to the blurring of foreign and domestic policy. Beginning in 1991, Presidents George H. W Bush and Bill Clinton negotiated the North American Free Trade Agreement (NAFTA) with Mexico and Canada, which, among other things, eliminated most tariffs and duties between the three countries. The treaty was accepted by a 61 to 38 **bipartisan** vote in the Senate. In recent years, however, presidents have preferred to use **executive agreements**, which do not require Senate approval, to finalize international agreements.[28] President Obama committed the United States to the Paris Climate Accord, an agreement to reduce greenhouse emissions, and the Trans Pacific Partnership, a major trade compact, using this method. Unfortunately for the supporters of these agreements, what one president agrees to, another president can disavow. Soon after taking office, Donald Trump removed the United States from both compacts. The Trump administration replaced the North American Free Trade Agreement (NAFTA) with a new agreement designed to encourage automobile manufacturing in the U.S. and environmental problems on the U.S. Mexico border.

The Domestic Presidency

The ability to effectively wage war and to negotiate treaties is beyond the capability of a large, multi-member institution such as Congress. It made sense, therefore, for the Framers of the Constitution to assign the roles of commander in chief and maker of treaties to the president with Congress retaining significant checks. When it comes to domestic policies, however, it is more accurate to say that the president's executive powers are shared with Congress rather than separated.[29]

Power to Nominate

The president has the power to appoint all federal judges (including justices of the Supreme Court); ambassadors to foreign nations; heads of cabinet-level agencies, such as the Secretaries of Agriculture, Commerce, and Homeland Security; and the heads of independent regulatory agencies, such as the Environmental Protection Agency and the Consumer Product Safety Commission. This gives the president power to influence the policies and the personnel of bureaucracy by appointing individuals who will carry out the president's goals. He or she can also fill government positions by rewarding campaign contributors and other political allies. However, most of these appointments are subject to the approval of the Senate. For its part, the Senate takes its duty to advise and consent seriously. Because the Constitution does not set any qualifications for service, the president may nominate anyone he or she chooses, but not everyone selected by the president is approved. For example, Andrew Puzder, Donald Trump's nominee for Labor Secretary, withdrew his nomination after Senators turned against him for hiring an undocumented maid.[30]

The president can shape the judicial branch by selecting judges who share his or her ideological outlook. The president can also make the judiciary more symbolically representative of the nation's population by appointing women and people of color to the federal bench. Because federal judges serve life terms, assuming "good behavior," the president's influence can last for some time. Once in office, however, judges can only be removed by Congress through the process of impeachment. This gives the federal judiciary considerable independence from the president. In addition, each of the president's nominees must be approved by the Senate. Senatorial courtesy gives senators who represent the state in which the judge will serve the ability to express their disapproval of the nominee. The president must consult with these senators prior to selection to avoid an embarrassing rejection. Once nominated, senators on the Judiciary Committee who oppose a nominee can delay the committee's review or attempt to derail the process by giving the nominee an unfavorable recommendation. The Senate rejected 147 judicial nominations using the fillibuster, 79 of which were President Obama's.[31] The Senate rubbed salt in the president's wounds when it refused to consider Obama's nomination to replace the late Antonin Scalia on the Supreme Court in the last year of his presidency. However, in 2017, Senate Republicans used their majority position to change the threshold for advancing Supreme Court nominations from 60 to a simple majority, thereby ending the use of the filibuster by the minority party to block Supreme Court nominations.

Legislative Power

A successful president uses his executive powers to make legislation consistent with his wishes. The Constitution asks the president to give Congress information on the condition of the country and recommend new policies for its consideration. Although some presidents have given this information in writing, the more recent tradition lets the president give a yearly nationally televised speech to a **joint session of the Congress.** We call this speech the "State of the Union" address. The speech allows the president to claim credit for the things he or she has done and gives him or her an opportunity to set the national agenda for the coming year. In President Obama's last State of the Union, he boasted that during his presidency the country recovered from the Great Recession and helped more people afford health care. Given that this was his last year in office, he limited his list of policy proposals, but he urged Congress to take military action against the Islamic State and asked the legislative branch to make progress in dealing with global climate change.

joint session of the Congress

A gathering of the members of both houses of Congress in the same session.

President George W. Bush delivering his State of the Union speech.

Rob Crandall / Shutterstock.com

During the first years of the Great Depression, President Franklin D. Roosevelt used his inaugural speech to evoke a sense of emergency and ask for wartime powers to initiate legislation designed to pull the country out of its economic decline. In his first 100 days in office, Roosevelt's administration got Congress to pass 15 major bills, including the National Industrial Recovery Act, which funded the building of large-scale projects such as dams, bridges, power plants, and hospitals; the Federal Emergency Relief Administration, which gave state and local governments funds to operate emergency relief programs; the Works Progress Administration, which employed millions of skilled and unskilled workers in the construction of public infrastructure projects; the Federal Deposit Insurance Corporation, which insured bank deposits and protected bank accounts; the Tennessee Valley Authority Act, which built dams to control floods, generate electricity, and boost economic development; and the Emergency Conservation Work Act, which created the Civilian Conservation Corps to provide jobs for unemployed young men.[32] The amount of legislation passed in 100 days set the standard for gauging the effectiveness of future presidents in their first months in office. However, historian Patrick Maney notes that only a few of these items originated in the White House and almost all had been debated for years.[33] Nevertheless, every candidate running for president promises quick and vigorous action in the first 100 days. According to Politifact, at the 100-day mark, President Trump had completed only six of the 103 promises he made during the campaign and all six were items that he could accomplish without the help of Congress.[34]

Franklin Delano Roosevelt National Memorial in Washington, D. C.

© Shutterstock, Inc.

veto

The ability to reject a bill or law made by a legislative body.

The president can also influence legislation by using his constitutional authority to **veto** acts of Congress. It seems like the president only uses the veto to reject legislation that he or she does not like, but vetoes are often part of a bargaining process between the president and Congress.[35] The president is not a member of Congress, but he or she can step into the process of lawmaking and modify almost any bill. The process involves the threat of a veto followed by negotiation to modify the bill, or the actual veto of a bill followed by its subsequent passage.

Passing legislation by majority vote is not easy, but overriding a veto, which requires a supermajority of at least 67 votes in the Senate and 218 votes in the House of Representatives, is more difficult. The possibility that members of

Congress will waste their time or come up with the votes to override the veto is often sufficient to cause them to modify a bill according to the president's wishes. Sometimes, all the president needs to do is express reservations about the pending legislation and hint that a veto is likely. If the president is clever, he or she will attempt to shape the legislators' beliefs about what they must do to keep him or her from carrying out his veto threat. In other words, the president can exaggerate preferences as well as criticize the parts of a bill he or she dislikes in the hope that what Congress ends up passing is closer to his or her real preferences. Although members of Congress are unsure about the president's true policy preferences, they do know that overriding a presidential veto is difficult and that their time is valuable. Consequently, even with legislation that is generally preferred, the president can make it more to his or her liking with a veto threat.

With veto bargaining, the president can influence legislation even though his pen stays on his desk. On the other hand, presidents attempt to modify legislation when they issue **signing statements** to go along with the bills they do sign.[36] Although not technically part of the bill, a signing statement is printed along with the bill to communicate to executive agencies how to apply the legislation according to the president's interpretation of the law. Signing statements may also contain the president's objections to certain provisions of the bill being signed. These signing statements are controversial. The Constitution does not mention them, and Article I, Section 7 limits presidential objections to bills that are vetoed and returned to Congress. In other words, unlike many of the states' governors, the president cannot veto parts of legislation or choose which parts of a bill to execute. The Supreme Court in Clinton v. City of New York (1998) rejected the **line-item veto** as unconstitutional. However, the court allows the president to reasonably interpret a law especially when its provisions are unclear or imprecise. As in other matters, it falls to the judicial branch to prevent the president from overstepping executive bounds.

Still, presidents since Ronald Reagan have used carefully worded signing statements to construe congressional intent in ways that better fit their agendas. For example, President George W. Bush signed a bill outlawing the torture of prisoners from Afghanistan and Iraq. In the statement, he declared that he viewed the ban "in a manner consistent with the constitutional authority of the President . . . as Commander in Chief."[37] The statement, he asserted, allows the executive to waive the ban and carry out harsh interrogation, including torture, if he believes a detainee has information that threatens national security. As a candidate for president, Barack Obama criticized Bush's actions but, as president, he did pretty much the same, but less frequently. For instance, he signed a law requiring the president to notify Congress at least 30 days before transferring any prisoner from Guantanamo Bay and to certify that such transfer would not threaten the interests of the country. But in signing the law, Obama stated that he believed the provision was unconstitutional because the president must be able "to act swiftly in conducting negotiations with foreign countries regarding the circumstances of detainee transfers."[38] Thus, he did not notify Congress when he traded the release of U.S. Army Sergeant Bowe Bergdahl for five prisoners being held at the facility.

Judicial Powers

The Constitution also gives the executive judicial powers, in that the president can grant reprieves or pardons of crimes against the United States. Some presidents have used this privilege more than others. For example, after the Civil War, Andrew Johnson granted amnesty to all Southerners who had participated in the war. Jimmy Carter pardoned all who had evaded the draft during the Vietnam War. Franklin Roosevelt granted 3,687 individual pardons during his three terms. By contrast, George W. Bush pardoned 176 individuals during his two terms, while Barack Obama pardoned 64. Donald Trump has pardoned political allies Dinesch D'Souza for violating campaign finance laws, Roger Stone for obstructing Congress, Paul Manafort for bank and tax fraud and witness tampering, Charles Kushner for tax evasion, and witness tampering and four military contractors found guilty of killing seventeen Iraqi civilians in Baghdad. He pardoned former Sheriff Joe Arpaio of Maricopa County, Arizona, for refusing a court order to refrain from racially profiling Latinas/os. He also pardoned Lewis "Scooter" Libby, former Vice President Dick Cheney's chief of staff, for out-

signing statements
Often included when the president signs a law to communicate to executive agencies how to apply the legislation according to the president's interpretation.

line-item veto
The power of the executive, usually a governor, to reject individual provisions of a bill rather than its entirety.

ing the identity of C.I.A agent Valerie Plame. Additionally, he pardoned conservative author Dinesh D'Souza for a violation of campaign finance laws. Perhaps the most famous pardon was Gerald Ford's pardon of Richard Nixon after Watergate "for all offenses against the United States which he . . . has committed or may have committed."[39]

former Sheriff Joe Arpaio of Maricopa County, Arizona, for refusing a court order to refrain from racially profiling Latinas/os. He also pardoned Lewis "Scooter" Libby, former Vice President Dick Cheney's chief of staff, for outing the identity of C.I.A agent Valerie Plame. Additionally, he pardoned conservative author Dinesh D'Souza for a violation of campaign finance laws. Perhaps the most famous pardon was Gerald Ford's pardon of Richard Nixon after Watergate "for all offenses against the United States which he . . . has committed or may have committed."[40]

Executive Power

The president's most fundamental power comes from the fact that the Constitution makes him or her the head of a vast bureaucracy consisting of more than 500 departments, agencies, authorities, corporations, and commissions employing more than 2.7 million civilian workers.[41] However, most of the bureaucracy was created by Congress through legislation that identifies these agencies' missions and gives them the authority to develop policies and methods to carry out Congress's wishes. For example, in 1970, Congress passed the Clean Air Act to protect public health by regulating air emissions from stationary and mobile sources. After the law was passed, bureaucrats from the Environmental Protection Agency wrote pollutant standards and implementation plans to interpret every page of the Act. These regulations were then approved by Congress. During implementation, Congress continued to make sure the agency was doing what the law requires through committee inquiries, hearings, reports, and other proceedings. During this time, the president was not free to redirect the agency or its funding away from the Act's goals. Other agencies are shielded from the president's direct control by means of independent commissions representing both parties or with staggered or lengthy terms of office.

In times of crisis, such as war, civil disturbance, economic depression or other national emergencies, presidents claim powers beyond those specified in the Constitution. Only the executive branch, the presidents argue, can meet the crisis because neither Congress nor the courts provides the energy and vigor of the presidency. President Abraham Lincoln suspended the right of habeas corpus for civilians arrested by the military during the Civil War. When a federal district court ruled that only Congress can suspend such rights, Lincoln simply ignored the order to turn the suspects over to civilian courts.[42] President Harry Truman commanded the seizure and operation of steel mills closed by a labor strike during the Korean War. After the terrorist attacks of September 11, 2001, President George W. Bush declared an emergency to call up National Guard and Reserve troops and bypass military personnel rules. Bush renewed the emergency order 17 times.[43] President Obama declared the swine flu outbreak a national emergency to allow hospitals to move emergency rooms offsite and protect their patients.[44] Congress often acquiesces to presidential initiatives under emergency conditions. In turn, the legislature's passivity sets precedents and establishes new presidential prerogatives.

As Congress creates new departments and agencies, it delegates authority to the executive branch and enhances the power of the president. Congress attempts to maintain control of its legislation through its oversight authority, but the president remains powerful because he or she is a unitary actor. As President George W. Bush said: "I listen to all voices, but mine's the final decision .... I am the decider, and I decide what's best."[45] In contrast, members of Congress must debate, compromise, and vote before making a final decision. Often, the legislation produced from such negotiation turns out to be vague and ambiguous, which allows executive branch officials to interpret the law and write the regulations according to the president's goals. This is often the case when quick action is needed. For example, in 2008, world financial markets plunged into a crisis fueled by the collapse of the investment bank Lehman Brothers and the subprime mortgage market. Congress responded by giving the president new powers to provide large bail-outs to financial institutions on the verge of collapse and prevent further foreclosures and evictions. Over time, a giant administrative apparatus surrounds the president to help him or her manage the economy and promote the health and welfare of the nation. Still, agencies can resist the president's initiatives. Bureaucrats have their own interests which are often tied to their personal careers, the mission of their agency, and the success of the programs they administer. Furthermore, they are often hired under civil service system, which protects them from being terminated for political reasons.

Executive Office of the President

The immediate staff of the president.

Managing a bureaucracy as large as the federal government is too demanding for one person, so in 1939 President Franklin Roosevelt created the **Executive Office of the President**. The office has a wide range of responsibilities from managing the president's communications to the executive residence. The office employs about 4,000 individuals, about half of whom have policy-making responsibilities.[46] The president has a good deal of control over the personnel of the office as very few of its top officials need to be confirmed by the Senate (the exceptions are the Director of the Office of Manage and Budget, the chair and members of the Council of Economic Advisors, and the U.S. Trade Representative).

Housed in the Eisenhower Executive Office Building and in the West Wing of the White House, the office represents the center of power in the executive branch. In the past, the president's cabinet secretaries served as primary advisors, but today, cabinet members are mostly responsible for operating their respective departments and performing ceremonial roles associated with the being a department secretary. The job of advising the president falls to the 100 or so special assistants in the west wing. Some of Joe Biden's notable cabinet nominees include Janet Yellen for Secretary of the Treasury, General Lloyd Austin for Secretary of Defense, Xavier Becerra for Secretary of Health and Human Services, Pete Buttigieg for Secretary of Transportation, Jennifer Granholm for Secretary of Energy, Alejandro Myorkas for Secretary of Homeland Security, and Katherine Tai as U.S. Trade Representative among others. Many of Trump's top advisors had short careers in the white house, including Chief of Staff Reince Priebus, Chief Strategist Steven Bannon, National Security Advisor Michael Flynn, Press Secretary Sean Spicer, and Deputy Chief of Staff Katie Walsh. All resigned within the first six months of the administration. Anthony Scaramucci, one of Trump's directors of communication, lasted only 10 days in office.

The White House is the official residence and workplace of the President of the United States.

© Shutterstock, Inc.

The office is also home the president's Council of Economic Advisors, the Council on Environmental Quality, the Office of National Drug Control Policy and the Office of Science and Technology Policy. The two most important officials in the White House (other than the president) are director of the Office of Management and Budget (OMB) and the White House Chief of Staff. The director of the OMB is important because executive branch agencies do not have independent authority to initiate major spending. Thus, the preparing of department budgets, regulatory proposals, and new policy initiatives makes the staff of the OMB personnel a part of every major decision because funding is what makes programs run successfully or not. In the past, budgets were developed from the bottom up as agencies determined what funds were needed to carry out their missions and included such estimates in their annual budget requests. Today the process is top-down, making the director of the OMB one of the most powerful people in the federal government.

The Executive Office of the President is headed by the chief of staff who selects and supervises key members of the staff, controls information, and manages the president's agenda. The chief of staff often speaks for the president in talks with Congress, members of the executive branch, and others outside of government. The chief also manages a key resource for white house staff: access to the president. In this regard, those working physically near the president have a distinct advantage. As Leon Panetta, President's Clinton's chief of staff, put it: "Presidents are like any other individual. They look for those that are in proximity to them to give them the best guidance. That's why the power frankly has gone from the cabinet to presidential assistants. Because they have proximity, they deal directly with the president."[47] Panetta once compared the White House advisors to a team of second-graders playing soccer, "because all of the kids wind up chasing the ball and not staying in their position, everybody wants to chase the ball. ... So the president was holding meetings in his office that sometimes included as many as twenty, thirty, forty assistants who were in the room, that's impossible, it can't operate that way."[48]

After weeks of turmoil, former Trump Chief of Staff Reince Priebus was replaced by the Secretary of Homeland Security and retired four-star Marine General John F. Kelly. Kelly's first order of business was to institute order. He regimented the flow of people and information to the president as Priebus had not done. Even Ivanka Trump, the president's daughter, required Kelly's permission to meet with the president.[49]

The president's chief of staff is also charged with managing the president's executive orders. In his first days in office, President Trump issued orders to modify the Affordable Care Act (aka "Obamacare"), hire 10,000 more immigration officers, direct funding to construct a wall along the Mexico-U.S. border, and suspend the entry of immigrants from seven Muslim-majority countries among other orders. Such orders are not new. President Thomas Jefferson ordered the 828 million square mile Louisiana Purchase from France and authorized the Lewis and Clark expedition to map and catalog the area's biology and establish trade with the Native American tribes. At the beginning of the Civil War, President Lincoln combined the state militias into a national Army, diverted unspent funds intended for other programs to enlarge the Army and Navy, instituted censorship of U.S. mail, and ordered a blockade of southern ports.[50] Among many other orders, President Franklin D. Roosevelt temporarily closed banks, forbid them from releasing gold coins, and commanded the internment of 70,000 Japanese Americans during World War II.[51]

Abraham Lincoln delivering the Gettysburg Address in 1863.

© Shutterstock, Inc.

executive orders

Orders given by the president which have the force of law.

As directives, **executive orders** have the force of law but are subject to judicial review by the federal courts. Interestingly, all the above executive orders (including Trump's) were considered constitutionally suspect. The most famous executive order, Lincoln's Emancipation Proclamation that freed slaves in the Confederate States, illustrates the problem. First, Lincoln's justification for the Proclamation was a war measure, an action he considered necessary to bring the Civil War to an end. However, like most of the president's constitutional prerogatives, war powers are vague. Freeing slaves in the Confederate States amounted to the seizure of property from citizens of an enemy nation. Since Lincoln refused to recognize the Confederacy as an independent nation, the Emancipation Proclamation violated the right of state governments to determine their own property laws (including their right to decide whether slaves were property) as a principle of federalism. Of course, the rebelling states were in no position to challenge the president in the federal courts; to do so would admit that they were still part of the government. After the war, however, the returning states would have asked the courts to declare the Proclamation unconstitutional and order the slaves to be returned to their owners. To avoid this risk, Lincoln pushed for the passage of the Thirteenth Amendment to the U.S. Constitution banning involuntary servitude (slavery) in the United States.

Most of the president's executive orders outside of crises involved the reorganization of structures or procedures of the executive branch. For example, President George W. Bush created the Department of Homeland Security as a permanent cabinet level department with an executive order. However, he did not create new missions or fund the department from scratch; only Congress can do that. Rather, Bush united existing federal agencies involved in national public safety that needed to work closely together during a national emergency. Still, the order would direct the largest reorganization of the federal government in more than 40 years. It would be made up of 22 agencies encompassing 240,000 employees ranging from air traffic controllers and cybersecurity analysis to chemical facility and border inspectors. It had a budget of up to $40 billion, the third largest in the federal government.[52] Executive orders also lack permanence because they can be reversed by subsequent presidents. On his second day in office, President Obama ordered the closing of the detention camp at Guantanamo Bay. The camp remains open, however, thanks to resistance from Congress. President Trump promised to keep it open to "load it up with some bad dudes."[53]

FIGURE 12.1 Significant Executive Orders

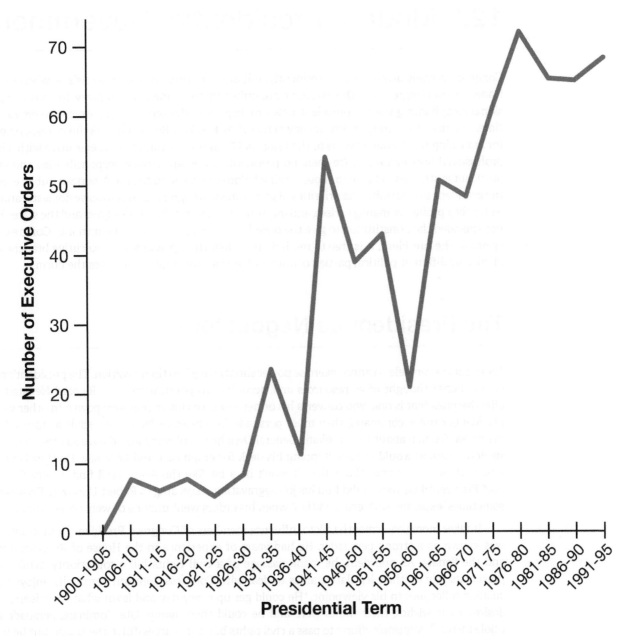

Based on William G. Howell, "The President's Powers of Unilateral Action: The Strategic Advantages of Acting Alone" PhD dis Stanford University 1999.

Although Trump ordered the rollback of the Affordable Care Act (ACA) in his second day in office, the president cannot fundamentally change a law passed by Congress or rescind its funding. Trump ordered the immediate construction of a border wall with Mexico, but the wall could not be built without Congressional approval of funding. Similarly, Trump was unable to order that federal funding be denied to so-called "sanctuary cities" or states that refuse to turn over undocumented immigrants to federal authorities. Trump's order to exclude refugees from seven Muslim-majority nations mostly caused confusion and protests at airports. The original order was blocked by the federal courts, although a revised order was later considered by the Supreme Court. Lastly, the president cannot order a 10-fold increase in the size of the country's nuclear arsenal without funding from Congress. Presidents reach for as much authority as Congress and the courts will allow, but if Congress fails to support his or her decisions, the president's orders often go unfulfilled.

12.2 Modern Presidential Government

Congress typically acquiesces to presidential initiatives in times of national crisis or when the top leadership in Congress and the executive are united by the same political party. In turn, Congressional compliance gives the president new privileges and the power of the executive grows over time. The rise of the modern presidency began after Franklin Roosevelt took direct responsibility for managing the economic crisis of the 1930s and Congress surrounded the executive with a large professional bureaucracy. Since then, no president can escape similar responsibilities and every president is stronger, relative to those serving before the 1930s. Today, the American public expects the president to determine the priorities of government, design programs to solve domestic and foreign policy problems, manage crises, and implement programs.[54] Still, Congress and the states have not amended the Constitution to give the president more power. Whatever authority Congress delegates to the president, it is free to rescind and, when the legislative and executive branches are divided by different political parties, conflict rather than cooperation becomes the norm.

The President as Negotiator

Presidents nevertheless cannot exercise power simply based on their position. The president's powers are better thought of as resources and, according to political scientist Richard Neustadt, an effective president is one who converts his or her resources into persuasive power. In other words, presidents cannot command; they must persuade. To illustrate, Neustadt recalls a story told by President Truman about the problems General Dwight Eisenhower would have as president. "He'll sit here, Truman would remark (tapping his desk for emphasis), and he 'll say, 'Do this! Do that!' And nothing will happen. Poor Ike—it won't be a bit like the Army. He'll find it very frustrating." President Eisenhower did find his job aggravating. According to Robert Donovan, Eisenhower sometimes "exploded with exasperation" when his orders went undone or were done wrong.[55]

It takes more than smooth talk to influence members of Congress. President Lyndon Johnson was known as a strong persuader. He had years of experience in the House of Representatives and the Senate. As president, he made passage of a civil rights bill a top priority. While most presidents rely on their legislative aides to deal with Congress, Johnson personally enjoyed persuading colleagues to his viewpoint. "He could get up every day and learn what their fears, their desires, their wishes, their wants were and he could then manipulate, dominate, persuade and cajole them."[56] Johnson's efforts to pass a civil rights bill were successful in the House, but he faced stiff opposition from fellow southerners in the Senate. When he met with his friend and mentor Senator Richard Russell, he threatened, "Don't' get in my way on this civil rights bill, because if you do, I'm gonna run you down."[57] Russell led a filibuster in the Senate nevertheless. Bringing debate to an end would require a vote of two-thirds of the senators, so Johnson turned to his rival, Republican Minority Leader Senator Everet Dirksen, and made a deal. Dirksen promised the three votes Johnson needed and the president agreed to appoint Dirksen's choices to the Federal Trade and Federal Communications Commissions. The negotiations paid off, as several Republican senators changed their votes and the bill passed. As Neustadt puts it, "The essence of a President's persuasive task with congressmen and everybody else is to induce them to believe that what he wants of them is within their own appraisal and their own responsibility requires them to do in their interest, not his."[58]

On the other hand, according to Neustadt, presidents will not get their way if they fail to bargain effectively. The contrast to Lyndon Johnson is Jimmy Carter, who was elected president after the Watergate Scandal in part because he was viewed as someone who was unknown and thus uncorrupted by Washington politics. When he came into office, he continued to stay aloof from the political leaders in Washington. Carter did not enjoy politicking with Congress. For example, at times, previous presidents lobbied members of Congress on the presidential yacht Sequoia during cruises on the Potomac River. David Gergen, director of communications for presidents Ford and Reagan, remembers, "You'd invite in some congressmen and you'd go out on the Sequoia and schmooze for an evening and have a few drinks, put your feet up, the spouses would be there. It was a way to get along and put down the troubles and partisanship of the day and try to build some friendships. Carter came in and saw the Sequoia as a symbol of wealth. He sold the Sequoia. Well, a lot of us thought it was a dumb thing to do; it's not that expensive and it's helpful. It is a way to show that you care; it's a way to build trust. This city ultimately works on trust and it's the people who trust each other that can build something together."[59]

Carter's main priority was the energy crisis. He and his staff crafted an energy policy that he presented to the American public on television. After the speech, House Speaker Thomas "Tip" O'Neill met with the president and gave him a list of 30 people he wanted him to call. But Carter refused, saying, "Energy is one of the great issues of our time; the American people know that. Congress is going to respond to the will of the people. I don't have to make those calls; that's not my nature." O'Neal added, "As bright as he was on the matter of the policy, he didn't know how to operate in the political field of Washington."[60] Carter served as an officer in the Navy's nuclear submarine program and had a reputation for technical competency and integrity. Had he been more willing to bargain, as per Neustadt, he would have been a better president. But times changed. Beginning in the 1970s, the traditional alliances that allowed President Johnson and Senate Majority Leader Dirksen to trade votes for appointments began to weaken.

The President Going Public

The size and complexity of government lead to an increase in the number of organized groups with a stake in national policy. For example, the above-mentioned 1970 Clean Air Act required the federal government to regulate the emission of air pollutants from stationary and mobile sources. This single piece of legislation led to the political mobilization of interests from automobile makers to oil and gas extractors to suppliers of chemicals to neighborhood dry cleaners, all wishing to soften the impact of regulations on their industry: presidents not only lack the time and energy to bargain with all groups, but effective bargaining requires some isolation from interested groups. When President Johnson and Minority Leader Dirksen traded votes on civil rights legislation for representation on regulatory commissions, they essentially made a private deal between two negotiators. Past presidents could barter across dissimilar issues over a long time frame. This requires that flexibility be given to leaders to make deals for which those making sacrifices would be paid back with unrelated benefits, trusting that today's favor could be redeemed months or years later.[61]

Changes in technology have made Washington politics more open. Before satellite communications, the national network news organizations like CBS, ABC, and NBC had a monopoly on news video, which they could withhold from local broadcasters until they showed it first. Satellites allowed local stations to download video transmissions for immediate broadcast and led to the proliferation of cable networks, some of whom specialize in political programing. Inexpensive cameras and access to the internet allows anyone to be a reporter, producer, and broadcaster of news. Today's technology makes it easier for groups to find common interests and to monitor what leaders in Washington are doing. Such changes also make it easier for the president to speak directly to the people.

Given the scope of such changes, persuasion through negotiation with a small group of key policy makers inside Washington is no longer an effective means for the president to achieve his or her policy goals. Today's presidents are more likely to communicate directly and make their case with the American people, who then pressure their legislators to support the president.[62] Going over the heads of Congress by appealing directly to their constituents is not new. President Theodore Roosevelt advocated the use of what he called the "bully pulpit," the president's position as the nation's only nationally elected official, to generate public support for his initiatives. He also used Thomas Edison's motion picture invention to film himself riding horses and chopping wood to create the image of an energetic executive. His fifth cousin, President Franklin Roosevelt, went on speaking tours and communicated directly with the American public through fireside chats broadcast to radios across the nation. Every president since Bill Clinton has set up a White House Communications Office to craft and deliver a coordinated communications strategy to promote the president's policy goals, respond to the press, and generally promote a positive image of the president. Recent presidents use social networks to communicate directly with the public. President Obama effectively used social media to raise money, organize local events, send out voting reminders, and respond to negative press in his 2008 and 2012 campaigns. In the White House, he continued to use Facebook, Instagram, Snapchat, Twitter, and other services to supplement the work of the Communications Office, earning him the title, "America's first social-media president."[63] In the 2020 presidential campaign, both candidates made extensive use of social media for good reason, according to the Pew Research Center: nearly 70 percent of Americans use some form of social media, most of whom check in on a daily basis.[64] President Trump used his Twitter account in the White House to promote his policy initiatives but also to attack and insult his opponents.[65]

Donald Trump speaking at a rally in Sacramento, CA.

Joseph Sohm / Shutterstock.com

The frequency with which presidents have been making direct public appeals has increased dramatically. President Franklin D. Roosevelt made less than 20 public appearances over a two-year period between 1933 and 1935, whereas President Reagan made about 70 over the same number of years. President George W. Bush made over 280 appearances in a six-year period between 2001 and 2007, while president Obama made almost 300 between 2009 and 2010.[66] Past presidential persuasion was about negotiation, creating an environment for give and take. Going public does more than change the target of persuasion: it is about going over the heads of members of Congress to their bosses—their constituents. Public presidential appearances are not random; they are often strategically scheduled at times and places to influence votes in Congress. The goal is to get district voters to support the president, but sometimes the president makes personal visits with the representatives' largest donors while in their districts. These contributors, who usually donate to the president as well, are frequently asked to call or write letters to the intransigent members.[67]

FIGURE 12.2 Presidential Public Appearances

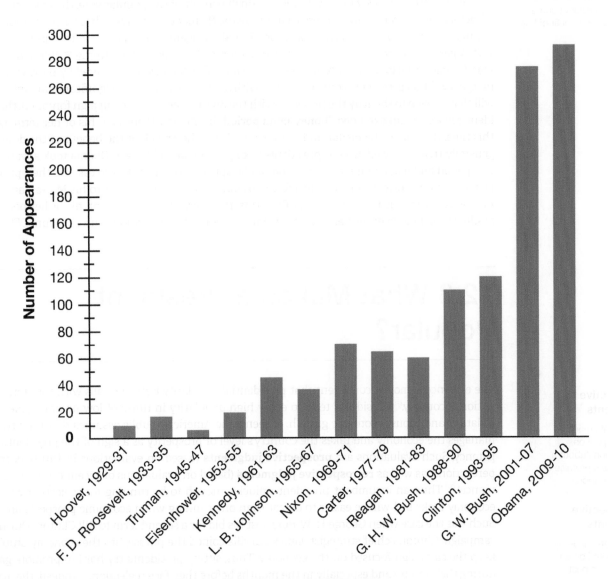

Data from Kernell, *Going Public.*

Paradoxically, going public works for the president because members of Congress are more independent today than in the past. Most members run their own campaigns and raise their own campaign funds through political action committees (PACs). The incumbents also win. In the last Congressional elections, 90 percent of the members of the House of Representatives and 91 percent of senators who sought re-election were successful.[68] Their independence draws their allegiances away from their party and the president, but also from the national welfare and toward the narrower interests of their districts. This local focus, however, leaves members vulnerable to a popular president. Under these circumstances, the president's popularity with the members' constituencies becomes an asset to be used as leverage to threaten and force concessions from the members of

Congress. But such coercion may be costly, especially if the president needs the members' votes on other issues. Threats build resentment and may invite retaliation in other matters. In going public, the president also risks the possibility that the people will not respond. If so, the president will lose credibility with Congress.

honeymoon period

The beginning period of a president's first term of office in which the public gives the president some license or the benefit of the doubt.

Still, a more popular president is a more powerful president. Unfortunately, the things that make a president popular are largely beyond his or her control. Certainly, presidents who win their elections by wide margins are more popular than presidents that barely win. Following the assassination of John F Kennedy in 1964, Johnson won 61 percent of the popular vote, the greatest margin of victory for any candidate in more than 100 years. No modern president has surpassed Johnson's popular vote victory, but in a three-way race, Ronald Reagan's 489 to 49 vote in the electoral college was larger. On the other hand, Richard Nixon after 1968, Jimmy Carter after 1976, Bill Clinton after 1992, George W, Bush after 2000, and Barack Obama after 2008 were hampered by narrow winning margins. Still, all presidents come into office with a "positivity bias" or a significant amount of good will that is given to them by the public.[69] With the divisiveness of the campaign forgotten, the president can expect an extended **"honeymoon period"** in the first months of his or her term. During this time, the public, the media, and Congress will give the president the benefit of the doubt and generally treat him well. Recent presidents George W. Bush and Barack Obama took advantage of this period and made numerous trips and public appearances to make the case for their priorities. Donald Trump, however, made only a few trips outside of Washington or to his Mar-a-Lago resort in Florida during his first months in office. Unfortunately for the president, his or her popularity gradually declines over time as criticism from the media and opposition sources mounts.[70]

12.3 What Makes a President Popular?

prospective judgments

Judgments made by voters based on assumptions about a candidate's promise of future behavior.

retrospective judgments

Judgments made by voters based on an incumbent's past behavior.

The evidence is mostly consistent that presidential popularity rises and falls with the state of the nation's economy.[71] Presidents tend to enjoy high popularity in times of low unemployment, low inflation, and robust economic growth. It seems the American public assumes that the president manages the economy and takes the country's level of prosperity as a sign of the president's competency. Such evaluations are **prospective judgments** (based on evaluations of future economic perceptions) as well as **retrospective judgments** (based on evaluations of recent economic performance).[72] Thus, an incumbent president unlucky enough to be running for reelection when the economy looks bad will be easier to defeat than one running when economic prospects are good. Such was the case when George H. W. Bush lost his bid for a second term to Bill Clinton. During the campaign, Clinton's chief strategist James Carville coined the phrase, "it's the economy, stupid," to keep the campaign focused on the economy. Thus, sitting presidents try hard to promote growth during their tenure and especially in the months before they face reelection.[73] Indeed, the average rate of income growth peaked in presidential election years under Republican presidents. For the Democrats, income growth rose during the second year of their four-year terms, then declined in the third and fourth years.[74] Unfortunately for the Democrats, their efforts at producing economic growth were ill-timed. They were given little credit by voters for income growth in non-election years, but punished for slow growth during the election years.

As the head of state and the personification of the nation, presidents also benefit from a "rallying effect" at times of national crisis. After the terrorist attacks on 9/11, George W. Bush's job approval rose from 30 to 85 percent. His approval ratings declined after the attack, but increased when the City of Baghdad fell to the Americans and increased again after Saddam Hussein was captured.[75] In the weeks after 9/11, Congress gave Bush the authority to invade Afghanistan to pursue Osama bin Laden and remove the Taliban from power. Congress also supported the president's decision to invade Iraq. It is understandable that Congress would defer to the president on military affairs and foreign policy. Following Bush's reelection in 2002, however, Congress also passed Bush's domestic initiatives unrelated to Afghanistan or Iraq, including proposed tax cuts, a comprehensive energy bill, funding to combat AIDS, and a controversial "partial birth" abortion bill. Congress also raised the government's debt limit by nearly $1 trillion. Popularity can be a potent ally for a president. It is no wonder presidents have often been charged with manipulating events to take advantage of this effect.

FIGURE 12.3 Presidential Approval Ratings Over Time

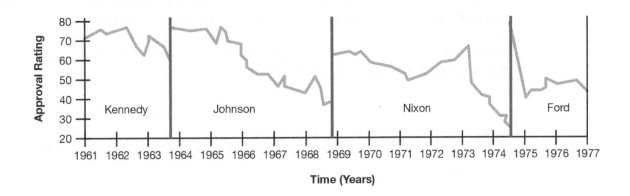

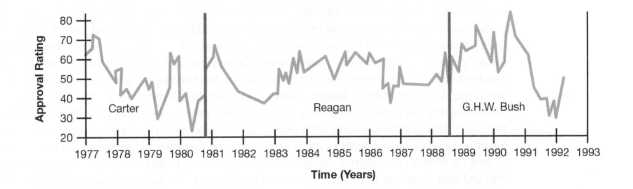

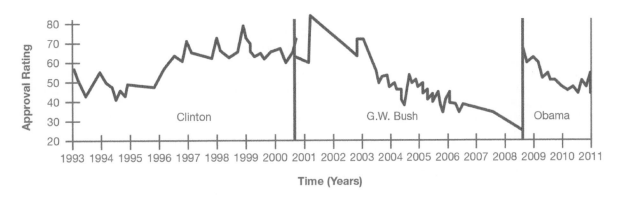

Still, rallying effects are usually short lived. President Johnson's popularity increased after he escalated the conflict in Vietnam into a full-scale war, but declined sharply as U.S. casualties multiplied. President Reagan's popularity increased, then declined after the invasion of Grenada. President George H. W. Bush was one of the most popular presidents after operation Desert Storm in 1991. He was so popular that several prominent Democrats declined to run against him in 1992, leaving the field to a little-known governor from Arkansas named Bill Clinton. However, Bush's approval ratings eroded rapidly as the country fell into recession and, in the end, he eventually lost his reelection bid. After the terrorist attacks in September 2001, George W. Bush reached record levels of popularity and was easily reelected in 2004 after the invasions of Afghanistan and Iraq. Yet, the casualties of war and his failure to find Saddam Hussein's weapons of mass destruction in the end made him one of the least popular presidents in U.S. history. Those presidents that remained popular did so because of a strong economy. Clinton remained popular in his second term despite enduring both scandals and impeachment. Similarly, Barack Obama left office relatively popular due to, among other things, a steadily recovering economy.

12.4 Presidential Success and Timing

If presidents can time their tenure in office with their party's control of Congress, they often find it easy to keep promises made during their campaigns. Franklin Roosevelt's famous explosion of legislation passed within his first 100 days in office was largely due to the Democrats' overwhelming majorities in both the House and the Senate. Similarly, Barack Obama could pass the Affordable Care Act largely because of his party's leadership and majorities in both houses of Congress. Unfortunately, since the 1980s, divided government, whereby one party controls one or both houses of Congress and the other party controls the presidency, has become more common than not. Recent presidents, including Ronald Reagan, George H.W. Bush, Bill Clinton, George W. Bush, and Barack Obama, mostly had to deal with a Congress controlled by the opposite party, which found it had little to gain politically by supporting the president. In these cases, the president's success in getting his or her agenda passed declines dramatically and the president is compelled to use veto power to bargain with an unreceptive Congress. When Democrats briefly controlled Congress between 1993 and 1994, President Bill Clinton vetoed no legislation, but issued 36 vetoes when party control shifted to the Republicans. Likewise, George W. Bush vetoed no bill during his first term of office, but vetoed 11 in his last two years after his party lost control of Congress.

FIGURE 12.4 Successful Votes Under United and Divided Government

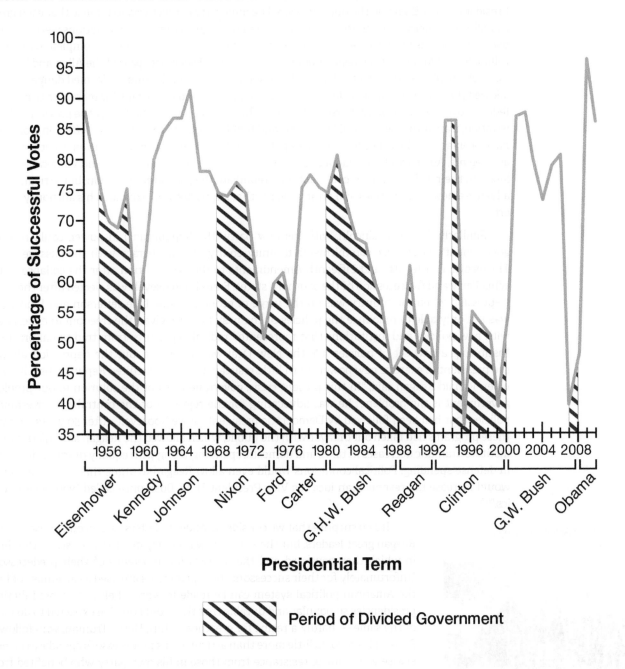

Presidential Term

Period of Divided Government

Based on Congressional Quarterly Weekly Report. FiscalNote, https://www.fiscalnote.com/.

Unified party control of government is no guarantee of presidential success, however. Lyndon Johnson's party maintained control of Congress throughout his presidency, yet he did not run for reelection in 1968 after large segments of his own party turned against him during the Vietnam War. Despite his considerable skill as a politician and majorities in both houses of Congress, he became another causality of war. Given President Donald Trump's long-standing disagreements with fellow Republicans in Congress, unified party control of government did not amount to much before the Republicans lost control of the House in 2018.

According to political scientist Steven Skowronek, presidential success or failure is also a function of the time in which a president governs.[76] The most successful presidents have served during times of reconstruction following economic depressions or periods of intense social conflict, especially if they were elected after the voting public rejected the failures of their immediate predecessors. For example, before President Jefferson and his party, the Democratic-Republicans, took office, the new country had split into factions with the Federalists, such as Alexander Hamilton and President John Adams, on the opposite side. The interparty conflict was so intense that each group thought the other was about to destroy the nation through bloodshed. Such notions were not terribly far-fetched, as they had recently witnessed a violent revolution in France, complete with heads rolling off guillotines. At the peak of political conflict, the Federalists passed the Alien and Sedition Acts, which allowed President Adams to imprison or deport immigrants he deemed dangerous and allowed the courts to imprison Jeffersonian pamphleteers and politicians for merely criticizing the federal government. When Jefferson took office, he could repudiate the acts of the previous administration, transform the political landscape, and build a legacy. Per Skowronek, Jefferson would not have been able to do so but for the failed policies of the preceding administration. In other words, as a regime, Adams and the Federalists were in the process of disintegration and vulnerable to collapse. In their wake, Jefferson could not only repudiate the past administration, but articulate and advance a new set of policies and arrangements that supported and expanded his authority to govern.

Similarly, Abraham Lincoln, with his new party (the Republicans) in power, could redefine government's most basic commitments to unity, equity, and democracy with the passage of the Thirteenth, Fourteenth, and Fifteenth Amendments to the Constitution after the collapse of the Whig Party and the secession of the southern states. Franklin Roosevelt was elected after the Great Depression when the country was on the verge of economic ruin. Like Jefferson and Lincoln, he was not only able to renounce the policies of the past, but was given the freedom to experiment with new policies and institutions that represented radical departures from traditional practices. Instituting a new set of policies like the New Deal was disruptive, but the depression allowed the president to exercise new powers with little resistance from discredited Republicans. Likewise, when Ronald Reagan said, "In this present crisis, government is not the solution to our problem; government is the problem," he was advocating for the rejection of the centralized government policies that had been followed by Democratic presidents since Roosevelt. After 50 years, many of these programs had fallen out of favor with the public, which allowed the Reagan administration to institute dramatic decreases in taxes and domestic spending, along with equally dramatic increases in defense spending. Political conditions would even allow Reagan to argue that decreasing taxes would increase tax revenues, an idea his Vice President H. W. Bush once called "voodoo economics."[77]

Abraham Lincoln at Antietam during the Civil War.

© Shutterstock, Inc.

It's no surprise that we consider presidents Jefferson, Lincoln, Roosevelt and Reagan great leaders, but their success was largely due to the crises of the times in which they governed and the political incompetence of their predecessors. Unfortunately for their successors, these presidents are used as examples of how the American political system can be made to work. Their successors inherited presidencies so popular and durable that they could only be expected to do more of the same — hardly a recipe for greatness. Thus, Harry Truman, who followed Roosevelt, could do little more than articulate his predecessor's agenda; to do otherwise would invite resistance from those in his own party who benefited from Roosevelt's legacy. The next outstanding president would have to wait for the right times and an unsuccessful predecessor to open the door to an opportunity for greatness.

Skowronek notes that Barack Obama spent most of his administration dealing with the legacies of the Reagan era and looking for opportunities to repudiate it. His presidency revitalized conservative opposition, first with the Tea Party and then through the Trump campaign. Candidate Hillary Clinton followed Obama's lead by insisting on a secular, more pragmatic approach to government, but she was defeated by Trump's promises to reconstruct Washington politics fundamentally, that is, to "drain the swamp" and "make America great again." Unfortunately for Trump, the Regan legacy may oppose large, intrusive government, but does not point to programs that solve people's problems, manage crises, or lead a massive bureaucracy. As much as Americans want their president to shake things up, they also want their executive to be a responsible manager. Moreover, the election was close enough that left Trump without a definitive mandate. Like all challengers, he framed his predecessor as a failure, but voters did not necessarily agree. According to Skowronek, Trump can't reconstruct presidential politics in the absence of a "consensus that what came before was a complete and systemic failure."

There have only been 45 presidents before President Biden and each has faced different situations within different social and political contexts. Like the many pundits who predicted a landslide victory for Biden in November 2020, political scientists and their theories can be wrong. Yet by conventional standards, prospects for creating a memorable legacy are not great. At the time of this writing, the president is faced with a pandemic, the rollout of a vaccine and an economy struggling to recover. During Ronald Reagan's time in office, the president's popularity made it difficult for Congress to oppose him. Today, most members of Congress have little to fear from opposing the president.   Fortunately, for President Biden, after the January 2020 runoff elections in Georgia, the Democrats now control both houses of Congress which awards them the chairs and majority votes on all of committees, giving him the opportunity to shape his administration, achieve his policy agenda and shape the nation's judiciary. If unemployment rates stay low and incomes remain stable, one would expect his prospects for reelection to be reasonably good."

12.5 What Can I Do?

When we wrote this feature for Chapter 11, we argued that voting mattered. Congress has the power to raise taxes, declare war, and make laws that will affect your life. The division of representation into 435 House districts and 100 Senate seats means your vote can make a difference because of the smaller numbers of people voting in each area relative to the population of the entire country. If you vote in primary elections and visit or write letters to your representative, your influence will be even greater. Because of its closeness to the people, the legislature is and should be the central representative institution in a democratic government. Yet, individual members' close attention to the people of their districts insulates them from the institution's unpopularity and makes it difficult for Congress to choose national over local interests.

At the presidential level, however, it is much harder to imagine one vote making a difference among the 160 million or so cast in a presidential election. Likewise, it's hard to argue that a few letters, tweets, or emails from a single citizen will influence the decisions of the president of the United States. Still, if you are opposed to the president's actions, adding your voice to others in social protest remains a viable option. As discussed previously, a president's popularity makes a great deal of difference to his or her success. The opposite of protesting, of course, is to support the president when opportunities present themselves.

On the eve of the 2016 election, many prominent Americans pledged to leave the country if Trump were to be elected. We doubt if more than a few followed through. Most Americans have a deep sense of attachment to their society, including its government. The fact that the president is the only nationally elected official makes him or her our only leader chosen to represent the entire population. In a democratic nation, this reason is sufficient to engender our loyalty, at least conditionally. We should give the president the benefit of the doubt and allow him or her some flexibility to lead the country. Because of its visibility and unitary character, the institution of the presidency promises to counter the deficiencies of the fragmented representation produced by Congress, better representing the national interest. Further, no other branch of government can deal effectively with a national crisis because none can provide the energy and vigor of a single executive. The president is also more likely to be responsive to unorganized interests.

The presidency makes up for some of the deficiencies we found in Congress, but the institution has developed pathologies of its own. In particular, reliance on presidential leadership equates to dependency on an individual leader. Presidents do not see themselves as mere clerks content to keep the machinery of the federal government humming efficiently. They expect to pursue "fame" by taking on "great and arduous enterprises" with an eye to securing eminence in American history.[78] This concern for reputation can drive presidents to represent faithfully, but also to justify their stewardship. In so doing, presidents sometimes deceive the public about what their government is doing, as Johnson did during the Vietnam War. They may also act counter to the law and cover up their actions, as Nixon did during the Watergate scandal. When things go poorly or when the president's popularity declines, our leaders are tempted to exaggerate or even manufacture crises to distract the public and gain more power as Congress acquiesces to their leadership. This often leads to adventurism in foreign affairs and threatens the security of the nation, not to mention the lives and well-being of our troops.

For our part, a frantic search for a great leader is not healthy in a democracy. In running for the presidency, winning is everything, so candidates evoke powerful symbols of nationalism, race, gender, class, and regionalism. They promise more than they can deliver given the limits of their constitutional powers. The press highlights the individual skills and capabilities each candidate will bring to the office, but it is difficult to predict future capabilities when the challenges are yet uncertain. Further, the effective exercise of executive power is contingent on factors beyond the president's control and often beyond the abilities of any individual. Today's members of Congress are more independent and less likely to go along with their party's leaders when they make deals with the president. This forces the president to go public and leads to take-it-or-leave-it politics rather than political negotiation and compromise. Yet, after each president inevitably fails to live up to our raised expectations, we fix blame on the person and begin looking for another champion.

12.6 What's the Alternative?

Congressional elections reflect the wishes of the voters in individual congressional districts or states. A presidential election is the only opportunity we have to express our attitudes about the condition of the nation and for a single leader to reflect those sentiments. Unfortunately, too often our rules for electing the president preclude this from happening. The problem is that the electoral college system allows the loser of the popular vote to be elected president. This has happened five times, which is 10 percent of all presidential elections, and twice in the last five presidential elections held since 2000. Indeed, the Electoral College is often on the edge of handing the presidency to the candidate with fewer votes. It happened in 2000 when Al Gore fell short of the presidency by only 537 votes. In 2004 a change of only 58,706 votes (.05%) in four states would have given the presidency to John Kerry instead of the popular vote winner George W. Bush. In 2016, Trump did win despite having 3 million fewer votes than Hillary Clinton but for 38,868 vote (.03%) in three states. And in 2020, Trump needed to flip only 33,139 (.02%) votes in Arizona, Georgia and Wisconsin to win over Joe Biden, despite Biden having 7 million more votes.[79] Such results are confusing, undemocratic, and undermine the legitimacy of the president.

When Americans vote for the president, they are actually voting for a slate of electors, generally chosen by the candidate's political party, in each state and the District of Columbia. These electors then choose the president. The electors are apportioned to each state according to the number of seats that state has in the House of Representatives plus its two Senate seats. The effect of giving each state two votes for its Senate seats gives states with small populations a disproportionate share of the electoral college vote (see Chapter 7 for more detail). The winner of the presidential election is not the candidate who wins the most votes cast in the general election; rather the winner is the candidate who garners an absolute majority of votes (270 or more) from the electors. Because this formula gives states with small populations a disproportionate share of the vote, it violates the democratic principle of equity embodied in the idea of one person, one vote. Barring a compelling reason why the votes of citizens in sparsely populated states should count more than those in densely populated states, the determination of electoral college votes should be based on population.

In 1964, the Supreme Court outlawed the distribution of representation in the upper houses of state legislatures by county rather than apportioning legislative seats by population in the case of Reynolds v. Sims. This decision moved state legislatures closer to the democratic ideal than the U.S. Congress. The effect of apportioning representation by population greatly increased the number of state legislators from urban and suburban areas in state senates and made the state legislatures more reflective of the state's population distribution. Choosing the president by popular election would be more reflective of the will of the people. Unfortunately, the Supreme Court cannot alter the manner of determining representation in the U.S. Senate, and thus the distribution of votes in the electoral college. The only way to make this change is through an amendment to the U.S. Constitution.

Endnotes

1. Buettner, Russ, Susanne Craig, and Mike Mcintire. "Trump's Taxes Show Chronic Losses and Years of Income Tax Avoidance." The New York Times. The New York Times, September 27, 2020. https://www.nytimes.com/interactive/2020/09/27/us/donald-trump-taxes.html.

2. Montgomery, David. "Trump Dramatically Changed the Presidency. Here's a List of the 20 Most Important Norms He Broke - and How Biden Can Restore Them." The Washington Post. WP Company, November 10, 2020. https://www.washingtonpost.com/graphics/2020/lifestyle/magazine/trump-presidential-norm-breaking-list/.

3. "100 Days of Trump Claims." The Washington Post. WP Company. Accessed January 2, 2021. https://www.washingtonpost.com/graphics/politics/trump-claims/.   -database/?utm_term=.27babcd5e58c&itid=lk_inline_manual_2&itid=lk_inline_manual_2.

4. Samuels, Brett. "Trump Ramps up Rhetoric on Media, Calls Press 'the Enemy of the People'." TheHill, April 5, 2019. https://thehill.com/homenews/administration/437610-trump-calls-press-the-enemy-of-the-people.

5. Kessler, Glenn. "Analysis | The Biggest Pinocchios of 2020." The Washington Post. WP Company, December 19, 2020. https://www.washingtonpost.com/politics/2020/12/18/biggest-pinocchios-2020/.

6. Hibbing, John R. 2020, The Securitarian Personality: What Really Motivates Trump's Base and Why It Matters for the Post-Trump Era, Oxford University Press, p. 23.

7. Goldberg, Jeffrey. "Trump: Americans Who Died in War Are 'Losers' and 'Suckers'." The Atlantic. Atlantic Media Company, September 3, 2020. https://www.theatlantic.com/politics/archive/2020/09/trump-americans-who-died-at-war-are-losers-and-suckers/615997/.

8. "Key Findings of the Mueller Report: ACS." American Constitution Society, July 24, 2019. https://www.acslaw.org/projects/the-presidential-investigation-education-project/other-resources/key-findings-of-the-mueller-report/.

9. Cornwell, Susan, David Morgan, and Richard Cowan. "Partisan Rancor on Display as Senators Argue Their Positions in Trump Impeachment Trial." Reuters. Thomson Reuters, February 4, 2020. https://www.reuters.com/article/us-usa-trump-impeachment/partisan-rancor-on-display-as-senators-argue-their-positions-in-trump-impeachment-trial-idUSKBN1ZY1BW.

10. Buchanan, Larry, Quoctrung Bui, and Jugal K. Patel. "Black Lives Matter May Be the Largest Movement in U.S. History." The New York Times. The New York Times, July 3, 2020

11. Rogers, Katie. "Protesters Dispersed With Tear Gas So Trump Could Pose at Church." The New York Times. The New York Times, June 2, 2020. https://www.nytimes.com/2020/06/01/us/politics/trump-st-johns-church-bible.html.

12. "Here's Everyone at the White House Rose Garden SCOTUS Event Now Called a Likely 'Superspreader.' Help Us ID Them All." USA Today. Gannett Satellite Information Network, October 21, 2020. https://www.usatoday.com/in-depth/news/investigations/2020/10/07/likely-rose-garden-covid-superspreader-white-house-drew-hundreds/3636925001/.

13. DataDhrumil. "National President: General Election Polls." FiveThirtyEight, January 2, 2021. https://projects.fivethirtyeight.com/polls/president-general/national/.

14. Kevin Schaul, Kate Rabinowitz. "2020 Turnout Is the Highest in over a Century." The Washington Post. WP Company, December 8, 2020. https://www.washingtonpost.com/graphics/2020/elections/voter-turnout/.

15. Thompson, Derek. "The Most Important Divide in American Politics Isn't Race." The Atlantic. Atlantic Media Company, November 10, 2020. https://www.theatlantic.com/ideas/archive/2020/11/2020-election-results-prove-density-destiny/617027/.

16. Huang, Produced Jon, Samuel Jacoby, Michael Strickland, and K. K. Rebecca. "Election 2016: Exit Polls." The New York Times. The New York Times, November 9, 2016.

17. "National Exit Polls: How Different Groups Voted." The New York Times. The New York Times, November 3, 2020. https://www.nytimes.com/interactive/2020/11/03/us/elections/exit-polls-president.html?action=click.

18. Gerhart, Ann. "Election Results under Attack: Here Are the Facts." The Washington Post. WP Company, December 9, 2020. https://www.washingtonpost.com/elections/interactive/2020/election-integrity/.

19. "Joint Statement from Elections Infrastructure Government Coordinating Council & the Election Infrastructure Sector Coordinating Executive Committees." Cybersecurity and Infrastructure Security Agency CISA. Accessed January 2, 2021. https://www.cisa.gov/news/2020/11/12/joint-statement-elections-infrastructure-government-coordinating-council-election

20. Matt Zapotosky, Devlin Barrett. "Barr Says He Hasn't Seen Fraud That Could Affect the Election Outcome." The Washington Post. WP Company, December 2, 2020. https://www.washingtonpost.com/national-security/barr-no-evidence-election-fraud/2020/12/01/5f4dcaa8-340a-11eb-8d38-6aea1adb3839_story.html.

21. Savage, Charlie. "Incitement to Riot? What Trump Told Supporters Before Mob Stormed Capitol," January 10, 2021. https://www.nytimes.com/2021/01/10/us/trump-speech-riot.html.

22. Edward S. Corwin, The President, Office and Powers: 1787-1957; History and Analysis of Practice and Opinion (New York: New York University Press, 1962), 229.

23. U.S. Const. art II, § 2.

24. Jon Stewart, America (The Book): A Citizen's Guide to Democracy Inaction (Allen Lane, 2004).

25. U.S. Const. art II, § 2.

26. Dan Lamothe, "Why the Navy's Tomahawk missiles were the weapon of choice in strikes in Syria," The Washington Post, April 06, 2017, accessed November 6, 2017, https://www.washingtonpost.com/news/checkpoint/wp/2017/04/06/why-the-navys-tomahawk-missiles-are-the-most-likely-option-for-a-strike-in-syria-against-assad/?utm_term=.2f95074a128e.

27. "Trump's Syria Airstrikes: Constitutional or Not?" PolitiFact, accessed October 26, 2018, https://www.politifact.com/truth-o-meter/article/2017/apr/07/trumps-syria-airstrikes-constitutional-or-not/.

28. Adam Yarmolinsky, The Military Establishment (New York: Harper & Row, 1973).

29. Richard E. Neustadt, Presidential Power and the Modern Presidents: the Politics of Leadership from Roosevelt to Reagan (New York: Free Press, 1991).

30. Alan Rappeport, "Andrew Puzder Withdraws From Consideration as Labor Secretary," The New York Times, February 15, 2017, accessed November 6, 2017, https://www.nytimes.com/2017/02/15/us/politics/andrew-puzder-withdrew-labor-secretary.html.

31. Louis Jacobson, "Harry Reid says 82 presidential nominees have been blocked under President Barack Obama, 86 blocked under all other presidents," PolitiFact, accessed November 6, 2017, http://www.politifact.com/truth-o-meter/statements/2013/nov/22/harry-reid/harry-reid-says-82-presidential-nominees-have-been/.

32. Kenneth T. Walsh, "The First 100 Days: Franklin Roosevelt Pioneered the 100-Day Concept," U.S. News, February 12, 2009, https://www.usnews.com/news/history/articles/2009/02/12/the-first-100-days-franklin-roosevelt-pioneered-the-100-day-concept.

33. Tamara Keith, "President Franklin D. Roosevelt Set 100-Day Standard," NPR, April 21, 2017, accessed November 6, 2017, http://www.npr.org/2017/04/21/525110119/president-franklin-d-roosevelt-set-100-day-standard.

34. "#PolitiFact100: Tracking Trump's promises in first 100 days," PolitiFact, accessed November 6, 2017, http://www.politifact.com/truth-o-meter/article/2017/apr/25/politifact100-tracking-trumps-promises-first-100-d/.

35. Charles M. Cameron, Veto Bargaining: Presidents and the Politics of Negative Power (Cambridge: Cambridge University Press, 2004).

36. Terry M. Moe and William G. Howell, "Unilateral Action and Presidential Power: A Theory," Presidential Studies Quarterly 29, no. 4 (1999): 850-73,doi:10.1111/1741-5705.00070.

37. Charlie Savage, "Bush could bypass new torture ban," Boston.com National News, January 04, 2006, accessed November 06, 2017, http://archive.boston.com/news/nation/articles/2006/01/04/bush_could_bypass_new_torture_ban/.

38. Karen Tumulty, "Obama circumvents laws with 'signing statements,' a tool he promised to use lightly," The Washington Post, June 02, 2014, accessed November 6, 2017, https://www.washingtonpost.com/politics/obama-circumvents-laws-with-signing-statements-a-tool-he-promised-to-use-lightly/2014/06/02/9d76d46a-ea73-11e3-9f5c-9075d5508f0a_story.html?utm_term=.2244d0697331.

39. "Gerald R. Ford: Proclamation 4311—Granting Pardon to Richard Nixon - September 8, 1974," The American Presidency Project, accessed November 6, 2017, http://www.presidency.ucsb.edu/ws/?pid=4696.

40. "Gerald R. Ford: Proclamation 4311—Granting Pardon to Richard Nixon - September 8, 1974," The American Presidency Project, accessed November 6, 2017, http://www.presidency.ucsb.edu/ws/?pid=4696.

41. "Data, Analysis & Documentation Federal Employment Reports," U.S. Office of Personnel Management, accessed November 6, 2017, https://www.opm.gov/policy-data-oversight/data-analysis-documentation/federal-employment-reports/historical-tables/executive-branch-civilian-employment-since-1940/ (includes the 600,000 + employees working for the postal service). "Postal Facts," USPS.com, https://about.usps.com/who-we-are/postal-facts/size-scope.htm.

42. Mr. Ryan Strasser, "Emergency Powers," Legal Information Institute, July 02, 2008, accessed November 6, 2017, https://www.law.cornell.edu/wex/emergency_powers.

43. Gregory Korte, "Special report: America's perpetual state of emergency," USA Today, October 23, 2014, accessed November 6, 2017, https://www.usatoday.com/story/news/politics/2014/10/22/president-obama-states-of-emergency/16851775/.

44. Obama declares swine flu national emergency," NBCNews.com. October 25, 2009, accessed November 6, 2017, http://www.nbcnews.com/id/33459423/ns/health-cold_and_flu/t/obama-declares-swine-flu-national-emergency/.

45. Sheryl Gay Stolberg, "The Decider," The New York Times, December 23, 2006, accessed November 6, 2017, http://www.nytimes.com/2006/12/24/weekinreview/24stolberg.html.

46. "American President: Administration of the White House," Miller Center of Public Affairs University of Virginia, accessed November 6, 2017, https://web.archive.org/web/20101117160520/http://millercenter.org/academic/americanpresident/policy/whitehouse.

47. The Shadow Government, produced by Gail Flannigan (2003; United States: Educational Film Center, 2003), VHS

48. The Shadow Government, produced by Gail Flannigan (2003; United States: Educational Film Center, 2003), VHS.

49. Glenn Thrush and Maggie Haberman, "Forceful Chief of Staff Grates on Trump, and the Feeling Is Mutual," The New York Times, September 1, 2017, accessed November 6, 2017, https://www.nytimes.com/2017/09/01/us/politics/john-kelly-trump.html.

50. "Executive Orders (J.Q. Adams 1826 – Trump 2018)," The American Presidency Project, accessed November 06, 2017, http://www.presidency.ucsb.edu/executive_orders.php?year=1862.

51. Ibid.

52. "The Storm," PBS, accessed November 6, 2017, http://www.pbs.org/wgbh/pages/frontline/storm/.

53. Connie Bruck, "Why Obama Has Failed to Close Guantánamo," The New Yorker, June 19, 2017, accessed November 6, 2017, https://www.newyorker.com/magazine/2016/08/01/why-obama-has-failed-to-close-guantanamo.

54. Edward S. Corwin, The President, Office and Powers: 1787-1957; History and Analysis of Practice and Opinion (New York: New York University Press, 1962).

55. Richard E. Neustadt, Presidential Power and the Modern Presidents: the Politics of Leadership from Roosevelt to Reagan (New York: Free Press, 1991), 9.

56. Lisa Jardine, "Lyndon B Johnson: The uncivil rights reformer," The Independent, January 20, 2009, accessed November 6, 2017, http://www.independent.co.uk/news/presidents/lyndon-b-johnson-the-uncivil-rights-reformer-1451816.html, quote attributed to Doris Kerns Goodwin.

57. From video Johnson treatement.

58. Richard E. Neustadt, Presidential Power and the Modern Presidents: the Politics of Leadership from Roosevelt to Reagan (New York: Free Press, 1991), 40.

59. "The People & The Power Game: Series Overview," Seeking Solutions with Hedrick Smith, accessed June 04, 2018, http://www.hedricksmith.com/site_powergame/files/overview.html.

60. Smith, Hedrick, Philip Burton, Jr, and David Saltman. The Power Game. Video. PBS Video: Maryland Public Television, 1988.

61. Samuel Kernell, Going Public: New Strategies of Presidential Leadership (Washington, D.C.: CQ Press, 2007).

62. Ibid.

63. Ian Bogost, "Obama Was Too Good at Social Media," The Atlantic, January 6, 2017, accessed November 6, 2017, https://www.theatlantic.com/technology/archive/2017/01/did-america-need-a-social-media-president/512405/.

64. Shannon Greenwood, Andrew Perrin, and Maeve Duggan, "Social Media Update 2016," Pew Research Center: Internet, Science & Tech, November 11, 2016, accessed November 6, 2017, http://www.pewinternet.org/2016/11/11/social-media-update-2016/.

65. Jasmine C. Lee and Kevin Quealy, "Introducing the Upshot's Encyclopedia of Donald Trump's Twitter Insults," The New York Times, January 28, 2016, accessed November 6, 2017, https://www.nytimes.com/2016/01/29/upshot/introducing-the-upshots-encyclopedia-of-donald-trumps-twitter-insults.html.

66. Samuel Kernell, Going Public: New Strategies of Presidential Leadership (Washington, D.C.: CQ Press, 2007).

67. Hedrick Smith, The Power Game: How Washington Works (New York: Ballantine Books, 1996).

68. "Reelection Rates Over the Years," OpenSecrets.org, accessed November 6, 2017, https://www.opensecrets.org/overview/reelect.php.

69. George C. Edwards, Presidential Influence in Congress (San Francisco: Freeman, 1980).

70. Robert S. Erikson and Kent L. Tedin, American Public Opinion: Its Origins, Content, and Impact (New York: Pearson/Longman, 2007).

71. Robert S. Erikson and Kent L. Tedin, American Public Opinion: Its Origins, Content, and Impact (New York: Pearson/Longman, 2007).

72. Robert S. Erikson, Michael B. MacKuen, and James A. Stimson, The Macro Polity (New York: Cambridge University Press, 2006).

73. Tufte (from American Public Opinion Chapter 4).

74. Larry M. Bartels, Unequal Democracy: The Political Economy of the New Gilded Age (Princeton: Princeton University Press, 2016).

75. Gallup and CBSNews/New York Times polls, February 4, 2001 to April 21, 2005.

76. Stephen Skowronek, The Politics Presidents Make: Leadership from John Adams to George Bush (Cambridge, Mass.: Belknap Press of Harvard University, 1997).

77. Steven Mufson, "Before Trump's tax plan, there was 'voodoo economics' and 'hyperbole'," The Washington Post, December 23, 2016, accessed November 6, 2017, https://www.washingtonpost.com/business/economy/before-trumps-tax-plan-there-was-voodoo-economics-hyperbole/2016/12/21/c37c97ea-c3d2-11e6-8422-eac61c0ef74d_story.html?utm_term=.f2d28746343a.

78. Stephen Skowronek, The Politics Presidents Make: Leadership from John Adams to George Bush (Cambridge, Mass.: Belknap Press of Harvard University, 1997).

79. Cooper, Ryan. "The Electoral College Is Only Getting Worse." The Week - All you need to know about everything that matters. The Week, November 30, 2020. https://theweek.com/articles/951953/electoral-college-only-getting-worse?

CHAPTER 13
Bureaucracy: Who Is Really Doing the Work?

Chapter Objectives

1. Understand what the federal bureaucracy is and how it developed.
2. Appreciate the implications of iron triangles and issue networks.
3. Consider the impact of bureaucratic culture and interagency politics.
4. Think critically about policy implementation and the principal-agent problem.
5. Recognize the role citizens can play in improving bureaucracy.

Introduction: Chain of Command

On the night of September 11, 2012, a group of heavily armed militants launched a coordinated attack on the U.S. diplomatic mission in Benghazi, Libya. The attackers fired into the main building, setting it on fire before all U.S. personnel could escape. Among those killed were Ambassador J. Christopher Stevens and Information Management Officer Sean Smith. Stevens' death marked the first time since 1979 that an American ambassador had been killed in the line of duty. Later that same night, attackers launched mortar rounds at a nearby CIA compound, killing two more Americans. How were the militants able to evade security and fire upon U.S.-held sites? Was our own government in some way responsible for the tragic deaths of four American civil servants?

The *Federal Register* is the daily newspaper of the Federal government. The paper is published every business day by the National Archives and Records Administration and contains federal agency regulations, proposed rules and public notices, executive orders, proclamations, and other presidential documents.

Federal Register: https://www.federalregister.gov/.

These questions have been at the center of debates and congressional hearings in the years following the Benghazi attacks. While the attacks have been attributed to anti-American militants linked to al-Qaeda, investigations have focused on the U.S. government's response to the violence and how it handled the public relations aspect of the attacks.

In his book *Essence of Decision: Explaining the Cuban Missile Crisis*, Graham Allison discusses the bureaucratic challenges policymakers and government leaders face. Different groups and individuals within the government have different goals, and sometimes those goals can be at odds. Breakdowns in communication occur, turf wars are common, and critical information can fall through the cracks. Many argue the attacks at the World Trade Center and the Pentagon on September 11, 2001, could have been prevented had there been better coordination among bureaucratic agencies.

Part of the delayed reaction from the White House during the Benghazi attacks stemmed from the fact that there were conflicting reports coming out of Libya. It was unclear who had committed the attacks, and whether they were the result of a spontaneous protest or premeditated. But as far as bureaucratic institutions are concerned, there were competing interests within the State Department and Department of Defense. In addition, there are allegations about a breakdown in communication within the State Department, meaning that possibly hundreds of email requests for additional security in Benghazi prior to the attacks never reached Secretary of State Hillary Clinton. It was Clinton's job to oversee all security details at U.S. embassies, consulates, and diplomatic missions. Does the hierarchical structure of bureaucracy mean that she was ultimately responsible for the attacks? In testimony before Congress in October 2015, Clinton accepted responsibility, saying: "I take responsibility for what happened in Benghazi [but] I was not going to second-guess" the diplomatic security professionals who made decisions on what to do in Libya prior to the attacks. She denied claims that she failed to increase security at the diplomatic compound, claiming she was never directly asked to do so.[1]

Questions remain about whether the attacks in Benghazi could have been prevented by some action on the part of the American bureaucracy. What the events demonstrate is the individual and collective shortcomings of government agencies. While the hierarchical structure and formal rules of bureaucracy make the chain of accountability fairly clear-cut, better coordinated responses and a greater synchronization of goals for various groups that deal with national security could perhaps help prevent the U.S. from finding itself in another Benghazi-like situation.

13.1 What Is Bureaucracy?

iron triangles

The close-knit relationships among agencies, interest groups, and congressional subcommittees.

issue networks

Clusters of interest groups, elected leaders, consultants, think tank institutes, and policy specialists who influence policy in a complex system of relationships.

Bureaucracy is all around you. It impacts the quality of the air you breathe, the import tax on the T-shirt you are wearing, the terms of your student loans, and the type of food you eat. While bureaucracy plays an important role in our day-to-day lives, for the most part, we do not choose or elect the people who work for the bureaucracy and make the decisions that have so much influence on us. In fact, at times it seems this area of government is the least democratic and the farthest from our control. Even the president and Congress do not have absolute power over the bureaucracy. And it is supposed to be that way. In order for the work of bureaucracy to be carried out efficiently and fairly, this sector of government should be insulated from pressure from politicians and the public. This institutional design protects us to be sure, but it has also allowed for the rise of **iron triangles** and tight knit **issue networks** between agencies, interest groups, and congressional subcommittees. These informal arrangements, also called subgovernments, develop among people and groups that become accustomed to working together over time. Subsequently, the actions of these networks often go unnoticed by the press or others outside of the individuals involved and are less likely to consider the preferences of average citizens.

In this chapter, we explore the features of bureaucracy in the United States, trace its historical development, and consider some of the challenges to bureaucratic efficiency.

Features of Bureaucracy

When trying to understand what bureaucracy is, it can be useful to think about government in this way: Congress is the institution the Framers of the Constitution intended to do the work, the president is who the American public thinks does the work, and the bureaucracy is who actually does the work. In fact, the main purpose of the federal bureaucracy is to carry out the policy decisions of the president and Congress.

A bureaucracy is a way of organizing people to do work, with those on the top giving orders and those on the bottom following them. The word comes from the French *bureau-* (desk) and the Greek *-cracy* (type of government structure). The term **bureaucracy** itself refers to any large, complex administrative structure that is characterized by a hierarchical organization, job specialization, and complex, formal rules. By definition, it is not privately owned. The German sociologist Max Weber laid out the model of bureaucracy with the following characteristics:[2]

- **Hierarchy**: There is a clear chain of command and accountability in which employees report to superiors or supervisors.
- **Specialization**: Tasks are divided and handled by expert and experienced staffs.
- **Rules**: Bureaucracies and bureaucrats (those who work in a bureaucracy) are governed by explicitly defined rules. These rules limit the discretion that bureaucrats have and ensure there are operating procedures in place to create standardization and predictability.
- **Merit**: Hiring and promotions are based on experience, scores on examinations, and/or other objective criteria.

Weber's model is considered the ideal for which bureaucracies should strive. The closer bureaucracies are to this ideal, the more likely they are to achieve **neutral competence**. Neutral competence refers to the principle that bureaucracy should be depoliticized and made more professional through having government work done by experts and based on explicit standards, rather than on personal judgments or party affiliations. Competence then refers to what you know rather than what you are, who you know, or who knows you. American government has not always followed the Weber model of bureaucracy. Part of the public's disillusionment and collective distrust of government organizations stems from the early history of hiring government workers.

bureaucracy

Any large, complex administrative structure characterized by a hierarchical organization, job specialization, and complex, formal rules. It is the various departments, agencies, bureaus, commissions, and other unites of government that carry out policies.

neutral competence

The principle that bureaucracy should be depoliticized and made more professional through having government work done by experts and based on explicit standards, rather than on personal judgments or party affiliations.

13.2 The Development of the Bureaucracy

The federal bureaucracy, meaning the various departments, agencies, bureaus, commissions, and other units that carry out national policies, is rooted in the Constitution, which gives Congress the authority to make laws and the president the duty to ensure that they are implemented. But what the Constitution does not do is provide guidance about the structure of the federal bureaucracy. The Framers did not detail the organization of cabinet departments, much less the independent agencies. Congress has subsequently created executive branch agencies with the authority to execute the laws it passes, and presidents have delegated some of their policymaking obligations to various subordinate agents.

At its founding, the United States had just three cabinet departments—Treasury, Defense, and State. It has since grown into a large collection of 15 cabinet-level departments and more than 2,000 departments, agencies, bureaus, and commissions comprising over 2.9 million nonmilitary employees. The Framers could not have foreseen the massive growth of government that was prompted by social, economic, and technological change. Each new bureau, agency, department, and commission reflects the plurality of American interests and values. For example, Congress established the Department of the Interior in 1849 to manage the nation's lands and natural resources, but also to deal with the Native American tribes. The Department of Agriculture was created by Abraham Lincoln and given cabinet status by Congress in 1887 to serve the needs of farmers. In 1903, Congress created the Department of Commerce and Labor "to foster, promote and develop" the mining, manufacturing, shipping, and fishing industries as well as transportation facilities. As various groups lobbied Congress for similar treatment, it responded by creating separate departments for Labor (1913), Housing and Urban Development (1965), Transportation (1966), Energy (1977), Education (1979), Health and Human Services (1979), and Veterans Affairs (1988). The latest cabinet level department, Homeland Security, was created to increase border security, cybersecurity, and disaster management in response to the suicide attacks on September 11, 2001. The agencies represent a practical response from Congress and presidents to implement their legislative and policy agendas by delegating authority to the bureaucracy.

FIGURE 13.1 The Federal Bureaucracy

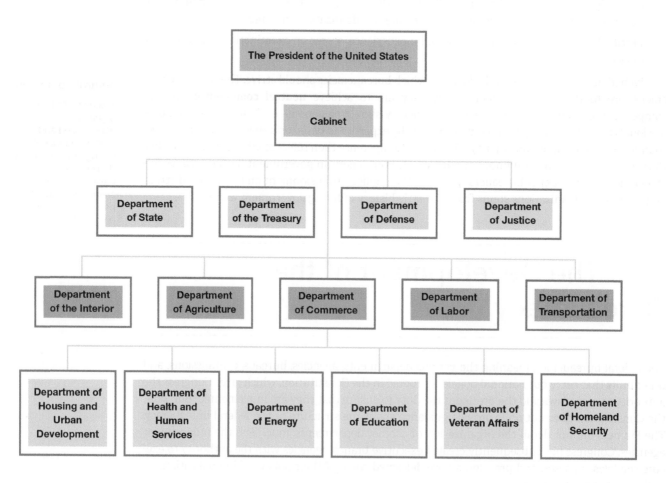

While the Framers envisioned the need to delegate to bureaucratic agencies, they did not detail how bureaucrats should be hired. Early American government focused on hiring individuals who were honest, competent, well-educated, and respected by their communities. While presidents retained the authority to dismiss officials at will, an informal system of tenure based on good behavior remained until the 1820s. The practice of hiring bureaucrats based on reputation became regarded as elitist and undemocratic. When President Andrew Jackson took office, he pushed for an end to informal tenure and argued that because the business of governing does not require experience, bureaucrats should **rotate in office**, meaning they should serve in a position for a short, fixed time and then move on to some other job, either in the public or private sector. Jackson sought to democratize the civil service, but his ideal of rotation in office also worked well to meet the very practical need of parties to reward their supporters with government positions. What developed, then, was a system of distributing jobs in bureaucratic organizations on the basis of party loyalty and personal connections to those in power. It was during this time that the notion of standard operating procedures came into use. The idea was that prescribed actions or procedures designed for routine operations would allow an inexperienced party worker to take the place of another without disrupting the smooth flow of government business.

> **rotate in office**
>
> The concept that bureaucrats should serve in a position for a short, fixed time and then move on to some other job, either in the public or private sector.

This cartoon that appeared in *Harper's Weekly* in April 1877 shows a statue of Andrew Jackson on a pig eating "plunder" while resting on the words "fraud," "bribery," and "spoils." One of President Jackson's first acts in office was to fire dozens of federal employees who had been hired by his predecessors. He replaced them with his supporters and friends.

Thomas Nast [Public domain] http://www.loc.gov/pictures/item/90710858/, via Wikimedia Commons. https://bit.ly/2G1EloG.

Patronage and the Spoils System

patronage

The practice of giving government jobs to friends and relatives of elected officials and to party loyalists.

spoils system

A hiring and promotion system based on knowing the right people.

The practice of giving government jobs to friends and relatives of elected officials and to party loyalists is known as **patronage**. In a patronage system, bureaucrats are hired as a reward for supporting successful candidates or because they have personal ties to the president or other officials. Until about 100 years ago, a person got a job with the government through the **spoils system**, a hiring and promotion system based on knowing the right people. The term takes its name from the saying, "To the victor belong the spoils of the enemy." In practice, it means those elected to office should be able to replace administrators with their own friends, family, and political supporters. The spoils system aligned with President Jackson's belief that any person of "normal" intelligence was fit to hold any government position and that government jobs should belong to the party elected by the people.

Distributing jobs on the basis of personal ties rather than expertise and experience generated incompetence, corruption, and inefficiency in many bureaucratic agencies. Congress ultimately reformed the way government jobs were filled and created the civil service system. The **civil service** refers to non-military government employees who are appointed on the basis of merit. Support for a civil service system increased dramatically as a result of the assassination of President James Garfield in 1881. Garfield was shot by Charles Guiteau because the gunman believed the president owed him a patronage position for his "vital assistance" in securing Garfield's election the previous year.[3] Garfield died two months later, and when Vice President Chester Arthur assumed the office of president, he pushed through legislation to reform the civil service. Arthur and Congress used the image of Garfield's assassin as a "disappointed office seeker" to garner support for reforming the inadequate civil service system, ultimately passing the Pendleton Civil Service Reform Act of 1883.

The cover of Puck Magazine on July 13, 1881, shows Charles Guiteau holding a gun in one hand and a note in the other that reads, "An Office or Your Life!" The caption under the cartoon read, "A Model Office Seeker" and quoted Guiteau as saying, "I am a lawyer, a theologian, and a politician." Guiteau believed he was responsible for Garfield's victory and demanded he be appointed ambassador to Paris. When Garfield refused, Guiteau shot him. Guiteau was hanged in 1882 for assassinating the president.

Published by Keppler & Schwarzmann, signed by James Albert Wales with his reversed initials (Library of Congress) [Public domain] http://www.loc.gov/pictures/item/92508892/, via Wikimedia Commons. https://bit.ly/2X4Qn64.

The **Pendleton Act of 1883** created a system in which federal employees were chosen on the basis of competitive examinations, thus basing hiring for federal positions on merit and ability. President Jimmy Carter improved the system when he urged Congress to pass the Civil Service Reform Act of 1978. Reforms included the creation of the Office of Personnel Management, the federal agency charged with the testing and hiring of most federal workers, and the Merit System Protection Board, which enforces the merit system in the federal bureaucracy. As a result, 93 percent of federal agencies today hire civil servants on the basis of the merit principle.

civil service

Non-military government employees who are appointed on the basis of merit.

Pendleton Act of 1883

Legislation that created a system in which federal employees were chosen on the basis of competitive examinations, thus basing hiring for federal positions on merit and ability.

The Hatch Act

In order to create a non-partisan civil service, government workers had to be insulated from the risk of being fired when a new party came to power. The **Hatch Act** (1939, amended most recently in 2012) limits the political activities of civil servants. Under the terms of the Hatch Act, civil servants are permitted to: 1) Vote in primary elections; 2) Contribute money to political parties; 3) Attend political rallies; and 4) Place bumper stickers on their personal property.

Bureaucracy and Democracy

Bureaucracy exists to carry out the decisions made by our political leaders. It is designed to ensure decisions made at upper levels of an organization are executed at lower levels with expertise and efficiency. When we pay income taxes, apply for student loans, or request food stamps, we deal with bureaucracy. In theory, bureaucracy is there to make our lives easier by providing structure, order, a clear set of rules, and a chain of command. This is so that when we need to get something done, we know exactly where to go, what forms to fill out, and with whom to speak. Much of the time, bureaucracy works efficiently, and we are satisfied with the outcome. But because bureaucracy is rules oriented with a rigid hierarchical system, we can also become frustrated by the many steps and length of time we endure to have our requests fulfilled. Many of the rules can seem unnecessary, and the regulations, constraints, forms, and hearings can be burdensome. We refer to these complex procedures and regulations as **red tape**, an idea that takes its name from the red tape with which English officials bound legal documents in the seventeenth century. While rules may make bureaucracy less efficient, they also increase **accountability**, the principle that bureaucratic employees should be answerable for their performance to supervisors all the way up the chain of command. Rules also help ensure decisions are implemented fairly. When we talk about fairness with respect to bureaucracy, what we mean is that bureaucrats should not privilege certain people or groups over others. Favors and special considerations should not be given to those with more money or with personal ties to policymakers or to bureaucrats themselves. Preferential treatment should also not be given to people on the basis of race, ethnicity, religion, gender, party affiliation, or sexual orientation. Fairness therefore requires a level of neutrality in bureaucracy.

Only the top-ranking officials in the federal government, such as cabinet secretaries, undersecretaries, and ambassadors to foreign countries are nominated by the president and confirmed by the Senate. These officials serve at the pleasure of elected officials. However, most bureaucrats, as we mentioned previously, were hired on the basis of merit through the civil service system. This practice allows the bureaucracy to treat citizens equally, but it also insulates the institution from political pressure. The same rules that protect federal employees from politics also make it difficult for elected officials and their appointees to weed out incompetent and unproductive workers. Thus, the civil service system must take great care in hiring to maintain quality. This feature makes it difficult for government to respond quickly to changing needs or to implement new programs by hiring more employees.

Hatch Act

Legislation that limits the political activities of civil servants. Under the terms of the Hatch Act, civil servants are permitted to: 1) Vote in primary elections; 2) Contribute money to political parties; 3) Attend political rallies; and 4) Place bumper stickers on their personal property.

red tape

A term that conveys the idea that the rules implemented by the bureaucracy are unnecessary and the regulations, constraints, forms, and hearings can be overly burdensome.

accountability

The principle that bureaucratic employees should be answerable for their performance to supervisors all the way up the chain of command, which help ensure that decisions are implemented fairly.

contempt of court

Willful disregard for the authority of a court of law.

Bureaucrats must not bring personal beliefs and preferences into their jobs. They are required to carry out policies made by the government. If they cannot fulfill those policies for whatever reason, they must remove themselves from their positions. But there are times when personal beliefs clash with governmental policies. This was the case with Kim Davis, the county clerk for Rowan County, Kentucky. Part of Davis's job as county clerk was to issue marriage licenses. When the U.S. Supreme Court made same-sex marriage legal in the *Obergefell v. Hodges* (2015) decision, county clerks were required by law to issue marriage licenses to same-sex couples. Davis has a moral objection to same-sex marriage and defied the federal court order to issue the marriage licenses. Davis began refusing to issue any licenses to anyone. Four couples filed a lawsuit against Davis and, in response, the U.S. District Court ordered Davis to issue licenses in compliance with the law. Davis continued to defy the court order and refused to issue marriage licenses, claiming that she was acting "under God's authority."[4] As a result of her defiance, she was arrested and held in **contempt of court** because of her willful disregard for the authority of a court of law. She was held in jail for five days. When she returned to work, Davis agreed to not interfere with her deputies, who had begun issuing licenses as directed by the court order.

The county registrar provides marriage licenses, which are required for any couple wishing to enter a legally recognized marriage. Marriage licenses were originally introduced to prevent interracial marriages.

© Shutterstock, Inc.

13.3 Major Elements and Roles of the Federal Bureaucracy

The federal government employs nearly 3 million people.[5] This number increases to 17 million if state and local public employees are included. Most of the civilians who are employed by the federal government work in the executive branch, the home of the federal bureaucracy. In this section, we look at how bureaucracy is organized and consider the various functions it performs.

FIGURE 13.2 Number of Federal Employees vs. State and Local Government Employees, 1939-2017
Source: Federal Reserve Bank of St. Louis

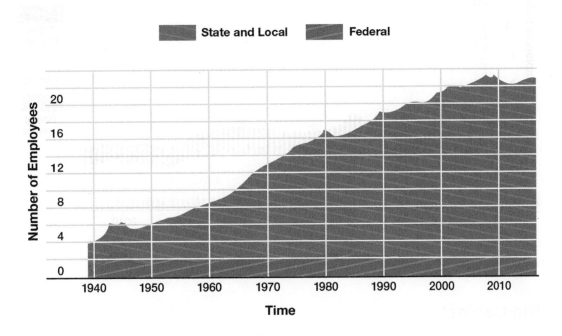

Based on "By the numbers, a story of the federal worker and the size of government." https://bit.ly/2CRT1T6.

Organization of the Federal Bureaucracy

The bureaucracy is comprised of four major groups of administrative agencies: the 15 cabinet departments; the independent agencies; independent regulatory boards and commissions; and government corporations.

FIGURE 13.3 Federal Employment 1939-2016
Note: Federal jobs have been a mostly downward trend for three decades. Source: Federal Reserve Bank of St. Louis.

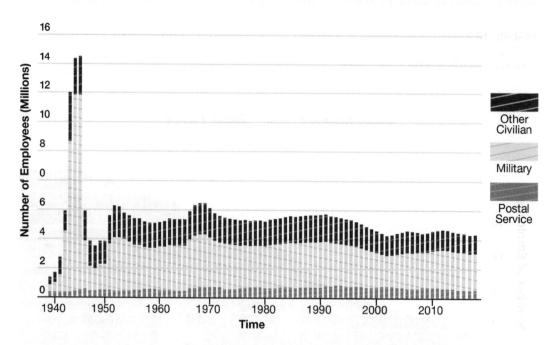

Based on "By the numbers, a story of the federal worker and the size of government."https://bit.ly/2CRT1T6.

The Cabinet

Cabinet

The presidential advisory body, traditionally composed of the heads of the 15 executive departments and other officers the president may choose.

The **Cabinet** is the presidential advisory body, traditionally composed of the heads of the executive departments and other officers the president may choose. The head of each department is known as the secretary, except for the Justice Department, which is headed by the attorney general. Together, the department secretaries serve as the president's cabinet. Department secretaries are appointed by the president with the approval of the Senate to provide advice on areas of government policy including national security, education, finance, and transportation. Cabinet members can be removed by the president. Removal can occur on the rare occasions when a member of the president's cabinet is said to have "gone native," that is, when a cabinet member places his or her department's priorities above the president's.

Independent Agencies

An **independent agency** is an agency created by Congress that operates outside the 15 executive departments in the cabinet. Independent agencies also have a narrower policy focus than the cabinet departments. While often referred to as "independent executive agencies," these agencies operate outside the executive departments (Cabinet), but are nonetheless considered part of the executive branch of government. These independent agencies exist outside of the Cabinet department structure for several reasons, including: 1) their functions do not fit well into any of the existing departments; 2) to insulate their officials from political pressures; 3) to make them more responsive to interest-group demands; and 4) their functions are sensitive. Examples of independent agencies include the CIA, the Environmental Protection Agency, and the Social Security Administration. Independent agencies are structured like the Cabinet departments with a single head administrator who is appointed by the president. While these agencies are independent of cabinet departments, they vary in their independence from the president. When Congress disagrees with the president, it can limit presidential control by creating agencies that have fixed term appointments that do not overlap with the president's. Congress can also remove financial oversight of the agency from the Office of Management and Budget (OMB).[6] Congress also insulates some independent agencies from judicial review, meaning that the decisions of some agencies can be challenged by the courts, while others cannot be.[7]

> **independent agency**
>
> An agency created by Congress that operates outside the 15 executive departments in the cabinet. Independent agencies also have a narrower policy focus than the cabinet departments.

Independent Regulatory Boards and Commissions

Independent regulatory boards and commissions are created to regulate important aspects of the nation's businesses, industry, and economy. An example is the Food and Drug Administration (FDA), an independent regulatory agency intended to promote public health by overseeing food and drug safety. Some of the regulatory agencies are bureaus within Cabinet departments like the FDA, which is located in the Department of Health and Human Services. All independent regulatory boards and commissions are set up to be quasi-legislative bodies that operate largely outside presidential control. The members of the boards and commissions are nominated by the president and are confirmed by the Senate for long, staggered terms. In order to protect the boards and commissions from political influence, Congress requires that they must be made up of members of both parties and that members cannot be removed for political reasons. The president also cannot fire the heads of regulatory boards and commissions. Members of these agencies often have extensive experience working in the industry they regulate while on the commission.

> **independent regulatory boards and commissions**
>
> Agencies created to regulate important aspects of the nation's businesses, industry, and economy.

Congress has an interest in keeping these agencies independent of presidential control because individual presidents can vary in their opinions of how much certain businesses and industries should be regulated. These opinions frequently follow partisan lines. Republicans, for example, believe in limited regulation, preferring instead to leave control of the industry to the market. As a result, Republican presidents tend to appoint business people sympathetic to the industry being regulated. While Republicans believe that individuals need minimal protection from the workings of a free and competitive market, Democrats prefer to protect the interests of workers and consumers. Thus, they tend to appoint agency heads who have experience and scientific expertise. While independent regulatory boards and commissions are intended to be insulated from political pressures, the commissions are said to be "captured" when they serve to unduly protect the interests of the industry they regulate (rather than the public interest).[8]

The Government Corporations

Government corporations provide services to the public that the private sector could, in theory, handle. These corporations are within the executive branch and operate under the control of the president. The president appoints their top officers with Senate confirmation. The Postal Service is an example of a government corporation. The business of delivering the mail was handled by a government corporation so that mail would reach even the most remote parts of the country where delivery service might not be profitable for a private company. Private companies such as UPS and FedEx that do provide mail delivery services, and do so with efficiency and competitive pricing, have put the U.S. Postal Service in crisis. The competition, combined with the reality that there is less demand for traditional postal services in the era of electronic communications, has led to downsizing by the Postal Service in an effort to save money.[9]

While these government corporations exist to generate revenue for the government and to serve the public interest, there is some debate about whether these corporations are compatible with the democratic government's requirement that all public agencies be accountable to the public. Because the public is relatively quiet in speaking up for its interests, government corporations tend to be more responsive to pressures from bureaucrats, interest groups, and congressional committees.

13.4 Roles of the Federal Bureaucracy

Bureaucrats are charged with implementing the laws and policies passed by Congress and the president. But not only does bureaucracy administer the laws, it also effectively determines compliance with laws. Most laws are written in vague language, which is subject to interpretation. For example, the Americans with Disabilities Act prohibits discrimination against individuals with disabilities in jobs, schools, transportation, and all places that are open to the general public. It requires all employers, schools, and service providers to provide reasonable accommodations to people with disabilities without causing undue hardship to the employer, school, or provider. But what qualifies as a disability? What constitutes "reasonable accommodation"? And who determines "undue hardship?" Other laws are vague because they were written in a hurry, amended at the last minute, or avoided addressing difficult questions in order to placate critics. In cases where these gaps exist, it falls to the bureaucrats to make judgments about *how* to implement a law or policy. Bureaucratic power can therefore be much broader, making issues of control and accountability critical. This power is embodied in two main roles that bureaucrats play: administration and rulemaking.

Bureaucracy as Administration

When bureaucrats act as administrators, they simply carry out laws made elsewhere in government. This occurs when the postal service delivers the mail on time or when the Internal Revenue Service collects the proper amount of taxes. We look to bureaucracy to provide these services professionally, neutrally, and efficiently.

Bureaucracy as Rulemaking

However, the idea that bureaucrats are unbiased or impartial may be unrealistic. Bureaucrats actually have a significant amount of influence when it comes to implementing government policies and laws. This independence is greatest when policies and laws leave room for interpretation as to how they should be carried out. Administrators frequently must use **bureaucratic discretion**, or their own judgment, to interpret and implement laws. For example, it falls to bureaucrats to decide how makers of packaged snacks and candies go about listing the calories on their products, how many park rangers to assign to the Grand Canyon, or whether the newest sugar substitute in soft drinks is safe to consume. The bureaucracy is tasked with writing the rules that determine compliance with the laws and policies passed by Congress. Once an agency has devised a rule, it sends the rule to the Office of Management and Budget (OMB). After approval from the OMB, the rule is published in the **Federal Register**, the daily journal of the federal government. Anyone who is interested in the rule can comment. The agency then reviews all the public comments, makes revisions, and proposes a **final rule** that, after being reviewed again by the OMB, gets published in the Federal Register.

Lobbyists work closely with agencies during the rule-making process to ensure that the interests of specific industries are protected. Competing interests can mean that the rules are never really final, however, and citizens, groups, and firms that do not agree with a rule can sue the agency for misinterpreting Congress' intent. This happened in October 2015 when a coalition of 24 states and a coal mining company sued the Obama administration over the Clean Power Plan, a coal plant emission rule that proposed a 32 percent cut in the power sector's carbon emissions by 2030 compared with 2005 levels. The litigants accused the Environmental Protection Agency (EPA) of overstepping its authority by ordering a significant transformation of states' electricity generation, moving away from fossil fuels like coal and toward lower-carbon sources like wind and solar power. Coal producers felt threatened by the rule, arguing that it would hurt their livelihood and raise power rates for consumers.[10] Each state has been assigned a specific emissions goal based on its unique circumstances, with flexibility in how the goals are met. In 2017, President Trump signed the Executive Order on Energy Independence, which calls for a review of the Clean Power Plan.[11]

Some cases are controversial enough that they gain public attention, but most rule-making happens behind the scenes and out of public view. The rules that bureaucracies make have a direct impact on our day-to-day lives. These rules affect unemployment benefits, air quality, and food supply. How democratic are these rules when the public is often unaware of them and they can be influenced by industries and clientele groups? We address this question in the next section.

13.5 Understanding Bureaucracies

Iron Triangles and Issue Networks

When executive branch agencies, groups, and congressional committees all depend on one another and are in close, frequent, "cozy" contact, they form iron triangles or subgovernments. The three legs are often composed of bureaucratic agencies, interest groups, and congressional subcommittees. The iron triangle is characterized by mutual dependency and extensive collective power in which each element shares key services and specialized information with the others to further their common goal. When this occurs, the triangle becomes relatively impermeable to intervention from Congress, the president, or the public.

bureaucratic discretion

Bureaucrats use their own judgment at times to interpret and implement laws.

Federal Register

The daily journal of the federal government.

final rule

The rule that emerges after an agency reviews all the public comments and makes revisions.

In Federalist No. 10, James Madison warned about the "mischiefs of faction" but argued that this mischief would be tempered by the diversity of interests in a large republic. What he did not foresee was the development of groups that would receive concentrated benefits from relatively closed networks operating for mutual support. Figure 13.4 illustrates the concept of how each point of the iron triangle is a relationship of reciprocation with the others.

FIGURE 13.4 The Iron Triangle

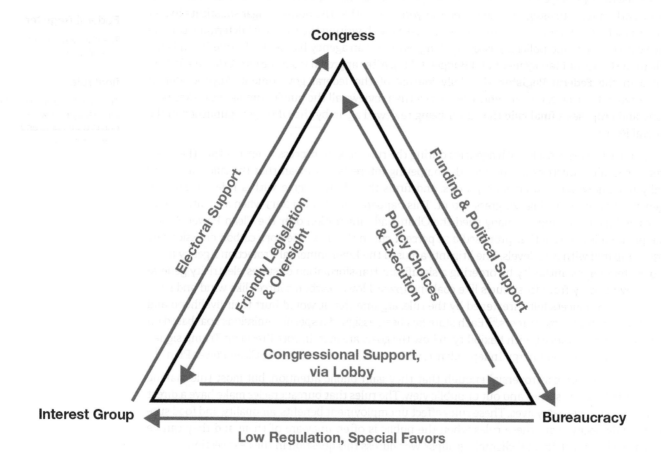

To better understand how iron triangles operate, consider the example of the corn industry. Yields of corn in the United States are extremely high. In fact, the United States produces so much corn that the market price is actually less than the cost of growing the corn. Economic theories of supply and demand say that when the price of an item falls below the cost of production, the supply needs to be scaled back. That is not what happens with corn in the United States. In order to sustain the flow of cheap corn, the government gives cash subsidies to farmers that make up the difference between their cost to produce the corn and the market price for the commodity. As a result, farmers have further increased the production of corn. Why does this happen?

There is a close-knit relationship, or iron triangle, between congressional agricultural subcommittees, corn processors, and the Department of Agriculture. In order to justify the existence of this iron triangle, we have invented new uses for corn. Corn now shows up in various forms in everything from food to cosmetics to cars. Farmers and processors obviously benefit from the fact that corn is so versatile. But the fact that corn is showing up in so many products, and in particular in the food we eat, can have negative consequences. Because corn is so cheap, the food products that use corn are inexpensive on a cost/calorie basis, so they can be offered as dollar menu items and in extremely large sizes (supersizes). This means that a family on a budget can make their money go further and their bellies feel fuller going through the drive-through of a fast food chain rather than walking into a grocery store and buying fresh vegetables and meat to cook. The availability of cheap corn and products such as high fructose corn syrup has increased the rates of obesity and diseases like diabetes.[12] Malnutrition and food insecurity have also increased in those countries whose own agriculture cannot compete with cheap U.S. corn.[13] The problem of illegal immigration to the Unites States is also compounded by the existence of the corn iron triangle. It is less expensive for consumers in countries like Mexico to buy U.S. corn than to purchase corn grown domestically. In fact, corn from the United States is sold in Mexico at 25 percent less than it costs to produce. Mexican farmers are deprived of their livelihoods, as they cannot compete with such prices.[14] Desperation drives many of them across the border illegally in search of work.

Relationships can actually be more complex than the iron triangle idea suggests and, in many policy areas, iron triangles have given way to "issue networks."[15] Iron triangles assume a relationship among a fixed interest group, a fixed agency, and a fixed congressional subcommittee. The notion of issue networks posits that the relationships do not always fit neatly into a fixed triangle. There are instead clusters of interest groups, elected leaders, consultants, think tank institutes, and policy specialists who influence policy in a complex system of relationships. The tobacco industry is a good example of an iron triangle that has morphed into an issue network.

Progress in tobacco control policy was halted for almost 30 years because cigarette manufacturers convinced key entities in each arm of the tobacco iron triangle that their interests aligned with those of the manufacturers. This began to change between 1997 and 2007. The agriculture arm of the triangle realized its interests no longer overlapped with the manufacturers as the result of a decline in demand for U.S. tobacco leaf by cigarette manufacturers, as well as national changes in the tobacco market structure. The political distancing of the former agricultural-manufacturer allies left room for tobacco control advocacy. In some tobacco-growing states, agricultural interests responded to national-level changes by "shifting from staunch advocacy for manufacturer positions on tobacco control towards neutral positions to better represent their farming constituency's interests."[16] The lack of opposition from these groups opened the iron triangle into an issue network that included public health groups, who would push for stronger tobacco control policies in tobacco-growing states.

Bureaucratic Culture

Bureaucracies are influenced by internal agency politics. These internal politics give rise to what is known as **bureaucratic culture,** or the accepted values, assumptions, and procedures of an organization. A certain way of thinking or doing things develops in any place of employment. Over time, roles become standardized and practices become ritualized. In many ways, bureaucratic culture is like any other workplace culture. Its consequences, however, can have important impacts. Before we address that, we need to understand the four main elements of bureaucratic culture.

bureaucratic culture

The accepted values, assumptions, and procedures of an organization.

Bureaucratic Behavior

Part of learning to function in a bureaucracy is learning the rules of the game. Because structures are hierarchical, the chain of command is quickly discerned and pleasing those in charge becomes a priority, sometimes at the expense of serving the public good. Obedience, cooperation, and conformity are rewarded in bureaucratic agencies. Standard operating procedures ensure uniformity in behavior. Bureaucrats, especially those working in specialized departments, also have a specific way of speaking known as **bureaucratese**. This formal language uses acronyms and other linguistic shortcuts by bureaucrats to convey information efficiently. While bureaucratese can ease the

bureaucratese

The formal language that bureaucrats use to convey information efficiently.

flow of information between specialists, it can decrease understanding of important policy matters for ordinary citizens who do not share the distinctive language. At worst, the careful selection of words and verb tenses can obscure meaning and serve the purpose of avoiding responsibility.

Specialization, Commitment, and Agency Point of View

Power in bureaucracy comes from expertise in a particular area or doing a particular job. Bureaucrats are valued for their highly specialized knowledge in specific policy areas. This specialization and expertise mean that bureaucrats are often better equipped than politicians and the public to make certain policy decisions. In specific organizations, bureaucrats share a commitment to the particular policy agenda of their agency. For example, bureaucrats in the National Institutes of Health (NIH) share a commitment to policy issues such as cancer research and disparities in access to health care. Policy commitment binds the organization together and ensures that everyone within the agency shares the same primary goals.

agency point of view

Identification with the organization.

More generally, bureaucrats develop an **agency point of view**, or identification with their organization. The phrase "where you stand depends on where you sit" applies here. Bureaucrats can become so committed to their agency's policy agenda, so tied to its rules and structures, and so indoctrinated in the belief of the value of expertise and specialization that they begin to see their own agency's work as being more important than the work of others. They identify so closely with the organization that their beliefs and values become shaped by the agency's mission. This commitment becomes so serious that it takes precedence for those working in a particular agency. That means that a bureaucrat at the NIH will prioritize health research over agricultural issues or national security.

Turf Wars

turf wars

When bureaucrats become entrenched in agency points of view and become so consumed with advancing their agency's policy goals, they can end up fighting for that position even when it may not lead to the best outcome for the country.

Bureaucratic culture breeds commitment, shared values, and loyalty. It also creates camaraderie and can raise morale. It ensures that individuals within an organization work collaboratively toward a common goal. But bureaucratic culture can also lead to **turf wars**. These frequently occur when bureaucrats become entrenched in agency points of view and become so consumed with advancing their agency's policy goals that they fight for that position even when it may not lead to the best outcome for the country. Agencies are concerned with protecting themselves and their programs, and they compete with others to capture as many federal resources as possible, ensure the survival of their organizations, and protect their policy jurisdictions. Turf wars are common between the State Department and the Department of Defense, with the former approaching national security issues from a diplomatic perspective and the latter responding with military strategies.

Were Hillary Clinton's emails classified? Where you stand depends on where you sit. For the CIA, you can never be too cautious. Because the agency is in the business of intelligence collection and analysis, its culture and procedures demand a conservative approach to classification. Much of its work is done clandestinely and in secret. It makes sense that the CIA would want to keep as much as possible classified. The State Department is different: it does much of its work in public and with other countries. The department often has to share sensitive information with foreigners and conducts diplomacy in public places like restaurants, parks, and on the telephone. Thus, the department has a different approach to secrecy and what information should be classified. For the CIA, classification is necessary for it to get its work done; for the State Department, classification can keep diplomats from being able to get their work done. Thus, the interpretation of the Clinton email scandal very much depends on what perspective one adopts.

Senior Airman Nichelle Anderson [Public domain], via Wikimedia Commons. https://bit.ly/2HD3vLQ.

These turf wars can also lead to a breakdown in communication, as we saw in the Benghazi example that opens this chapter. Turf wars and bureaucratic culture also likely played a role in the failure of law enforcement and intelligence agencies to prevent the events of September 11, 2001. According to her testimony before the Senate Judiciary Committee in June 2002, former FBI agent Colleen Rowley claims that her office in Minneapolis knew that a suspected terrorist was trying to take flying lessons. When field officers in her office tried to get warrants to search the suspect's computer, they were accused of going over the heads of their superiors and were denied. Bureaucratic culture and turf wars also kept the FBI and the CIA from sharing critical information. Between them, the agencies had enough information leading up to the attacks to piece together the puzzle and "connect the dots."

The commission investigating the 9/11 terrorist attacks found that federal agencies were unprepared and failed to respond effectively. Communication among agencies broke down in crucial moments and, in some cases, government officials intentionally circumvented bureaucratic operating procedures.

Anthony Correia / Shutterstock.com

Part of the reason they failed to share information has to with their individual cultures. The FBI is a law enforcement agency that, prior to 9/11, was focused on after-the-fact investigations and convictions rather than on terrorism prevention.[17] The CIA instead focuses on clandestine activities to acquire intelligence and information about non-American groups. It is concerned with plans and intentions and rewards building relationships rather than recognizing individual achievements. The difference in culture between the two agencies is such that they almost speak entirely different languages, making the sharing of information that much more difficult.[18] Because of agency expertise and specialization, Congress, the president, and the public look to bureaucracy to recognize and interpret early warning signals. When the bureaucratic experts fail, the results can be catastrophic.

13.6 Policy Implementation and the Principal-Agent Problem

In previous chapters, we have discussed the fact that the policies the government provides depend on who is in power (and what their preferences are) and on the kinds of political institutions that are in place. In these discussions, we have assumed a direct, uninterrupted link between voter preferences, the government that is elected, and the policies implemented. In the real world, this is not necessarily the case. While government devises and enacts the policies, it relies on the bureaucracy to implement them. Quite apart from the challenges of iron triangles and issue networks, the government does not have absolute control over the bureaucrats because of the problems of delegation and monitoring.

If the government decides it would be good to have cleaner air, it can pass legislation to provide for smog tests and fuel efficiency standards, but it has to delegate someone (other than legislators) to go around and make sure the cars are being tested and that fuel efficiency standards are being met.

If the government wants to improve schools, it can pass legislation that provides for teacher review and standardized student testing, but it has to delegate someone (other than legislators) to make sure that teachers are being reviewed in a meaningful way and that tests are being developed and administered to students.

The point is that the government can make laws and issue policies, but it is dependent on the bureaucracy to whom it must delegate the responsibility of implementing these policies. And as we have covered earlier in the chapter, agencies have bureaucratic discretion when it comes to how these laws and policies will be implemented. The analytical crux of the issue is called the **principal-agent problem**. This arises any time that one person (the principal—in this case, Congress) hires or entrusts someone else (the agent—the bureaucracy) to do a task for them. If the principal could perfectly monitor what the agent was doing and sanction the agent if the agent were not doing a good job, then there would not be a principal-agent problem. However, principals and their agents rarely have exactly the same interests. Given different interests, the principal must expend time and effort to monitor the behavior of the agent.

This is a very important problem in politics. It is also an issue in our everyday lives. Consider the following example. Let's say the authors of this textbook have just completed the manuscript, and they would like to hire a student as a research assistant to help with the index. Let's say they agree to pay the student $15 an hour. The student agrees to work as long as it takes to finish the index. The authors' goal, of course, is to have a comprehensive and useful index completed as quickly and cheaply as possible. The student's goal is to produce a quality product, but he or she also wants to make money, which means taking as much time as possible. The student may also enjoy going for coffee, working slowly, and making phone calls, all "on the clock." The authors could monitor the student, say by looking over his or her shoulder or locking the student in a room with a camera. But if the authors had the time to watch over the student, they would not have needed to hire the student in the first place. And locking the student in a room is not really practical and probably not legal. The problem that results stems from what economists call **asymmetric information**: the student knows how hard he or she is working, but the authors do not.

And the problem is more complicated still. Suppose the authors think the job should take 30 hours and are prepared to pay $450. After 30 hours, the student tells the authors that because of a computer crash, he or she needs another 10 hours to finish the job. How should the authors respond? The problem is the student's performance is a function of two things: effort (for which the authors want to pay him or her) and luck (which neither the authors nor the student can control). If the student underperforms and does not get the job done in the allotted time, the authors have no way of knowing if this underperformance was caused by lack of effort or bad luck. It is not just the information that is asymmetric (the student knows how much he or she has worked and the authors don't); it is also that the work product (the only thing the authors can observe) is a function of a combination of effort and luck. Even if the student genuinely works hard, bad luck might get in the way. The authors want to reward the hard work and not penalize the bad luck, but how can they be sure it is bad luck and not low effort? The answer is that they can't.

Problems like this frequently arise. A farm hires a manager to run his farm and the yield is low. Is this because the manager did not work hard or because of poorly timed rains? The president orders the Drug Enforcement Agency to make war on drugs, yet the crime rate stays the same. Is this because the agency was lax or because a crack cocaine surge engulfed the nation's cities? The government contracts with a company to build a road, and it goes way over budget. Is this because the company took too much profit or because of unforeseen expenses? An added wrinkle in the last example is the company will have incentives to behave in ways that increase costs it will not have to bear. For example, engaging in risky construction practices might save the company money but might result in costly repairs, which the government will have to pay to perform. The construction company will pocket the savings. Thus, the company bears none of the risk and reaps all the

principal-agent problem

The problem that arises when Congress entrusts the bureaucracy to do a task. Congress is unable to perfectly monitor what the bureaucracy is doing.

asymmetric information

The idea that the bureaucratic agent has more information such that Congress does not have complete information about how hard the bureaucracy is working.

moral hazard

A situation in which one party bears little of the risk and reaps most of the potential gains while the other party incurs most of the cost.

potential gains in what economists call **moral hazard.** The issue of moral hazard was relevant when, in 2008, the U.S. Treasury decided to bail out banks in the financial crisis. Bail outs were necessary to stabilize the economy. However, bailing out banks that made risky loans sends the message that, next time, if you make a risky loan and it works out, you get to keep the profits, but if it goes bad, the government will step in and pay you back.

In sum, the policy implementation problem holds that while government enacts the policies, it has to rely on the bureaucracy to implement them. When it does so, it encounters the principal-agent problem. President Richard Nixon's "war on drugs" illustrates the fact that agency loss is a more serious problem for government because of the complexity of societal problems and the difficulty of measuring the performance of public agencies. Should the Drug Enforcement Agency target drug users to pad the number of arrests and make the president happy, or should it take on the more difficult task of catching the dealers or suppliers of illegal drugs? How does the government deal with this?

In sum, the crux of the policy implementation problem is that government enacts the policies, but it has to rely on the bureaucracy to implement them. When it does so, it encounters the principal-agent problem. President Richard Nixon's "war on drugs" illustrates the fact that agency loss is a more serious problem for government because of the complexity of societal problems and the difficulty of measuring the performance of public agencies. Should the Drug Enforcement Agency target drug users to pad the number of arrests and make the president happy, or should it take on the more difficult task of catching the dealers or suppliers of illegal drugs? How does the government deal with this?

The government has responded in part by creating the General Accounting Office (GAO), an independent, nonpartisan agency that works for Congress. Often called the "congressional watchdog," the GAO investigates how the federal government spends taxpayer dollars. The government also addresses the principal-agent problem by encouraging bureaucracies to compete with each other for limited federal resources and offering performance bonuses. In addition, the government has outsourced or privatized some jobs. The advantage of this is that private firms can be sued in court if they do meet the terms of their contracts. None of these are perfect remedies because the underlying conditions of the principal-agent problem cannot be eliminated. It is important to study the policy formation process, but we cannot assume that policies formed are policies enacted.

13.7 Who Does the Bureaucracy Work For?

Issues of oversight and monitoring, closed iron triangles, and issue networks raise the important question: for whom does the bureaucracy work? It is charged with implementing the laws and policies determined by government and, in doing so, provides essential services and benefits to the public. But just how responsive is the bureaucracy to government? How responsive is it the American public? In this final section, we consider the relationship between bureaucracy, the president, Congress, and citizens.

The President

According to the Constitution, the president should control the bureaucracy. As you learned in the previous chapter, one of the president's jobs is bureaucrat in chief. The president is vested with **overhead democracy**: the people elect the president, who controls the bureaucracy from the top.

The president has five main powers in dealing with the bureaucracy: appointment power, budget, veto power, government restructuring, and power of the office of the president.

overhead democracy

The people elect the president, who controls the bureaucracy from the top.

Appointment Power

The president appoints the heads and the next layer or two of undersecretaries for the Cabinet and for several of the independent agencies. The president tries to minimize agency problems by nominating qualified and competent individuals to head executive branch agencies. The Senate further scrutinizes these individuals during the confirmation process. Recent presidents have sought to expand their control by increasing the number of their appointees at the top levels of agencies, especially those agencies whose goals are not aligned with the administration's policy agenda.[19]

Budget

Bureaucratic agencies submit their budget requests to the Office of Management and Budget, which can lower or raise departmental budget requests. The budget, which is then sent on to Congress, is a good indication of the president's policy objectives and priorities. Congress, however, has the power to add on, cut back, or reject completely the president's budget requests. This often happens, especially when strong interest group and congressional support coincide with agency requests.

Veto Power

One of the most important presidential powers is the veto. Presidents can use the veto to defeat legislation, but they can also use it to influence the bureaucracy. For agencies eager to protect their resources and ensure their survival, complying with the president's policy requests to avoid any backlash that may result from a veto may be in their best self-interest.

Government Restructuring

The president can reorganize the bureaucracy, create new agencies, fold some agencies into others, and eliminate organizations all together. This restructuring needs to have congressional approval, but it is another way for the president to exert control and signal his or her policy preferences.

Power of the Office

Presidents can use the presidential office and the power and influence that comes from being the highest ranking American to persuade bureaucracies to support presidential initiatives.

While the president has authority over the bureaucracy, the relationship between the president and bureaucracy has historically been defined by frustration. President John Kennedy expressed this when he said, "Dealing with bureaucracy is like trying to nail jelly to the wall." When

President Nixon attempted to reorganize the bureaucracy, the *New York Times* observed that, "The President is bound and determined to run the Government. On the evidence of past experience, such an effort is laudably, but almost laughably, optimistic. Other Administrations have sought to harness the mixed allegiances of the vast department bureaucracies, answerable in fact to Congress and their own special constituencies as well as the White House."[20]

The reality is that it can take a long time for a presidential directive to be put into action. This is due in part to the structure of bureaucracy and in part to the fact that the bureaucracy's different perspectives and goals can often clash with the president's agenda.

Bureaucracy and Congress

congressional oversight

The process through which Congress monitors agency rule making, enforcement, and implementation of laws and policies.

Although it was not designed to be this way, Congress actually has more control over the bureaucracy than the president does. This power does not derive from the Constitution, but instead from the informal relationships that have developed over time and have become institutionalized by the existence of iron triangles and issue networks. Congress has the power of **congressional oversight** through which it monitors agency rule making, enforcement, and implementation of laws and policies. It uses this power to conduct hearings to make sure its laws and policies are being faithfully executed. More often, its committees and subcommittees use their investigative powers to follow-up on complaints received from citizens, businesses, and other institutions regarding the actions of the agencies within their policy domain. Bureaucratic oversight is significant because agency heads will precondition their actions according to congressional wishes to prevent their agencies from being investigated. Congress' most important power over the bureaucracy is formal. Congress funds bureaucratic operations and passes the laws that agencies implement. Congress also has the last say because it writes the laws and has the power to deny funding to any agency or program that resists its directives.

Still, members of Congress can be divided on their policy agendas and priorities. When these divisions occur, congressional control over the bureaucracy can be less effective. Bureaucratic agencies are most sensitive and responsive to those congressional committees that deal with the same goals that they do. The preferences of congressional committees and subcommittees may not reflect the interests of Congress as a whole, and so when bureaucratic agencies are responsive to particular committees and subcommittees, they may be ignoring Congress, the president, and the public.

Bureaucracy and the Public Interest

Bureaucracy is an institution designed to link the government and the people. The people delegate to government the task of passing laws and policies that will keep order and provide public benefits. The government then delegates to bureaucracy the task of implementing those laws and policies that will keep order and provide public benefits. The public should therefore be at the very center of all that bureaucracy does. The bureaucracy should serve the public and be answerable to the public. But when it comes to policymaking and implementation, the bureaucracy is frequently criticized for not being responsive to the public interest. Average citizens and consumers are not well organized and may not even know they will be affected by a law until it has already been implemented. Much of what the bureaucracy does is too technical for direct public involvement, or the policy making process is so obscure that ordinary citizens are effectively excluded. Most of the time, citizens are willing to delegate control to the bureaucracy. But when the bureaucracy missteps, becomes mired in scandal and mistakes, or engages in fraudulent activity, public mistrust and criticism rear their heads and the public is quick to charge the bureaucracy as corrupt and unresponsive.

It is true that iron triangles and issue networks can have negative consequences on society's well-being, but in defense of bureaucracy, it is not always easy to determine what the public interest is. Is public interest the majority preference? If so, what happens to the minority? Again, we see that the political conflict between diversity of values and scarcity of resources is critical to defining public interest and public good.

To truly have our finger on the pulse of public interest, more citizens need to be involved in the policy process. The reality is that those who are most vocal, are best organized, and have the greatest financial support are the ones most likely to be heard by the bureaucracy. Perhaps one way to make the bureaucracy more responsive to public interest is to bring more people into the policymaking process. One of the benefits of the expansion of government and the increase in the number of bureaucratic agencies is that there are many points of entry for citizens who want to be involved in public policy. People can seek employment in the public sector at multiple levels of government, with the greatest number of jobs being available at the state and local level.

But it is not necessary to be employed by the bureaucracy to have more access to policy implementation. In response to demands that the bureaucracy be more accessible to the public, Congress passed the **Freedom of Information Act** (FOIA) in 1966. The Act gives citizens access to agency and department deliberations. While there are some documents and information that are kept classified for reasons such as national security concerns, FOIA facilitates full or partial disclosure of government files. To further increase transparency, the government passed **sunshine laws**, which make meetings, records, votes, deliberations, and other official actions open to public attendance, participation, and/or viewing. These laws also require government meetings to be held with sufficient advance notice and at times and in places that are accessible to the public (with exceptions for emergency meetings).

The Freedom of Information Act provides the public the right to request access to records held by government agencies, such as food safety reports and the provision of health care. The public can request the disclosure of any information as long as it does not fall under one of nine exemptions, such as personal privacy, national security, and law enforcement.

Do research and determine if you need to make a FOIA request, then get ready.

FOIA.gov: https://www.foia.gov/#agency-search.

Freedom of Information Act

A 1966 law that gives citizens access to agency and department deliberations.

sunshine laws

Legislation passed in 1976 that makes meetings, records, votes, deliberations, and other official actions open to public attendance, participation, and/or viewing. These laws also require government meetings to be held with sufficient advance notice and at times and in places that are accessible to the public (with exceptions for emergency meetings).

If the bureaucracy is working to become more transparent and it is easier for the public to get involved in the policy process, why do so few Americans seek access to the bureaucracy? Politicians and the media have a tendency to promote negative images that convey the idea that bureaucracy is big, top-heavy, bloated, too complex, and too closely tied to special interests. As a result, the public does not have a favorable opinion of the bureaucracy or the government.

For bureaucracy to improve, the public must be involved. This is one area of government in which your participation can have a direct, positive impact. If we want the bureaucracy to be more responsive and to better serve our interests, there are some simple actions we can take. We need to have realistic expectations about what the government can do and the services it can provide, but if we have an issue of concern, we should contact bureaucratic agencies and voice our opinions. When we vote for elected officials, we should think about the bureaucratic appointments they are likely to make and how these appointments will impact the policies that will be implemented. Citizens can increase responsiveness by taking advantage of opportunities for gaining access to bureaucratic decision-making.

13.8 What Can I Do?

A vibrant, functioning bureaucracy is essential for a healthy democracy. As you learned in this chapter, bureaucracy is responsible for implementing the policies passed by the officials and representatives we elect to government. If you want to be involved in that implementation process and play a role in addressing pressing issues from poverty to homeland security, consider working for the government. The fastest growing area of government is at the state and local levels. Between 2014 and 2024, the state and local sector is projected to add 756,100 jobs to reach almost 19.9 million. This increase is more than three times the number of jobs added in the previous 10 years. Federal government jobs are expected to decrease during that same period to reach just over 2.3 million jobs by 2024. The decline in federal employment by about 1.5 percent is by far the largest decline in any sector of the economy and reflects cuts in government spending as well as reduced consumer and business use of the Postal Service.[21] Many jobs that were historically federal government positions are becoming responsibilities of state and local governments. Some federal government industries will continue to grow, however, as shown in Table 13.1.

TABLE 13.1 Federal Industries Expected to Grow 2014-2024

	Number of Jobs	Overall Growth of Sector
Automotive	227,000	11%
Education	100,030	11%
Advanced Manufacturing	9,000	12%
Aerospace	22,000	13%
Energy	19,000	16%
Information Technology	90,000	16.50%
Biotechnology	12,000	18.30%
Health Care	93,117	26.80%
Homeland Security	96,000	42%

Information compiled from CareerVoyages.gov and 2006-16 BLS Projections.

In addition to the availability of jobs, average government salaries are competitive with the private and nonprofit sectors. Many of the government's top jobs pay annual salaries that range from $117,000 to $177,000, and starting salaries are often comparable to the private sector. Salaries increase quickly based on education and experience. Table 13.2 shows the average salary and quartiles of the executive branch of the federal workforce for occupational categories.

TABLE 13.2 Average Federal Employee Salary by Occupational Category, 2015

Occupational Category	Average Salary
Professional	$104,593
Administrative	$92,356
Technical	$51,022
Clerical	$40,530
Other White Collar	$62,540
Blue Collar	$54,184.00
Unspecified	$101,531

Based on "Salary Information for the Executive Branch: Fiscal Year 2017." United States Office of Personnel Management https://www.opm.gov/policy-data-oversight/data-analysis-documentation/federal-employment-reports/reports-publications/salary-information-for-the-executive-branch.pdf

You can improve your chances of moving up by pursing a relevant graduate degree, such as a master's in public administration or a master's in public policy. But since there are government jobs suited to every interest and skill, you could find a mathematics, physics, engineering, or medical background relevant to your work. Benefits for government employees, such as health insurance, retirement, and job security, are competitive and often superior to other sectors. You do not have to live in Washington, D.C., to work for the government. In fact, only 10 percent of government employees work in the D.C. area. California alone has more federal employees than Washington, D.C. You could be based in your home city or state or even work outside the United States, as more than 50,000 federal employees do.

13.9 What's the Alternative?

For many, the word bureaucracy has come to be synonymous with frustration, inefficiency, and waste. The bureaucratic structure can make things move slowly and, at times, it seems like there is a lack of communication across and between the various hands of government. The public often feels disconnected as it tries to navigate the maze of government regulations and paperwork. Almost every presidential election since 1980 has seen candidates debate over the size of the federal government, with politicians making promises to cut bureaucratic red tape and reduce the size of government. Many in the public share the belief that government has become too large, too expensive, and too overreaching. In response to these concerns, many political leaders began to demand reform of the bureaucracy and a "reinvention" of government. It is true that government is large. Navigating all the agencies, programs, rules, and procedures can be challenging and often frustrating. So how can we reform bureaucracy to make it more efficient and responsive to the public?

The Clinton administration made reforming bureaucracy one of its primary policy objectives and established the National Partnership for Reinventing Government to create government that "works better and costs less." The Partnership called for community-owned, competitive (both internally and externally), results-oriented, customer-driven, and market-oriented reforms. Few of these recommendations were actually implemented, however, because reforming bureaucracy means having to reconcile the interests of both the legislative and the executive branches. Each branch is suspicious that in trying to reform government, the other is trying to gain greater control. It can be difficult, therefore, to get the necessary support to implement reforms.

Bureaucracy could be made more efficient, accountable, and effective through termination, devolution, and privatization. Reducing programs is one certain way to reduce the size of government, but this rarely happens because voters benefit from the services of particular programs and would potentially object to their elimination. The number of rules implemented by regulatory agencies could be reduced, which comes with its own costs and benefits. Deregulation can speed up transactions and cut back on red tape, but it can also lead to less oversight, inequality, and negative externalities such as environmental damage and compromises on health and safety standards. Government power can also be devolved—that is, power could be shifted from the federal government to state and local governments, thereby reducing the size and scope of the federal bureaucracy. Activities traditionally carried out by bureaucratic agencies could become the responsibility of private companies under contracts between these companies and the government. Privatization of this type would allow programs to remain on the federal budget and be supervised by the government, but could potentially lead to greater efficiency as private firms competed for government contracts. The outsourcing of government raises new questions about accountability, however, as many of the mechanisms for holding the government accountable to the public do not apply to private firms. Privatization of government activities is further complicated by the fact that private contractors donate millions of dollars each year to political campaigns. These donations may limit the willingness of members of Congress to scrutinize the business practices of contractors who contribute to their campaigns. Reforming bureaucracy requires presidential and congressional vigilance in the defense of the public interest. Privatization and the outsourcing of government jobs may complicate this responsibility.

Ultimately, if government is going to be reinvented, then bureaucrats have to be held accountable to their customers: the American public. We do not vote for bureaucrats, so how, then, can we hold them accountable? Most bureaucratic appointments are made using the merit system. There are concerns that once a person is employed, he or she becomes complacent and inflexible, as there are no requirements that he or she be held accountable for their work. To make bureaucrats accountable, we could limit the term of their appointments so that when the term expires, the employee must be reviewed before being rehired. The problem with this suggestion, however, is that it may stifle innovation and encourage compliance as employees concerned with being rehired will be reluctant to challenge the status quo. Other reforms include the suggestion of rotating employees between agencies and from outside. This practice could help bring new ideas to agencies, limit thinking from an agency point of view, and broaden perspectives. Rotating employees, however, does mean that agencies may become more inefficient in the short term as these individuals learn the rules and procedures of the new agency. While it is challenging to come up with strategies to reform government, it is critical that we continue the conversation about reinventing government and ensuring bureaucratic accountability to maximize efficiency and responsiveness. Reinvention promotes an entrepreneurial attitude that can create innovation, efficiency, and progress, which can eliminate red tape and streamline public services.

Despite our frustration with bureaucracies and the realization that reforms are necessary, government programs have had positive impacts on many of our lives. Some credit for the good that government does should go to the agencies that make these programs work. Bureaucracy is essential to the functioning of our society: It does the heavy lifting of government and helps address medical concerns, carry out justice, clean up the environment, educate our youth, and provide economic support. Bureaucratic agencies are there to help us, and that is exactly what they do the vast majority of the time. In making his case for bureaucracy, Charles Goodsell notes that, "A good bureaucracy is indispensable to a free society, a democratic polity, and a capitalist economy. The freedom to wander the streets at night, for example depends on competent law enforcement. The ability to vote governments out of office without disruption requires a reliable administrative apparatus. A prosperous business community demands good schools, highways, health departments, post offices, and water and sewer systems."[22] Even those aspects of bureaucracy that frustrate us the most can actually benefit us. Consider, for example, the regulations put in place by the Food and Drug Administration in order to secure approval for new medications. Those regulations slow down the process of getting access to new drugs, but they also protect us. When it comes to safety issues, we are especially grateful for bureaucracy and government regulations and frequently call for greater oversight of certain sectors like the food industry. An effective and functioning bureaucracy also minimizes opportunities for corruption. The hierarchical structure and numerous rules and procedures can work to promote equal treatment of all and access to services, regardless of political clout or personal connections.

Endnotes

1. "Full text: Clinton testifies before House committed on Benghazi," *The Washington Post*, October 22, 2015, https://www.washingtonpost.com/news/post-politics/wp/2015/10/22/transcript-clinton-testifies-before-house-committee-on-benghazi/.

2. *Max Weber*, eds. H.H. Gerth and C. Wright Mills (Oxford University Press, New York: 1946), 196-99.

3. *Civil Service 2014*, Funk & Wagnalls New World Encyclopedia.

4. Alex Blinder and Richard Pérez-Peña, "Kentucky Clerk Denies Same-Sex Marriage Licenses, Defying Court," *The New York Times* (New York City, New York), September 1, 2015.

5. "Data Retrieval: Employment, Hours, and Earnings (CES)," Bureau of Labor Statistics, April 4, 2017, http://www.bls.gov/webapps/legacy/ces-btab1.htm.

6. William G. Howell and David E. Lewis, "Agencies by Presidential Design," *Journal of Politics* 64 (2002): 1094-1114.

7. Dennis D. Riley, *Controlling the Federal Bureaucracy* (Philadelphia: Temple University Press, 1987), 139-142.

8. Marver H. Bernstein, *Regulating Business By Independent Commission* (Princeton University Press, 1955). Theodore J. Lowi, *The End Of Liberalism: Ideology, Policy, And The Crisis Of Public Authority* (New York City, New York: W.W. Norton & Co., Inc., 1969).

9. Emily Stephenson, "Postal Service Downsizing Plan Cuts 35,000 Jobs," MSNBC, February 22, 2012, http://www.msnbc.msn.com/id/46501840/ns/business-us_business/.

10. Timothy Cama, "Two Dozen States Sue Obama Over Coal Plant Emissions Rule," The Hill, October 23, 2015, http://thehill.com/policy/energy-environment/257856-24-states-coal-company-sue-obama-over-climate-rule.

11. "Complying with President Trump's Executive Order on Energy Independence," United States Environmental Protection Agency, https://www.epa.gov/energy-independence.

12. Michael I. Goran, Stanley J. Ulijasek, and Emily E. Ventura, "High Fructose Corn Syrup and Diabetes Prevalence: A Global Perspective," *Global Public Health* (2012): 1-10.

13. Carmen G. Gonzalez, "Markets, Monocultures, and Malnutrition: Agricultural Trade Policy Through an Environmental Justice Lens," *Michigan State Journal of International Law*, vol. 14 (2006).

14. Tina Rosenberg, "Why Mexico's Small Corn Farmers Go Hungry," *The New York Times* (New York City, NY), March 3, 2002.

15. J. Skok, "Policy Issue Networks And The Public Policy Cycle: A Structural-Functional Framework For Public Administration," *Public Admin Review* 55 no. 4 (1995):325–332.

16. Sarah Sullivan and Stanton Glantz, "The Changing Role of Agriculture In Tobacco Control Policymaking: A South Carolina Case Study," *Social Science & Medicine* 71 no. 8 (2010): 1527–1534.

17. "The 9/11 Commission Report: Final Report on the National Commission on Terrorist Attacks Upon the United States, Executive Summary," 9-11 Commission, https://www.9-11commission.gov/report/

18. Donald F. Kettl, *System Under Stress: Homeland Security and American Politics* (Washington: C.Q. Press, 2004).

19. David E. Lewis, "Staffing Alone: Unilateral Action and the Politicization of the Executive Office of the President, 1988-2004," *Presidential Studies Quarterly* 35 (2005): 496-514.

20. Jack Rosenthal, "Nixon's Reorganization," *New York Times* (New York City, NY) December 23, 1972.

21. For more information, see "Industry employment and output projections to 2024," Bureau of Labor Statistics, December 2015, https://www.bls.gov/opub/mlr/2015/article/industry-employment-and-output-projections-to-2024.htm.

22. Charles Goodsell, *The Case for Bureaucracy: A Public Administration Polemic, 4th ed.* (Washington, D.C.: CQ Press, 2004), 157.

CHAPTER 14
The Federal Courts: Unelected but Powerful

Chapter Objectives

1. Describe how the judicial system operates and the role it plays in democratic societies.
2. Understand the origins of judicial review and the path to the Supreme Court.
3. Examine the relationship between the courts and the Constitution and reflect on how judges decide cases.
4. Explore the role that the Supreme Court plays in American democracy.
5. Evaluate the extent to which the courts uphold the ideals of justice and equality.

Introduction: Rap Music and Free Speech

The Supreme Court is the highest court in the United States and handles cases that arise under the Constitution and the laws of the nation. The Court is charged with ensuring "Equal Justice Under Law" and serves as the final arbiter of justice.

© Shutterstock, Inc.

When Anthony Elonis's wife took their children and left him, the 28-year-old turned to Facebook to express his anger. In a series of increasingly dark posts, Elonis used rap-style lyrics to describe shooting up kindergarten classes, dismembering his former wife, harming his co-workers, and brutally killing police officers and an FBI investigator. He wrote things like: "There's one way to love you but a thousand ways to kill you. I'm not going to rest until your body is a mess soaked in blood and dying from all the little cuts."[1] His former wife was terrified by these posts and obtained a protective order. Elonis was later arrested on December 8, 2010, and charged with five counts of violating a federal law that prohibits transmitting "any threat to injure the person of another" across state lines. Elonis asked that his case be dismissed, arguing at his trial that his Facebook comments were not true threats. He claimed that he was an aspiring rap artist and that he was expressing himself artistically and therapeutically to deal with recent events in his life. Even though his ex-wife and the others, including the FBI agent, may have perceived his posts as threats, Elonis stated it was not his intention to threaten or to cause any harm. He asserted that he did not mean what he said in a literal sense, and he did not have subjective intent to threaten anyone. The court denied his motion to dismiss the case and ruled that what mattered was not the intent of the post, but the perceptions of threat. Elonis was convicted on four counts and was sentenced to 44 months in prison. He appealed his conviction to the U.S. Court of Appeals for the Third Circuit, which affirmed the district court's ruling. Elonis then appealed to the U.S. Supreme Court, arguing it was not his intent to threaten anyone and that his First Amendment right to free speech was at stake. The U.S. Supreme Court agreed to hear the case and consider the issue of whether a conviction of threatening another person under the federal anti-threat statute requires proof that the defendant meant what he said in a literal sense.

For the Supreme Court, this case was about language and intent, freedom of speech on social media, and the history and essence of rap music. As some rap music scholars described to the court in an amicus brief, rap has gotten a bad reputation in the courts because most courts just do not understand it. Rap has its roots in a long tradition of black American storytelling and verbal competition and "privileges exaggeration, metaphor, and above all, wordplay. ... Ambiguity is prized, meaning is destabilized, and gaps between the literal and figurative are intentionally exploited."[2] What this argument suggests is that the "reasonable listener" test depends on whether the listener has any knowledge of rap as a complex artistic and political form of expression. Moreover, according to rap music experts, rap lyrics should not be taken as literal, but instead as demonstrations of the virtuosity of the lyricist.

Rap music experts had to be called in to provide context because most Supreme Court justices are not very familiar with the music. Consider that the average age of Supreme Court justices is over 69 and, while some may know rap better than others, none at the time had ever grappled with rap lyrics as speech. Moreover, none had ever had to consider the issue as it relates to freedom of expression on social media outlets like Facebook. Rap lyrics have been used as evidence in hundreds of cases across the country, and most courts tend to view rap as autobiographical and as confessions rather than as an art form. But the issues presented in *Elonis v. United States* were more complicated: what was at stake was the question of intent of threat versus the perception of threat. For the Supreme Court, when it handed down its ruling, intent was everything. In an 8-1 decision, the Court reversed Elonis's conviction. The Court did not rule on First Amendment rights, but instead on lack of evidence to demonstrate Elonis's intent to carry out the actions described in his posts. The decision was a victory for Elonis, for rap music, for free speech on social media, and for artistic expression. The case also illustrates the power of the courts to make determinations about what we can say, how we can say it, and where we can say it.

Like the president and Congress, the Supreme Court has shaped and defined American politics. It has made rulings that protected slavery (*Dred Scott v. Sanford*, 1857); institutionalized segregation (*Plessy v. Ferguson*, 1896); defended the internment of Japanese Americans (*Korematsu v. the United States*, 1944); ordered the desegregation of schools (*Brown v. the Board of Education*, 1954); legalized abortion (*Roe v. Wade*, 1973); influenced the results of a presidential election (*Bush v. Gore*, 2000); and legalized same-sex marriage (*Obergefell v. Hodges*, 2015). Judicial authority is broad and continues to expand. While the judicial branch was established as a check on the executive and legislative branches, the question emerges whether that check has now become too powerful. If we consider that Supreme Court justices are unelected officials with lifetime appointments who have the power to overturn legislation, how does the institution fit into a democratic framework? These are questions we will consider in our exploration of the judiciary.

On June 26, 2015, the Supreme Court handed down a landmark opinion in *Obergefell v. Hodges*, ruling that same-sex couples may exercise the fundamental right to marry in all 50 states and that there is no lawful basis for a state to refuse to recognize a lawful same-sex marriage performed in another state on grounds of its same-sex character. In the majority opinion, Justice Anthony Kennedy wrote, "It would misunderstand these men and women to say they disrespect the idea of marriage. Their plea is that they do respect it, respect it so deeply that they seek to find its fulfillment for themselves. Their hope is not to be condemned to live in loneliness, excluded from one of civilization's oldest institutions. They ask for equal dignity in the eyes of the law. The Constitution grants them that right."[3]

Rena Schild / Shutterstock.com

We begin the chapter by examining the U.S. court system in comparative perspective. We describe the role of the courts in interpreting the Constitution and explain the development of judicial review. We trace the evolution of increasing judicial authority and focus on some important cases. We then explore how cases make their way to the Supreme Court and the impact the Court's decisions have had on national culture and the American people.

14.1 The American Judicial System

Woodrow Wilson once characterized the Supreme Court as a constitutional convention in continuous session. He meant that the judiciary branch is continuously reviewing the language of the Constitution and applying it to present-day politics. When it comes to resolving political conflict and deciding who gets what, when, and how, the courts weigh in with what is written in the Constitution and how it should be interpreted. Of course, the Constitution provides limited guidance on many of the issues we face today. The framers could not have predicted, for example, that there would come a time when the judicial branch would have to rule on a case about social media and rap music as free speech. In situations where the Constitution does not offer specific guidelines, the courts must read what the document says about similar issues and decide how to apply what is in the Constitution to the case at hand. Even when the Constitution does address a particular topic, it addressed that topic at the time it was written more than 230 hundred years ago. Again, the judicial branch considers the applicability and relevance of what was written in the document all those years ago to today's context.

litigation

The conduct of a lawsuit.

The legislative branch writes the laws, the executive implements the laws, and the Judiciary decides whether these laws are constitutional. One of the foundations of the American political system is the rule of law. Laws serve important functions in democratic societies. They provide security and order, they manage political conflict, they safeguard our rights, they distribute public goods, and they help promote norms of justice and equality. In the United States, we rely on laws and our legal system to advance our goals. **Litigation**, also known as the conduct of lawsuits, is an ever-present feature of American life. State courts receive an annual criminal caseload of 15 million cases; traffic violations comprise an additional 44 million cases.[4] U.S. federal courts of appeals open about 355,000 cases a year and almost 1 million cases are filed in bankruptcy courts.[5] As illustrated in Figure 14.1, the number of cases filed in federal courts has actually decreased in recent years, but the fact remains that more than 60 million cases are filed in U.S. courts every year.

FIGURE 14.1 Appeals Court Cases Filed

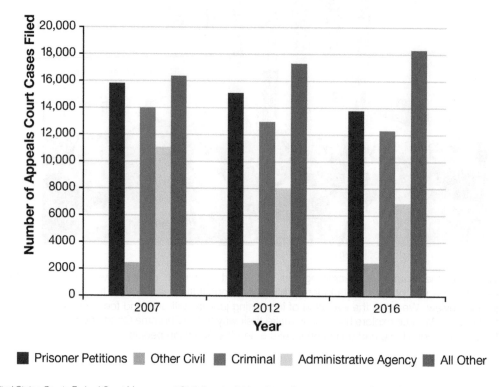

United States Courts Federal Court Management Statistics. Available at https://www.uscourts.gov/statistics-reports/analysis-reports/federal-court-management-statistics.

adversarial system

The type of judicial system that exists in the United States, in which opposing attorneys lead and represent the interests of their clients. Judges serve as relatively passive and detached referees and do not challenge the evidence presented by the attorneys.

The American legal system is rooted in British common-law and adversarial traditions. In an **adversarial system**, opposing attorneys take the lead and represent the interests of their clients. Judges serve as relatively passive and detached referees who do not challenge the evidence presented by the attorneys. This type of system differs from an inquisitorial one in which judges are required to take a more active role in discovering and evaluating evidence, questioning witnesses, and intervening when deemed necessary.

The American Legal System in Comparative Perspective

The United States is one of the few countries in the world where judges play so large a role in policy-making. In other democracies, such as Britain, Parliament is supreme. While the American judicial branch has significant power, other nations' courts have played similar roles in determining political outcomes. Consider, for example, the case of presidential elections in Kenya in August 2017. Kenya is an emerging democracy in which political institutions are still developing legitimacy and authority. A major test of the authority of the Kenyan courts came when claims were made that the elections had been compromised and the results could not be trusted. About 10 days before the elections, one of the election officials was kidnapped, tortured, and murdered. Concerns were raised that the kidnappers had succeeded in gaining access to the ballot system and were able to rig the elections. The case was brought to the Kenyan Supreme Court which, in an unprecedented move, declared the results of the election null and void and ordered that there be a new round of elections in October 2017. The Kenyan justices ruled against the sitting president who had won the original election in August, and they were subsequently praised for advancing democratic ideals. It can be useful to compare the American political system with other systems in order to evaluate the roles played by our institutions and to think critically about the relationship between democracy and the power wielded by our branches of government.

The most important power of the American judicial branch is **judicial review**. Judicial review establishes the right of federal courts to determine the constitutionality of laws and executive decisions. It is the primary tool that the judiciary uses to check and balance the legislative and executive branches of government. In most other democracies, judicial review means little. In the United Kingdom, for example, judges do not have the authority to strike down legislation. Some countries such as Australia, Canada, Germany, and India have stronger judicial review. The judiciary in these countries can rule on the constitutionality of laws, but there is variation across these legal systems and how they understand judicial review.

judicial review

Established in *Marbury v. Madison*, this process gives federal courts the right to determine the constitutionality of laws and executive decisions. It is the primary tool that the judiciary uses to check and balance the legislative and executive branches of government.

The Judicial Process and Interpreting the Constitution

The Constitution is sometimes ambiguous and interpreting it can be challenging. In some cases, the Constitution provides very clear guidelines for how a law should be understood and applied. In other cases, the Constitution does not speak directly to an issue or a particular context, as was true in the case that is described at the beginning of the chapter. What happens when the Constitution does not tell policymakers what to do? Who decides how the law should be interpreted and applied?

In fact, there is a lot of debate over how it should be interpreted. Two schools have developed around the different ways to read the document. **Originalism** (also known as strict constructionism) suggests that judges should be bound by the *wording* of the Constitution. **Activist** or loose constructivism holds that judges should consider the *underlying principles* of the Constitution. This is not a liberal versus conservative division: a judge can be liberal and an originalist, while a conservative judge can be an activist. It is true, however, that today most originalists tend to follow conservative ideologies while activists tend to be liberal. But the decision to adopt an activist or constructionist approach is more likely to reflect a justice's view of the status quo than an ideological position.[6] Justices are also likely to be influenced by their personal, educational, and professional backgrounds as well as their party affiliations. Most judges advocate using **judicial restraint**, which holds that the courts should only interfere with the *elected* branches (that is, the legislative and executive branches) as a last resort.

originalism

Also known as strict constructionism. Holds that judges are bound by the wording of the Constitution.

activist

Also known as loose constructivism. Holds that judges should consider the underlying principles of the Constitution.

judicial restraint

Suggests that the courts should only interfere with the elected (legislative and executive) branches as a last resort.

14.2 The Development of the Federal Courts

Alexander Hamilton referred to the judiciary as the "least dangerous" and the "weakest" branch of government. The courts, he reasoned, lack influence over "the sword" (the president controls the military) and "the purse" (Congress controls the national budget).[7] Yet, as we will see in this chapter, the judicial branch has acquired increasing powers over time and has the authority to rule on a variety of issues that affect our freedom. It is the Court's role and responsibility to interpret the Constitution and, as such, it has the authority to strike down laws, rules, and regulations that it finds violate the Constitution. When Hamilton referred to the judiciary as the least dangerous branch of government, he was likely not expecting judicial review to play such a large role in policy-making. The ruling in the landmark case *Marbury v. Madison* soon undermined Hamilton's guarantee that the other two branches would reign supreme over the courts.

The Establishment of Judicial Review

Marbury v. Madison began when John Adams lost the 1800 election. During his last hours as president, Adams made several "midnight appointments" that put some of his supporters in key judicial positions. When new President Thomas Jefferson took over, he objected to these last-minute appointments. He did not share many of the appointees' political views and preferred to fill the positions with men of his own choosing. Jefferson directed his Secretary of State James Madison to **not** deliver the appointment letters. One of the undelivered letters was for William Marbury, who was to be justice of the peace for the District of Columbia. The Judiciary Act of 1789 established this position. Moreover, under this act, some cases—such as those involving direct orders to government officials—could be referred to the Supreme Court. Thus, Marbury invoked the Judiciary Act and petitioned the Supreme Court to order Madison to deliver his appointment letter. The stakes were high for the Court, as it was being asked to rule in a politically charged case. John Marshall, the chief justice of the Supreme Court at the time, faced a difficult decision. If the Court ruled in favor of Madison, it would be accepting Jefferson's defiance and increasing executive authority. If it ruled in favor of Marbury, then it risked alienating the newly elected president and there was no guarantee that Jefferson would not just ignore the Court's decision and continue to refuse to deliver the commission. In this scenario, the Court's legitimacy would be significantly undermined and its importance diminished. Marshall's ultimate decision proved brilliant. He resolved the conflict in a way that was acceptable to both sides and at the same time expanded the power of the Court. The Supreme Court ruled that Congress, in drafting the Judiciary Act of 1789, had made a mistake in granting the Supreme Court the authority to decide the question of direct orders to government officials. The Court determined that according to its interpretation of the Constitution, the Supreme Court would only rule on cases that were appealed from the lower courts. But the Constitution said nothing about what would happen if Congress passed a law (like the Judiciary Act of 1789) that conflicted with the constitutional duties granted to the branches of government. Marshall greatly expanded judicial authority when he asserted that in a case like this, where the Constitution does not provide specific guidance, "it is emphatically the province and duty of the judicial department to say what the law is."[8] With the ruling in *Marbury v. Madison*, Marshall established judicial review, which gives the Court the authority to interpret the Constitution, a power that was not mentioned in the Constitution itself. Even though the Court had sided with him, Jefferson denounced the "despotism" by which the unelected court had taken the power of judicial review from elected officials. But there was nothing Jefferson could do except to defy the court, which he did not want to do. In ruling the Judiciary Act to be unconstitutional, Marshall permanently increased the powers of the judicial branch. After *Marbury v. Madison*, whenever questions about interpreting the Constitution arose, it was the Supreme Court that decided.

The Expansion of Judicial Authority

The expansion of judicial authority began with *Marbury v. Madison* and continued to develop as the court took a more active role in resolving conflicts about the division of power between the federal governments and the states. While most of the Framers of the Constitution likely anticipated judicial review, none expected it to be so central to policy-making. The traditional view of judicial authority held that judges would find and apply existing law. As a result, the Framers believed the courts would be neutral, nonpartisan, and politically passive. Alexander Hamilton wrote in *Federalist 78* that the independence of the courts is critical to the "steady, upright and impartial administration of the laws." This view did not foresee judges actually making law by interpreting the Constitution in new ways. It was this view that Hamilton was invoking when he described the judiciary as the least dangerous branch of government. Over time, the view shifted as the courts became active participants in policy-making and a partner in the American government on par with the other two branches. The courts began to not only apply the law, but to actually make the law. This new role evolved through early cases like *McCulloch v. Maryland* (1819), in which the Court determined that interstate commerce should be placed under the authority of federal law, and *Dred Scott v. Sandford* (1857), in which the Court decided that blacks were not U.S. citizens and that federal law prohibiting slavery in the North was unconstitutional. During the Civil War era, when a dominant issue was determining the circumstances under which the economy could be regulated by the federal government or by the states, the Court ruled on the constitutionality of government regulation of business and labor. The Supreme Court also ruled on the legality of racial segregation and determined that separate but equal was constitutional. As the country focused on questions of political liberty in the twentieth century and beyond, the Court was active in defining rights. It established the tradition of deferring to Congress in economic cases. It also helped the nation define discrimination, interpret the right to privacy, evaluate the rights of the accused, and decide who should be allowed to marry. As judicial authority has expanded, the branch that was predicted to be the least dangerous has evolved into a powerful institution with significant influence on our rights and liberties.

The Supreme Court's decision in the Dred Scott case hardened the rivalry between the North and South and paved the way for the Civil War. The Court ruled that slaves were not U.S. citizens and therefore could not bring suit against their "owners."

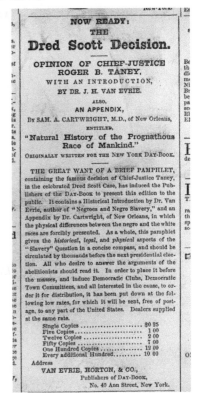

© Shutterstock, Inc.

Ten Supreme Court Cases You Should Know

Several Supreme Court cases have defined or redefined American politics and shaped national culture. We have explored many of these cases in other parts of the book, particularly in the chapters on civil liberties and civil rights. If there is any common thread that links these cases, it is that they all represent moments of intense political conflict during which the Court stepped in to determine what the Constitution would say about the issue. Here we present a list of 10 important Supreme Court cases. This list is by no means exhaustive or even representative of the top most important cases. But the cases chosen illustrate that the U.S. federal courts have addressed a wide range of issues including civil rights, separation of powers, elections, gender, and religion. The Court has made decisions about some of the most controversial and divisive questions in American society, and these cases demonstrate the extensive reach of the judicial branch into politics and society.

1. *Marbury v. Madison* (1803)

   This landmark case discussed earlier in this chapter established judicial review, essentially giving the judicial branch its power to rule on the constitutionality of decisions made by the other two branches of government.

2. *McCulloch v. Maryland* (1819)

   In 1816, Congress chartered The Second Bank of the United States to control the amount of unregulated money issued by state banks. Many states believed the national government was overstepping its bounds. One of these states, Maryland, imposed a tax in 1818 on all banks not chartered by the state. James W. McCulloch, a cashier at the Baltimore branch of the U.S. National Bank, refused to pay the tax. Maryland filed suit against McCulloch. The case reached the Supreme Court, which, in a unanimous decision, declared that Congress had the power to charter a bank and that Maryland could not tax the bank. The Court noted that Congress had powers that were not enumerated in the Constitution and that, while states retained the power of taxation, "The Constitution and the laws made in pursuance thereof are supreme . . . they control the Constitution and laws of the respective states, and cannot be controlled by them."[9]

3. *Dred Scott v. Sandford* (1857)

   For many constitutional historians, the Dred Scott decision was the worst decision in the history of the U.S. Supreme Court. The case involved Dred Scott, who had been a slave in Missouri. He later lived with his owner in Illinois and in an area of the Louisiana Territory where slavery was prohibited. When his owner died after they moved back to Missouri, Scott sued his owner's family for his freedom, claiming that because he had lived in free states, he should be a free man. He lost in the Missouri courts and appealed to the Supreme Court, which ruled on the question of whether Dred Scott was free or a slave. In a 7-2 decision, the Court ruled that Dred Scott was a slave. Citing Articles III and IV of the Constitution, the Court argued that only citizens of the United States could be citizens of a state. Because he had been a slave, Dred Scott could not be a citizen of the United States and therefore could not sue in U.S. courts. The Court also decided that Congress did not have the authority to prohibit slavery in the territories, meaning that slavery could not be restricted in any part of the country.

4. *Plessy v. Ferguson* (1896)

   In 1892, Homer Plessy, who was 7/8 white and 1/8 black, sat in the car reserved for whites on a train in Louisiana. Plessy refused to move when ordered to do so by the conductor and was subsequently arrested. The case reached the Supreme Court, which had to decide whether Louisiana's law mandating racial segregation on its trains was a violation of the equal protection clause of the Fourteenth Amendment. In a 7-1 decision, the Court ruled that the Louisiana law was constitutional and separate facilities for blacks and whites were allowed as long as those facilities were equal. Segregation itself was not found to constitute unlawful discrimination.

5. *Korematsu v. U.S.* (1944)

   This case concerned Presidential Executive Order 9066 that, during World War, II gave the military the authority to move Japanese Americans into internment camps from areas deemed critical to national defense and vulnerable to espionage. During World War II, Presidential Executive Order 9066 and congressional statutes gave the military authority to exclude citizens of Japanese ancestry from areas deemed critical to national defense and potentially vulnerable to espionage. Fred Korematsu refused to leave his home in San Leandro, California, arguing that his Fourteenth Amendment rights were being violated. The Supreme Court was asked to rule whether the president and Congress had gone beyond their war powers by restricting the rights of Japanese Americans. The Court decided in a 6-3 ruling that national security concerns justified discrimination against Korematsu.

6. *Brown v. Board of Education* (1954)

   The parents of Linda Brown sued the school board in Topeka, Kansas, in order to be able to send their daughter to an all-white school that was closer to their home than the all-black school. By the time the case reached the Supreme Court, it had been joined by four others from different states, all concerning the question of segregation in public schools on the basis of race. The issue before the Court was whether segregation in public education based solely on race violated the Equal Protection Clause of the Fourteenth Amendment. In a unanimous ruling, the Court overturned *Plessy v. Ferguson* and held that "separate but equal" facilities are unconstitutional. The Court also argued that segregation in public schools based on race had a significantly detrimental effect on the education and growth of black children.

7. *Lemon v. Kurtzman* (1971)

   In 1968 and 1969, Pennsylvania and Rhode Island, respectively, adopted statutes that allowed the use of state funds for non-secular, non-public education, including teachers' salaries, textbooks, and instructional materials. Citizens in Pennsylvania and Rhode Island filed suit arguing that the statute violated the First Amendment's separation of church and state. In Pennsylvania, the district court ruled in favor of the state's motion to dismiss the case; in Rhode Island, the district court found in favor of the citizens and ruled that the statute violated the First Amendment. Lemon had a child in Pennsylvania public school and led the appeal to the Supreme Court, which was asked to decide whether statutes that provide funding for non-public, non-secular schools violate the Establishment Clause of the First Amendment. The Court ruled 8-1 in favor of Lemon and held that a statute must past a three-pronged test to avoid violating the First Amendment's Freedom of Religion. This decision led to the Lemon Test, which requires a statute to have a secular legislative purpose; its primary effect cannot promote or inhibit religion and it must not foster "excessive government entanglement with religion."[10] The Court found that the Pennsylvania and Rhode Island statutes had secular legislative purposes: they were state initiatives to ensure that minimum secular education requirements were being met in the non-public schools.

8. *Roe v. Wade* (1973)

   Jane Roe wanted to terminate her pregnancy by abortion. Roe was a resident of Texas, where abortions were prohibited except to save the pregnant woman's life. The question before the Supreme Court was whether a woman had the constitutional right to terminate her pregnancy by abortion. The Court ruled 7-2 in favor of Roe, arguing that a woman's right to an abortion falls within the right to privacy and is protected by the Fourteenth Amendment. The decision established the trimester framework, allowing a woman to terminate a pregnancy at any time in the first trimester, and leaving it to the states to determine restrictions in the second and third trimesters. As the result of the Court's decision, 46 states had to rewrite their laws regarding abortion. The issue remains an important source of political conflict in the nation today.

9. *Bush v. Gore* (2000)

On December 8, 2000, Florida's Supreme Court ordered a manual recount of contested ballots cast in the November presidential elections. Every county in Florida was also ordered to begin manually recounting all "under-votes" (ballots which did not indicate a vote for president) because the number of contested ballots called into question the outcome of the election. Presidential candidate George W. Bush and his running mate, Richard Cheney, filed an appeal with the Supreme Court to stop the recount. The issues before the Supreme Court were whether the Florida Supreme Court had violated the Constitution by making new election law and whether manual recounts violated the Equal Protection and Due Process Clauses of the Constitution. The Supreme Court decided in favor of Bush and held that even if the recount were fair in theory, it violated the Equal Protection Clause in practice because the clause guarantees voters that their ballots cannot be devalued by "later arbitrary and disparate treatment."[11] The way that the recount would be conducted would vary from ballot to ballot, precinct to precinct, and county to county, and there was not enough time to standardize a recount.

10. *Obergefell v. Hodges* (2015)

This case is the consolidation of six lower-court cases originally representing 16 same-sex couples. The cases started in Michigan, Ohio, Kentucky, and Tennessee, where the couples sued their relevant state agencies to challenge bans on same-sex marriage or refusal to recognize same-sex marriages that took place in states where they were legal. The plaintiffs argued that their Fourteenth Amendment rights of Equal Protection and Due Process had been violated. In all cases, the courts ruled in favor of the plaintiffs. The decisions of the lower courts were reversed by the U.S. Court of Appeals for the Sixth Circuit, which found that state bans on same-sex marriage and refusal to recognize marriages performed in other states did not infringe on the couples' Fourteenth Amendment rights. The issue was appealed to the Supreme Court, which was asked to decide whether the Fourteenth Amendment requires a state to license a marriage between two people of the same sex and whether the amendment requires a state to recognize a same-sex marriage that was licensed and executed in another state. The Court ruled 5-4 in favor of Obergefell and held that the Due Process Clause of the Fourteenth Amendment guarantees the right to marry and that this right applies to same-sex couples just as it does to opposite-sex couples. The Equal Protection Clause of the Fourteenth Amendment also guarantees the right of same-sex couples to marry because the denial of that right would deny same-sex couples equal protection under the law.

14.3 Federalism and the American Courts

There are two court systems in the United States—federal and state—that operate at the same time in the same geographic areas but have different jurisdictions (see Figure 14.2 and Figure 14.4). The dual system is characterized by rules and procedures that determine who wins and who loses in court.

FIGURE 14.2 The Dual Court System

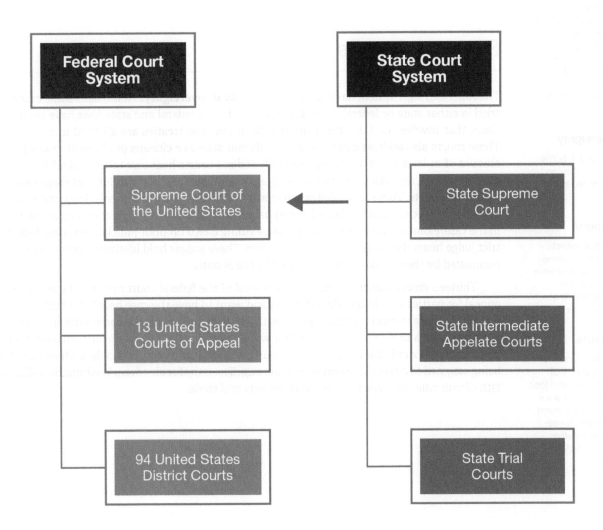

State Courts

appellate courts

Cases that begin in state trial courts can be appealed to state appellate courts. From there, they can be appealed to state supreme courts. Both the state and federal systems have appellate courts. The outcome of a trial in a lower court can be appealed or brought to an appellate court to be heard again. The highest appellate court in the states is the state supreme court; at the federal level, there are intermediate level appeals courts for each district and the U.S. Supreme Court, which is the nation's highest court of appeal.

dual sovereignty

A system in which some court cases can be tried in either state or federal court.

district courts

These courts establish facts in a case, examine the evidence, and make a ruling based on prior judicial decisions. There are 94 district courts.

circuit courts

These are the 13 courts that serve as courts of appeal for parties who lose in district court and want to have their cases heard at a higher level. These courts decide whether district courts made the correct rulings.

State courts do most of the legal heavy lifting. These courts rule on a wide variety of issues that arise under state law, from murder and sexual assault to medical malpractice and antitrust questions. Cases typically begin in state trial courts and can be appealed to state **appellate courts**. From there, they can be appealed to state supreme courts. Both the state and federal systems have appellate courts. The outcomes of trials in lower courts can be appealed or brought to an appellate court to be heard again. The highest appellate court in the states is the state supreme court; at the federal level, there are intermediate level appeals courts for each district, and then the U.S. Supreme Court, which is the nation's highest court of appeal. Though it happens only rarely, cases that started in local and state courts can be appealed all the way up to the U.S. Supreme Court. Such cases, however, must raise a question of federal law before they can be resolved by the federal courts. Many of the most significant Supreme Court rulings were made on cases that began in state court, such as *Dred Scott v. Sandford* and *Roe v. Wade*.

Federal Courts

The American legal system has what is known as **dual sovereignty**. That means some cases can be tried in either state or federal court, for example, if both federal and state laws have been broken. Cases that involve the U.S. Constitution, federal law, and treaties are all tried in federal courts. These courts also address cases involving different states or citizens of different states (when an amount of at least $75,000 is being disputed). Federal courts hear cases that deal with issues such as immigration, terrorism, freedom of religion, and intellectual property. Most of these cases begin in **district courts**. There are 94 district courts in the country: each state has at least one, while some larger states (such as California and Texas) have as many as four. District courts establish the facts in the case, examine the evidence, and make a ruling based on prior judicial decisions. A single district judge hears the cases and makes a decision. These judges hold lifetime appointments and are nominated by the president and confirmed by the Senate.

Thirteen **circuit courts** occupy the next level of the federal court system. These are courts of appeal for parties who lose in district court and want to have the case heard at a higher level. The purpose of these courts is to decide whether the district court made the correct ruling. Three judges hear each case and rule on the record that was established by the lower court without a jury and without cross-examining witnesses. The courts are organized geographically, with eleven of them being assigned to a specific region (see Figure 14.3). The 12th Circuit covers Washington, D.C., and the 13th Circuit rules on cases that deal with patents and trade.

FIGURE 14.3 U.S. Courts of Appeals and District Courts

Graphic Boundaries
of United States Courts of Appeals and United States District Courts

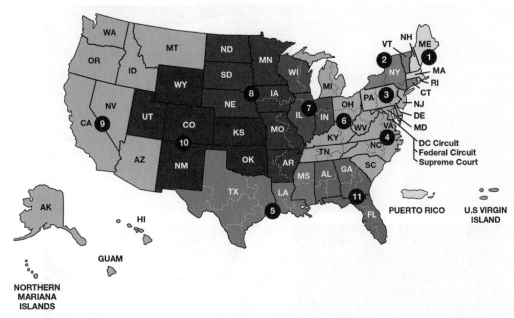

United States Courts: https://www.uscourts.gov/sites/default/files/u.s._federal_courts_circuit_map_1.pdf.

Federal courts also include several specialized courts that handle military cases, bankruptcy issues, and tax law. The Foreign Intelligence Surveillance Court (FISC) was created in 1978 to oversee requests for surveillance warrants of suspected spies. Judges in these courts are nominated by the president and confirmed by the Senate, but they do not serve lifetime appointments.

FIGURE 14.4 Jurisdictions of the Supreme Court and Lower Courts

Supreme Court

- Highest court in the federal system
- Nine Justices, meeting in Washington, D.C.
- Appeals jurisdiction through *certiorari* process
- Limited original jurisdiction over some cases

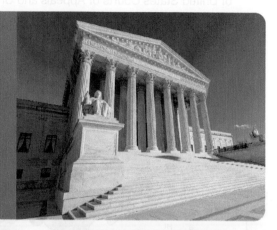

Courts of Appeal

- Intermediate level in the federal system
- 12 regional "circuit" courts, including D.C. circuit
- No original jurisdiction; strictly appellate

District Courts

- Lowest level in the federal system
- 94 judicial districts in 50 states & territories
- No appellate jurisdiction
- Original jurisdiction over most cases

Images from © Shutterstock, Inc.

14.4 The Supreme Court in Action

The Road to the Supreme Court

The Supreme Court chooses the cases it wants to hear on appeal. Most of these cases begin in district courts (see Figure 14.5). Losing parties in the lower courts are allowed to file a petition with the Supreme Court stating the facts of the case and detailing why it is critical for the Court to hear it. In order to be eligible for consideration by courts at all levels, a case must meet three conditions: 1) the case must involve a *legitimate controversy*, that is, there must be an actual (rather than a hypothetical) dispute between the parties; 2) the parties filing the case must have *standing*: they must prove that an actual harm has already occurred; and 3) the Court's proceedings must still affect the issue at hand; *mootness* refers to a case that is no longer relevant by the time it is received by a federal court. If the issue has already been resolved, then the courts have the option of declaring a case moot and throwing it out. An example of this is *Roe v. Wade* (1973) when a federal court dismissed the case because Jane Roe, who was petitioning the court for the right to terminate her pregnancy, had already delivered the baby by the time the case reached the court. The Supreme Court reviewed this decision and, even though the issue no longer affected Jane Roe at that time, the Court agreed to hear it on the basis that because pregnancies would always conclude before a court could reach a decision (because it can take so long for cases to work their way through the appeals process).

In 1973, the Supreme Court ruled in the landmark case *Roe v. Wade* that most laws against abortion violate the constitutional right to privacy. The decision, one of the most controversial in the history of the Supreme Court, overturned all state laws outlawing or unduly restricting abortion.

Rena Schild / Shutterstock.com

If the above conditions have been met, and if it the case deals with a constitutional question that will affect a significant number of people, a party—or petitioner—who has lost in a lower court can file a petition for certiorari (from Latin meaning "to be informed of") with the appellate court. The petition details why the case cannot be decided in any other court or through any other appellate process. It also identifies the case and discusses the questions to be reviewed, the relevant laws to be applied, a brief statement of the facts related to the issues, and any other materials required by statute.

solicitor general

A presidential appointee who supervises the litigation of the executive branch. When the federal government is a party in a case, the solicitor general represents the government in court.

This petition gets sent to the Supreme Court, but before the justices can vote on which cases to hear, the cases must first get reviewed by several of the youngest, least experienced lawyers in the United States—the 36 law clerks who are assigned to serve the nine individual justices. There are typically four clerks per justice. These clerks are an elite group of recent law school graduates who generally spend one year in a lower court clerkship for a district court judge or in a state supreme court before applying to be Supreme Court clerks. It is the clerks who do the first reading of the annual petitions and select just a few that they believe the Court should consider. The justices look at this winnowed down group of cases. Then, in a closed conference room and beginning with the Chief Justice and continuing by seniority, they vote out loud whether to hear each case. Many factors influence which cases the Court will hear. Interest groups and other governmental bodies may draw attention to particular issues, making cases that address them more likely to be considered by the Court. The **solicitor general** may also influence the Court's decision to hear a case. The solicitor general is appointed by the president and supervises the litigation of the executive branch. When the federal government is a party in a case, it is the solicitor general, or someone from that office, who represents the government in court. The Supreme Court hears 70 to 80 percent of cases in which the U.S. government is a party.

rule of four

At least four Supreme Court justices must agree to hear a case in order for a writ of certiorari to be issued.

writ of certiorari

The request, issued by the Supreme Court, for a lower court to send its official records of a case to the Supreme Court.

The **rule of four** dictates that at least four Supreme Court justices must be in agreement to hear a case. Once the justices have agreed, the Court issues a **writ of certiorari** requesting the official records from the lower court that heard the case. Only about 1 percent of the 80,000 appeals that are made annually to the Court are granted certiorari.

The Court rarely offers insight into why it chooses to hear certain cases over others. What we do know, however, is that there is a pattern to the types of cases the Court picks. For example, the Court is most likely to choose to hear cases in which two lower courts decide the legal question differently. It is also more likely to hear cases in which a lower court ruling conflicts with an existing Supreme Court decision, and where the issues raised by the case could have significance beyond the two parties involved. This latter component explains why the Supreme Court rarely hears sexual harassment cases. One important exception to this was *Jones v. Clinton* (1997) in which Paula Jones, who worked in Bill Clinton's office when he was governor of Arkansas, accused the then-governor of sexual harassment. Because the suit was filed when Clinton was already president, the Court decided to hear the case to determine whether a sitting president could be immune from a civil lawsuit while in office. In one of the rare times the Court has used its power of judicial review against the president, it ruled that the president was, in fact, not immune from a lawsuit while in office. This decision allowed Jones's case to proceed and led to Clinton's impeachment by the House of Representatives. The Senate subsequently acquitted Clinton of charges made by the House.

The Court does not automatically agree to hear all cases that present pressing societal challenges. In 2017, for instance, the Court sent a case dealing with a transgender high school student back to the lower courts. The student had petitioned to be allowed to use the school bathrooms that align with the student's gender identity. The Supreme Court's action meant that it was up to the lower court to decide whether federal law should treat discrimination on the basis of gender identity as equivalent to sex discrimination.

While the Court is influenced by a variety of factors, it ultimately has sole discretion to decide which cases it wants to hear. The Court can choose to ignore standing and mootness and ultimately pick those cases that it finds most urgent. While it can choose which cases to hear, the Court is limited in its ability to set its own agenda. It must wait for cases to make their way up from the lower courts, rather than dictate which issues it will consider.

FIGURE 14.5 Road to the Supreme Court

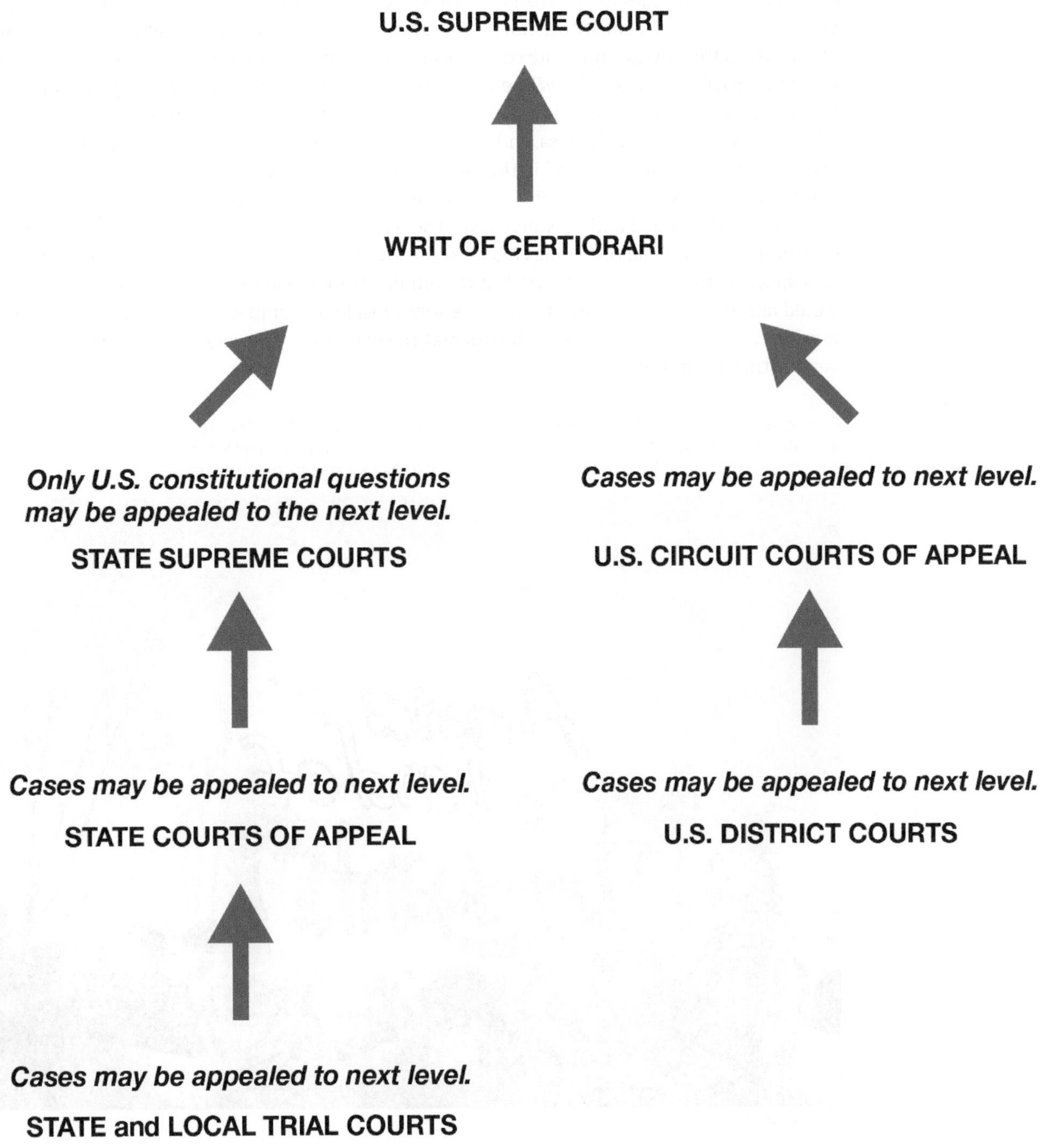

U.S. SUPREME COURT

WRIT OF CERTIORARI

*Only U.S. constitutional questions
may be appealed to the next level.*

STATE SUPREME COURTS

Cases may be appealed to next level.

U.S. CIRCUIT COURTS OF APPEAL

Cases may be appealed to next level.

STATE COURTS OF APPEAL

Cases may be appealed to next level.

U.S. DISTRICT COURTS

Cases may be appealed to next level.

STATE and LOCAL TRIAL COURTS

President Donald Trump's travel ban is a recent and relevant example of how a case makes its way to the Supreme Court. In January 2017, a week after he was sworn in, Trump issued an executive order temporarily banning travel from seven majority-Muslim countries (Iraq, Iran, Syria, Yemen, Libya, Sudan and Somalia) for 90 days in order for the U.S. government to review and strengthen its vetting procedures. The order also suspended worldwide refugee entry into the United States. The travel ban was highly controversial and was immediately met with protests and legal challenges. A week after the order was issued, a federal judge in Seattle, Washington, issued a nationwide restraining order blocking the travel ban. The White House responded that the federal government would challenge the judge's decision and that courts are powerless to review a president's assessment of national security.[12] A federal appeals panel in San Francisco unanimously refused to reinstate the ban. The three-judge panel found that the order did not advance national security and determined that the administration had shown "no evidence" that anyone from the seven nations had committed terrorist acts in the United States.[13] The court also stated that judges play a critical role in a constitutional democracy: "It is beyond question that the federal judiciary retains the authority to adjudicate constitutional challenges to executive action."[14] In response to the initial legal challenges, the White House issued a new travel ban that dropped Iraq from the list of targeted countries, provided explicit exemptions for legal permanent residents and for those who already have a valid U.S. visa, and removed the indefinite restriction on Syrian refugees being allowed admission. Also included in the new order was a list of who may qualify for a waiver to the ban, which could be determined on a case-by-case basis. Before the policy could take effect, two federal judges in Maryland and Hawaii blocked the ban. The case then went to the 4th and 9th Circuit Courts and each upheld the rulings made by the lower courts. At this point, the Trump administration appealed to the Supreme Court, but the administration had to make changes to the order so it would not expire in the meantime. In June 2017, President Trump wrote on Twitter that, "The Justice Dept. should have stayed with the original Travel Ban, not the watered down, politically correct version they submitted to S.C."

Protesters rallying against President Trump's travel ban in Washington, D.C. The highly controversial proposed legislation was intended to promote national security by banning entry into the United States for citizens from several predominantly Muslim countries. It also sought to block the entry of Syrian refugees.

Rena Schild / Shutterstock.com

The Supreme Court allowed a limited version of the ban to go into effect in late June 2017 and agreed to hear the government's appeal of the lower court rulings. The limited ban put into effect by the Supreme Court could apply only to refugees and travelers who do not have a "bona fide" relationship to a person or entity in the United States. Debate ensued about what constituted a "bona fide" relationship, and the 9th Circuit Court of Appeals ultimately blocked the government from denying entry to extended family members of a person in the United States. The court also determined that the government cannot ban refugees who have formal assurances from resettlement agencies or who are in the U.S. Refugee Admissions Program, a decision that was quickly overturned by the Supreme Court.[15] The Supreme Court agreed to hear the full case in April 2018 and, in late June 2018, the Court upheld President Trump's ban in a 5-4 ruling, thereby rejecting the constitutional question of whether the ban violates immigration law as well as the First Amendment's Establishment Clause.

How the Supreme Court Decides

Once the Court has accepted a case, a date is set to hear oral arguments. The Supreme Court is open for business for nine months, beginning on the first Monday in October, and arguments are usually scheduled during this period on Monday, Tuesday, and Wednesday mornings. These sessions are free and open to the public, but seating is limited and on a first-come, first-seated basis. Before the hearing, the parties not involved in the case submit written briefs that detail their arguments. Other parties may also submit briefs supporting a particular side in the case. These are called **amicus curiae briefs** (from the Latin meaning "friend of the court"). The Court must give its permission to accept an amicus briefs and usually grants 85 percent of all requests. Once these briefs have been submitted, oral arguments may begin. There is no jury present or witnesses called. No photos are allowed, so sketches are the only images we have of the proceedings. Each side's lawyers have 30 minutes to make their case and the justices can interrupt at any time with questions. The judges may make mini-speeches of their own, and while they can interrupt the lawyers presenting their cases, no one interrupts a Supreme Court justice, even if the lawyer's 30 minutes are dwindling away. Most justices concede, however, that the written briefs submitted by the parties matter far more than the oral arguments.

amicus curiae briefs

From the Latin "friend of the court." Before a Supreme Court hearing, the parties not involved in the case submit written briefs detailing their arguments. Other parties may also submit "friend of the court" briefs supporting a particular side of the case.

Conference Procedures and Written Decisions

After oral arguments are heard, the Supreme Court will consider the cases on its docket during conferences that typically take place on Thursday or Friday afternoons when the Court is in session. These conference sessions are closed to the public and even to the clerks. The justices sit at a conference table, with the most recently appointed justice seated closest to the door. The junior justice opens the door only for staff delivering materials relevant for the next case to be considered. In these conferences, the justices discuss the cases they heard in oral arguments. The chief justice speaks first and votes last. The chief justice also selects the judge who will write the **majority opinion** on each case. The majority opinion is the official statement of the Supreme Court that details its ruling on a particular case. If another justice wishes, he or she can draft a **concurrent opinion** explaining why he or she voted in favor of the majority opinion. If justices do not agree with the majority decision, they can write a **dissent** that outlines why they voted against the majority.

In making its decisions, the Court puts the facts of the case in the context of the Constitution and uses **stare decisis**, the rulings or precedents established in previous cases. The Court can decide that previous decisions were wrong and choose to overrule them. There are cases, however, that do not have precedents or a body of previous rulings. There are also cases that do not have a clear constitutional answer. In these cases, the justices on the Supreme Court are left to interpret the Constitution and apply it to the case as they see fit. It is here where the debate between activists and originalists arises. Some justices (the activists) see the Constitution as a living, flexible document, while others (the originalists) are bound by the wording of the Constitution. While there can be significant conflict between activists and originalists, the Court does make unanimous decisions on some cases. In fact, the usual trend is for the justices to vote 9-0 or to be split 5-4. These vote splits have been the trend since 1995. We rarely see justices voting 6-3 or 7-2. This pattern is likely due to the fact that many of the cases do not have an ideological component. Absent an ideological concern, the justices either do not bother to express their disagreements or think that the appearance of cooperation makes the Court look better in the eyes of the public. If there is an ide-

majority opinion

The official statement of the Supreme Court, which details its ruling on a case.

concurrent opinion

A document that outlines why a Supreme Court justice voted in favor of the majority opinion.

dissent

A document that outlines why a Supreme Court justice voted against the majority opinion.

stare decisis

The rulings or precedents established in previous cases that the Supreme Court uses to make its decisions.

ological question, that is where the court does split between activists and originalists.[16] Where there is agreement on cases, collegiality and peer pressure may also play a role. Justices can have a lot of influence on each other; additionally, the broader legal community of academics, lawyers, members of Congress, and interest groups may influence the justices.

Almost every case is decided in the same term in which the oral arguments were heard. In fact, the Court usually makes a decision within three months of hearing an oral argument,[17] though in some very rare situations, the case can be debated for more than six months. There is a trend for so-called big cases to be decided closer to the end of June when the Supreme Court is about to close session for the year.[18] A couple of possibilities explain this trend. It may be that in writing what they think will be a major decision, justices and their clerks take more time revising until the last moment with the hope of promoting their legacies and reputations. Another possibility is that important cases may cluster at the end of term in order to diffuse media coverage and potentially critical commentary about a particular case.

14.5 Judicial Selection

Judges have a significant amount of power to interpret the law rooted in the nation's common-law tradition. The selection of judges is critical to definitions of what is legal and permissible. The type of court to which they are being appointed determines how judges are selected.

State Level

At the state court level, judges are chosen through one of four methods: partisan elections; non-partisan elections; merit selection; and gubernatorial or legislative appointments. The majority of states (31) elect judges. Seventeen allow the governor to make appointments, and two leave it up to the state legislature. While most judges start their legal careers as lawyers, some states do not require any formal training (such as law school) before judges can be appointed. The terms of office range from six to 12 years in elected courts and from six years to lifetime tenure in appointed courts. The states of Massachusetts, New Hampshire, and Rhode Island grant lifetime tenure.

Given that we elect members of the other two branches of government, why don't all states allow for judicial elections? The answer has to do with the fact that judges are supposed to be above politics and should weigh evidence without political pressure. Elections might comprise a judge's ability to defend the minority when he or she feels an obligation to win majority favor in the voting booth. Research shows that elected judges give harsher sentences at the end of their electoral cycle when they are facing reelection out of fear that lenient sentences would allow their opponents to portray them as soft on crime.[19] Campaign contributions also can compromise a judge's ability to remain unbiased. Fear of corruption and judges being "bought" further contribute to concerns about electing justices. Despite these dangers, many states insist that government by the people means that judges have to be accountable to the public.

Federal Level and the Supreme Court

At the federal level, the Constitution specifies that judges be nominated by the president, confirmed by the Senate, and serve lifetime appointments. The Constitution does not, however, provide any guidelines for the qualifications of federal judges. Both the executive and legislative branches have an interest in appointing justices who will advance their political agendas and resolve political conflicts in ways that align with their ideologies. The biggest prize, of course, is the Supreme Court.

When it was originally constituted in 1789, there were just six members on the Supreme Court. The number expanded to seven in 1807, then to nine in 1837, and 10 in 1863. With the Judiciary Act of 1869, the number was set at nine, and it has remained at that number ever since. Franklin Roosevelt tried to expand the court to 13 justices with his "court-packing plan." This plan was part of his strategy to gain political control of the court in order to get his New Deal policies implemented. The Senate rejected his plan by a 70-20 vote.

Because it is composed of nine justices, the ability to appoint someone to the Supreme Court is an important feather in the cap of any president. The great stake that all Americans have in what the Supreme Court does means it is in the interest of the president to try to shape the Court and have an influence on how it rules. This influence helps advance the president's policy agenda and seal his legacy. As a result, the process of selecting Supreme Court justices is a highly partisan and extremely political process. When it comes to choosing a Supreme Court justice, it is not necessarily a question of finding the most experienced, best-qualified person for the job. Party affiliation, ideology, and personal and professional relationships all matter. The president makes a nomination based on advice from party leaders, staff, influential members of Congress, and others. The nomination goes to the Senate Judiciary Committee for an investigation, hearing, and vote. The process concludes with a confirmation vote in the full Senate. Presidents have to balance their preferences for an appointee who shares their ideology with the need to select someone who will pass the hearings and be acceptable to the Senate. Presidents use the nominations to try to please their base of supporters and win the favor of certain interest groups. Members of the Senate also want to confirm justices who share their political ideologies and will advance the interests of their parties. As a result of these various interests, confirmation hearings can be divisive. The Senate can also refuse to even investigate a presidential nominee. When Justice Antonin Scalia died in 2016, President Barack Obama nominated Merrick Garland to fill the vacancy. The Republican majority in the Senate refused to hold a hearing or vote on the nomination, arguing it was Obama's final year in office and that it should be left to the next president to make the appointment. This decision was controversial, particularly because Garland was a moderate and because Obama's action was not unprecedented: six so-called lame duck presidents filled Supreme Court seats in their last years of office, even though their successors had been elected. As President Obama stated, he had a constitutional duty to nominate a successor to Scalia and as president, "your job doesn't stop until you are voted out or until your term expires."[20] Garland's nomination expired in February 2017. President Donald Trump nominated Neil Gorsuch, an originalist much like Scalia, and in April 2017, Gorsuch was confirmed by the Senate and sworn in as an associate justice of the Supreme Court.

Diversity on the Supreme Court

President Obama nominated Justice Sonia Sotomayor to the Supreme Court in 2009, making her the first Latina to serve on the Court. President Obama chose Sotomayor not only because she is "an inspiring woman" with the intellect and capacity to be impartial, but also because, he said, she has the life experience and ability to relate to ordinary Americans.

Official White House photo by Pete Souza from Washington, DC (Flickr) [Public domain], via Wikimedia Commons By Official White House photo by Pete Souza from Washington, DC (Flickr) [Public domain], via Wikimedia Commons https://commons.wikimedia.org/wiki/File:Obama_and_Sotomayor.jpg

Until recently, only older white men held Supreme Court seats. Today, one-third of the justices are women. Federal courts as a whole continue to be dominated by white males: the number of women on the courts has grown over time, but only a small percentage of the total number of judges are minorities.[21] (See Figure 14.6 and Figure 14.7.) Presidents have worked to increase racial and gender diversity on the courts and have made appointments that reflect this goal. Yet, the courts' composition is hardly reflective of the country's demographics. Does this matter? According to Supreme Court Justice Sonia Sotomayor, it does. Before she was appointed to the Court, Sotomayor stated that, "I would hope that a wise Latina woman with the richness of her experience would more often than not reach a better conclusion than a white male who hasn't lived that life."[22] She based her argument on the idea that justices are inevitably shaped by their experiences and their backgrounds. These experiences inform their values, perspectives, and ultimately their judicial decisions. Some Americans may feel better represented by justices who share their socioeconomic, racial, and/or religious background. Some may want courts that better reflect the demographic composition of the nation. Others may argue that we should appoint the best justices possible, regardless of their backgrounds, and that because the courts are intended to be neutral and unbiased, justice will prevail regardless.

FIGURE 14.6 Racial and Ethnic Diversity and the Courts

New Article III Judges by Race or Ethnicity, 1940-2017

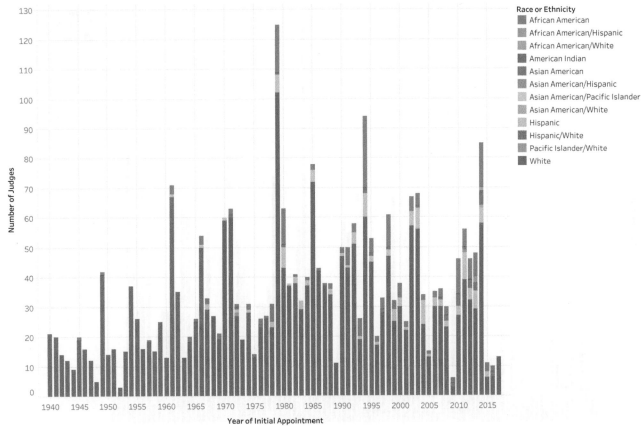

Federal Judicial Center: https://www.fjc.gov/history/exhibits/graphs-and-maps/race-and-ethnicity.

FIGURE 14.7 Gender Diversity and the Courts

New Article III Judges by Gender, 1920-2017

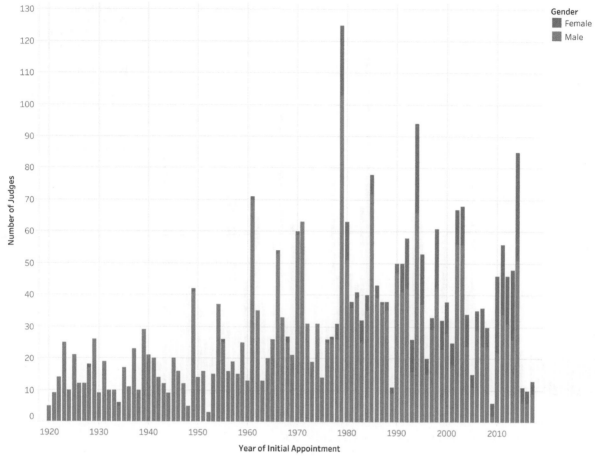

Federal Judicial Center: https://www.fjc.gov/history/exhibits/graphs-and-maps/gender.

14.6 Democracy and the Courts

The judiciary has come to play an important role in the American political system. While we may not always agree with the rulings of the courts, we accept that the courts are examples of democracy at work. Citizens see the courts as symbol of American justice and as guardians of the Constitution. After the controversial *Bush v. Gore* (2000) ruling, citizens, even those who had hoped for a different outcome, respected the Court's decision, and George W. Bush was sworn in as president without protest. There are times when the other branches do not agree with the Court, but still implement its decision as the law of the land. This was the case after the *Brown v. the Board of Education* (1954), when the Court ruled that schools must desegregate. President Dwight Eisenhower did not agree with the Court's decision, yet when the Arkansas governor acted in defiance of the law and moved in the state's National Guard to keep black students from entering their high school in Little Rock, Eisenhower was quick to send in federal troops to put the National Guard under federal control. The justices themselves have a great deal of respect for the democratic process. They want to make sure their decisions are significant and fair: thus, they take their roles as decision-makers seriously.

Former First Lady Michelle Obama toured the *Brown v. Board of Education* historic site. Speaking on the occasion of the 60th anniversary of the ruling, Mrs. Obama said: "The truth is that *Brown v. Board of Education* isn't just about our history, it's about our future. … No matter what you do, the point is to never be afraid to talk about these issues, particularly the issue of race, because even today, we still struggle to do that. This issue is so sensitive, so complicated, so bound up with a painful history, and we need your generation to help us break through. We need all of you to ask the hard questions and have the honest conversations because that is the only way we will heal the wounds of the past and move forward to a better future." [23]

The White House from Washington, DC (P051614CK-0038) [Public domain], via Wikimedia Commons https://bit.ly/2UwVRUL.

Checks and Balances on the Federal Courts

As we have discussed, the courts have the power to make policy by interpreting the Constitution and legal precedents. They also have the power to extend the reach of existing law and apply it to new areas and issues. While the judiciary has a lot of influence on democracy in the United States, there are checks on judicial power.

Public Opinion and the Courts

The citizens do not elect federal justices. The reason for this is the belief that the courts should not be accountable to public opinion. Supreme Court justices and other federal judges are appointed to life terms: they cannot be impeached or removed from their positions unless they have committed a serious crimes. As mentioned earlier, this protected tenure insulates them from the partisan battles in the other two branches and from the passions of the citizens. If the courts were accountable to voters, there would be the tendency to make decisions based on popularity instead of the Constitution and legal precedents. Courts are protected in order to make decisions they believe are right but that may not be popular with the public. When the Court ruled in *Brown v. The Board of Education* (1954), public opinion was still in favor of school segregation.

Even though the structure of the judiciary protects the courts from public opinion and the courts have ruled against popular beliefs, justices are not immune to politics or public opinion. While judges are not elected by the public, they do seem to sometimes respond to public opinion.

Some justices, such as Chief Justice John Roberts, seem to be concerned with how the court is perceived by the public.[24] Why do justices care what the public thinks? One answer may be that public opinion may influence which judges are nominated for seats on the court. A second reason may be that the judges want their decisions to be seen as institutionally legitimate and upheld by the other branches of government who are accountable to voters. Third, justices with more moderate ideological views may be more likely to be influenced by the opinions of others. They may be particularly susceptible to changing beliefs in society and mindful of making decisions that align with public attitudes on issues. On some issues, courts may wait to see how the public is responding and then base their decisions on citizens' views and perceptions. This seemed to be the case with same-sex marriage: many courts, such as those in New York and the District of Columbia, ruled that same-sex marriage is legal after a process which allowed citizens to discuss and weigh arguments for and against these marriages.

Congress and the Courts

Congress's primary check on the courts comes with its role in the confirmation of judges and in impeachment proceedings. The president nominates justices, but the Senate must vote to confirm the president's choices. Congress can remove from office justices convicted of bribery, treason, or other high crimes and misdemeanors. The House of Representatives determines the rationale for the charges, and the Senate then holds a trial. Article III of the Constitution establishes the Supreme Court. It gives Congress the authority to determine the numbers of justices who sit on the Supreme Court. In addition, Congress can revise legislation declared unconstitutional and can amend the Constitution. If Congress disagrees with how the Court has interpreted the Constitution, lawmakers can create a law that essentially nullifies the Court's ruling. The Supreme Court cannot react until another lawsuit addressing the issue makes its way to the Court.

The Executive and the Courts

Statue at the Trail of Tears Memorial and Museum in Pulaski, Tennessee, commemorating the experience of Native American tribes when, between 1838 and 1839, 15,000 Cherokees were taken from their ancestral homes in Georgia and placed on a forced march to Oklahoma. More than 4,000 died en route.

JNix / Shutterstock.com

The power of the judiciary extends only as far as the executive branch is willing to enforce it. There are, however, only a handful of cases in which presidents did not enforce a Supreme Court decision. One such example was Andrew Jackson's refusal to carry out the Supreme Court's ruling on the removal of Cherokee Indians from Georgia. Cherokees had lived for nearly 40 years on land in Georgia that they held through a treaty with the federal government. When gold was discovered in the territory, the Georgia legislature seized the land and, in doing so, defied the federal treaty. President Jackson sided with Georgia and supported the removal of the Cherokees. The Cherokees sued and the case eventually reached the Supreme Court, which ruled in *Worcester v. Georgia* (1832) that the seizure of Cherokee lands was illegal. Jackson refused to enforce the Court's ruling, arguing "[Supreme Court Chief Justice] John Marshall made his decision, now let him enforce it."[25] Jackson negotiated an agreement with the Cherokees and sent troops to move them west of the Mississippi River. Thousands died along the way and those who did reach their destination realized they in fact had no land on which to settle. The story of the "resettlement" of the Cherokees, known as the Trail of Tears, is one of the greatest tragedies in American history. The story also illustrates that the power of the Court is merely the power to persuade. Unless the Court's decisions are upheld and enforced by the other branches of the political system, they are just words.

14.7 The Politics of the Apolitical Branch

bakdc / Shutterstock.com

The judicial branch defines the boundaries of permissible conduct. It checks the powers of the president and Congress through judicial review, making sure that the actions of the elected branches of government are constitutional. It also serves as a referee between national and state governments. Established as a neutral and impartial arbiter for justice, the judiciary is not immune from political conflict. The Supreme Court often weighs in on some of the most divisive issues facing the country. Moreover, many landmark cases cause deep divisions within the Court about how to interpret the Constitution and how to balance the tension between differences in values and scarcity of resources.

The political process affects how courts make decisions. While judges may be shielded from some aspects of politics, individual political ideologies, interactions with the executive and legislative branches, and pressure from interest groups bring politics into the courts.

The courts play a critical role in the political system. They are the gatekeepers of the Constitution and an important link between the intent of the nation's founders and the realities of the present day.

14.8 What Can I Do?

The judiciary is a powerful institution in American politics whose influence has evolved and grown over time. The nation's founders viewed the judicial branch as necessary to the functioning of democracy. Many share this view: they see the courts as central to justice and as champions in the defense of our liberties and the promotion of our rights. There are others, however, who take a more critical approach to the judiciary and argue that it wields too much influence, especially with regard to the elected branches of government. They worry that the lifetime appointments and protected tenure mean that justices are not accountable to the people and therefore undermine the very definition of democracy. What happens if these unelected, long-serving officials make bad policy decisions? What if their decisions overturn the actions of the people's elected representatives? In response to these concerns, some argue that judges should limit their activities to ligation between two parties and avoid making decisions on any major policy issues. By limiting their activities in this way, justices would not overstep their bounds and interfere with the work of the elected branches of government that are accountable to the people. If you are worried about the policy making power of the Supreme Court, remember that the Constitution envisioned a democratic system in which the Court would actively participate. While the U.S. government is for the people and by the people, the majority should not necessarily have control over every policy decision. Sometimes the majority supports policies that advance discrimination and violate civil rights, as was the case in 1954 when the Court ruled against popular opinion and ended segregation in schools in *Brown v Board of Education*.

While the courts have advanced civil rights in many cases, minorities, poor Americans, and marginalized groups have not always been treated equally. It is important to be aware of the valid concerns about inequalities that remain in the dispensation of justice.

Because you cannot elect Supreme Court justices, you cannot exercise your democratic rights in the voting booth. But you can still engage and have your opinions heard. As we discussed in this chapter, the Supreme Court does respond to public opinions. So get involved. Participate in marches and protests, write letters and make phone calls to your elected representatives, and take a public stance on the issues that matter to you. If you are interested in more directly participating in the judiciary, you could go to law school, become a lawyer, become a judge, and contribute to the system from within.

14.9 What's the Alternative?

The Framers of the Constitution could have chosen to have a weak judicial branch and make Congress supreme, similar to the British Parliament, whose laws cannot be overturned by any court in the land. The legislature would have absolute authority when it comes to passing laws and deciding on their constitutionality. In the United Kingdom, however, Parliament has both legislative and executive powers and is therefore institutionally sovereign in a way that the U.S. Congress is not. If Congress were the final arbiter of constitutional interpretation, it would assume executive powers and we would have a parliamentary system rather than a presidential democracy.

Another alternative is that the United States could have a system in which a consensus of states could rule on the constitutionality of laws. The problem with consensus, however, is that it can break down easily and lead to war.

It is difficult to conceive of an alternative to the judicial branch that would be able to avoid all dissension and resolve every dispute in a way that would be acceptable to all sides. If politics is about who gets what, when, and how, then political conflict between differences in values and scarcity of resources is an inevitable feature of democracy. The judicial branch plays a critical role in helping establish the rules that define the political process in the United States. The federal government is built on a triad, with each branch of the triad created to prevent the others from becoming too powerful. The loss of any one branch would cripple the balance of power and weaken democracy. While it is flawed and rightly subject to criticism, the judicial branch keeps the wheels of government turning as the nation works to uphold the ideals espoused in the Constitution.

Endnotes

1. *Elonis v. United States*, 575 U.S. ___ (U.S. 2015)

2. "Amici Curiae Brief of the Marion B. Brechner First Amendment Project And Rap Music Scholars (Professors Erik Nielson And Charis E. Kubrin) In Support Of Petitioner," Ars Technica, August 18, 2014, http://cdn.arstechnica.net/wp-content/uploads/2014/08/elonisrap.pdf.

3. *Obergefell et al. v. Hodges, Director, Ohio Department of Health, Et Al.*, No. 14–556 (2015).

4. "Data from the National Center for State Courts," National Center for the State Courts, http://www.ncsc.org/Sitecore/Content/Microsites/PopUp/Home/CSP/CSP_Intro.

5. "Federal Judicial Caseload Statistics, 2016," United States Courts, http://www.uscourts.gov/statistics-reports/federal-judicial-caseload-statistics-2016.

6. Andrew Cohen, "Psst...Justice Scalia...You Know, You're an Activist Too," *The New York Times*, April 19, 2005, https://www.nytimes.com/2005/04/19/opinion/psst-justice-scalia-you-know-youre-an-activist-judge-too.html.

7. Alexander Hamilton, "Federalist no. 78," The Avalon Project, http://avalon.law.yale.edu/18th_century/fed78.asp.

8. *Marbury v. Madison*, 5 U.S. (1 Cranch) 137 (U.S 1803).

9. *McCulloch v. Maryland*, 17 U.S. (4 Wheat.) 316 (1819).

10. *Lemon v. Kurtzman*, 403 U.S. 602 (1971).

11. *Bush v. Gore*, 531 U.S. 98 (2000).

12. Dahlia Lithwick, "Is Trump's Second Immigration Ban Unconstitutional?: Assessing the Legal Challenges to the New Executive Order," Slate, March 10, 2017, https://slate.com/news-and-politics/2017/03/is-trumps-second-immigration-ban-unconstitutional.html.

13. Adam Liptak, "Court Refuses to Reinstate Travel Ban, Dealing Trump Another Legal Loss," *The New York Times*, February 9, 2017, https://www.nytimes.com/2017/02/09/us/politics/appeals-court-trump-travel-ban.html.

14. Ibid.

15. Melanie Zanona, "Timeline: Trump's Travel Ban's Road to the Supreme Court," The Hill, September 17, 2017, http://thehill.com/homenews/administration/350932-timeline-trump-travel-bans-road-to-the-supreme-court.

16. Eric Posner, "Why does the court usually decide cases either 9–0 or 5–4?" Slate, July 1, 2014, http://www.slate.com/articles/news_and_politics/the_breakfast_table/features/2014/scotus_roundup/supreme_court_2014_why_are_most_cases_either_9_0_or_5_4.html,

17. Lee Epstein, William M. Landes, And Richard A. Posner, "The Best For Last: The Timing Of U.S. Supreme Court Decisions," *Duke Law Journal* 64, no. 6 (March 2015): 993.

18. Lee Epstein, William M. Landes, And Richard A. Posner, "The Best For Last: The Timing Of U.S. Supreme Court Decisions," *Duke Law Journal* 64, no. 6 (March 2015): 993. According to the article's authors, a big case is identified by front-page coverage in The New York Times; front-page and other coverage in four national newspapers (The New York Times, Los Angeles Times, The Washington Post, and Chicago Tribune); the number of amicus curiae briefs filed in a case; and the number of subsequent citations by the Supreme Court to its decision in a case.

19. Pamela Torn, "Criminal Punishment and Politics: Elected Judges Take Tougher Stance Prior to Elections," Berkeley Haas Newsroom, October 18, 2012, http://newsroom.haas.berkeley.edu/criminal-punishment-and-politics-elected-judges-take-tougher-stance-prior-elections/.

20. Stephen Collinson, "Obama: SCOTUS nominee will be 'indisputably' qualified," CNN Politics, February 16, 2016, http://www.cnn.com/2016/02/16/politics/barack-obama-antonin-scalia-replacement/index.html.

21. "Demography of Article III Judges," Federal Judicial Center, https://www.fjc.gov/history/exhibits/graphs-and-maps/gender.

22. UC Berkeley, "Judge Sonia Sotomayor's 2001 address to the 'Raising the Bar' symposium at the UC Berkeley School of Law," UCBerkeleyNews https://www.berkeley.edu/news/media/releases/2009/05/26_sotomayor.shtml.

23. Morgan Whitaker, "First Lady: Brown v. Board not just about history, but future," MSNCB, May 14, 2016, http://www.msnbc.com/politicsnation/michelle-obama-brown-v-board-of-ed-anniversary-speech-topeka-kansas

24. Charles Lane, "Slimy Leaks about John Roberts at Supreme Court," *The Washington Post*, July 3, 2012, https://www.washingtonpost.com/blogs/post-partisan/post/slimy-leaks-about-john-roberts-at-supreme-court/2012/07/03/gJQAPq9mKW_blog.html?utm_term=.d723f8976e88.

25. Stephen Breyer, "University of Pennsylvania Law School Commencement Remarks," SupremeCourt.gov, May 19, 2003, https://www.supremecourt.gov/publicinfo/speeches/viewspeech/sp_05-19-03.

CHAPTER 15
Domestic Policy: Taking Care of Things at Home

Chapter Objectives

1. Understand how public policy is made and evaluated.
2. Discuss the policy-making process from agenda setting to evaluation.
3. Assess generic public policy solutions.
4. Describe monetary and fiscal economic policies.
5. Explore major social welfare policy programs.

Introduction: Should the Tax on Alcohol be Increased?

Bar-hopping can be fun. It can lead to friendship, or even a love relationship. Intoxication feels good, relieves tension, and loosens inhibitions. Alcoholic drinks not only quench thirst, they taste good and can make a nice complement to a satisfying meal. And what would holiday celebrations be without a little booze? Evidence suggests that light consumption of alcohol among older adults improves health and extends life due to its anti-cholesterol effects.[1] However, excessive drinking can lead to serious health and social problems. Alcohol can lead to acts of violence, injury, unprotected sex, and death. Some of these harms fall on the drinker, but many of the costs of drinking are paid by friends, family, and the public.

econometric research

The application of statistical methods and economic data in research.

elasticity

Changes in demand in response to price or income.

© Shutterstock, Inc.

The most serious health concern regarding alcohol consumption involves public safety. Alcohol is involved in two of every five deaths from automobile accidents and about one-third of all injury deaths.[2] About 88,000 deaths per year are related to alcohol consumption, making it the third leading cause of preventable death in the United States (resulting in $249 billion in losses in 2010.)[3] Alcohol impairs attention and information processing, reduces peripheral vision, and impairs the ability to track objects.[4] Contrary to popular belief, drinking alcohol decreases the likelihood of surviving an accident.[5] Perhaps the most sorrowful statistic is that for each 100 alcohol-impaired drivers who die in accidents, another 77 victims die with them.[6] The consumption of alcohol reduces inhibitions and triggers aggressive behavior in some people, leading to bar fights, violence at sporting events, date rape, and domestic battery. Impaired judgment causes one to discount the consequences of his or her actions such that immediate urges hold greater importance.[7] Such "courage in a bottle" can lead to violence but also to greater injury, because alcohol numbs the senses and makes injuries less painful. In addition, drinkers may be easy prey to assaulters and rapists. Among teens, the use of alcohol decreases the likelihood of using birth control measures.[8] Over time, excessive drinking is related to disorders of the gastrointestinal tract, damage to the pancreas and kidneys, and scarring of the liver (cirrhosis), which does the work of metabolizing alcohol. Liver damage can lead to nutritional deficiencies and impair one's immune system, resulting in greater susceptibility to infection.[9] About 21,000 Americans die from alcoholic liver disease annually.[10]

Should the government do something about the public health problems associated with alcohol? Economist Philip J. Cook thinks so. In his book, *Paying the Tab: The Costs and Benefits of Alcohol Control,* Cook found that the consumption of alcoholic beverages was influenced by price. The higher the price of alcohol, the less consumption, even among those who drink heavily on a regular basis. During World War I, for example, Cook found that several countries rationed alcohol to divert its use for military purposes, while other countries instituted prohibition. In each case, deaths due to liver cirrhosis declined dramatically. Other studies show that even small increases in the state excise taxes on alcohol lead to statistically significant reductions in cirrhosis mortality. The public policy insight is that if the price of alcohol can be increased through taxation, the quantity demanded by consumers will decline. Why? Because people have multiple demands on their limited incomes. Adding a federal excise tax on alcohol will reduce consumption and lead to reductions in rates of accidents, violence, and other unwanted social behavior.

© Shutterstock, Inc.

Pooling decades of data reflecting differences in prices from the 50 states and reviewing findings from half a century of **econometric research**, Cook concluded that a small increase in taxation can reduce the average alcohol consumption of a large population even though the price increase would affect the decisions of only a fraction of drinkers. Economists measure the responsiveness of demand to price in terms of **elasticity**, the change in the amount demanded associated with a 1 percent increase in price. The effect of a 1 percent increase in the price of beer, for example, results in a -0.74 price elasticity. In other words, a 1 percent increase in the price of a six-pack from $7 to $7.07 would result in a reduction in sales of almost three-fourths of 1 percent annually. Who would forgo buying beer to save a measly 7 cents? Not many people–just 7.5 per 1000 on average–but a 10 percent increase (from $7 to $7.70) would affect 10 times more people, or 7.5 people per 100 on average, and so on.[11]

Estimates of price elasticity also provide a basis for predicting whether increased prices would reduce the negative effects of alcohol consumption. Using a 30-year panel of state-level data, Cook and his colleagues found that an increase of 10 cents per ounce of ethanol (the primary ingredient in alcoholic beverages) would result in a 3.4 percent reduction in overall mortality rates, saving tens of thousands of lives each year.[12] Based on extensive research, the Environmental Protection Agency estimates the value of a single life at $7.4 million (adjusted for inflation) when evaluating environmental regulations.[13] Losses from less serious injuries, property damage, unwanted pregnancies, and decreased worker productively would also be reduced. Higher prices would also help some people with dependency to control excessive drinking. Higher taxes would also enhance public revenues. The additional money could be used to pay for the treatment of alcoholism, some other worthy purpose, or to reduce other taxes. Survey research also shows that a majority of the public favors increasing taxes on alcohol if the revenues are used for treatment of alcoholism or for prevention programs.[14] Furthermore, state and federal taxes haven't been raised for some time, which means that the real value of excise taxes on alcohol has declined. Increased taxes on alcohol wouldn't affect the one-third of adults who don't drink alcohol, and the effect on moderate drinkers with healthy incomes would hardly be noticeable. But heavy or binge drinkers would be substantially affected (which is the point), as would be the entire liquor industry, including beer, wine, and spirit makers as well as bars, restaurants, hotels and other industries that profit from the sale of alcohol.

Cook's policy analysis makes clear that higher alcohol taxes would improve the health and safety of the public and save a substantial number of victims' lives taken by drunk drivers. But, higher prices would also impinge on the legitimate enjoyment of alcoholic beverages. Holiday celebrations may be a little less festive and the positive effects of moderate alcohol consumption on the health and life expectancy in older drinkers will be a little less evident. Taxation also fails to distinguish responsible from irresponsible drinking behavior, such as when a group of friends drinks at home, designates a driver when clubbing, or uses a taxi or ride-sharing service. Taxation may also result in substitutions; for example, drinkers may turn to marijuana as an alternative means of intoxication. Higher prices will affect lower income drinkers more than those with higher incomes or greater wealth. Increasing taxes on alcohol would also result in lost jobs and profits in the liquor industry and related businesses and would result in lost tax revenue. And what about the words, "Life, liberty and the pursuit of happiness"? Are adults not the best judge of their own interests?[15] Is government the right place to turn when the public benefits from changes in individual behavior? Can losses in freedom and happiness be measured and compared with lost lives, wages, property damage, and medical costs? If so, where do we draw the line between greater public health and safety and less individual freedom or happiness? What, then, is the cost-effective alcohol policy?

In this chapter and the next, we will attempt to analyze what the American government does in response to pubic problems and what that tells us about our politics and society. We analyze public policies in terms of the problems that are addressed, the goals or objectives the policies are meant to achieve, the tools or methods used to address problems, and the institutional and political processes that produced them. The economic policy section highlights the problems as well as the goals and tools of economic policy, including fiscal, regulatory, monetary, taxing, and spending. The social policy section does the same for health and welfare policies. We discuss foreign policy in the next chapter.

15.1 Making and Evaluating Public Policy

The making of public policy is complex because values like health, safety, freedom, and happiness are hard to quantify. Various segments of society value each of these differently, which make trade-offs difficult. Those opposed to controls on alcohol dislike the loss of enjoyment and jobs, while people in favor of regulation may have lost loved ones to drunk drivers and wish to prevent further loss of life. Finding the best solution is rarely easy. Taxing alcohol to recover the policy effects lost to inflation is the solution favored by Philip Cook, but there are other alternatives, such as making bar owners liable for the actions of their customers if they serve visibly intoxicated patrons.

Members of the Jefferson Country Historical Society reenacting a Nineteenth-century temperance demonstration in Port Townsend, Washington, March 18, 2006.

The Old Major / Shutterstock.com

It is important to keep in mind that not all social problems are a concern of government. Federal taxes on alcohol were not always implemented to address health or moral problems; rather, they were mostly viewed as a means to raise revenue for the federal government. Indeed, the first tax on distilled spirits was originally justified by Congress to pay the Revolutionary War debt. However, the tax caused resentment among western farmers, proved difficult to collect, and was revoked by 1802. The tax was instituted again to help pay for the Civil War, and by the time the United States entered World War I in 1917, taxes on alcohol amounted to as much as 30 percent of all federal tax revenue.[16] The passage of the Sixteenth Amendment allowed for the imposition of the federal income tax, which decreased the federal government's dependence on the alcohol tax and cleared the way for Prohibition via the Eighteenth Amendment.[17] Prohibition was due to the efforts of the temperance movement (a social movement against alcohol), but it lasted only 13 years before it was repealed by the Twenty-first Amendment. Much of the support for the repeal of Prohibition was due to declining federal revenues during the Great Depression and the perceived opportunity to recover jobs and tax revenues. It wasn't until the 1980s that a concern for public safety led to a national standard for driving under the influence (the .08 blood-alcohol level) and a minimum drinking age of 21 years.

Policy solutions are seldom final. They may fail to reflect a consistent understanding of the social problem. They are constantly changing due to social or economic conditions or changes in political leadership. Policy speeches given by politicians and others can be heard. Legislation, the opinions of judges, and the regulations and memoranda written by administrators and elected officials can be read, but these things are not policy by themselves. Public policies can be inferred only from the actions of national, state, and local institutions and officials over time. For example, the next chapter on foreign policy begins with President John F. Kennedy's decision to blockade Cuba as a way of compelling the Soviet Union to remove nuclear missiles from the island without triggering a nuclear war. That decision wasn't America's foreign policy; it was just one episode among many in a long sequence that determined U.S. policy toward the Soviet Union during the Cold War. Public policy is not something that can be captured by a single event or decision. It is the guiding principle behind the decisions, actions, laws, and programs of government. Like politics, public policy is complex and sometimes elusive.

The Policy-Making Process

Making public policy is a process. It is a series of actions undertaken by government intended to achieve a specific end. Beyond intentions, policy can be what is actually accomplished. In other words, policy is the cumulative effect or outcomes of the actions and decisions of all those who make and implement public policy. It is useful to think of this as a cycle or logical sequence of continuous events. Because solutions to public problems are rarely complete, the policy process is best thought of as continuous rather than a strictly ordered series of actions with a definable beginning, middle, and end (see Figure 15.1). Changing social and economic conditions constantly bring new information and demands that spur reconsideration and revision of existing policies. The process is depicted as a sequence, but in the real world, the stages often overlap, are skipped, or are repeated out of order.

FIGURE 15.1 The Policy Process Cycle

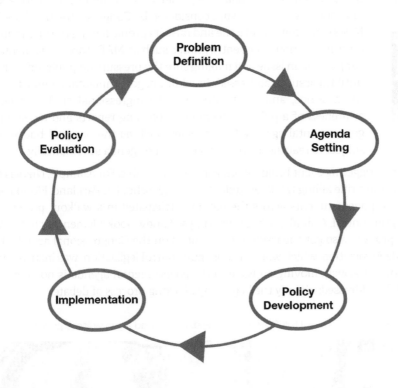

Agenda Setting

The first stage of the policy process is getting the issue on the governmental agenda. Moving an issue that can become the subject of public policy to the institutional agenda is a critical step. As you can imagine, public officials have a multitude of issues with individuals, interest groups, and businesses clamoring for attention. As mentioned already, federal taxes on alcohol were not originally thought of as a response to health or moral problems. The concern for alcohol as a public safety rather than a moral concern began in 1980 after Candy Lightner's 13-year-old daughter was killed by a drunk driver as the girl was walking to a church carnival. The driver had a history of drunk driving..[18] Lightner's tragic loss motivated her to organize a politically effective grassroots organization called Mothers Against Drunk Driving (MADD). After much lobbying, California's governor appointed a commission on drunk driving and added Lightner to the commission. Later, President Ronald Reagan would appoint her to a presidential Commission on Drunk Driving. With help from the 395 local chapters of MADD, Lightner and the commissions promoted several programs, including the establishment of roadside testing and the setting of a national minimum drinking legal age.[19] Without Lightner and her organization, the issue of drunk driving may not have become part of the federal government's agenda.

© Shutterstock, Inc.

Not all individuals and groups have an equal chance of moving an issue to the governmental agenda. The president, for example, can, with a single speech or post on Twitter, get issues considered by Congress. *The New York Times* or Fox News can publicize an issue and raise its profile among the public and move Congress into action. Frequently, groups such as MADD are instrumental in building support for an issue and making sure the pressure on public officials is sustained until the issue is addressed. In addition, governmental administrators, advisory commissions, and White House and congressional staff members can raise awareness of a pubic problem by publishing reports and moving issues to the governmental agenda. Other issues, such as the national budget or programs subject to reauthorization, make it to the agenda automatically.

At times, a triggering event brings an issue before the pubic. For example, Nikolas Cruz opened fire with an assault rifle killing 17 fellow students at a high school in Parkland, Florida on Valentine's Day 2018. In response, students across the nation participated in a walkout protesting Congress' inaction on gun control. A similar school shooting at Sandy Hook Elementary in Connecticut and subsequent protests also got the issue of gun control on the Congressional agenda. However, the National Rifle Association, which works against gun control legislation, was instrumental in killing the legislation. Obviously, moving an issue to the governmental agenda is no guarantee that the problem will be addressed: it's only the beginning of a long process of debate.

Students from Stoneman Douglas High School in Parkland, Florida lead a gun violence protest.

Louis.Roth / Shutterstock.com

Policy Formation

After an issue makes it to the governmental agenda, it is shaped and may be given legal status. Policy can take many forms, including legislation from Congress or other legislatures; legal opinions from the courts; and various methods of executive orders, regulations, and memoranda from presidents, governors, and other executives, as well as the bureaucracy. Much of policy formation is a political process affected by institutional rules and behavior. Thus, the policy formation process in Congress is different from that of the president and the executive branch and different again from the courts. During this time, policy is defined, information is collected and discussed, alternatives for dealing with the problem are analyzed, and the preferred choice is made. Policy formation is not complete after a legislature passes a law and it is signed by the executive. Because legislation is often vague or ambiguous, it is turned over to the bureaucracy, which promulgates rules and regulations, or the new law works its way into the courts where laws are interpreted.

We cover the national policy institutions and their influences in our chapters on Congress (Chapter 11), the presidency (Chapter 12), the bureaucracy (Chapter 13) and the courts (Chapter 14). Congress and the president are open to outside influences including political parties (Chapter 8), interest groups (Chapter 9), and the media (Chapter 10), but constituent influences that come in the form of public opinion (Chapter 6) and voting (Chapter 7) are especially important. Advisors, funders, colleagues, and professional staff are also influential in shaping policy.

Policy makers have access to many sources of information and expertise as they formulate public policy proposals. The Government Accountability Office, the Congressional Budget Office, and the Congressional Research Service provide research for Congress in addition to the 20,000 people who serve the several hundred congressional committees and subcommittees.[20] The president is advised by the White House staff but also by the Office of Management and Budget, the Council of Economic Advisors, the Council on Environmental Quality, and the National Security Council. Interests groups such as MADD provide technical information and background as well as information about whether a solution is likely to be politically feasible.

Policy analysis is often thought of as a rational process in which all possible options are weighed according to their costs and benefits before the best policy is selected. Much of this was done in Philip Cook's analysis of the best way to manage the public costs of drinking alcohol. His formal analysis began by setting goals, such as the efficient use of public funds, the preservation of life, the freedom to enjoy alcoholic beverages, and finding a policy solution that would be politically and administratively feasible. He developed and analyzed policy alternatives to increasing taxes on alcohol, including raising the minimum drinking age or increasing penalties for drinking and driving. In the end, he chose what his research indicated was the most cost-effective solution. While much policy is analyzed rationally, it is not always possible to satisfy everyone's goals or interests. Often the policy chosen is the result of compromise whereby the different interests involved are satisfied with less than what they originally wanted. Frequently, the most politically feasible options are the ones close to current practice. Hence, evidence shows that policy changes incrementally, in small steps, rather than through radical departures from the status quo.

Policy Implementation

Once policy formulation is complete, the next stage is policy implementation, which involves getting the funds, people, offices, and methods for administering a program. This is the beginning of activity as the policy decisions and goals embodied in legislation or executive orders are translated into rules and regulations and carried out by a variety of people, businesses, government agencies, and non-profit organizations. A large variety of agencies and individuals are involved in implementing policy and each has some influence. Administrators, for example, normally have some discretion in interpreting the rules and regulations, deciding on agency priorities, allocating funds, and choosing methods to carry out programs. Such decisions often reflect the political philosophy and preferences of the administrators as well as the time-honored traditions of the agency.

Often, the federal government develops partnerships with private institutions to implement federal policy. For example, federal health care policy is implemented by private and public hospitals, nursing homes, insurance companies, doctors, nurses, therapists, and many others. Recall also from our chapter on federalism (Chapter 3) how the federal government used grants-in-aid to get state and local governments to adopt the use of breathalyzers for administering roadside tests for drunk driving and accept a national standard of .08 percent blood alcohol concentration (BAC) or higher as proof of intoxication. In practice, most policy is made during implementation. The process is ongoing as agencies and programs depend on a continuing supply of money to operate and carry out policy implementation. Dealing with the question of how much money the government devotes to each of its programs is a way of revisiting society's problems and revising its goals. Often, program goals are revised according to how much money is available.

Evaluation

Policy evaluation determines if the policy works as intended. It involves judging a program's success in terms of its goals. For example, Philip Cook's proposal of increasing the federal excise tax on alcohol (if implemented) would be evaluated in terms of reductions in alcohol-related traffic accidents, cirrhosis fatalities, bar fights, assaults, rapes, and unwanted pregnancies. These costs can be measured by the number of lives saved, injuries avoided, and by savings in hospital and worker productivity costs. However, Cook also wanted to minimize losses in terms of freedom and enjoyment of alcohol as well as the possible health enhancing effects for older drinkers, so he wanted to find a politically and administratively feasible policy solution. This proves to be much more difficult to measure. To fully evaluate the program, the costs of administering the policy (collecting the tax from makers of alcoholic beverages) as well as public and private costs due to lost jobs, lost enjoyment, and health benefits would have to be estimated and subtracted from the benefits gained.

Ideally, policy evaluation should come after the policy is implemented. In practice, however, policies are evaluated almost immediately by citizens, the media, political parties, and interest groups. The rollout of the Affordable Care Act (aka Obamacare), for example, was judged a failure after it became apparent that the government's website, which was supposed to make it easy to apply for and purchase health insurance over the internet, could not handle the demand and technical requirements of the program. With the deadline looming, the website crashed almost immediately, leaving thousands of people without information or a place to apply to the program. Like other aspects of the policy process, evaluation is political as well as technical. Those who opposed the ACA were keen to conclude it was a failure. Indeed, opposition in the House of Representatives tried to use the failed rollout to defund the Act, which led to a 16-day government shutdown in October 2013. On the other hand, proponents of the program used the issue as evidence that the demand for the program was underestimated and the program should be expanded. It was too soon to tell if the ACA had failed or succeeded, but because goals of such a program are many and difficult to measure, evaluation inevitably becomes part of the political process. Legislation often requires annual audits or after-the-fact policy analysis to see if the program is working. The idea is to inject some objectivity into policy evaluation.

15.2 Generic Policy Solutions

sanctions

Penalties, such as fines or imprisonment, for disobeying a law.

Enforcement of public policy is often associated with coercion. At the extreme, the punishment for purposefully inflicting harm on another person can involve a prison term proportional to the harm inflicted. Long prison terms for driving under the influence may act as a deterrent to would-be offenders and prevent them from harming others while in prison. However, there are many methods other than coercion that governments can use to implement policy. After the passage of the Eighteenth Amendment, the production, transport, and sale of alcohol was banned and **sanctions** (penalties) were put in place to enforce the policy. But prohibition was a failure and the Amendment was eventually repealed. Other policy tools for controlling the negative effects of alcohol consumption, such as raising the price of alcohol through taxation, have proven to be effective while preserving some personal freedom and the choice to consume alcohol. Public policies can be implemented by freeing or stimulating markets, taxing or spending, supplying goods and services through government, or supplying education, information, and persuasion. In the following sections we consider a sampling of some of the more common methods of enforcing public policies. Keep in mind that it is not always clear the government should involve itself in a public problem. For example, laws requiring automobile drivers and passengers to wear seat belts and motorcyclists to wear helmets can be justified because they save lives, but the costs of non-compliance fall mostly on the user. In other words, limiting individual choice is often necessary to keep someone from harming others, but seat belt and helmet laws mostly protect the wearers, who may not want to protect themselves. Preserving choice and freedom should be considered desirable even if there is some cost to the public. Public problems and their solutions are usually complex. Policy tools should be narrowly tailored to fit specific causes and contexts.

Freeing or Stimulating Markets

Often the best approach is to rely on the efficiency of markets to provide society with needed goods and services. In some cases, this implies deregulation, such as when President Jimmy Carter signed the Airline Deregulation Act of 1978. This removed many of the controls protecting airline routes, the entry of new carriers into the market, and air fares. As a result of the Act, some smaller cities and towns lost airline services, the salaries of airline pilots and employees fell, and airline unions were weakened. However, increased competition caused airline fares to drop dramatically as the number of carriers and routes increased. In sum, the winners vastly outnumbered the losers as low-cost carriers such as Southwest Airlines expanded air travel to thousands of middle- and lower-income individuals. This contributed to the development of a wider range of aircraft types and manufactures. The removal of prohibition of alcohol and the legalization of gambling and marijuana in some states is a form of deregulation that comes from a realization that criminalization of certain activities is ineffective and leads to the development of black markets and other criminal activity.

Privatization, whereby a government agency contracts with a private company to provide a good or service that was previously carried out by government, is also a way to free up markets that often results in greater efficiency. For example, instead of the federal government building housing projects for low-income families, it now gives those families in need of shelter a **voucher** that can be used to rent an apartment in the private housing market. Food stamps (now EBT cards) given to low-income families are vouchers that can be used like cash to buy groceries in most markets. They replaced government surplus food commodities like cheese and peanut butter that were provided to low-income families and individuals in need of food. Some communities are issuing vouchers so families can purchase educational services at private institutions in districts with failed public schools.

voucher

An authorization for a disbursement of cash or credit. As a method of implementing public policy, it is usually given to qualified individuals to exchange for goods or services such as food or housing.

Governments can also create new markets, such as when the federal government allowed companies required to meet air pollution standards to buy, sell, trade, or bank emission allowances. Such permits encourage efficient companies to pollute below allowable standards and sell permits to companies with older plants who find it too difficult or costly to meet new emission standards. This allows older plants to remain in business while the permit system leads to an overall reduction in emissions.

Regulation

The traditional method of implementing public policy is by establishing laws or rules backed by sanctions designed to coerce behavior. Criminal codes are a prime example. When people violate laws enacted to protect the public health, safety, morals, or welfare, those found guilty may be fined or sent to prison. Regulation can be costly because, after rules are established, compliance must be monitored, such as when the police establish checkpoints to test drivers for intoxication or when inspectors enforce safety regulations for buildings during construction. In determining whether rules and regulations have been violated, the government must also observe procedures designed to protect the rights of the accused. The court system (Chapter 14) is designed to prevent the government from depriving any individual or corporation of life, liberty, or property without due process of law. In 2016, the Office of Management and Budget estimated the annual direct and indirect costs of 129 major regulations from 2005 to 2015 in the range of $74 billion to $110 billion. The same report estimated the benefits of of the same regulations at between $269 billion to $872 billion, far outweighing the costs.[21]

cartelization

Agreements among producers to limit or control production in order to fix prices and increase profits.

Natural monopolies, such as electricity, transportation, communication, water, and sewer utilities are a problem because the limited number of firms leads to monopoly pricing and **cartelization** (agreements among producers to limit production and increase prices). In such cases, price regulation by government is often required to ensure adequate supply at a reasonable price.

Taxing and Spending

Government can use its power to tax and spend to induce or modify behavior rather than coerce. The idea is to use taxes to increase the cost of items that are too plentiful from a society's perspective or to subsidize things that are too scarce. In theory, to avoid higher prices due to taxation, consumers and firms can choose to limit their consumption voluntarily. This is the idea behind raising taxes to reduce the harms imposed on society due to excessive consumption of alcohol. The same technique is used to increase the price of cigarettes to reduce addiction and lung cancer. Through taxation, the policy is implemented at lower costs than by setting and enforcing regulation. Government intervention and the costs of administration are minimized.

tax expenditures

Government spending accomplished through the tax code by allowing exemptions, dedications, or credits for select activities or people.

Tax policy in the form of income tax deductions and credits can be and is used to lower the costs of items the government wants citizens to purchase. One of the most popular tax deductions is the mortgage interest deduction. Currently, taxpayers can deduct the interest paid on their first and second mortgages up to a total of $1 million from their income taxes.[22] Proponents of the mortgage interest rate deduction claim that it promotes home ownership and stimulates the home building industry. However, the lost revenue costs the federal government some $77 billion and mostly benefits the more affluent members of society, who are generally better able to take advantage of **tax expenditures**.[23] On the other hand, the earned income tax credit benefits low-income working families with children. The credit is refundable, meaning that for very low-income families, the tax credit can increase one's tax refund even if one's tax liability is zero. In other words, they receive a check even though they owe no taxes. Thus, the earned income tax credit provides a substitute for cash assistance for low-income working families distributed by the state welfare office. The government avoids the administrative costs.

Supplying Goods and Services through Government

In some cases, the private market is unable to provide a service that the public needs. Military defense is an example of a public good that is needed yet is not provided by the private marketplace.[24] The problem is that, once produced, national security cannot be divided such that it can be sold in the marketplace. In addition, one person's enjoyment of the benefits of national security doesn't diminish or detract from another person's enjoyment. For this reason, public goods such as military defense, public health, police and fire protection, disease control, public roadways, clean air and water, and air-traffic control are not supplied by markets and must be provided by government. Indeed, the federal government has been supplying services such as building roads, bridges, dams, and waterways through the Army Corps of Engineers since the beginning of the country. Similarly, the Centers for Disease Control and Prevention provides essential public health services when it protects the population from emerging infectious diseases.

Information and Persuasion

Government can improve the functioning of markets by providing information. The theory is that market exchanges work better if the buyer and the seller have the same information about the quality of good or service being traded. Unfortunately for the buyer, the seller usually has better information about the product or service and has an incentive to hide negative information. This is the idea behind the surgeon general's warning on packages of cigarettes that smoking causes lung cancer, heart disease, emphysema, and possible complications for pregnancy. The label is needed because consumers, especially teenagers, have difficulty recognizing the long-term effects of using this product—that smoking causes addiction and, eventually, a slow, painful death.

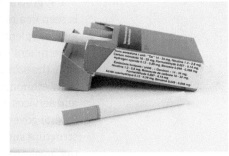
© Shutterstock, Inc.

The Food and Drug Administration (FDA) requires a label on most packaged foods detailing the calories, fat, sodium, carbohydrates, protein, and other nutrition facts contained in a standard serving. The FDA also requires disclosure of possible side effects of drugs and evidence that the product works before it can be sold. Labeling is an attractive policy option because it provides helpful information to the consumer or anyone who comes in contact with a potentially harmful product. However, services such as those offered by plumbers, contractors, doctors, and others defy labeling. In this case, licensure helps provide information about the level of skill or training of the professional that a consumer needs to make an informed decision. Organizational report cards, whereby the government provides performance ratings on restaurant sanitation, schools, health insurance programs, and hospitals, are becoming increasingly popular.

15.3 Economic Policy

Many of the generic policy tools mentioned above are used by government to help markets operate more efficiently. Indeed, government makes it possible for the economy to function by providing a legal and social framework to do business. The judicial system, for example, not only establishes order by catching and punishing criminal behavior, but settles disputes over contract violations and injuries caused by employer negligence or malfeasance. The government establishes and protects property rights (which allows people to accumulate wealth) but also sets rules for market exchange. The National Institute of Standards and Technology establishes standard weights and measures for everything from length and mass to temperature and time, allowing for an orderly and fair marketplace. The U.S. Securities and Exchange Commission protects investors from false or misleading information, insider trading, and accounting fraud. The Consumer Product Safety Commission protects consumers from unsafe products, while the Food and Drug Administration does the same for food, drugs, and medical devices. Public schools and universities create an educated labor force. The government also regulates market competition when it enforces anti-trust laws that break-up or prevent monopolies.

The goals of economic policy are many. Indeed, looking over the last few paragraphs, one wonders if all policy is economic policy. However, at its core, the goal of economic policy is to produce and maintain a strong, prosperous, and growing economy. This usually means developing programs designed to keep people employed and prices stable while maintaining economic opportunity and avoiding high levels of inequality. Of course, economists, public officials, political parties, and the public disagree about how much, and in what ways, government should be involved in the economy. To make matters more complicated, some of the goals of economic policy may be contradictory. For example, most economists believe that sustaining full employment causes high rates of inflation or price instability. Other public policies affect the economy. For example, many conservatives believe that policies to prevent global warming will hamper economic growth. On the other hand, environmentalists argue that new technologies designed to curb carbon dioxide emissions will create jobs in new sustainable industries.

A growing economy normally means an increase in the production of goods and services and is seen in a rise in the country's gross domestic product. During times of robust economic growth, jobs are plentiful and people's incomes increase. At the same time, public revenues increase and government can make more public goods and services available. On the other hand, during a recession, the economy slows or even contracts, unemployment is high, and consumer spending is low. Slow economic growth also causes governmental revenues to decline. As revenues fall, programs and services are likely to be cut when people need them most. To maintain a strong economy, the federal government uses monetary and fiscal policies. State and local governments develop infrastructure such as highways, bridges, ports, and airports to spur future growth. They also provide tax breaks to entice companies to locate in their area.

Monetary Policy

The Federal Reserve Board

AgnosticPreachersKid [CC BY-SA 3.0 (https:// creativecommons.org/licenses/by-sa/3.0)], from Wikimedia Commons. https://bit.ly/2sWzQ6l.

Monetary policies attempt to control the entire economy by managing the availability of money to banks through the Federal Reserve System (Fed), the central bank of the United States. The bank is controlled by a board of governors appointed by the president and confirmed by the Senate. To ensure that it makes its decisions free from politics, the Fed is an independent agency. Monetary policy is made by the Federal Open Market Committee, which consists of the seven members of the Board of Governors and the presidents of five of the 12 Reserve Banks.

To manage the amount and accessibility of money that banks have available to lend, the Fed uses three general policy approaches. First, it controls the flow of credit by lending to its member banks. Making more credit available helps businesses to expand and hire more people, which helps the economy expand. If, on the other hand, the Fed believes the economy is growing too fast and inflation is looming, it can make credit less available to slow the economy. The Fed does this by determining the interest rate it charges its member banks (the discount rate), thereby influencing rates that member banks charge each other (the federal funds rate). Second, the Fed can increase or decrease the amount of money in circulation by either selling or buying back securities, such as Treasury bills, thereby increasing or decreasing the supply of money. To expand the economy, the Fed increases the amount of money in the hands of the public; to slow economic growth and inflation, it decreases the supply. Lastly, the Fed can influence interest rates by adjusting the amount of money it requires banks to have on reserve. The lower the reserve requirement, the more money banks have available to lend and vice versa.

Fiscal Policy

The sheer amount of money the federal government collects and spends has a significant impact on the national economy. Fiscal policy is the federal government's influence on the economy as the sum of all the federal government's taxing and spending policies. The federal budget is formulated and passed by Congress and signed by the president as a series of funding bills. The bills reflect the priorities of the government, but also economic theories about how taxing and spending will affect the national economy. **Keynesian economic theory** predicts that decreasing taxes and increasing spending on government programs will increase the money people have to spend to buy goods and services. The increased consumer demand in turn encourages firms to produce more and increase employment. Such spending during a recession will counter its negative effects by keeping employment stable and stimulating the economy. If the economy is growing too fast, the government can reduce spending and increase taxes to slow things down.

Keynesian approaches that lower taxes on the middle- and lower-income populations and increase spending on social programs or infrastructure development, such as the building and repair of roads and bridges, are favored by Democrats. Republicans, on the other hand, favor spending for things like military weapons and border security while advocating tax cuts for corporations and investors. In general, the government is under pressure to produce a **balanced budget**, in which revenues are equal to expenditures, in order to avoid a **budget deficit**. However, both parties stimulate the economy during recessions by spending more money than the government collects through taxes, thereby creating a deficit. Fiscal policy thus becomes contentious when recessions are looming due to the future costs of deficit spending, when the annual budget is due, and when government is divided among the two political parties.

Keynesian economic theory

An economic theory that suggests governments should increase demand through increased spending to boost economic growth.

balanced budget

A governmental budget in which the revenues collected through taxes are equal to expenditures.

budget deficit

A governmental budget in which expenditures exceed revenues collected through taxes.

FIGURE 15.2 Composition of Fiscal Year 2018 Federal Budget (Billions of Dollars)
Source: Budget of the United States Government FY 2018. ©2017. AAAS.

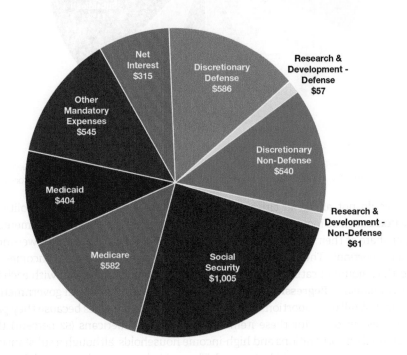

Based on "Guide to the President's Budget: Research and Development FY 2018." https://www.aaas.org/news/guide-presidents-budget-research-and-development-fy-2018.

The federal government spends most of its revenues for national defense and retirement programs, including Social Security, Medicare, and Medicaid. Social Security and Medicare are earned-benefit programs in which spending levels are determined by eligibility rules outside of the appropriations process. They are considered **mandatory spending**. These programs ease the negative effects of recessions by keeping money in the pockets of citizens and preventing the demand for goods and services from falling to depression levels. Congress does not decide how much to spend on Social Security and Medicare each year; rather, the eligibility rules are reviewed periodically, resulting in another politically contentious process. Spending for the Medicaid program is also determined by eligibility rules but the costs of the program are shared by the 50 states (although the federal government provides most of the money). Defense spending, on the other hand, is considered **discretionary spending** and can change from year to year. Congress can only use its discretionary spending programs to manage its fiscal policy, which represents only about 30 percent of the federal budget.

FIGURE 15.3 2017 Federal Outlays

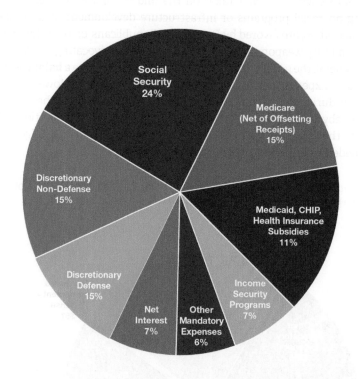

Based on "Policy Basics: Introduction to the Federal Budget Process." Center on Budget and Policy Priorities. November 08, 2018. Accessed February 14, 2019. https://www.cbpp.org/research/policy-basics-introduction-to-the-federal-budget-process.

Tax policies do not affect all citizens equally and are a major source of political conflict. **Progressive taxes** such as income taxes are designed to require the wealthier segments of society to pay a larger share of their income based on their greater ability to pay, while lower-income families pay smaller portions. The value of a dollar also decreases with higher incomes; that is, as incomes rise, the amount of satisfaction and happiness that individuals gain with each increase in their incomes diminishes. **Regressive taxes**, such as excise taxes the federal government places on tobacco and alcohol, fall disproportionately on those with lower incomes because they pay a higher percentage of their incomes for these items in taxes. Most Americans (52 percent) think taxes should be increased on corporations and high-income households, although a substantial minority (24 percent) think their taxes should be lowered. That said, there are substantial differences in attitudes toward taxation among party identifiers. A large majority (69 percent) of Democrats believe taxes on corporations should be increased, while only 32 percent of Republicans think taxes should be increased on large businesses and corporations.[25]

It should be no surprise that most Americans believe their taxes are too high.[26] However, relative to other countries with well developed economies, the total national tax rate (total federal taxes, including mandatory Social Security and Medicare insurance contributions) that the U.S. citizen pays is less than the global average. The Organization for Economic Cooperation and Development (OECD) used standardized data from 39 countries since 2008 and found that, in the United States, a married couple who both work (one at the average wage, the other at two-thirds of the average) and have two kids pay 20.1 percent of their income in taxes. This ranks 30th among the nations studied.[27] Such comparisons are difficult, however. Other countries have higher tax burdens because their social welfare programs (Social Security and Medicare in the United States) offer more generous benefits. At the same time, the OECD data do not include state and local taxes, nor do they include proportions of Social Security and Medicare taxes paid by employers.

FIGURE 15.4 OECD Tax Rates by Country

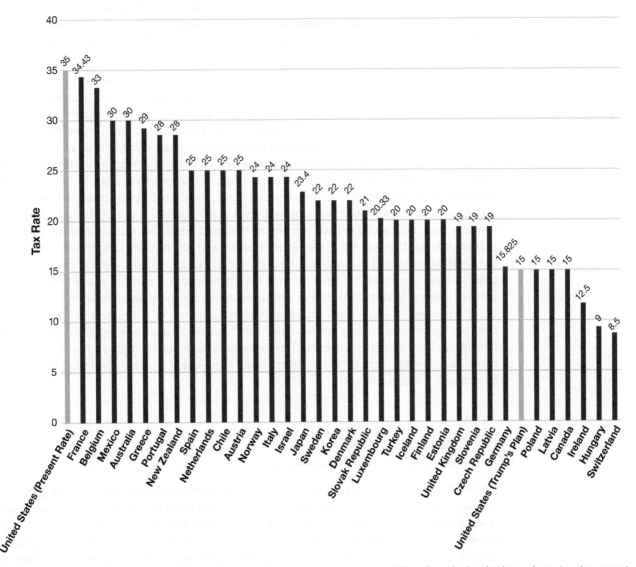

Based on "Under Trump's plan, business taxes in the US would be among the lowest in the developed world." http://www.businessinsider.com/trump-tax-plan-corporate-tax-rate-oecd-countries-2017-4.

15.4 Social Policy

contributory programs

Social programs that require recipients to contribute some cash in exchange for benefits they receive.

non-contributory programs

Social programs normally reserved for the poor that do not require recipients to contribute cash in exchange for benefits.

Most of the estimated $4 trillion federal budget of 2017 was spent on social welfare programs. This did not mean, however, that all or even most of the money went to help those living in poverty; rather, most social programs transfer income from working to middle-class elderly citizens for health care and retirement benefits. The Social Security program, which provides cash assistance to retired people, amounted to slightly more than 24 percent of the federal budget, while Medicare expenditures amounted to another 15 percent of the budget. Both of these are **contributory programs**, or "mandatory savings," in which current taxpayers now working contribute a percentage of their income in exchange for benefits they will receive after reaching retirement age. By contrast, the largest non-social policy federal spending category is for national defense, which uses about 15 percent of the federal budget. Only 8 percent of federal funds are devoted to traditional "welfare" or **non-contributory programs** that aid poor families with children based on income eligibility, such as the Supplemental Nutrition Assistance Program (formerly food stamps), Temporary Assistance for Needy Families, and Medicaid.[28]

The goals of social policy are to reduce the risks and insecurities of life and help families escape poverty. Stock markets crash, companies go bankrupt–taking worker pension funds with them–and whole economies slump. Joblessness, illness, disability, aging, miscalculation, bad luck, and laziness happen. People do not always make the best decisions for themselves, so it is important to provide help to fellow citizens who need temporary assistance or who are too old to work. Like a set of insurance programs, social policy reduces the risk of unfortunate outcomes by pooling funds across a large population and redistributing them to people in need. Because some people receive more benefits than they contribute in taxes, social policy is controversial and social programs are almost always hard won. Indeed, the United States was one of the last of the western democracies to offer social welfare. For most of the country's history, the government avoided social policies, leaving them instead to the jurisdiction of local government and private charities. It took the Great Depression to impress upon Americans the need for national welfare. Americans believed that hard work and sacrifice were the only keys to economic security, but self-reliance could not produce jobs and businesses could not survive when the economy was in collapse. During this time, the unemployed looked to their extended families, churches, charities, and local government for help, but widespread poverty overwhelmed the capacity of local agencies to provide relief. There had always been poverty in America. The Depression, however, brought a large percentage of formerly middle-class citizens into poverty, and they began making demands on the federal government for help.

Social Security

One the first of the national policies designed to help with the effects of poverty during the Depression was the Social Security Act of 1935, one of President Franklin Roosevelt's New Deal programs. It was designed to provide retirement benefits, unemployment insurance, and aid to widows, mothers with dependent children, the physically handicapped, and victims of industrial accidents. Social Security remains today to provide cash benefits to maintain a minimal income to retirees on the basis of their contributions to payroll taxes paid over their careers. However, it is not a personal savings program in which the government invests contributions and distributes them to the recipients during retirement. Rather, Social Security is a pay-as-you-go system whereby today's workers pay for benefits collected by today's retirees. In turn, future retirees will be paid by future workers. In other words, Social Security transfers or redistributes income across generations from relatively young workers to the elderly retirees. In most cases, retired workers receive more money from the program than they contributed while working.[29]

Approximately 63 million Americans will receive about $1 trillion in Social Security benefits this year. It is the single largest federal government program. Nearly 90 percent of Americans over the age of 65 receive benefits. For most, it provides the largest component of their yearly income. The average monthly benefit for retired workers in 2017 was $1,404. Twenty-three percent of married and 43 percent of unmarried elderly recipients depend on Social Security for 90 percent of their yearly incomes.[30] The program has been successful in keeping the elderly out of poverty and is overwhelmingly popular.[31] Because of its popularity, it is extremely difficult to reform. National politicians refer to Social Security as the untouchable "third rail" of politics—so called because, like most subway systems that use an electrified third rail to power the trains, if you touch it, you will die. The senior citizens who make up most of the program's beneficiaries are the most likely group to vote in the United States . The American Association of Retired Persons, with its 40 million members, vigorously defends the program.

Changing demographics have made Social Security vulnerable. In 1945, the program had only 5 million beneficiaries, but as the population and the number of beneficiaries has grown, the number of workers contributing to the program has declined. In 1960, the ratio of workers paying into the program was 5 to 1 for each person retired and collecting benefits. Today there are only about 2.9 workers per retiree and, by 2030, there will be only 2.1 workers supporting each retiree.[32] The Congressional Budget Office projects that the program's trust fund will be depleted by 2029. From then, benefits would need to be reduced by almost 30 percent to keep the program balanced if nothing changes.[33]

Proposals designed to keep Social Security benefits constant range from increasing taxes on individuals, increasing the maximum income that can be taxed, increasing the age at which one can start collecting benefits, delaying cost of living adjustments, and reducing benefits. Privatizing the program by allowing individuals to invest some of their social security taxes in private investment, which may result in a higher return than the low-risk government investments, has also been discussed, but the proposal remains unpopular among retirees.[34] Any privatization scheme would also be very expensive. Options that allow workers to divert funds into private investments would deplete reserves sooner than 2029. However, the obligations of the existing system to the already retired will continue, requiring the government to spend even more on the program. Furthermore, the stock market losses in 2008 serve as a warning about the risks associated with privatization.

Medicare

Medicare is a federal health care program created for people who are 65 and older, and certain younger people with disabilities or permanent kidney failure requiring dialysis or transplant. Different parts of Medicare cover specific services: for example, Medicare Part A is the core program that includes hospital charges, with individuals responsible for deductibles and copayments; Part B is supplemental insurance; and Part C provides insurance through managed care programs.[35] The program was created in 1965 and was the largest expansion in social policy since the New Deal. Like the Social Security program, it is a contributory program in which workers contribute through a payroll tax matched by their employers. Medicare does not have its own hospitals, nor does it employ doctors to provide care. Instead, the government reimburses enrolled private health care providers who give services to recipients, just like other health insurance programs. The program determines fees of "reasonable costs" that physicians, hospitals, nursing homes, and home services should charge for a given procedure and pays 80 percent of that amount. Considering restrictions, co-payments and deductibles, the program historically covers about two-thirds of the health care costs of the elderly. Retirees can purchase supplemental coverage (Part B) for expenses not covered by the main plan. In 2003, the Medicare Prescription Drug, Improvement, and Modernization Act was passed by Congress to provide discounts for routine prescription drugs depending on the plan selected.[36]

There were more than 55 million Medicare beneficiaries in 2015, a number expected to rise as more members of the baby boom generation reach the eligibility age of 65. Currently, total spending on Medicare is about $400 billion annually, or 15 percent of the federal budget, and is projected to climb to 17.5 percent by 2027. Like the Social Security program, Medicare also has a trust fund which is projected to be depleted by 2029. In 2010, the Independent Payment Advisory Board (IPAB), consisting of 15 full-time experts appointed by the president and confirmed by the Senate, was created to help slow the growth in Medicare spending. Since then, the share of Medicare spending on hospital inpatient services has fallen by one-third. The average annual growth in per capita spending also declined. The program was also expected to grow slower than private insurance programs.[37] However, in 2017, the U. S. House of Representatives passed legislation to repeal the IPAB. As of this writing, no members of the board have been appointed and the board is not operational.

Medicaid

The same amendments to the Social Security Act that created the Medicare program in 1965 also established the Medicaid program. Whereas Medicare is a national program that provides hospitalization and other health insurance for persons aged 65 and over, Medicaid is shared by the national and state governments. It provides health insurance to low-income people who are aged, blind, or disabled; to poor families with children; and to certain pregnant women and children. The federal government establishes eligibility standards, the services to be provided (including physician, inpatient, and outpatient hospital services) and most of the financing. State governments design and administer the program and provide some financing. Unlike Social Security and Medicare, Medicaid is a non-contributory program. Recipients do not contribute a percentage of their income in exchange for benefits.

The federal government pays most of the program costs based on a matching rate that requires more affluent states to pay a greater share of program costs. On average, 43 percent of traditional Medicaid costs are paid by the state governments, while the rest is covered by the national government.[38] The states have the flexibility to add additional services, such as medications, vision, and psychiatric care. While the program is designed to provide health care for the poor, coverage is available to many people who are not poor, including those living in families with incomes up to 138 percent of the federal poverty level. However, 18 states, mostly in the South and Midwest, rejected the Medicaid expansion even though the federal government would pick up 100 percent of the cost for the first 3 years and 90 percent thereafter.[39] Medicaid also covers expensive long-term care in nursing homes, or through personal or adult day care for the elderly with chronic or disabling conditions. These elderly and disabled recipients account for only 25 percent of Medicaid cases, yet account for more than 65 percent of program spending.[40] Nationwide, Medicaid accounts for about half of all spending for long term care services.[41]

FIGURE 15.5 Status of State Action on Medicaid Expansion

The states that have elected each option are as follows: Adopted: AK, HI, CA, NV, AZ, UT, NM, CO, ID, OR, WA, ID, MT, ND, NE, MN, IA, AR, LA, IL, IN, KY,OH,MI, VA, MD, PA, NY, NJ, DE, CT, RI, MA, VT, NH, and ME. Not Adopted: WY, SD, WI, MO, KS, OK, TX, TN, MS, AL, GA, FL, SC, and NC.

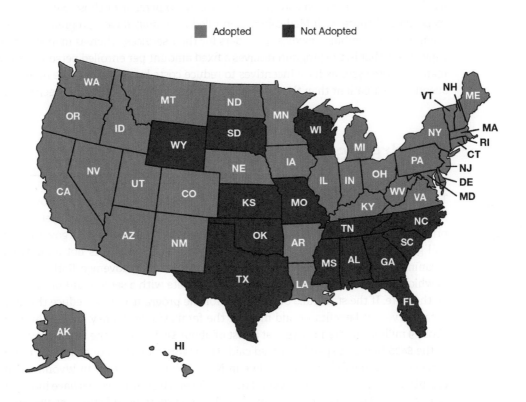

Henry J. Kaiser Family Foundation: https://www.kff.org/.

Medicaid provides health insurance and services to more than 68 million Americans, at a total cost to the federal government of about $400 billion, or about 10 percent of the federal budget. Although the states contributed only about one-third of the costs, on average they devote about 22 percent of their budgets to Medicaid, making the program the largest single expenditure program for the state governments.[42] The program has also grown due to the increasing number of Americans without private health insurance and increasing program eligibility and poverty rates. The average annual state Medicaid benefits per recipient in 2014 ranged from $10,392 in North Dakota to $3,691 in South Carolina.[43] Like the Medicare program, Medicaid does not have its own doctors, hospitals, or clinics. Again, the government acts like a private insurance company, reimbursing providers (physicians, hospitals, nursing homes, and home services) for "reasonable costs." However, fee-for-service rates reimbursed by Medicare tend to be higher than Medicaid rates for similar services, leading to difficulties for Medicaid recipients to find doctors that will accept the lower fees. The Kaiser Family Foundation discovered that reimbursement rates for Medicaid amounted to two-thirds of those of Medicare reimbursements for equivalent services.[44]

In 2010, President Obama worked with Democratic majorities in Congress to pass the Affordable Care Act (ACA). The Act provided Medicaid coverage for families with incomes up to 138 percent of the federal poverty level in states that chose to participate in the expansion and subsidized private health insurance coverage for many others. One study found that the Medicaid expansion alone reduced uncompensated care of patients without insurance by 30 percent in the states that adopted the new program, while uncompensated care remained the same in states that declined to expand the program.[45] The ACA also included a provision that insurers allow parents to keep their children on their plans up to age 26, which, according to a study by the Department of

Health and Human Services, helped 6.1 million young Americans and reduced the number of young adults without health insurance from 3 million to 1 million.[46]

The Medicaid program has also gone the way of many insurance programs by moving from fee-for-service to managed care providers. Today, 90 percent of those with private insurance and 70 percent of those with Medicaid are enrolled in managed care programs.[47] Fee-for-service programs simply reimburse medical providers for their services, whereas managed care programs are capitulated; that is, the program receives a fixed amount per enrolled person. The difference is that managed care systems have incentives to reduce costs by delivering care more efficiently. If they spend less per patient than the fixed amount the program receives, they keep the surplus.

Children's Health Insurance Program

entitlement program

A program that is mandatory and determined by the number of eligible recipients.

The Children's Health Insurance Program (CHIP) was created in 1997 to provide health insurance for middle class families with incomes too high to qualify for Medicaid, yet not enough to afford private insurance. The program is shared between the federal and state governments, with the federal government providing about 70 percent of the funding. It is not an **entitlement program**, meaning that not all people who qualify for the program get coverage. Rather, CHIP is a block grant in which the federal government provides each state with a set amount of money that is matched by the state. If the state runs out of funds for the program, it must reduce the number of families it can serve, cut benefits, or add more of the families' own money. Currently the program serves about 9 million children per year at a cost of about $13 billion to the federal government, compared to the $400 billion it spends on Medicaid. The states set eligibility standards that range from 400 percent above the federal poverty line in New York to 175 percent in Wyoming. The average state eligibility is 255 percent of the federal poverty level. Thirty-four states have incorporated CHIP into their existing Medicaid programs, making the two programs indistinguishable and giving children in those states full Medicaid benefits.[48] At the federal level, cigarette taxes provide the main source of revenue. However, unlike Medicaid, Congress must reauthorize the CHIP program every few years.

Temporary Assistance for Needy Families

The best way to describe the Temporary Assistance for Needy Families (TANF) program is to contrast it with the program it replaced—Aid to Families with Dependent Children (AFDC). AFDC was a federal program shared with states established in 1935 as part of the Social Security Act. The program was designed to help the "deserving poor," which at that time meant white single mothers with children who had been widowed or abandoned by their husbands. Black mothers were not originally eligible to receive benefits.[49] Assistance was in the form of cash, but language in the legislation that would have required states to provide "reasonable subsistence compatible with decency and health" was removed, as was most federal oversight.[50] By 1994, the average need per person was $688 per month, but the average grant was only $450.[51] It was an entitlement program that guaranteed benefits based on eligibility, but in practice it operated like a local charity. Local case workers were free to authorize assistance only to children they deemed to be in "suitable homes." They could deny benefits to "illegitimate" children or children of color, or reduce benefits for any number of reasons. Since the states could choose to participate in the program, eight states had no program. Several states would routinely discontinue coverage during seasons when low-wage labor was short. By 1960, an estimated 8 percent of children nationally were in need of assistance, but only 3 percent received assistance.[52]

Also by the 1960s, the National Welfare Rights Organization and other civil rights groups began to defend the rights of welfare recipients. By filing court cases challenging the administration of the AFDC program, advocates eliminated surprise inspections as unwarranted searches, removed provisions that punished children if their mothers engaged in sexual relations, rendered unconstitutional requirements that families establish state residency before receiving benefits, and struck down the states' ability to terminate benefits prior to a hearing. By this time, some states expanded benefits to children up to 18 (if they attended school), allowed benefits for foster children, and the federal government increased its share of program costs to 50 percent.

After nearly 30 years of slow growth, the number of cases increased dramatically from 2 million in 1960 to more than 10 million by 1972, prompting some to believe that cultural change had caused the upsurge in caseloads.[53] The composition of recipients also changed by this time. The "deserving" white widows were being replaced by divorced or separated women as well as mothers who had never been married. The cash assistance program had become increasingly unpopular, especially among conservatives. In the late 1970s, Ronald Reagan famously evoked the image of the welfare queen: "She used 80 names, 30 addresses, 15 telephone numbers to collect food stamps, Social Security, veterans' benefits for four nonexistent deceased veteran husbands, as well as welfare. Her tax-free cash income alone has been running $150,000 a year," despite having no systematic evidence that recipients were cheating the system.[54] By the late 1980s, most Americans felt that "welfare benefits make poor people dependent and encourage them to stay poor."[55]

Instead of fixing AFDC, the program was replaced by TANF in 1996 when President Bill Clinton declared an end to "welfare as we know it."[56] His actions were motivated, in part, to take the issue away from his party's Republican opponents, who for years had been attacking Democrats for helping indolent mothers get cash while avoiding work, discouraging marriage while giving single mothers financial incentives to have additional children. Republicans also accused Democrats of encouraging fraud and illegal immigration while creating inter-generational dependency. In the minds of the American public, opposition to AFDC was also correlated with race—with stronger opposition consistently related to negative attitudes toward race despite evidence that minorities have never accounted for more cases than white recipients.[57]

TANF was created by the aptly named Personal Responsibility and Work Opportunity Reconciliation Act. The program is designed to help poor families but also to counter the perceived deficiencies of the AFDC program by promoting work, encouraging marriage, and reducing out-of-wedlock pregnancies. The entitlement program was replaced by fixed-sum block grants to the states who were also given increased flexibility to determine eligibility and benefit standards. The states also had more flexibility in determining how the program was to be designed, implemented, and evaluated. Should a recession cause unemployment to increase and applications for assistance to climb, states would be compelled to deny and reduce benefits. Unlike Social Security, under which beneficiaries receive cost-of-living adjustments, the block grants would fail to keep up with inflation and therefore decline in real value over time. TANF also eliminated most of the requirements that the federal government approve state plans.

The nature of assistance under TANF would change dramatically. Most notably, under TANF, cash benefits would be eliminated for the most part and be replaced by **in-kind assistance** to find work or provide work-related assistance, including for job training, day-care, and transportation. The states were required to move recipients off the welfare rolls with the goal of having 50 percent of adult recipients working at least 30 hours a week by 2002.[58] Recipients were limited to a total of five years of federal funding and the states were allowed to impose shorter limits if they wished. Teenage parents were required to live with their parents. In the last year of AFDC, 14 million people were helped by the program, but by 2015, the states reduced their TANF cases to 1.6 million families comprising 4.1 million people, 2.9 million of whom were children.[59] Meanwhile, the number of families with children in poverty increased from 12.2 million in 2000 to 14.1 million by 2016.[60] In constant dollars, the average total cash assistance to needy families would decline by 300 percent from 1987 to 2009.[61] In addition, 15 states would impose drug tests as part of their applications screening, spending millions in the process. Missouri, for example, spent $336,297 to identify 48 abusers among nearly 40,000 TANF recipients. Another 15 states prohibited higher benefits to families with newborn children under the assumption they were produced to claim more cash from the program.[62] Total federal and state spending for TANF remains about $31 billion in contrast to the

in-kind assistance

Assistance given in goods, commodities, or services instead of cash.

$550 billion state and local spending for Medicaid, $400 billion federal spending for Medicare, and $1 trillion for Social Security. Clearly, the country prefers to help the elderly and disabled more than poor children.

15.5 Trade-Offs Between Economic and Social Welfare

Among policy leaders there is a common belief that a trade-off exists between economic policies that produce economic growth and social welfare policies that care for the poor, elderly, and disabled. Phrased in more concrete terms: Does taxing middle- and upper-income citizens to pay for programs that help the unfortunate discourage wage earners and entrepreneurs from working their hardest to produce wealth? Can economic and social welfare policies reflect both a goal to encourage a robust free market economy and a concern for those the market leaves behind? Such a balance seemed possible in the 1950s and 1960s when high levels of progressive taxation coincided with high levels of employment and economic equality.[63] Since then, federal economic policy has focused on freeing businesses from regulation and encouraging investment by lowering income taxes on the very rich. In terms of economic prosperity, the results have been mixed. Since the 1980s, tax cuts, deregulation, and reduced federal spending spurred economic growth and reduced the federal deficit (temporarily), but the tax cuts fueled rising rates of inequality, increased the federal deficit, and deregulation produced economic bubbles on Wall Street that burst and sent the economy into recession. Despite being more productive, the average worker earns about the same today as in the year 2000, while the median family income declined by 6 percent between 2000 and 2010. Between 1979 and 2007, the top 1 percent of wage earners increased their incomes by 156 percent while claiming 60 percent of all wealth. Wage inequality is about the level it was just before the Great Depression.[64]

It seems that it is possible to take good things like tax cuts and deregulation too far. On the other hand, programs like unemployment insurance, Social Security, Medicare and Medicaid not only cushion the economic and social effects of a recession, but keep them from developing into full-blown depressions by stabilizing demand. Free markets reward those with marketable talents, as well as those born into wealth. In contrast, free markets can be disastrous for individuals with low intelligence, those with few marketable skills, and those born into poverty. The precise balance between policies that produce economic growth and social welfare is elusive, but ultimately it comes down to political choices. In the past, liberals in the Democratic Party used their power to regulate business and soak the affluent to generate revenues to fix social problems. Lately, they have turned their efforts more toward market-based policies such as emission allowances and enhancing equal opportunity through college loans and grants and by defending affirmative action policies. The economy under Democratic presidents has actually produced higher job growth, corporate profits, investments, stock market returns, and lower unemployment than under Republican presidents.[65] Conservative Republicans continue down the path of deregulating business and reducing taxes and the size of government as an homage to the free market, even at the cost of exacerbating the effects of environmental pollution, global warming, and social inequality. The policies of both parties have intensified income and wealth inequality. It's probably too optimistic to wish for an ideological synthesis, but both parties should insist on policies that promote economic growth without making environmental degradation or social inequality worse. For Democrats, this would mean a continued respect for economic growth, deregulation, and efficient government, but with a reminder that affluent societies have always redistributed incomes through taxation to promote greater economic opportunity and reduce inequality. Republicans, for their part, should realize markets produce winners and losers, often arbitrarily, and that regulation, progressive taxation, and helping the unfortunate need not always harm economic efficiency.

15.6 What Can I Do?

In many ways, public policy is what politics is all about. As political scientist Harold Lasswell once wrote: "Politics is who gets what, when, how." What you want are policies that make life better and presumably the "who" is you or people you care about, so questions remain about when and how. In previous chapters we've suggested ideas in this feature about how to get what you want from government and politics, but the bottom line from all these suggestions is engagement with your fellow citizens in the political process. Whether that means formulating an opinion, voting, joining a group or political party, or even running for and occupying a political office, you must join in and become part of something greater than yourself.

Public policy profoundly shapes your life. For example, the great majority (70 percent) of students like you attend an institution of higher education created and supported by state government. You pay tuition, but the money you give covers only a portion of the actual costs of college. The rest comes from taxes collected from taxpayers across the state. When recessions appear or when the state needs to pay for other things, such as prisons or health care, it has less money to spend on higher education and tuition must rise to make up the difference. State governments don't want to cut funding for higher education, but tuition allows states to pass the costs on to users like you, which is much harder to do with prisons and health care. States used to cover 30 to 50 percent of the cost of college, but now that proportion is down to less than 20 percent. To slow or reverse this process, you need to work with your fellow students and others to compete for scarce resources. Getting your issue on the government's agenda is a critical step, but so is coming up with cost-effective solutions and pushing for their implementation. The University of California Riverside is considering getting rid of tuition altogether and taking a 5 percent share of students' salaries after they graduate. That would eliminate worries about how to pay for college, but 5 percent of one's salary could add up to a lot of money. Universities can save students money by offering more online classes, making textbooks available electronically, making class transfers from less expensive community colleges easier, having fewer required courses that create bottlenecks and slow graduation rates, or offering more classes during summer to speed graduate rates. Left on their own, college administrators may increase revenues by making classes larger, replacing full-time staff with part-time instructors, or accepting more international of out-of-state students who pay higher tuition. The policy choices could make a difference in the quality of education produced. Making a good college accessible to more students is good public policy. When the education level of workers in a society rises, that community becomes more competitive, attracts jobs with higher salaries, innovates for the market, and benefits from higher tax revenue. Education makes societies more efficient and more prosperous.

15.7 What's the Alternative?

In Chapter 3, we found that federalism encourages state leaders to think about what is best for their own states rather than of the national good. This thinking is profoundly shaped by their position within the American system of government, a place they share with other states. Within this order, state governments provide a wide range of public policies, including education, highway construction and, in cooperation with the federal government, health and welfare programs. Since each state has the freedom to set its own levels of spending for these services, the states become a market for public goods among which businesses and residents "shop" when deciding to relocate. They will move to the state that offers services and levels of taxation that match their preferences. As "sellers" of public goods, states compete with others for business and residents by offering quality services at the lowest levels of taxation. Federalism thus encourages state governments to understand their polices in terms of economic efficiency. This persuades states to invest in infrastructure and education, which boost economic development but it discourages states from in engaging in social welfare programs. This is because they benefit those least needed by the economy (the poor) while requiring increased taxation on business and middle- and upper-class residents. Social welfare programs can put a state at an economic disadvantage relative to others. States avoid attracting the poor from other states by keeping their welfare benefits at or below the levels of neighboring states, leading to a progressive decline in benefits across the entire country. The implications of this logic are clear: the federal government must take the primary responsibility for social welfare policies that care for the less fortunate in our society. Unfortunately, in times of fiscal austerity, one of the easiest ways to reduce federal government spending is to shift responsibility for welfare programs to the states, which speeds the race to the bottom.

Endnotes

1. Philip J. Cook, *Paying the Tab* (Princeton, New Jersey: Princeton University Press, 2016).

2. Ibid.

3. "Alcohol Facts and Statistics," National Institute on Alcohol Abuse and Alcoholism, accessed April 13, 2018, https://www.niaaa.nih.gov/alcohol-health/overview-alcohol-consumption/alcohol-facts-and-statistics.

4. Ralph Hingson and Michael Winter, "Epidemiology and Consequences of Drinking and Driving," *Alcohol Research and Health* 27, no. 1 (2003): 63-78.

5. Leonard Evans, *Traffic Safety* (Bloomfield, MI: Science Serving Society, 2006).

6. David Leo Weimer and Aidan R. Vining, *Policy Analysis: Concepts and Practice* (Boston: Longman, 2010), Chapter 16.

7. Peter R. Giancola, "Executive Functioning and Alcohol-Related Aggression," *Journal of Abnormal Psychology* 113, no. 4 (2004): 541-55, doi:10.1037/0021-843x.113.4.541.

8. Philip J. Cook, *Paying the Tab* (Princeton, New Jersey: Princeton University Press, 2016).

9. Marlene Oscar-Berman and Ksenija Marinkovic, "Alcoholism and the Brain: An Overview," National Institute on Alcohol Abuse and Alcoholism, accessed April 13, 2018, https://pubs.niaaa.nih.gov/publications/arh27-2/125-133.htm.

10. "Alcohol Use," Centers for Disease Control and Prevention, January 20, 2017, accessed April 13, 2018, https://www.cdc.gov/nchs/fastats/alcohol.htm.

11. Philip J. Cook, *Paying the Tab* (Princeton, New Jersey: Princeton University Press, 2016), 72.

12. Philip J. Cook, *Paying the Tab* (Princeton, New Jersey: Princeton University Press, 2016), 170.

13. "Mortality Risk Valuation," United States Environmental Protection Agency, February 8, 2018, accessed April 13, 2018, https://www.epa.gov/environmental-economics/mortality-risk-valuation.

14. Ibid.

15. In Cook's defense, he considered all these and many more issues in his cost-benefit analysis.

16. Philip J. Cook, *Paying the Tab* (Princeton, New Jersey: Princeton University Press, 2016), 15.

17. Ibid, note 4 page 15.

18. James B. Jacobs, *Drunk Driving An American Dilemma* (Chicago: University of Chicago Press, 2013).

19. Philip J. Cook, *Paying the Tab* (Princeton, New Jersey: Princeton University Press, 2016), 99.

20. Michael Kraft and Scott Furlong, *Public Policy* (Los Angeles: SAGE, 2012).

21. "2016 Draft Report to Congress on the Benefits and Costs of Federal Regulations and Agency Compliance with the Unfunded Mandates Reform Act," Executive Office of the President, 2016, https://obamawhitehouse.archives.gov/sites/default/files/omb/assets/legislative_reports/draft_2016_cost_benefit_report_12_14_2016_2.pdf.

22. "Mortgage Interest Tax Deduction Calculator," Bankrate, accessed April 13, 2018, https://www.bankrate.com/calculators/mortgages/loan-tax-deduction-calculator.aspx.

23. Ilya Somin, "Mortgage Interest Deduction Mostly Benefits the Rich - End It," The Hill, November 9, 2017, accessed April 13, 2018, http://thehill.com/opinion/finance/358922-mortgage-interest-deduction-mostly-benefits-the-rich-end-it.

24. See Chapter 1 and chapters on Federalism, Public Opinion, Citizen Participation and Voting, Congress, Political Parties, for more on the nature and implications of pubic goods.

25. Hannah Fingerhut, "More Americans Favor Raising than Lowering Tax Rates on Corporations, High Household Incomes," Pew Research Center, September 27, 2017, accessed April 13, 2018, http://www.pewresearch.org/fact-tank/2017/09/27/more-americans-favor-raising-than-lowering-tax-rates-on-corporations-high-household-incomes/.

26. "Taxes," Gallup, Inc., accessed April 13, 2018, http://news.gallup.com/poll/1714/taxes.aspx.

27. Drew DeSilver, "Among Developed Nations, Americans' Tax Bills Are Below Average," Pew Research Center, October 24, 2017, accessed April 13, 2018, http://www.pewresearch.org/fact-tank/2017/10/24/among-developed-nations-americans-tax-bills-are-below-average/.

28. Arlie Russell Hochschild, *Strangers in Their Own Land: Anger and Mourning on the American Right* (New York: New Press, 2018), Appendix C.

29. Louis Jacobson, "Medicare and Social Security: What You Paid Compared with What You Get," PolitiFact, accessed October 26, 2018, https://www.politifact.com/truth-o-meter/article/2013/feb/01/medicare-and-social-security-what-you-paid-what-yo/.

30. "Fact Sheet: Social Security," Social Security Administration, https://www.ssa.gov/news/press/factsheets/basicfact-alt.pdf

31. Michael Kraft and Scott Furlong, *Public Policy* (Los Angeles: SAGE, 2012), Chapter 9 Note 10.

32. "Worker-to-Beneficiary Ratio in the Social Security Program," Peter G. Peterson Foundation, August 15, 2017, accessed April 13, 2018, https://www.pgpf.org/chart-archive/0004_worker-benefit-ratio.

33. "CBO's 2016 Long-Term Projections for Social Security: Additional Information," Congressional Budget Office, October 27, 2017, accessed April 13, 2018, https://www.cbo.gov/publication/52298.

34. "Public Divided on Social Security Privatization." Gallup, Inc., January 5, 2005, accessed April 13, 2018, http://news.gallup.com/poll/14530/public-divided-social-security-privatization.aspx.

35. "What's Medicare?" Medicare.gov, accessed April 13, 2018, https://www.medicare.gov/sign-up-change-plans/decide-how-to-get-medicare/whats-medicare/what-is-medicare.html.

36. Michael Kraft and Scott Furlong, *Public Policy* (Los Angeles: SAGE, 2012), Chapter 8 Note 22.

37. Juliette Follow Cubanski and Tricia Neuman, "The Facts on Medicare Spending and Financing," The Henry J. Kaiser Family Foundation, February 16, 2018, accessed April 13, 2018, https://www.kff.org/medicare/issue-brief/the-facts-on-medicare-spending-and-financing/.

38. "The Difference Between Medicare and Medicaid Reimbursement," RevCycleIntelligence, July 17, 2017, accessed April 13, 2018, https://revcycleintelligence.com/features/the-difference-between-medicare-and-medicaid-reimbursement.

39. Kevin B. Smith and Alan Greenblatt, *Governing States and Localities* (Los Angeles: Sage, 2018), Chapter 15.

40. Virginia Gray, Russell L. Hanson, and Thad Kousser, *Politics in the American States: A Comparative Analysis* (Los Angeles: Sage/CQ Press, 2018): Chapter 11.

41. Michael Kraft and Scott Furlong, *Public Policy* (Los Angeles: SAGE, 2012), Chapter 8.

42. National Association of State Budget Officers 2011, 43 ROM.

43. "Medicaid Spending per Enrollee (Full or Partial Benefit)," The Henry J. Kaiser Family Foundation, June 9, 2017, accessed April 13, 2018, https://www.kff.org/medicaid/state-indicator/medicaid-spending-per-enrollee/?currentTimeframe.

44. "Examining Differences Between Medicare, Medicaid Reimbursement," RevCycleIntelligence, July 17, 2017, accessed April 13, 2018, https://revcycleintelligence.com/news/examining-differences-medicare-medicaid-reimbursement.

45. "Uncompensated Care Dropping Fast in Medicaid Expansion States," *Governing*, accessed April 13, 2018, http://www.governing.com/topics/health-human-services/gov-uncompensated-care-dropping-fast.html.

46. "Health Coverage Under the Affordable Care Act," *Journal of the American Medical Association* 308, no. 24 (2012): 2556, doi:10.1001/jama.2012.128713.

47. Virginia Gray, Russell L. Hanson, and Thad Kousser, *Politics in the American States: A Comparative Analysis* (Los Angeles: Sage/CQ Press, 2018), Chapter 11.

48. Ramona-Elena Irimia and Marc Gottschling, "Taxonomic Revision of Rochefortia Sw. (Ehretiaceae, Boraginales)," *Biodiversity Data Journal* 4: E7720 (2016): Figure 2f, doi:10.3897/bdj.4.e7720.figure2f.

49. Dorothy Roberts, *Killing the Black Body: Race, Reproduction, and the Meaning of Liberty* (New York City, New York: Pantheon Books., 1997), Chapter 5.

50. "Aid To Dependent Children: The Legal History," Social Welfare History Project, February 26, 2018, accessed April 13, 2018, https://socialwelfare.library.vcu.edu/public-welfare/aid-to-dependent-children-the-legal-history/.

51. Alana Semuels, "The End of Welfare as We Know It," *The Atlantic*, April 1, 2016, accessed April 13, 2018, https://www.theatlantic.com/business/archive/2016/04/the-end-of-welfare-as-we-know-it/476322/.

52. "Aid To Dependent Children: The Legal History," Social Welfare History Project, February 26, 2018, accessed April 13, 2018. https://socialwelfare.library.vcu.edu/public-welfare/aid-to-dependent-children-the-legal-history/.

53. *Governing the States*, Chapter 15.

54. "Ronald Reagan Campaign Speech, January 1976," SoundCloud, accessed April 13, 2018. https://soundcloud.com/slate-articles/ronald-reagan-campaign-speech.

55. "Poverty Is Perceived as Increasing And State of the Poor Unimproved," *The New York Times*, August 23, 1989, accessed April 13, 2018, https://www.nytimes.com/1989/08/23/us/poverty-is-perceived-as-increasing-and-state-of-the-poor-unimproved.html.

56. Bill Clinton, "Opinion | How We Ended Welfare, Together," *The New York Times*, August 22, 2006, accessed April 13, 2018, https://www.nytimes.com/2006/08/22/opinion/22clinton.html.

57. Robert A. Moffitt and Peter T. Gottschalk, *America Becoming: Racial Trends and Their Consequences, Volume II* (National Academies Press: OpenBook, 2001), https://www.nap.edu/read/9719/chapter/8.

58. Michael Kraft and Scott Furlong, *Public Policy* (Los Angeles: SAGE, 2012).

59. "The Temporary Assistance for Needy Families (TANF) Block Grant: Responses to Frequently Asked Questions," Congressional Research Service, December 12, 2018, https://fas.org/sgp/crs/misc/RL32760.pdf.

60. "Children in Poverty (100 Percent Poverty) | KIDS COUNT Data Center," KIDS COUNT Data Center: A Project of the Annie E. Casey Foundation, accessed April 13, 2018, https://datacenter.kidscount.org/data/tables/43-children-in-poverty-100-percent-poverty#detailed/1/any/false/870,868,35,15,11/any/321,322.

61. "Table 7-3. Federal and State Expenditures on Cash Assistance Under Aid to Families with Dependent Children and TANF: FY1987 to FY2009," U.S. House of Representatives Committee on Ways and Means, https://greenbook-waysandmeans.house.gov/sites/greenbook.waysandmeans.house.gov/files/2011/documents/Table 7-3. Federal and State Expenditures on Cash Assistance under Aid to Families with Dependent Children and TANF.pdf.

62. Rachel Black and Aleta Sprague, "The 'Welfare Queen' Is a Lie," *The Atlantic*, September 28, 2016, accessed April 13, 2018, https://www.theatlantic.com/business/archive/2016/09/welfare-queen-myth/501470/.

63. In 1960 the top marginal tax rate in 1960 was 91 percent. Nick Kasprak, "Some Historical Tax Stats," Tax Foundation, January 17, 2017, accessed April 13, 2018, https://taxfoundation.org/some-historical-tax-stats/.

64. "Key Findings," State of Working America, accessed April 13, 2018, http://www.stateofworkingamerica.org/fact-sheets/key-findings/.

65. Arlie Russell Hochschild, *Strangers in Their Own Land: Anger and Mourning on the American Right* (New York: New Press, 2018), Appendix C.

CHAPTER 16
Foreign Policy: Engaging in the Global Community

Chapter Objectives

1. Identify what national security policy is.
2. Trace the evolution of U.S. foreign policy from isolationism to internationalism.
3. Distinguish key policymaking actors in U.S. foreign policy.
4. Discuss various tools and strategies of foreign policy.
5. Think critically about foreign policy challenges facing the U.S.

Introduction: Finger on the Button

During the Cuban Missile Crisis in October 1962, the Executive Committee of the National Security Council held a series of closed-door discussions in the White House Cabinet Room to determine how to respond to evidence of Soviet warships off the coast of Cuba and in striking distance of U.S. territory.

Cecil Stoughton. White House Photographs. John F. Kennedy Presidential Library and Museum, Boston.

On October 22, 1962, at the height of the Cold War, President John F. Kennedy broadcast a special message to the nation from the Oval Office. In calm and collected tones, he told the American public he was preparing to use military force to neutralize a perceived threat to national security. Americans listened to their president speak, believing that the country was on the brink of nuclear war. In his speech, Kennedy shared the news that six days before, on October 13, he had been briefed that the pilot of an American U-2 spy plane making a high-altitude pass over Cuba on

October 14, 1962, had photographed a Soviet SS-4 medium-range ballistic missile being assembled for installation. This meant there were nuclear armed missiles being installed within striking distance of the nation—just 90 miles off the Florida coast—and within reach of targets on the east coast of the United States. The discovery of the missiles in the nation's back yard fundamentally altered the dynamics of the nuclear rivalry between the United States and the Union of Soviet Socialist Republics (USSR), which until this moment had been dominated by the United States. The country's leaders were plunged into a crisis that would last 13 days and would call on them to use every tool of statecraft before they ultimately reached a solution with the Soviets. This 13-day period became known as the Cuban Missile Crisis and marked the first—and so far only time—the country has been so close to nuclear war.

The story of the Cuban Missile Crisis is one of the most interesting and frightening chapters in U.S. foreign policy. It involved the world's most advanced weapons technology, fundamental ideological differences, and a political and military standoff in which the leaders of the United States, the USSR, and Cuba stared each other down for 13 tense days.

For Kennedy, the presence of Soviet missiles so close to home was unacceptable. Immediately after he was briefed on the situation, he assembled the ExComm, a group of his closest advisers. Behind closed doors and away from the public eye, the ExComm considered its options. The priority was to protect national security by getting rid of the missiles without triggering a nuclear war. They considered every foreign policy tool and strategy, from a bombing attack on the missile sites to a full-scale invasion of Cuba. After extensive discussions and careful deliberation, Kennedy and the ExComm ultimately decided on a more measured approach: first, the U.S. Navy would establish a blockade of Cuba to prevent the Soviets from delivering additional weapons; second, Kennedy would issue an ultimatum that the existing missiles be removed. It was with that ultimatum that the world edged closer to the brink of nuclear war. The crisis came to a head on October 24 when Soviet ships heading toward Cuba approached the line of U.S. navy ships enforcing the blockade. Had the Soviets crossed the line, they would have likely initiated a military confrontation that would have quickly escalated to nuclear attacks. Fortunately, Khrushchev blinked first and the Soviets stopped before crossing the blockade. While the blockade seemed to have worked, the question of the remaining missiles in Cuba remained. The standoff continued. Then, on October 27, an American spy plane was shot down over Cuba. An invasion force was prepared in Florida and a sense of impending doom hung over the Soviets and Americans alike.

When it looked like military strategies were likely going to lead to an outright war, Kennedy and Khrushchev opted to use other tools in their political arsenals. Throughout the crisis, the two leaders had communicated via letters and telegrams. On October 26, Khrushchev sent a message to Kennedy. The Soviet leader offered to remove the missiles in Cuba if the United States agreed to not invade Cuba. The U.S. agreed and, the next day, Khrushchev said he would dismantle the missiles in Cuba if the U.S. removed its missiles in Turkey. Again, but in private this time, Kennedy agreed and the crisis was finally over. In 1963, a "hot line" telephone was installed between Washington and Moscow to ensure that the two nations would never come so close to nuclear war. The two sides signed treaties related to their nuclear arsenals. Even though the Cuban Missile Crisis ended peacefully, the Cold War continued. Both the United States and the USSR competed for nuclear supremacy, developing new technology and intercontinental ballistic missiles capable of reaching each other's territory from their home countries.

The Cuban Missile Crisis provides important insights about foreign policy goals and the tools of statecraft. In this chapter, we will examine how the United States develops its foreign policy, determines its priorities, and executes its goals on the international stage.

16.1 Foreign Policy Explored

Foreign policy refers to a country's relations with other nations in the international community. The interactions among countries are guided by each nation's national interests. In the United States, foreign policy has always been driven by the attempt to provide absolute security. The United States defines **national security** as the process by which the nation manages its territory, political autonomy, resources, and people. National security is manifested along various dimensions that include: 1) **military security**, which focuses on the strength and effectiveness of the country's armed forces; 2) **economic security**, which considers the productive use of human and natural resources, financial assets, technology, and foreign markets; 3) **political security**, which ensures the stability and legitimacy of political values and freedoms at home and for American citizens living abroad; 4) **societal security**, which refers to the durability of civil society, interest groups, and the media; and 5) **environmental security**, which protects and secures global natural resources and promotes sustainable development. The United States utilizes various tools of statecraft to safeguard its national security and ensure that the government's relationships with other nations advance its interests.

The Evolution of U.S Foreign Policy

In order to understand the development of American foreign policy, it is important to examine the key historical events that shaped the country's interests and priorities. The concern for national security can be traced to the burning of Washington, D.C., in the War of 1812. On August 24, 1812, a British force invaded and occupied Washington and set fire to a number of government buildings, including the White House (known then as the Presidential Mansion) and the Capitol. The burning was in retaliation for the recent American attacks on Port Dover in Canada and marks the only time in U.S. history that the nation's Capitol has been invaded by a foreign country. President James Madison was in office at the time of the burning, and he and his officials fled the city after being warned that an attack was imminent. The invasion lasted just 24 hours and ended when a heavy thunderstorm extinguished the fires and sent the British back to their ships, which had been badly damaged by the storm. The Americans were able to regain control of the city and the country experienced a surge of nationalism. Americans rose to protect Washington, D.C., as the seat of government. What had been a loose collection of states were suddenly united by a common sense of pride in the nation's capital and the shared goal to defend it from future attacks. The country realized it needed to turn its attention from consolidating power at the domestic level to developing a coherent foreign policy. This policy has evolved and changed over time and can be divided into four eras.

foreign policy

A country's relations with other nations in the international community.

national security

The process by which the nation manages its territory, political autonomy, resources, and people.

military security

Focuses on the strength and effectiveness of the country's armed forces.

economic security

The productive use of human and natural resources, financial assets, technology, and foreign markets.

political security

Ensures the stability and legitimacy of political values and freedoms at home and for American citizens living abroad.

societal security

The durability of civil society, interest groups, and the media.

environmental security

Protects and secures global natural resources and promotes sustainable development.

1800-1914: Period of Isolation

Monroe Doctrine

A U.S. foreign policy strategy that declared the country would stay out of European affairs as long as Europe stayed out of the Western Hemisphere.

isolationism

Foreign policy strategy that advocates neutrality and avoidance of direct involvement in the activities of other nations.

unilateralism

A foreign policy strategy that refers to taking independent action without consulting other countries. It also avoids joining alliances and signing treaties.

expansionism

A policy that calls for the spreading of U.S. borders to the Pacific Ocean while extending the nation's influence in the Pacific, Asian, and Caribbean basins.

Manifest Destiny

The nineteenth-century doctrine or belief that the United States was destined to expand its dominion and spread democracy and capitalism across the North American continent.

The early keystone of American foreign policy was the **Monroe Doctrine**, which stated that the United States would stay out of European affairs as long as Europe stayed out of the Western Hemisphere. In his annual message delivered to Congress in December 1823, President James Monroe declared: "The American continents ... are henceforth not to be considered as subjects for future cowers," thereby warning European nations that the United States would not tolerate further colonization or puppet monarchs. This doctrine was the cornerstone for the three policies that dominated American foreign policy during this time: isolationism, unilateralism, and expansionism. As a foreign policy, **isolationism** advocates neutrality and avoidance of direct involvement in the activities of other nations. **Unilateralism** refers to taking independent action without consulting other countries. It also means avoiding joining alliances and signing treaties. **Expansionism** is a policy that calls for the spreading of the United States' borders to the Pacific Ocean while extending the nation's influence in the Pacific, Asian, and Caribbean basins. This territorial and political expansion was justified by the theory of "**Manifest Destiny**," the nineteenth century doctrine or belief that the United States was destined to expand its dominion and spread democracy and capitalism across the North American continent.

One of the ways in which the United States expanded its influence was through land acquisition. In 1803, President Thomas Jefferson made the Louisiana Purchase when he bought most of the land west of the Mississippi River and north of the Arkansas River from France. Fifty years later in 1853, the United States made the Gadsden Purchase (named for James Gadsden, the U.S. ambassador to Mexico at the time) and agreed to pay Mexico $10 million for a 29,670 square mile portion of Mexico that would become part of Arizona and New Mexico. In 1867, President Abraham Lincoln purchased Alaska from Russia, thereby ending Russia's presence in North America and securing U.S. access to the northern Pacific Rim.

The United States expanded its domestic and global power through a series of land purchases and territorial cessions. Early territorial acquisitions were driven by the nineteenth-century philosophy of Manifest Destiny, the notion that the United States was destined to expand and spread democracy and capitalism across North America.

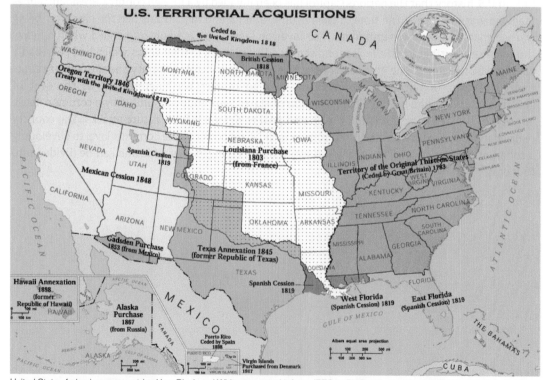

United States federal government (en:User:Black and White converted it from JPEG to PNG and retouched it) [Public domain], via Wikimedia Commons. https://commons.wikimedia.org/wiki/File:U.S._Territorial_Acquisitions.png.

The United States also extended its reach through wars of expansion. The nation engaged in a series of wars in an effort to consolidate its borders, including the Mexican War (1846-48), the Indian Wars (1876-1890), and the Spanish-American War (1898). It was the Spanish-American War fought between the United States and Spain that announced the nation's arrival on the global stage as an important player in world politics. The war ended Spanish colonial rule in the Americas and resulted in the acquisition of new lands in the western Pacific and Latin America, such as Puerto Rico, Cuba, Guam, the Philippine Islands, and the Hawaiian Islands.

The Rise of the U.S. as a World Power: 1914-1941

While the Spanish American War set the stage for the emergence of the United States as a global actor, it was World War I that signaled its power. The United States joined World War I reluctantly: at the beginning, the nation resisted involvement, invoking the policy of isolationism and its commitment to not get entangled in affairs beyond its borders. But as pressure began to mount from both England and Germany to enter the war on their respective sides, the U.S. abandoned its isolationist principles and allowed itself to enter the war on the side of the Allied or Entente Powers—England, France, Russia, and later Italy. It joined in the fight against the Central Powers—Germany, the Austro-Hungarian Empire, the Ottoman Empire, and Bulgaria.

The Zimmerman Telegram was a secret correspondence sent by the German Foreign Office in January 1917 that proposed an alliance between Germany and Mexico against the United States. The United States' decision to abandon its policy of isolationism and enter World War I is frequently linked to the Zimmerman Telegram, coupled with Germany's unrestricted submarine warfare.

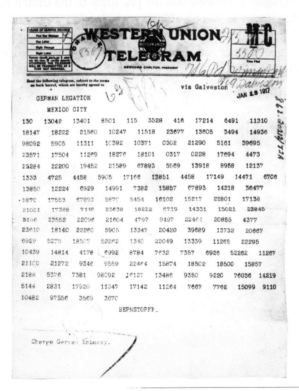

Department of State. Office of the Secretary. *Telegram from Secretary of State Robert Lansing to the American Embassy, London: Zimmermann Telegram as Received by the German Minister to Mexico.* Textual record. March 1, 1917. File Unit: 862.20212 / 57 through 862.20212 / 311, 1910 - 1963. https://catalog.archives.gov/id/302025 (accessed January 16, 2019).

Zimmermann Telegram

A communication that was intercepted and decoded by British intelligence on January 16, 1917, that outlined a secret wartime alliance through which Germany would provide Mexico with military and economic assistance for a Mexican attack against the United States. In exchange, Mexico would be free to annex territory in Texas, New Mexico, and Arizona.

League of Nations

A collective security organization conceived by President Woodrow Wilson in his Fourteen Points address to Congress in January 1918, in which he called for a "general association of nations … formed under specific covenants for the purpose of affording mutual guarantees of political independence and territorial integrity to great and small states alike."

alliance

A union for mutual benefit to foster international cooperation, provide security to its members, and ensure a lasting peace by committing member nations to come to each other's defense in the case on attack.

Two specific events occurred that pulled the United States out of isolationism and into the war. The first of these was the unrestricted submarine warfare by the German Navy that commenced on February 1, 1917, a policy that allowed their boats to torpedo ships regardless of military status or country of origin. The second event was the **Zimmermann Telegram**, a communication intercepted and decoded by British intelligence on January 16, 1917, that outlined a secret wartime alliance through which Germany would provide Mexico with military and economic assistance for a Mexican attack against the United States. In exchange, Mexico would be free to annex territory in Texas, New Mexico, and Arizona. President Woodrow Wilson learned of the telegram on February 26 and the next day he proposed to Congress that the nation begin arming its ships in preparation for a German attack. When the American public found out about the telegram, opinions shifted firmly in favor of U.S. entry into World War I. Some of the nation's pro-isolationist supporters argued that the telegram was fake, but on March 3, German foreign secretary Arthur Zimmermann admitted that he had written the telegram, thereby dismissing questions of its authenticity. The telegram was the last straw for American neutrality, as it was evidence of a direct threat against American territorial security. This threat, coupled with the German Navy's unrestricted warfare, propelled the nation toward war. On April 4, 1917, Wilson asked Congress for a declaration of war against Germany and, two days later on April 6, the United States formally entered the conflict.

After the United States helped the Allied Powers win World War I in 1918, the country retreated to its policy of isolationism. The United States refused to sign the Treaty of Versailles that ended the war and failed to join the **League of Nations**, a collective security organization conceived by President Wilson himself in his Fourteen Points address to Congress in January 1918. In that speech, Wilson called for a "general association of nations … formed under specific covenants for the purpose of affording mutual guarantees of political independence and territorial integrity to great and small states alike." The League of Nations was the precursor to the United Nations (U.N.) and, like the U.N., required its signatories to join an **alliance** or union for mutual benefit to foster international cooperation, provide security to its members, and ensure a lasting peace by committing member states to come to each other's defense in the case of an attack. The United States also failed to assist in the rebuilding of Europe after the war and did nothing to stop the rise of Hitler and Mussolini in the 1930s.

The End of Isolationism, 1941-1947

The U.S. policy of isolationism permanently ended on December 7, 1941 with the bombing of Pearl Harbor. The attack on the U.S. military base in Honolulu, Hawaii, by Japanese forces signaled that the oceans were no longer a safe buffer against foreign attack. American soldiers, sailors, and civilians killed in the attack numbered 2,403, and another 1,000 were wounded. The day after, on December 8, President Franklin D. Roosevelt asked Congress to declare war on Japan. Three days later, Japan's allies, Germany and Italy, declared war against the United States, and Congress responded by declaring war on them.

The United States again joined the Allied powers of Britain, France, and Russia against the Axis powers: Germany, Italy, and Japan. After the war ended in victory for the Allies with the 1945 U.S. nuclear bombing of Hiroshima and Nagaski in Japan, the United States did not return to isolationism.

Just before 8 a.m. on December 7, 1941, Japanese forces attacked Pearl Harbor, a U.S. naval base near Honolulu, Hawaii. More than 2,400 Americans died, 1,000 were wounded, and almost 20 American naval vessels and more than 300 airplanes were destroyed. The next day, President Franklin D. Roosevelt asked Congress to declare war on Japan. The United States had officially entered World War II.

Front page of the *Honolulu Star Bulletin*, December 7, 1941. History on the Net: https://www.historyonthenet.com/pearl-harbor-ultimate-guide-dec-7-1941-attacks/.

The Modern Era, 1947-Present

The United States emerged from World War II as a global superpower. It played a leading role in the rebuilding of Europe after the war and in the development of the **United Nations** (U.N.) in 1945. The U.N. is an international security organization that brings together its 193 member states to share in global governance to maintain peace, uphold international laws and norms, and promote sustainable development. In addition to helping establish this global alliance, the United States implemented the **Marshall Plan**, also known as the European Recovery Program, which helped rebuild a devastated Europe after the war by channeling $13 billion into the continent between 1948 and 1951.

As World War II was ending in 1945, the Allied powers decided they would divide Germany into four occupation zones: the Soviet Union would have control over the eastern part of the country; the United States, Britain, and France would govern the western part. From 1945 to 1949, France, Britain, and the United States occupied their zones and transformed the western section into a democracy. Berlin was located entirely within the Soviet controlled part of Germany, but the Allied powers divided the city into similar sections, with the Soviets taking the eastern half and the Allies taking the western area. This division of Berlin would prove critical in future Soviet-American relations. In asserting its global influence, the United States also led the Allies in the occupation and rehabilitation of Japan from 1945 to 1952 and introduced military, political, economic, and social reforms.

United Nations

An international security organization founded in 1945 to bring together its 193 member states to share in global governance to maintain peace, uphold international laws and norms, and promote sustainable development.

Marshall Plan

A U.S. economic recovery program implemented to rebuild a devastated Europe after World War II by channeling $13 billion into the continent between 1948 and 1951.

The Manifestation of U.S. Global Power

Since its emergence as a major world power, the United States' foreign policy has been shaped by several significant events, including the Cold War, Vietnam, and the War on Terror.

The Cold War

Cold War

An ideological war between the United States and the USSR in which the two sides did not confront each other on a battlefield in a traditional "hot war," but instead engaged in a clash of ideas while supporting proxies in various conflicts.

proxy wars

Skirmishes and hostilities generally fought by smaller countries allied with the United States and the USSR during the Cold War.

Truman Doctrine

Issued by President Harry Truman in 1947 to send a firm message to countries in Europe who were considering an alliance with the Soviets. With the goal of containing Soviet geopolitical expansion, the doctrine was further developed in 1948 when the United States pledged to provide financial support to Greece and Turkey.

The Soviet Union also emerged from World War II as a strong power. While they had been allies during the war, the USSR's communist government was in direct opposition to the United States' democratic, capitalist ideals. The United States valued private ownership and a free market economy with limited government intervention, whereas the Soviet government owned production and maintained tight control on supply and demand, setting the prices for goods and services. The goal of the communist model was to decrease the income gap between the rich and the poor and bring about economic equality. The capitalist model instead sought to encourage innovation and entrepreneurship. The two systems were inherently at odds with each other and these ideological differences led quickly to the **Cold War,** a war in which the countries did not confront each other on a battlefield in a traditional "hot war," but instead engaged in a clash of ideas characterized by **proxy wars**. These were skirmishes and hostilities generally fought by smaller countries allied with the United States and the Soviet Union. The fact that the two superpowers did not meet directly on the battlefield did not mean the Cold War was peaceful. On the contrary, it was a period marked by crises, any of which could have led to global nuclear war. In 1947, President Harry Truman issued the **Truman Doctrine**, which sent a firm message to countries in Europe who were considering an alliance with the Soviets. With the goal of containing Soviet geopolitical expansion, the doctrine was further developed in 1948 when the United States pledged to provide financial support to Greece and Turkey. The onset of the Cold War is often traced to the Truman Doctrine and the sentiments expressed in it became the foundation of an American foreign policy rooted in a "you're either with us or against us" mentality. This meant that countries either supported the United States and upheld its democratic principles or they were considered enemies.

From June 1948 to May 1949, the United States and the USSR confronted each other in the Berlin Blockade, one of the first major crises of the Cold War. The Soviets were angered by the recently introduced Deutsche mark as the currency in West Berlin, and so they sought to starve the Western allies out by blocking access to the sectors of the city under Western control. In response, the United States and its allies organized the Berlin airlift and, from June 26, 1948 until September 30, 1949, they flew over 200,000 flights to supply West Berlin with all of its necessities, including food, fuel, cars, and medicine. In May 1949, the Soviet Union lifted the blockade of West Berlin after realizing that the airlift was clearly succeeding and that the Allies were unlikely to yield to Soviet demands. The Berlin Blockade demonstrated that the Soviet Union and United States had fundamentally incompatible ideas about how to promote political and economic recovery and reforms in postwar Europe.

Between 1950 and 1953, the United States was involved in the Korean War, which pitted North Korea (supported by China and the Soviet Union) against South Korea (supported by the United States). The war, which was the first military conflict of the Cold War, started on June 25, 1950, when 75,000 North Korean soldiers crossed the 38th parallel, the latitude border between the communist-backed Democratic People's Republic of Korea to the north and the pro-democratic Republic of Korea to the south. American troops soon entered the war on the side of South Korea in an effort to push back and contain communism. For the United States, this was a global struggle between the East and West, communism and democracy. It was understood to be the first step of the broader Soviet plan to spread communism and take over the world. "If we let Korea down," President Truman said, "the Soviet[s] will keep right on going and swallow up one [place] after another."[1] When it became clear the war was not going to end with an outright victory for South Korea, and amid fears that the fighting could lead to World War III, the United States was eager to reach a settlement with North Korea. After two years of negotiations and after 5 million soldiers and civilians had been killed in the fighting, the two sides signed an armistice in July 1953. The agreement allowed prisoners of war to repatriate if they wanted; gave South Korea an additional 1,500 square miles of territory by drawing a new border near the 38th parallel; and demarcated a 2-mile-wide "demilitarized zone" that remains in place today.

In Europe, the division of Berlin remained a serious point of contention between the Soviet Union and the United States. People were fleeing from East Germany through West Berlin in droves: on August 12, 1961, alone, 2,400 refugees fled—the largest number of people to leave East Germany in a single day. That night, Khrushchev gave the East German government permission to stop the flow of refugees by closing the border. It took just two weeks for the East German army and police force to build a makeshift wall with barbed wire and concrete. This wall would become the **Berlin Wall** that would divide East and West Berlin. It became a symbol of the global division between communism and democracy. Before the wall was constructed, Berliners could move freely from one side to the other; after the wall was in place, one could only move from East to West Berlin through one of three checkpoints. Travelers were rarely allowed across the border. The makeshift wall was eventually replaced by an 11- to 13-foot tall mass of reinforced concrete with an enormous pipe along the top that made climbing over it nearly impossible. The wall was patrolled on the East German side by trip-wire machine guns, soldiers with orders to shoot on sight, and vicious dogs. Over 100,000 tried to escape over the wall; between 5,000-10,000 succeeded. Almost 200 people died trying to cross the wall, but between 1961 and 1989 when the wall came down, more that 5,000 East Germans managed to cross the border by flying in hot air balloons, scaling the barbed wire, driving at high speeds through weaker parts of the wall, and crawling through sewers. The wall was by no means an effective solution to the ideological conflict between the United States and the Soviet Union, but as U.S. President John F. Kennedy said, "A wall is a hell of a lot better than a war."[2]

The threat of nuclear war loomed large during the Cold War. The United States had developed the atomic bomb first and used it in World War II when it bombed Hiroshima and Nagasaki. To this day, the United States is the only country to have launched a nuclear attack against another nation. The Soviet Union tested its first atomic bomb in 1949, setting off an arms race between the Soviets and the Americans that would become a defining feature of the Cold War. The closest the two superpowers came to nuclear war was in 1962 with the Cuban Missile Crisis, which is described at the beginning of this chapter. One of the most compelling reasons why the Cold War did not turn into a hot war was because nuclear weapons and the threat of mutual annihilation kept the two sides from taking actions that would escalate tensions to that level.

In this image, residents of Berlin await a cargo plane carrying food during the Berlin Blockade of 1948-49. In what was the first major crisis of the Cold War, the Soviet Union blocked access routes on the Western side of Berlin. The United States, along with its allies France and the United Kingdom, organized the Berlin Airlift to deliver supplies.

United States Air Force. *USAFE Celebrates 65th Birthday*. https://bit.ly/2DMBhdE.

Berlin Wall

A wall that divided East and West Berlin and became a symbol of the global division between communism and democracy.

bipolarism

Idea that the world was divided into two spheres of influence defined by opposing economic and political systems: communism (the eastern sphere) and democracy/capitalism (the western sphere).

containment

Theory that asserted that actions must be taken to prevent spheres of influence from expanding.

domino theory

The idea that if one country fell to communism, the nations surrounding it would also fall like a standing line of dominos.

deterrence

A Cold War policy of discouraging action by instilling fear of the consequences.

mutual assured destruction

Cold War theory by which both the United States and the Soviet Union knew that a nuclear attack by one would be met by a nuclear response from the other and that neither side would likely survive a nuclear war.

security dilemma

The notion that as one state takes steps to increase its security, it decreases the security of other states.

U.S. foreign policy during the Cold War was dominated by three theories: bipolarism, containment, and deterrence. The notion of **bipolarism** held that the world was divided into two spheres of influence defined by opposing economic and political systems: communism (the eastern sphere) and democracy/capitalism (the western sphere). The theory of **containment** asserted that actions must be taken to prevent these spheres of influence from expanding. The fear of expansion and the need for containment came in part from the **domino theory**, the idea that if one country fell to communism, the nations surrounding it would also fall like a line of standing dominos. The domino theory contributed directly to the U.S. decision to intervene in both the Korean and Vietnamese wars. Because the threat of nuclear annihilation loomed over Soviet-American interactions during the Cold War, U.S. foreign policy was focused on preventing the Soviets from launching a nuclear attack against the United States and its allies. The theory of **deterrence** was thus invoked and enacted through measures like **mutual assured destruction**, by which both sides knew that a nuclear attack by one would provoke a nuclear response by the other and that neither side would likely survive a nuclear war. The arms race or competition for nuclear superiority was driven by deterrence and by the **security dilemma**. Any defensive actions taken by the Soviets were perceived by the United States to be for offensive purposes. The United States, therefore, built up its own offensive capabilities to defend against and deter a Soviet attack. The Soviets, seeing the U.S. build-up of arms and interpreting this as an offensive maneuver, also built up its military capabilities, thereby confirming U.S. fears that the Soviets were preparing for an attack. The security dilemma refers to the notion that as one state takes step to increase its security, it decreases the security of other states. Figure 16.1 illustrates the security dilemma.

FIGURE 16.1 The U.S.-U.S.S.R. Security Dilemma

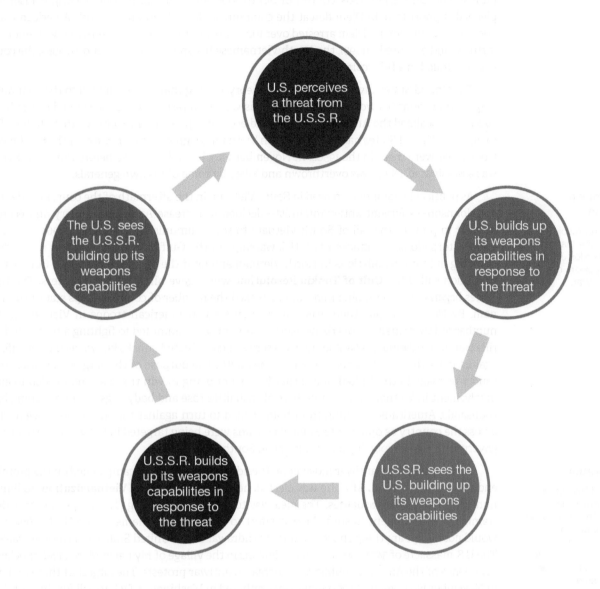

The three Cold War theories led the United States to form a series of alliances with countries that pledged support in efforts to contain communism. One of the most important of these was The North Atlantic Treaty Organization, or **NATO**, founded in April 1949 as an intergovernmental military alliance between the United States and countries in Western European to prevent further Soviet expansion into Eastern and Western Europe. The alliance was complemented by the South East Asian Organization (SEATO), a union between the United States and its allies to contain communist expansion into Southeast Asia. While NATO is still active today, SEATO expired in 1977.

Vietnam

The United States' membership in SEATO provided the legal justification for intervention in Vietnam. Before World War II, Vietnam had been a French colony. When World War II ended and European countries was struggling to hold onto their colonies, pro-communist forces in northern Vietnam seized the opportunity to start a war and end French rule. The communist forces successfully defeated the French at the Battle of Dien Bien Phu in 1954, and an agreement was reached at the Geneva Peace Convention a few months to divide the country temporarily into North and

NATO

The North Atlantic Treaty Organization, founded in April 1949 as an intergovernmental military alliance between the United States and countries in Western European to prevent further Soviet expansion into Eastern and Western Europe.

South. The treaty called for the reunification of the country in 1956 but, in 1955, the anti-communist Ngo Dinh Diem took control of South Vietnam, and U.S. President Dwight Eisenhower pledged support to help Diem defeat the communist North Vietnamese. With American training and military equipment, Diem arrested over 100,000 communist sympathizers, many of whom were tortured and executed. In 1957, the North Vietnamese began fighting back and, by 1959, the country was embroiled in a full-scale civil war.

The United States invoked the domino theory, fearing that if Vietnam fell to the communists, neighboring countries would be likely to fall as well. As a result, President Kennedy, Eisenhower's successor, escalated the American military and economic presence in South Vietnam to help Diem. By 1962, the United States had 9,000 troops in Vietnam, a significant increase over the 800 American troops that were there in the 1950s. In November 1963, just a few weeks before President Kennedy was assassinated, Diem was overthrown and killed by some of his own generals.

Gulf of Tonkin Resolution

Congressional resolution passed in 1964 that gave President Lyndon Johnson broad war powers during the Vietnam War.

As political instability increased in South Vietnam in the aftermath of the coup, President Lyndon Johnson—a fervent anti-communist—decided to increase American military and economic support to prevent the fall of South Vietnam to the communists. On August 2, 1964, North Vietnamese torpedo boats attacked two U.S. warships in the Gulf of Tonkin. Johnson responded by bombing military installations in North Vietnam and used the incident to secure a Congressional resolution called the **Gulf of Tonkin Resolution**, which gave him broad war powers. The United States began regular bombing raids and increased the number of combat troops stationed in Vietnam. By November 1967, there were more than 500,000 American troops in Vietnam, and the number of U.S. casualties was rising. North Vietnam was committed to fighting a protracted guerrilla war, and in January 1968, it launched a series of coordinated attacks known as the Tet Offensive against more than 100 cities and towns in the South. The purpose of this large-scale attack was to send a message to the United States that it was not going to win this war and needed to end its involvement in Vietnam. As the numbers of casualties rose and body bags began returning by the thousands, Americans watching from home began to turn against the war. Protests were staged across the country as opponents claimed civilians were being targeted in the war and that the U.S. government was supporting a dictatorship in South Vietnam.

Vietnamization

The policy of limiting the number of American casualties. The idea was to begin withdrawing U.S. troops and provide the training and equipment to shift the war effort to the South Vietnamese.

In response to the antiwar movement, President Richard Nixon campaigned on the promise to end the war in Vietnam. After he was elected, he began a process of "**Vietnamization**" to limit the number of American casualties. The idea was to begin withdrawing U.S. troops and provide the training and equipment to shift the war effort to the South Vietnamese. The North Vietnamese would not accept anything short of a total withdrawal of the United States and the war waged on. The U.S. massacre of 347 to 504 unarmed civilians in the village of My Lai in March 1968 shocked the conscience of the American public, who increased antiwar protests. The largest of these took place in November 1969, when 250,000 Americans gathered in Washington, D.C., to call for the withdrawal of troops from Vietnam. Protests across the country increased, particularly on college campuses. It was at one of these protests in May 1970 at Kent State University in Ohio when National Guardsmen shot and killed four students. Instead of withdrawing completely in response to the antiwar movement, Nixon expanded the air war to protect ground troops. The United States also engaged in a secret war in Cambodia and Laos to destroy North Vietnamese supply bases.

The bombing attacks did not deter the North Vietnamese, but by 1972, after a failed attack in South Vietnam, they were willing to begin negotiations. U.S. Secretary of State Henry Kissinger drafted a peace accord, and by early 1973, the South Vietnamese government signed what would become the Paris Peace Agreement. U.S. forces soon withdrew completely from Vietnam, but fighting in the country continued until April 30, 1975, when communist forces captured the city of Saigon and renamed it Ho Chi Minh City. Vietnam was unified in 1976 as the Socialist Republic of Vietnam, but more than two decades of fighting had claimed 2 million Vietnamese lives, wounded 3 million more, and left 12 million refugees. The country's political and economic infrastructure had been destroyed. It would take years for the nation to rebuild.

For the United States, the Vietnam War was the longest in its history. It was also one of its greatest foreign policy failures. In all, 58,200 Americans died in Vietnam and about 300,000 were wounded. The war cost the U.S. about $120 billion and led to widespread inflation. As it waged on, the war became increasingly unpopular and contributed directly to the lack of support of future U.S. incursions beyond its borders. The United States was no longer seen as invincible and returning soldiers were met with protests and criticism. Opponents of the war blamed them for killing innocent civilians, while supporters of the war blamed them for losing. Coupled with the scandal of Watergate, the Vietnam War produced a generation of Americans more wary of trusting the government.

This image shows a U.S. soldier with Charlie Company setting a fire during the My Lai Massacre in Vietnam on March 16, 1968. During one of the brutal incidents of violence committed against unarmed civilians during the Vietnam War, U.S. forces killed more than 400 Vietnamese women, children, and old men, slaughtered livestock, raped an unknown number of women and young girls, and burned the village of My Lai. The Vietnamese did not fire a single shot against the American soldiers. The U.S. army covered up the massacre for more than a year, and when the American press shared details of what happened, widespread outrage and protests erupted against the Vietnam War, both at home and abroad.

Ronald L. Haeberle [Public domain], via Wikimedia Commons. https://bit.ly/2B8waCH.

The End of the Cold War

While Nixon was focusing on the war in Vietnam, he was also trying to relax tensions with the Soviet Union and Communist China. This period of relaxed tensions between the United States and the Soviet Union became known as **détente**. As part of détente, President Nixon visited Moscow, and in May 1972, he and Soviet leader Brezhnev signed a series of arms control agreements intended to prevent accidental military clashes. Détente ended with the presidency of Jimmy Carter who, while he supported improved relations with the Soviets, also pressed for a military buildup and a human rights campaign. Hostilities between the two countries resumed in 1979 with the Soviet invasion of Afghanistan and the Iran hostage crisis.

détente

Period of relaxed tensions between the United States and the Soviet Union.

President Ronald Reagan was a staunch anti-communist who believed that the only way to end the Cold War was through a massive increase in military preparations and weapons buildup. The Soviet Union lost the war in Afghanistan; that loss, combined with trying to keep up with the arms race, ultimately led to economic collapse. Soviet leader Mikhail Gorbachev introduced a series of democratic reforms known as glasnost and the communist government began to fall. The Berlin Wall came down in November 1989 and, just as its construction had been a symbol of the battle between East and West, its fall signaled the end of the Cold War and the beginning of a wave of democracy that would spread across countries in the Soviet sphere of influence. By 1991, the Soviet Union had dissolved into 15 independent republics.

On December 8, 1987, President Regan and Soviet General Secretary Gorbachev signed the Intermediate-Range Nuclear Forces (INF) Treaty in the East Room of the White House. The treaty required the United States and the Soviet Union to eliminate all of their nuclear and conventional ground-launched ballistic and cruise missiles, as well as their launchers, with ranges of 500-1,000 km (short-range) and 1,000- 5,500 km (intermediate range). With the treaty, the Cold War superpowers had agreed for the first time to decrease their nuclear arsenals, abolish intermediate range nuclear weapons, and allow inspections for verification of compliance.

White House Photographic Office [Public domain] https://catalog.archives.gov/id/198588, via Wikimedia Commons. https://commons. wikimedia.org/wiki/File:Reagan_and_Gorbachev_signing.jpg.

Since 1989 and the collapse of the Soviet Union, the United States has been the global world superpower. As such, other nations in the international system look to America to provide leadership and military and economic support when hostilities erupt. There are currently nine countries that possess nuclear weapons capabilities as illustrated in Table 16.1. The United States continues to advocate for nuclear nonproliferation through arms control agreements that would reduce the global stockpiles of nuclear weapons. While the United States is the sole superpower, new challenges to American superiority exist from a variety of sources and continued dominance is not a given.

TABLE 16.1 Global Nuclear Warheads Inventories, 2018

Country	Total Nuclear Warheads
Russia	6,850
United States	6,550
France	300
China	280
United Kingdom	215
Pakistan	145
India	135
Israel	80
North Korea	15
Total	14,570

Data from Arms Control Association, https://www.armscontrol.org/factsheets/Nuclearweaponswhohaswhat, Accessed on Jan. 19, 2018.

The War on Terror

One of the greatest threats to national security comes from terrorism. U.S. foreign policy during the Cold War revolved around the idea that nuclear war with the Soviet Union was the most serious threat to national security. The Mutual Assured Destruction (MAD) strategy was developed to avert the risk of war and was enacted through an extensive anti-missile defense system. In the aftermath of the Cold War and in the absence of traditional state enemies, MAD no longer seems applicable, as terrorists are not deterred by the threat of mutual destruction.

Since the end of the Cold War, the United States has been fighting a war on terror. Events on September 11, 2001, stand out as among the most significant in the war on terror, but the bombing of Pan Am Flight 73 over Lockerbie, Scotland, in 1988; the bombings of U.S. embassies in Dar Es Salaam, Tanazania, and Nairobi, Kenya, in 1998; and the bombing of the USS Cole in Yemen in 2000, among others, all made it clear that the greatest challenge to U.S. security comes not from other countries, but from terrorist groups. Terrorism can be understood as asymmetric warfare, with a weaker group challenging a larger power, often a state. The expression "one person's terrorist is another person's freedom fighter" captures the idea that sometimes, terrorism is seen as the only option for a group struggling to address its grievances and advance its goals against a larger, more powerful opponent. Terrorism by definition targets civilians with the objective of striking fear into them, thereby making them mistrust the state's ability to defend them. This mistrust, terrorists hope, will weaken the state's capacity to govern and will ultimately compel the state to change its policies vis-à-vis the group represented by the terrorists. Terrorist groups today are sophisticated with regard to financing and communication. While the number of attacks is actually decreasing, their deadliness is increasing. Figure 16.2 shows the primary methods used for terrorist attacks worldwide in 2016.

FIGURE 16.2 Primary Methods Used for Terrorist Attacks Worldwide, 2016

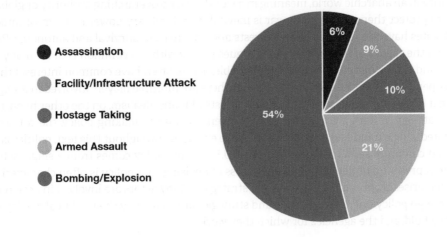

- ● Assassination
- ● Facility/Infrastructure Attack
- ● Hostage Taking
- ● Armed Assault
- ● Bombing/Explosion

Data from U.S. Department of State, https://www.state.gov/j/ct/rls/crt/2016/272241.htm.

Powell Doctrine

Developed in 1988 by Gen. Colin Powell, this doctrine determined that: any U.S. involvement in affairs beyond its borders must be in its national interests; clear military and political objectives must exist as well as a clear exit strategy; there must a high likelihood of winning and there must be public and Congressional support; and military action must come as a last resort after all other options have been explored.

Bush Doctrine

Replaced the Powell Doctrine after 9/11 and called for preventive strikes, that is, action taken to preempt a credible threat not yet executed. These preventive strikes could be military, economic, or social.

In the immediate aftermath of the Cold War, when it was understood that policies like containment and deterrence were no longer appropriate, the **Powell Doctrine** emerged as the United States' primary foreign policy strategy. Developed in 1988 by Gen. Colin Powell, who was Reagan's chairman of the Joint Chiefs of Staff, the Powell Doctrine was based on lessons learned in Vietnam and refined later by the first Gulf War. The Powell Doctrine determined that: any U.S. involvement in affairs beyond its borders must be in its national interests; clear military and political objectives must exist as well as a clear exit strategy; there must be a high likelihood of winning; there must be public and Congressional support; and military action must come as a last resort after all other options have been explored. After 9/11, the United States replaced the Powell Doctrine with the **Bush Doctrine**, a strategy outlined by President George W. Bush in a commencement speech at West Point in 2002. The Bush Doctrine echoed the Truman Doctrine in declaring that countries were either with the United States or against it. This time, however, the division was not between communist and capitalist countries but between states that supported and sponsored terrorists and those that did not. The Bush Doctrine called for preventive strikes, that is, action taken to preempt credible threats not yet executed. These preventive strikes could be military, economic, or social. They could also involve removing leaders who threaten U.S. national security, such as Iraqi President Saddam Hussein.

One of the key strategies for combatting terrorism has been spreading democracy and extending American political and economic influence. The war on terror has also been waged by improving homeland security and counterinsurgency operations, modernizing the nation's weapons system, preventing the proliferation of weapons of mass destruction, and focusing on cybersecurity.

16.2 Key Ideas and Players in U.S. Foreign Policy

realism

A theory that argues the state is the dominant and unitary actor in foreign policy. States will seek to maximize their security and power, and their interests are generally in conflict with the interests of other states.

liberalism

A theory that holds there are many types of actors involved in formulating foreign policy and, as such, no single interest dominates. Wealth is the common goal for many actors whose common interests can lead to cooperation.

One of the most important theories in foreign policy is **realism**. Realism holds that the pursuit of power is the goal of politics and that states are first and foremost concerned with ensuring their own security in an anarchic world, meaning in a world with no overarching authority or global government to protect them. For realists, war is inevitable and military power is the most important tool that states have to safeguard their interests and ensure their survival and autonomy. Realism differs from the theory of **liberalism**, which argues that wealth is a common goal for many actors in politics and that, while conflict is always possible, actors often have common interests that can lead to cooperation. Liberalism also suggests that there are multiple players involved in foreign policy and that decisions and actions reflect the interests of many. Realism, on the other hand, tells us that the state is a unitary actor, meaning that when it comes to making policy, the country acts with a united, single mind and purpose. As we have explored throughout this text, politics is about conflict and compromise. While the outcome of U.S. foreign policy comes from a single actor and appears to represent a united interest, the process of devising that policy is often characterized by conflict that arises from competing goals and strategies. Many actors are involved in designing the nation's foreign policy, and their interests and strategies are shaped by their political ideologies, the offices they hold, and the agencies for which they work.

President

The president is often understood to be the most important player in the foreign policy process. Presidents come into office with foreign policy agendas on which they have campaigned frequently during their elections.. They benefit from being the chief of state and by being the figurehead for the country. This position gives them legitimacy and prestige in the eyes of other countries in the international system. The nation's public also gives the president legitimacy and authority when it comes to foreign policy, in large part because of the powers granted by the Constitution. The president is not only the head of state, but is also the Commander-in-Chief of the U.S. military and the chief diplomat. That means the president has control of U.S. armed forces and diplomatic relations, two of the most significant tools of statecraft. Despite the formal and implied powers granted to the president, he or she still has to operate in a democratic system where power is shared among the branches of government and where the will of the people must also be taken into account. President Barack Obama, for example, was welcomed by many as an American leader whose Kenyan roots would prompt him to put Africa higher on the U.S. foreign policy agenda. The reality was, however, that Obama was constrained by the system and by competing interests that did not prioritize U.S.-African relations. His own policy interests were therefore checked and balanced by the other actors. The president can sign **treaties** or agreements with other countries, provided that two-thirds of the Senate approves. To get around the issue of Senate approval, the president has the option of signing an executive agreement with other nations. Executive agreements are considered *politically* binding, while treaties ratified by Congress are *legally* binding.

Where presidents do have more of an influence on foreign policy is during crises when time constraints and the need for an immediate response give the executive broader responsibilities. Congress tends to be less involved during crises, particularly because it can be much more difficult to reach consensus among a large group compared to a small team of the president and advisers. The role that the president plays in crisis decision-making was evident in the Cuban Missile Crisis, the Iranian Hostage Crisis, and in the decision in 2003 to go to war in Iraq.

treaties

Agreements with other countries that are legally binding.

Other Actors in the Executive Branch

The president works closely with other key actors in the executive branch to make foreign policy. The **National Security Council** (NSC) plays an important advisory role to the president. Established in 1947, the NSC consists of the president, vice president, and secretaries of state and defense. The Joint Chiefs of Staff and the director of national intelligence sit on the council as advisers. The president appoints a **National Security Adviser** (NSA), who coordinates the NSC and serves as the president's main counselor on foreign policy and national security. The NSA is often the closest and most trusted adviser to the president.

National Security Council

Advises the president on issues of foreign policy. Established in 1947, it comprises the president, vice president, and secretaries of state and defense along with the Joint Chiefs of Staff and the director of national intelligence (who sit on the council as advisers).

National Security Adviser

Presidential appointee who coordinates the National Security Council and serves as the president's main counselor on foreign policy and national security.

Secretary of State

Head of the State Department who sits on the president's Cabinet and executes several foreign policy roles. The Secretary of State is fourth in the presidential line of succession.

Secretary of Defense

Head of the Department of Defense, who advises the president on defense and military operations. The president appoints the secretary, who must be a civilian. This requirement ensures that the military is under the authority of civilians.

Joint Chiefs of Staff

Part of the Department of Defense made up of the nation's chief military officers from the Army, Navy, Marine Corps, and Air Force, and headed by a chair appointed by the president. The Joint Chiefs of Staff advise the president, Secretary of Defense, the Homeland Security Council, and the National Security Council on military matters.

Central Intelligence Agency

Agency that oversees foreign intelligence gathering and carries out classified and often covert operations to advance U.S. national security goals.

Director of National Intelligence

The president's main intelligence adviser, who coordinates the activities of the intelligence community.

While the NSC helps determine the policy agenda, the Department of State manages foreign affairs. The State Department was the first department established by the Constitution, and its head is fourth in the presidential line of succession. The president appoints its head, the **Secretary of State,** who sits on the president's Cabinet and executes several foreign policy roles. The first and perhaps most visible of these roles is the operation of American embassies and consulates around the world. These posts provide services for Americans living abroad, assist U.S. travelers, issue visas to visitors to the United States, and grant asylum to refugees. The State Department also sends representatives to international meetings and negotiates treaties and executive agreements with other nations. Employees of the State Department include foreign service officers, who staff the embassies and consulates, report on issues happening overseas, and represent the United States abroad. The most senior foreign service officer at an embassy is the ambassador. Some ambassadors are appointed by the president in exchange for political support during the presidential campaign, while other ambassadors are career diplomats who have advanced through the system.

The State Department handles the country's diplomatic affairs, while the Department of Defense handles its military relations. Headquartered in the Pentagon, the Department of Defense manages U.S. soldiers and equipment. The **Secretary of Defense** heads the department and advise the president on defense and military operations. The president appoints the secretary, who must be a civilian. This requirement ensures that the military is under the authority of civilians.

Part of the Department of Defense is the **Joint Chiefs of Staff**. It is made up of the nation's chief military officers from the Army, Navy, Marine Corps, and Air Force, and is headed by a chair appointed by the president. The Joint Chiefs of Staff advises the president, Secretary of Defense, the Homeland Security Council, and the NSC on military matters.

Another player that helps shape foreign policy is the intelligence community. Information used to determine foreign policy decisions and strategies is collected and analyzed by the intelligence community, which then reports back to the president and the secretaries of state and defense. More than a dozen agencies make up the intelligence community that, until recently, was led by the head of the **Central Intelligence Agency** (CIA). The CIA oversees foreign intelligence gathering and carries out classified and often covert operations to advance U.S. national security goals. As a result of reports about 9/11 and breakdowns in communication within the intelligence community, the role of the director of the CIA was limited to only directing the CIA instead of the entire community. There is now a **Director of National Intelligence** who is the president's main intelligence adviser and coordinates the activities of the intelligence community. The National Counterterrorism Center was also established to focus specifically on gathering terrorism-related intelligence.

In the aftermath of 9/11, the Department of Homeland Security was also created to help prevent attacks against the United States. Several existing agencies, such as the Transportation Security Administration (TSA), Immigration and Naturalization Services (INS), and the Federal Emergency Management Agency (FEMA) all now sit within the Department of Homeland Security.

Other cabinet departments have foreign policy interests, including economic policy as it relates to commerce, trade, and foreign aid. Agencies such as the Treasury Department, the Commerce Department, the Department of Labor, and the Department of Agriculture help determine export/import relations, the promotion of American goods and food abroad, the delivery of humanitarian aid, and the impact of trade on jobs in the United States.

Congress

Though less visible than the president and the executive branch, Congress is an important foreign policy actor. The Constitution gives Congress the power to make treaties, declare war, and spend money. Despite these foreign policy related powers, Congress has traditionally focused more on domestic politics while the president has played a greater role in foreign affairs. The size and competing interests in Congress impede the body from making decisions with regard to foreign policy, particularly when there are time constraints. The most important congressional power as it relates to foreign policy and the greatest source of conflict between the executive and legislative branches on international politics is its power to declare war. While the president can commit troops abroad, only Congress can issue a formal declaration of war. Presidents will try to get around this by committing troops but not calling the mission a war. They did this, for example, in Korea (1950), Vietnam (1965), the Persian Gulf (1990), Afghanistan (2001), and Iraq (2003). In response to the increasing number of troops sent to Vietnam without a formal declaration of war, Congress passed the **War Powers Act of 1973**. The act states that: 1) the president must inform Congress when troops have been committed into hostilities; 2) troops cannot be committed for more than 60 days without congressional approval (though an additional 30 days is allowed for troop withdrawal); and 3) Congress, with a concurrent resolution in both houses, has the authority to withdraw troops who have been committed without a declaration of war. The Wars Powers Act has not stopped presidents from committing troops abroad without congressional approval. They have avoided the 60-day clock by reporting to Congress in a way that is "consistent but not pursuant to" the act. Presidents have also played with words, claiming that some interventions did not constitute "hostilities" because ground troops were not committed. Such was the case in 2011 when President Obama sent U.S. forces to topple Libyan leader Muammar Gaddafi from power. But perhaps the most critical constraint on the War Powers Act is that once American troops have been sent into action by the president, it is unlikely that Congress would call them back. To do so would constitute a major loss of prestige and legitimacy in the eyes of the international community and would reveal an underlying lack of agreement and coherence within U.S. foreign policy.

War Powers Act of 1973

Congressional act that states that: 1) the president must inform Congress when troops have been committed to hostilities; 2) troops cannot be committed for more than 60 days without congressional approval (though an additional 30 days is allowed for troop withdrawal); and 3) Congress, with a concurrent resolution in both houses, has the authority to withdraw troops who have been committed without a declaration of war.

16.3 Setting the Foreign Policy Agenda

Each of the actors we have described plays an important role in setting the nation's foreign policy agenda and determining its strategies. But these foreign policy decision makers do not operate in a political vacuum; rather, they determine their interests and strategies in the context of political debates in society.

Domestic Influences on Foreign Policy

The United States' foreign policy agenda is the product, in large part, of domestic influences and preferences. The country's relationships with other nations are often determined by domestic coalition formation.

Interest Groups

In Chapter 9, we discussed the role that interest groups play in American politics. We defined interest groups as coalitions of people who share a common interest in the outcome of a particular political issue and who organize themselves to try to influence that outcome. When it comes to foreign policy, we often see interest groups form along ethnic lines. Ethnic groups can become interest groups when they are concerned about issues relating to their ancestral nations outside the United States. These groups have effective lobbying presences in Congress and are successful in large part because the majority of Americans do not have strong interest in issues affecting the ethnic groups' homeland. As a result, even a small ethnic group can have significant influence in setting the foreign policy agenda. For example, Cuban Americans have largely shaped U.S. policy toward Cuba; similarly, Jewish Americans have a considerable influence on relations with Israel and the Middle East.

Interest groups can also form around business concerns. These groups argue that what is good for their businesses (often defined by profit margins) is good for the United States. They frequently influence U.S. trade policies with other nations. They can also influence the country's positions on global issues and the strategies it implements to pursue its interests. This effect is evident in the so-called military-industrial complex.

Military-Industrial Complex

military-industrial complex

The relationship between the government, weapons manufacturers, and research institutions.

The **military-industrial complex** refers to the relationship between the government, weapons manufacturers, and research institutions. These entities work together to supply the country's armed forces. The term military-industrial complex was first used by President Eisenhower in 1961 when, in his farewell speech, he warned that this network was gaining too much influence in American society and that militarization would ultimately erode democracy. He blamed the military-industrial complex for the arms race with the Soviet Union during the Cold War. Those who stood to profit from the production of weapons were calling the shots at the expense of the general public's interest in peace.

The various constituencies of the complex have an interest in military spending. There are industries that produce weapons and war materials that profit from government contracts; military officers who advance their careers around new weapons systems; and research institutions that fund scientists through grants for military studies. The practice of the revolving door in politics means executives from military industries are often appointed to government positions and charged with making decisions about the country's military spending. Once their time in office has ended, these executives frequently return to their companies, but they maintain their relationships with influential contacts in government. Military industries such as Lockheed Martin are generous political campaign contributors, particularly to candidates who vote on military budgets.

Public Opinion

Interest groups will try to influence public opinion on foreign policy. In the United States, the attitudes of citizens regarding foreign policy decisions do seem to have some influence. An unpopular war, for example, can force a leader from office, as was the case with President Johnson and Vietnam. But in general, public opinion has less of an impact on foreign policy than it does on domestic policy. Decision makers have fewer constraints when it comes to making foreign policy, and it is important for the nation to present a unified front on the world stage. In addition, there may be a need to keep information secret from the public, at least in the short term, to protect national security. As a result, there may be a democratic deficit in foreign policy: the decisions that are made by the government may not reflect the usual debates and reconciling of conflicting interests that are part of the political process. Instead, the foreign policy agenda may be set in large part by those in power. In the United States, the public enters the foreign policy process to provide support and legitimacy for interests and strategies that have already been determined. There may be, then, an inherent incompatibility between democracy and foreign policy. In the nineteenth century, Alexis de Tocqueville, one the greatest modern democracy theorists, argued that democracies were destined to be inferior to other regime types when it comes to foreign policy.[3] Because they are subject to the constraints of public opinion and the need for consensus, he argued, democracies are incapable of producing rational foreign policy, which demands technical expertise, discretion, and competence. Authoritarian regimes, on the other hand, can make decisions independent of the public's will and behind closed doors. These regimes, therefore, may have an advantage in international politics.

Despite these concerns, there is an **attentive public**, or a minority of the population that stays informed about international issues. This attentive public is comprised of people in business, journalists, lobbyists, and academics who constitute a foreign policy elite who influence decision making. The government also adopts certain foreign policies to generate public approval and consolidate power domestically. This strategy is evident when the government engages in war at time when the nation faces challenges at home. It capitalizes on the **rally around the flag** effect when the public's support of the government increases in times of international crisis. The rally around the flag effect is short-lived, however, and wanes as the number of casualties rises.

Media

The news media have had a profound effect on foreign policymaking. In Chapter 10, we discuss the CNN effect and the capacity of news cameras to set the policy agenda. It is debatable whether the government leads the cameras to generate support for decisions it has already made or whether the cameras lead the government by drawing attention to an issue, but it is clear that real time news coverage gives the domestic public a front row seat to foreign policy decision making. The media receives and sends signals and, in doing so, can pressure politicians to respond promptly to news stories. It is unlikely, however, that the news media dictate the response. The news media can shape the conversation around foreign policy and function as an accelerant, but decision-making power rests with the policymakers. The media can also be an instrument of the government, used to promote **propaganda**, or information selected, designed, and sometimes distorted to influence the beliefs of an audience. The aim of propaganda in the context of foreign policy is to promote a favorable image of the United States abroad. While the government often relies on the media through radio broadcasts, movies, television, and pamphlets to transmit propaganda, study abroad programs, student exchanges, and initiatives like the Peace Corps are also used to promote a favorable image of the United States.

The newsworthiness of a story from the media's perspective and the policy priorities of the government are connected in a relationship of mutual influence: it can be difficult to determine where one ends and the other begins.

16.4 Tools of Statecraft

The various actors involved with foreign policy making work to develop the nation's **grand strategy**, that is, a statement of U.S. goals in world politics and the means to achieve them. This grand strategy guides all areas of the country's international relations and determines how the Pentagon, White House, and military are organized and prioritized. The first step in building a grand strategy is identifying U.S. global objectives. These objectives often stem from national security, broadly defined. For example, national security can be defined along political, military, and/or economic lines. Next, available resources and perceived threats are assessed in order to determine

attentive public

A minority of the population that stays informed about international issues. This attentive public comprises people in business, journalists, lobbyists, and academics who constitute a foreign policy elite with influence on decision making.

rally around the flag

The public's support of the government increases in times of international crisis.

propaganda

Information selected, designed, and sometimes distorted to influence the beliefs of an audience.

grand strategy

A statement of U.S. goals in world politics and the means to achieve them.

capacity and review options. Finally, a grand strategy is proposed and implemented using various tools of statecraft. Figure 16.3 illustrates the strategic matrix. Examples of grand strategies include containment and deterrence during the Cold War and the neoconservative plan to use preventive force to defeat terrorism and promote democracy.

FIGURE 16.3 The Strategic Matrix

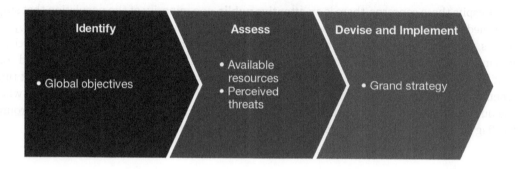

A successful grand strategy is one that protects and advances the United States' national interests and contributes to the enhancement and preservation of its power and status while, at the same time, does not harm the power and status of other nations. It works to avoid conflict, and where this is not possible, it seeks to minimize the damage to the nation's power and prestige. The successful execution of a grand strategy is due in large part to the foreign policy instruments used to implement it.

Diplomacy

diplomacy

The formal communications and negotiations between countries.

Diplomacy refers to the formal communications and negotiations between countries. The State Department conducts most of the United States' diplomatic relations. The United States has an extensive diplomatic presence throughout the world. Almost every country has a U.S. embassy and an embassy of its own in Washington, D.C. These embassies are staffed by diplomats, or foreign service officers (FSOs), whose job it is to represent the United States abroad, promote and defend American interests, gather information about what is happening in the foreign country, assist Americans living abroad, and conduct negotiations with foreign leaders.

While diplomatic channels were once the only way in which foreign countries could communicate, technological advancements in communications and transportation have made diplomacy less relevant. Foreign leaders can speak to each other easily on the phone or online and can travel anywhere in the world to be available within hours to attend meetings or negotiations. The rise of shuttle diplomacy, that is, the ease with which foreign leaders can travel to deal directly with each other, is diminishing the need for professional diplomats.

A different type of political tool that foreign policy makers can use involves **covert operations** or undercover actions, in which the United States is intimately involved but appears to have no role. The actions are carried out in secret, often by the CIA. They can take various forms, such as efforts to assassinate foreign leaders (for example, Fidel Castro in Cuba and Patrice Lumumba in the Democratic Republic of Congo); regime changes in governments that do not support the United States (e.g., the overthrow of Mohammed Mosaddeq in Iran in 1953 and Salvador Allende in Chile in 1973); and promoting and encouraging foreign civil unrest to protect American business interests (for example, the overthrow of democratically elected President Jacobo Arbenz Guzmán in Guatemala in 1954 in order to protect the United Fruit Company). The secrecy of these covert operations undermines the democratic process of debate and accountability, as the public has no idea and therefore no say in what is happening. In 1980, President Carter signed the Intelligence Oversight Act, which was intended, at a minimum, to keep Congress informed about secret operations. But the Act does not apply to actions carried out by the Department of Defense. This loophole has meant that covert options carried out by the Special Operations Command, which is under the Defense Department's jurisdiction and is responsible for most undercover activity today, have continued unabated.

covert operations

Undercover actions in which the United States is intimately involved but appears to have had no role.

Economic Instruments

Foreign policymakers rely on **foreign aid** and **economic sanctions** to implement their strategies. Foreign aid is economic assistance provided to other nations, often poorer ones or those who have suffered a natural disaster or crisis. The aid is given in the form of grants, loans, or technical assistance. The Marshall Plan applied to European nations in the aftermath of World War II is an example of a foreign aid. The United States often directs aid to development projects and invests in education, health care, and infrastructure abroad in order to advance its own national interests and promote global stability. While most Americans assume that 26 percent of the federal budget goes to foreign aid, the reality amounts to about 1 percent, putting the United States at the bottom of the list of countries that give aid.[4] Many of the grants the United States gives come with the condition that the grant be used to buy U.S. goods and services.

In addition to aid, the government relies on economic sanctions to advance its interests. Economic sanctions are restrictions on trade imposed on one nation by another as punishment. The United States has utilized sanctions in its relations with Iran, Cuba, and Russia, for example, in an effort to alter policies in those countries. Economic sanctions have mixed results. On one hand, they do send a strong signal to countries that the United States does not approve of their actions. On the other hand, unless other nations join in and support the sanctions, the restrictions often have limited impact. Moreover, trade restrictions can harm domestic businesses and ultimately deprive U.S. companies of significant export earnings.

foreign aid

Economic assistance provided to other nations, often poorer ones or those who have suffered a natural disaster or crisis, in the form of grants, loans, or technical assistance.

economic sanctions

Restrictions on trade imposed on one nation by another as punishment.

free trade

Promotes keeping tariffs and trade barriers to a minimum to allow for the free flow of goods across borders. Free trade aims to keep prices low for consumers and expand markets for producers.

protectionism

Trade policy that prioritizes the needs of domestic producers and advocates trade policies that allow them to compete with foreign producers in domestic markets.

The nation's economic relations with other countries manifest themselves through international trade policies. Globalization has introduced new debates about trade issues. These debates focus on a key dimension: free-trade v. protectionism. **Free trade** promotes keeping tariffs and trade barriers to a minimum to allow for the free flow of goods across borders. Free trade aims to keep prices low for consumers and expand markets for producers. **Protectionism** instead prioritizes the needs of domestic producers and advocates trade policies that allow them to compete with foreign producers in domestic markets. Debate about trade policies was initiated in negotiations for the North American Free Trade Agreement, known as NAFTA, which was drafted in 1993 to improve trade relations between the United States, Canada, and Mexico. It was hoped that the agreement would boost the economies of all three countries, and side agreements were worked out to protect some U.S. producers from adverse effects. Critics of the agreement argue that it has resulted in a loss of jobs in Mexico and has harmed domestic producers in the United States. Other trade agreements, such as the Trans Pacific Partnership (TPP) signed in February 2016 by Australia, Brunei, Canada, Chile, Japan, Malaysia, Mexico, New Zealand, Peru, Singapore, and Vietnam, illustrate the challenges of drafting international trade pacts. The United States supported the TPP to increase American influence in Asia and to check China's military and economic ambitions, but President Trump withdrew the nation from the agreement in January 2017, citing concerns that the terms of the agreement did not treat the U.S. fairly.[5]

Military Tools

defense strategy

The organization and deployment of a nation's armed forces to protect the country against threats from other nations.

One of the most important components of American foreign policy is the nation's **defense strategy**, or the organization and deployment of its armed forces to protect the United States against threats from other nations. The U.S. defense strategy promotes national security, the ultimate goal for any country's international affairs. This defense strategy is supported through the deployment of American troops worldwide and by a massive defense budget. The United States spends more on its military than any other country in the world. The defense budget is just under $600 billion, which is more than the budgets of the next nine countries combined (see Table 16.2). As of 2017, the United States controls about 800 military bases outside of the 50 states and Washington, D.C., and has a military presence in over 156 countries.[6] For many people in the world, the face of America is the face of its military personnel.

TABLE 16.2 Military Budget of the United States in Comparative Perspective

Country	Military Spending in 2015	Most Powerful Countries Rank
U.S.	$596 billion	1
China	$215 billion	3
Saudi Arabia	$87 billion	9
Russia	$66 billion	2
U.K.	$55 billion	5
India	$51 billion	14
France	$51 billion	6
Japan	$41 billion	7
Germany	$39 billion	4
South Korea	$36 billion	10

Data from Stockholm International Peace Research Institute

Since abandoning its policy of isolationism at the end of World War II, the United States has been continuously involved in conflicts overseas to protect and advance its national security interests. The number of military personnel on active duty has decreased in the past 60 years, but the military's reach has not. As of 2018, American troops are engaged in conflicts in Afghanistan, Iraq, Syria, Yemen, Niger, Somalia, Jordan, Thailand, and elsewhere. In addition, there are 37,813 more troops serving on secret assignments in places listed as "unknown." There are also American troops stationed in Japan and South Korea to defend against North Korea and China, if necessary, and troops in Germany, Britain, and Turkey to protect NATO allies.[7] Figure 16.4 shows U.S. troop deployments worldwide. When the United States engages in conflict, these incursions tend to be small scale and destruction is minimal. It has been the nation's policy to use armed conflict only after other strategies have failed. The United States attempts **coercive diplomacy** as a first step, threatening to use force if the other nations do not reverse or change their actions. Coercive diplomacy is often effective, as was the case in the Cuban Missile Crisis, and it can prevent large-scale war. In order to be successful, coercive diplomacy must be accompanied by clear and credible demands, severe penalties, coherent plans, and a flexible approach. It also has to provide a way for the other side to back down without losing face. If coercive diplomacy fails, either because other countries attempt to call the United States' bluff or because those nations believe that military conflict is inevitable, then armed violence may be the only option. Coercive diplomacy failed to prevent the 1991 and 2003 U.S. wars in Iraq.

> **coercive diplomacy**
>
> The threat of force if other nations do not reverse or change their actions.

FIGURE 16.4 U.S. Troops Deployment Worldwide

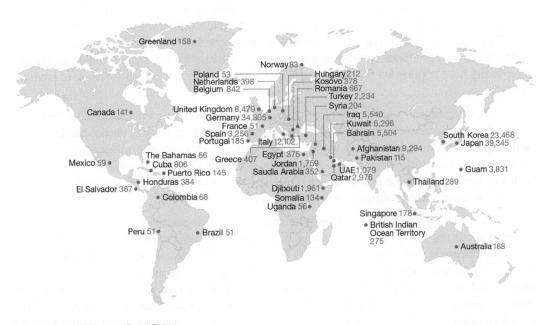

Data from DoD, SIPRI, (2015 Data), Politico.

National security in the United States depends not only on having an effective, well-trained and well-armed military capable of rapid response, but also international cooperation to promote dialogue and understanding. The United States shares the global commitment to transparency and strong international institutions that enforce agreements and maintain peaceful relations among nations.

16.5 Challenges to U.S. Foreign Policy

As the United States navigates its foreign policy in the twenty-first century, there are several key transnational issues it must contend with beyond national defense and the global economy. Challenges presented by environmental concerns, immigration, and weapons proliferation are among the global problems demanding attention of U.S. foreign policymakers as they negotiate agreements and policies that advance American national security interests.

global commons

The earth's ecosystem of human, animal, and plant life.

Environmental concerns and threats to the **global commons**, that is the earth's ecosystem of human, animal, and plant life, are at the top of the world's foreign policy agenda. Policies have been implemented to reduce air and water pollution, preserve forests, and promote more efficient energy use. But managing the global commons is difficult because of national self-interest. For the United States, the regulations in place as the result of environmental agreements put limits on industries and raise costs of production. The United States is the world's second largest air polluter[8] and the largest consumer of oil, but remains reluctant to join treaties that would reduce emissions. The Kyoto Protocol, an attempt to curb pollution by requiring nations to reduce greenhouse gas emissions, was voted down by Congress as the result of concerns about free riding by developing countries, such as China and India. The United States withdrew from the Paris Agreement, an international environmental policy implemented in November 2016 to strengthen the global response to the impacts of climate change. The United States is the only country to reject the climate accord. President Trump said his duty to protect the American people required withdrawal from the agreement.[9] Foreign policy with regard to the environment reflects continued disagreements in the United States over fuel prices, efficiency, and domestic politics with automakers and labor unions. These issues have at times led the nation to prioritize business demands at the expense of environmental protection.

Immigration presents another foreign policy challenge. Border security is an important concern, as Trump has vowed to erect a highly controversial wall along the U.S.-Mexico border to prevent illegal immigration and stop drug trafficking. There already exists 643 miles of fence between the two countries, which was completed by 2010 by the Army Corps of Engineers. Immigration is both a domestic and foreign policy issue and requires the United States to develop responses that address the cause of the problem as well as solutions to mitigate it.

As the United States manages its relationships with other countries, it remains focused on concerns about the proliferation of weapons of mass destruction and the buildup of small arms. The United States is also concerned about the proliferation of nuclear weapons as evidenced by its foreign policies with Iran and North Korea. In negotiating international arms treaties, the country must balance concerns about national security with domestic interests. The United States, for example, resists more stringent global measures to restrict the sale of small arms because of the nation's Second Amendment right to bear arms. Multilateral agreements about weapons in space are also complicated by the United States' opposition to limits on its free access to outer space. The country maintains a dominant position in the global arms market and leads the world in arms sales.[10]

The United States must continue to balance domestic pressures with foreign policy goals as it looks to the future. There are many access points in the foreign policy decision-making process for groups to intervene and promote particular interests at the expense of the national interest. These groups can be businesses, bureaucratic agencies, ethnic lobbies, and other domestic actors who have a stake in the outcome of U.S. relations with other countries. The U.S. public is frequently uninterested in foreign policy, which gives these groups even greater dominance and latitude in shaping the policy agenda. The history of foreign policy in the United States has been marked by periods of isolationism and internationalism, and the country continues to alternate between engaging and detaching from world affairs. Other countries, such as China and Russia, are emerging to challenge U.S. global dominance. In response, the United States must be aware of its world image and carefully manage the global order it has helped craft.

16.6 What Can I Do?

Most Americans are uninterested or disengaged from foreign policy. As a result, their influence on international policy making is limited. By following the news and making an investment in understanding global affairs, you can increase the impact you have on foreign policy. You can join a group that feels strongly about a particular global issue and you can advocate for specific policies. You can also devote your time and resources to public goods such as the environment and work to overcome collective action problems.

There are also numerous job opportunities within the foreign policy sector. You could intern at the State Department or Pentagon, for example. You could join the military. Or you could apply to be a foreign service officer representing the United States at an embassy or consulate abroad. To be considered for a career in the foreign service, you must first take a written exam. If you pass that test, you would be invited to participate in an oral exam offered on specific dates that may be held in another city or state compared to where you live. This oral exam is highly competitive and only a select few pass. Those who do succeed go through extensive background checks, security clearances, and medical examinations. If these generate favorable results, you would be invited to participate in training in Washington, D.C., and then deployed to a diplomatic post where you would serve for several years before being dispatched to another location. It is an exciting and dynamic career, one that requires you to move every few years and represent U.S. interests and goals first and foremost.

16.7 What's the Alternative?

As we watch the United States negotiate the foreign policy arena, there may be reason to criticize the country for being overly engaged or not sufficiently engaged. We may also disagree with specific policies pursued by the United States. But whatever issues we may have with how it conducts itself on the global stage, it is unlikely that the United States could withdraw completely from foreign affairs and return to a position of isolationism. While U.S. power is not what it was during the Cold War, the nation remains the world's leader. Other countries continue to look to the United States to preserve and protect the global order.

While isolationism is not a viable alternative, a foreign policy guided by investments in education, health care, innovation, and worker empowerment could prove critical to the nation's world standing and ability to compete internationally. The United States could also pursue a policy of offshore balancing, that is, focusing on efforts to maintain its dominance in the West and counter potential powers in Europe, Northeast Asia, and the Persian Gulf.[11] Promoted by political scientists John Mearsheimer and Stephen Walt, this strategy encourages other nations to provide their own defense rather than waiting for the United States to intervene. The United States could then be more selective about where and when it gets involved, thereby minimizing domestic opposition at home and abroad and increasing its chances of emerging in a dominant position and being seen as an ally. The United States is in a unique geographic position to be able to engage in offshore balancing. Its natural borders provided by oceans on two sides protect the nation. The United States also has a large population, a well-developed economy, and a nuclear arsenal, all of which contribute to protect the territory. Offshore balancing would be an alternative to the current U.S. strategy that positions the United States as the nation that must use its power and prestige to promote free markets and democratization. This strategy commits the United States to multiple places around the world without increasing the resources required to fulfill these commitments effectively. Other states may be threatened by U.S. power and occupation, and may work to undermine U.S. efforts by developing weapons of mass destruction or supporting terrorist activities. When such efforts fail, U.S. security can be threatened and diminished. Offshore balancing would instead utilize the United States' advantageous geographic positions, recognize the power of nationalism, and refrain from imposing American values on other states.

As the United States' foreign policy evolves and adapts to current challenges, whatever strategy the country pursues, the nation must balance competing domestic interests and preferences. This balancing will continue to occur within the context of protecting and advancing national security.

Endnotes

1. Melvyn Leffler, *The Preponderance of Power* (Stanford, California: Stanford University Press, 1992).

2. W.R. Smyser, *Kennedy and the Berlin Wall: A Hell of A Lot Better than a War* (Latham, MD: Rowman and Littlefield Publishers, Inc., 2010).

3. Alexis De Tocqueville, *Democracy in America* (Project Gutenberg: 2006), https://www.gutenberg.org/files/815/815-h/815-h.htm.

4. Poncie Rutsch, "Guess How Much Uncle Sam's Money Goes to Foreign Aid. Guess Again!" NPR, February 10, 2015, https://www.npr.org/sections/goatsandsoda/2015/02/10/383875581/guess-how-much-of-uncle-sams-money-goes-to-foreign-aid-guess-again.

5. Ylan Q. Mui, "Withdrawal from Trans-Pacific Partnership shifts U.S. role in world economy," *The Washington Post* (Washington, D.C.), January 23, 2017.

6. David Vine, "List of U.S. Military Bases Abroad, 2017," Digital Research Archive, May 14, 2017, https://dra.american.edu/islandora/object/auislandora:55685.

7. The Editorial Board, "America's Forever Wars," *The New York Times*, October 22, 2017, https://www.nytimes.com/2017/10/22/opinion/americas-forever-wars.html.

8. China is the largest emitter of CO2. See "When It Comes to Climate Change, National Interests Outweigh Individual Mandates," Stratfor Worldview, January 2, 2015, https://worldview.stratfor.com/article/when-it-comes-climate-change-national-interests-outweigh-international-mandates.

9. Robinson Meyer, "Did President Trump Just Make the Planet Hotter?" *The Atlantic* (Boston, MA) June 1, 2017.

10. Data available from the Stockholm International Peace Research Institute.

11. John J. Mearsheimer and Stephen M. Walt, "The Case for Offshore Balancing: A Superior U.S. Grand Strategy," *Foreign Affairs*, (July/August 2016).

APPENDIX A
The Constitution of the United States

We the People of the United States, in Order to form a more perfect Union, establish Justice, insure domestic Tranquility, provide for the common defence, promote the general Welfare, and secure the Blessings of Liberty to ourselves and our Posterity, do ordain and establish this Constitution for the United States of America.

A.1 Article I

Section. 1. All legislative Powers herein granted shall be vested in a Congress of the United States, which shall consist of a Senate and House of Representatives.

Section. 2. The House of Representatives shall be composed of Members chosen every second Year by the People of the several States, and the Electors in each State shall have the Qualifications requisite for Electors of the most numerous Branch of the State Legislature.

No Person shall be a Representative who shall not have attained to the Age of twenty five Years, and been seven Years a Citizen of the United States, and who shall not, when elected, be an Inhabitant of that State in which he shall be chosen.

Representatives and direct Taxes shall be apportioned among the several States which may be included within this Union, according to their respective Numbers, which shall be determined by adding to the whole Number of free Persons, including those bound to Service for a Term of Years, and excluding Indians not taxed, three fifths of all other Persons. The actual Enumeration shall be made within three Years after the first Meeting of the Congress of the United States, and within every subsequent Term of ten Years, in such Manner as they shall by Law direct. The Number of Representatives shall not exceed one for every thirty Thousand, but each State shall have at Least one Representative; and until such enumeration shall be made, the State of New Hampshire shall be entitled to chuse three, Massachusetts eight, Rhode Island and Providence Plantations one, Connecticut five, New York six, New Jersey four, Pennsylvania eight, Delaware one, Maryland six, Virginia ten, North Carolina five, South Carolina five, and Georgia three.

When vacancies happen in the Representation from any State, the Executive Authority thereof shall issue Writs of Election to fill such Vacancies.

The House of Representatives shall chuse their Speaker and other Officers; and shall have the sole Power of Impeachment.

Section. 3. The Senate of the United States shall be composed of two Senators from each State, chosen by the Legislature thereof, for six Years; and each Senator shall have one Vote.

Immediately after they shall be assembled in Consequence of the first Election, they shall be divided as equally as may be into three Classes. The Seats of the Senators of the first Class shall be vacated at the Expiration of the second Year, of the second Class at the Expiration of the fourth Year, and of the third Class at the Expiration of the sixth Year, so that one third may be chosen every second Year; and if Vacancies happen by Resignation, or otherwise, during the Recess of the

Legislature of any State, the Executive thereof may make temporary Appointments until the next Meeting of the Legislature, which shall then fill such Vacancies.

No Person shall be a Senator who shall not have attained to the Age of thirty Years, and been nine Years a Citizen of the United States, and who shall not, when elected, be an Inhabitant of that State for which he shall be chosen.

The Vice President of the United States shall be President of the Senate, but shall have no Vote, unless they be equally divided.

The Senate shall chuse their other Officers, and also a President pro tempore, in the Absence of the Vice President, or when he shall exercise the Office of President of the United States.

The Senate shall have the sole Power to try all Impeachments. When sitting for that Purpose, they shall be on Oath or Affirmation. When the President of the United States is tried, the Chief Justice shall preside: And no Person shall be convicted without the Concurrence of two thirds of the Members present.

Judgment in Cases of Impeachment shall not extend further than to removal from Office, and disqualification to hold and enjoy any Office of honor, Trust or Profit under the United States: but the Party convicted shall nevertheless be liable and subject to Indictment, Trial, Judgment and Punishment, according to Law.

Section. 4. The Times, Places and Manner of holding Elections for Senators and Representatives, shall be prescribed in each State by the Legislature thereof; but the Congress may at any time by Law make or alter such Regulations, except as to the Places of chusing Senators.

The Congress shall assemble at least once in every Year, and such Meeting shall be on the first Monday in December [Modified by Amendment XX], unless they shall by Law appoint a different Day.

Section. 5. Each House shall be the Judge of the Elections, Returns and Qualifications of its own Members, and a Majority of each shall constitute a Quorum to do Business; but a smaller Number may adjourn from day to day, and may be authorized to compel the Attendance of absent Members, in such Manner, and under such Penalties as each House may provide.

Each House may determine the Rules of its Proceedings, punish its Members for disorderly Behaviour, and, with the Concurrence of two thirds, expel a Member.

Each House shall keep a Journal of its Proceedings, and from time to time publish the same, excepting such Parts as may in their Judgment require Secrecy; and the Yeas and Nays of the Members of either House on any question shall, at the Desire of one fifth of those Present, be entered on the Journal.

Neither House, during the Session of Congress, shall, without the Consent of the other, adjourn for more than three days, nor to any other Place than that in which the two Houses shall be sitting.

Section. 6. The Senators and Representatives shall receive a Compensation for their Services, to be ascertained by Law, and paid out of the Treasury of the United States. They shall in all Cases, except Treason, Felony and Breach of the Peace, be privileged from Arrest during their Attendance at the Session of their respective Houses, and in going to and returning from the same; and for any Speech or Debate in either House, they shall not be questioned in any other Place.

No Senator or Representative shall, during the Time for which he was elected, be appointed to any civil Office under the Authority of the United States, which shall have been created, or the Emoluments whereof shall have been encreased during such time; and no Person holding any Office under the United States, shall be a Member of either House during his Continuance in Office.

Section. 7. All Bills for raising Revenue shall originate in the House of Representatives; but the Senate may propose or concur with Amendments as on other Bills.

Every Bill which shall have passed the House of Representatives and the Senate, shall, before it become a Law, be presented to the President of the United States; If he approve he shall sign it, but if not he shall return it, with his Objections to that House in which it shall have originated, who shall enter the Objections at large on their Journal, and proceed to reconsider it. If after such Reconsideration two thirds of that House shall agree to pass the Bill, it shall be sent, together with the Objections, to the other House, by which it shall likewise be reconsidered, and if approved by two thirds of that House, it shall become a Law. But in all such Cases the Votes of both Houses shall be determined by yeas and Nays, and the Names of the Persons voting for and against the Bill shall be entered on the Journal of each House respectively. If any Bill shall not be returned by the President within ten Days (Sundays excepted) after it shall have been presented to him, the Same shall be a Law, in like Manner as if he had signed it, unless the Congress by their Adjournment prevent its Return, in which Case it shall not be a Law.

Every Order, Resolution, or Vote to which the Concurrence of the Senate and House of Representatives may be necessary (except on a question of Adjournment) shall be presented to the President of the United States; and before the Same shall take Effect, shall be approved by him, or being disapproved by him, shall be repassed by two thirds of the Senate and House of Representatives, according to the Rules and Limitations prescribed in the Case of a Bill.

Section. 8. The Congress shall have Power To lay and collect Taxes, Duties, Imposts and Excises, to pay the Debts and provide for the common Defence and general Welfare of the United States; but all Duties, Imposts and Excises shall be uniform throughout the United States;

To borrow Money on the credit of the United States;

To regulate Commerce with foreign Nations, and among the several States, and with the Indian Tribes;

To establish an uniform Rule of Naturalization, and uniform Laws on the subject of Bankruptcies throughout the United States;

To coin Money, regulate the Value thereof, and of foreign Coin, and fix the Standard of Weights and Measures;

To provide for the Punishment of counterfeiting the Securities and current Coin of the United States;

To establish Post Offices and post Roads;

To promote the Progress of Science and useful Arts, by securing for limited Times to Authors and Inventors the exclusive Right to their respective Writings and Discoveries;

To constitute Tribunals inferior to the supreme Court;

To define and punish Piracies and Felonies committed on the high Seas, and Offences against the Law of Nations;

To declare War, grant Letters of Marque and Reprisal, and make Rules concerning Captures on Land and Water;

To raise and support Armies, but no Appropriation of Money to that Use shall be for a longer Term than two Years;

To provide and maintain a Navy;

To make Rules for the Government and Regulation of the land and naval Forces;

To provide for calling forth the Militia to execute the Laws of the Union, suppress Insurrections and repel Invasions;

To provide for organizing, arming, and disciplining, the Militia, and for governing such Part of them as may be employed in the Service of the United States, reserving to the States respectively, the Appointment of the Officers, and the Authority of training the Militia according to the discipline prescribed by Congress;

To exercise exclusive Legislation in all Cases whatsoever, over such District (not exceeding ten Miles square) as may, by Cession of particular States, and the Acceptance of Congress, become the Seat of the Government of the United States, and to exercise like Authority over all Places purchased by the Consent of the Legislature of the State in which the Same shall be, for the Erection of Forts, Magazines, Arsenals, dock Yards, and other needful Buildings; —And

To make all Laws which shall be necessary and proper for carrying into Execution the foregoing Powers, and all other Powers vested by this Constitution in the Government of the United States, or in any Department or Officer thereof.

Section. 9. The Migration or Importation of such Persons as any of the States now existing shall think proper to admit, shall not be prohibited by the Congress prior to the Year one thousand eight hundred and eight, but a Tax or duty may be imposed on such Importation, not exceeding ten dollars for each Person.

The Privilege of the Writ of Habeas Corpus shall not be suspended, unless when in Cases of Rebellion or Invasion the public Safety may require it.

No Bill of Attainder or ex post facto Law shall be passed.

No Capitation, or other direct, Tax shall be laid, unless in Proportion to the Census or Enumeration herein before directed to be taken.

No Tax or Duty shall be laid on Articles exported from any State.

No Preference shall be given by any Regulation of Commerce or Revenue to the Ports of one State over those of another; nor shall Vessels bound to, or from, one State, be obliged to enter, clear, or pay Duties in another.

No Money shall be drawn from the Treasury, but in Consequence of Appropriations made by Law; and a regular Statement and Account of the Receipts and Expenditures of all public Money shall be published from time to time.

No Title of Nobility shall be granted by the United States: And no Person holding any Office of Profit or Trust under them, shall, without the Consent of the Congress, accept of any present, Emolument, Office, or Title, of any kind whatever, from any King, Prince, or foreign State.

Section. 10. No State shall enter into any Treaty, Alliance, or Confederation; grant Letters of Marque and Reprisal; coin Money; emit Bills of Credit; make any Thing but gold and silver Coin a Tender in Payment of Debts; pass any Bill of Attainder, ex post facto Law, or Law impairing the Obligation of Contracts, or grant any Title of Nobility.

No State shall, without the Consent of the Congress, lay any Imposts or Duties on Imports or Exports, except what may be absolutely necessary for executing it's inspection Laws; and the net Produce of all Duties and Imposts, laid by any State on Imports or Exports, shall be for the Use of the Treasury of the United States; and all such Laws shall be subject to the Revision and Controul of the Congress.

No State shall, without the Consent of Congress, lay any Duty of Tonnage, keep Troops, or Ships of War in time of Peace, enter into any Agreement or Compact with another State, or with a foreign Power, or engage in War, unless actually invaded, or in such imminent Danger as will not admit of delay.

A.2 Article II

Section. 1. The executive Power shall be vested in a President of the United States of America. He shall hold his Office during the Term of four Years, and, together with the Vice President, chosen for the same Term, be elected, as follows:

Each State shall appoint, in such Manner as the Legislature thereof may direct, a Number of Electors, equal to the whole Number of Senators and Representatives to which the State may be entitled in the Congress: but no Senator or Representative, or Person holding an Office of Trust or Profit under the United States, shall be appointed an Elector.

The Electors shall meet in their respective States, and vote by Ballot for two Persons, of whom one at least shall not be an Inhabitant of the same State with themselves. And they shall make a List of all the Persons voted for, and of the Number of Votes for each; which List they shall sign and certify, and transmit sealed to the Seat of the Government of the United States, directed to the President of the Senate. The President of the Senate shall, in the Presence of the Senate and House of Representatives, open all the Certificates, and the Votes shall then be counted. The Person having the greatest Number of Votes shall be the President, if such Number be a Majority of the whole Number of Electors appointed; and if there be more than one who have such Majority, and have an equal Number of Votes, then the House of Representatives shall immediately chuse by Ballot one of them for President; and if no Person have a Majority, then from the five highest on the List the said House shall in like Manner chuse the President. But in chusing the President, the Votes shall be taken by States, the Representation from each State having one Vote; a quorum for this Purpose shall consist of a Member or Members from two thirds of the States, and a Majority of all the States shall be necessary to a Choice. In every Case, after the Choice of the President, the Person having the greatest Number of Votes of the Electors shall be the Vice President. But if there should remain two or more who have equal Votes, the Senate shall chuse from them by Ballot the Vice President.

The Congress may determine the Time of chusing the Electors, and the Day on which they shall give their Votes; which Day shall be the same throughout the United States.

No Person except a natural born Citizen, or a Citizen of the United States, at the time of the Adoption of this Constitution, shall be eligible to the Office of President; neither shall any Person be eligible to that Office who shall not have attained to the Age of thirty five Years, and been fourteen Years a Resident within the United States.

In Case of the Removal of the President from Office, or of his Death, Resignation, or Inability to discharge the Powers and Duties of the said Office, the Same shall devolve on the Vice President, and the Congress may by Law provide for the Case of Removal, Death, Resignation or Inability, both of the President and Vice President, declaring what Officer shall then act as President, and such Officer shall act accordingly, until the Disability be removed, or a President shall be elected.

The President shall, at stated Times, receive for his Services, a Compensation, which shall neither be increased nor diminished during the Period for which he shall have been elected, and he shall not receive within that Period any other Emolument from the United States, or any of them.

Before he enter on the Execution of his Office, he shall take the following Oath or Affirmation:—"I do solemnly swear (or affirm) that I will faithfully execute the Office of President of the United States, and will to the best of my Ability, preserve, protect and defend the Constitution of the United States."

Section. 2. The President shall be Commander in Chief of the Army and Navy of the United States, and of the Militia of the several States, when called into the actual Service of the United States; he may require the Opinion, in writing, of the principal Officer in each of the executive Departments, upon any Subject relating to the Duties of their respective Offices, and he shall have Power to grant Reprieves and Pardons for Offences against the United States, except in Cases of Impeachment.

He shall have Power, by and with the Advice and Consent of the Senate, to make Treaties, provided two thirds of the Senators present concur; and he shall nominate, and by and with the Advice and Consent of the Senate, shall appoint Ambassadors, other public Ministers and Consuls, Judges of the supreme Court, and all other Officers of the United States, whose Appointments are not herein otherwise provided for, and which shall be established by Law: but the Congress may by Law vest the Appointment of such inferior Officers, as they think proper, in the President alone, in the Courts of Law, or in the Heads of Departments.

The President shall have Power to fill up all Vacancies that may happen during the Recess of the Senate, by granting Commissions which shall expire at the End of their next Session.

Section. 3. He shall from time to time give to the Congress Information of the State of the Union, and recommend to their Consideration such Measures as he shall judge necessary and expedient; he may, on extraordinary Occasions, convene both Houses, or either of them, and in Case of Disagreement between them, with Respect to the Time of Adjournment, he may adjourn them to such Time as he shall think proper; he shall receive Ambassadors and other public Ministers; he shall take Care that the Laws be faithfully executed, and shall Commission all the Officers of the United States.

Section. 4. The President, Vice President and all civil Officers of the United States, shall be removed from Office on Impeachment for, and Conviction of, Treason, Bribery, or other high Crimes and Misdemeanors.

A.3 Article III

Section. 1. The judicial Power of the United States shall be vested in one supreme Court, and in such inferior Courts as the Congress may from time to time ordain and establish. The Judges, both of the supreme and inferior Courts, shall hold their Offices during good Behaviour, and shall, at stated Times, receive for their Services a Compensation, which shall not be diminished during their Continuance in Office.

Section. 2. The judicial Power shall extend to all Cases, in Law and Equity, arising under this Constitution, the Laws of the United States, and Treaties made, or which shall be made, under their Authority;—to all Cases affecting Ambassadors, other public Ministers and Consuls;—to all Cases of admiralty and maritime Jurisdiction;—to Controversies to which the United States shall be a Party;—to Controversies between two or more States;—between a State and Citizens of another State;—between Citizens of different States;—between Citizens of the same State claiming Lands under Grants of different States, and between a State, or the Citizens thereof, and foreign States, Citizens or Subjects.

In all Cases affecting Ambassadors, other public Ministers and Consuls, and those in which a State shall be Party, the supreme Court shall have original Jurisdiction. In all the other Cases before mentioned, the supreme Court shall have appellate Jurisdiction, both as to Law and Fact, with such Exceptions, and under such Regulations as the Congress shall make.

The Trial of all Crimes, except in Cases of Impeachment, shall be by Jury; and such Trial shall be held in the State where the said Crimes shall have been committed; but when not committed within any State, the Trial shall be at such Place or Places as the Congress may by Law have directed.

Section. 3. Treason against the United States shall consist only in levying War against them, or in adhering to their Enemies, giving them Aid and Comfort. No Person shall be convicted of Treason unless on the Testimony of two Witnesses to the same overt Act, or on Confession in open Court.

The Congress shall have Power to declare the Punishment of Treason, but no Attainder of Treason shall work Corruption of Blood, or Forfeiture except during the Life of the Person attainted.

A.4 Article IV

Section. 1. Full Faith and Credit shall be given in each State to the public Acts, Records, and judicial Proceedings of every other State. And the Congress may by general Laws prescribe the Manner in which such Acts, Records and Proceedings shall be proved, and the Effect thereof.

Section. 2. The Citizens of each State shall be entitled to all Privileges and Immunities of Citizens in the several States.

A Person charged in any State with Treason, Felony, or other Crime, who shall flee from Justice, and be found in another State, shall on Demand of the executive Authority of the State from which he fled, be delivered up, to be removed to the State having Jurisdiction of the Crime.

No Person held to Service or Labour in one State, under the Laws thereof, escaping into another, shall, in Consequence of any Law or Regulation therein, be discharged from such Service or Labour, but shall be delivered up on Claim of the Party to whom such Service or Labour may be due.

Section. 3. New States may be admitted by the Congress into this Union; but no new State shall be formed or erected within the Jurisdiction of any other State; nor any State be formed by the Junction of two or more States, or Parts of States, without the Consent of the Legislatures of the States concerned as well as of the Congress.

The Congress shall have Power to dispose of and make all needful Rules and Regulations respecting the Territory or other Property belonging to the United States; and nothing in this Constitution shall be so construed as to Prejudice any Claims of the United States, or of any particular State.

Section. 4. The United States shall guarantee to every State in this Union a Republican Form of Government, and shall protect each of them against Invasion; and on Application of the Legislature, or of the Executive (when the Legislature cannot be convened), against domestic Violence.

A.5 Article V

The Congress, whenever two thirds of both Houses shall deem it necessary, shall propose Amendments to this Constitution, or, on the Application of the Legislatures of two thirds of the several States, shall call a Convention for proposing Amendments, which, in either Case, shall be valid to all Intents and Purposes, as Part of this Constitution, when ratified by the Legislatures of three fourths of the several States, or by Conventions in three fourths thereof, as the one or the other Mode of Ratification may be proposed by the Congress; Provided that no Amendment which may be made prior to the Year One thousand eight hundred and eight shall in any Manner affect the first and fourth Clauses in the Ninth Section of the first Article; and that no State, without its Consent, shall be deprived of its equal Suffrage in the Senate.

A.6 Article VI

All Debts contracted and Engagements entered into, before the Adoption of this Constitution, shall be as valid against the United States under this Constitution, as under the Confederation.

This Constitution, and the Laws of the United States which shall be made in Pursuance thereof; and all Treaties made, or which shall be made, under the Authority of the United States, shall be the supreme Law of the Land; and the Judges in every State shall be bound thereby, any Thing in the Constitution or Laws of any State to the Contrary notwithstanding.

The Senators and Representatives before mentioned, and the Members of the several State Legislatures, and all executive and judicial Officers, both of the United States and of the several States, shall be bound by Oath or Affirmation, to support this Constitution; but no religious Test shall ever be required as a Qualification to any Office or public Trust under the United States.

A.7 Article VII

The Ratification of the Conventions of nine States, shall be sufficient for the Establishment of this Constitution between the States so ratifying the Same.

A.8 Bill of Rights

Article the third [Amendment I]

Congress shall make no law respecting an establishment of religion, or prohibiting the free exercise thereof; or abridging the freedom of speech, or of the press; or the right of the people peaceably to assemble, and to petition the Government for a redress of grievances.

Article the fourth [Amendment II]

A well regulated Militia, being necessary to the security of a free State, the right of the people to keep and bear Arms, shall not be infringed.

Article the fifth [Amendment III]

No Soldier shall, in time of peace be quartered in any house, without the consent of the Owner, nor in time of war, but in a manner to be prescribed by law.

Article the sixth [Amendment IV]

The right of the people to be secure in their persons, houses, papers, and effects, against unreasonable searches and seizures, shall not be violated, and no Warrants shall issue, but upon probable cause, supported by Oath or affirmation, and particularly describing the place to be searched, and the persons or things to be seized.

Article the seventh [Amendment V]

No person shall be held to answer for a capital, or otherwise infamous crime, unless on a presentment or indictment of a Grand Jury, except in cases arising in the land or naval forces, or in the Militia, when in actual service in time of War or public danger; nor shall any person be subject for the same offence to be twice put in jeopardy of life or limb; nor shall be compelled in any criminal case to be a witness against himself, nor be deprived of life, liberty, or property, without due process of law; nor shall private property be taken for public use, without just compensation.

Article the eighth [Amendment VI]

In all criminal prosecutions, the accused shall enjoy the right to a speedy and public trial, by an impartial jury of the State and district wherein the crime shall have been committed, which district shall have been previously ascertained by law, and to be informed of the nature and cause of the accusation; to be confronted with the witnesses against him; to have compulsory process for obtaining witnesses in his favor, and to have the Assistance of Counsel for his defence.

Article the ninth [Amendment VII]

In Suits at common law, where the value in controversy shall exceed twenty dollars, the right of trial by jury shall be preserved, and no fact tried by a jury, shall be otherwise re examined in any Court of the United States, than according to the rules of the common law.

Article the tenth [Amendment VIII]

Excessive bail shall not be required, nor excessive fines imposed, nor cruel and unusual punishments inflicted.

Article the eleventh [Amendment IX]

The enumeration in the Constitution, of certain rights, shall not be construed to deny or disparage others retained by the people.

Article the twelfth [Amendment X]

The powers not delegated to the United States by the Constitution, nor prohibited by it to the States, are reserved to the States respectively, or to the people.

A.9 Additional Amendments to the Constitution

Amendment XI [Proposed 1794; Ratified 1798]

The Judicial power of the United States shall not be construed to extend to any suit in law or equity, commenced or prosecuted against one of the United States by Citizens of another State, or by Citizens or Subjects of any Foreign State.

Amendment XII [Proposed 1803; Ratified 1804]

The Electors shall meet in their respective states, and vote by ballot for President and Vice President, one of whom, at least, shall not be an inhabitant of the same state with themselves; they shall name in their ballots the person voted for as President, and in distinct ballots the person voted for as Vice President, and they shall make distinct lists of all persons voted for as President, and of all persons voted for as Vice President, and of the number of votes for each, which lists they shall sign and certify, and transmit sealed to the seat of the government of the United States, directed to the President of the Senate;—The President of the Senate shall, in the presence of the Senate and House of Representatives, open all the certificates and the votes shall then be counted;—The person having the greatest number of votes for President, shall be the President, if such number be a majority of the whole number of Electors appointed; and if no person have such majority, then from the persons having the highest numbers not exceeding three on the list of those voted for as President, the House of Representatives shall choose immediately, by ballot, the President. But in choosing the President, the votes shall be taken by states, the representation from each state having one vote; a quorum for this purpose shall consist of a member or members from two thirds of the states, and a majority of all the states shall be necessary to a choice. And if the House of Representatives shall not choose a President whenever the right of choice shall devolve upon them, before the fourth day of March next following, then the Vice President shall act as President, as in the case of the death or other constitutional disability of the President.—The person having the greatest number of votes as Vice President, shall be the Vice President, if such number be a majority of the whole number of Electors appointed, and if no person have a majority, then from the two highest numbers on the list, the Senate shall choose the Vice President; a quorum for the purpose shall consist of two thirds of the whole number of Senators, and a majority of the whole number shall be necessary to a choice. But no person constitutionally ineligible to the office of President shall be eligible to that of Vice President of the United States.

Amendment XIII [Proposed 1865; Ratified 1865]

Section. 1. Neither slavery nor involuntary servitude, except as a punishment for crime whereof the party shall have been duly convicted, shall exist within the United States, or any place subject to their jurisdiction.

Section. 2. Congress shall have power to enforce this article by appropriate legislation.

Amendment XIV [Proposed 1866; Ratified 1868]

Section. 1. All persons born or naturalized in the United States, and subject to the jurisdiction thereof, are citizens of the United States and of the State wherein they reside. No State shall make or enforce any law which shall abridge the privileges or immunities of citizens of the United States; nor shall any State deprive any person of life, liberty, or property, without due process of law; nor deny to any person within its jurisdiction the equal protection of the laws.

Section. 2. Representatives shall be apportioned among the several States according to their respective numbers, counting the whole number of persons in each State, excluding Indians not taxed. But when the right to vote at any election for the choice of electors for President and Vice President of the United States, Representatives in Congress, the Executive and Judicial officers of a State, or the members of the Legislature thereof, is denied to any of the male inhabitants of such State, being twenty one years of age, and citizens of the United States, or in any way abridged, except for participation in rebellion, or other crime, the basis of representation therein shall be reduced in the proportion which the number of such male citizens shall bear to the whole number of male citizens twenty one years of age in such State.

Section. 3. No person shall be a Senator or Representative in Congress, or elector of President and Vice President, or hold any office, civil or military, under the United States, or under any State, who, having previously taken an oath, as a member of Congress, or as an officer of the United States, or as a member of any State legislature, or as an executive or judicial officer of any State, to support the Constitution of the United States, shall have engaged in insurrection or rebellion against the same, or given aid or comfort to the enemies thereof. But Congress may by a vote of two thirds of each House, remove such disability.

Section. 4. The validity of the public debt of the United States, authorized by law, including debts incurred for payment of pensions and bounties for services in suppressing insurrection or rebellion, shall not be questioned. But neither the United States nor any State shall assume or pay any debt or obligation incurred in aid of insurrection or rebellion against the United States, or any claim for the loss or emancipation of any slave; but all such debts, obligations and claims shall be held illegal and void.

Section. 5. The Congress shall have power to enforce, by appropriate legislation, the provisions of this article.

Amendment XV [Proposed 1869; Ratified 1870]

Section. 1. The right of citizens of the United States to vote shall not be denied or abridged by the United States or by any State on account of race, color, or previous condition of servitude.

Section. 2. The Congress shall have power to enforce this article by appropriate legislation.

Amendment XVI [Proposed 1909; Questionably Ratified 1913]

The Congress shall have power to lay and collect taxes on incomes, from whatever source derived, without apportionment among the several States, and without regard to any census or enumeration.

Amendment XVII [Proposed 1912; Ratified 1913]

The Senate of the United States shall be composed of two Senators from each State, elected by the people thereof, for six years; and each Senator shall have one vote. The electors in each State shall have the qualifications requisite for electors of the most numerous branch of the State legislatures.

When vacancies happen in the representation of any State in the Senate, the executive authority of such State shall issue writs of election to fill such vacancies: Provided, That the legislature of any State may empower the executive thereof to make temporary appointments until the people fill the vacancies by election as the legislature may direct.

This amendment shall not be so construed as to affect the election or term of any Senator chosen before it becomes valid as part of the Constitution.

Amendment XVIII [Proposed 1917; Ratified 1919; Repealed 1933 (See Amendment XXI, Section 1)]

Section. 1. After one year from the ratification of this article the manufacture, sale, or transportation of intoxicating liquors within, the importation thereof into, or the exportation thereof from the United States and all territory subject to the jurisdiction thereof for beverage purposes is hereby prohibited.

Section. 2. The Congress and the several States shall have concurrent power to enforce this article by appropriate legislation.

Section. 3. This article shall be inoperative unless it shall have been ratified as an amendment to the Constitution by the legislatures of the several States, as provided in the Constitution, within seven years from the date of the submission hereof to the States by the Congress.

Amendment XIX [Proposed 1919; Ratified 1920]

The right of citizens of the United States to vote shall not be denied or abridged by the United States or by any State on account of sex.

Congress shall have power to enforce this article by appropriate legislation.

Amendment XX [Proposed 1932; Ratified 1933]

Section. 1. The terms of the President and Vice President shall end at noon on the 20th day of January, and the terms of Senators and Representatives at noon on the 3d day of January, of the years in which such terms would have ended if this article had not been ratified; and the terms of their successors shall then begin.

Section. 2. The Congress shall assemble at least once in every year, and such meeting shall begin at noon on the 3d day of January, unless they shall by law appoint a different day.

Section. 3. If, at the time fixed for the beginning of the term of the President, the President elect shall have died, the Vice President elect shall become President. If a President shall not have been chosen before the time fixed for the beginning of his term, or if the President elect shall have failed to qualify, then the Vice President elect shall act as President until a President shall have qualified; and the Congress may by law provide for the case wherein neither a President elect nor a Vice President elect shall have qualified, declaring who shall then act as President, or the manner in which one who is to act shall be selected, and such person shall act accordingly until a President or Vice President shall have qualified.

Section. 4. The Congress may by law provide for the case of the death of any of the persons from whom the House of Representatives may choose a President whenever the right of choice shall have devolved upon them, and for the case of the death of any of the persons from whom the Senate may choose a Vice President whenever the right of choice shall have devolved upon them.

Section. 5. Sections 1 and 2 shall take effect on the 15th day of October following the ratification of this article.

Section. 6. This article shall be inoperative unless it shall have been ratified as an amendment to the Constitution by the legislatures of three fourths of the several States within seven years from the date of its submission.

Amendment XXI [Proposed 1933; Ratified 1933]

Section. 1. The eighteenth article of amendment to the Constitution of the United States is hereby repealed.

Section. 2. The transportation or importation into any State, Territory, or possession of the United States for delivery or use therein of intoxicating liquors, in violation of the laws thereof, is hereby prohibited.

Section. 3. This article shall be inoperative unless it shall have been ratified as an amendment to the Constitution by conventions in the several States, as provided in the Constitution, within seven years from the date of the submission hereof to the States by the Congress.

Amendment XXII [Proposed 1947; Ratified 1951]

Section. 1. No person shall be elected to the office of the President more than twice, and no person who has held the office of President, or acted as President, for more than two years of a term to which some other person was elected President shall be elected to the office of the President more than once. But this Article shall not apply to any person holding the office of President when this Article was proposed by the Congress, and shall not prevent any person who may be holding the office of President, or acting as President, during the term within which this Article becomes operative from holding the office of President or acting as President during the remainder of such term.

Section. 2. This article shall be inoperative unless it shall have been ratified as an amendment to the Constitution by the legislatures of three fourths of the several States within seven years from the date of its submission to the States by the Congress.

Amendment XXIII [Proposed 1960; Ratified 1961]

Section. 1. The District constituting the seat of Government of the United States shall appoint in such manner as the Congress may direct:

A number of electors of President and Vice President equal to the whole number of Senators and Representatives in Congress to which the District would be entitled if it were a State, but in no event more than the least populous State; they shall be in addition to those appointed by the States, but they shall be considered, for the purposes of the election of President and Vice President, to be electors appointed by a State; and they shall meet in the District and perform such duties as provided by the twelfth article of amendment.

Section. 2. The Congress shall have power to enforce this article by appropriate legislation.

Amendment XXIV [Proposed 1962; Ratified 1964]

Section. 1. The right of citizens of the United States to vote in any primary or other election for President or Vice President, for electors for President or Vice President, or for Senator or Representative in Congress, shall not be denied or abridged by the United States or any State by reason of failure to pay any poll tax or other tax.

Section. 2. The Congress shall have power to enforce this article by appropriate legislation.

Amendment XXV [Proposed 1965; Ratified 1967]

Section. 1. In case of the removal of the President from office or of his death or resignation, the Vice President shall become President.

Section. 2. Whenever there is a vacancy in the office of the Vice President, the President shall nominate a Vice President who shall take office upon confirmation by a majority vote of both Houses of Congress.

Section. 3. Whenever the President transmits to the President pro tempore of the Senate and the Speaker of the House of Representatives his written declaration that he is unable to discharge the powers and duties of his office, and until he transmits to them a written declaration to the contrary, such powers and duties shall be discharged by the Vice President as Acting President.

Section. 4. Whenever the Vice President and a majority of either the principal officers of the executive departments or of such other body as Congress may by law provide, transmit to the President pro tempore of the Senate and the Speaker of the House of Representatives their written declaration that the President is unable to discharge the powers and duties of his office, the Vice President shall immediately assume the powers and duties of the office as Acting President.

Thereafter, when the President transmits to the President pro tempore of the Senate and the Speaker of the House of Representatives his written declaration that no inability exists, he shall resume the powers and duties of his office unless the Vice President and a majority of either the principal officers of the executive department or of such other body as Congress may by law provide, transmit within four days to the President pro tempore of the Senate and the Speaker of the House of Representatives their written declaration that the President is unable to discharge the powers and duties of his office. Thereupon Congress shall decide the issue, assembling within forty eight hours for that purpose if not in session. If the Congress, within twenty one days after receipt of the latter written declaration, or, if Congress is not in session, within twenty one days after Congress is required to assemble, determines by two thirds vote of both Houses that the President is unable to discharge the powers and duties of his office, the Vice President shall continue to discharge the same as Acting President; otherwise, the President shall resume the powers and duties of his office.

Amendment XXVI [Proposed 1971; Ratified 1971]

Section. 1. The right of citizens of the United States, who are eighteen years of age or older, to vote shall not be denied or abridged by the United States or by any State on account of age.

Section. 2. The Congress shall have power to enforce this article by appropriate legislation.

Amendment XXVII [Proposed 1789; Ratified 1992; Second of twelve Articles comprising the Bill of Rights]

No law, varying the compensation for the services of the Senators and Representatives, shall take effect, until an election of Representatives shall have intervened.

Index